Human Development Report 2014

Sustaining Human Progress:
Reducing Vulnerabilities and Building Resilience

Empowered lives.
Resilient nations.

Published for the
United Nations
Development
Programme
(UNDP)

Human Development Reports 1990–2014

Regional Human Development Reports: Over the past two decades, regionally focused HDRs have also been produced in all major areas of the developing world, with support from UNDP's regional bureaus. With provocative analyses and clear policy recommendations, regional HDRs have examined such critical issues as political empowerment in the Arab states, food security in Africa, climate change in Asia, treatment of ethnic minorities in Central Europe and challenges of inequality and citizens' security in Latin America and the Caribbean.

National Human Development Reports: Since the release of the first national HDR in 1992, national HDRs have been produced in 140 countries by local editorial teams with UNDP support. These reports—some 700 to date—bring a human development perspective to national policy concerns through local consultations and research. National HDRs have covered many key development issues, from climate change to youth employment to inequalities driven by gender or ethnicity.

Copyright © 2014
by the United Nations Development Programme
1 UN Plaza, New York, NY 10017, USA

ISBN 978-92-1-126368-8
eISBN 978-92-1-056659-9

A catalogue record for this book is available from the British Library and the Library of Congress.

Printed in the United States by PBM Graphics, an RR Donnelley Company, on Forest Stewardship Council® certified and elemental chlorine-free papers. Printed using vegetable-based inks.

Editing and production: Communications Development Incorporated, Washington DC, USA
Information design and data visualisation: Accurat s.r.l., Milan, Italy

For a list of any errors or omissions found subsequent to printing, please visit our website at http://hdr.undp.org

Human Development Report 2014 Team

Director and lead author
Khalid Malik

Research and statistics
Maurice Kugler (Head of Research), Milorad Kovacevic (Chief Statistician), Eva Jespersen (Deputy Director), Subhra Bhattacharjee, Astra Bonini, Cecilia Calderon, Alan Fuchs, Amie Gaye, Sasa Lucic, Arthur Minsat, Shivani Nayyar, Pedro Martins, Tanni Mukhopadhyay and José Pineda

Communications and publishing
William Orme (Chief of Communications), Botagoz Abreyeva, Eleonore Fournier-Tombs, Anna Ortubia, Admir Jahic, Brigitte Stark-Merklein, Samantha Wauchope and Grace Sales

National Human Development Reports
Jon Hall (Head of Team), Christina Hackmann and Mary Ann Mwangi

Operations and administration
Sarantuya Mend (Operations Manager), Mamaye Gebretsadik and Fe Juarez-Shanahan

Foreword

The 2014 Human Development Report—*Sustaining Progress: Reducing Vulnerabilities and Building Resilience*—looks at two concepts which are both interconnected and immensely important to securing human development progress.

Since the United Nations Development Programme's (UNDP) first global *Human Development Report (HDR)* in 1990, most countries have registered significant human development. This year's Report shows that overall global trends are positive and that progress is continuing. Yet, lives are being lost, and livelihoods and development undermined, by natural or human-induced disasters and crises.

However, these setbacks are not inevitable. While every society is vulnerable to risk, some suffer far less harm and recover more quickly than others when adversity strikes. This Report asks why that is and, for the first time in a global *HDR,* considers vulnerability and resilience through a human development lens.

Much of the existing research on vulnerability has considered people's exposure to particular risks and is often sector-specific. This Report takes a different and more holistic approach. It considers the factors which contribute to risks to human development and then discusses the ways in which resilience to a broad group of evolving risks could be strengthened.

This approach is particularly important in our interconnected world. While globalization has brought benefits to many, it has also given rise to new concerns, manifest at times as local reactions to the spillover effects of events far away. Preparing citizens for a less vulnerable future means strengthening the intrinsic resilience of communities and countries. This Report lays the groundwork for doing that.

In line with the human development paradigm, this Report takes a people-centred approach. It pays particular attention to disparities between and within countries. It identifies the 'structurally vulnerable' groups of people who are more vulnerable than others by virtue of their history or of their unequal treatment by the rest of society. These vulnerabilities have often evolved and persisted over long periods of time and may be associated with gender, ethnicity, indigeneity or geographic location—to name just a few factors. Many of the most vulnerable people and groups face numerous and overlapping constraints on their ability to cope with setbacks. For example, those who are poor and also from a minority group, or are female and have disabilities, face multiple barriers which can negatively reinforce each other.

The Report considers the way in which vulnerabilities change during our lives—by taking a 'life cycle approach'. Unlike more static models, this analysis suggests that children, adolescents and the elderly each face different sets of risks which require targeted responses. Some periods of life are identified as particularly important: for example, the first 1,000 days of a child's life or the transition from school to work or from work to retirement. Setbacks at these points can be particularly difficult to overcome and may have prolonged impacts.

Based on analysis of the available evidence, this Report makes a number of important recommendations for achieving a world which addresses vulnerabilities and builds resilience to future shocks. It calls for universal access to basic social services, especially health and education; stronger social protection, including unemployment insurance and pensions; and a commitment to full employment, recognizing that the value of employment extends far beyond the income it generates. It examines the importance of responsive and fair institutions and increased social cohesion for building community-level resilience and for reducing the potential for conflict to break out.

The Report recognizes that no matter how effective policies are in reducing inherent vulnerabilities, crises will continue to occur with potentially destructive consequences. Building capacities for disaster preparedness and recovery, which enable communities to better weather—and recover from—shocks, is vital. At the global level, recognizing that risks which are transborder in nature require collective action, the Report calls for global commitments and better international governance.

These recommendations are both important and timely. As UN Member States prepare to conclude negotiations on the post-2015 development agenda and launch a set of sustainable development goals, the evidence collected and analysed in this Report, and the human development perspective on which it is based, are particularly valuable. Eradicating poverty, for example, will be a central objective of the new agenda. But, as this Report argues, if people remain at risk of slipping back into poverty because of structural factors and persistent vulnerabilities, development progress will remain precarious. The eradication of poverty is not just about 'getting to zero'—it is also about staying there.

Achieving UNDP's vision to help countries achieve the simultaneous eradication of poverty and significant reduction of inequalities and exclusion and to promote human and sustainable development, requires a deep appreciation of the concepts of vulnerability and resilience. Unless and until vulnerabilities are addressed effectively, and all people enjoy the opportunity to share in human development progress, development advances will be neither equitable nor sustainable.

This Report aims to help decisionmakers and other development actors lock in development gains through policies which reduce vulnerability and build resilience. I recommend it to all who wish to see sustained development progress, especially for the most vulnerable people in our world.

Helen Clark

Helen Clark
Administrator
United Nations Development Programme

Acknowledgements

The 2014 *Human Development Report* is the product of a collective effort by the United Nations Development Programme (UNDP) Human Development Report Office (HDRO) and many valued external advisors and contributors. However, the findings, analysis and policy recommendations of this Report, as with previous Reports, are those of the authors alone and do not represent the official viewpoint of UNDP, nor that of its Executive Board. The UN General Assembly has officially recognized the *Human Development Report* as "an independent intellectual exercise" that has become "an important tool for raising awareness about human development around the world."[1]

We are pleased that H.E. Ms. Ellen Johnson Sirleaf, President of Liberia, Bill Gates, Stephen Hawking, James Heckman, Rajendra Pachauri, Juan Somavia, Joseph Stiglitz and M.S. Swaminathan have made special contributions to the Report. We are also most grateful to the authors of papers commissioned for this 2014 Report: Connie Bayudan; Des Gasper and Oscar Gomez; Andrew Fischer; Thomas Hale; Khalil Hamdani; Abby Hardgrove, Kirrilly Pells, Jo Boyden and Paul Dornan; Naila Kabeer; Inge Kaul; William Kinsey; Samir KC, Wolfgang Lutz, Elke Loichinger, Raya Muttarak and Erich Striessnig; Rehman Sobhan; Adam Rose; Till von Wachter; Mary E. Young; and Ashgar Zaidi.

During the preparation of the Report, HDRO received invaluable insights and guidance from our distinguished Advisory Panel, including Hanan Ashrawi, Edward Ayensu, Cristovam Ricardo Cavalcanti Buarque, Michael Elliott, Patrick Guillaumont, Ricardo Hausmann, Nanna Hvidt, Rima Khalaf, Nora Lustig, Sir James Alexander Mirrlees, Thandika Mkandawire, José Antonio Ocampo, Rajendra Pachauri, Samir Radwan, Rizal Ramli, Gustav Ranis, Frances Stewart, Akihiko Tanaka and Ruan Zongze.

We would also like to thank HDRO's statistical panel, which provided expert advice on methodologies and data choices related to the calculation of the Report's human development indices: Jose Ramon Albert, Sir Anthony Atkinson, Birol Aydemir, Rachid Benmokhtar Benabdellah, Wasmalia Bivar, Grant Cameron, Nailin Feng, Enrico Giovannini, D.C.A. Gunawardena, Peter Harper, Yemi Kale, Hendrik van der Pol and Eduardo Sojo Garza-Aldape.

The Report's composite indices and other statistical resources rely on the expertise of the leading international data providers in their specialized fields, and we express our gratitude for their continued collegial collaboration with HDRO. James Foster, Stephan Klasen and Conchita D'Ambrosio contributed critical reviews of the Report's composite indices. To ensure accuracy and clarity, the Report's statistical analysis have also benefitted from the external review of statistical findings by Sabina Alkire, Adriana Conconi, Maria Emma Santos, Kenneth Harttgen, Hiroaki Matsuura, Claudio Montenegro, Atika Pasha and Jackie Yiptong.

The consultations held around the world during preparation of the Report relied on the generous support of many institutions and individuals who are too numerous to mention here. Events were held between April 2012 and February 2014 in Addis Ababa, Almaty, Brussels, Geneva, Islamabad, Managua, New York and Tokyo.[2] Support from partnering institutions, including UNDP country and regional offices, listed at http://hdr.undp.org/en/2014-report/consultations, is acknowledged with much gratitude. Equally, the annual HDRO Conference on Measuring Human Progress has allowed us to pursue a systematic dialogue with key partners from government, academia and civil society on our indices and their improvements.

Many of our UNDP colleagues around the world—as members of the HDRO Readers Group and the Executive Group—provided invaluable insights into the preparation and final drafting of the report. We would especially like to thank Adel Abdellatif, Pedro Conceição, Samuel Doe, George Ronald Gray Molina, Heraldo Muñoz, Selim Jehan, Natalia Linou, Abdoulaye Mar Dieye, Magdy Martinez-Soliman, Stan Nkwain, Thangaval Palanivel, Jordan Ryan, Turhan Saleh, Ben

Slay, Mounir Tabet, Antonio Vigilante and Mourad Wahba.

Colleagues at Helpage, the United Nations Children's Fund and the International Labour Organization also offered much valued insights and commentary. Laurent Thomas and Neil Marsland from the Food and Agriculture Organization of the United Nations also generously shared their expertise.

Special thanks to the Governments of France (AFD) and Germany (BMZ) for their financial contributions to the Report, and to the Government of Japan (JICA) for their support to the East Asia Regional Consultation.

We are much indebted to our team of fact-checkers and consultants, which included Akmal Abdurazakov, Melissa Mahoney, Agnes Zabsonre and Simona Zampino.

Our interns Caterina Alacevich, Ruijie Cheng, Bouba Housseini, Yoo Rim Lee, Élisée Miningou, Ji Yun Sul, Petros Tesfazion and Lin Yang also deserve recognition for their dedication and contribution. The Report has been blessed with many 'friends of HDRO' who have gone out of their way to help strengthen it. We benefited much from the critical readings of the draft report and related textual contributions by James Heintz, Shiva Kumar, Peter Stalker and Frances Stewart. We are very grateful to Amartya Sen and Joseph Stiglitz for their review and feedback on the report.

In particular we would like to acknowledge the highly professional work of our editors at Communications Development Incorporated, led by Bruce Ross-Larson, with Joe Caponio, Christopher Trott and Elaine Wilson, and of designers Federica Fragapane, Michele Graffieti and Gabriele Rossi of Accurat Design.

Most of all, I am as always profoundly grateful to Helen Clark, UNDP's Administrator, for her leadership and vision, and to the entire HDRO team for their dedication and commitment in producing a report that strives to further the advancement of human development.

Khalid Malik
Director
Human Development Report Office

Notes

1   UN Resolution 57/264, 30 January 2003.
2   Participants are listed and acknowledged at http://hdr.undp.org/en/2014-report/consultations.

Contents

FIGURES

MAP

TABLES

"Human progress is neither
automatic nor inevitable . . ."

Martin Luther King, Jr.

Overview

Charles Dickens's classic *Tale of Two Cities* explored the many contrasting realities—"the best of times, the worst of times"—of 18th century Paris and London. While the contemporary world is a very different place, it displays similar contrasts—some acute and some arguably more complex.

As successive *Human Development Reports* have shown, most people in most countries have been doing steadily better in human development. Advances in technology, education and incomes hold ever-greater promise for longer, healthier, more secure lives.[1] Globalization has on balance produced major human development gains, especially in many countries of the South. But there is also a widespread sense of precariousness in the world today—in livelihoods, in personal security, in the environment and in global politics.[2] High achievements on critical aspects of human development, such as health and nutrition, can quickly be undermined by a natural disaster or economic slump. Theft and assault can leave people physically and psychologically impoverished. Corruption and unresponsive state institutions can leave those in need of assistance without recourse. Political threats, community tensions, violent conflict, neglect of public health, environmental damages, crime and discrimination all add to individual and community vulnerability.

Real progress on human development, then, is not only a matter of enlarging people's critical choices and their ability to be educated, be healthy, have a reasonable standard of living and feel safe. It is also a matter of how secure these achievements are and whether conditions are sufficient for sustained human development. An account of progress in human development is incomplete without exploring and assessing vulnerability.

Traditionally, the concept of vulnerability is used to describe exposure to risk and risk management, including insuring against shocks and diversifying assets and income.[3] This Report takes a broader approach, emphasizing the close links between reducing vulnerability and advancing human development. We introduce the concept of *human vulnerability* to describe the prospects of eroding people's capabilities and choices. Looking at vulnerability through

a human development lens, we draw attention to the risk of future deterioration in individual, community and national circumstances and achievements, and we put forward policies and other measures to prepare against threats and make human development progress more robust going forward.

We particularly emphasize systemic and perennial sources of vulnerability. We ask why some people do better than others in overcoming adversity. For example, almost everywhere, women are more vulnerable to personal insecurity than men are. We also ask what structural causes leave some people more vulnerable than others. People experience varying degrees of insecurity and different types of vulnerability at different points along the life cycle. Children, adolescents and older people are inherently vulnerable, so we ask what types of investments and interventions can reduce vulnerability during sensitive transitional periods of the life cycle.

This Report makes the case that the sustained enhancement of individuals' and societies' capabilities is necessary to reduce these persistent vulnerabilities—many of them structural and many of them tied to the life cycle. Progress has to be about fostering resilient human development. There is much debate about the meaning of resilience, but our emphasis is on *human resilience*—ensuring that people's choices are robust, now and in the future, and enabling people to cope and adjust to adverse events (chapter 1).

Institutions, structures and norms can either enhance or diminish human resilience. State policies and community support networks can empower people to overcome threats when and where they may arise, whereas horizontal inequality may diminish the coping capabilities of particular groups.

This Report explores the types of policies and institutional reforms that can build resilience into the fabrics of societies, particularly for excluded groups and at sensitive times during the life cycle. It examines universal measures that can redress discrimination and focuses on the need for collective action to resolve vulnerability that stems from unresponsive national institutions and the shortcomings of global governance.

Why discuss vulnerability now?

Human vulnerability is not new, but it is increasing due to financial instability and mounting environmental pressures such as climate change, which have a growing potential to undermine progress in human development. Indeed, since 2008 there has been a deceleration in the growth of all three components of the Human Development Index in most regions of the world (chapter 2). It is critical to deal with vulnerability now to secure gains and prevent disruptions to continuing progress.

The world is changing rapidly. The scope and scale of connectivity and related insecurities are accelerating, as are the threats of contagion and exposure to natural disasters and violent conflict. National policy space to enhance coping capabilities is becoming more and more constrained as globalization deepens. In an increasingly interconnected world what was once local is often now global as well, due to international trade, travel and telecommunications. Globally integrated supply chains, for instance, have brought efficiency gains. But disruptions at one point of the chain can trigger serious local problems elsewhere. The types of public goods, both national and global, that are needed to build long-term coping capabilities and resilient societies are underprovided. Across the world people feel insecure.

With the lead-up to the post-2015 agenda and the development of a set of sustainable development goals, this is also a time of reflection for the international community and an opportunity for change and new forms of global cooperation. As UN Secretary-General Ban Ki-moon underlined in his July 2013 address to the United Nations General Assembly, the world has "to pay particular attention to the needs and rights of the most vulnerable and excluded."[4] He called for a new vision that can

bring together the full range of human aspirations and ensure "a life of dignity for all". This Report about vulnerability informs the global debate and offers recommendations for how to achieve new goals and build more-resilient societies.

Reducing both poverty and people's vulnerability to falling into poverty must be a central objective of the post-2015 agenda. Eliminating extreme poverty is not just about 'getting to zero'; it is also about staying there. This can be achieved only with a renewed focus on vulnerability and human development. It requires ensuring that those lifted from extreme deprivation benefit from sustained public support that strengthens their social and economic resilience and greatly reduces the systemic sources of their vulnerability.

There is positive news as well. As the Report acknowledges (in chapter 2), average loss of human development due to inequality has declined in most regions in recent years, driven mainly by widespread gains in health. But disparities in income have risen in several regions, and inequality in education has remained broadly constant. Declines in inequality should be celebrated, but offsetting growing income disparities with progress in health is not enough. To tackle vulnerability, particularly among marginalized groups, and sustain recent achievements, reducing inequality in all dimensions of human development is crucial.

Unless more-vulnerable groups and individuals receive specific policy attention and dedicated resources across all dimensions of human development, they are in danger of being left behind, despite continuing human progress in most countries and communities. Without national and global policies and institutions to reduce persistent and systemic vulnerability, the post-2015 development agenda will remain inadequate in addressing the complexity and scale of future challenges.

Who is vulnerable—and why?

Most people everywhere are vulnerable to shocks to some degree—natural disasters, financial crises, armed conflicts—as well as to long-term social, economic and environmental changes. Economic weaknesses are undermining the social contract even in advanced industrialized societies, and no country anywhere will be immune to the long-term effects of climate change.

Yet some people are much more vulnerable than others. And in many cases discriminatory social norms and institutional shortcomings exacerbate this vulnerability, leaving certain groups without the household, community and state support needed to boost their coping capacities. These groups and the institutions and norms that weaken their capabilities and restrict their choices are the main focus of this Report.

Those living in extreme poverty and deprivation are among the most vulnerable. Despite recent progress in poverty reduction, more than 2.2 billion people are either near or living in multidimensional poverty. That means more than 15 percent of the world's people remain vulnerable to multidimensional poverty. At the same time, nearly 80 percent of the global population lack comprehensive social protection.[5] About 12 percent (842 million) suffer from chronic hunger,[6] and nearly half of all workers—more than 1.5 billion—are in informal or precarious employment.[7]

In many cases the poor—along with, for example, women, immigrants, indigenous groups and older people—are structurally vulnerable. Their insecurity has evolved and persisted over long periods to create divisions—in gender, ethnicity, race, job type and social status—that are not easily overcome. People who are structurally vulnerable may be as capable as others but may still face additional barriers to overcoming adverse conditions. For example, people with disabilities often lack easy access to public transportation, government offices and other public spaces such as hospitals, which makes it more difficult to participate in economic, social and political life—or to seek assistance when faced with threats to their physical well-being.

Many face overlapping structural constraints on their ability to cope—for example, people who are poor and from a minority group, or women with disabilities. Three-quarters of the world's poor live in rural areas, where agricultural workers suffer the highest prevalence of poverty. They are caught in intractable cycles of low productivity, seasonal unemployment and low wages and are particularly vulnerable to changing weather patterns. Disenfranchised ethnic and religious minorities are vulnerable to discriminatory practices, have limited access to formal justice systems and suffer from the legacy of past repression and prejudice. And while indigenous peoples make up about 5 percent of the world's population, they account for some 15 percent of the world's poor, with as many as a third of them in extreme rural poverty.[8] Worldwide, more than 46 percent of people ages 60 and older live with a disability, facing severe challenges to full participation in society, further heightened by discriminatory social attitudes.[9]

Climate change poses grave risks to all people and all countries, but again, some are subject to more-grievous losses than others are. Between 2000 and 2012 more than 200 million people, most of them in developing countries, were hit by natural disasters every year, especially by floods and droughts.[10] The 2011 *Human Development Report* showed how continuing failure to slow the pace of global warming could jeopardize poverty eradication, because the world's poorest communities are the most vulnerable to rising temperatures and seas and to other consequences of climate change.[11]

Life cycle vulnerability receives particular attention in this Report. Capabilities accumulate over an individual's lifetime and have to be nurtured and maintained; otherwise they can stagnate and even decline. Life capabilities are affected by investments made in preceding stages of life, and there can be long-term consequences of exposure to short-term shocks. A setback in early childhood, for instance, can have serious ramifications throughout the rest of a person's life, including the chances of holding onto a job, the uncertainties associated with growing older and the transmission of vulnerability to the next generation. This Report notes the cumulative nature of vulnerability and the need for timely and continuous policy interventions. Particular attention is needed at sensitive periods—investments in early childhood education, a focus on employment opportunities for youth and support for older people enhance life capabilities.

Despite recent progress in poverty reduction, more than 2.2 billion people are either near or living in multidimensional poverty

The challenge is not just to keep vulnerable populations from falling back into extreme difficulty and deprivation. It is to create an enabling environment for their continuing human development advancement in the decades to come

The challenge is not just to keep vulnerable populations from falling back into extreme difficulty and deprivation. It is to create an enabling environment for their continuing human development advancement in the decades to come. This calls for understanding poverty and deprivation as multidimensional phenomena requiring universal policies for extending rights and services to all, with special attention to equal opportunities, life cycle capabilities and access for those who are excluded. Such mutually reinforcing interventions can build societal resilience and strengthen human agency. The most successful antipoverty and human development initiatives to date have taken a multidimensional approach, combining income support and job creation with expanded health care and education opportunities and other interventions for community development.

There are policy steps to close the gaps between people and among countries and to build greater resilience and capabilities for those who would otherwise remain persistently vulnerable. Policies that prevent devastation caused by hazards, promote the extension of the benefits of prosperity to all and build broader societal resilience can collectively protect and sustain human progress. Yet none of them falls automatically into place. They are the outcomes of vigorous collective action, equitable and effective institutional responses, and far-sighted leadership—local, national and global. All society ultimately benefits from greater equality of opportunity. And unless these multidimensional and intersecting vulnerabilities are recognized and systematically reduced, continuing progress in human development could be interrupted or even reversed.

Human security and human development

Twenty years ago the *Human Development Report* introduced the notion of human security as an integral aspect of human development. This Report is closely aligned with the human security approach, but with a focus on vulnerability and how it threatens to undermine achievements in human development. In this context, there is an emphasis on the imperatives for reducing disparities and building

social cohesion, particularly through actions that address social violence and discrimination.

Conflict and a sense of personal insecurity have pervasive adverse impacts on human development and leave billions of people living in precarious conditions. Many countries in the bottom tier of the Human Development Index are emerging from long periods of conflict or still confront armed violence. More than 1.5 billion people live in countries affected by conflict—about a fifth of the world's population.[12] And recent political instability has had an enormous human cost: About 45 million people were forcibly displaced due to conflict or persecution by the end of 2012—the highest in 18 years—more than 15 million of them refugees.[13] In some areas of West and Central Africa lawlessness and armed conflict continue to threaten human development advances, with long-term repercussions for national progress. And in a number of countries in Latin America and the Caribbean, despite high human development achievements, many people feel threatened by rising rates of homicide and other violent crimes.

Women everywhere experience vulnerability in personal insecurity. Violence violates their rights, and feelings of personal insecurity restrict their agency in both public and private life. Expanding freedoms and human security, then, is also about supporting measures that bring about changes in institutions and norms that reduce interpersonal violence and discrimination. Improvements in personal security can have a profound impact on actual and perceived vulnerability of individuals and communities and on their sense of security, empowerment and agency.

Higher incomes alone are not enough to reduce vulnerability to conflict and personal insecurity. Persistent vulnerability, which generally can be allayed only over longer periods, requires multiple policy interventions and norm shifts that build tolerance and deepen social cohesion.

Building resilience

People's well-being is influenced greatly by the larger freedoms within which they live and by their ability to respond to and recover from adverse events—natural or human-made. Resilience underpins any approach to securing and sustaining human development. At its core, resilience is about ensuring that state, community and global institutions work to empower and protect people. Human development involves removing the barriers that hold people back in their freedom to act. It is about enabling the disadvantaged and excluded to realize their rights, to express their concerns openly, to be heard and to become active agents in shaping their destiny. It is about having the freedom to live a life that one values and to manage one's affairs adequately. This Report highlights some of the key policies, principles and measures that are needed to build resilience—to reinforce choices, expand human agency and promote social competences. It also indicates that achieving and sustaining human development progress can depend on the effectiveness of preparedness and response when shocks occur.

Committing to universalism

A common commitment—national and global—towards universal provision of social services, strengthening social protection and assuring full employment would constitute a profound societal and political decision that would lay the foundation for building long-term resilience, for countries and for their citizens as individuals. Such a commitment would boost the ability of individuals, societies and countries to resist and recover from setbacks, while recognizing that some are more exposed to risks and threats than others and need additional support.

Universal provision of social services. Universal access to basic social services—education, health care, water supply and sanitation, and public safety—enhances resilience. It is not only desirable—it is also possible at early stages of development. And recent experience—for example, in China, Rwanda and Viet Nam—shows that it can be achieved fairly fast (in less than a decade).

Universal provision of basic social services can raise social competences and reduce structural vulnerability. It can be a powerful force for equalizing opportunities and outcomes. For instance, universal high-quality public

education can mitigate the gaps in education of children from rich and poor households. Intergenerational transmission of capabilities such as education within families can perpetuate the benefits in the long run. Universal policies also promote social solidarity by avoiding the disadvantages of targeting—social stigma for recipients and segmentation in the quality of services, as well as failure to reach many of the vulnerable.[14]

One commonly held misconception is that only wealthy countries can afford social protection or universal basic services. As this Report documents, the evidence is to the contrary. Except for societies undergoing violent strife and turmoil, most societies can—and many have—put in place basic services and social protection. And they have found that an initial investment, of just a small percentage of GDP, brings benefits that far outweigh the initial outlay.

Take South Africa's Child Support Grant, which cost 0.7 percent of GDP in 2008–2009 and reduced the child poverty rate from 43 percent to 34 percent. Or Brazil's Bolsa Família programme, which cost 0.3 percent of GDP in 2008–2009 and accounted for 20–25 percent of the reduction in inequality.[15] Countries enjoying rapid economic progress, such as those in East Asia, have benefited from greater coverage and better health, education and employment investments. And they did so even with limited revenues and resources at their disposal.

The case for universal provision of basic social services rests first and foremost on the premise that all humans should be empowered to live lives they value and that access to certain basic elements of a dignified life ought to be delinked from people's ability to pay. While ways of delivering such services may vary with circumstances and country context, common to all successful experiences is a single idea: The state has the primary responsibility to extend social services to the entire population, in a basic social contract between citizens and state.

Strengthening social protection. Social protection, including unemployment insurance, pension programmes and labour market regulations, can offer coverage against risk and adversity throughout people's lives and especially during sensitive phases. By providing an additional and predictable layer of support, social protection programmes help households avoid selling off assets, taking children out of school or postponing necessary medical care, all detrimental to their long term well-being. Further, the distribution networks and mechanisms for administering social protection programmes can also be used to provide short-term emergency responses and assistance during crises such as natural disasters and droughts.

Many social protections have positive spinoff effects. Unemployment insurance improves the working of labour markets by allowing the unemployed to choose jobs that better match their skills and experience rather than forcing them to simply take the first job that comes along. Income support to households has been shown to encourage labour market participation by providing resources to enable people to search for better opportunities, including allowing members of the household to migrate to find jobs. Some contend such support may reduce the incentive to get back to work. Much depends on the design of the policy. Nevertheless, there is considerable evidence that labour market regulations have a net benefit and are able to reduce inequality.

Social protection is feasible at early stages of development and can even bring about other benefits such as stimulating spending and reducing poverty. Social protection offsets output volatility by reducing fluctuations in disposable income. Strong universal social protection policies not only improve individual resilience, they also bolster the resilience of the economy as a whole.

Assuring full employment. As this Report shows, the social value of employment goes far beyond a salary. Universal access to decent jobs is a key part of building resilience across a society. Work is a means of livelihoods, in strengthening human agency, in providing social connections and in the larger value for providing security for families and communities. Unemployment tends to be associated with an increase in crime, suicide, violence, drug abuse and other social problems that can increase personal insecurity. Jobs foster social stability and social cohesion, and decent jobs strengthen people's abilities to manage shocks and uncertainty. Yet few countries, developed or developing, pursue full employment as an overarching societal or economic goal. Expanding jobs should guide public policy. Labour market policies are needed that help workers regain employment—for example, through temporary employment schemes or by acquiring employable skills. Employment generation programmes can be fully integrated into broader policy objectives, such as building infrastructure and connectivity, using expanded public works programmes, including providing cash for work for the poor and unemployed.

For developing countries faced with the challenges of underemployment, active labour market policies are not enough, considering that most jobs are in the informal economy—more than 40 percent in two-thirds of the 46 emerging and developing countries with available data.[16] Pursuing full employment and reducing employment-related vulnerability in these countries require policies that promote job-creating growth and that extend a social protection framework for all in both the formal and informal sectors.

In some ways a structural transformation of the economy is in order to provide more jobs—using targeted policies that support the development of strategic sectors and activities. This may entail macroeconomic policies that go beyond an exclusive focus on price stability and debt management. Global cooperation can also help ensure that intensifying global competition does not result in a 'race to the bottom' in terms of labour standards, but rather in an agreement to push for full and decent employment for all.

Responsive institutions and cohesive societies

Building human resilience requires responsive institutions. Adequate policies and resources are needed for providing adequate jobs, health care and education opportunities, especially for the poor and vulnerable. In particular, states that recognize and take actions to reduce inequality among groups (so called horizontal inequality) are better able to uphold the principle of universalism, build social cohesion and prevent and recover from crises.

Persistent vulnerability is rooted in historic exclusions—women in patriarchal societies, Black people in South Africa and the United

> For developing countries faced with the challenges of underemployment, active labour market policies are not enough, considering that most jobs are in the informal economy

States, and Dalits in India encounter discrimination and exclusion due to longstanding cultural practices and social norms. Responsive and accountable institutions of governance are critical to overcoming the sense of injustice, vulnerability and exclusion that can fuel social discontent. Civic engagement and collective mobilization, in turn, are also indispensable for ensuring that states recognize the interests and rights of vulnerable people.

States can intervene to reduce horizontal inequality with a mix of policy interventions. Direct interventions such as affirmative action may work to immediately address historic injustices, but its long-term impact is ambiguous. And it cannot always fix the structural drivers behind persistent inequality. Policies are needed that respond in the short term and promote long-term and sustainable access to social services, employment and social protections for vulnerable groups. These may include formal incentives and sanctions such as preventative laws. For example, rights-based laws can lead to considerable improvements for vulnerable groups, who are empowered with legal recourse and public scrutiny when institutions fail them.

Changing norms to build tolerance and deepen social cohesion is also a necessary and often overlooked aspect of building resilient societies. More-cohesive societies are better at protecting people from adversity and may be more accepting of policies based on the principle of universalism. Lack of social cohesion is correlated with conflict and violence, especially in situations of unequal access to resources or benefits from natural wealth, and with the inability to deal effectively with rapid social or economic change or the impact of economic or climate-related shocks. Indeed, pursuing the broad goals of equity, inclusion and justice reinforces social institutions and in turn deepens social cohesion.

Campaigns and messages that seek to alter people's perceptions are indispensable in ensuring social change. Laws, policies and educational and normative measures are most meaningful when people are engaged and have mechanisms to hold institutions accountable. In this sense, state responsiveness requires openness, transparency and accountability to the poor and excluded, as well as the promotion of a positive dynamic between governance institutions and civic participation.

Crisis prevention and response

Natural and human-made disasters are inevitable, but efforts can be made to mitigate their effects and to accelerate recovery. Opportunities can be taken to 'build back better'. Indeed, the 2004 tsunami led directly to the Indian Ocean Tsunami Warning System. But for disaster preparedness and response frameworks to enhance resilience, they need to be designed from a systems approach that extends beyond immediate threats and shocks to address underlying causes and longer term impacts.

In the case of natural disasters, prevention and response frameworks can include, as laid out in the Hyogo Framework for Action, improving risk information, strengthening and establishing early warning systems, integrating disaster risk reduction into development planning and policies, and strengthening institutions and mechanisms for response. Planning for preparedness and recovery can be pursued at all levels—global, regional, national and community—and can be enhanced by information sharing and solidarity in action. This is easier when governments and communities are prepared. When policies are oriented towards emergency response, mitigation can be overlooked, and shocks can re-emerge with potentially larger impacts and greater subsequent costs of protection. Emergency response efforts are important and necessary, but resilience requires comprehensive efforts to build preparedness and response capacities.

Intrastate conflict as well as internal civil unrest continues to impose enormous costs on development in affected countries. A combination of causes can be identified for these types of conflict. However, one common characteristic is that these causes, from exclusionary policies and elite rent-seeking to unaddressed social grievances, all contribute to social discord or, at the very least, impeding the minimum of social harmony and cohesion that would be conducive to resilient development outcomes, something discussed more extensively in chapters 3 and 4. In communities and countries vulnerable to conflict and violence, programmes that enhance social cohesion can underpin prevention and recovery efforts.

Policies and institutions that fight exclusion and marginalization, create a sense of belonging, promote trust and offer the opportunity of upward mobility can reduce the potential for conflict. Increasing public awareness and access to information can generate public support for peace and less contentious politics. Involving credible and objective intermediaries and mediators can build trust and confidence among conflicted and polarized groups and consensus on issues of national import, ranging from the conduct of elections to the elements of a new constitution. Local committees and citizen groups can build trust at the community level and lay the foundation for 'infrastructures for peace'. Investing in jobs and livelihoods can help communities and individuals recover from crises in the short term and increase resilience to the challenges of future crises.

Global action for the 'world we want'

Globalization has brought countries together and provided new opportunities. But it has also increased the risk that adverse events will be transmitted more rapidly. Recent events have exposed huge gaps in how globalization is managed on issues ranging from food security to energy access, from financial regulation to climate change. These cross-border challenges are likely to continue in coming decades, with global governance architectures short on capacity to prevent or minimize shocks. Policymakers and leaders may find themselves unprepared for the sheer speed and scale of these changes.

New and emerging threats call for national, global and cross-border responses, resources and leadership. Collective action is needed that can prioritize issues, extend cooperation across silos organized around particular problems, and bring together states, international organizations, civil society and the private sector in common support of building more-resilient global systems. In particular, collective action is needed, in the form of a global commitment to universalism, to better facilitate the provision of global public goods and to reduce the likelihood and scope of transnational shocks

> Collective action is needed, in the form of a global commitment to universalism, to better facilitate the provision of global public goods

by fixing shortcomings in global governance architectures.

Global commitment to universalism

National measures—for the universal provision of social services, for universal social protection and for full employment—are more easily enacted when global commitments are in place and global support is available. Such a commitment should be part of the post-2015 agenda. Including elements of a global social contract in the agenda could open up policy space at the national level for states to determine the approaches for building employment and providing social services and protections that work best in their particular contexts, but global agreements are essential because they can instigate action and commitment and generate financial and other support.

Policy norms that depict public provision of social protections as positive instruments can enable states to adopt and implement policies and programmes that protect people inside their territories. A set of norms that emphasize universalism could embolden states to make a commitment to universal protections for labour that reduce the likelihood of exploitative work conditions while encouraging minimum social protections for workers as well as for those who are unable to work.

Today, only 20 percent of people worldwide have adequate social security coverage, and over 50 percent lack any type of social security.[17] The sustainable development goals present an opportunity for the international community and individual states to advance a positive view of the public domain and push forward the principle of universalism—in public provision of social services, including at a minimum universal access to health care and education, and for full employment and social protections. These are all essential elements of more-sustainable and -resilient human development.

Better facilitation of the provision of global public goods

Many global public goods have social value and can reduce vulnerability but are undervalued by markets. Their underprovision, ranging from communicable disease control to adequate global market regulation, fosters shocks that have regional and global reach. As the world's interdependence expands and deepens, the manifestation of vulnerability from the underprovision of global public goods grows.

Multilateral efforts to facilitate cooperation and provide some of these goods seem weak in the face of the challenges and vulnerabilities. And they are weak in the face of the momentum of markets, the pace of commodification and the power of private interests. International rules and norms often reflect private interests rather than providing public goods and prioritizing social interests.[18] Global public goods and universal social goods that would correct or complement markets for more-inclusive and -sustainable growth remain, in large part, underprovided.

Minimum levels of social protection and commitments to the provision of social services are important public goods that can be included in the sustainable development goals to enhance the capabilities people have to cope with adverse shocks. But there are also public goods that are needed to reduce the likelihood of crises, such as fostering climate stability or reducing the likelihood of yet another financial crisis. Progress has been made in the past—for example, the eradication of smallpox. The task now is to extend this kind of collective effort to the provision of other types of vulnerability-reducing public goods.

Fixing shortcomings in global governance architectures

There is a mismatch between governance mechanisms and the vulnerability and complexity of global processes. Many international institutions and structures were designed for a post–Second World War order, and reforms have not reflected changing power relations. Meanwhile, new regimes, such as those for global intellectual property rights, often benefit elites disproportionately. Governance systems are not only short on offering protections and enhancing capabilities; in some cases they are producing new vulnerabilities. In many respects the shortcomings of global governance architectures in reducing vulnerability stem from deep asymmetries of power, voice and influence. Agendas and policies underrepresent the interests and needs of the least developed countries and the people most vulnerable—for example, unskilled workers, immigrants and older people. Those with the least capacity to cope with shocks and adjust to the speed of change are the least involved in creating the regulations, norms and goals of global governance.

The list of global challenges is long, and at times responses may seem out of reach, but we know that markets can be better regulated, financial and trade systems adjusted, and environmental threats reduced. Certain adjustments can be made across global issue areas to increase the likelihood that states will act collectively and to ensure cohesiveness in global governance. These are first-order changes that make policy and institutional progress more likely on specific problems.

First, is the imperative to ensure equitable participation of developing countries in global governance so that the needs of more-vulnerable countries, including in particular the least developed countries and small island developing states, are not marginalized. Second, participation can be extended to include perspectives from the private sector and civil society to ensure support for global collective action among states. Third, collective action is most effective if it is inclusive, with decisions being made in representative institutions, not in ad hoc groupings of countries like the Group of 20 or in selective meetings where decisionmaking lacks transparency. Finally, greater coordination and cooperation among global governance institutions in different issue areas can reduce spillovers and better align goals.

This Report emphasizes the potential of collective action to restructure global systems in a way that instils new capabilities in people rather than generating new vulnerabilities and adding to existing insecurity. Widespread cooperation among states, international institutions, the private sector and civil society is possible. Global governance systems have to break the link between globalization and vulnerability—and this is more likely to occur when global policies and decisionmaking are inclusive, accountable and coordinated.

Key messages

This Report seeks to improve understanding and raise awareness about how reducing

Governance systems are not only short on offering protections and enhancing capabilities; in some cases they are producing new vulnerabilities

The intersecting or overlapping vulnerabilities arising from economic, environmental, physical, health and other insecurities magnify the adverse impact on freedoms and functions

vulnerability and building resilience are essential for sustainable human development. In doing so, it makes the following central points:

- *Vulnerability threatens human development—and unless it is systematically addressed, by changing policies and social norms, progress will be neither equitable nor sustainable.*

  While almost all countries have improved their levels of human development over the past few decades, recent gains have not been smooth. Progress has taken place in a context of growing uncertainty due to deeper and more-frequent shocks. From greater financial instability to high and volatile commodity prices, from recurrent natural disasters to widespread social and political discontent, human development achievements are more exposed to adverse events.

  Hundreds of millions of poor, marginalized or otherwise disadvantaged people remain unusually vulnerable to economic shocks, rights violations, natural disasters, disease, conflict and environmental hazards. If not systematically identified and reduced, these chronic vulnerabilities could jeopardize the sustainability of human development progress for decades to come. Shocks from multiple causes are inevitable and often unpredictable, but human vulnerability can be reduced with more-responsive states, better public policies and changes in social norms.

- *Life cycle vulnerability, structural vulnerability and insecure lives are fundamental sources of persistent deprivation—and must be addressed for human development to be secured and for progress to be sustained.*

  Different aspects of vulnerability can overlap and reinforce persistent deprivations. Life cycle vulnerability—from infancy through youth, adulthood and old age—can affect the formation of life capabilities. Inadequate investments in sensitive phases of life create long-term vulnerability. Similarly, vulnerability embedded in social contexts generates discriminatory behaviours and creates structural barriers for people and groups to exercise their rights and choices, perpetuating their deprivations. And fear for physical security in daily life has deeper ramifications for securing or sustaining progress.

The intersecting or overlapping vulnerabilities arising from economic, environmental, physical, health and other insecurities magnify the adverse impact on freedoms and functions. This makes it much more difficult for individuals and societies to recover from shocks. Recovery pathways and public policies must incorporate measures that build resilience and stabilizers to respond to and cope with future challenges.

- *Policy responses to vulnerability should prevent threats, promote capabilities and protect people, especially the most vulnerable.*

  Most vulnerabilities remain persistent—a consequence of social marginalization, insufficient public services and other policy failures. Persistent vulnerability reflects deep deficiencies in public policies and institutions, societal norms and the provision of public services, including past and present discrimination against groups based on ethnicity, religion, gender and other identities. It also reveals state and societal inability or unwillingness to anticipate and protect vulnerable people against severe external shocks, many of them predictable in kind, if not in precise timing or impact.

  Building resilience thus requires boosting the capacity of individuals, societies and countries to respond to setbacks. People with insufficient core capabilities, as in education and health, are less able to exercise their agency to live lives they value. Further, their choices may be restricted or held back by social barriers and other exclusionary practices, which can further embed social prejudice in public institutions and policies. Responsive institutions and effective policy interventions can create a sustainable dynamic to bolster individual capabilities and social conditions that strengthen human agency—making individuals and societies more resilient.

- *Everyone should have the right to education, health care and other basic services. Putting this principle of universalism into practice will require dedicated attention and resources, particularly for the poor and other vulnerable groups.*

  Universalism should guide all aspects of national policies—to ensure that all groups

The Post-2015 Agenda: Addressing vulnerabilities and building resilience

Two years from the 2015 deadline, Africa's progress on the Millennium Development Goals remains uneven. Remarkable advances have been made in some areas, such as net primary school enrollment, gender parity in primary education, the representation of women in decision-making, some reduction in poverty, immunization coverage, and stemming the spread of HIV/AIDS.

Notwithstanding this progress, there is ample room for more good news. Some areas have been neglected when they should have been put upfront, for example malaria, the number one killer of children in sub-Saharan Africa and many other places in the world. Additionally, the goal for school enrollment did not take into account the need for quality education.

Over the past decade, Africa has made great strides in instituting political and economic reforms that are starting to bear fruits. These future successes are, however, vulnerable to many factors that are not within Africa's control but can be redressed through collective engagement and a new international development partnership. Although some parts of the continent still grapple with political instability, this is now a rarity, no longer the rule. The new global development agenda that will be agreed upon in 2015 presents an opportunity for Africa to take stock of these challenges and our position in the world.

Economic transformation is a particular priority on my continent. It will help us to reduce our vulnerability to social, economic and environmental shocks, but it is not a priority for Africa alone. The recent economic meltdown that plunged the world into recession, the widening gap between rich and poor with its attending inequalities that fuel social unrest, and the rising scourge of youth unemployment, as well as global environmental threats created by negative economic policies, clearly show that transformation is needed everywhere, not just in Africa.

When the UN High-Level Panel on Post-2015 met in Liberia in January 2013, under the general theme of "economic transformation," we identified six key areas which we believed must form part of a transformative agenda: the pursuit of inclusive growth that reduces inequalities; the promotion of economic diversification and value addition; the creation of a stable, enabling environment for the private sector and free enterprise to flourish; the necessity to change our production and consumption patterns to protect our ecosystems; the creation and strengthening of fair and transparent institutions; and, finally, the necessity to create equal opportunities for all.

There are opportunities today that can make the transformation not only plausible but very affordable. We live in an era where rapid technological change, especially empowered by the information revolution, is deepening the integration of the world economy, changing the structure of jobs, offering new economic opportunities for all countries, facilitating green growth and enabling many low-income countries to leapfrog through economic transformation.

We have the means and capacities to effect changes. The current global consultations on a Post-2015 Development Agenda bode well for a world with a common vision, with opportunities and shared responsibilities. Africa will contribute to develop a world where no one is left behind, where all have equal opportunity to prosper, and a world where we show respect for our environment.

and sections in society have equality of opportunity. This entails differential and targeted treatment for unequal or historically disadvantaged sections by providing greater proportional resources and services to the poor, the excluded and the marginalized to enhance everyone's capabilities and life choices.

Universalism is a powerful way of directly addressing the uncertain nature of vulnerability. If social policies have a universal aim, not only do they protect those who currently experience poverty, poor health or a bout of unemployment, but they also protect individuals and households who are doing well but may find themselves struggling if things go wrong. Further, they secure certain basic core capabilities of future generations.

- *Strong universal social protection not only improves individual resilience—it can also bolster the resilience of the economy as a whole.*

Nearly all countries at any stage of development can provide a basic floor of social protection. They can progressively expand to higher levels of social protection as fiscal space allows. A lower income country might start with basic education and health care and later expand to offer cash transfers or basic labour protection. A higher income country with already well established basic education, health care and conditional cash transfer programmes might expand eligibility for unemployment insurance to traditionally excluded populations, such as agricultural or domestic workers, or expand family leave policies for new parents to include fathers.

- *Full employment should be a policy goal for societies at all levels of development.*

When employment is either unattainable or with very low rewards, it is a major source of vulnerability with lasting repercussions for individuals and for their families and communities. It is time to recognize that the opportunity to have a decent job is a fundamental aspect of building human capabilities—and, equally, to see full employment

Providing meaningful employment opportunities to all adult job-seekers should be embraced as a universal goal, just as education or health care

as smart, effective social policy. Providing meaningful employment opportunities to all adult job-seekers should be embraced as a universal goal, just as education or health care. Full employment should be an agreed societal goal, not simply as a matter of social justice and economic productivity, but as an essential element of social cohesion and basic human dignity.

Decent work that pays reasonable wages, involves formal contracts preventing abrupt dismissals and provides entitlements to social security can enormously reduce employee vulnerability, although less so in recessions. Reducing employment vulnerability is then hugely important from the perspective of reducing human vulnerability in general. Yet this is clearly difficult to do. The importance of realizing decent and full employment has long been recognized, but large-scale unemployment and underemployment continue in most countries.

- *The effects of crises, when they occur, can be lessened through preparedness and recovery efforts that can also leave societies more resilient.*

Sudden onset of hazards and crises, from natural disasters to violent conflicts, often occur with destructive consequences for human development progress. Building capacities in preparedness and recovery can enable communities to withstand these shocks with less loss of life and resources and can support faster recoveries. Efforts to build social cohesion in conflict areas can lead to long-term reductions in the risk of conflict, while early warning systems and responsive institutions lessen the impacts of natural disasters.

- *Vulnerabilities are increasingly global in their origin and impact, requiring collective action and better international governance.*

Pollution, natural disasters, conflicts, climate change and economic crises do not respect political boundaries and cannot be managed by national governments alone. Today's fragmented global institutions are neither accountable enough nor fast enough to address pressing global challenges. Better coordination and perhaps better institutions are needed to limit transnational shocks and urgently respond to our changing climate as an integral part of the post-2015 agenda. Stronger, responsive and more-representative global governance is essential for more-effective global action. Much can be done to improve global and national responses to crises, to prevent such crises from occurring and to reduce their magnitude.

- *A global effort is needed to ensure that globalization advances and protects human development—national measures are more easily enacted when global commitments are in place and global support is available.*

An international consensus on universal social protection would open national policy space for better services for all people, reducing the risk of a global 'race to the bottom'. Elements of a global social contract would recognize the rights of all people to education, health care, decent jobs and a voice in their own future. The global agenda must seek to address vulnerability and strengthen resilience comprehensively. Whether they are pursued in defining new sustainable development goals or in the broader post-2015 discussions, a formal international commitment would help ensure universal action.

"Human rights are violated not only by terrorism, repression or assassination, but also by unfair economic structures that create huge inequalities."

Pope Francis I

1.

Vulnerability and human development

"Human development is a process of enlarging people's choices. The most critical ones are to lead a long and healthy life, to be educated and to enjoy a decent standard of living." —*Human Development Report 1990*[1]

"Vulnerability is not the same as poverty. It means not lack or want but defencelessness, insecurity and exposure to risks, shocks and stress." —Robert Chambers[2]

On Sunday, 26 December 2004, an earthquake off Sumatra triggered one of the worst disasters in recorded history. Some 230,000 people in 14 countries died, with incalculable damage to livelihoods and communities. Almost a decade later many people continue to struggle to regain their lives.

Adverse shocks can come from many directions. Environmental changes can lead to natural disasters such as floods and droughts. Economic shocks can lead to lost jobs through recession or worsening terms of trade. Health shocks can lead to reduced incomes—as well as rising medical expenses—for households. Wars and civil conflict can have pervasive negative impacts on human development.

One way to reduce vulnerability is to prevent disasters. The way the world tackles climate change or organizes global financial systems can be critically important for reducing the frequency and magnitude of shocks. When prevention is not possible, the effects can be mitigated by building preparedness and response capabilities. Natural disasters cannot be prevented, but environmental systems and seismic activity can be monitored, and early warning systems can save lives. When the Eyjafjallajökull volcano erupted in Iceland in 2010, there was no loss of life: Ongoing monitoring of seismic activity provided advance warning, rescue services and emergency plans were put into effect to evacuate the local population overnight and the airspace in some 20 countries was closed. And when cyclone Phailin struck India in October 2013, the death toll was less than 50, thanks to global storm tracking systems and the advance evacuation of a million people; by contrast, there were 10,000 deaths the last time a similar super cyclone struck the area in 1999.[3]

Vulnerability can also be reduced by building resilience among both people and communities. Some resilience building is threat-specific, such as changing land use laws to prevent people from living in flood-prone areas. Other resilience building is more systemic and longer term, endowing people and societies with the skills to weather and recover from many different shocks. Social cohesion can profoundly affect many aspects of life, from disaster recovery to the quality of government. Education and investment, especially for the very young, can equip people to adapt when a financial crisis or natural disaster takes away their livelihood. And social protection and responsive institutions can ensure that those who need help receive it fairly, thus lessening the adverse impacts that might flow on to future generations.

Human vulnerability is about the prospect of eroding human development achievements and their sustainability. A person (or community or country) is vulnerable when there is a high risk of future deterioration in circumstances and achievements. Of course, we all live in an uncertain world, and it may never be possible to reduce such risks to zero. Everyone, rich or poor, is vulnerable to some extent. But this Report focuses on the possibility of *major* deterioration in conditions, which may take people down to unacceptably bad conditions—poverty and destitution—or worsen the conditions of those already suffering low human development.

How far shocks translate into reduced human development depends on people's ability to cope with shocks as well as on the assistance that they may receive. People's ability to cope and adjust is referred to here as *human resilience* (box 1.1). Most people are resilient to some degree—they can adjust to minor shocks, for example. But how far they can adjust to large or persistent shocks without a major sacrifice and

BOX 1.1

Towards human resilience: concepts and definitions

Resilience is used in different ways by different disciplines. In ecology and the natural sciences resilience was traditionally understood as a property that allows a system to recover its prior state after suffering a shock.[1] The term has now come to be seen, not without some controversy, in more dynamic terms. The Intergovernmental Panel on Climate Change defines resilience as the "ability of a system and its component parts to anticipate, absorb, accommodate, or recover from the effects of a hazardous event in a timely and efficient manner."[2] A related concept, *social resilience,* is defined as the capacity of individuals or groups to secure favourable outcomes under new circumstances and, if need be, by new means.[3]

Given its origin in the study of natural systems and engineering, resilience, as traditionally defined, does not adequately address empowerment and human agency or the power-related connotations of vulnerability.[4] A group or community may be resilient at the expense of another group.[5] Assessments of the resilience of systems must take into account possible tradeoffs and asymmetries among different groups and individuals within the system.

A human development approach to resilience focuses on people and their interactions, where power and social position are important factors. Resilience is to be built at the level of both individuals and society—in terms of their individual capabilities and social competences.

Resilience also encourages a better understanding of systems, the interaction of components and the feedback loops involved. It is important to consider the architecture and internal logic of systems, especially since some systems may themselves be sources of vulnerability.[6] It can be also be useful to understand what happens when different system components interact and how their interaction can lead to unintended or unpredictable consequences.[7] For example, a study of climate-related disasters would do well to include rural-urban and migration dynamics.

While most people are vulnerable to some extent, this Report focuses on those who are particularly vulnerable to severe deterioration in well-being and human development. How far shocks translate into reduced human development depends on people's ability to adjust and cope with shocks, and this ability of people to cope and adjust may be termed *human resilience.*

Vulnerability can be reduced by preventing shocks or by building resilience at the individual and community levels. Due to the constructs of society, some people face restricted choices and capabilities. Human resilience is about removing the barriers that hold people back in their freedom to act. It is also about enabling the disadvantaged and excluded groups to express their concerns, to be heard and to be active agents in shaping their destinies.

Notes

1. Holling 1973; Miller and others 2010. 2. IPCC 2012, p. 2. 3. Hall and Lamont 2013. 4. Cannon and Muller-Mahn 2010. 5. Households and communities may sometimes strengthen their resilience only at the expense of their own well-being or self-esteem; see Béné and others (2012). 6. Stiglitz and Kaldor 2013a. 7. Gallopín 2006.

loss of human development varies according to their circumstances. The required adjustment depends on the nature of the shock and the circumstances of those affected. Those who are better placed and find it easier to adjust are more resilient.

This Report develops two basic propositions. One is that people's vulnerability is influenced considerably by their capabilities and social context. The other is that failures to protect people against vulnerability are mostly a consequence of inadequate policies and poor or dysfunctional social institutions. And while almost anyone can be vulnerable to some event or shock, this Report focuses on those particularly vulnerable to changes in personal circumstances and external shocks, especially from persistent or systematic threats to human development, such as climate change, violence and societal barriers that prevent people from exercising their full ability to act.

Two central theses of this Report are that sustainably enhancing and protecting individual choices and capabilities and societal competences are essential and that human development strategies and policies must consciously aim to reduce vulnerability and build resilience. A better understanding of vulnerability and resilience from a multidimensional human development perspective allows for a deeper analysis of the key factors and policies that explain why some individuals, communities or countries are more resilient to adverse events and respond better to them.

In this vein, this Report seeks to answer some critical questions:

- Who are the most vulnerable? Which groups are inherently or structurally vulnerable?
- How can vulnerability be reduced and human resilience increased?
- Are there architectural or systemic issues to address, particularly at the global level, so that human development progress can be more secure?

A human development perspective

This Report takes a human development perspective to vulnerability and goes beyond a narrow interpretation of vulnerability as exposure to risk. This viewpoint underlines the role of people's capabilities in minimizing adverse consequences from shocks and persistent threats. It also unearths important factors underlying vulnerability, such as exclusion and discrimination that would not be evident from a risk-based approach alone. The structural causes underlying vulnerability are key to understanding why some groups and people are systematically worse off when disaster strikes or even in leading secure lives, free from violent threats.

A risk-based approach would recommend policies such as insurance to manage risk. While these policies are important, a human development approach points to a broader canvas of policies that build the strength of individuals and societies—and suggests fundamental principles that can be followed and built into specific polices for reducing vulnerability and building resilience.

People with higher human development, notably with good health and education, are more resilient than those who are malnourished, without education and thus in a weaker position to change their activity or location in reaction to adverse shocks. Owning assets enables people to protect their core capabilities by using these assets when circumstances deteriorate. But the social context and power relations have a large bearing on people's vulnerability. Minorities or people with disabilities, for instance, even those healthy and educated, may feel vulnerable if they cannot express their concerns openly, if the political system does not take their voices seriously or if institutions do not serve them well. Similarly, the nature of the risks—especially when persistent or systemic—matter in shaping specific vulnerabilities. Rising sea levels, for example, present a long-term risk to coastal communities.

To protect well-being or minimize losses when circumstances change, people or households may make a range of adjustments, including changing their location, activity or spending, using their assets or borrowing. The set of choices available depends on a person's capabilities, position in society and age as well as several other factors. Some groups, such as the poor and the near poor, may not have much savings or many assets to fall back on. When adversity strikes, they have to resort to harmful coping strategies such as cutting back on food

or reducing spending on health or children's education.[4]

Human resilience means that people can exercise their choices safely and freely—including being confident that the opportunities they have today will not be lost tomorrow. While being less vulnerable often goes hand in hand with being more resilient, resilience is more than just a mirror of vulnerability. It may be possible to reduce vulnerability by lowering the incidence of shocks and threats. But society's resilience may remain unaffected unless other measures are also applied. Active policies to build community, to remove barriers to individual expression and to strengthen norms to help others in need all might be needed to build resilience. A useful way to view this relationship is as going 'from vulnerability to resilience'.

People's vulnerability to particular shocks depends not only on their own resilience but also on others' treatment of those who suffer from adverse events. Institutions that can provide support to those in adversity include a range of social and government institutions that may be local, national or international. Social institutions are those in which people act collectively; they exclude profit-making market institutions and the state.[5] Important social institutions include family networks (including global family networks), community organizations and nongovernmental organizations. The strength of support from social institutions depends on prevalent norms—for instance, how far providing aid during adversity is regarded as a social obligation—and on their social competences or ability to provide support.[6]

A human development approach is incomplete unless it incorporates vulnerability and resilience in the analysis. Sustained progress in human development is a matter of expanding people's choices and keeping those choices secure. The world has experienced progress in human development for some time. But increasingly this progress seems threatened by uncertainty and by persistent inequality and climate change. Understanding vulnerability and resilience in their fuller sense becomes necessary to define the policies and actions that can sustain progress.

This was recognized in the 1994 *Human Development Report (HDR)* on human security.

A human development approach is incomplete unless it incorporates vulnerability and resilience in the analysis

Human security was defined then as having two main aspects: "It means safety from the constant threats of hunger, disease, crime and repression. It also means protection from sudden and hurtful disruptions in the patterns of our daily lives—whether in our homes, in our jobs, in our communities or in our environment."[7]

In the 1994 *HDR* and in the later Ogata and Sen Commission on Human Security, doing well in human security is interpreted as implying both that a good level of human development has been achieved and that people are relatively secure against hazards arising from the economy, ill health, violence and environmental deterioration.[8] This year's Report, while closely aligned with the human security approach, puts the major focus on vulnerability—on the threats to achievement in human development and the ways to reduce them. This is a more direct way of handling such a complex issue, especially since the human security approach has been interpreted in a variety of ways since 1994. Some have confined human security to security from physical assault for individuals,[9] while others have used the term to embrace almost any aspect of development.[10] The approach to vulnerability here is broader than the first interpretation but not as wide-ranging as the second. It encompasses vulnerability to any type of adverse event that could threaten people's capabilities and choices.

A major motivation for this focus is the view that despite progress on human development in many countries and in many respects (chapter 2), vulnerability for many people is high and perhaps rising. There has been an increase in natural hazards associated with climate change and in economic fluctuations associated with globalization and the recession of the late 2000s. Employment insecurity in particular seems to have been rising in both rich and poor countries,[11] while threats from global health pandemics remain high. In some parts of the world—especially in the Middle East and parts of Africa—political violence is a major threat, while terrorist incidents have led to a global nervousness. Finding policies that will reduce such threats, increase human resilience and protect people when they confront hazards is an urgent priority from a human development perspective.

The concepts of vulnerability and resilience add much to the human development approach by looking not just at achievements but also at risk and uncertainty. Through them, we can explore the potential downsides of any given level of human development and design policies to protect it and make progress more resilient. Through a different lens, they emphasize sustainable and secure human development. When individuals face vulnerability and when their lives are persistently restricted in the wake of a shock, their capabilities may be harmed over the long term. And these worsened conditions, particularly for children and women, can have intergenerational consequences.

Vulnerable people, vulnerable world

Vulnerability, as a concept, can seem overly broad and abstract. After all, most people and most societies at different levels of development are vulnerable in many ways to adverse events and circumstances, not all of which can be anticipated or prevented. Economic weaknesses undermine the social contract even in advanced industrialized societies today, and no country or community anywhere is immune to the long-term effects of climate change. But vulnerability as a concept can become less abstract when broken down into who is vulnerable, what are they vulnerable to and why (figure 1.1).

Who is vulnerable?

In principle, everyone is vulnerable to some adverse event or circumstance, but some people are more vulnerable than others. One way of identifying groups who are vulnerable to adverse shocks or events is to think of thresholds; this also allows for some degree of measurement. People are vulnerable to poverty if they are "below or at risk of falling below a certain minimally acceptable threshold of critical choices across several dimensions, such as health, education, material resources, security."[12] These thresholds are likely to vary according to the level of development.

Poverty and vulnerability are linked, multidimensional and, at times, mutually

FIGURE 1.1

Who is vulnerable to what and why?

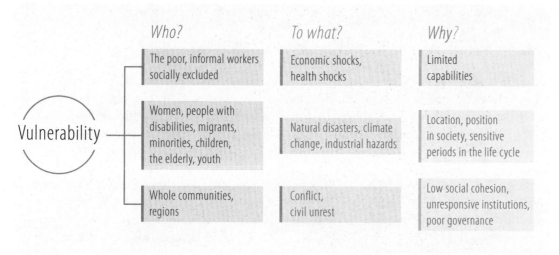

Source: Human Development Report Office.

reinforcing. But they are not synonymous. While vulnerability is generally an important aspect of being poor, being rich is not the same as not being vulnerable. Both poverty and vulnerability are dynamic. The rich may not be vulnerable all the time or throughout their lives just as some of the poor may not remain poor all the time.

But the poor are inherently vulnerable because they lack sufficient core capabilities to exercise their full agency. They suffer from many deprivations. They not only lack adequate material assets, they tend to have poor education and health and to suffer deficiencies in other areas. Equally, their access to justice systems may be constrained.[13] They tend to be intrinsically vulnerable.

The poor already fall below the critical poverty threshold. If people are vulnerable when they face a high risk of falling below the threshold, the poor—already below it—are all vulnerable. This is true by definition, but it is more than a question of definition alone. Anyone lacking the essentials for a minimally acceptable life is truly vulnerable.

More than 2.2 billion people are vulnerable to multidimensional poverty, including almost 1.5 billion who are multidimensionally poor.[14] Three-quarters of the world's poor live in rural areas, where agricultural workers suffer the highest incidence of poverty, caught in a cauldron of low productivity, seasonal unemployment and low wages.[15] Globally, 1.2 billion people (22 percent) live on less than $1.25 a day. Increasing the income poverty line to $2.50 a day raises the global income poverty rate to about 50 percent, or 2.7 billion people.[16] Moving the poverty line in this way draws in a large number of people who are potentially vulnerable to poverty and reduced circumstances. In South Asia 44.4 percent of the population, around 730 million people, live on $1.25–$2.50 a day.[17] Many who recently joined the middle class could easily fall back into poverty with a sudden change in circumstances.

Worldwide the proportion of the income poor and the multidimensionally poor has been declining, but this does not necessarily mean that their vulnerability has been reduced (chapter 3). Sizeable portions of the population are close to the poverty threshold (the "near poor"), and such a clustering implies that idiosyncratic or generalized shocks could easily push a large number of people back into poverty.

But vulnerability extends further. Ill health, job losses, limited access to material resources, economic downturns and unstable climate all add to people's vulnerability and economic insecurity, especially when risk mitigation arrangements are not well established and social protection measures and health systems are not sufficiently robust or comprehensive.

According to the International Labour Organization (ILO), only a third of countries worldwide—with about 28 percent of the global population—provide comprehensive social protection for their citizens.[18]

With limited social protection, financial crises can quickly lead to profound social crises. Indonesia's poverty rate shot up from 11 percent to 37 percent during the Asian financial crisis in the late 1990s.[19] Similarly, the 2007–2008 world financial crisis led to a sharp jump in the number of working poor. The ILO estimates that there were 50 million more working poor in 2011. Only 24 million of them climbed above the $1.25 income poverty line over 2007–2011, compared with 134 million between 2000 and 2007.[20]

Work is one of people's main sources of security. Jobs provide and sustain livelihoods, but even more important to reducing vulnerability is access to decent jobs, with the requisite social protections. Several forces have come together to make finding decent jobs more difficult in the current environment. One is globalization, which has put pressure on social compacts, reducing some of the built-in national 'shock absorbers'.[21] Added to this is the strong belief in self-correcting markets, particularly flexible labour markets, and in macroeconomic policies that focus more on price stability than on full employment. When crises hit, rising unemployment and limited or even absent social protections heighten economic insecurity and vulnerability.

Enhancing capabilities—in health, education and the command over resources—addresses vulnerability by empowering people to overcome threats when and where they arise. But a higher level of capabilities alone may not be enough—women may feel insecure regardless of their education. Nor do people function alone—how individuals relate to each other or in groups can determine how they protect people during crises. Whether restrictive norms and values hold back certain groups (such as women and minorities) or a lack of cohesion in society constrains collective action, both influence how people and communities respond to risk and threats.

There is an intrinsic issue of equity here as well—risks are generally greater for the poor than for the rich. Poor people and poor countries are particularly subject to vulnerability. They face larger shocks, they are less adaptable and they receive less compensation (or none) when crises occur.

Vulnerability to what?

What risks do people and societies face, and what has changed in recent years to make people feel more vulnerable (box 1.2)? Analysts argue that some risks appear to be intensifying, especially those connected to the environment and climate change and to the growing connectivity among countries, which challenges the remit of national policy.[22] With global warming, vulnerability becomes more acute as a result of climate instability, reflected in changing weather patterns and the greater frequency and intensity of natural disasters. As the 2011 *HDR* highlights, these growing threats most affect poor people and poor communities: 98 percent of those killed and affected by natural disasters are from developing countries.[23] By 2025 more than half the people in developing countries may be vulnerable to floods and storms.[24] Moreover, the threats of environmental changes are becoming chronic—as with decades of drought in the Sahel.[25] And environmental systems are becoming less resilient, as with the reduced regenerative value of forest fires in the United States.

Growing vulnerability and threats cut across borders.[26] Natural, financial and other shocks in one country can have global reach, jeopardizing development progress in communities and countries around the world. International financial instability, regional pandemics, climate-related disasters, armed conflicts and failures to enforce international norms and standards frequently have a direct bearing on individual capabilities and social competences across the world.

Transborder vulnerabilities are not new. Communities and individuals, organizations and firms have always been threatened by disruptive external events such as natural and human-made disasters, economic booms and busts, and communicable diseases. But most would agree that the connectivity networks that link disparate communities have never been greater than they are today. The result is

With limited social protection, financial crises can quickly lead to profound social crises

BOX 1.2

Shocks and threats to human development

The threats to human development come from many different directions.[1]

Economic risks

Millions of households live uncertain and insecure lives, facing a constant threat of shocks to their income and well-being. Lacking private savings, financial assets and sufficient protection through national policy, these households are exposed to financial crises and natural disasters. Economic insecurity can be high in developing countries, where a large proportion of employment is in the informal economy, lacking coverage from social insurance. The informal sector accounts for 25–40 percent of annual output in developing countries in Africa and Asia.[2] But economic vulnerability is not a problem in developing countries only. Due to the slow recovery from the global economic crisis, many people in rich countries continue to face tremendous insecurity. In 2014 unemployment is expected to be more than 11 percent in France, around 12.5 percent in Italy and close to 28 percent in Greece and Spain, with even higher rates among young people—almost 60 percent in Spain.[3]

Inequality

The 85 richest people in the world have the same wealth as the 3.5 billion poorest people.[4] Between 1990 and 2010 income inequality in developing countries rose 11 percent.[5] Inequality in health and education has been declining but remains high, particularly in some regions. Sub-Sahara Africa has the highest inequality in health outcomes, and South Asia has the highest inequality in education.[6] Inequality is a considerable threat to human development, particularly because it reflects inequality of opportunity.[7] And beyond a certain threshold, it harms growth, poverty reduction and the quality of social and political engagement.[8] High inequality also diminishes a shared sense of purpose and facilitates rent-seeking by influential groups.[9] Rent-seeking, directed towards getting a larger share of the pie rather than increasing its size, distorts resource allocation and weakens the economy.[10] Inequality impedes future human development by reducing investment in basic services and public goods, lowering the progressivity of the tax system and raising the prospect of political instability.[11] High inequality between groups is not only unjust but can also affect well-being and threaten political stability. When specific groups are discriminated against, resources and power are not distributed based on merit, and talented people are held back. Such group inequality fuels dissatisfaction and grievances.[12]

Health risks

Health shocks can be some of the most destabilizing to households and society, and hunger and malnutrition add to the high risks of poverty-related health threats. In India paying for health care has become a major source of impoverishment for the poor and even the middle class. Ill health of the main wage earner can push households into poverty and keep them there.[13]

Recent data suggest that more than 40 percent of hospital patients either borrow money or sell assets and that close to 35 percent fall into poverty because of having to pay for their care.[14] And making the lives of everyone vulnerable, not just the poor, are the HIV/AIDS epidemic, the accelerating spread of malaria and tuberculosis, the rapid spreads of dengue and swine flu, and the increasing threats of bioterrorism.

Environment and natural disasters

Global risks connected to the environment and climate change appear to be intensifying. Climate change will produce more droughts in arid regions and more-frequent and more-intense hurricanes, typhoons and other extreme weather phenomena. It will also lead to rising sea levels, flooding, water scarcity in key regions, the migration or extinction of plant and animal species, and the acidification of oceans.[15] Other environmental threats arise from extensive industrialization and rapid urbanization. In every country there are growing problems of scarce water, poor sanitation, degraded land, eroded soil, polluted air and threats to biodiversity. Climate change is adding to the variability in farm incomes and insecurity in livelihoods that depend on ecosystems.[16] For example, pastoral communities in Western Niger have experienced the effects of prolonged drought combined with overgrazing, leading to the conversion of open woodland with perennial grasses to a mosaic of bare ground and unpalatable shrubs.[17]

Food insecurity

High volatility in the prices and availability of food are of particular concern, given the large impact on poor people and poor countries. Following the 2008 global economic crisis, food price spikes and recession slowed the decline in the number of people worldwide suffering from hunger, which the Food and Agriculture Organization of the United Nations estimated at 842 million people in 2012.[18] This serves as powerful commentary on the inadequacy of global efforts to eliminate hunger and reduce deprivations more broadly.

Physical insecurity

Conflict and war inflict shocks on society and human security. Greatly threatening lives and livelihoods are outbreaks of communal violence, attacks by terrorist groups, fights between street gangs and protests that turn violent. And criminal and domestic violence adds to personal insecurity. The World Health Organization estimates that about 4,400 people die every day because of intentional acts of violence.[19] Of the estimated 1.6 million who died from violence in 2000, almost half were suicides, nearly a third homicides and a fifth war-related (most of them men). In some conflicts civilians are targeted and mutilated as a deliberate strategy to demoralize communities and destroy their social structures. Rape is often an expression of power and brutality against communities.[20]

Notes
1. For a comprehensive list and full coverage, see World Economic Forum (2014). 2. World Bank n.d. 3. OECD 2013d,f. 4. Fuentes-Nieva and Galasso 2014. 5. UNDP 2014. 6. HDRO data (see table 3 in *Statistical annex*). 7. This is inequality stemming from factors and circumstances beyond the scope of individual responsibility, such as race and socioeconomic background. See Roemer (1993) and Van de Gaer (1993). 8. UNDP 2014. 9. It is arguably also a result of that behaviour since rent-seeking redistributes resources from those at the bottom to those at the top. 10. Stiglitz 2012b. 11. Pineda and Rodríguez 2006b; Bénabou 2000; Alesina and others 1996. 12. Stewart, Brown and Mancini 2005. 13. Narayan and Petesch 2007. 14. Raman and Björkman 2000. 15. IPCC 2013. 16. UNDP 2011a, 2012a. 17. Sinclair and Fryxell 1985; Tshimpanga 2011. 18. FAO, IFAD and WFP 2013. 19. Krug and others 2002b. 20. Krug and others 2002a.

a deep and entirely new form of interdependence, with the actions of every human being having the potential to affect the life chances of others around the globe as well as those of future generations.

A highly integrated global system has fuelled investment, trade and economic growth, but shocks can be contagious. When global supply chains get disrupted, it affects far more people than those in the country where the shock originated, as the 2011 Tohoku earthquake and tsunami show. The 1997 Asian financial crisis had devastating consequences in the region and beyond. And the 2008 bank failures in New York shook financial capitals everywhere and led to a still lingering global recession with long-term effects. Countries and individuals are ill-equipped to respond to global shocks, and some of the policy responses adopted so far appear to be generating new vulnerabilities.[27]

A connected world also creates global demands for workers with different skills. Such job creation is positive and generally improves people's lives. Today there are more than 200 million migrants around the world, a generally vulnerable community with limited formal protections. Many migrants—if not most—have precarious rights and face uncertain futures. They have to reconcile the loss of dignity, the disruption of families and even the potential for violence with the prospect of earning more.

People around the world are getting more connected, facilitated by social media. Thanks to Facebook and Twitter, newly connected communities trade ideas and knowledge in a way that could not have been imagined just a few years ago. But as the 2013 *HDR* noted, many people—especially the young, who are more educated and social media savvy—are pressing for better, more-secure jobs and to be treated with dignity. They are challenging governments everywhere to do better. A force for change clearly, but as the recent years testify, social and political change can produce unsettled conditions, even conflicts, if not well managed.

The why of vulnerability

This Report analyses systemic and overarching vulnerability that reduces individuals' ability to manage their affairs and that weakens the foundations of society. It looks at groups of people who are structurally the most vulnerable and tries to understand why that is so. It also develops the concept of life capabilities, examining how vulnerability changes over a life cycle. This life cycle approach points to sensitive transition periods of life when support is necessary and assesses how vulnerabilities may interact and compound as people age.

Structural vulnerability is rooted in people's position in society—their gender, ethnicity, race, job type or social status—and evolves and persists over long periods. A fuller understanding of such vulnerability implies that people who are otherwise endowed with equal capabilities may still face differing barriers based on who they are, where they live or what they do.

The poor are one such structurally vulnerable group. But poor people are not the only group that can be categorized in this way. Political and economic discrimination exists in countries across different levels of the Human Development Index. Minority and socially excluded groups experience high horizontal inequality and often suffer discrimination in access to jobs, justice and services.[28] The Minorities at Risk Project identifies more than 283 minority groups in more than 90 countries who suffer varying degrees of political and economic exclusion, ranging from neglect to repression.[29] Indigenous peoples in particular experience weak protection of their property rights,[30] exposing them to risk of expropriation and exploitation.

People experience many vulnerabilities from economic, environmental, physical, health and other insecurities. Overlapping structural vulnerabilities can magnify the adverse impact on freedoms and functioning quite substantially. Take older people. With ageing comes a higher probability of being disabled. Worldwide, more than 46 percent of people ages 60 and older live with a disability.[31] When vulnerabilities overlap, individuals find it much more difficult to recover from shocks to their lives—or to convert new opportunities into capabilities. Poor households in particular express fears about losing or not finding a job, about their children's falling sick, about not being able to send their children to school and about facing a loss of dignity.

Such vulnerability results in widespread and persistent disparities in the capabilities of excluded groups and in the indicators of their well-being. For instance, while indigenous peoples make up about 5 percent of the world's population, they account for 15 percent of the world's poor and 33 percent of the world's extreme rural poor.[32] And in most regions political exclusion restricts women's voice and ability to shape the laws and policies that affect their lives. Only in Cuba and Rwanda does the share of women in parliament match their share in the population.[33]

These vulnerabilities are not evenly distributed across the life cycle. They are especially acute from infancy to early childhood, when susceptibility to disease, social disruption and lapses in learning and nurturing is greatest. Quality health care and intellectual stimulation early on can set a child on a higher life path to advancing human capabilities. Adolescence presents opportunities and vulnerability in the social and education spheres and in physical and psychological health. The elderly depend on caregivers, accessible public services and often economic assistance. The concept of *life cycle* or *life capabilities* captures these key transitions and what they imply for policies to reduce vulnerabilities.

Choices and capabilities

Vulnerability reflects threats to choices and capabilities. If human development is about widening choices, human vulnerability stems quintessentially from a restriction of the choices critical to human development—choices for health, education, command over material resources and personal security.

Individuals tend to feel more vulnerable when they have few and less certain options. Women who are economically independent tend to be less vulnerable than those who depend on others for sustenance. Similarly, illiterate and unskilled workers are more vulnerable than well educated people because they have fewer work options. Deeply indebted households are likely to be more vulnerable to exploitation and less able to protect themselves in adversity.

Choices depend on capabilities. An individual's capabilities—all the things a person can do or be—determine the choices a person can make. People are vulnerable when they lack sufficient core capabilities, since this severely restricts their agency and prevents them from doing things they value or coping with threats.

Vulnerability is multifaceted and dynamic. An exclusive focus on economic vulnerability, defined narrowly as low and irregular earnings, is not enough. Viewing human vulnerability in the space of capabilities, choices and freedoms makes it possible to analyse the full range of vulnerabilities. Income deprivation is clearly not the only source of vulnerability. A person with high income but no opportunity to participate politically is not poor in the usual sense but may be highly vulnerable to discrimination and neglect. Equally, a well-off person can be vulnerable to violent attack, but having resources can reduce that person's vulnerability, since richer people can better protect themselves against many adversities.

Unemployed people entitled to receive social security or unemployment benefits may be less vulnerable to the loss of income, but unemployment has other serious effects on their lives. There is plenty of evidence that the value of a job far exceeds the wages received,[34] so unemployment reaches beyond the loss of income. Its effects include psychological harm (such as a loss of work motivation and self-confidence), the attrition of skills, increases in ailments and illnesses (and even death), disruptions in family relations and social life, and social exclusion.[35]

Viewing vulnerability in the context of capabilities and choices focuses attention on the important relationship among human vulnerability, personal differences, environmental diversities, social variations, relational perspectives and resource distributions within households. Vulnerability may depend on a person's age, gender, social roles, location, epidemiological atmosphere and other variations over which there is little or no control.[36]

Age and disability in particular are important facets of vulnerability. Children tend to be intrinsically more vulnerable than others. During a stampede, flood or hurricane they are more vulnerable to injury and death than adults are. Similarly, older people and those with disabilities living in high-rise apartments

If human development is about widening choices, human vulnerability stems quintessentially from a restriction of the choices critical to human development

are more vulnerable in the event of a building fire than adults and young people who can run down the stairs. Young people are more vulnerable to high-risk behaviours—for example, by falling prey to enticing advertisements that promote cigarettes and alcohol.

Even if individuals have a similar income or education, their vulnerability will depend on whether they can participate in society equally, mediated by race, religion or ethnicity. The quality of institutions therefore influences vulnerability and the ability to cope with crises.

Both real and perceived threats affect behaviour. Fear of violent assault is of particular concern to women everywhere. The term *bodily integrity* gives concrete meaning to this vulnerability.[37] Witness the brutal rape in Delhi that grabbed headlines worldwide in 2012 and highlighted what women in many societies fear in their daily lives. Being educated or having a high income is not enough to overcome such a threat to bodily integrity.

Perhaps no other aspect of human security is so vital to people as their security from physical violence, which can derail the perceived value of human progress. Even in Latin America and the Caribbean, with high human development, many people fear that progress is being threatened by rising levels of homicides and other violent crime. In large parts of West and Central Africa armed conflict and lawlessness threaten to reverse human development gains, with long-term repercussions for national progress.

The presence and threat of violence are more likely to exist in the lives of the poor and the socially excluded, more likely to affect the choices and freedoms of women and more likely to touch those who have fewer resources and capabilities to settle disputes through negotiations. Violence is an exercise of power to restrict choices and freedoms through physical harm and threats. It is also a means to enforce social and cultural norms.[38]

Another key security is economic. In today's world large numbers of people face economic insecurity and fear not making ends meet. In developing countries half to three-quarters of nonagricultural employment is in the informal economy.[39] In the absence of job security and social protection

informal workers lead unpredictable and precarious lives, vulnerable to abuse and corruption, often by the very law enforcement and civic authorities who should be protecting them In developed countries the impacts of the global financial crisis linger. Greece, Ireland and Italy have yet to recover from their 2008 economic downturns.[40] The United States may have recovered much of its GDP growth, but many people remain in long-term unemployment.[41] And an entire generation of young people face a future of high job and financial insecurity.[42]

Economic security and personal security are linked. People feel secure when they have jobs with sufficient social protections—and when they are confident about the future. Full employment reduces crime and increases well-being generally.[43] By contrast, high unemployment fuels uncertainty and inflicts a sense of hopelessness. Equally, long-standing unequal treatment and denials of rights feed into deep discrimination, and at times groups or communities seek to redress long-established inequities through violent means. In India estimates range from a tenth to a third of districts having insurrection movements or armed struggles in one form or the other by such dissident groups as the Naxalites and other Maoist groups.[44] Horizontal inequality and unmet basic rights are often the causes of group violence.[45]

Policies and collective action

A core aspect of human development is having the freedom to live a life that one values, to manage one's affairs adequately. Higher capabilities, particularly in education, advance human agency—people's capacity to make choices. It is a type of freedom—the freedom to act. But higher capabilities may not be enough. To have full agency, people also need to be free of social, institutional and other constraints that inhibit their ability to act. While empowerment is quintessentially individual, a useful analogy can also be drawn for societies. If social cohesion is not strong and there is ethnic and other fragmentation, a society's capacity for collective action is much reduced in responding to adverse events.

Perhaps no other aspect of human security is so vital to people as their security from physical violence, which can derail the perceived value of human progress

As highlighted earlier, this Report is about tackling deep, systemic vulnerability and examining policies and social institutions that empower people and build stronger foundations for more-resilient people and societies. It does not attempt to identify policy fixes that respond to specific risks or to overcome inadequacies of specific systems in managing risks, such as those dealing with natural disasters.

National governments have a central responsibility to help the vulnerable, especially if other institutions fail to do so, but the extent to which they meet this responsibility varies considerably. In socially cohesive societies, governments as well as social institutions tend to play a bigger role.[46] Social institutions support vulnerable people where social cohesion is strong. In divided societies social institutions may be very supportive within a particular group but less so across groups. International support (official and nonofficial) also helps, with finance and resources generally in response to major disasters, say, after tsunamis, hurricanes or wars.

National policies and international action are interdependent. Global rules, norms and collective action at times influence and may determine the scope and efficacy of national responses to major crises. They may even produce new vulnerabilities. Although an integrated global system has brought many benefits—fuelling investment, trade and economic growth—it has also heightened vulnerability. Shocks in one part of the world—financial, natural or otherwise—can be readily transmitted to other parts of the world. There is, as yet, no analogy at the global level to the implicit social contracts in many developed and some developing countries that commit states to protecting people's well-being, through social insurance and unemployment benefits, when people's economic and social circumstances are hurt.

Not only individuals are vulnerable. Communities, regions and countries can also be vulnerable. Some countries suffer more and have larger shocks (economic, environmental, political) than others, and some countries are more resilient than others—better able to sustain their human development in the face of such shocks. As with individuals, poor countries are generally more vulnerable than rich ones, suffer from larger shocks and are less resilient. Compared with individuals in rich countries, individuals in poor countries tend to be more vulnerable, to have lower social competences and to have governments with fewer resources to protect them from adversity.

Governments may be aware of these issues, but markets are blind to them. The operation of markets may reduce vulnerability—by increasing production, economic growth and incomes—but they also clearly heighten vulnerability, by neglecting public goods and human insecurity in the quest for efficiency and profit. Markets must thus be regulated and supplemented if vulnerability is to be reduced. Public goods can make markets function better and deliver more sustainable outcomes, nationally and globally. So governments and social institutions have to regulate, monitor and complement the market.

Prevention, promotion and protection

Policies and related measures can help in addressing the big issues that leave people and communities vulnerable in three broad areas: prevention, promotion and protection (figure 1.2). The interest here is in policies that help across the three areas and make both individuals and societies more resilient. A commitment to universal education may help in two or all three areas by enhancing individual capabilities, contributing to social cohesion and reducing deprivations. In turn, expanding the space for diverse voices to be heard—and reflected in policies—enables individuals and societies to address their particular concerns and promote equal life chances, laying the base for secure and sustained development.

Preventing shocks. Policies to prevent conflict, improve economic stability, reduce the impact of environmental shocks and halt the spread of disease can help reduce the incidence and size of shocks. Such national actions as having stable macro-policies, reducing disease through immunizations and reducing the likelihood of floods can help prevent shocks. By contrast, reducing global volatility in capital flows or food prices and preventing large increases in carbon dioxide emissions require collective global action. Without it, national polices may have limited value.

Prevention can anticipate future trends. Take the rise in obesity. On current trends there

Public goods can make markets function better and deliver more sustainable outcomes, nationally and globally. So governments and social institutions have to regulate, monitor and complement the market

FIGURE 1.2

Policies for reducing vulnerability and building resilience

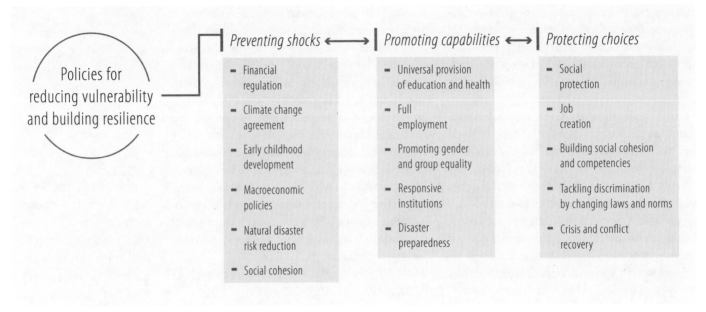

Source: Human Development Report Office.

will be more than twice as many obese people worldwide in 2030 as in 2008—1.12 billion compared with 0.5 billion—greatly increasing vulnerability to ill health.[47] Determined policy is needed now to prevent these numbers from rising sharply. Or take the life cycle approach to capability formation. The right investments at the right time, especially during the sensitive periods of early childhood and adolescence, can reduce future vulnerability. In most cases prevention is also cost-effective.

Another broad concern in preventing adverse shocks is high and rising inequality. If certain thresholds are crossed, high inequality can lead to alienation, social unrest and vulnerability across large sections of the population.[48] High inequality can lead to erosion of social competencies, and 'tipping' points' may be reached beyond which societal degeneration is inevitable.[49]

Promoting capabilities. Better social and economic policies can advance core capabilities, which directly improve human resilience. So can reducing societal or other barriers to the ability of individuals and communities to act in the face of adversities (through better norms and laws and the protection of rights). The second may require policies to reduce or overcome

restrictions on opportunities and the exercise of choices, say, by eliminating discrimination, improving gender equality and giving rights to immigrants (chapter 4). Of course, specific policies to address different vulnerabilities will always be important, but the greater interest here is in foundational policies that reduce vulnerabilities across society.

Protecting choices. Policies may seek to prevent shocks and make individuals and societies more resilient. But adverse events—human-made or otherwise—will still occur. Some people, unable to cope with shocks, will need help. Economic downturns and the pressures of globalization, even if well managed, will still create unemployment. The sudden death of the main breadwinner makes even well endowed households immediately vulnerable. Policy responses may involve health insurance, social protection and active labour and job creation programmes. Being supported by the household or community also protects choices and overall well-being.

Principles underlying policies

Drawing on ideas governing human development and the promotion of equal life chances, we advance four guiding principles for designing and implementing policies to reduce vulnerability and enhance resilience: embracing universalism, putting people first, committing to collective action and coordinating states and social institutions. Taking into account that a variety of approaches and perspectives are needed to reduce vulnerability, depending on the types of adverse events people face, these principles can move development in a more sustainable and resilient direction.

Embracing universalism. All individuals are equally valuable and entitled to protection and support. So there has to be a greater recognition that those most exposed to risks and threats, children or people living with disabilities, may require additional support to ensure that their life chances are equal to others'. Universalism may thus require unequal entitlements and attention. Equal consideration for all could thus demand unequal treatment in favour of the disadvantaged.[50]

The basic idea of human development is promoting equal life chances for all, based on the Kantian principle that all people are of equal worth,[51] as enshrined in the UN Charter. All humans need to be empowered to live lives they value. Both economic and social policies influence people's life chances and capabilities. Pursuing the broader goals of equity and justice reinforces social competences and deepens social cohesion. How far policies and responsive systems of governance succeed in advancing the prospects of most members of society will determine whether social solidarity is enhanced and fragmentation and stigma can be avoided.

Putting people first. Reducing vulnerabilities calls for renewing the core message of human development as 'putting people first'—a message promoted consistently in all *HDRs* since the first in 1990. All public policies, especially macroeconomic ones, must be seen as means to an end, not as ends in themselves. Policymakers must ask some basic questions. Is economic growth improving the lives of people in areas that really matter—from health, education and income to basic human security and personal freedoms? Are people feeling more vulnerable? Are some people being left behind? And, if so,

who are they, and how can such vulnerabilities and inequities be best addressed?

The notion of putting people first is not just about people-centred policies. It is also about policies that people influence, so all members of society have full rights as citizens and have a voice that is heard in developing policies. Reducing vulnerability requires that the voice of the disadvantaged be heard clearly. Empowering all citizens is a powerful tool for reducing risks. As Amartya Sen observed, "Famines are easy to prevent if there is a serious effort to do so, and a democratic government, facing elections and criticisms from opposition parties and independent newspapers, cannot help but make such an effort. Not surprisingly, while India continued to have famines under British rule up to independence, . . .[with a democratic government after independence] they disappeared."[52]

Putting people first has implications for policies and measures: The two are inextricably linked because "what we measure affects what we do; and if our measurements are flawed, decisions may be distorted."[53] As all *HDRs* have argued, focusing narrowly on GDP and its growth is misleading. Economic growth is important, not for itself but for what it enables a country and people to do with the resources generated. Growth that does not generate sufficient jobs—jobless growth—cannot be treated on a par with growth that does.[54] Jobs are a source of dignity and self-worth. Higher quality or decent jobs contribute to social cohesion and political stability.[55] For example, austerity in Europe is severely straining social structures, with larger burdens borne by the young and the old,[56] even after conceding the need to reduce fiscal deficits.

The Human Development Index—a composite measure of income, education and health—was presented in 1990 as an alternative to GDP. Its widespread adoption reflects countries' desire to understand whether, how and why people are doing better. Since its introduction, human development measures of inequality, gender and poverty have been added to the arsenal.

All these measures assess achievement in human development, but they do not incorporate measures of vulnerability. This requires looking beyond achievements to hazards and

Equal consideration for all could demand unequal treatment in favour of the disadvantaged

fluctuations, especially those affecting the more deprived groups such as the poor and the near poor (box 1.3). This Report does not propose a new measure of human vulnerability. Policies to reduce vulnerability require going beyond averages to gauge how secure the benefits are and how well they are distributed and to measure how poverty and deprivation are declining, whether there are enough decent jobs and whether social protections are adequate to

BOX 1.3

Measuring vulnerability

The past 40 years have seen considerable work on measuring vulnerability. Researchers have proposed measuring several types of vulnerability, many covered in this Report. Some work has focused on specific vulnerabilities: to natural disasters, to income poverty or to food price volatility. Others take a broader systemic approach to assess the vulnerability of an economy or environment to shocks. But little has been done to assess the vulnerability and sustainability of human development achievements.

Much of the early work on vulnerability focused on natural disasters in the 1970s. A landmark study showed that the incidence of natural disasters and fatalities was increasing and that the burden of death fell disproportionately on developing countries.[1] One of the authors developed the concept of vulnerability as both external (exposure to risks) and internal (people's capacity to cope).[2] More recent frameworks, such as the *World Risk Report,* have added a third component, adaptation (capacities for long-term societal change).[3]

Whereas poverty can be directly observed, vulnerability cannot: it is essentially a measure of what might happen in the future. Measuring vulnerability to poverty is generally aimed at the likely sources of vulnerability and who is vulnerable. A study in Ethiopia, for example, examined the impact and potential interactions of health, education and consumption among the poor, finding that those with both chronic undernutrition and illiteracy are more vulnerable to poverty and more like to stay longer in deep poverty.[4]

The United Nations Development Programme's Macroeconomic Vulnerability Assessment Framework assesses a country's capacity to cope with a crisis in the short term and to identify policy areas that need to be strengthened to build longer term resilience.[5] It considers the sources and transmission channels of vulnerability as well as coping mechanisms.

The Economist Intelligence Unit's Global Food Security Index, which measures vulnerability to hunger, comprises measures of affordability, availability, quality and safety. Some 870 million people globally have no secure source of food: That number is not changing rapidly, with an average of just 2.5 million people a year emerging from food insecurity.[6] The Institute for Economics and Peace's Global Peace Index assesses states' vulnerability to conflict and aggregates 22 indicators of violence or the absence of violence in a society. A sibling measure, the Positive Peace Index, measures national attitudes, institutions and structures to determine their capacity to create and maintain a peaceful society.[7]

Broader approaches include work that seeks to assess environmental and economic vulnerability. The Secretariat of the Pacific Community, for example, developed the Environmental Vulnerability Index, which comprises three pillars: hazard (such as extreme climatic events), resistance (such as land area) and damage (such as endangered species).[8]

The United Nations uses economic vulnerability in defining the least developed countries: low-income countries "suffering from structural impediments to sustainable development . . . manifested in a low level of human resource development and a high level of structural economic vulnerability." It uses a structural economic vulnerability index to reflect the risk posed by shocks along with gross national income per capita and a human assets index. The economic vulnerability index includes indicators of shocks (natural and external), such as the instability of exports and agricultural production and victims of natural disasters, alongside measures of exposure to shocks, such as the share of population in low coastal zones. It highlights the high vulnerability of the least developed countries and small island developing states and shows that vulnerability is decreasing more slowly in least developed countries than in other developing countries.[9]

Considering a society's overall vulnerability to loss of human development or well-being is more challenging still. Experimental work by the Organisation for Economic Co-operation and Development defined vulnerability to future loss of well-being when people lack "assets which are crucial for resilience to risks." It proposed a set of indicators to assess a society's vulnerability based on access to different types of capital: economic (poverty), human (education) and social capital (support networks) as well as collective assets, such as essential services.[10]

These approaches, though different, have some ideas in common. First, overall risk is defined by the interaction of the chance of something happening (exposure) and its likely impact if it does (vulnerability). Second, the analysis and measurement of vulnerability are more tractable when looking separately at exposure to risk and ability to cope or adapt. Third, vulnerability is itself a multidimensional concept that can include measures of people's capacity both to cope (in terms of skills, assets or capabilities) and to adapt over the longer term.

These approaches all take a narrower perspective on vulnerability than is used in this Report and generally measure vulnerability to a particular type of threat (economic shocks, hunger, natural disasters). So they may be useful in providing partial measures of vulnerability, but they do not assess the broad systemic vulnerability that is the focus of this Report. Nor do they shed very much light on the ways the very systems themselves can generate vulnerability.

There is clearly a lot more thinking to be done and much to be learned from existing work. This Report does not propose new measures, preferring instead to focus on embedding vulnerability firmly within the human development approach, which might then pave the way for new measurement work.

Notes
1. O'Keefe, Westgate Wisner 1976. 2. Wisner and others 2004. 3. Alliance Development Works 2012. 4. Kwak and Smith 2011. 5. UNDP 2011d. 6. See http://foodsecurityindex.eiu.com. 7. See http://economicsandpeace.org/research/iep-indices-data/global-peace-index. 8. See www.sopac.org/index.php/environmental-vulnerability-index. 9. UNDESA 2013a. 10. Morrone and others 2011.

help individuals and societies cope with adverse events (chapter 2). Together, they provide a checklist to judge whether public policies are people-driven and whether broader human development goals are being adequately met.

Committing to collective action. Meeting today's challenges requires collective action (chapters 4 and 5). When people act collectively, they marshal their individual capabilities and choices to overcome threats, and their combined resilience deepens development progress and makes it more sustainable. The same can be said of states acting collectively to reduce vulnerabilities to transborder threats by provisioning global public goods. Despite the many uncertainties that surround us, one thing seems clear: A positive vision of the public domain will depend in large measure on the successful provisioning of public goods, both national and global.

All this is feasible. Financial systems can be better regulated. Trade talks can be unblocked, as the recent World Trade Organization agreement at Bali testifies.[57] Corporate conduct around the world can be subject to common codes and standards. Climate change can be mitigated. But only if citizens and states everywhere recognize the value of cross-border collaboration and global public goods—and accept that people's well-being cannot be left to the vagaries of the market or to national responses alone.

A shared planet where individual decisions have the ability to influence others and the future of all humankind requires accepting and promoting social norms that embody mutual responsibility for each other. It also requires global, national and local obligations to prevent vulnerability and assist those who suffer from adverse events. The historic Millennium Declaration signed by 189 countries in 2000 and the Millennium Development Compact a little later are probably the clearest expressions of such global solidarity. Whether expressed in global conversations among governments on the sustainable development goals or in a growing sense of ecological citizenship at the Rio + 20 Global Conference in June 2012, this solidarity needs to be further nurtured and interpreted in the context of vulnerability, as a collective responsibility to help others in need.[58]

Coordinating between states and social institutions. It is also time to look at broader architectural questions and revisit the dynamic between states and markets, and between countries and global forces, to examine the scope of private and public spaces. Today's vulnerability is deep-seated and systemic. Global connections across multiple fronts have melted large parts of the formerly more separate national policy domains into one large and still expanding global public domain. Yet this domain has been dominated by excessive belief in the value and adequacy of unfettered markets. Polanyi's caution—about the social destruction that unregulated markets can cause—is as relevant today as when he wrote *The Great Transformation* in 1944.[59] Required now is his anticipated response of state intervention to protect people and societies from the perils of believing in self-regulating markets.

Individuals cannot flourish alone. Indeed, they cannot function alone. When they are born, family provides their life support. In turn, families cannot function independent of their societies. Policies to improve social norms, social cohesion and social competences become important so that governments and social institutions can act in concert to reduce vulnerabilities. And when markets and systems themselves produce vulnerabilities, governments and social institutions must guide markets to limit vulnerability and help people where markets fail to do so.

Policies are only as good as their results. No matter how elegant policies appear on paper, they are effective only if they work in practice. Many factors can affect a political economy, and some, such as social cohesion or citizen trust in government, are touched on in this Report. Beyond these specific concerns, however, the quality of governance is important for the effectiveness of policies. People everywhere want government to work better—to deliver quality services, to have less corruption and to increase commitment to the rule of law. This Report does not attempt to discuss such major ideas in depth other than to highlight that they are extremely important for human development outcomes.

*   *   *

Over the last decades most countries have made considerable progress in human development. But rising or high vulnerability raises

> When people act collectively, they marshal their individual capabilities and choices to overcome threats, and their combined resilience deepens development progress and makes it more sustainable

the prospect of those human development achievements being eroded, the need to consider whether those achievements are secure and sustainable and the need to identify policies to reduce vulnerability and build resilience. Chapter 2 documents how large numbers of people are doing much better, particularly over the last decade, in terms of different aspects of well-being. It also points to the growing evidence of recent slowdown in this progress and the context of growing uncertainty and risks. When looking at progress, we emphasize the need to look closely at whose well-being is being assessed and to put people first in policymaking. Expanding people's choices now and securing them for the future require understanding the threats that people face and the underlying factors that shape vulnerability.

"Human beings the world over need freedom and security that they may be able to realize their full potential."

Aung San Suu Kyi

"Any fool can make things bigger, more complex, and more violent. It takes a touch of genius—and a lot of courage—to move in the opposite direction."

Albert Einstein

2.

State of human development

Almost all countries have improved human development over the past few decades, and billions of people are now doing substantially better. The 2013 *Human Development Report (HDR)* revealed that more than 40 developing countries—with the majority of the world's population—had greater HDI gains than would have been predicted given their situation in 1990.[1] Life expectancy at birth has increased due to lower infant and child mortality, fewer deaths due to HIV/AIDS and better nutrition. Education levels have risen on stronger investments and political commitment. Multidimensional poverty has been considerably reduced, though wide variation across countries and regions remains.

We cannot take these achievements for granted, however. There is evidence that the overall rate of progress is slowing—and this is worrying. We also have to ask a basic question: Whose prosperity are we observing? We need to look beyond averages and income thresholds to gather a more comprehensive view of how improvements in well-being are distributed among individuals, communities and countries. We also need to assess whether the gains are secure and the progress is sustainable. In short, we need a deeper understanding of the dynamics of vulnerability and inequality.

The recent gains have not followed a smooth path. From greater financial instability to high and volatile commodity prices, from recurrent natural disasters to widespread social and political discontent, uncertainty is an increasingly common feature of our world. And interdependence among countries has widened and deepened. Decisions and events in one part of the world trigger shocks elsewhere, especially as markets integrate and people communicate instantaneously. The international transmission of shocks—such as food price hikes, financial crises, natural disasters and armed conflicts—creates a sense of precariousness, even helplessness. Countries and individuals are not firmly in charge of their own destinies and thus are vulnerable to decisions or events elsewhere. That is why it is so vital to reduce the vulnerability to systemic and persistent threats that can endanger present and future human development. Sustaining and accelerating human development will clearly require greater domestic and international policy ambition.

Progress of people

Human development is about equal life chances for all. It involves not only expanding capabilities to broaden people's present choices—to live healthy, productive and safe lives—but also ensuring that these choices do not compromise or restrict those available to future generations. The focus on people has implications for measuring progress and formulating policies. It calls for a broader frame of analysis and a re-examination of the policy tools available. Measurement and policy are inextricably linked since "what we measure affects what we do; and if our measurements are flawed, decisions may be distorted".[2]

Uneven and slowing progress in human development

Since 1990 the Human Development Index (HDI) has been an important measure of progress—a composite index of life expectancy, years of schooling and income. This year's Report presents HDI values for 187 countries. The global HDI is now 0.702, and most developing countries are continuing to advance, though the pace of progress remains highly uneven (table 2.1).

The lowest regional HDI values are for Sub-Saharan Africa (0.502) and South Asia (0.588), and the highest is for Latin America and the Caribbean (0.740), followed closely by Europe and Central Asia (0.738). The very high human development group—as measured by the HDI—has a value of 0.890, considerably higher than that of the medium and low human development groups. But lower human development groups continue to converge with the higher levels.[3]

While all regions are registering improvement, signs of a slowdown are emerging—as measured by the growth rate of HDI values (figure 2.1).[4] Although four of the six regions

TABLE 2.1

Human Development Index and components, 2010 and 2013

Human development group or region	Human Development Index value		Life expectancy at birth (years)		Mean years of schooling (years)		Expected years of schooling (years)		Gross national income per capita (2011 PPP $)	
	2010	2013	2010	2013	2010	2013	2010	2013	2010	2013
Very high human development	0.885	0.890	79.7	80.2	11.7	11.7	16.2	16.3	38,548	40,046
High human development	0.723	0.735	73.9	74.5	8.1	8.1	13.1	13.4	11,584	13,231
Medium human development	0.601	0.614	67.1	67.9	5.5	5.5	11.3	11.7	5,368	5,960
Low human development	0.479	0.493	58.2	59.4	4.1	4.2	8.7	9.0	2,631	2,904
Arab States	0.675	0.682	69.7	70.2	6.2	6.3	11.7	11.8	15,281	15,817
East Asia and the Pacific	0.688	0.703	73.5	74.0	7.4	7.4	12.3	12.5	8,628	10,499
Europe and Central Asia	0.726	0.738	70.7	71.3	9.6	9.7	13.3	13.6	11,280	12,415
Latin America and the Caribbean	0.734	0.740	74.2	74.9	7.9	7.9	13.8	13.7	12,926	13,767
South Asia	0.573	0.588	66.4	67.2	4.7	4.7	10.6	11.2	4,732	5,195
Sub-Saharan Africa	0.468	0.502	55.2	56.8	4.8	4.8	9.4	9.7	2,935	3,152
World	0.693	0.702	70.3	70.8	7.7	7.7	11.9	12.2	12,808	13,723

PPP is purchasing power parity.
Source: Human Development Report Office calculations.

FIGURE 2.1

While all regions are registering improvement on the Human Development Index, signs of a slowdown are emerging

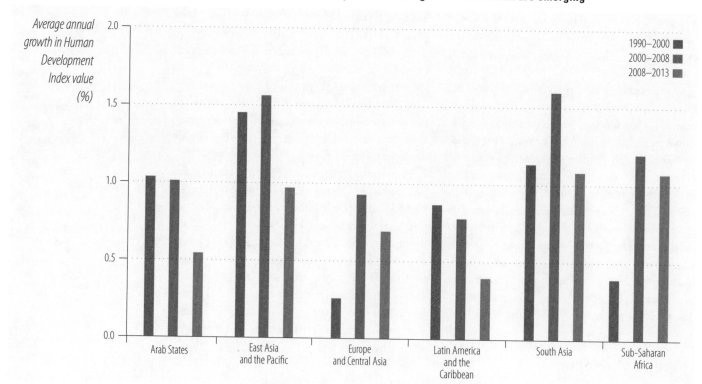

Note: Population-weighted panel for 99 developing countries.
Source: Human Development Report Office calculations.

registered faster gains in 2000–2008 than in the 1990s, progress in all regions slowed in 2008–2013. This was particularly noticeable in the Arab States and in Latin America and the Caribbean—where average annual growth dropped by about half—as well as in Asia. The global financial and economic crisis appears to have had a widespread impact.

The deceleration is evident in all three components of the HDI. Growth in gross national income (GNI) per capita has declined, particularly in the Arab States and in Europe and Central Asia. Growth rates of life expectancy at birth have recently declined in most regions—especially in Asia—though they increased in Sub-Saharan Africa. And since 2008 the growth of expected years of schooling has also declined.

All four human development groups have experienced a slowdown in HDI growth (figure 2.2). In fact, the very high human development group had been progressing more slowly even before the global crisis. The low human development group, by contrast, accelerated in 2000–2008, but progress subsequently declined, due largely to a decline in the growth of years of schooling. Despite achievement in primary education—with gross enrolment ratios averaging 100 percent—it may be harder to move more pupils to the secondary level and beyond. In this group of countries 43 percent of children enrolled in primary education do not complete it, while gross enrolment ratios in secondary education average only 39 percent. The implication: The transition from primary to secondary and higher education is unacceptably low. Stronger investments are needed to prevent future vulnerabilities.

Movements between human development groups can be tracked for 141 countries (figure 2.3).[5] Of the 47 countries in the low human development group in 1990, 16 are now in

FIGURE 2.2

All four human development groups have experienced a slowdown in growth on the Human Development Index

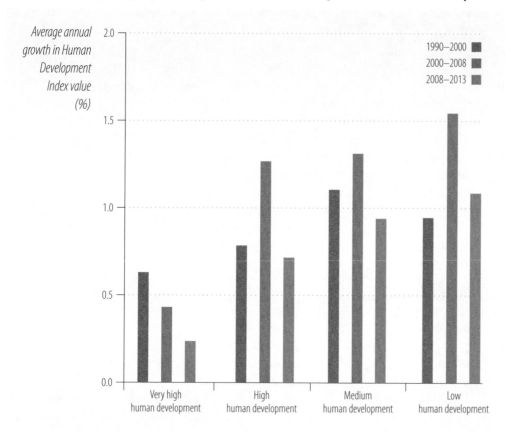

Average annual growth in Human Development Index value (%)

Legend: 1990–2000, 2000–2008, 2008–2013

Very high human development · High human development · Medium human development · Low human development

Note: Population-weighted panel for 141 developed and developing countries.
Source: Human Development Report Office calculations.

FIGURE 2.3

Progress to higher human development groups since 1990

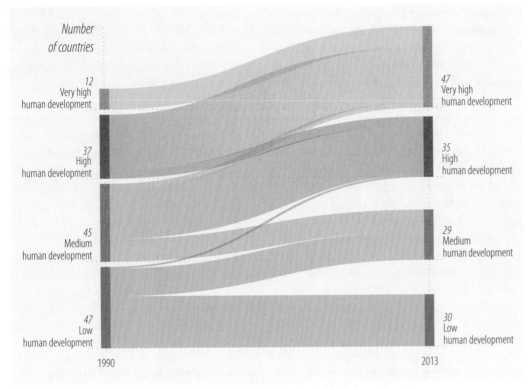

Number
of countries

12
Very high
human development

37
High
human development

45
Medium
human development

47
Low
human development

47
Very high
human development

35
High
human development

29
Medium
human development

30
Low
human development

1990   2013

Note: Human development groups are defined using 2013 cutoff values. Data are for 141 developed and developing countries.
Source: Human Development Report Office calculations.

the medium group and 1 is in the high group (China), and of the 45 countries in the medium human development group in 1990, 29 are now in the high human development group and 3 (Argentina, Croatia and Saudi Arabia) are in the very high human development group. Impressively, 32 countries that were in the high human development group in 1990 (nearly 90 percent of them) are now in the very high human development group.

Some countries perform far better in human development than in income alone—as seen in the large differences in GNI per capita and HDI rankings (table 2.2). High positive differences in rank are mainly in East Asia and the Pacific and in Europe and Central Asia, while negative differences predominate in the Arab States and Sub-Saharan Africa. Countries with positive differences tend to have a higher HDI value, and the majority have moved to a higher human development group. They also have lower inequality and a lower proportion of poor and near poor people. Generally, they started with fairly

low inequality and reduced it further, partly through strong investments in people's health and education as well as through spending on social protection.

Better access to health services has reduced maternal and child mortality and, more generally, improved quality of life. Increasing literacy rates and skills development has been crucial to boosting people's capabilities as well as their employability and productivity. Social protection measures, such as cash transfer programmes and other forms of income support, have been protecting the most vulnerable from shocks. All these aspects are fundamental to advancing human development.[6]

Continuing inequality in human development

One of the main drags on development is deep and chronic inequality, which restricts choices and erodes the social fabric. Large disparities in income, wealth, education, health and other dimensions of human development persist across the world, heightening the vulnerability of marginalized groups and undermining their ability to recover from shocks. People clustered at the bottom of the socioeconomic distribution are not there randomly. They lack a sufficient range of capabilities to enable them to live a fulfilling life, and they typically are the most vulnerable to health risks, environmental calamities and economic shocks.

The 2010 *Human Development Report* introduced the Inequality-adjusted HDI, a measure of inequality that takes into account how each country's progress is distributed in the three HDI dimensions—life expectancy, years of schooling and income.[7] It goes beyond traditional income-based measures of inequality to consider disparities in education and health.

Reported here is the loss in HDI value due to inequality, which measures the difference between HDI and the Inequality-adjusted HDI in percentage terms. Based on data for 94 developing countries, the average loss due to inequality has declined in most regions—except East Asia and the Pacific (figure 2.4). The highest loss is in Sub-Saharan Africa (34 percent), followed by South Asia (29 percent), the Arab States (26 percent) and Latin America and the Caribbean (25 percent). The lowest loss is in Europe and Central Asia (13 percent).

Among the HDI components, the average inequality was 19 percent for health (down from 23 percent in 2010), 27 percent for education (about the same as in 2010) and 23 percent for income (up from 21 percent in 2010). For health the highest inequality was in Sub-Saharan Africa (37 percent), followed by South Asia (25 percent). However, both regions have made substantial progress, possibly due to vaccination campaigns and better nutrition that greatly reduced under-five mortality. For education the highest levels of inequality were in South Asia (42 percent), the Arab States (41 percent) and Sub-Saharan Africa (37 percent). There has been limited progress in reducing disparities in education, except in Europe and Central Asia.[8]

For income the greatest inequality is in Latin America and the Caribbean (36 percent), followed by Sub-Saharan Africa (28 percent). Income inequality declined in Latin America and the Caribbean, although it seems to have

TABLE 2.2

Highest positive differences between gross national income per capita rank and Human Development Index rank, by human development group, 2013

	Gross national income per capita rank	Human Development Index rank	Difference
Very high human development			
New Zealand	30	7	23
Australia	20	2	18
Korea, Republic of	33	15	18
Ireland	28	11	17
Poland	51	35	16
High human development			
Georgia	116	79	37
Sri Lanka	103	73	30
Tonga	127	100	27
Fiji	114	88	26
Ukraine	109	83	26
Medium human development			
Samoa	134	106	28
Tajikistan	157	133	24
Palestine, State of	129	107	22
Vanuatu	153	131	22
Kiribati[a]	154	133	21
Low human development			
Rwanda	171	151	20
Madagascar	174	155	19
Zimbabwe	175	156	19
Solomon Islands	172	157	15
Nepal[b]	158	145	13

a. Kyrgyzstan is also a medium human development country with a rank difference of 21.
b. Kenya and Togo are also low human development countries with a rank difference of 13.
Source: Human Development Report Office calculations (based on table 1 in *Statistical annex*).

increased in South Asia and Sub-Saharan Africa. Overall, the declining inequality in HDI has been driven mainly by health, since inequality in income appears to have risen in several regions and inequality in education has remained broadly constant.

The 2013 *HDR* found a negative relationship between inequality and human development.[9] Inequality reduces the pace of human development and can even bring it to a halt. Although overall inequality in HDI has recently declined, it is not sufficient to offset

FIGURE 2.4

The average loss in the Human Development Index due to inequality has declined in most regions

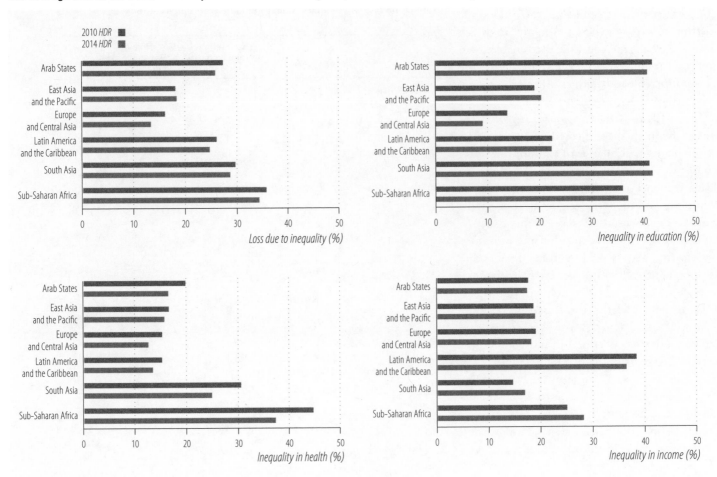

Note: The 2010 *HDR* reflects inequality in 2000–10, and the 2014 *HDR* reflects inequality in 2003–13. Population-weighted panel for 94 developing countries.
Source: Human Development Report Office calculations.

TABLE 2.3

Countries with rising or falling income inequality by region, 1990–2012

Region	Rising inequality	Falling inequality	No trend[a]	Total
Africa	13	19	3	35
Asia	18	10	3	31
Latin America and the Caribbean	4	14	2	20
Europe, North America, Oceania and Japan	30	8	6	44
Total	65	51	14	130
Percentage of countries	50.0	39.2	10.8	100.0
Percentage of total population	70.6	25.3	4.1	100.0

a. Inequality remained relatively constant or fluctuated without a clear upward or downward trend during the period.
Source: UNDESA 2013b.

growing income disparities with progress in health and education. To tackle vulnerability and sustain recent achievements, it is crucial to reduce inequality in all dimensions of human development.

Although income disparities among countries have been declining over the past 20 years as emerging economies have narrowed the gap with developed countries, inequality within many countries has increased worldwide (table 2.3).[10] This is particularly noticeable in the most developed regions, such as Eastern Europe, and in Asia. Where inequality declined, notably in Latin America and the Caribbean, it has been due mainly to the expansion of education and public transfers to the poor.[11]

These two trends—declining income inequality among countries and rising inequality within countries—virtually cancel each other out, suggesting that global income inequality (among the world's citizens) remains stubbornly high.[12] The poorest two-thirds of the world's people are estimated to receive less than 13 percent of world income, while the richest 1 percent amass nearly 15 percent.[13]

Beyond income, about half the world's wealth is owned by the richest 1 percent of the population, with the richest 85 people collectively holding the same wealth as the poorest half of the world's population.[14] Globalization, technological progress, deregulation of labour markets and misguided macroeconomic policies are likely to create and sustain these large gaps in income and wealth.

Tackling inequality is important to reduce vulnerability and sustain progress. Rising income inequality in developed and developing countries has been associated with higher economic volatility and slower progress in human development.[15] High and persistent inequality also makes it harder to reduce poverty. Evidence suggests that a 1 percent increase in national income reduces income poverty 4.3 percent in the most equal societies but just 0.6 percent in the least equal.[16] Inequality matters not only for those at the poorest end of the distribution, but for society as a whole—as it threatens social cohesion and hampers social mobility, fuelling social tensions that can lead to civil unrest and political instability. Large income disparities can even undermine democratic values, if wealthy individuals influence political agendas (say, by securing tax breaks for top income earners and cutbacks in social services) or try to shape social perceptions (through the media).

Revisiting economic progress

A country's economic status and performance can look much less impressive when adjusted for income distribution. GNI per capita is higher in the United States than in Canada, but the reverse is true for inequality-adjusted GNI per capita. Botswana, Brazil and Chile also have large adjustments to GNI per capita due to high inequality (figure 2.5).

The United Kingdom's performance is also less impressive after adjusting for inequality.

In the 1980s mean household income grew 3.2 percent a year, but adjusting growth with the Gini coefficient reduced it to only 2.1 percent.[17] This is similar to the adjusted growth of 2 percent in the 1990s, a lacklustre decade. Over 1961–2010 the adjustment reduces the average annual growth in mean household income from 1.9 percent to about 1.5 percent.

Another way to evaluate progress is to track the growth in consumption for the poorest 40 percent of the population. By this measure, some countries have done well. In Bolivia, Brazil and Cambodia consumption growth for the poorest 40 percent has been faster than that for the population as a whole (figure 2.6). But in countries where inequality has been high or rising—as in China, Malaysia and Uganda—growth in consumption for those at the poorest end of the distribution has been slower than for the population as a whole.

Gender inequality

Women experience many kinds of disadvantage and discrimination in health, education and employment. To highlight these disparities, this Report presents HDI values separately for women and men for 148 countries. Worldwide the female HDI value averages about 8 percent lower than the male HDI value. Among regions, the largest gap is in South Asia (17 percent). The gap is small (3 percent) in the very high human development group but about 17 percent in the low human development group. Slovakia has achieved gender parity, while female HDI values are slightly higher than male values in 15 countries (see table 3 in *Statistical annex*).

The Gender Inequality Index for 149 countries reveals the extent to which national achievements in reproductive health, empowerment and labour market participation are eroded by gender inequality. Unlike the HDI, a higher Gender Inequality Index value indicates poor performance. Values range from an average of 0.317 for Europe and Central Asia to 0.575 for Sub-Saharan Africa and from an average of 0.197 for the very high human development group to 0.586 for the low human development group. Slovenia outperforms all

Inequality matters not only for those at the poorest end of the distribution, but for society as a whole—as it threatens social cohesion and hampers social mobility, fuelling social tensions that can lead to civil unrest and political instability

FIGURE 2.5

A country's economic status and performance can look much less impressive when adjusted for income distribution

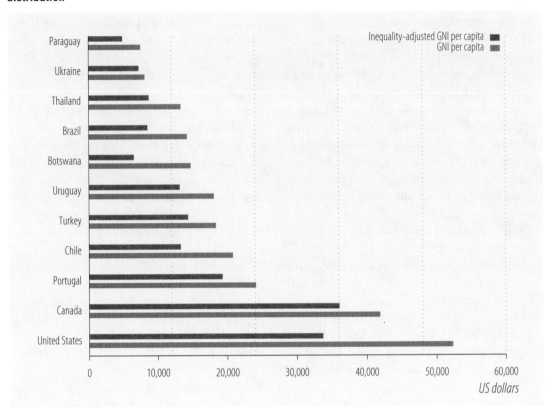

Note: The inequality-adjusted GNI per capita uses the Atkinson index. Data are for 2013.
Source: Human Development Report Office calculations.

other countries (0.021), while Yemen has the highest value (0.733).

Globally, women are disadvantaged in national political representation. On average, they occupy 21 percent of seats in national parliaments. In Latin America and the Caribbean they do better, with around 25 percent of seats. In Arab States parliaments they hold less than 14 percent of seats.

Poor reproductive health services are a major contributor to gender inequality, especially in developing countries. For example, the maternal mortality ratio is 474 deaths per 100,000 live births in Sub-Saharan Africa. Maternal deaths naturally have serious implications for babies and their older siblings left without maternal care, who could be trapped in low human development throughout their life cycle. Adolescent births could also lead to debilitating human development outcomes for young mothers and their babies. In Sub-Saharan Africa there are 110 births per 1,000 women ages 15–19.

The deficits in education are wide as well. On average, 60 percent of women ages 25 and older have at least some secondary education, compared with 67 percent of men. This discrepancy is particularly large for the low human development group (15 percent versus 29 percent). And South Asia has the largest gender gap in education (15 percentage points). The very high human development group has near gender parity at this level (about 86 percent versus 88 percent).

Women also lag behind men in labour market participation (51 percent compared with 77 percent). The situation is less promising for women in the Arab States, where 25 percent of women of working age participate in the labour market, compared with 73 percent of men. Labour force participation rates tend to be higher among women in Sub-Saharan Africa because women are more often than not forced to eke a living in the informal sector.

FIGURE 2.6

In countries where inequality has been high or rising, growth in consumption for the poorest 40 percent of the population has been slower than for the population as a whole

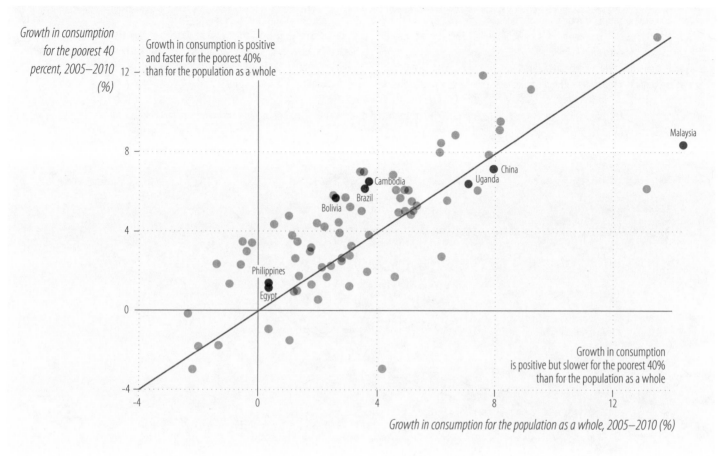

Source: Narayan, Saavedra-Chanduvi and Tiwari 2013.

Poverty

Typical measures of poverty are based on income or consumption, which register important dimensions of deprivation but provide only a partial picture. People can be deprived of many things beyond income. They may have poor health and nutrition, low education and skills, inadequate livelihoods and poor household conditions, and they may be socially excluded.

Some of these broader aspects of poverty are captured in the concept of multidimensional poverty. In 104 developing countries 1.2 billion people had an income of $1.25 or less a day.[18] But the multidimensional poverty headcount for 91 developing countries was an estimated 1.5 billion people—as measured by the Multidimensional Poverty Index (MPI).[19]

According to the MPI, which was introduced in the 2010 *HDR* to measure deprivations in the three HDI dimensions—health, education and living standards—2.2 billion people live in multidimensional poverty or near-poverty (out of 10). The MPI measures not only the proportion of people deprived but also the intensity of deprivation for each poor household, providing a more comprehensive picture (see chapter 3).

The proportion of multidimensionally poor people is usually higher than the proportion living on less than $1.25 a day. In Cambodia 47 percent of the population were in multidimensional poverty in 2010, but only 19 percent lived on less than $1.25 a day. But in Brazil and Indonesia income poverty is higher. Moreover, while in many countries both multidimensional poverty and income poverty have decreased, the rate of progress varies widely

BOX 2.1

Looking at disposable income

Material living standards can be better monitored, particularly during economic downturns, through measures of household income and consumption rather than GDP (see figure). For example, while GDP fell sharply (by 5.7 percent) in the euro area in 2008 and 2009, household disposable income stayed at precrisis levels. This can be attributed at least partly to automatic social protection stabilizers and discretionary measures that protected household income in the first few years of the crisis. Equally, household disposable income rose less quickly than GDP in the precrisis period up to 2007. So moving away from standard income measures can change the perspective on economic and social progress. But disposable income also has disadvantages, because it assumes that tax regimes and social benefits are comparable across countries.

While GDP fell sharply in the euro area in 2008 and 2009, household disposable income stayed at precrisis levels

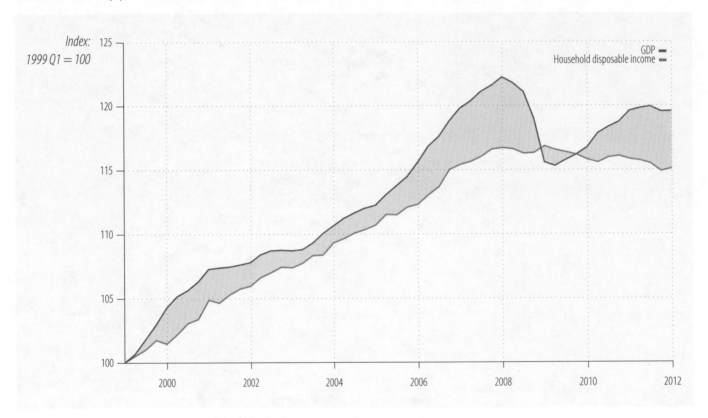

Note: Household disposable income is measured in real terms using the deflator for the seasonally adjusted household final consumption expenditure. GDP is measured in real terms using the GDP deflator.
Source: Atkinson 2013.

(figure 2.7). The multidimensional poverty headcount declined faster than income poverty in Indonesia, while the opposite was true in Peru.

Vulnerable employment and stagnant wages

Economic growth that does not generate sufficient decent employment is unlikely to foster human development. The 1993 *HDR* called attention to jobless growth, where output increases but employment lags far behind.[20] The issue seems to have resurfaced. Unemployment rose considerably after the 2008 crisis. An analysis of 65 countries showed that in more than two-thirds of them the employment rate had not returned to the precrisis level by the end of 2012. In some, such as Ireland and Spain, the long-term unemployment rate rose at least 20 percentage points over 2007–2012.[21] Globally, about 200 million people are now unemployed.

Despite strong productivity growth, real wages have been fairly stagnant. Between 2000 and 2011 real wages increased only 5 percent in developed economies and 15 percent in Latin America and the Caribbean, and they declined in the Middle East. In Asia, however, they grew a remarkable 94 percent. As a consequence, labour's share of GNI has declined in many parts of the world. For 16 developed countries with data, labour's average share fell from about 75 percent of GNI in the mid-1970s to about 65 percent in the years preceding the global economic and financial crisis.[22]

Decent and well paid jobs are essential to improve living standards. Even with recent improvements, the share of workers in vulnerable employment remains very high in Sub-Saharan Africa and South Asia—at about 77 percent of total employment (table 2.4). Nearly half the world's working population continues to be in vulnerable employment, trapped in insecure and low-paid jobs. High working poverty rates suggest that income from labour remains below what is required to secure decent living standards. Progress may have been impressive in several regions, but 40 percent of workers in Sub-Saharan Africa and 24 percent of workers in South Asia still live in households earning less than $1.25 a day per person.

Employment has also become more precarious in several developed countries, with many more workers on temporary and part-time contracts. And stagnant real wages have hindered improvements in living standards. In most developing countries vulnerable employment continues to be the norm. Wage employment in the formal sector is available

FIGURE 2.7

While in many countries both multidimensional and income poverty decreased over 2005–2012, the rate of progress varies widely

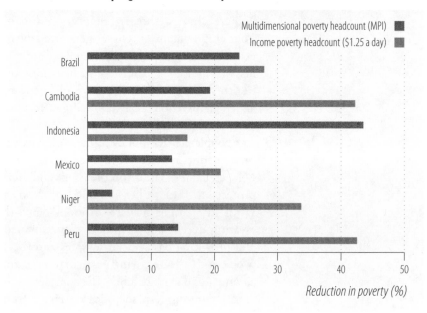

Source: Human Development Report Office calculations.

TABLE 2.4

Vulnerable employment and working poverty, 2010 and 2012

	Vulnerable employment[a] (% of total employment)		Working poor[b] (% of total employment)	
	2010	2012	2010	2012
World	53.1	49.2	26.6	12.3
Developed economies and European Union	11.2	10.1	..	..
Other Europe[c] and Commonwealth of Independent States	23.8	19.7	5.0	1.7
East Asia	58.4	48.9	31.2	5.6
South-East Asia and the Pacific	65.2	61.1	33.7	11.7
South Asia	81.3	76.9	43.9	24.4
Latin America and the Caribbean	35.8	31.5	7.8	3.5
Middle East	33.5	27.0	1.4	1.8
North Africa	42.1	41.4	9.5	6.4
Sub-Saharan Africa	81.8	77.2	56.7	40.1

a. Sum of own-account workers and contributing family workers.
b. Employed people living in a household that earns less than $1.25 a day per person.
c. Refers to non-EU countries in Central and South-Eastern Europe.
Source: ILO 2013d.

to only a few, while the majority of the population engages in unpaid or own-account work—such as subsistence farming and street trade—which is often associated with greater vulnerability to shocks (chapters 3 and 4). Poor employment outcomes generate adverse economic effects, but they can also lead to a loss of acquired capabilities (such as skills and health status), restrict choices and freedoms, affect the psychological well-being of individuals and fuel social discontent.

A people-centred policy framework needs to be aligned with macroeconomic and structural policies, labour market interventions and social protection. These policies should be geared towards stimulating inclusive economic growth, creating decent and productive employment and providing basic social services and social protection—while paying particular attention to equity and sustainability. The complex problems facing modern societies require a fresh look at the types of policies that can create synergies to foster and sustain human development (box 2.2).

Securing and sustaining human development

Over the years there has been much debate about what sustainability means and about what measures can track sustainable progress—or the lack of it. In 2012 the United Nations Conference on Sustainable Development in Rio took a broad view that sustainable progress must cover all three dimensions that affect people's life chances—social, economic and environmental.

Protecting the environment can be viewed as a good in itself, but Amartya Sen and others have argued that a more fruitful approach is to focus on the sustainability of people and their choices.[23] Human beings have always depended on the bounty and resilience of the natural world. But it is clear that the future is precarious, thus increasing people's vulnerabilities. Environmental degradation and climate change threaten the long-term survival of humanity. The challenge of sustaining progress is thus about ensuring that present choices and

BOX 2.2

Macroeconomics and austerity

In the years preceding the global financial crisis, the public finances of most developed countries were in fairly good shape. Government deficits were falling, and debt was either stable or declining. Then the economic recession triggered automatic stabilizers, such as unemployment benefits, and required fiscal stimulus packages that contributed to higher public spending. Some governments took responsibility for huge private sector debts, especially from troubled banks. Tax revenues dwindled in the slowdown. The combined trends of rising debt and falling GDP sharply increased fiscal deficits and public debt–to-GDP ratios.

Despite early signs of an economic recovery, thanks in part to counter-cyclical fiscal policies, many governments—especially those in Europe—quickly shifted their policy focus to austerity measures. Austerity programmes have, among other things, contributed to a drastic drop in public investment in Europe. Between 2008 and 2012 public gross fixed capital formation fell 65 percent in Ireland, 60 percent in Greece and Spain, 40 percent in Portugal and 24 percent in Italy. Overall, public investment in the euro area (17 countries) declined from €251 billion in 2009 to €201 billion in 2012—a 20 percent nominal decline. This, after a steady declining trend in investment as a share of GDP since the 1970s. Budget cuts are also affecting the delivery of public services. Between 2009 and 2011 health spending declined in a third of Organisation for Economic Co-operation and Development (OECD) countries—including Greece, Ireland, Portugal and the United Kingdom. The outcomes? Lower spending on prevention programmes, reductions in the supply of health

services, increases in direct out-of-pocket payments and wage cuts in hospitals. The crisis also inverted the long-term trend of rising investment in education. In 2011–2012, 15 OECD countries cut their education budgets.

This disproportionate focus on public spending and debt diverts attention from a deeper and more fundamental question: how to achieve inclusive and sustainable long-term growth? Austerity creates a vicious cycle. Cuts to growth-enhancing public expenditures—such as capital investment and social spending—weaken the tax base and increase the need for social assistance, aggravate fiscal deficits and debt and lead to further austerity measures. The cuts also undermine future human development and risk reversing hard-won gains. And they are likely to amplify inequality, which in itself is an obstacle to sustained growth and increases the risk of economic and financial crises.

Macroeconomic policy matters for human development. It influences the quantity and quality of employment, the level of social protection and the provision of public services. There is growing evidence that current macroeconomic policies—especially in developed countries—encourage volatility in output and exchange rates, increase inequality and thus undermine human development. This is due largely to an excessive focus on price stability and the poor timing of austerity policies that exacerbate problems of public and private debt and do little to lay the basis for economic recovery. It is time to reassess the rationale for austerity measures and refocus policy efforts on boosting investments for sustained long-term growth.

Source: EC 2013a,b; Berg and Ostry 2011a; Kumhof and Rancière 2010; Karanikolos and others 2013; Nayyar 2012; OECD 2013c,e; Välilä and Mehrotra 2005.

capabilities do not compromise the choices and freedoms available to future generations.[24] While sustainability can be tracked through adjusted net savings and ecological footprints, these measures do not adequately reflect the dynamic nature of the choices available to people. An important aspect of this framing is that, in addition to requiring greater attention to the tensions that exist between present and future choices, it also highlights the need to protect human development gains from negative shocks and adverse events.

The 2011 and 2013 *HDRs* argued that environmental disasters could not only slow human development but even throw it into reverse. Climate change could become the single biggest hindrance to the ambitions of the sustainable development goals and the post-2015 development agendas.[25] Environmental threats highlight potential tradeoffs between the well-being of current and future generations. If current consumption surpasses the limits imposed by our planetary boundaries, the choices of future and current generations will be seriously compromised.[26]

Whether a country or a community is on a sustainable development path depends on its position relative to local and global thresholds. A local threshold relates to the resources available within the boundaries of a country, while a global threshold takes a broader perspective by considering planetary boundaries. For instance, a country's consumption of a natural resource might be well within its local threshold—due to resource abundance within its borders—but its per capita consumption might exceed the global threshold. Crossing these thresholds can have damaging consequences within and across borders, so it is important to explore how to balance these local and global boundaries.

The universalist principle provides a good starting point for combining equity in the use of environmental and other resources within and across generations. Science provides an idea of the global thresholds for specific resources, while social justice requires that everyone have an equal claim to the resource available for use by the current generation. This enables us to identify countries on unsustainable development pathways, particularly on certain environmental indicators.

Although the environment is a key dimension affecting the choices of current and future generations, it is not the only one. Economic, social and political factors also expand or restrict choices. Nonetheless, fairly well established thresholds of global environmental sustainability enable more formal assessments.

Many countries, especially those in the high human development groups, now follow unsustainable development paths.[27] Of 140 countries with data, 82 have ecological footprints above global carrying capacity. As a result, the world per capita footprint is substantially higher than the global sustainability threshold. Carbon dioxide emissions by 90 of 185 countries exceed the global threshold, and their emissions are large enough to push global per capita emissions above global sustainability. Fresh water withdrawals by 49 of 172 countries with data also exceed the global threshold. Overall, correlation is positive between higher HDI achievements and unsustainable ecological footprints and emissions, while water consumption is unsustainable across developing and developed countries.[28]

The world's ecological footprint of consumption is currently larger than its total biocapacity, that is, the biosphere's ability to meet human demand for material consumption and waste disposal (figure 2.8). The very high human development group, in particular, has a very large ecological deficit—as its ecological footprint is significantly larger than available biocapacity.

While human development requires the expansion of choices currently available to people, it is also important to consider the impact on the choices of future generations—for intergenerational equity. Human development should not come at the cost of future generations. To secure and sustain human development and avert dramatic local and global repercussions, bold and urgent action on environmental sustainability is crucial.

Global threats to human development

Economic, social and environmental shocks have a major impact on people's lives and are a key challenge to sustaining and advancing human development. Unpredictable changes in

Economic, social and environmental shocks have a major impact on people's lives and are a key challenge to sustaining and advancing human development

FIGURE 2.8

The world's ecological footprint of consumption is currently larger than its total biocapacity

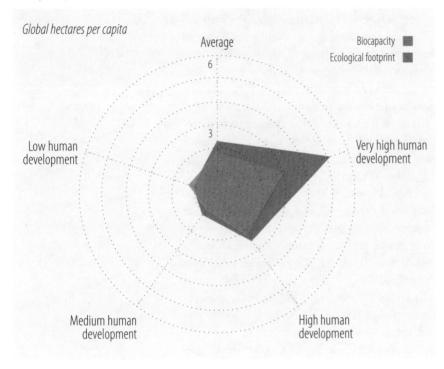

Note: Data are for 2010.
Source: Global Footprint Network 2014 and Human Development Report Office calculations.

market conditions, the environment and social perceptions can have dramatic destabilizing effects—restricting current and future choices of individuals and households and hampering the progress of entire societies. For instance, sharp swings in prices and economic activity—as seen in the global economic and financial crisis of 2007–2008 and the growing volatility of commodity prices since 2007—threaten people's livelihoods and social cohesion, while creating a climate of uncertainty that affects decisionmaking and risk-taking.

In recent years financial asset prices, commodity prices and capital flows have been particularly volatile.[29] In addition, social and political instability erupted from North Africa to Latin America, even in countries that had good or rapidly improving standards of living. While not attempting to be comprehensive or exhaustive, the rest of this chapter analyses four interconnected global threats that can increase vulnerability and undermine progress in human development: financial instability, food price volatility, natural disasters and violent conflict.

Financial instability

Over the past few decades the world has suffered deeper and more frequent financial crises that have spread rapidly to other economic sectors, creating uncertainty, affecting livelihoods and threatening social stability. In the most recent crisis global unemployment increased by nearly 30 million between 2007 and 2009, while current unemployment estimates remain far above precrisis levels.[30] Economic shocks can have long-term negative consequences, especially if they trigger a vicious cycle of low human development and conflict.[31] Natural disasters and political shocks—such as droughts and coups d'état—usually have strong negative impacts on human development. But financial shocks—such as banking crises—are the most probable trigger of HDI downturns.[32] The number of countries affected by banking crises appears to be higher in periods of high international capital mobility. Between 1950 and 1980, when capital controls were common, few countries had banking crises. But after capital flows were liberalized and financial markets further integrated, the incidence of banking crises soared (figure 2.9).[33] The Nordic banking crisis in the early 1990s, the Asian financial crisis in 1997 and the recent global financial crisis exemplify this growing instability.

Although the poorest countries were more insulated from the initial financial shock—due to their limited integration in global capital markets—they were extremely vulnerable to secondary transmission channels, such as declining external demand for their exports and lower foreign investment. Developing countries traditionally are less able to cope with large economic shocks and usually take longer to recover from crises. For instance, the volatility of GDP growth is often higher in the poorest countries—except in recent years—and the proportion of years spent in deep recession is also higher for them, due partly to their undiversified economic structures and limited policy space.[34]

Economic crises often generate unemployment and hardship, but economic booms can enhance inequality—which may contribute to the next crisis.[35] Indeed, inequality can be both a cause and a consequence of macroeconomic instability.[36] A more equitable distribution of

Measuring human progress

The accomplishments of the Millennium Development Goal (MDG) era have been stunning: To take just one example, the number of children who die each year has gone down by almost half, from more than 12.4 million to 6.6 million. That doesn't quite hit the two-thirds target included in MDG 4, but it's a great thing for humanity.

With the MDGs set to expire in 2015, the development community is starting to consider the next set of global goals and how to build on the current progress. The Secretary-General of the United Nations convened a High Level Panel on the subject, and one of the priorities it highlighted is a 'data revolution'. According to the panel, to accelerate the pace of improvements, development organizations and developing-country governments need access to more and better data.

Few people believe in the power of data as much as I do. In fact, I wrote the Bill & Melinda Gates Foundation's annual letter in 2012 about the importance of measurement. In my experience, the management slogan "What gets measured gets done" holds true. The mere act of tracking key indicators makes it much more likely that changes in those indicators will be positive. Second, analysing development statistics yields lessons that improve outcomes over time. For example, the recent proliferation of excellent community-based health systems in developing countries has a lot to do with the clear evidence that frontline workers get results.

Once there's consensus on the importance of data and the need for a data revolution, the next step is more debate on the specific contents of that revolution.

One priority is to rationalize the ongoing data collection processes. Currently, the supply of data is extremely fragmented, so different players often count the same things multiple times in slightly different ways while neglecting

to gather other useful statistics altogether. The answer is not to collect every conceivable piece of data on economic and human development, which would increase costs and lead to gridlock. We need a coordinating mechanism whereby the development community and the developing countries themselves agree on a limited list of indicators that are worth tracking carefully.

A second priority is investing in developing countries' ability to collect data over the long term: in the end, development data is only valuable if used in-country by policymakers. We should not launch a data revolution based on a huge infusion of money to gather a trove of data at a single point in time, as the next set of global goals takes effect. Instead, for a truly lasting revolution, we need to help countries hire and train more experts and invest in their own systems for tracking data that matter to them for years to come. Part of this will involve giving serious consideration to how digital technology can improve data collection in countries where current techniques are decades old. For example, using a global positioning system instead of a tape measure and a compass to estimate agricultural yields can speed up the work by more than a factor of 10.

A third priority is making sure that data on human development is widely available, informs public policy, and increases accountability. This means giving citizens, civil society, donors, entrepreneurs, and parliamentarians full access to government data, no matter what the data suggest. It also means making sure experts use the data that's available to make better policy decisions.

The benefit of a data revolution is that it will have an impact on every single priority in global development and health. With better data, countries will get better at every single goal they set, whether it's saving children's lives, increasing agricultural yields, or empowering women. Ultimately, better data can mean a better life for billions of people.

FIGURE 2.9

Since the liberalization of capital flows and greater financial integration in the 1980s, the incidence of banking crises has soared

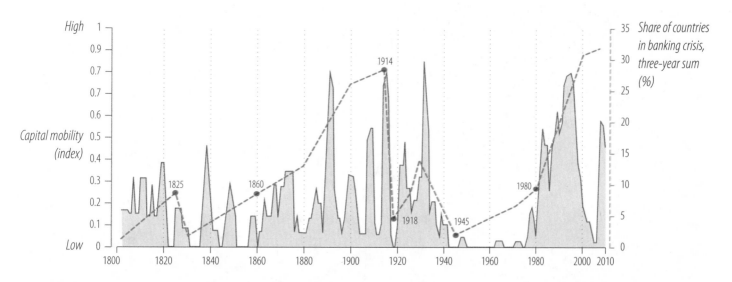

Source: Reinhart 2012.

income can boost economic growth and promote greater social and political stability. Low income inequality has been associated with longer growth spells and thus greater economic sustainability.[37]

Food price volatility

Food price volatility has become a growing threat to food security and thus to human development. Agricultural prices are inherently variable, but food prices have fluctuated considerably and unexpectedly since 2007 (figure 2.10).[38] High and volatile food prices can have long-term consequences on the physical and mental well-being of individuals, as poor households are forced to switch to cheaper but less nutritious food, cut portion sizes and even forgo meals. They may also need to work longer hours or give up other spending on health or education. Although high prices benefit food producers and food-exporting countries, they hurt poor consumers. In addition, greater price uncertainty also affects smallholders and traders.

Between 1960 and 1990 food prices broadly declined—as technological advances enabled agricultural yields to grow faster than demand. In the near future, however, they are likely to remain high and volatile. Why? Because population growth and rising incomes in emerging and developing economies are pushing demand to record levels. Growing demand for biofuels also plays a role. Meanwhile, supply is constrained by soil degradation, climate change and low investment in agriculture, especially the neglect of research and extension services. Prices are likely to be more volatile as a consequence of the higher frequency of extreme weather events, the financialization of commodity markets and the volatility in exchange rates.

Natural disasters

More frequent and intense environmental disasters are destroying lives, livelihoods, physical infrastructure and fragile ecosystems. They can impair human capabilities and threaten human development in all countries—especially in the poorest and most vulnerable.[39] Higher income and socioeconomic status are associated with greater ability to absorb losses and higher resilience. Women, people with disabilities and racial and ethnic minorities may face greater barriers to recovering from disasters, partly because they have fewer personal assets and unequal access to support.[40] Children, women and the elderly are particularly vulnerable.[41]

FIGURE 2.10

Food prices have fluctuated considerably and unexpectedly since 2007

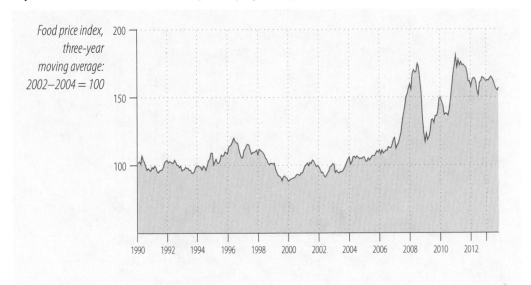

Source: FAO 2013.

Meeting the Zero Hunger Challenge

The Zero Hunger Challenge, launched in 2012 by the Secretary-General of the United Nations, integrates a zero food loss and waste challenge and a 100 percent sustainable food system challenge. How can this be accomplished? Let me cite the case of India.

Over 70 years ago, the Indian sub-continent witnessed a serious famine in the Bengal region that led to the death of more than 3 million children, women and men. India's population was then 300 million; it is now over 1.2 billion. In 2013, India witnessed a historic transition from the famine conditions of 1943 to a legal commitment to provide, at a very low cost, the minimum essential calories to over 75 percent of the population from home grown food. The challenge now is to sustain the right to food commitment in an era of climate change, which can be characterized by unfavourable alterations in temperature, precipitation and sea level.

The Indian experience shows that the challenge can be met through a six-pronged strategy consisting of:

- Attention to soil health enhancement, and conservation of prime farm land for agriculture.
- Rain water harvesting, aquifer recharge and conjunctive use of ground water, surface water, treated waste water and sea water. Sea water constitutes 97 percent of the global water resource, and it is now possible to promote sea water farming systems involving halophytes and aquaculture.
- Spreading appropriate technologies and the needed inputs.
- Credit at low interest and effective group and individual insurance.
- Assured and remunerative marketing.
- Providing farmers with small holdings the economy and power of scale through cooperatives, self-help groups, producer companies and contract farming.

Through a science-based marriage of nutrition and agriculture, agricultural remedies can be provided for nutritional maladies. For achieving nutrition security, there is a need for concurrent attention to under-nutrition or calorie deprivation, protein hunger, and hidden hunger caused by the deficiency in the diet of micronutrients like iron, iodine, zinc, vitamin A and vitamin B12. Protein deficiency can be alleviated through enhanced production and consumption of pulses (grain legumes), milk and eggs. Micro-nutrient deficiencies can be addressed through the popularization of biofortified crops. Micronutrient-enriched varieties are becoming available in several crops, such as rice, beans and wheat. The United Nations has designated 2014 as the International Year of Family Farming, and efforts should be made by developing countries to make every family farm a biofortified farm. We also should aim to train one woman and one man in every village in nutrition literacy to serve as Community Hunger Fighters.

Factors like clean drinking water, sanitation, primary healthcare and nutritional literacy have to be addressed for achieving nutrition security for all. Above all, priority to assisting small farm families to produce and earn more is the best way of overcoming poverty and malnutrition. The Indian Food Security Act has several interesting features worthy of emulation. Some of these include adopting a life cycle approach with special attention to the first 1,000 days in a child's life and designating the eldest woman in the household as the recipient of the subsidized food. Thus, the critical role women play in household food security is recognized under this Act.

In most developing countries the livelihood security of more than 50 percent of the population depends on crop and animal husbandry, inland and marine fisheries, forestry and agro-forestry, and agro-processing and agri-business. Under such conditions, if agriculture goes wrong, nothing else will have a chance to go right. Recent trends in food prices indicate that the future belongs to countries with grains and not guns.

Natural disasters are increasing in frequency and intensity. Between 1901 and 1910 there were 82 recorded disasters, but between 2003 and 2012 there were more than 4,000. Even allowing for better recording, the increase is substantial. Particularly worrying is the much greater incidence of hydrological and meteorological disasters (figure 2.11). Although fatalities from natural disasters appear to be declining, the number of people affected is increasing.

The frequency and severity of heat waves, floods, droughts and heavy precipitation have been linked to climate change. These extremes inflict exceptionally high economic and social costs. Moreover, there is growing scientific evidence that human action is responsible for warming the atmosphere and oceans, rising sea levels and some climate extremes.[42] Global warming increases the likelihood of severe, pervasive and irreversible impacts.[43] So, some of these weather extremes could be potentially prevented, or at least lessened. Climate change and environmental degradation are major threats to human development. Action to reduce these vulnerabilities, including a global agreement on climate change negotiations, will be fundamental to securing and sustaining human development.

Violent conflict

Armed conflicts impose enormous costs on individuals, communities and countries. In addition to the loss of lives, they destroy livelihoods, generate insecurity and disrupt social services, institutions and markets. Conflicts can also cause large population displacements. By the end of 2012 around 45 million people were forcibly displaced due to conflict or

FIGURE 2.11

Between 1901 and 1910 there were 82 recorded natural disasters, but between 2003 and 2012 there were more than 4,000

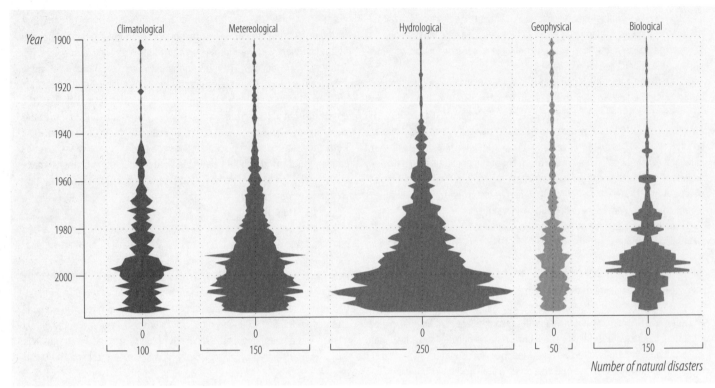

Note: The main types of disasters include extreme temperatures and droughts (climatological), storms (meteorological), floods (hydrological), earthquakes (geophysical) and epidemics (biological).
Source: CRED 2013.

persecution—the highest in 18 years—with 15.4 million of them refugees.[44] Displaced populations separated from their jobs, assets and social networks are highly vulnerable to further violence, disease, poverty and natural disasters and have impaired ability to cope with adversity.

Internal and nonstate armed conflicts account for the vast majority of conflicts worldwide (figure 2.12).[45] The number of nonstate conflicts has risen recently, and although the total number of internal conflicts is declining, the number of internationalized internal conflicts is on the rise. Interstate conflicts have declined due partly to the end of the colonial wars and the Cold War. Armed conflicts occur for different reasons and in very different contexts. But deficits in development, unaddressed grievances (including past conflicts) and natural resource rents are common threads in the majority of armed conflicts.

Civil unrest has been fuelled by a growing perception that policymaking has not prioritized people's needs or listened to their voices, which should be taken as an important call for better governance. This requires greater accountability and responsiveness of governments to the concerns of their citizens. Profound transformations are needed—beyond changes in government, as the Arab Spring illustrated—to open the political space and enable agency. Growing economic and social tensions—emerging from increasing inequality and a lack of economic opportunities—are likely to continue to fuel social unrest.[46]

Several global factors can fuel conflicts and enhance fragility, such as transnational organized crime, international markets in military goods and security services, and the spread of radical extremism. Addressing these sources of vulnerability will be crucial to promote peace and advance human development.[47]

The world has always been subject to uncertainty and unpredictability. But the growing frequency and severity of economic and environmental shocks threaten human

FIGURE 2.12

Internal and nonstate armed conflicts account for the vast majority of conflicts worldwide

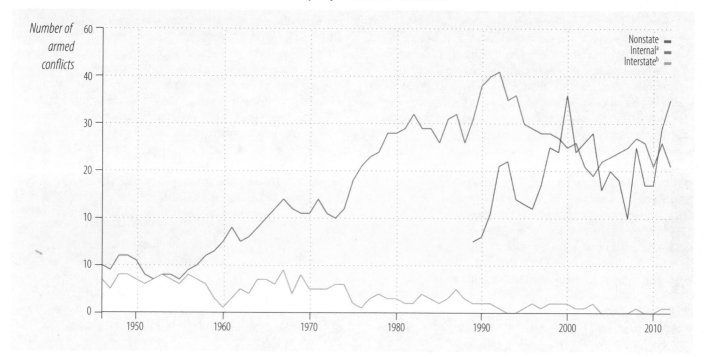

a. Includes internationalized internal conflicts.
b. Includes extrasystemic conflicts.
Source: UCDP and PRIO 2013; UCDP 2013.

development. That makes it vital to adopt bold national and international policies to reduce the vulnerability of individuals, communities and countries and to increase their resilience (chapters 4 and 5).

*   *   *

Despite continuing progress in human development, many people remain vulnerable to shocks that undermine their ability to live a healthy and fulfilling life. The next chapter identifies specific population groups that are particularly vulnerable to systemic threats and the mechanisms through which these vulnerabilities affect human development.

Dealing with climate change

Addressing vulnerabilities and building resilience would need to deal with the impacts of climate change, which could become progressively serious if mitigating emissions of greenhouse gases (GHG) is either delayed or inadequate in magnitude. The recently completed Working Group I report by the Intergovernmental Panel on Climate Change (IPCC) as part of the Fifth Assessment Report clearly establishes that each of the last three decades has been successively warmer at the Earth's surface than any preceding decade since 1850. In the Northern Hemisphere, 1983–2012 was likely the warmest 30-year period of the last 1,400 years.

The rate of sea level rise since the mid-19th century has been larger than the mean rate in the previous two millennia. Over 1901–2010 the global mean sea level rose by 0.19 meters. Projections indicate that for the highest GHG concentration scenario, sea level rise would lie between 0.52 to 0.98 meters by 2100 and between 0.58 and 2.03 meters by 2200. This clearly would severely test the resilience and adaptive capacities of societies in low-lying coastal areas and small island states. It is also likely that mean sea level rise will contribute to upward trends in extreme coastal high water.

The length, frequency and intensity of warm spells or heat waves will increase over most land areas. Based on emission scenarios, a 1-in-20 year hottest day is likely to become a 1-in-2 year event by the end of the 21st century in most regions. And the frequency of heavy precipitation or the proportion of total rainfall from heavy falls will increase in the 21st century over many areas of the globe. A nearly ice-free Arctic Ocean in September is likely before mid-century in the highest GHG concentration scenario. Correspondingly, temperature increases relative to 1986–2005 are projected to be in the range of 2.6°C to 4.8°C for 2081–2100.

Some of the expected changes from climate change will be abrupt, leaving less time for adaptation. A large fraction of anthropogenic climate change from CO_2 emissions is irreversible on a multicentury to millennial time scale. For example, depending on the scenario, about 15 to 40 percent of emitted CO_2 will remain in the atmosphere longer than 1,000 years. It is also virtually certain that global mean sea level rise will continue beyond 2100, with sea level rise due to thermal expansion to continue for many centuries. Sustained mass loss by ice sheets would cause larger sea level rise, and some part of the mass loss might be irreversible. There is high confidence that sustained warming greater than some threshold would lead to the near-complete loss of the Greenland ice sheet over a millennium or more, causing a global mean sea level rise of up to 7 metres. Current estimates indicate that the threshold is greater than about 1°C but less than about 4°C. The Fourth Assessment Report stated that under the SRES scenarios, the coastal population could grow from 1.2 billion people in 1990 to 1.8–5.2 billion people by the 2080s, depending on assumptions about migration. With increases in global population, the number of people vulnerable to sea level rise will also likely increase.

Actions that range from incremental steps to transformational changes are essential for reducing risks from climate extremes. Social, economic and environmental sustainability can be enhanced by disaster risk management and adaptation approaches. A prerequisite for sustainability in the context of climate change is addressing the underlying causes of vulnerability, including the structural inequalities that create and sustain poverty and constrain access to resources.

The most effective adaptation and disaster risk reduction actions are those that offer development benefits in the relative near term as well as reductions in vulnerability over the longer term. There are many approaches and pathways to a sustainable and resilient future. However, limits to resilience are faced when thresholds or tipping points associated with social and natural systems are exceeded, posing severe challenges for adaptation. Consequently, global society has to be aware that neither mitigation nor adaptation alone can avoid all climate change impacts. Adaptation and mitigation can complement each other, and together can significantly reduce the risks of climate change.

"There can be no keener revelation of a society's soul than the way in which it treats its children."

Nelson Mandela

"A stone thrown at the right time is better than gold given at the wrong time."

Persian proverb

3.

Vulnerable people, vulnerable world

Almost everyone feels vulnerable at some point in life. But some individuals and some groups are more vulnerable than others due to varying exposure to social and economic conditions and at different stages of their life cycles, starting at birth. This Report is concerned with people facing the possibility of major deterioration in their circumstances as a result of adverse events. The interest is in examining how individual and social characteristics condition the impacts that people feel in response to persistent shocks and risks more generally. By focusing on enduring and systemic vulnerability, we then ask who is vulnerable and why. This leads us to examine some of the critical underlying factors that generate these impacts.

People with limited core capabilities, such as in education and health, are less able to easily live lives they value. And their choices may be restricted or held back by social barriers and other exclusionary practices. Together, limited capabilities and restricted choices[1] prevent them from coping with threats. At certain stages of the life cycle, capabilities may be restricted due to inadequate investments and attention at the appropriate times, yielding vulnerabilities that may accumulate and intensify. Consider how the lack of development of cognitive and noncognitive skills in early childhood affects labour outcomes and even drug and alcohol use later in life.[2] Among the factors that condition how shocks and setbacks are felt and tackled are circumstances of birth, age, identity and socioeconomic status—circumstances over which individuals have little or no control.

This chapter highlights life cycle vulnerabilities and structural vulnerabilities (as well as their intersections). It also looks at how security influences choices and affects some groups more than others, with a focus on personal insecurity.

- *Life cycle vulnerabilities* refer to threats that individuals face across different stages of their life—from infancy through youth, adulthood and old age. Focusing on life cycle vulnerabilities and the formation of life capabilities draws attention to sensitive phases when a person may be particularly susceptible. Inadequate attention during such periods can limit capabilities and heighten vulnerability. Earlier and continual investments make the formation of life capabilities more robust. This approach helps in identifying interventions and policies that build human resilience, a subject for the next chapter.

- *Structural vulnerabilities* are embedded in social contexts. Such a focus draws attention to individual and group characteristics, including group identity, that are associated with a higher vulnerability to adverse circumstances. The reduced ability to bounce back can be traced to inadequate investments in building capabilities not only today, but throughout the entire life cycle, to disability, to geographical remoteness or other isolation, or to societal barriers that prevent people from realizing their potential even if they otherwise have similar capabilities (such as discrimination and the exclusion of women).

Social institutions including norms shape the capabilities and choices that are afforded to individuals. Norms such as discrimination against certain groups, weak rule of law and systems of recourse, and settling of disputes through violence can severely curtail the freedoms that individuals enjoy. Structural factors can also subject people or groups to multiple disadvantages. Group-based discrimination and exclusion exist across multiple dimensions—political participation, health care, personal security and education, to name a few—and generate chronic and overlapping vulnerabilities for minorities and other excluded groups by limiting their capabilities and their potential role in the larger society.

- *Group violence and insecure lives.* Vulnerability adds an important dimension to any assessment of human development and its progress. Human development is about not only expanding choices, but also whether those choices are secure and likely to exist in the future. Making choices freely can be impaired by personal insecurity and fear of violence. Violence restricts choices and freedoms through physical harm and threats and flourishes in countries with weak states, limited governance and poor social institutions. Violence is also associated with high poverty and inequality. Women and sexual, ethnic and religious minorities—as well as other groups and communities that face social discrimination—are more likely to experience personal insecurity and threats of violence, perceived or actual.

Whether societies are cohesive can influence how individuals and communities respond to persistent and pervasive shocks. A lack of social cohesion coupled with high inequality threatens human development achievements by skewing institutions and eroding the social contract.[3] Beyond a certain threshold, inequality exacerbates rent-seeking, which impedes growth, slows poverty reduction and limits the quality of social and political engagement. Of course, the relationship also goes the other way, since rent-seeking activities may lead to increased inequality.[4] Inequality also impedes human development by reducing investment in basic social services and public goods and by increasing political instability.[5] Cohesive and more-equal societies do better in most aspects of human development, including responding to threats and challenges.[6] People are more secure when states function well and when social cohesion is strengthened by protecting all rights and advancing norms that boost tolerance and inclusiveness. Such states also tend to have strong social institutions that create space for individuals and groups to feel secure in expressing their concerns, in claiming their rights to support and protection and in building alliances for collective action.

Life capabilities and life cycle vulnerabilities— interdependent and cumulative

Capabilities are built over a lifetime and have to be nurtured and maintained; otherwise they can stagnate. Many of people's vulnerabilities (and strengths) are the result of their life histories, with past outcomes influencing present exposure and ways of coping.[7] The formation of life capabilities has two features.

- First, life capabilities at any stage of life are path-dependent—that is, they are affected by investments in the preceding stages of life. They are also subject to an ecological relationship and affected by the interplay among the immediate environment, the community and society.

- Second, short-term shocks frequently have long-run consequences. Individuals may not automatically bounce back from what appears to be a transitory shock (hysteresis). For instance, a setback in early childhood can have serious ramifications throughout the rest of a person's life, including the chances of holding onto a job, the uncertainties associated with growing older and the transmission of vulnerabilities to the next generation. Some effects can be reversed, but not always[8]; reversal is context-specific and not necessarily cost-effective.[9]

When investments in life capabilities occur earlier, future prospects are better (see the solid blue line in figure 3.1). The opposite is also true—the lack of timely and continuing investments in life capabilities can heavily compromise an individual's ability to achieve full human development potential (see the solid red line in figure 3.1). Later interventions can help individuals recover—but usually only partially—and move to a higher human development path (see the dashed blue lines in figure 3.1).

Structural vulnerabilities—arising from such factors as gender, ethnicity and intergroup inequality (see next section)—interact with life cycle dynamics to place certain groups of children, youth, working people and older adults at greater risk. An example is the intergenerational transmission of vulnerability from disadvantaged parents to their children. This interaction is influenced by the social context and the degree of human agency. Since people do not suffer crises passively, they have a major role in shaping their destinies. This active role, or agency, of the individual and collective is most easily realized in societies that create space for citizens to express their views, voice their concerns and make reasoned decisions about the types of lives they want to live.

The extent to which the public can engage with states or take direct action to reduce vulnerability goes beyond democratization in the institutional sense. Even in democracies elite

When investments in life capabilities occur earlier, future prospects are better

FIGURE 3.1

When investments in life capabilities occur earlier, future prospects are better

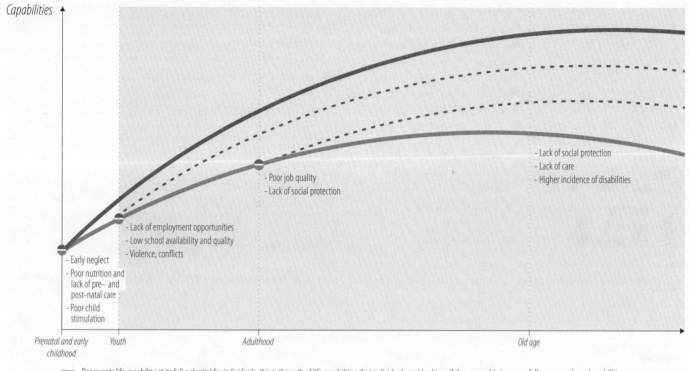

Capabilities

- Early neglect
- Poor nutrition and lack of pre- and post-natal care
- Poor child stimulation

- Lack of employment opportunities
- Low school availability and quality
- Violence, conflicts

- Poor job quality
- Lack of social protection

- Lack of social protection
- Lack of care
- Higher incidence of disabilities

Prenatal and early childhood   Youth   Adulthood   Old age

■■■ Represents life capability at its full potential for individuals; this is the path of life capabilities that individuals could achieve if they were able to successfully manage the vulnerabilities they are likely to face during sensitive periods along their life cycle.

■■■ Shows that when individuals fail to overcome vulnerabilities at any sensitive period, their life capabilities are likely to end up on a lower path.

• • • Later interventions could help individuals recover—but usually only partially—and move to a higher path.

Source: Human Development Report Office calculations.

capture of political systems can narrow the scope of public discussion and reduce opportunities for critical examination of a society's values and priorities.

Early childhood—building strong foundations to break the intergenerational cycle of deprivation

The foundational period is early childhood—a window of opportunity for resolving early inequity and achieving inclusive and sustainable social and economic development (box 3.1). The global population of children under age 5 is 659 million (9.1 percent of the total). The regions with the highest shares of children in the total population are Sub-Saharan Africa (16.2 percent), the Arab States (12 percent) and South Asia (10.5 percent; figure 3.2). By 2050 the global share is expected to drop to 7.9 percent, with the largest drop in South Asia (to 6.9 percent). By 2050 only the Arab

States and Sub-Saharan Africa will have above-average shares of children under age 5.[10]

By providing basic health care, adequate nutrition, and nurturing and stimulation in a caring environment, interventions in early childhood development help ensure children's progress in primary school, continuation through secondary school and successful entry into adulthood and engagement in the workforce.[11]

Events in early life affect the development of the brain's circuitry, the dynamic gene–environment interactions and the programming of the body's immune, neurological and endocrine systems. This has implications for subsequent trajectories of human development.[12] Both the architecture of skills (coping abilities and cognitive and noncognitive competences) and the process of skill formation are strongly influenced by neural circuits that develop as a result of dynamic interactions between genes and early-life environments and experiences. In other words,

Human development and early childhood development

Recent research on the economics, psychology and neuroscience of human development is converging to a deeper understanding of how we become who we are. This Report offers guidelines on how this knowledge should guide policy.

Multiple abilities shape flourishing lives. Policymakers need to move beyond a one dimensional focus of measuring human development by scores on achievement tests, like the Programme for International Student Assessment, and consider a much broader array of essential life skills.

The early years are important in creating human capacities. Policymakers need to act on the knowledge that skills beget skills, that flourishing lives have strong early foundations and that substantial gaps in skills emerge before children start school. This Report offers guidance on effective strategies of human development starting in the womb and continuing through old age.

Investments in early childhood development can play an important role in reducing the role of the accident of birth in determining life outcomes. The most productive investments foster parenting, attachment and interactions between parents and children. Good parenting is far more important than cash. An economically advantaged child subject to low-quality parenting is more disadvantaged than an economically disadvantaged child with a parent who cares and guides the child wisely.

The new science of early childhood shows that what is socially fair can be economically efficient. High-quality supplements to family life that foster beneficial parent–child interactions and stimulate children have high economic returns that more than pay for themselves. Quality early childhood development can be an important contributor to a successful national economic development strategy.

FIGURE 3.2

The regions with the highest shares of children under age 5 in the total population are Sub-Saharan Africa, the Arab States and South Asia

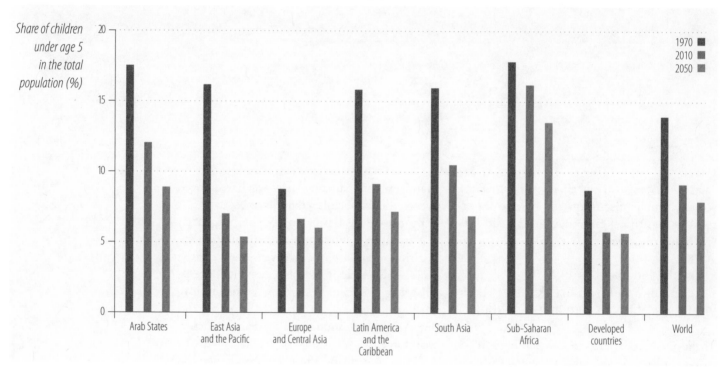

Source: Human Development Report Office calculations based on Lutz and KC (2013).

the environment can affect individuals differently depending on their genetic endowments, and the same genetic endowment produces different outcomes depending on the environment.[13] This interaction follows hierarchical rules in a sequence of events, such that later attainment is built on foundations laid earlier.

Cognitive, social, emotional and language competences are interdependent, since all are shaped by early experiences and all contribute to the formation of lifelong capabilities (figure 3.3).[14] As a result, stresses in early life—such as socioeconomic deprivation, disruptive care giving and harsh parenting—tend to be associated with difficulties in adult life, including the incidence of chronic diseases. Studies from New Zealand and the United States have linked childhood abuse and other adversities

FIGURE 3.3

Cognitive, social, emotional and language competences are interdependent, since all are shaped by early experiences and all contribute to the formation of lifelong capabilities

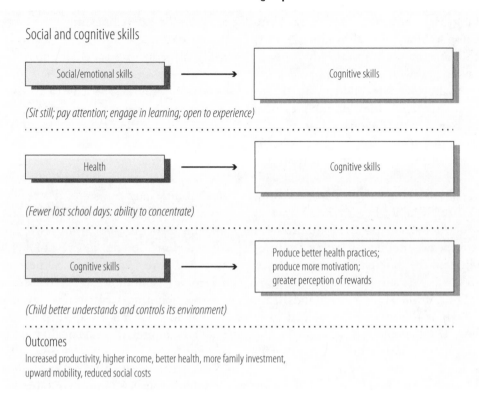

Source: Heckman 2013.

with a range of health problems, including coronary artery disease, high blood pressure, type 2 diabetes, obesity and cancer—as well as with such mental and behavioural problems as depression, alcoholism, smoking and other substance abuse.[15]

Infants and young children across the world, exposed to innumerable risks, are extremely vulnerable to the effects of inadequate access to health care or education, clean drinking water or proper sanitation and food.[16] The longer the exposure to harsh conditions or deprivations, the greater the burden on the body's stress response system.[17]

But it is a mistake to assume that abilities are fixed. Multiple abilities, both cognitive and noncognitive, develop continuously from the early years onwards in a variety of learning situations to foster further learning and performance. Many of these processes interact.[18] For example, academic motivation not only boosts education outcomes, but is also likely to reduce drug and alcohol use, both of which are associated with crime. Enhanced personality

traits such as academic motivation can promote learning, which in turn boosts achievement. But in the other direction, aggressive, antisocial or rule-breaking behaviours can lead to crime and poor labour market outcomes.[19]

Too often, poverty disrupts the normal course of early childhood development—more than one in five children in developing countries lives in absolute income poverty and is vulnerable to malnutrition.[20] In developing countries (where 92 percent of children live) 7 in 100 will not survive beyond age 5, 50 will not have their birth registered, 68 will not receive early childhood education, 17 will never enrol in primary school, 30 will be stunted and 25 will live in poverty.[21] Inadequate food, sanitation facilities and hygiene increase the risk of infections and stunting: close to 156 million children are stunted, a result of undernutrition and infection.[22] Undernutrition contributes to 35 percent of deaths due to measles, malaria, pneumonia and diarrhoea.[23] The impact is greatest if the deprivation is in early childhood.[24] Children are also affected if their mothers are poor, have low levels of education or suffer from depression or high levels of stress, perhaps as a result of violence, poor housing or a lack of services.

Lacking basic nutrition, health care and stimulation to promote healthy growth, many poor children enter school unready to learn, and they do poorly in class, repeat grades and are likely to drop out. For children who survive, poverty and undernutrition during preschool years account for a subsequent loss of more than two school grades. Even at age 6, or by the time of school entry, a poor child may already be at a disadvantage (figure 3.4).[25] Gaps in skills open early. For example, word accumulation begins very early in life. In the United States at age 36 months the verbal skills of children from different socioeconomic backgrounds differ markedly, and the differences, or trajectories, for verbal skills, are still present at age 9 (box 3.1).[26] Those from poor backgrounds learn more slowly if their parents have had little education. In Colombia and Mexico semantic verbal fluency is strongly associated with parental education.[27]

Good adult–child interactions in the early years are essential stimulation for brain development and do not necessarily depend on money.[28] In fact, parents' communication with their children and their sensitivity to children's emotional needs can limit the effects of low socioeconomic status on children's cognitive and socioemotional development.[29]

Economic downturns can also disrupt children's education development—especially when their parents lose their jobs. The Indonesian crisis in 1998 led to a 5–8 percentage point decline in enrolment among children ages 13 and 14,[30] and the crises in post-Soviet and Central Asian countries reduced enrolment 3–12 percentage points.[31]

When educational attainment is reduced, vulnerabilities are transmitted across generations by limiting children's future learning and employment opportunities.[32] Poverty and undernutrition during preschool years are associated with a more than 30 percent loss in income.[33] Conditions experienced before age 18, including structural vulnerabilities such as poverty and group inequality, contribute to about half the inequality in lifetime earnings.[34]

Violence, neglect and conflict also damage early childhood development. Children in the Gaza Strip have three times the emotional and behavioural problems of middle-class Canadian

FIGURE 3.4

Poor children are already at a vocabulary disadvantage by age 6, as shown in the case of Ecuador

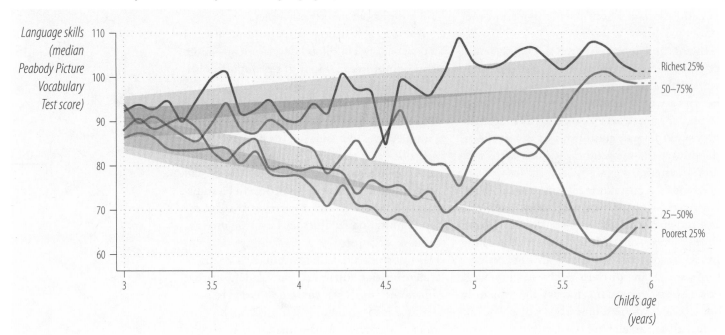

BOX 3.1

Meaningful differences: 30 million more words

Children's early exposure to language in relation to family status and income makes a difference. Evidence from the United States highlights the importance of good parent–child interaction and stimulation, especially for children in poorer socioeconomic settings, and the critical roles of families and communities (see table and figure). Children's success depends on the quality of early home environments.

Cumulative vocabulary experiences for children in the United States

Family socioeconomic status	Words heard per hour	Words heard by age 4
Welfare	616	13 million
Working class	1,251	26 million
Professional	2,153	45 million

Gaps open early before entering school—vocabulary

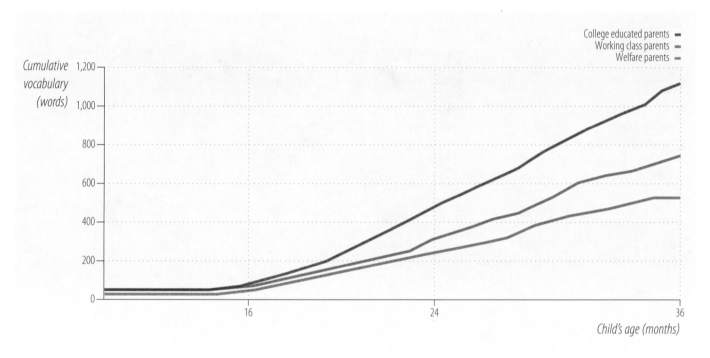

Source: Hart and Risley 1995.

children.[35] And children who witness their mothers being beaten by intimate partners are more likely than others to grow up to become victims or perpetrators of violence.[36]

At particular risk of sexual abuse are children with disabilities and those who are psychological or cognitively vulnerable[37]—those who live in communities where unemployment and substance abuse are rampant—or are abandoned, trafficked or forced to work outside the home.[38] Children raised in institutions may also suffer profound deprivation that damages brain development.[39] Even schools may be sources of insecurity. Indeed, when parents fear for the physical and sexual safety of daughters, they are likely to keep them out of school.[40]

Alleviating the worst effects of poverty and deprivation, and breaking the intergenerational cycle of poverty, gives children a better chance.

Navigating vulnerabilities during youth

Youth—ages 15–24—is a key period of transition when children learn to engage with society and the world of work.[41] In many countries the number of young people is rising. The global youth population is 1.2 billion (17.6 percent of the total population), and the regions with the highest shares of young people in their population are Sub-Saharan Africa (20.2 percent), the Arab States (19.6 percent) and South Asia (19.6 percent). By 2050 the share of young people in the total population is expected to drop to 13.8 percent, with the largest drop in East Asia and the Pacific (from 17.3 percent in 2010 to 10.7 percent in 2050).[42] Country data also show that the share of young people in the total population is expected to fall in most regions by 2050 (map 3.1).

Governments will need to ensure sufficient employment opportunities for young people or face social and political unrest. Recent social upheavals show that a mismatch between increasingly educated young people and employment opportunities can yield alienation and despair. The International Labour

MAP 3.1

The share of young people in the total population is expected to fall in most regions between 2010 and 2050

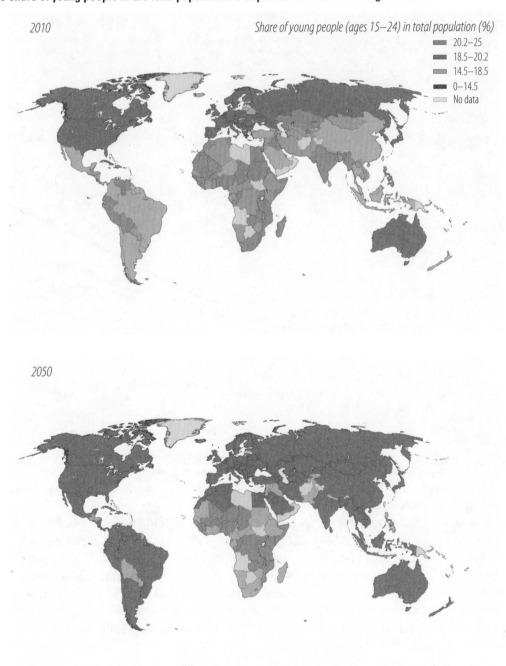

Note: These maps are stylized and not to scale. They do not reflect a position by the United Nations Development Programme on the legal status of any country or territory or the delimitation of any frontiers.
Source: Human Development Report Office calculations based on Lutz and KC (2013).

Organization's projection for job creation in the Middle East is flat, which could lead to a continuing mismatch between opportunities and aspirations.[43]

Young people around the world are especially vulnerable to marginalization in the labour market because they lack work experience, social networks, job search abilities and the financial resources to find employment. So they are more likely to be unemployed, underemployed or employed on more precarious contracts. Youth unemployment rates, almost always higher than those for adults, are also more sensitive to macroeconomic shocks.[44] In 2012 the global youth unemployment rate was an estimated 12.7 percent—almost three times the adult rate.[45] When a crisis hits, young people are more likely to experience joblessness than adults are, and the gap between youth and adult unemployment rates remains wide, even after the economy has begun to recover.[46]

Many social and economic challenges facing young people today, including unemployment, must be understood in the interaction between unique demographic trends and specific economic contexts.[47] As a consequence of the large decline in fertility rates,[48] in many developing countries the share of young people in the total population has increased over the past 40 years, creating a 'youth bulge'. This presents an opportunity to foster human development, as the labour force grows[49] with better educated and potentially more-productive workers. But the growing youth labour force has not been matched by increasing productive employment opportunities. Today's high youth unemployment rate is a considerable loss of human development potential that not only threatens economic progress,[50] but also raises the risk of social unrest, violence and crime.[51]

Ambitious policies are critical for meeting young people's expectations in the labour market. Under an 'ambitious policy' scenario, global youth unemployment would be less than 5 percent by 2050[52] due to the dual effect of fewer young people entering the labour market and higher economic growth. However, there are important regional heterogeneities. Under a 'business as usual' scenario the gap would continue to grow, particularly in Sub-Saharan Africa.[53] But ambitious policies (fast track education policies and accelerated economic growth) would close the gap in supply and demand for young workers for South Asia and reduce it for Sub-Saharan Africa (figure 3.5). In South Asia the gap would be closed by 2050 due to the dual effect of education policies on population dynamics (which will reduce the number of young people that enter the labour market) and higher economic growth. For Sub-Saharan Africa additional policies to raise the employment intensity of growth would be needed to close the gap.

Young people are also vulnerable as they face changes in their physical, cognitive, social, gendered and emotional lives. For example, adolescents could risk being out of school and out of work, limiting their engagement in society. Some are forced to work, are trafficked for sex or become undocumented migrants. These experiences are shaped by the socioeconomic environment. In many countries young people are seeing their choices limited by economic insecurity, technological change, political uprisings, conflict (box 3.2) and climate change—which can transform enthusiasm and entrepreneurship into frustration and despair.

Young people's social transitions are also shaped by broader structural factors, such as poverty, gender and inequality, as well as local practices. In some regions social change and the expansion of formal education are altering the opportunities for and constraints on young people's social transitions to adulthood. For example, young people are marrying later and delaying having children.

Investing earlier in the life cycle has proven effective in improving outcomes for adolescents later in life. But if substantial deprivation occurs in childhood, there is potential for long-term losses.[54] A recent study looked at 15-year-olds who experienced a food shortage at age 12. In Peru they were 60 percent less likely to have a healthy body mass index; in Ethiopia and Andhra Pradesh, India, they scored lower in cognitive achievement; in Viet Nam and Andhra Pradesh they reported lower self-rated health; and in Ethiopia and Peru they reported lower subjective well-being.[55]

Typically, the opportunities are better in urban areas.[56] In Andhra Pradesh 25 percent of young people are no longer in school in rural areas, compared with 15 percent in urban areas. Girls were needed for work at home or on family land, while boys had left school,

Recent social upheavals show that a mismatch between increasingly educated young people and employment opportunities can yield alienation and despair

FIGURE 3.5

Fast track education policies and accelerated economic growth would eliminate the gap in supply and demand for young workers in South Asia and narrow it in Sub-Saharan Africa between 2010 and 2050

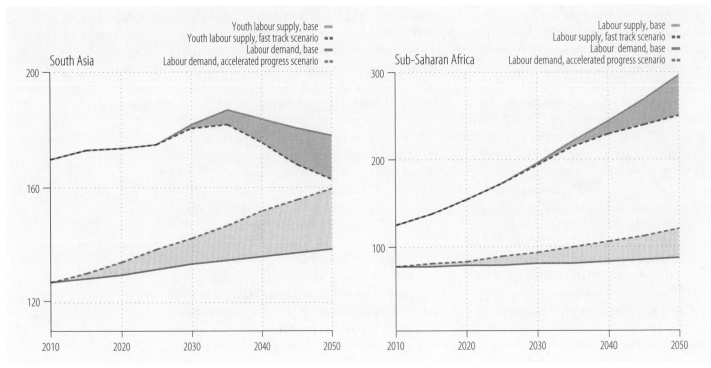

Source: Human Development Report Office calculations based on Lutz and KC (2013) and Pardee Center for International Futures (2013).

either to work for pay or because of schooling's perceived irrelevance or poor quality. Young people from Scheduled Castes and Scheduled Tribes were twice as likely to have left school. Urban families also have more variety in education institutions.[57]

Gender inequality shapes the school experience of young people. In rural Ethiopia 15-year-old girls in the lowest wealth quintile scored on average 2.1 of 20 on a math test, whereas 15-year-old boys averaged 7.4. In rural Viet Nam 15-year-old girls averaged 9.4, whereas 15-year-old boys averaged 18.1.[58]

The onset of puberty opens other vulnerabilities, with different ramifications for boys and girls.[59] A major concern is teenage pregnancy—which brings medical risks to mother and child, increases the rate of maternal depression and lowers the mother's education and employment status.[60] Premature pregnancy also has implications for young men, imposing financial and social obligations they are not yet ready to handle.[61] There are similar concerns about early marriage—often arranged for young people who have limited social and economic

options.[62] But in most parts of the world, marriage of young girls is arranged as part of taking care of their material needs and those of their families. The practice of early marriage tends to continue when the social and economic options of young women are limited.

These and other local customs and sociocultural practices shape young people's social transitions to adulthood. For example, young men may have intergenerational obligations that shape their social transitions, such as caring for ageing parents.

Young adults are also particularly vulnerable to violence,[63] which can lead to exclusion, hopelessness, a lack of purpose in life and, particularly among girls, increased anxiety, depression and post-traumatic stress.[64] Based on homicide rates, the problem is greatest in Latin America, where the rate is higher than 70 per 100,000.[65] For each young person killed, 20–40 more are believed to sustain injuries requiring hospital treatment. Homicide rates, highest for men ages 15–29, tend to decline with age, whereas the much lower rates for woman remain largely unchanged during the life cycle (figure 3.6).[66]

BOX 3.2

Somalia: conflict and youth exclusion

Deprivation, exclusion and grievances are particularly widespread during conflicts. They are fuelled by underdevelopment and poverty and uneven power distributions and inequality between groups that result in multiple exclusions and competition for resources. In Somalia young people experience exclusion in three dimensions—sociocultural, economic and political—and a lack of opportunities. As a result, they become both victims and sources of conflict. Caught between conflict and poverty, they are jobless and voiceless. To capture their deprivations and frustrations, and highlight the potential of energy and enthusiasm for change, the 2012 *Somalia National Human Development Report: Empowering Youth for Peace and Development* engaged youth to hear their opinion of their situation.

In all Somali regions young people experience a disconnect between education and employment opportunities that prevents social and economic empowerment (see figure). They also perceive few opportunities to

participate in society or express their needs and aspirations. This feeling is particularly strong in South Central Somalia, the most conflict-affected region. The lack of voice, choice and options forces young people to engage in violence and conflict. Motives are financial as well as nonfinancial, out of a need for personal security or related to identity, status and revenge.

Combining these results in a new youth frustration index, Somalia scores 3.96 out of 5 points (where 5 is the most frustrated). With the lack of employable skills, the lack of employment opportunities, the lack of voice and the lack of recreational activities as the most relevant causes for frustration, it is clear that young people feel undervalued and excluded from various parts of society.

Despite their challenges, young people in Somalia still have hopes and aspirations for the future, indicating the importance of giving them voice in their society and according them a role in peace building.

Youth perceptions of exclusion and coping strategies

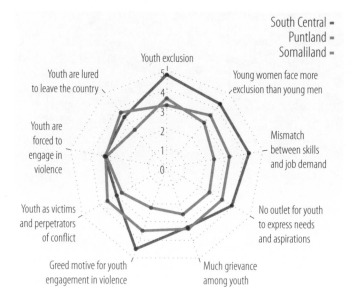

Youth frustration and underlying causes

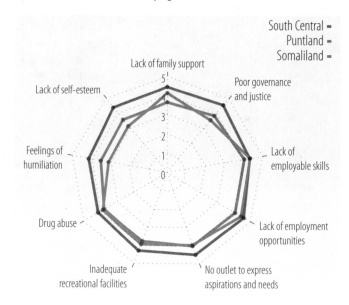

Source: UNDP 2012e.

Young people are at particular risk of being coerced or manipulated into criminal activity by gangs and criminal groups managed by adults. In environments with high youth unemployment, gangs offer an occupation, a sense of identity and belonging and a platform to protest against society.

Adulthood and work—more than just money

Adults are expected to provide for themselves and their families through paid and unpaid labour. Those with jobs are often considered less vulnerable. Yet many are exposed to precarious employment or unemployment. In 2012 more than 200 million adults worldwide were unemployed. Vulnerable employment accounts for more than half of total employment and is particularly high in South-East Asia (61 percent), South Asia (77 percent) and Sub-Saharan Africa (77 percent).[67] Even those employed may be earning very little. In 2011, 397 million people ages 15 and older were estimated to be employed but living in households with less than $1.25 per person a day. The regions with

FIGURE 3.6

In Latin America and the Caribbean homicide rates for men, highest for men ages 15–29, tend to decline with age, whereas the much lower rates for woman remain largely unchanged

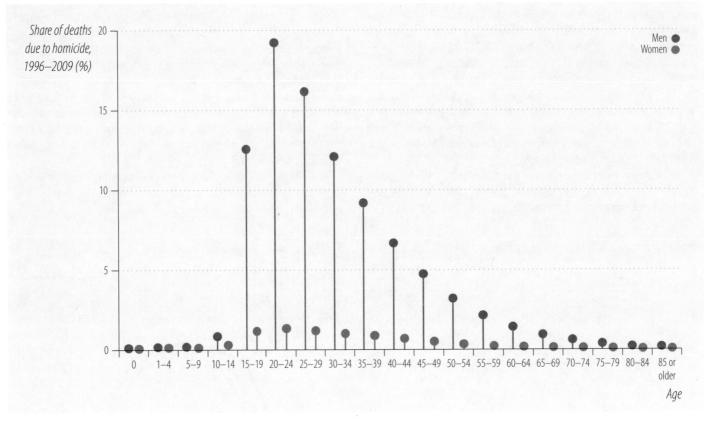

Source: UNDP 2013b.

the highest rate of these working poor as share of total employment are South Asia (25.7 percent) and Sub-Saharan Africa (41.7 percent).[68]

Work provides more than wages. Employment, especially decent employment, is associated with dignity and status—and with stable and cohesive communities and societies. Stable employment brings benefits for society—enabling the workforce to retain experience, knowledge and productivity, thus enhancing economic performance.[69] Full employment also contributes to social cohesion, particularly by improving the well-being of girls. Increased employment of women helps change perceptions of the 'value' of girls and encourages investment in their education and health. It also helps reduce poverty.

The recent economic crisis led to relatively long unemployment spells for many workers. Since the last quarter of 2007 in a majority of 42 countries with data, a high proportion of unemployed were out of work for 12 months

or more.[70] Even if economic downturns are short, individuals can be subject to 'scarring', with lasting negative consequences. In developed countries a loss of employment results in a 10–25 percent reduction in earnings, and this decline can last 5–20 years.[71] Large losses of earnings from an unexpected job displacement have also been found in developing countries,[72] where economic crises have large negative effects on earnings, household consumption and poverty.[73]

The lack of a decent job can have serious consequences beyond the loss in income. The stresses of layoffs and episodes of unemployment can reduce life expectancy as a result of health problems such as strokes or heart attacks.[74] Bouts of unemployment are also associated with high rates of depression and alcoholism.[75] And there is a gender bias. In the United Kingdom women ages 60 and older are more likely than men of the same age to have a low income, and women who have had lower

Valuing the dignity of work

In today's world defending the dignity of work is a constant uphill struggle. Prevailing economic thinking sees work as a cost of production, which in a global economy has to be as low as possible in order to be competitive. It sees workers as consumers who because of their relative low wages need to be given easy access to credit to stimulate consumption and wind up with incredible debts. Nowhere in sight is the societal significance of work as a foundation of personal dignity, as a source of stability and development of families or as a contribution to communities at peace. This is the meaning of 'decent work'. It is an effort at reminding ourselves that we are talking about policies that deal with the life of human beings not just bottom line issues. It is the reason why the International Labour Organization constitution tells us "Labour is not a commodity."[1] And we know that the quality of work defines in so many ways the quality of a society. So we must begin by helping the working poor step out of poverty and informality into quality livelihoods, self-employment or a formal job. And that's what our policies should be about: keeping people moving into progressively better jobs with living wages, respect for worker rights, nondiscrimination and gender equality, facilitating workers organization and collective bargaining, universal social protection, adequate pensions and access to health care. This is what millions of human beings are telling us worldwide: "Give me a fair chance at a decent job and I'll do the rest; I don't want charity or handouts." It will take longer and require different emphasis in developing and developed countries, but all societies face decent work challenges, particularly in the midst of the global crisis that still haunts us.

Why is this so difficult? There are many converging historical and policy explanations, but there is a solid underlying fact: in the values of today's world, capital is more important than labour. The signs have been all over the place—from the unacceptable growth of inequality to the shrinking share of wages in GDP. We must all reflect on the implications for social peace and political stability, including those benefitting from their present advantage. Pope John Paul II reminded us "All must work so that the economic system in which we live does not upset the fundamental order of the priority of work over capital, of the common good over the private interest." As Gandhi said, "There is enough for everybody's needs, not for everybody's greed."

But things are changing. Many emerging and developing countries have shown great policy autonomy in defining their crisis responses, guided by a keen eye on employment and social protection, as this Report advocates. Policies leading to the crisis overvalued the capacity of markets to self-regulate; undervalued the role of the State, public policy and regulations and devalued respect for the environment, the dignity of work and the social services and welfare functions in society. They led into a pattern of unsustainable, inefficient and unfair growth. We have slowly begun to close this policy cycle, but we don't have a ready-made alternative prepared to take its place. We are moving into a rather lengthy period of uncertainty with no obvious source of global policy leadership: A period more of muddling through than forceful global decision making. This is an extraordinary political opportunity and intellectual challenge for the United Nations System. Coming together around a creative post-2015 global vision with clear Sustainable Development Goals can be a first step into a new policy cycle looking at what a post-crisis world should look like. And beyond the United Nations, we need to listen. There is great disquiet and insecurity in too many societies. From polls and elections to people in the streets and increasingly vocal social movements a clear message to governmental and business leaders is coming through: "Your policies are not working for a great majority of us."

And that's why the insistence of this Report on reclaiming the role of full employment, universal social protection and the road to decent work is so important. It builds on the existing consensus of the largest meeting of Heads of State and Government in the history of the United Nations. In their 2005 Summit they stated that "We strongly support fair globalization and resolve to make the goals of full and productive employment and decent work for all, including for women and young people, a central objective of our relevant national and international policies as well as our national development strategies."[2] So, at least on paper, the commitment is there in no uncertain terms.

Let me finish with one example of the changes necessary for which I believe there is widespread consensus. Strong real economy investments, large and small, with their important job-creating capacity must displace financial operations from the driver's seat of the global economy. The expansion of short-term profits in financial markets, with little employment to show for it, has channelled away resources from the longer term horizon of sustainable real economy enterprises. The world is awash in liquidity that needs to become productive investments through a regulatory framework ensuring that financial institutions fulfil their original role of channelling savings into the real economy. Also, expanding wage participation in GDP within reasonable inflation rates will increase real demand and serve as a source of sustainable development growth. Moving from committed minimum wage policies to a much fairer distribution of productivity gains and profits should be a point of departure.

Dreams or potential reality? We shall see, but no doubt this is what politics and social struggles will be all about in the years to come.

Notes
1. ILO 2010a. 2. UN 2005.

---

status or part-time work generally get a lower occupational pension.[76]

Many of the working poor are in nonstandard employment—involuntary part-time and temporary work in advanced countries and informal employment in developing countries. Ideally, employment rates rise, and the incidence of nonstandard employment falls over time (see the category 1 countries in figure 3.7). However, the majority of countries with data saw unemployment and nonstandard employment both increase between 2007 and 2010[77] (see the category 4 countries in figure 3.7).[78]

Informal employment, a particular challenge for developing countries, accounts for more than 40 percent of total employment in

FIGURE 3.7

For most countries with data nonstandard employment increased between 2007 and 2010, while overall employment fell

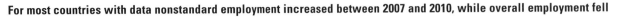

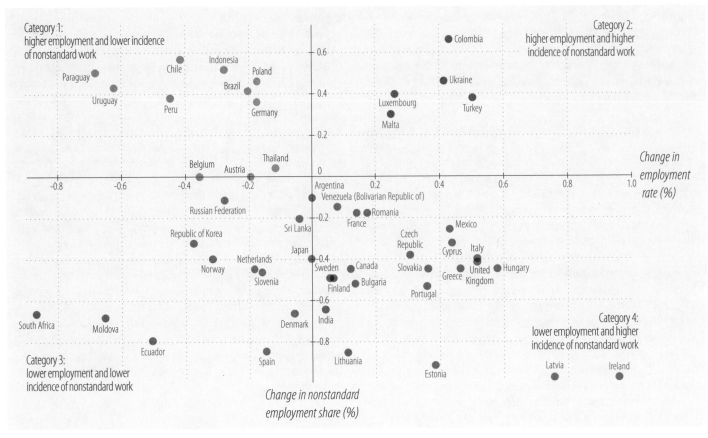

Source: ILO 2012c.

two-thirds of the 41 emerging and developing countries with data.[79] Definitions vary widely, but informal employment generally lacks social, legal or regulatory protection.[80] Those in informal employment earn less on average than those in formal jobs do.[81]

The vulnerabilities of those in informal employment go beyond low and volatile earnings. The ability to cope with adverse shocks is compromised by the lack of formal social protection, and vulnerabilities are compounded when individuals working informally face harassment by public authorities. Many in part-time or temporary jobs face similar problems: They may not have the same protections or benefits, such as health insurance, as permanent full-time employees.

Nearly half the world's workers are in vulnerable employment, trapped in insecure jobs usually outside the jurisdiction of labour legislation and social protection. Over the years, in response to economic volatility and repeated

crises, employers are increasing their reliance on part-time or temporary employment.[82] Among developing regions the share of vulnerable employment is highest in South Asia and Sub-Saharan Africa (77.5 percent in 2011).[83]

When one household member loses a job, the others may try to compensate.[84] In some cases, if a male worker loses his job, more women may seek work to make up for this. But during an economic downturn women may withdraw from the labour force. And when a crisis squeezes household resources, women are likely to increase their time spent in unpaid work.[85] Increases in women's labour force participation may intensify conflicts within the household: Women who enter paid work can experience more domestic violence.[86]

When adults lose their jobs, children are also affected.[87] In developing countries adverse economic conditions can reduce school enrolment rates by up to 12 percentage points.[88] In addition, children may leave school in order to work—eroding their chances of escaping poverty in the future.

Better employment outcomes generate social benefits that extend beyond the individual.[89] Societies in which everyone has access to employment opportunities that meet a basic standard of decency tend to have fewer conflicts, stronger social networks and a greater sense of fairness and justice.[90] These outcomes affect the degree of social cohesion within a country and tend to make institutions function better—creating an environment that supports human development. There are also implications for social expenditure, as public health expenditures may increase following large episodes of job loss.[91]

Ageing with dignity—an elusive reality for many

The global population of people ages 60 and older is more than 500 million (close to 8 percent of the total). Europe and Central Asia has the highest share of older people in the total population among developing country regions (11.4 percent; figure 3.8). By 2050 the share of older people in the total population is expected to double to 15.5 percent, with the largest increase in East Asia and the Pacific (from 7.4 percent in 2010 to 22.2 percent in 2050). By 2050 only Sub-Saharan Africa is expected to have a share of older people below 5 percent.[92]

Poverty and social exclusion are problems for those who are ageing, especially because roughly 80 percent of the world's older population does not have a pension and relies on labour and family for income.[93] And as people age, they generally become physically, mentally and economically more vulnerable.[94] Poverty in old age is more often chronic, since the lack of economic opportunities and security during earlier life accumulates into vulnerability in

Better employment outcomes generate social benefits that extend beyond the individual

FIGURE 3.8

By 2050 the share of people ages 60 and older in the world's population is expected to double to 15.5 percent, with the largest increase in East Asia and the Pacific

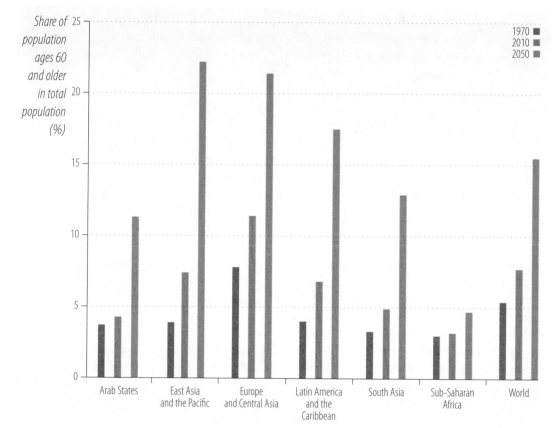

Source: Human Development Report Office calculations based on Lutz and KC (2013).

old age. The cumulative disadvantages during younger life also imply the transfer of poverty from one generation to another. For example, in Bangladesh nearly a third of the general population lives in a household with an older person, while many more people in other households are part of a network of support to, and from, older people.[95]

Low income is not the only thing that increases vulnerability among older people; additional disadvantages can compound their inability to cope, as when a loss of income is accompanied by illness and disability that deplete financial resources. Reduced capacity to earn a personal income and contribute to the household income—even indirectly—has clear implications for the dignity and empowerment of older people within the family. Even when older people are supported by their families with food and shelter, the fact that they do not have their own resources may affect their autonomy and capacity to exercise choice and lead to them to be seen potentially as a burden.[96]

Untimely death of a partner, inadequate access to affordable physical and health care, exclusion from participation in society, homelessness, loss of autonomy, institutionalization, lack of social contacts and loneliness—all add to the vulnerabilities of older people. They may also face a restricted social and physical environment, which when combined with diminished personal capabilities can hold back older people from taking advantage of opportunities available to them and from being resilient to threats that affect them.

Poverty in old age has a strong gender dimension. Women's life expectancy is longer than men's, so women may spend more time in poverty than men. Women are more likely to lose their partner and less likely to remarry. Lower education and the need to combine work with childcare means that women are more likely to work in the informal sector. Older women, especially widows and those without children, are particularly vulnerable, both economically and socially.[97] They may be subject to vilification and abuse and live in conditions of abandonment.[98]

Most older people and people living in households with an older person face higher poverty rates. In Organisation for Economic Co-operation and Development countries the old-age poverty rate is higher than the average for the whole population (13.5 percent versus 10.6 percent),[99] and older women are more likely than older men to be poor (figure 3.9). The situation is similar in many developing countries. In the Dominican Republic, El Salvador, Guatemala, Honduras and Paraguay more than 40 percent of the population ages 60 and older is poor.[100]

With ageing comes a higher probability of living with a disability. Worldwide, more than 46 percent of people ages 60 and older live with a disability,[101] and whether living with a disability or not, 15–30 percent of older people live alone or with no adult of working age.[102] Abuse of older people is quite extensive. A 2011–2012 survey of 36 countries found that 43 percent of older people fear violence and mistreatment.[103]

Older people are also major caregivers to their partners and grandchildren, and increasingly to their parents too. Particularly in countries with a high prevalence of HIV/AIDS, grandparents are usually the ones caring for AIDS orphans.[104] The situation is similar for migrants. Some 69 percent of Bolivian migrants who moved to Spain left their children at home, usually with grandparents. In rural China grandparents care for 38 percent of children under age 5 whose parents have gone to work in cities.[105]

Structural vulnerabilities

Where social and legal institutions, power structures, political spaces, or traditions and sociocultural norms do not serve members of society equally—and where they create structural barriers for some people and groups to exercise their rights and choices—they give rise to structural vulnerabilities. Structural vulnerabilities are often manifested through deep inequalities and widespread poverty, which are associated with horizontal or group inequalities based on socially recognized and constructed group membership.[106] Structural vulnerabilities are perpetuated by exclusion, low human development and people's position in society, reducing their ability to cope with downside risks and shocks.

The poor, women, minorities (ethnic, linguistic, religious, migrant or sexual), indigenous peoples, people in rural or remote areas

Poverty in old age has a strong gender dimension

or living with disabilities, and countries landlocked or with limited natural resources tend to face higher barriers, sometimes of a legal nature, to build capabilities, exercise choices and claim their rights to support and protection in the event of shocks. And even if laws do not explicitly discriminate, the absence of effective policies can leave people excluded and vulnerable. Group (or horizontal) inequalities and exclusion limit the political influence of some groups, even if they are the majority of the population, as with the poor. Horizontal inequalities can lead to elite capture of policies that favour certain groups and not society as a whole.[107] This magnifies vulnerabilities for the excluded by limiting the quantity and quality of public services they receive.

Some groups may also be more exposed to certain risks and have less capability and intrinsic ability to cope with shocks. The exposure of some groups and the way society treats their inherent characteristics produce adverse outcomes.[108] Shocks also create new vulnerabilities or new groups of vulnerable people. For example, about 200,000 people are expected to live with a long-term disability as a result of injuries sustained during the January 2010 earthquake in Haiti.[109] It can be argued that it was not the earthquake itself that affected such a huge amount of people; it was its interaction with the country's vulnerability.[110]

Poverty and vulnerability

Although linked and often mutually reinforcing, poverty and vulnerability are not synonymous. People who are poor are more vulnerable than others in society because for the most part the risk of adverse shocks is greater for the poor than for others, as is well documented for environmental shocks.[111]

Some 1.2 billion people live on less than $1.25 a day, and 2.7 billion live on less than $2.50 a day (figure 3.10).[112] Moreover, 1.5 billion people live in multidimensional poverty, and almost 0.8 billion live in near-poverty,[113] so some 2.2 billion live with two or more critical deprivations. These numbers are declining, but many people live just above the poverty threshold. So, idiosyncratic or generalized shocks could easily push them back into poverty. The share of people just above the poverty threshold

FIGURE 3.9

In Organisation for Economic Co-operation and Development countries the poverty rate tends to be higher for older people than for the population as a whole and higher for older women than for older men

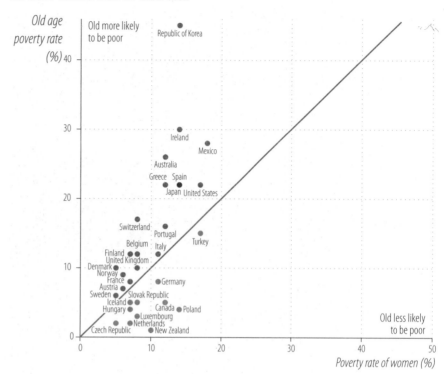

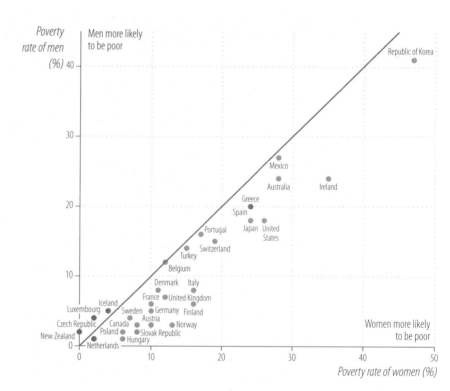

Note: Data are for 2008.
Source: OECD 2011b.

FIGURE 3.10

Some 1.2 billion people live on less than $1.25 a day, and 1.5 billion people live in multidimensional poverty

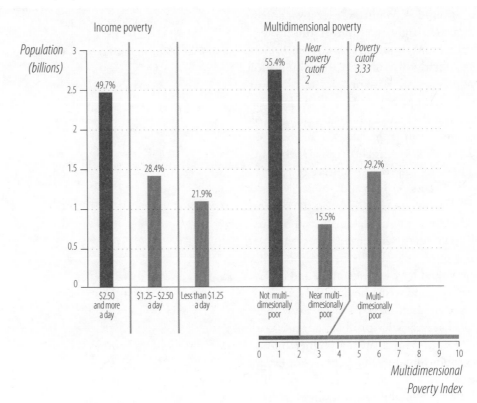

Source: Multidimensional poverty, Human Development Report Office calculations based on various household surveys, including ICF Macro Demographic and Health Surveys, United Nations Children's Fund Multiple Indicator Cluster Surveys and several national household surveys; income poverty, Human Development Report Office calculations based on data from the World Bank's World Development Indicators database.

(either income or multidimensional) is largest in South Asia, Sub-Saharan Africa, and East Asia and the Pacific (table 3.1).

Multidimensional poverty has a strong geographical component, since it tends to be highest in rural areas. In Somalia it affects 60 percent of the population in urban households and over 95 percent of the population in rural households. In Burkina Faso 43 percent and 94 percent, in Niger 56 percent and 96 percent and in Ethiopia 54 percent and 96 percent.

In many countries multidimensional poverty is also more likely among female-headed households and those that include a person age 60 or older. Another important factor is the presence of young children. In Bolivia, for example, the overall proportion of the population in multidimensional poverty is 12 percent, but in households with at least one child under age 5 it is 34 percent. The corresponding proportions are 21 percent and 42 percent in Ghana,

7 percent and 19 percent in Peru and 4 percent and 11 percent in the Syrian Arab Republic.

Vulnerability increases when poverty interacts with other household conditions.[114] Poor people are more likely to live in areas vulnerable to the impacts of climate change, whether in low-lying coastal regions at greatest risk of inundation from rising sea levels or on marginal land subject to increasing dryness and drought from climate change.[115]

Poor people are vulnerable since they generally lack access to savings, borrowed funds or other assets they can draw on to meet unforeseen contingencies. Faced with a job loss or other income shock, they resort to more harmful coping strategies such as cutting back on food or reducing spending on health or children's education.[116] Even with a higher income, households may not be or even feel much less vulnerable, and despite progress over recent decades in both developed and developing countries, individuals feel economically less secure.[117]

TABLE 3.1

Income and multidimensional poverty, by region

Region	Number of countries in sample	Income poverty headcount (%)	Near income poverty (%)	Number of countries in sample	Multidimensional poverty headcount (%)	Intensity of deprivation (%)	Near multi-dimensional poverty (%)
Arab States	10	6.5	36.4	9	15.5	48.4	8.7
East Asia and the Pacific	11	12.7	25.1	10	6.4	44.7	16.2
Europe and Central Asia	15	1.4	6.0	15	1.8	37.3	4.5
Latin America and the Caribbean	20	5.7	7.0	14	6.7	42.8	9.5
South Asia	8	30.6	44.4	7	53.4	50.8	17.9
Sub-Saharan Africa	40	50.9	27.8	36	59.6	55.0	16.2

Source: Multidimensional poverty, Human Development Report Office calculations based on various household surveys, including ICF Macro Demographic and Health Surveys, United Nations Children's Fund Multiple Indicator Cluster Surveys and several national household surveys; income poverty, Human Development Report Office calculations based on data from the World Bank's World Development Indicators database.

Recent austerity measures have increased poverty in more than half of European countries, and the groups most at risk are children, immigrants and people from a migrant background, ethnic minorities and people with disabilities.[118]

The impacts of natural disasters are disproportionately high among lower income groups, older people and people with disabilities. During the 2005 Mumbai floods the poorest households were the most vulnerable. Though the losses may not appear large in absolute terms, the average loss incurred by households roughly equalled the average household's savings. The ability to recover and reconstruct in the aftermath of the floods was impaired by the depletion of household savings and loss of household assets.[119] The 2001 earthquakes in El Salvador reduced the income per capita of the most affected households by a third.[120] In Bangladesh, in major flooding events in certain years, up to 7.5 million hectares of crops were damaged, hurting mostly the poor.[121]

During and after disasters children from poor households are particularly vulnerable to malnutrition and other long-term consequences. The 1982–1984 drought in Zimbabwe increased the probability of child stunting and delayed the school enrolment of children by an average of 3.7 months, which worsened their performance at school up to 16 years after the disaster. In Ethiopia between 2002 and 2006, 90 percent of the households in the poorest income quintile experienced at least one risk of shocks to adverse events, while many reported multiple risks, with an average of 4.2 risks per household.[122] Family responses to shocks include eating less, reducing household assets and accumulating debt, all likely to have long-term consequences for children's development. Income shocks have major impacts on the school attendance and performance of children from poor households.[123]

The effect of disasters on people and communities is conditioned not only by their capabilities and competences, but also by their asset base—their financial and natural capital. For example, considerable degradation of the ecosystem could threaten the livelihoods of the rural communities that depend directly on natural resources: access to marine biodiversity, nontimber forest products and small-scale or subsistence crop and stock farming. How vulnerable these communities are is determined by the condition of the natural resource base for current and alternative economic activities, the regimes for managing those resources and how close natural ecosystems are to tipping points past which productivity can no longer be restored. Environmental degradation and natural resource impoverishment are major threats. In 2011 agricultural workers accounted for 40 percent of the world's economically active population, 60 percent of them in low Human Development Index countries. Two-thirds of the extreme poor are in rural areas, their livelihoods heavily dependent on agriculture and natural resources. Land degradation and water scarcity are major concerns. By 2025 water scarcity is expected to affect more than 1.8 billion people—hurting agricultural workers and poor farmers the most.[124]

Gender

Globally, women suffer the most pervasive discrimination. Legal systems emerge from rich and diverse cultural traditions, but in some countries customary and religious laws prevail over civil laws that might protect women's human rights. Laws can explicitly discriminate against women in matters of family, marriage, economic rights and violence (figure 3.11). They may also limit women's rights to land ownership and require spousal consent for women's access to contraception and family planning.

Women may also face discrimination from social institutions—such as early marriage, discriminatory inheritance practices, higher burdens of unpaid care work, violence against women (box 3.3), son preference and restrictions on access to public space and productive resources. Infringing on women's rights,

discrimination from social institutions also leads to poorer human development outcomes. Primary school completion averaged more than 15 percent lower in the 21 countries where social institutions were deemed the most discriminatory against women than in other developing countries, and child malnutrition rates and maternal mortality ratios were twice as high.[125] The number of malnourished children averages 60 percent higher in countries where women do not have the right to own land and 85 percent higher in countries where women lack any access to credit. Maternal mortality ratios are also generally higher in countries where women have less control over their physical integrity.

Economic downturns are associated with a nearly fivefold increase in female infant mortality compared with male infant mortality.[126] The recent global economic crisis has resulted in an estimated 30,000–50,000 additional infant deaths in Sub-Saharan Africa, mostly among the poor and overwhelmingly female.[127]

In most countries women are free to engage in political activity, but in only two, Cuba and Rwanda, does the share of women in parliament match or exceed their share in the population. In Rwanda's 2013 parliamentary election 51 of

FIGURE 3.11

Several countries have laws that discriminate against women in family, economic activities, violence and other matters

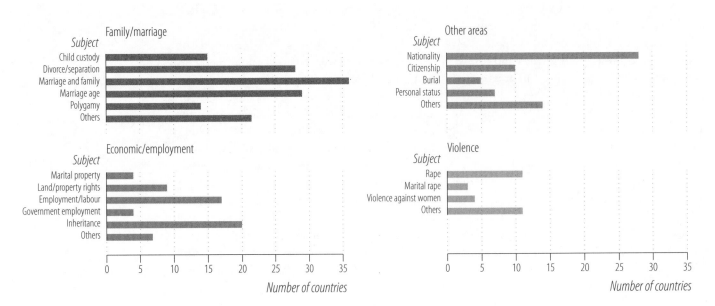

Source: Equality Now 2011.

BOX 3.3

Violence against women

Events in 2012 and 2013 drew global media attention to the epidemic proportions of violence against women. Malala Yousafzai was shot by the Taliban in Pakistan, a young student was fatally gang-raped in India and there were reports of rape and other sexual harassment of women at Tahrir Square in Cairo. These events are reminders that structural violence against women remains endemic across the world and poses huge challenges to women's participation in societal life and to community safety and security more broadly.

About a third of women worldwide will experience sexual or other physical violence in their lifetime, primarily by an intimate partner (who will also be responsible for nearly 40 percent of all femicides—this may extend to honour and dowry-related killings),[1] described as structural 'relational vulnerabilities' embedded within specific categories of social relations.[2] A recent World Health Organization analysis suggests that 7.2 percent of the world's women—or 1 in 14—is subjected to nonpartner sexual violence.[3]

Gallup data from surveys in 143 countries in 2011 suggest a gender-based fear of violence. Women not only felt less safe than men in every country, but the gender gap in perception of threats did not correspond to income: Double-digit gaps were found in many middle- and high-income countries.[4]

Correlation between intimate partner violence and poverty is strong and positive, and there are regional patterns in prevalence. Women in Africa are almost twice as likely to experience violence as women in low- and middle-income Europe. In South-East Asia women are almost eight times more likely to experience violence by a current or former partner than by someone else.

Public campaigns and mobilization have led to changes in civil and criminal justice, with legislation and judicial rulings that assert women's protection. Many countries have legal and other resources to support victims and their children and have passed civil remedies including restraining order legislation

to protect partners against their abusers. But changes to social norms and the law are often incremental and hard fought. The amendments to the Criminal Law in India following recent rape cases[5] do not criminalize marital rape,[6] highlighting both the scope and limits of law as an agent of social change.

Violence affects women's ability to participate in economic activity outside the home. In Mexico the primary reason women dropped out of the labour force was threats and violence by disapproving husbands.[7] In India actual or threatened violence by husbands prevents many women from participating in meetings of self-help groups.[8] Interventions that emphasize social norms (acceptance of gender violence) and reduction of psychosocial barriers (shame, guilt, resentment and prejudice) can reduce violence against women and more broadly increase women's empowerment. An example is Yo quiero, Yo puedo (I want to, I can) in Mexico, Focusing on individuals as the starting point, the programme increases its ownership and sustainability by conceiving personal agency and intrinsic empowerment as both a process and a state.

Less attention has been devoted to the intangible impacts on women's freedom of movement, emotional well-being and capacity for imagination and thought, all key dimensions of human capability.[9] Along with the assault on the personhood, dignity and sense of worth that all violence inflicts on its victims, the consequences of violence against women also reflect its systemic character—that it is not randomly distributed across the population but directed at a particular group by virtue of their identity as a subordinate group. As Iris Marion Young puts it, "The oppression of violence consists not only in direct victimization but in the daily knowledge shared by all members of the oppressed group that they are liable to violation, solely on account of their group identity. Just living under the threat of attack . . . deprives the oppressed of freedom and dignity, and needlessly expends their energy."[10]

Notes
1. WHO 2013. 2. Kabeer, Mumtaz and Sayeed 2010. 3. WHO 2013. 4. Gallup 2013. 5. Parliament of India Rajya Sabha 2013. 6. Harvard Law and Policy Review 2013. 7. Funk, Lang and Osterhaus 2005. 8. Sen 1998; Kabeer and others 2012. 9. Nussbaum 2005. 10. Young 1990, p. 62.
Source: Chalabi and Holder 2013; Kabeer 2014; Pick and Sirkin 2010.

---

80 seats (64 percent) were filled by women.[128] But in about 60 percent of countries with data, women account for less than 20 percent of parliamentary seats. Better representation of women in political life can greatly improve the position of women generally. Rwanda now has some of the most progressive laws in Africa to empower women and protect them from violence. Laws and policies alone are insufficient to eradicate discrimination, but they can be important first steps.

Natural disasters and climate change often heighten inequality and discrimination, including those that are gender-based.[129] But women's empowerment and agency can reduce such vulnerabilities. For example, three weeks after the 2004 Indian Ocean tsunami, a group of poor female villagers who survived the 1993 and 2001 earthquakes in Latur (Maharashtra) and Kutch (Gujarat) actively supported the recovery efforts by travelling to Tamil Nadu to show their solidarity with women like themselves and sustain the rehabilitation process.[130]

Ethnic groups and minorities

Indigenous peoples constitute around 5 percent of the world's population but account for 15 percent of the world's income poor and for more than 30 percent of the world's extremely poor in rural areas.[131] They tend to have poor educational attainment, unequal opportunities and unequal access to land and other productive assets.[132] In Latin America the average income of indigenous workers is about half that of nonindigenous workers.[133]

In Europe one of the most vulnerable groups is the Roma. In 2011 around 30 percent of

Roma lived on less than $4.30 a day, compared with 9 percent of the non-Roma population (figure 3.12). Despite numerous national and regional initiatives to improve their conditions, they continue to suffer the effects of social exclusion and the limited access to basic services associated with it.[134]

Disabilities

People living with disabilities face physical barriers to claiming rights and exercising choices. They often lack easy access to public transportation, government offices and other public spaces such as hospitals, making it more difficult to participate in economic, social and political life—or to seek assistance when faced with threats to their physical well-being. Particularly vulnerable among people with disabilities are those in poverty. People with disabilities are also more likely than the general population to be victims of violence.[135] And they may be less able to work and so are generally poorer than the rest of the population. Further, people with disabilities that impair their ability to communicate are also more likely to be victims of abuse, including that by caregivers.

People with disabilities are particularly exposed at times of natural disasters and violent conflict. Cognitive, intellectual or physical impairments can reduce their capacity to access information or act on it.[136] They can be left behind during evacuations or be turned away by shelters and refugee camps on the grounds that they might need complex medical care. The disaster risk reduction community needs to widen the participation of people with disabilities—and address the environmental barriers and constraints they face.[137]

The vulnerabilities that disabilities generate depend on other social, economic and demographic factors. For instance, people with disabilities are also more likely to have less ability to work and thus are poorer than their counterparts without disabilities. Indeed, people with disabilities have lower employment rates.[138] Evidence from the World Health Survey for 51 countries shows employment rates of 52.8 percent for men with disabilities and 19.6 percent for women with disabilities, compared with 64.9 percent for men without disabilities and

> People with disabilities are particularly exposed at times of natural disasters and violent conflict

FIGURE 3.12

In 2011 poverty rates among Roma households were much higher than among non-Roma households

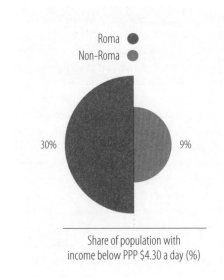

Roma ●
Non-Roma ●

30%   9%

Share of population with
income below PPP $4.30 a day (%)

Source: Human Development Report Office calculations based on UNDP, World Bank and EC (2011).

29.9 percent for women without disabilities.[139] But addressing the barriers and vulnerabilities of people with disabilities can unlock their potential and benefit society as a whole.

Migrants

Most international migrants, who account for over 3 percent of the world's population, have fewer rights and less protection, even when they are documented, than citizens and have less access to social protection.[140] Typically they are excluded from social and public life and, lacking voting rights, have little influence over policies that affect them—even though they might be contributing to the host country's economic progress. Their vulnerability overlaps with other structural vulnerabilities. For example, the number of women migrating is increasing. Today women account for half the international migrant population, reaching 70–80 percent in some countries, and they suffer from a higher exposure to exploitation and abuse in human trafficking.[141]

Forced migration due to conflict is another source of vulnerability, as the Syrian crisis dramatically shows. Even though refugees are a small part of the migrant population—around 10.5 million people in 2011—the armed

Disability and vulnerability

As a theoretical physicist I understand very well the concept of vulnerability: there is little in the cosmos that is not susceptible to harm. Even the very universe itself may someday come to an end.

Humanity has always been vulnerable to different challenges. And there can be no doubt that great scientific discoveries—from penicillin to the periodic table, from evolution to electricity—have helped us to understand our world, reduce our vulnerability, and build more resilient societies.

But, despite great and varied progress, vulnerable people and vulnerable groups of people remain—none more so than the disabled. The United Nations estimates that over a billion people live with some form of disability and they are disproportionately represented among the world's poorest and at greater risk of suffering from violence, disaster, catastrophic health expenses, and many other hardships.

The vast majority of people with disabilities have a hard time simply surviving, let alone living lives they have reason to value, to use the lexicon of human development. However, disability need not be an obstacle to success. I have had motor neurone disease for nearly all my adult life, but it has not prevented me from having a prominent career in theoretical physics and a happy family life.

I realize of course that in many ways I have been fortunate. My success in theoretical physics has ensured that I've been able to live a life I value.

I have benefited from first-class medical care. I can rely on a team of assistants who enable me to live and work in comfort and dignity. My house and workplace have been made accessible to me. Computer experts have supported me with an assisted communication system and a speech synthesizer, which allow me to compose lectures and papers and to communicate with different audiences.

People with disabilities are vulnerable because of the many barriers we face: attitudinal, physical, and financial. Addressing these barriers is within our reach and we have a moral duty to do so. Beyond that moral duty we would do well to remember the many other reasons to act. Legislation introduced to assist the disabled today will benefit nearly everyone at some point: almost all of us will be impaired at some time in life or care for someone who is. Inventions, such as optical character recognition and brain-controlled technology, have many other benefits beyond helping people with disabilities.

But most important, addressing these barriers will unlock the potential of so many people with so much to contribute to the world. Governments everywhere can no longer overlook the hundreds of millions of people with disabilities who are denied access to health, rehabilitation, support, education, and employment—and never get the chance to shine.

---

conflict displaced around 5 million people from the area (more than 255,000 of them between December 2012 and January 2013 alone).[142]

Vulnerable countries and geography

Efforts to tackle the vulnerability of individuals and communities must bear in mind their country's vulnerability. A major rationale for special treatment of countries is their structural vulnerability, which depends on outside factors not easily managed by domestic policy. For example, the least developed countries have been defined as poor countries suffering from structural weaknesses to growth. They are more likely than others to remain poor. Landlocked developing countries and small island developing states are two other groups of countries facing major structural challenges.

This Report discusses many of the structural vulnerabilities countries face, including how greater interconnectedness brings new vulnerabilities. Most of the analysis and evidence on country vulnerability concentrates on environmental or natural disasters, such as earthquakes or volcanic eruptions, and climatic shocks

(box 3.4)—or on external economic events, such as slumps in external demand and terms of trade shocks.

Group violence and insecure lives

The 1994 *Human Development Report (HDR)* introduced the concept of human security, opening with the statement "The world can never be at peace unless people have security in their daily lives."[143] Conceptions of security require a view of the human person that includes physical and psychological vulnerability, strengths and limitations, including limitations in the perception of risk.[144]

In 2000 about 4,400 people died every day because of intentional acts of self-directed, interpersonal or collective violence.[145] And many thousands more are affected in some way by acts of violence. In addition, huge costs are incurred in treating victims, supporting shattered families, repairing infrastructure and prosecuting perpetrators and as a result of lost productivity and investment.[146]

People's perceptions of threats offer feedback on policy efforts and shed light on the

BOX 3.4

Disaster resilience—Japan's experience

In the past five years alone the world has witnessed an earthquake in Haiti (2010), a heat wave in the Northern Hemisphere (2010), a tsunami in Japan (2011), a drought in East Africa (2011–2012) and a typhoon in the Philippines (2013). These adverse natural events have caused large human casualties and had considerable economic costs. Human development progress has been weakened by these impacts and, in some cases, hard-won gains have been reversed.

Japan is a disaster-prone country that can provide important insights on disaster resilience. In 2011 a powerful earthquake off the east coast of Japan triggered large tsunami waves that killed more than 15,000 people and caused extensive damage to economic and social infrastructure. It also led to a nuclear disaster in Fukushima. But despite the large loss of human life and record financial costs—estimated at $210 billion—the impact could have been dramatically worse. The Tohoku earthquake, estimated at magnitude 9.0, was the world's fourth strongest since records began in 1900, and the ensuing tsunami waves reached heights of up to 40 metres and travelled up to 10 kilometres inland.

Japan's early warning system prevented a much larger death toll. As soon as seismic activity was detected, alerts were broadcast by television, radio and mobile phone networks. This enabled many people to prepare and mitigate the impact, such as moving to higher ground, while the country's rail network and factories quickly came to a halt—thus avoiding greater damage. Emergency sirens, clearly marked evacuation routes and public education programmes were also critical in saving lives. Strict building codes ensured that tall buildings withstood the earthquake, while forested green belts and concrete barriers provided some protection against the tsunami.

State institutions have traditionally engaged with local communities to improve disaster preparedness and devise evacuation plans. Japan's long-standing investments in technology and public awareness were essential to averting an even bigger disaster.

Even if debates in Japan about preparedness and recovery have been critical, the case of Japan highlights that risk is inherently a development concern and that comprehensive risk reduction and recovery must be integral components of overall governance. Early warning systems, evacuation routes, strict building codes and engagement with local communities all need to stem from institutional, legal and governance systems that prioritize disaster risk reduction and recovery.

In March 2015 the third UN World Conference on Disaster Risk Reduction will take place in Sendai, one of the cities affected by the 2011 Tohoku earthquake and tsunami. The conference will allow member states to review the implementation of the Hyogo Framework for Action and adopt a post-2015 framework for disaster risk reduction. The framework, a 10-year plan to build the resilience of countries and communities to disasters agreed at the 2005 World Conference on Disaster Reduction, has five key priorities for action: make disaster risk reduction a priority, know the risks and take action, build understanding and awareness, reduce risk, and be prepared and ready to act.

Nonetheless, building disaster preparedness takes time, requiring significant long-term investments in education, technology and infrastructure, as well as adequate institutions and regulatory frameworks. Learning from recent experiences with disasters will be crucial to build a forward-looking global agenda that enables resilient and sustainable human development.

Source: UNISDR 2012a; Fraser and others 2012.

burden of fear in their lives.[147] The 2005 Costa Rica *HDR* and 2013 Latin America *HDR* show how people's lives are restricted as they avoid going out at night or travelling due to fear of violence.[148] The existence of gangs has been found to correlate with lower support for formal mechanisms of social control and regulation, which further opens the way for criminal groups to be the sole sources of protection.[149] Persistent horizontal inequality experienced along political, economic and social dimensions can create conditions that promote acts of physical violence that threaten human development for large numbers of people, including some specific groups. Homicide and armed violence occur most frequently in poverty-stricken urban areas characterized by lack of employment, poor standards of housing, overcrowding and low standards of education and social amenities. Homicides are more common in the poorer areas of cities with high inequalities, ranging from New York City

to Rio de Janeiro, and in the more unequal American states and cities and Canadian provinces. Research corroborates these connections between violence and inequality.[150] However, violence and crime are associated not only with increases in inequality, but also with the presence of firearms and drugs, seen to explain some of the very high levels of violence in some middle-income countries of South and Central America, where inequality has been falling in recent years.

As chapter 2 points out, violent conflict— and mostly intrastate conflict as well as internal civil unrest—continues to impose enormous costs on development in affected countries. A combination of causes can be identified for these types of conflict. One common characteristic is the fact that the causes—from exclusionary policies and elite rent-seeking to unaddressed social grievances—all contribute to social discord or, at the very least, impede the social harmony and cohesion conducive to resilient development outcomes, something discussed more extensively in chapter 4.

A 'socially cohesive' society is one that works towards the well-being of all its members, fights exclusion and marginalization, creates a sense of belonging, promotes trust and offers its members the opportunity of upward mobility.[151] Lack of these attributes is often correlated with conflict and violence, especially in situations of unequal access to resources or benefits from natural wealth, or with the inability to deal effectively with rapid social or economic change or the impact of economic or climate-related shocks.

Inequality in access to resources and outcomes that coincides with cultural differences can become mobilizing agents that end in a range of political upheavals and disturbances. This is not only because of the resentments of the excluded and deprived. Unrest and conflict can also erupt if the privileged take actions to ensure that the underprivileged do not make demands for more resources or political power.[152]

Almost all countries have groups that suffer from social exclusion,[153] which occurs when institutions systematically deny some groups the resources and recognition that would enable them to fully participate in social life.[154] Horizontal inequality and social exclusion can endure over long periods and may be associated with denial of rights and unequal access to social services by some groups. In some cases the persistent inequalities and prolonged deprivations last centuries.[155]

There is evidence of some correlation between group inequalities and violent conflict, which becomes more likely when political and socioeconomic and political inequalities are reinforcing.[156] For example, the probability of conflict rises significantly in countries with severe economic and social horizontal inequality. Similarly, violent conflict is more likely to occur when development is weaker and religious polarization is greater.[157] While there are many examples of peaceful multicultural societies, cultural ties can be a powerful source of mobilization and potential conflict when they interact with strong economic and political deprivations.[158] In addition, sharp increases in group inequality raise the likelihood of tension and conflict.[159]

How governments respond to protests explains how social exclusion can induce some groups to take to violence, even if they start as peaceful protests. Peaceful protests in which the state limits protesters' space and protection can either generate little change and more frustration or face violent and exclusionary actions by the state, unifying protesters and transforming what were mainly peaceful protests into violence.

Institutions, especially well functioning state institutions, have an important function in creating a cultural space where various groups can exchange ideas peacefully and where people can start to incorporate the views of others into their own understanding of the world. This could be very important for peaceful conflict resolution, indicating a large role in violent conflict prevention.[160]

Inclusive and representative institutions can reduce the potential for conflict, since they can take action to counter exclusion, changing practices in the way public goods and services are delivered. Examples of policies to reduce horizontal inequality include improving the group ownership of land via redistribution of government-owned land, forcible purchases and restriction on ownership in Fiji, Namibia, Malaysia and Zimbabwe. Other examples refer to public sector employment quotas (India, Malaysia and Sri Lanka and the requirement for balanced employment in the private sector in South Africa).[161]

Armed conflict is an important vulnerability for human development, for its aggregate effects not only on society but on some specific groups. In Kashmir exposure to violence *in utero* and in infancy was shown to have reduced children's height. Children in areas affected by insurgency were 0.9–1.4 standard deviations shorter than children less affected by insurgency. The effect was stronger for children born during peaks in violence.[162]

Conflicts also force people to flee their homes and livelihoods. Women and children account for 80 percent of the world's refugees and displaced persons.[163] Between 2012 and 2013 more than 1 million people fled their countries of origin due to conflict and persecution, mainly from eastern Democratic Republic of the Congo, Mali, Sudan and the Syrian Arab Republic.[164] Altogether, the Office

Inequality in access to resources and outcomes that coincides with cultural differences can become mobilizing agents that end in a range of political upheavals and disturbances

of the United Nations High Commissioner for Refugees records nearly 36 million people of concern.[165]

Deaths from cross-border wars have come down markedly since a peak in 1995, to some 320,000 a year. Yet armed conflicts continue to be a major impediment to human development, especially for low Human Development Index countries.[166] In 2012 there were 37,941 conflict-related deaths worldwide from 41 conflicts.[167] Conflicts disrupt essential public services such as basic health care[168] and education, doing permanent harm to people throughout their lives, with lasting health problems for entire generations of children in conflict zones often held back from completing primary school. In addition, violent conflict can cause immense psychological distress.[169] Loss of family and community, loss of homes and livelihoods, displacement and disruption can have severe mental health consequences, which affect many household decisions, including migration.[170]

In some conflicts civilians are targeted and mutilated as a deliberate strategy to demoralize communities and destroy their social structures; rape has been used as a deliberate weapon as an act of humiliation and revenge against the enemy as a whole.[171] For example, estimates of the number of women raped during the conflict in Bosnia-Herzegovina ranged from 10,000 to 60,000.[172]

"In a country well governed, poverty is something to be ashamed of. In a country badly governed, wealth is something to be ashamed of."

Confucius principle

"It took me quite a long time to develop a voice, and now that I have it, I am not going to be silent."

Madeleine Albright

4.

Building resilience: expanded freedoms, protected choices

This Report has discussed persistent threats to human development and the nature of vulnerability. It has also discussed how individuals are more vulnerable during certain critical junctures in their lives than at other times and how social contexts can render some individuals more vulnerable than others. Crises in the form of natural disasters and violent conflict deplete the capacities and material assets of entire communities, rendering them even more vulnerable. Policies to reduce vulnerability must account for these factors.

Enhancing resilience requires more than reducing vulnerability—it calls for empowerment and for fewer restrictions on the exercise of agency—the freedom to act. It also requires strong social and state institutions that can support people's efforts to cope with adverse events. Well-being is influenced greatly by the context of the larger freedoms within which people live. Societal norms and practices can be prejudicial or discriminatory. So enhancing the freedom to act requires addressing such norms and transforming them.

Chapter 1 presented fundamental principles that need to inform policy choices. Based on these principles, this chapter highlights key national policies that can reduce vulnerability and enhance resilience—at both the individual and society levels. By no means comprehensive, these policies include universal provision of basic services, addressing life cycle vulnerabilities, promoting full employment, strengthening social protection, addressing societal inclusion and building capacity to prepare for and recover from crises.

Several considerations underlie the focus on these policies. First, each addresses vulnerability in multiple dimensions. For instance, universal provision of basic social services can promote opportunities across the board by delinking basic entitlements from the ability to pay for them. Similarly, high employment has a large, positive impact on people's well-being while reducing violence and boosting social cohesion.

Second, these policies are interconnected, with strong synergies among them. Development pathways that are not informed by voices of all stakeholders are neither desirable nor sustainable. But when societies create

space for all voices to be heard, policymakers are more likely to be attentive to the concerns and needs of minorities and other vulnerable groups. And people can be both the agents and the beneficiaries of progress. Such societies are also more likely to attach a high priority to job creation and universal social policy. Indeed, if full employment expands the tax base, it also creates greater fiscal space for providing quality social services.

Third, these policies address vulnerability at different points in an individual's life cycle and at different points in a country's development pathway. Well designed social services can ensure that children receive care and education in the most critical phase of life and that older people receive appropriate care when they need it. Full employment policies smooth the critical transition for young people from education to employment. These policies also set up virtuous cycles that sustain national development pathways. Countries as diverse as the Republic of Korea and Sweden have reaped the benefits of an educated workforce on their path to industrialization.

The types of policies discussed here are likely to take time in building the resilience of people and societies. Can specific actions in the short run accelerate that resilience and protect future choices and capabilities? Chapter 3 took the position that a broad perspective is needed in examining the drivers of vulnerability. Inevitably, the response has to be across the board and long in term. But short-term actions can be better aligned with longer term needs.

Persistent shocks need determined public policies over the long haul, but response systems can facilitate better short-run adjustments to adverse events in ways that protect choices and

Broadening our thinking on vulnerability

The United Nations has long emphasized human security, in all of its dimensions.[1] When I was chief economist of the World Bank, we surveyed thousands of poor people throughout the world to ascertain what was of most concern to them, and at the top of the list (along with the obvious concerns about a lack of income and insufficient voice in the matters that affected their lives) was insecurity—vulnerability.[2]

At its basic level, vulnerability is defined as an exposure to a marked decrease in standard of living. It is of special concern when it is prolonged, and when standards of living fall below critical thresholds, to a point of deprivation.

Economists' traditional single-minded focus on GDP has led them to lose sight of vulnerability. Individuals are risk-averse. The realization that they are vulnerable thus leads to large welfare losses—even before they face the consequences of a shock itself. The failure of our systems of metrics to adequately capture the importance of security to individual and societal well-being was a key criticism of GDP by the International Commission on the Measurement of Economic Performance and Social Progress.[3]

If we are to formulate policies to reduce vulnerability, it is essential to take a broad view about what creates such vulnerability. Individuals and societies are inevitably exposed to what economists call 'shocks', adverse events that have the potential to lead to marked decreases in living standards. The larger the shocks, the greater their depth and duration, and the greater vulnerability, other things equal. But individuals and societies develop mechanisms for coping with shocks. Some societies and economies have done a better job of enhancing the capacity to cope with shocks than others. The greatest vulnerabilities arise in societies that have allowed themselves to be exposed to large shocks, but have left large fractions of their populations without adequate mechanisms for coping.

Vicious spirals

When we think of vulnerability, we inevitability think of vicious downward spirals. Robust systems have good shock absorbers: an individual experiencing an adverse shock quickly recuperates. One of the functions of bankruptcy laws is to give those with excessive debts a fresh start. It may not fully solve a debtor's problems, but at least it prevents the individual from being dragged down in a mountain of debt. Unfortunately, in many societies around the world, large fractions of the population are still highly vulnerable, highly exposed to these downward vicious spirals—and in some cases, matters are getting worse.

There are many channels for these downward spirals to operate. Individuals with inadequate income are less likely to eat well, and that means they are more likely to suffer from illness. But once sick, they cannot afford adequate health care; and that means, in societies without adequate public provision of medical services, an accident or illness can be the beginning of the end. Without adequate health care, they are at risk of significant diminution in earning power; reduced earnings lowers further their ability to afford health care.

Recent research has shown how the mental energies of the poor are disproportionately addressed to the here and now—the exigencies of survival. They can't think strategically; they can't plan for the long term. So, it

is no surprise that they fail to make decisions (including investments) that might raise them out of poverty.

Economic vulnerabilities

Global attention is inevitably focused on those who suffer from a natural disaster—from a tsunami, a flood or an earthquake. But economic disasters are just as devastating as natural disasters.

Changes in the global economy in recent decades have created many more vulnerabilities. The interlinks of banks and countries have increased the probability of financial contagion, of the kind that occurred in the financial crisis of 2008. These events showed how important regulations are in finance—including circuit breakers and capital controls. The devastation that the crisis wreaked on the global economy—shrinking economies and plunging millions into poverty—underlines that these are not just questions for the banking industry. They are important priorities for human development more generally.

Not only have changes increased the exposure to risk, they have also reduced the mechanisms that societies use to help the most vulnerable cope. This is especially true in developing countries, where strong social bonds and family ties have traditionally been at the center of social protection. But in many countries, these bonds have weakened faster than national public systems of social protection have been put into place.

How policies have increased vulnerability

One of the central criticisms of Washington consensus policies is that they systematically led to increases in vulnerability—both by increasing the shocks to which individuals and economies were exposed and by reducing the coping mechanisms. Policies such as capital market liberalization (associated with large fluctuations in flows of money in and out of countries) exposed developing countries increasingly to shocks from abroad. Financial market liberalization and deregulation led to greater domestic shocks—to credit and asset bubbles that inevitably broke. Weakening of systems of social protection simultaneously weakened automatic stabilizers, and some financial policies led to automatic destabilizers—so that the effects of any shock were amplified. At the same time, the policies weakened the capacity of large fractions of the population to cope with the shocks that these economies were experiencing. The Washington Consensus policies were often accompanied by a weakening of systems of social protection; the adverse effect on vulnerability should be obvious.

Thus, these 'reforms' increased the vulnerability both of individuals and of the economic system as a whole. For example, the often lauded switch from defined benefits to defined contributions increased individual and systemic vulnerability.

Even in developed countries, however, many argued that to compete in a world of globalization, there had to be cutbacks in the welfare state and in the systems of social protection, leaving those at the bottom and middle more vulnerable.

The Washington Consensus policies often also resulted in greater inequality, and those at the bottom will inevitably be more vulnerable, unless the government undertakes active protective measures.

(continued)

Broadening our thinking on vulnerability (continued)

Inequality and vulnerability

One of the biggest contributors to vulnerability—something that has adverse effects on many of the other factors mentioned—is inequality, and it is a contributor in many ways. Inequality causes instability, increasing the frequency of big swings in the economy.[4] Extremes of inequality mean that larger fractions of the population are in poverty—with a lower ability to cope with shocks when they occur. Extremes of economic inequality inevitably lead to political inequality—with the result that governments are less likely to provide the systems of social protection that can protect those at the bottom from the consequences of large shocks.[5] We need to begin thinking of inequality not just as a moral issue—which it is—but also as a fundamental economic concern, integral to thinking about human development and especially relevant to any analysis of vulnerability.

Limiting vulnerability

Some interventions to limit vulnerabilities are well known and have long fallen within the ambit of human development. These include improvements to education and social protection. In this perspective, education is important not just because it enables individuals to live up to their potential, not just because it leads to increases in productivity: it also enhances the ability of individuals to cope with shocks. More educated individuals can more easily move, for instance, from one job to another. While the beneficial effects of such policies may be obvious, they continue to be crucial.

But there are others that are not as obvious. Many aspects of our economic system are implicitly part of risk absorption—in other words, they help mitigate vulnerability. Having a bankruptcy law that protects ordinary citizens (debtors)—rather than trying to extract as much as possible from the most disadvantaged to the advantage of creditors, as the American system does—is extremely important. Good bankruptcy laws enable individuals to get a fresh start.

Income-contingent education loans can help families break out of a poverty trap, to begin a climb upward. And good systems of social protection affect, as noted, not just the well-being of those facing stress but the overall performance of the economic system.

Vulnerability has multiple causes and consequences. Reducing vulnerability is a key ingredient in any agenda for improving human development. But if we are to succeed in reducing vulnerability, we need to approach it from a broad systemic perspective.

Notes
1. Ogata and Sen 2003. 2. Narayan and others 2000. 3. Stiglitz, Sen and Fitoussi 2010. 4. The International Monetary Fund has called attention to this; see Berg and Ostry (2011b). 5. There are, of course, many other pernicious effects of inequality, emphasized in Stiglitz (2012b). Inequality is linked to lower growth, undermines democracy, increases social friction and erodes trust.

minimize longer term impacts. Take the Bolsa Família initiative in Brazil, a cash transfer programme that aims to minimize adverse longer term impacts by keeping children in school and protecting their health.[1] The impact of a sharp rise in food prices in 2008 following the global financial crisis was mitigated by higher transfer payments. Beyond that, not much else can be done other than ad hoc emergency relief, which however well designed is not best over the long term. Pending more-comprehensive social protection arrangements, cash transfer programmes can be started relatively easily, and their budget impact can be limited if there is an infrastructure to draw on, as in Brazil. Such programmes need to be designed to ensure that capabilities—especially those of the next generation—are protected.

Universal provision of basic social services

Universalism implies equal access and opportunities to build core capabilities. Universal access to basic social services—education, health care, water supply and sanitation, and public safety—enhances resilience. Universalism is a powerful way of directly addressing the uncertain nature of vulnerability. Social policies that have a universal aim not only protect those who currently experience poverty, poor health or a bout of unemployment; they also protect individuals and households that are doing well but may find themselves struggling if things go wrong. And they secure certain basic core capabilities of future generations.

Universal coverage of basic social services is not only imperative—it is also possible at early stages of development. And recent evidence shows that it can be achieved in less than a decade. Furthermore, universal provision of basic social services is better than targeting, which leads to social stigma for recipients and segmentation in the quality of services, as those who can afford to opt out of receiving public services do so.

Universal provision of basic social services can raise social competences through several channels. It can be a powerful force to equalize opportunities and outcomes—and a powerful enabler of societal empowerment. Universal public education can mitigate the gap in the quality of education that children from rich and poor households receive. Intergenerational transmission of capabilities such as education within families can perpetuate the benefits in the long run. Universal policies also promote social solidarity.[2]

The case for universal provision of basic social services then rests, first and foremost, on the premises that all humans should be empowered to live lives they value and that access to certain basic elements of a dignified life ought to be delinked from people's ability to pay. The UN Secretary-General's 2013 report, "A Life of Dignity for All", states that one of the prerequisites for the post-2015 sustainable development agenda is a "vision of the future firmly anchored in human rights and universally accepted values and principles, including those encapsulated in the Charter, the Universal Declaration of Human Rights and the Millennium Declaration."[3] The September 2010 Millennium Development Goal Summit outcome document states, "promoting universal access to social services and providing social protection floors can make an important contribution to consolidating and achieving further development gains."[4]

A commitment to universal provision of social services requires a profound societal and political decision. It reflects on the nature of society that people want. While ways of delivering such services may vary with circumstances and country context, common to all successful experiences is a single idea: The state has the primary responsibility to extend social services to the entire population, in a basic social contract between people and their state.

At a more policy-oriented level, looking at budgets alone is insufficient; how and when they are deployed are equally critical. More resources may well be required to extend basic social services to all, but modest investments at the right time can go a considerable way in reducing vulnerability. Budgets need to join legal and other measures to equalize access to services and opportunities.

Universal or targeted coverage

Recent decades have seen a global shift in the politics of social spending, changing the emphasis from development to poverty alleviation.[5] As a result, there has been greater stress on targeting social spending for the poor rather than for all. Targeted services were considered more efficient, less costly and more effective in ensuring redistribution. But historical evidence presents a more nuanced picture. Universal provision has in many instances been associated with greater poverty reduction, greater redistribution and lower inequality, something of a paradox since targeted benefits are theoretically more redistributive.[6] A key factor is that when benefits are narrowly targeted, the middle class and elites are less willing to fund them through taxes. If provision is universal, however, elites are more willing to fund services, and some of the inefficiencies in redistribution are offset by the larger pool of available funds.[7]

In the European welfare states, universal coverage of social insurance has been driven by the expectations and demands of the middle class.[8] Similarly, universal provision of education and health care in the Nordic countries was sustainable because of the high quality of education and health care from which all could benefit. This ensured that the middle class was willing to fund their provision with taxes. Because of this, there have been calls for a politics of solidarity—engaging universalist principles to create a stake for the middle class in social provision and thus to build a coalition between the poor and the nonpoor.[9] Targeting can undermine such solidarity, giving rise to two-track systems: underfunded low-quality services for the poor and better quality commercial services for the middle classes and the rich.

Universalist principles in social policy have been known and practised in several countries for years. Aspirationally, they have been included in country constitutions and recognized in the Universal Declaration of Human Rights. But many countries, in different geographic areas and at all stages of development, have yet to commit to universal provision of basic social services. An enduring concern has been finding adequate resources to fund universal provision. For example, there is a tacit assumption that economic growth producing higher incomes is a prerequisite for universal health care. Worries about reduced fiscal space have heightened since the 2008 financial crises—even in developed countries—leading to austerity measures.[10] Yet income alone need not constrain universal social policies. While resource

The case for universal provision of basic social services rests, first and foremost, on the premises that all humans should be empowered to live lives they value and that access to certain basic elements of a dignified life ought to be delinked from people's ability to pay.

constraints are a valid concern, mobilizing resources, restructuring the fiscal space, reprioritizing spending and improving the efficiency of service delivery through better institutional design can create more options.

Universal provision is feasible, even at early stages of development

Three stylized facts emerge from a study of the conditions in selected countries that adopted principles of universalism. First, the principles were generally adopted before the countries industrialized and became affluent. Second, they were adopted under a range of political systems—from autocracies to highly functional democracies. Third, universal coverage took many years, in some cases decades, for the early adopters to achieve, not so for several recent adopters. But the gains from expanded coverage start to accrue long before coverage is universal.

In Costa Rica, Denmark, the Republic of Korea, Norway and Sweden the first step towards universal provision of basic social services was taken at relatively low income per capita. Costa Rica adopted comprehensive measures on education investments, public health and social security in the constitutional amendment of 1949, in the immediate aftermath of a violent political struggle after which democracy emerged, when its GDP per capita was $2,123 in 1990 international dollars. Sweden (in 1891) and Denmark (in 1892) enacted sickness insurance laws at a GDP per capita of $1,724 and $2,598 respectively. Norway enacted a mandatory workers compensation law in 1894 when its GDP per capita was $1,764. The Republic of Korea had already made large gains in education by the early 1960s, when its GDP per capita was less than $1,500.[11] Ghana initiated universal health coverage in 2004 when its income per capita was $1,504—the coverage is not complete yet, but reductions in out-of-pocket expenditures have been large.[12] These countries started putting in place measures of social insurance when their GDP per capita was lower than India's and Pakistan's now (figure 4.1).

When Sweden made schooling compulsory for all children in 1842, its GDP per capita ($926) was lower than the current GDP per capita of all the countries in South Asia. So high national income is not a prerequisite for taking the first steps towards broad-based investment in providing basic social services. Investment in public services preceded growth takeoffs in all the countries just discussed.

The earliest measures towards widespread—if not universal—education, health care and social protection were adopted under a range of different political conditions (figure 4.2). In France and the Nordic countries a spirit of egalitarianism and a solidarity view of welfare as a right of citizenship preceded the adoption of welfare measures. Germany initiated education for the masses under Prussian rule. The Republic of Korea invested heavily in education even as a newly independent country in the late 1940s and continued to expand access to education during political turmoil and war.[13] Sri Lanka, which shares a colonial history similar to that of India and the rest of the subcontinent, achieved nearly universal education and health care despite years of militancy and war.

While the transition to universal coverage took time for the early adopters, the more recent adopters have made faster gains. Even though compulsory education and social protection were mandated in Denmark, Norway and Sweden in the late 19th century, the various schemes became truly universal more than 10 years after the Second World War, between 1955 and 1963. The Republic of Korea's near-universal primary education and high secondary and tertiary education took some five decades to achieve.[14] In comparison, China, Rwanda and Viet Nam went from very low health care coverage to nearly universal coverage within a decade.[15]

Sometimes severe shocks can set back progress in human development, including efforts to achieve universal coverage of basic social services, but the right short-term response can prevent long-term damage. In the aftermath of the East Asian crises in the late 1990s, Indonesia, the Republic of Korea, Malaysia, Thailand and other economies were reeling from market failures and the shock of capital flight. The resultant job losses and decline in growth output meant that large sections of the working population lost earnings, with immediate impacts on household spending and consumption and direct repercussions for health and education.

While resource constraints are a valid concern, mobilizing resources, restructuring the fiscal space, reprioritizing spending and improving the efficiency of service delivery through better institutional design can create more options

FIGURE 4.1

Several countries started putting in place measures of social insurance when their GDP per capita was lower than that of most countries in South Asia today

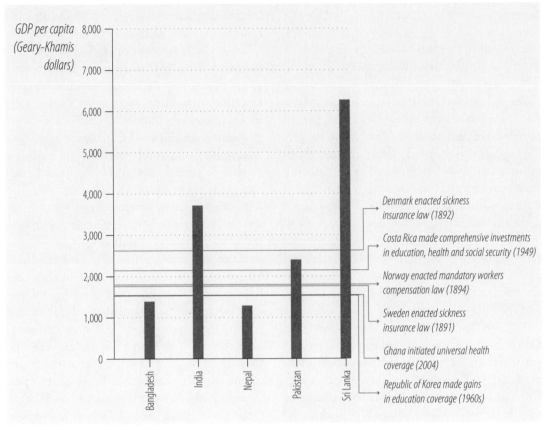

Source: Calculations based on Maddison (2010).

On closer examination, the countries responded differently to the crises.[16] Indonesia's leadership was constrained by political uncertainty, and there was a decline in public spending on the social sectors. Ongoing social unrest meant that informal community networks were not as resilient or resourceful. Household spending on health and education also declined, leading to higher illness and school dropout rates.[17] The Thai government implemented assistance measures for employment, health and education.[18] But executing such a response in Indonesia was more difficult. The difference in these two experiences is often pinned to the different levels of proactive policies by the government.[19]

Macro and other benefits

Expanded provision of basic public services can reduce poverty and inequality even before coverage is universal. The design and reach of social policies will affect inequality in people's lifetime earning power. In Mexico between 1997 and 1998 the Oportunidades programme reduced the poverty rate 17 percent. In Brazil the Bolsa Família programme has been linked to a 16 percent decline in extreme poverty.[20] In Europe consolidation of universal provision coincided with a decline in income inequality, giving rise to associations between the size of social expenditure and the reduction in inequality, termed the 'size-redistribution thesis'.[21]

Several studies have since shown that institutional design rather than amount of spending may have driven outcomes.[22] Indeed, countries can achieve better coverage and quality for the resources they spend on providing basic social services. And innovative sources of finance can be tapped to fund universal provision. For instance, Bolivia introduced a universal old age pension in 1997 and funded it partially through

FIGURE 4.2

Evolution of health protection coverage as a percentage of total population in selected countries

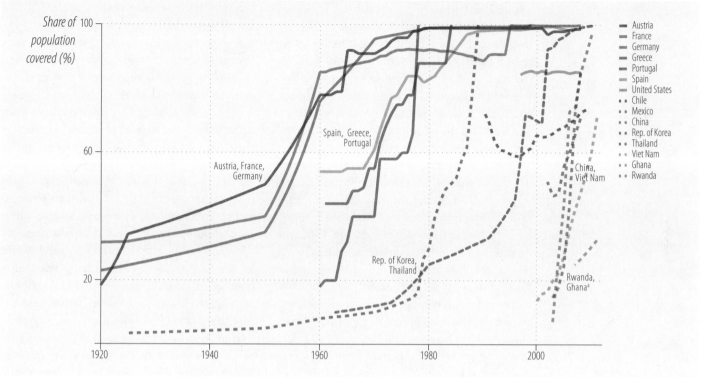

a. Estimated.
Source: ILO 2011b.

---

resources from privatizing public enterprises. In 2007 the qualifying age was reduced from 65 to 60, and taxes on hydrocarbon sales became the main source of funding.[23]

Social spending has been associated with poverty reduction in the population as a whole and among subgroups.[24] With a poverty line at 50 percent of median equivalent income, the Nordic countries reduced poverty 80–90 percent among families with children through redistribution in the mid-1990s.[25] Other European countries—notably Belgium, France, Germany, the Netherlands and Spain—also reduced poverty more than 50 percent among families with children. Non–means tested entitlements in Sweden reduced poverty by close to 72 percent, independent of the level of means-tested benefits.[26] In Argentina a universal child allowance, introduced in 2009 and covering 85 percent of children, reduced poverty 22 percent and extreme poverty 42 percent.[27]

Universalism in social policy can also contribute to economic growth, thus setting up a virtuous cycle of growth and human development. In East Asia in particular, rapid gains in education and training enabled countries to leverage the new knowledge-driven global economy. Universal provision affects development outcomes through a range of channels, including improvements in human resources that might contribute to growth, thus setting up a virtuous cycle. For instance, countries that reaped demographic dividends have usually had better education outcomes prior to takeoff. While there is no one-to-one correspondence between human development and economic growth, the latter increases a country's command over resources and is thus important for development.

Expanded education and health care have enabled several countries to reap demographic dividends.[28] In the Republic of Korea, for example, the child dependency ratio ranged between 74 percent and 81 percent through the 1960s, increasing until 1966 but then falling consistently to 22 percent by 2011. The country's economic takeoff starting in the mid-1960s was also preceded by large-scale achievements in education. In 1945 most of the population had no schooling, and less than 5 percent had secondary or higher education, but by 1960 primary enrolment had increased 3-fold (with 96 percent of school-age children in grades 1–6), secondary enrolment more than 8-fold and higher education 10-fold. By the early 1990s the high school graduation rate was 90 percent. This education revolution continued through political instability, poverty and war, and the country had universal education before its economic takeoff.

China presents a more complex picture. Through the 1960s the child dependency ratio was above 70 percent. It started declining in the mid-1970s, just before the reforms of 1978, and by 2011 had fallen to 26 percent. In 1982, the earliest year with data, adult female literacy was 51 percent.[29] By 2000 it was 87 percent and by 2010 more than 91 percent. In 1997, the most recent year with data, primary completion was 94 percent and for women, 92 percent. Primary enrolment became universal around 2007. As a result, the growth of the manufacturing sector over the last two decades was fuelled not just by a growing labour force, but also by an educated and productive labour force.

But in recent decades China has seen an erosion in health care coverage and social protection. From 1950 through the 1970s health care was nearly universal—thanks to the public health network and urban and rural health insurance schemes. But after 1978 a shift to market-oriented mechanisms and increasing costs of medical care, combined with the collapse of the rural cooperative health care system, left large sections of the population (including urban groups) without affordable care. In 2009 a blueprint for health system reform was announced, with the goal of establishing universal coverage of all urban and rural residents.[30] By the end of 2013, 99 percent of China's rural population was said to have access to health care through the new rural cooperative medical insurance scheme.[31]

Universal social policy is not uniform in its implementation. Providing access to marginalized and excluded groups, including the poor and the vulnerable, requires additional efforts and resources. Implementing policies with universal intent often starts by gathering the 'low-hanging fruit', as evident in policies

to move the poor closest to the poverty line over it. Avoiding this false choice will require starting at the 'last mile'—aiming to provide access to basic services that meet the needs of the poorest and the most vulnerable first.

A second issue is quality. Although most countries are close to universal primary school enrolment, school completion at that level is far from universal. Moreover, children in public schools often receive very poor quality education: Where public and private schooling systems coexist, a systematic difference in quality may emerge if public schooling is underfunded. The quality of health care that people can access (by paying) and what is included in universal health coverage can also make a large difference in outcomes. When public education has adequate funding, it competes favourably with privately provided education.[32] Expanding coverage thus requires a clear assessment of the appropriate balance between public and private spaces in delivering these basic services. A 'mixed' system tends to segment the provision of services—the rich and the middle class tend to opt out of publicly provided education, leading to a weaker commitment to providing quality education in the publicly organized system.

Addressing life cycle vulnerabilities—timing matters

Covering all individuals implies that social services are needed at different points in the life cycle, particularly at sensitive junctures in a person's life, including early childhood and the transitions from youth to young adulthood and from adulthood to old age, to build lifetime resilience. Timing the interventions is critical—since failing to support the development of capabilities at the right time is costly to fix later. Early childhood development provides a good example of how universalism helps support investments in human capabilities across the life cycle.

The focus here is on early childhood development. Another key transition is from youth to young adulthood. Most salient for young people are school-to-work transitions and precarious employment. (Employment policies are treated in the following section, and pensions and disability insurance, in the section on social protection.)

Early childhood development provides a good example of how universalism helps support investments in human capabilities across the life cycle

Ideally, governments should integrate health, education, family and social protection services for children and families throughout their lives. However, it is common for fewer resources to be available for early childhood development and for social spending per capita to increase with age.[33] Spending on health, education and welfare that increases over the life cycle does not nurture and support capability development during the crucial early years (figure 4.3).

Sweden is a rare model where the government allocates expenditures towards earlier years,[34] thus reflecting the crucial investments during the prenatal and postnatal sensitive period of brain development (figure 4.4). In launching or scaling up large national programmes, four ingredients deserve special consideration: pre- and post-natal care; parent education and training; income; and nutrition. As chapter 3 highlighted, brain growth is extremely rapid during the earliest years and tends to flatten after them. But the budget allocations in public social services are lowest in the earliest years and increase later (see figure 4.3).[35]

The advantages gained from effective early interventions are best sustained when followed by continued investments in high-quality education. Early childhood development interventions alone are not sufficient. Later complementary investments in lifetime learning during adolescence, adulthood and old age are necessary to ensure that individual capabilities can develop to their full potential. But current policies of education and job training are often not appropriately focused and tend to emphasize cognitive skills over social skills, self-discipline, motivation and other 'soft skills' that determine success in life.

Education performance stabilizes at a young age (around 7–8), and family environments can shape inequalities (figure 4.5).[36] Particularly important are interactions with parents and caregivers.[37] The degree and quality of these interactions—including play, vocal exchanges, facial expressions and physical contact—correlate with a child's later behaviour, cognitive abilities and emotional development.[38] Much of this care is unpaid and nonmarket work.

Infancy and early childhood are among the most formative periods in a person's life. Investments in children—of time, money and

FIGURE 4.3

Spending on health, education and welfare that increases over the life cycle does not nurture and support capability development during the crucial early years

Source: Karoly and others 1997.

FIGURE 4.4

Early childhood investment: the Swedish example

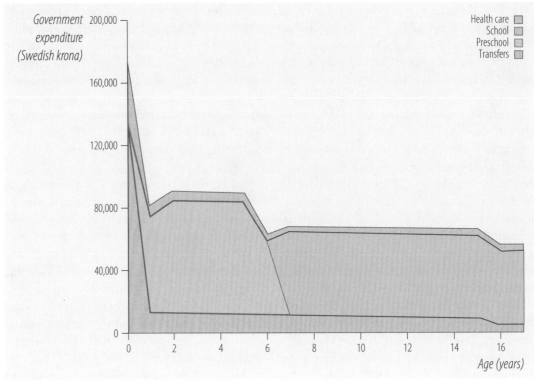

Source: Dalman and Bremberg 1999.

other resources—expand their choices further down the road, enhance capabilities and lead to sustainable improvements in human development. But children who are born into poverty, go hungry and receive inadequate care tend to perform worse in school, have poorer health and are less likely to get a decent job. And as adults they invest too little in their own children, perpetuating vulnerability across generations. When households are subject to persistent shocks, programmes such as Bolsa Família and Oportunidades can reduce the probability that children will be pulled out of school or suffer malnourishment.

Parents and caregivers in low-income and impoverished households may have to spend more time in paid work to make ends meet and thus have less time to invest in children. Adults in better resourced households have more money—and often more time. This helps explain correlations between socioeconomic status and early childhood development.[39] It also points to the benefits of universal access to early childhood development measures in equalizing opportunities.

Promoting full employment

Full employment as an objective was central to macroeconomic policies in the 1950s and 1960s. It disappeared from the global agenda during the era of stabilization that followed the oil shocks of 1973 and 1979. It is now time to return to that commitment so that progress can be robust and easily sustained. Universalism is frequently discussed with regard to social policies—such as health, education, childcare and income support. But it also applies to labour markets—ensuring that everyone has access to decent opportunities for paid employment. Not everyone will choose to engage in paid employment, but universalism implies that they should have the option to do so. Universal access to decent employment opportunities is often articulated in terms of full-employment policies. Not only does full employment extend universalism to the labour market, it also supports the provision of social services. Indeed, full employment was important for sustaining the Nordic model, since high employment helped

FIGURE 4.5

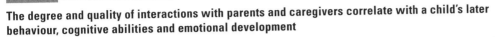

The degree and quality of interactions with parents and caregivers correlate with a child's later behaviour, cognitive abilities and emotional development

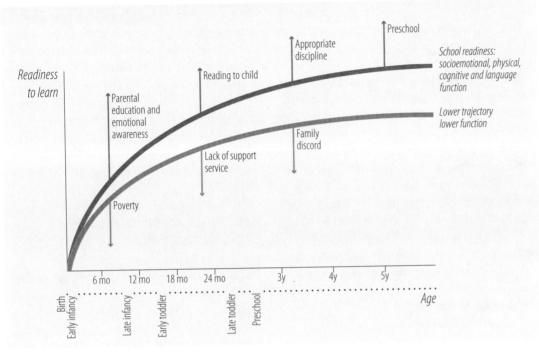

Source: Young 2014.

ensure adequate tax revenues to finance universal provision.

Full employment is also desirable for its social benefits. Unemployment entails high economic and social costs, leading to a permanent loss in output and a decline in labour skills and productivity. The loss of production and associated tax revenue can require higher public spending to support unemployment insurance. Long-term unemployment is also a serious threat to health (physical and mental) and to the quality of life (including children's education). And unemployment tends to be associated with an increase in crime, suicide, violence, drug abuse and other social problems. Therefore, the social benefits of a job far exceed the private benefit—the wage.

Jobs foster social stability and social cohesion, and decent jobs strengthen people's ability to manage shocks and uncertainty. Jobs, as a means of livelihood, strengthen human agency and have larger value for families and communities. Secure employment has a high psychological value as well.

Yet few countries, developed or developing, pursue full employment as an overarching societal or economic goal. Macroeconomic policies almost everywhere now focus on price stability and debt management. Globally connected financial markets are quick to penalize countries if they believe these objectives are not being adequately pursued. Even in theory, markets cannot deliver on full employment due to informational barriers and other labour market frictions. And unregulated markets make it particularly difficult to produce desirable labour outcomes.

A stronger national commitment to full employment and active public policies should be geared towards creating and protecting jobs. It is worth recalling that the 1995 Copenhagen commitment to full employment was added to the Millennium Development Goals as target 1.B in 2008. Expanding and conserving jobs rather than destroying them should now guide creative and active labour market policies. Unemployment benefits and work injury compensation, however useful, are reactive, dealing mainly with the effects of economic vulnerabilities. Active labour market policies seek to overcome these vulnerabilities by helping workers regain employment

Expanding and conserving
jobs rather than destroying
them should now guide
creative and active
labour market policies

through temporary employment schemes or by imparting employable skills. For instance, Singapore places a high premium on job stability in economic downturns by providing wage subsidies to employers (rather than providing unemployment benefits to workers) that increase wages at the lower end of the distribution.

But for developing countries faced with underemployment, active labour market policies are not enough. Pursuing full employment requires policies that promote pro-poor growth and create a social security framework. It also requires macroeconomic policies that go beyond an exclusive focus on price stability and debt management. Typically, developing countries have little formal unemployment—in fact, unemployment is generally a status that only better-off people can afford. These countries also face pressing challenges of creating many new jobs in the next years to accommodate youth spikes in their populations.

There are promising employment initiatives around the world—from China's strong commitment to high growth in order to absorb new entrants to the labour force to India's National Rural Employment Guarantee Scheme to secure work as a basic right of all citizens. The examples highlight the opportunities in vigorously pursuing full employment as a strategic objective, at different stages of development, to reduce vulnerability and build the resilience of people and societies.

In the past decades, however, macroeconomic frameworks in most developing countries have had a one-dimensional focus on price stability rather than on full employment, leading to low growth and high unemployment.[40] The shortcomings are also evident in developed countries. By further depressing aggregate demand when it needs to be boosted, fiscal austerity may be inappropriate as a macroeconomic policy because it exacerbates the impact of economic downturns on unemployment (box 4.1). Decent work that pays reasonable wages, involves formal contracts that prevent abrupt dismissals and brings entitlements to social security can do much to reduce employee vulnerability, but less so in recessions. Reducing vulnerable employment is thus hugely important for reducing human vulnerability in general. The importance of realizing

decent and full employment has long been recognized, yet widespread unemployment and underemployment continue in most countries due to the prolonged deployment of macroeconomic policies that have been insufficiently countercyclical.

All these policy areas are interrelated, and a comprehensive approach to addressing labour market deficiencies will require a coordinated effort. This will require structural transformation of the economy, with movement into higher productivity and higher value-added activities—using targeted policies that support the development of strategic sectors and activities.[41]

Developing countries require particular policies

Pursuing full employment in developing countries requires different approaches. Traditional policies, such as those highlighted above, are more appropriate to developed countries. Such policies make only a small contribution to reducing the vulnerability of employment, helping the minority in the modern formal sector. The long-run objective then is to secure structural change so that modern formal employment gradually incorporates most of the workforce, as has happened in developed countries and many emerging countries, such as China and the Republic of Korea. Such a transformation involves movement out of agriculture into industry and services, supported by investments in infrastructure, education and training, as the successful economies show.[42]

Policies supporting structural transformation, increasing formal employment and regulating conditions of work are thus needed to reduce employment vulnerability in the medium to long run, but they will be insufficient to tackle the vulnerabilities of the majority of the workforce in the short run. So policies are also essential to address the vulnerabilities—and secure the livelihoods—of the mass of the workforce that will remain in traditional and informal activities in the short run.

First, a host of interventions can contribute over the medium to long term, including micro-credit schemes, support for new and improved small-scale technologies, assisting

BOX 4.1

Macroeconomic policies for full employment

Full employment was pursued and mostly attained in the mid-20th century in Europe and North America. The East Asian economies achieved similar results during their high growth era in the 1970s and 1980s. High savings and high aggregate investment (both above 30 percent of GDP) produced inclusive growth that transformed the structure of their economies and led to full employment.[1]

In many other developing countries, however, most jobs remain vulnerable and precarious. The poor, with little or no social security, cannot afford to be unemployed but must accept whatever work and wages are available, often in the informal sector. The objective is full decent employment—moving towards higher productivity, higher value added, higher quality and better remunerated forms of employment. Generally this means moving out of agriculture into other sectors of the economy. So policies need to address land reform and the insecurity of labour transitioning out of agriculture. Full employment also has implications for fiscal policy. For example, since the mid-1990s increases in urban formal employment and rising wages in China have been financed by rising provincial government fiscal deficits.[2] Similarly, India uses tax revenues to finance the National Rural Employment Guarantee Scheme.

During economic downturns a countercyclical fiscal stimulus can raise aggregate demand. Macroeconomic policy should thus embrace multiple targets (not just the inflation rate) and multiple instruments (not just monetary policy) complemented with universal social protection that not only mitigates vulnerabilities among the population, but also stabilizes the economy in the face of shocks. In some developing countries, however, countercyclical policies may not be the first step if there are structural impediments to job creation.

In developed economies three policy approaches have traditionally aimed at restoring full employment—which needs to be explicitly acknowledged as an important objective of economic policy and incorporated into macro policy, both fiscal and monetary. First, a Keynesian approach to macro policy allowed budget deficits to rise during recessions, and monetary policy was guided by the employment objective as well as price stability. In the recent recession some developed countries (the United States and initially the United Kingdom) and several middle-income developing countries did adopt Keynesian deficit policies.[3]

Second, to facilitate structural change and reduce the employment vulnerability it brings, research and development policies can promote technology innovation to develop new sources of employment, increase workforce education and provide more training and retraining, as well as unemployment benefits as people change sectors.

Third, emphasis on upgrading to new activities diminishes the need for labour market reforms, which generally involve less employment security and lower wages. Indeed, minimum wages should be raised to encourage the move into higher productivity activities.[4] In general, the labour market reforms of the neoliberal model need to be carefully re-evaluated from the perspective of reducing employment vulnerability. Together, these three approaches to policy will contribute to reducing the vulnerability of employment in high- and middle-income countries.

Notes
1. Muqtada 2010. 2. Fang, Yang and Meiyan 2010. 3. Jolly and others 2012. 4. Raising minimum wages was a response to the crisis in Brazil and has contributed to improving wages and income distribution (Berg 2009).

---

small farmers with technology, credit and markets, and so on. And social and institutional innovations can support improved conditions. Farmer cooperatives, women's forestry groups and many others can improve productivity and increase the bargaining strength and thus the terms of trade and incomes of very poor producers.[43]

Second, responses to short-term shocks can improve the support that people in very low-income activities receive in general and during adversity in particular. They include cash transfers (conditional or unconditional), pensions for older people (which contribute to the well-being of the family), nutrition support through food subsidies and school needs, communal cooking and feeding programmes and low-cost insurance schemes. Locally administered cash transfers can support households when the main earners are ill, as can free medical services.

Third, direct job creation programmes can help those facing vulnerable employment. Some provide permanent employment at low wages for poor households. Others are temporary, introduced during recessions or in post-conflict situations as a short-term response to periods of particularly precarious employment outcomes. Both types of scheme, if on a sufficient scale, reduce employment vulnerability. Examples include[44]:

- The Indian National Rural Employment Guarantee Scheme guarantees every rural household 100 days of work a year at a reasonable wage.[45]
- Argentina's Jefes y Jefas de Hogar Desocupados, introduced in 2001 in response to an economic crisis, included 2 million beneficiaries by the end of 2003.[46]
- Food-for-work schemes in Bangladesh have provided extensive poverty alleviation since 1975, particularly for rural workers during the slack seasons. Each year they have provided 100 million workdays for 4 million people.[47]
- The Indonesian Padat Karya, introduced in 1998–1999 in response to the financial crisis,

provided employment for those who lost their jobs.[48]

- Nepal's Emergency Employment Programme, targeted at marginal communities, extended to roughly 5 percent of the population to meet the post-conflict need for employment and a peace dividend.[49]

Some groups face larger labour market risks and uncertainties, and it will be important to invest in their skills development and education.[50] Addressing residential segregation, improving transportation and lowering the cost of getting to better jobs will integrate labour markets and increase accessibility of employment opportunities.[51] Providing information about available opportunities and connecting those searching for better employment with new opportunities make labour markets work better. Those in informal employment, many of whom are self-employed, will need better access to credit and markets. All this will require public investment.

As development proceeds, workers move from low-productivity but stable and diversified rural livelihoods to less predictable forms of income, including wages and salaries.[52] Rather than exacerbating insecurity through flexible labour market policies, public policy needs to first focus on making it easier for people to transition into decent jobs with some autonomy. This will allow them to adopt a livelihood in response to socioeconomic structural change that is more in line with their skill sets and employment expectations, as seen in China and the Republic of Korea.

More universal social security and social provisioning help populations shifting out of agriculture and rural subsistence prepare for negative economic events and deal with the employment precariousness in the development process. Social security regimes are integral to—not optional for—enhancing people's capabilities and societies' competences during transition.[53]

Encouraging this shift and creating widespread productive employment require more-effective strategies of economic development, including greater public investment in infrastructure, development of human capabilities, active promotion of innovation and strategic policies for trade, particularly exports.

Some countries in East Asia have facilitated a rapid transition out of agriculture (box 4.2). In the Republic of Korea the share of the labour employed in the primary sector (mostly agriculture) fell from 30 percent in 1980 to 9 percent in 2006. In Malaysia it fell from 55 percent in the 1960s to 16 percent in 2000. And in China it fell from almost 84 percent in 1952 to 81 percent in 1970 to 69 percent in 1980 to 60 percent in 1990 to 50 percent in 2000 and to 37 percent in 2010.[54] The pace of these transitions is remarkable.

Transitions have been slower in, say, Brazil, where the primary sector's labour share fell from about 29 percent to 20 percent between 1980 and 2006, and much slower in India, where it barely fell between 1960 and 2005, stuck around 70 percent.[55] India's failure to transition into industry has to be remedied—jobs in business process outsourcing are a boon for the balance of payments but hardly for mass employment.

Success might be deemed as avoiding a situation in which the bulk of transitioning labour ends up in insecure informal employment, as in much of Latin America, where

---

BOX 4.2

Policy successes in East Asia

The varied policy measures in East Asia have generally not fallen into the mould of flexible labour market reforms and purely market-based approaches to solving employment problems. They are better characterized as industrial development through state interventions coupled with measures to enhance livelihood or employment security and avoid excessive social dislocation and unrest (among other aims).

State-led industrial policy created the conditions for labour to transition to more productive, higher value added and fairly formalized employment outside agriculture. Monetary policies to sustain aggregate demand for maximum employment included tolerance for moderate inflation. State ownership of the banking sector in the Republic of Korea and later in China allowed for the financing of industrial policy and employment-generating activities such as infrastructure construction, neither of which is necessarily profitable in the short term. Trade, macroeconomic, financial and industrial policies all increased the quality and quantity of jobs. Fiscal policies were similarly directed towards employment creation.

workers are highly urban and informal. For about 1 billion of the world's people,[56] the precarious livelihoods of those operating outside the labour market and engaged in self-subsistence cannot be enhanced in the long run without expanded decent employment. In the short run social protection that covers the whole population is essential to protect those whose livelihoods are in peril during the transition (see below).

Preserving employment

Various countries have boosted employment security for more-vulnerable workers through targeted labour market interventions. Since the 1980s Singapore has temporarily reduced mandated employer social security contributions to minimize job losses during economic downturns.[57] In 2009 the government introduced a one-year jobs credit scheme that helped businesses preserve jobs during the recession. Its 2013 budget included a wage credit scheme to raise the wages of lower income workers. Employers thus have an incentive to share productivity gains with all employees.

China has practised a degree of wage equalization across state employment in urban areas, increasing real wages nationwide since the 1990s. This presumably also raised wages in the nonstate sector, in both corporate and informal employment. European countries have also offered subsidies to employers to hire unemployed workers. In 2003 Germany subsidized roughly 6 percent of transitions out of unemployment for middle-age people.[58] The pay of the subsidized workers was not much different from that of their unsubsidized counterparts, but because subsidized workers tended to keep their jobs, their cumulative wages were substantially higher.[59] Subsidized employment also generated more tax and social security income and reduced the cost of unemployment benefits.

Yet some groups can be difficult to employ even in a healthy economy—particularly young people or the long-term unemployed. To address this, the United States offers workers an earned income tax credit that provides extended benefits if they have families with children. Combining wage support and social transfers, the system has a strong antipoverty

impact. Chile introduced an employer-side and training-linked wage subsidy programme in 1991. Under its Chile Joven programme, employers that hire and train unemployed young people received a subsidy to cover the training costs.[60] Some evidence indicates that three months after receiving training half the participants retained employment—usually in positions related to their training.

At least 10 Organisation for Economic Co-operation and Development (OECD) countries have policies for workers with disabilities. In 1998 Denmark, as an extension of its active social policy, introduced Flexjob, which offers wage subsidies to enable employers to retain the long-term sick or disabled on the job. Although there is little research into Flexjob's effectiveness, one study found that the scheme had substantial, positive employment effects over 1994–2001.[61]

Strengthening social protection

Social protection[62] can offer cover against risk and adversity throughout people's lives and especially during critical phases and transitions. By providing an additional and predictable layer of support, it can help households avoid coping strategies that take children out of school, postpone necessary medical care or require selling assets, all detrimental to long-term well-being. And the distribution networks and mechanisms for administering social protection programmes can convey social safety net benefits in the event of a natural disaster.

Social protection not only is a doable proposition at early stages of development, but it also brings about other benefits such as stimulating aggregate demand when needed and reducing poverty. Social protection dampens fluctuations by offsetting output volatility through disposable income compensation (chapter 2).

Strong universal social protection policies improve individual resilience and bolster the resilience of the economy, as in Europe following the 2008 global economic crisis, when GDP per capita declined more than 5 percent.[63] The Nordic countries, with more-comprehensive social policies, did better, with higher productivity than the rest of Europe

Social protection can offer cover against risk and adversity throughout people's lives and especially during critical phases and transitions

in 2010 and an employment rate of 51 percent of the population. In comparison, in the United Kingdom and Ireland productivity was down 12 percent and employment 9 percent. Employment rates were lower in all parts of Europe, though labour productivity in continental Europe matched that of the Nordic countries. On unemployment, the Nordic countries also did much better on average than other OECD countries in Europe (figure 4.6). Only Austria, Luxembourg, the Netherlands and Switzerland had lower unemployment rates than the Nordic countries before and after the crisis.

Short-run actions can bolster resilience within the long-run human development policy framework

Most of this chapter focuses on reducing vulnerability and building resilience over the long term—that is, human development policies that bring about systemic improvement. However, when crises happen, governments also need to react immediately. How can they best do so without harming longer term human development?

A useful taxonomy, in a 2011 review,[64] divides post-crisis policies into two groups: those that mitigate the impact of a crisis (such as reducing working hours to maintain employment or facilitating emergency credit) and those that promote recovery over the longer term (such as investment in education or changing agricultural practices to adapt to climate change). For some policies there might be a tradeoff: Some mitigation policies might slow recovery over the longer term. A rarely heard criticism of the Indian National Rural Employment Guarantee Programme is that the easy availability of work may discourage workers from moving to more-productive sectors of the economy, thus harming longer term growth prospects.[65] Particular thought should be given to win-win policies that both mitigate the impact and promote recovery.

Of course finding win-win policies is not always so easy, nor is having a plan in place necessarily enough. The capabilities to implement a plan may not exist. What actions can actually

FIGURE 4.6

Following the 2008 global economic crisis unemployment rates were lower in Nordic countries than elsewhere in Europe

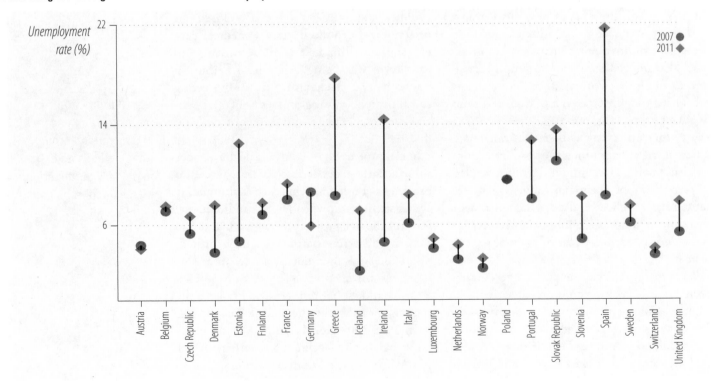

Source: Human Development Report Office calculations based on OECD (n.d.).

be implemented will depend on their cost and the capacity of institutions. As the review notes, "When government budgets decline, as often happens during crises, the more relevant question is what policies to preserve, rather than what additional policies to undertake",[66] and so interventions must be both feasible and flexible. Preparedness, it notes, is key—and takes longer. Setting up institutions or new policies, such as safety nets, during a crisis is both difficult and time-consuming.

Health care, including reproductive health care, needs priority in a crisis because of its long-term and intergenerational consequences, and this often requires difficult decisions when both resources and capacity are lacking. And so several minimum thresholds exist to guide decisionmakers, such as the Minimal Initial Service Package for Reproductive Health, though research shows mixed success because of such issues as inadequate training.[67]

Brazil's Bolsa Família and Mexico's Oportunidades are other examples of win-win policies. Three lessons could be highlighted in strengthening the link between short-run actions and longer term policies in bolstering resilience. First, a social infrastructure should be in place so that distribution networks can be readily accessed when a crisis hits. Second, conditional transfer payments might be helpful in protecting education and health status, especially for young people, and in reducing intergenerational consequences. Third, social support that starts with coverage of key vulnerable groups could become a basis for a more comprehensive social floor in the future.

A social infrastructure serves as an operational framework that public institutions can use to transfer payments to people in need. And since formal social protection systems take time to develop, the basic infrastructure of such programmes as Bolsa Família allows resources to be transferred quickly and effectively. When fluctuations and adverse events happen, these resource transfers protect poor people and other vulnerable groups.

While persistent shocks and hazards call for comprehensive policies over the long haul, emergency response systems can be designed to facilitate short-run adjustments to adverse events in ways that protect long-term choices. For instance, Bolsa Família was adapted to cover short-term emergency situations as well. Increased conditional transfers following the 2008 global financial crisis protected basic consumption levels, and the conditional nature of the transfers in turn protected the formation of long-term capabilities by keeping children in school and protecting their health status.

As more-comprehensive social protection arrangements emerge (see below), cash transfer programmes can be feasible in terms of both budget and social infrastructure. Part of these programmes' success is that they are designed to protect capabilities. In addition, they can be rapidly scaled up to mitigate the adverse consequences of a short-run shock such as a sudden recession or food price spike, as in Brazil following the 2008 crisis.

Similar examples exist elsewhere. In 2009, struck by the great global recession, Thailand's GDP fell 2.3 percent. Despite this, 2007–2010 socioeconomic surveys reveal that real consumption per capita rose relative to 2008 for most groups, including poor people, urban and rural households, men, women and children. The losers were residents of Bangkok who worked in exporting sectors, especially those ages 20–29 and those working in sales and services. During the recession school enrolment rates did not fall, and durable goods purchases actually rose.

In 2008 the Thai government cut taxes by 40 billion baht, offered emergency loans (totalling 400 billion baht), reduced energy prices and introduced transportation subsidies (at a cost of 50 billion baht). Then, in 2009 it introduced a first stimulus package that extended the earlier policies and put in place a supplementary budget worth 117 billion baht: Checks for 2,000 baht were sent to low-income households, allowances of 500 baht were sent to pensioners, and public education was made free through age 15. Half the appropriated money had been disbursed by May 2009, and the effect is believed to have been pro-poor.[68]

The displays of societal resilience in Brazil and Thailand are rooted in the placement of short-run measures to complement long-run policies.

While persistent shocks and hazards call for comprehensive policies over the long haul, emergency response systems can be designed to facilitate short-run adjustments to adverse events in ways that protect long-term choices

Built-in stabilizers

Automatic stabilizers and countercyclical policies can support living standards during economic contractions, as in Europe since the onset of the great recession in 2008. The Nordic countries increased the share of GNI going to disposable income, even as GNI was falling because countercyclical policies maintained living standards. But in some European countries—primarily those with low public social expenditure as a share of GDP[69]—living standards (as measured by disposable income) fell.[70]

Public social spending can smooth output fluctuations. As OECD research has shown, several European countries were shielded from the full impact of the 2008 global economic crisis due to the mitigating effects of social transfers, tax-benefit systems and fiscal stimulus policies.[71] For example, Norway and Sweden were cushioned from many of the effects of falling disposable incomes, and their faster recovery was thanks to cost-efficient delivery of social services, expansionary monetary policy, good management of resource revenues (in Norway) and automatic stabilizers in fiscal policy (in Sweden). Because Finland is in the euro area, it could not use interest rate cuts (as Sweden did) and thus suffered higher unemployment. Norway, faced with tepid growth, expanded its government budget in 2013. The pressure towards lower and more-unequal incomes was alleviated by tax benefits and social transfers as automatic stabilizers (rise in social transfers and falls in income taxes during recessions). The detrimental effects of crisis on poverty is conditional on the levels of social spending. Social protection can have a mitigating effect, as countries with high spending on health and education were more resilient in the face of financial crises.[72] It is safe to conclude that the human cost of recession was lower in countries with universal social protection.

Social protection policies include unemployment insurance, pension programmes and labour market regulations—such as minimum wage laws or health and safety standards. One argument against them is that they may generate unintended consequences. Some contend that minimum wage laws may reduce the incentive to create new jobs and that unemployment

insurance may reduce the incentive to get back to work.[73] Much depends on the design of the policy. But there is considerable evidence that labour market regulations have a net benefit and reduce inequality.[74] Many social protections have positive spinoff effects. Unemployment insurance makes labour markets work better by allowing the unemployed to choose jobs that better match their skills and experience rather than forcing them to take the first job that comes along.[75] Income support to households encourages labour market participation by providing resources that enable people to search for better opportunities, including allowing members of the household to migrate to find jobs.[76]

In developed countries social insurance provides short-term and in some cases medium- or even longer term income replacement. On the benefit side this income replacement covers short-term employment losses. But given the increasing likelihood that the duration of such losses might extend longer than expected and the fact that unemployment (and not wage loss) is typically insured, the benefits may be too short and too small.

The principle of combining economic development with social insurance programmes was demonstrated by the successful East Asian late industrializers. They were hugely successful at both rapidly reducing fertility and generating employment—allowing them to benefit from the demographic dividend. How? Through a combination of proactive industrial policy and universal social policies in education and health (although not in social welfare, which remained minimal until the 1990s, distinct from European welfare states). A key element of the state-led industrial policy was that it was rooted in nationally owned firms, regulated capital accounts and a dual objective of promoting competitiveness and generating employment.

The rapid universalization of health and education helped generate employment and support industrialization. Extensive land reform and the rapid expansion of the education system above the primary level were also pursued as part of the development strategy.

Following the 2008 global economic crisis, some countries adopted measures to increase employment and social protection,

Social protection can have a mitigating effect, as countries with high spending on health and education were more resilient in the face of financial crises thus stabilizing aggregate domestic demand and protecting vulnerable populations. The International Labour Organization suggests that such social protection measures created or saved 7–11 million jobs in Group of 20 countries in 2009.[77]

Social protection floors

In 2009 the Social Protection Floor Initiative set forth a global framework for universal access to essential social transfers and services, such as health care, primary education, pensions, unemployment protection and childcare.[78] The initiative takes the view that nearly all countries at any stage of development can provide a basic floor of social transfers, including through better cross-sectoral coordination. It also encourages countries to progressively expand to higher levels of social protection as fiscal space allows.[79] A lower income country might start with basic education and health care and later expand to offer cash transfers or basic labour protection. A higher income country with well established basic education, health care and conditional cash transfers might expand eligibility for unemployment insurance to traditionally excluded populations, such as agricultural or domestic workers, or expand leave policies for new parents to include fathers.

Social protection floor policies reduce poverty. The International Labour Organization has estimated that in Tanzania universal old age pensions and child benefits for school-age children would reduce poverty rates 35 percent among the entire population and 46 percent among households with children and the elderly.[80]

The approach to social protection depends on country circumstances and resources and varies according to level of development. Additional levels of social protection, such as conditional cash transfers aimed at disadvantaged households, add an additional, if relatively small, cost to a social protection programme. The Indian Employment Guarantee Fund cost about 0.3 percent of GDP in 2008.[81]

Providing basic social security benefits to the world's poor would cost less than 2 percent of global GDP.[82] The International Labour Organization's 2010 estimates of the cost of providing a basic social floor—universal basic old age and disability pensions, basic childcare

benefits, universal access to essential health care, social assistance and a 100-day employment scheme in 12 low-income African and Asian countries—ranged from more than 10 percent of GDP in Burkina Faso to less than 4 percent of GDP in India.[83] Current domestic resources covered less than 5 percent (Pakistan) of estimated total expenditures on basic social protection. But if basic social protection grew to account for 20 percent of government spending, domestic resources would cover 30 percent (Burkina Faso) to 100 percent of the total cost (India, Pakistan and Viet Nam). A basic social protection package is affordable so long as low-income countries reallocate funds and raise domestic resources, coupled with support by the international donor community.[84]

Addressing societal inclusion

In the presence of horizontal inequality specific measures are required to reach the whole population. A mix of policy interventions has been tried to address horizontal inequality: direct interventions (such as affirmative action), indirect measures (such as preventive laws and sanctions) and broader inclusion (through normative and education shifts). Social institutions reinforce government policy through greater coordination and stronger accountability. When civil society mobilizes to articulate the interests of the citizenry, there is a better connection between the needs of the population and the policies of government.

Persistent vulnerability is rooted in historic exclusions. For example, Black people in South Africa and the United States and Dalits in India have suffered grievous wrongs, and women across patriarchal societies continue to encounter discrimination and exclusion due to longstanding social norms and cultural practices. Many countries have tried affirmative action policies or special measures.[85] Norms and laws that favour members of these groups to improve their chances for equal opportunity can make society fairer and more inclusive.

Cohesive societies tend do better than less cohesive societies in most aspects of human development (figure 4.7).[86] How do societies redress deep divisions and historically rooted exclusions? By improving the availability of basic social

In 2009 the Social Protection Floor Initiative set forth a global framework for universal access to essential social transfers and services, such as health care, primary education, pensions, unemployment protection and childcare

BOX 4.3

Reducing vulnerability through responsive institutions

A key facet of vulnerability is often an inability to influence decisions that affect one's life: decisions are instead made by more-powerful actors, who may neither understand the situation of the vulnerable nor necessarily have their interests at heart.[1] To address this, states require the capacity to recognize the concerns of the vulnerable and react to them through appropriate interventions. This requires, among other things, giving the poor and marginalized a greater voice in decisionmaking[2] and opportunities for recourse when rights are violated or discrimination is encountered. Research suggests that women are more likely than men to suffer from negligence, petty corruption and harassment when they engage with state institutions.[3]

Simply understanding the technical cause of a vulnerability is not enough to design policies to reduce it. Rather, the processes that created the risk in the first place must be identified, and the political incentives and will to tackle them must be present. Political freedoms are a key part of this, as Jean Drèze and Amartya Sen underlined when discussing the role of the media in holding governments to account during famines.[4] Direct representation, social movements, and union and civil society pressures also shape policy and political processes in the broader political economy and are important for representing the interests of vulnerable groups.

There is some evidence to suggest that state institutions can become more responsive to the needs of the poor[5] and vulnerable when:

- Public administrations implement policies efficiently and are transparent, accountable and responsive to users. This curbs corruption and harassment, and the power of the state is used proactively to allocate resources for public actions benefiting poor people. Some encouraging examples include civil service reforms in Botswana and South Africa, where reforms in ministries and rationalized departments strengthened service delivery and effectiveness.[6]

- Legal systems are pro-poor when they assign and defend rights and are accessible to poor people. Promising interventions in this context have occurred in Cambodia, with the establishment of the Arbitration Council, a national statutory alternative dispute resolution body, and in Mozambique, with the implementation of the progressive land law, which has helped improve poor people's access to land.[7]

- Central and local governments are aligned to ensure the delivery of public services to all and to minimize the scope for capture by elites or dominant groups. Various forms of decentralization are under way across countries, which have tried to respond to the needs and interests of excluded communities. For example, the Philippines has long tried to address the rights of indigenous people in Palawan and their claim on the forest resources, and the Local Government Code of 1991 provided an opportunity for them to interact with government institutions and participate in forest management.[8]

- Governments generate political support for public action against poverty by creating a climate favourable to pro-poor action, facilitating the growth of poor people's associations and increasing poor people's political capacity. Such social movements and political activism propelled Brazil's ruling party to undertake pro-poor policies and helped set the agenda for political leadership in post-apartheid South Africa.[9]

- Political regimes honour the rule of law, allow the expression of political voice and enable the participation of vulnerable people in political processes.[10] A case in point is the peaceful democratic transition in Bolivia that brought into power the country's indigenous majority after a long history of exclusion.

Nonetheless, the challenges in building responsive institutions are manifold: from weak political will to inadequate capacities and funding of public institutions, including the civil service and courts. Improving accountability through transparency measures such as India's Right to Information Act can expose corruption and graft and boost efficiency. Increasing opportunities for participation, through such processes as participatory budgeting and greater representation in government, can give the excluded greater voice.

All too often governments respond to fiscal pressures at times of volatility and crises with austerity measures that limit social spending. As discussed in chapters 1 and 2, these measures often take the greatest toll on the most vulnerable, who are already under pressure. And during the good times the extra revenue from an economic boom is often returned as tax cuts rather than being used to build up social protection reserves for the next downturn or being invested in building broader institutional capacity and systemic resilience.

Adequate provisioning alone, however, may not suffice: Institutions themselves have to be designed to respond to the needs of all, not just the dominant in society. While national institutions are a product of a country's history and politics, those that often work best in different settings enable participation and accountability,[11] are more capable of representing the diversity in their populations,[12] are amenable to peaceful transitions of power[13] and are able to maintain the independence and integrity of institutions like the judiciary[14] and civilian control of the military[15] through a separation of powers and a system of checks and balances.[16] These features are important during times of stability but are particularly important for the protection of the rights of the vulnerable during crises.

Yet whatever the form institutions take in different societies, protecting citizen rights remains seen primarily as the responsibility of the nation state. But this may not be enough in an increasingly globalized world, where people in one part of the world can be threatened by events and actions elsewhere. Building responsive institutions at the national level requires a parallel effort at the international level to support and reinforce them.

Notes
1. UN 2012a. 2. Mearns and Norton 2010. 3. UNDP 2012d. 4. Drèze and Sen 1989. 5. World Bank 2000. 6. UNECA 2010. 7. UN General Assembly 2009. 8. Seitz 2013. 9. Heller 2014. 10. UNSSC 2010. 11. McGee and Gaventa 2011. 12. Temin 2008. 13. DFID 2010. 14. UNOHCHR 2003. 15. Sulmasy and Yoo 2007. 16. Waldron 2013.

services, strengthening employment policies and extending social protection. Yet these broader universal policies may not target specific exclusions and horizontal inequality of marginalized groups, particularly when social norms and laws do not protect the rights of specific groups that face discrimination in public life, including those in political institutions and in markets.

Societies respond in different ways to pressures, setbacks and disasters. Some demonstrate

FIGURE 4.7

Cohesive societies tend do better than less cohesive societies

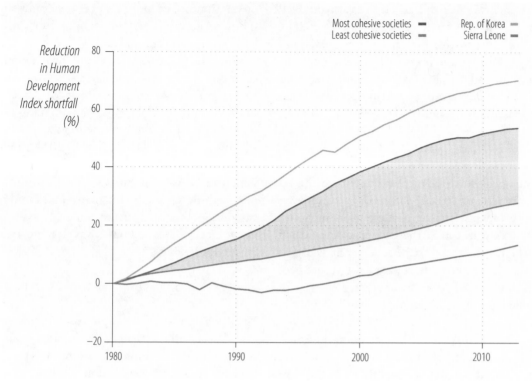

Most cohesive societies ▬   Rep. of Korea ▬
Least cohesive societies ▬   Sierra Leone ▬

Reduction in Human Development Index shortfall (%)

Source: Easterly, Ritzen and Woolcock 2006 and Human Development Report Office estimates.

greater resilience and resources to cope with and recover from crises. Others find themselves in vicious traps that deepen and broaden the impacts of such crises. Certain macro variables can have a major impact on societies' ability to manage such pressures and shocks, including economic inequality, the degree of social fragmentation and the adequacy of institutions, three aspects that interact. Social cohesion can therefore shape the quality and competency of institutions, which in turn influences how and whether pro-people policies are devised and implemented.[87]

Direct measures to redress group inequality

Direct measures are commonly thought of as affirmative action, which includes targets, quotas and preferential treatment to improve the discriminated group's access to jobs, assets, services, government contracts and political representation. Such policies are immediate though sometimes controversial ways of dealing with historic injustices, since the long-term

impact is ambiguous—they can be seen as perpetuating social cleavages, increasing stigma and risking elite capture and reverse discrimination. They address some symptoms of discrimination but are not always able to fix the structural drivers behind persistent inequality. Such measures work best when broader pro-poor policies and sunset clauses are in place to prevent reverse discrimination.

Brazil—the numbers look better

Brazil is attempting to reduce racial disparities[88] for its Afro-Brazilian and mixed-race population, which constitutes more than half of its 200 million people, by implementing affirmative action policies in education.[89] In August 2012 it passed a law mandating quotas for preferential entry for Afro-Brazilian and mixed-race students, proportional to their weight in the local population (such as 80 percent in Bahia state in the northeast and 16 percent in Santa Catarina in the south), to the country's 59 federal universities and 38 federal technical schools. In 1997, 2.2 percent of Black or mixed-race students ages 18–24 attended universities; in 2012, 11 percent did.[90] The number of posts reserved in federal universities for underprivileged Brazilians has also doubled under the legislation—from 30,000 to 60,000. Education institutions have used goals and quotas for underrepresented groups, including women and people of colour, to increase their diversity and create opportunities for underrepresented and vulnerable groups.

South Africa—hard to isolate a direct link

Employment policies that encourage the recruitment of female or minority candidates have increased their participation in South Africa's workforce. The end of apartheid left behind a labour market that was racially organized, with skilled jobs reserved for White people and unskilled jobs for other groups, with systematic discrimination against Black people, women and people with disabilities.[91]

Against this backdrop, democratic South Africa unveiled affirmative action policies to redress labour market inequality. The 1998 Employment Equity Act offered incentives for firms to hire people from historically disadvantaged groups as skilled workers. A 2009 study documented the success in reducing both unemployment and poverty in skilled and semi-skilled jobs.[92]

Attributing these improvements to affirmative action policies remains contested. Critics argue that these direct efforts have had only a marginal impact on reducing employment or wage gaps and that these improvements could be linked to overall efforts to improve access and quality of education for Africans and to the employment effects of accelerated economic growth.[93] Uncontested, however, is that these broader efforts and more-specific initiatives have together improved South Africa's record in redressing structural labour force imbalances, reduced the sense of historic injustice and improved the participation of historically excluded and disadvantaged groups.

Malaysia—dealing with some unintended consequences?

Some observers have critiqued direct measures for being misguided and mismatched to the deeper structural problems that need to be addressed.[94] For example, the positive discrimination policies favouring the ethnic Malays, or Bumiputras, in Malaysia over the dominant Chinese and minority Indian populations have improved their access to education and jobs and helped them more fully realize their economic potential. Yet Malaysia's Chinese and Indian minority citizens chafe at 70 percent quotas in university admissions, flocking instead to private and foreign schools and often staying away from the country. In 2011 about 1 million Malaysians had left the country, which has a total population of 29 million, most ethnic Chinese and many highly educated.[95] Some 60 percent of skilled Malaysian emigrants cited social injustice as an important reason for leaving.

Context is crucial

While there can be no single absolute answer on whether affirmative action reduces group disparities, the examples show that proactive policies can improve conditions for vulnerable groups and in particular contexts. The key is that such direct measures are not merely standalone interventions but are an intrinsic part of a broader commitment to ameliorate the conditions of the disadvantaged and remedy the particularities of specific group exclusions. Success is most common in mutually reinforcing contexts, where policy interventions are embedded in larger pro-poor efforts, bolstered by formal incentives and sanctions such as laws and supplemented by shifts in public opinions and social norms.

Laws and norms: tackling discrimination and influencing behaviour

Historically rooted discrimination is embedded in social interactions in the public domain, which can either enable the success of affirmative interventions or undermine their implementation.[96] The reason is that private decisions and public policies are shaped by personal and societal preferences, material and other explicit incentives (laws) and social sanctions or rewards (norms).[97]

Changed laws and norms can also encourage desirable behaviour. For example, public

While there can be no single absolute answer on whether affirmative action reduces group disparities, the examples show that proactive policies can improve conditions for vulnerable groups and in particular contexts advocacy and legal restrictions were instrumental in the United States in changing norms and reducing the consumption of tobacco. Similarly, promoting hygienic practices such as hand washing and using bednets to reduce malaria transmission have helped improve public health. Social marketing strategies for behavioural change—applying private sector advertising, marketing and communications—have increasingly spurred public health victories by bringing about changes in individual and group behaviour.

Norm-based messages and campaigns seek to alter people's perceptions of what constitutes 'acceptable' or 'desirable' behaviour or values among their peers.[98] They can determine the legitimacy and effectiveness of policy interventions, making them broad-based and credible, especially when they seek to challenge existing hierarchies and change power relations.[99] Targeting public values and behaviour is indispensable in ensuring the effectiveness and sustainability of social change.

Addressing violent conflict by transforming norms and extending inclusion efforts

Building on the lessons from conflict countries, the international community has tried to integrate security and development interventions—to reinforce community security through social cohesion. A wide range of state and civil society actors collectively develop coordinated responses to threats at the community level and build an enabling environment at the national level. These social cohesion and community security approaches emphasize increasing participatory engagement, improving service delivery, reducing social exclusion through enhanced relations between social groups and strengthening democratic governance.[100]

In Guatemala's Santa Lucia Municipality, a Citizen Security Commission coordinated an action plan that banned carrying guns in bars, controlled alcohol sales, improved street lighting, introduced community-based policing, reclaimed public spaces and addressed vagrancy. Within two years the homicide rate dropped from 80 per 100,000 people to less than 50. Given this success, a new national law established the National Security Council to coordinate the reform of the security sector and

mandates the development of citizen security plans in each municipality. Similarly, the Safer Communities Project in Croatia piloted an approach that identified the lack of recreational facilities for young people as contributing to insecurity. An old playground was refurbished as a meeting place for young people and includes a skateboard park and activity grounds. In a highly divided post-conflict community of Croatians and Serbs, this has become a meeting place for young people from both sides and has helped build bridges between these clashing communities.[101]

Civil society mediation with states and markets

People mobilize, even in the face of insurmountable challenges and embedded inequality, to improve on situations and make social institutions more relevant to their needs. Civil society has been effective in holding states politically accountable for delivering pro-poor development. But this is possible only when there are opportunities for participation with transparency and accountability. An empirical review of 96 countries suggests that participatory political regimes mediate social conflicts more effectively and induce compromise among citizen groups. The review argues, "Democracy makes us less selfish and more public spirited."[102] Another econometric study of 82 developed and developing countries concluded that state capacity to undertake effective policy action is not an issue of technocratic competence and political will alone.[103] The political space for decisive public action is also greatly influenced by social cleavages and conflict. Such social divides can lead to varying levels of trust in public institutions and influence their performance.

Individuals can exert greater pressure by mobilizing as groups—producer groups, worker associations or social movements. They can take collective action and bargain more effectively either within markets or with their employers or the state. Economically vulnerable groups often organize collectively—whether as businesses, smallholder farmers, pastoralists or fisher folk. They can promote fair trade products or support cooperative movements for local producers. New forms of collective action

Norm-based messages and campaigns seek to alter people's perceptions of what constitutes 'acceptable' or 'desirable' behaviour and new civic energies now engage politically at the local level—for participatory budgeting processes in Porto Alegre, Brazil, for the Right to Information Act in India and for social audits, which have increased the transparency and accountability of local authorities disbursing public funds for relief schemes.

A key aspect of state–civil society interaction is how civil society influences pro-people policies and outcomes. Brazil embarked on development and democratic consolidation with the backdrop of inequality, racial and ethnic divides. The government implemented a mix of policy interventions aimed at boosting the job market, targeting government spending and cash transfers, expanding universal primary schooling and redressing gender and racial disparities. Infant mortality was cut almost in half between 1996 and 2006, and the proportion of girls in primary school rose from 83 percent to 95 percent between 1991 and 2004. Brazil's efforts to reduce its longstanding inequality by promoting income redistribution and universal access to education, health care, water supply and sanitation services also improved child nutrition, resulting in a large reduction in child stunting for the poorest 20 percent of the population.[104]

Throughout these efforts, Brazil's civil society remained autonomous of political parties, having fostered a range of participatory institutions and processes that influence public policy and hold the state apparatus accountable for local results. In Brazil's Landless Workers Movement (Movimento dos Trabalhadores Sem Terra, or MST), cooperatives organized settlements on expropriated land for roughly a million families, with hundreds of MST-built schools enabling tens of thousands of people to learn to read and write.[105] MST's support was crucial in bringing the Workers Party to power in 2002, which led to greater expenditure on basic services, cash transfers and expanded access to education. In 2001–2007 the poorest six deciles that previously accounted for 18 percent of income accounted for 40 percent of total income growth, and the Gini coefficient of inequality fell from 0.59 in 2001 to 0.53 in 2007.[106]

And in Bangladesh civil society has grown over the decades into one of the world's largest nongovernmental organization sectors, driven in response to the country's numerous challenges, including its frequent natural disasters. Nongovernmental organizations have found a niche in the gap between society and state, seeking to promote people's welfare through grassroots initiatives. They also serve as important service delivery mechanisms and implementing partners, especially during environmental disasters and devastation, for programmes ranging from relief and rehabilitation to microcredit loans to women's empowerment. While the expansion of civil society in Bangladesh is reflective of on-the-ground realities, it also raises questions about the links with political society and the state. The resources being placed towards building more-effective and -sustainable state institutions remain wanting—and civil society has evolved faster and with greater capacity and reach than the formal institutions responsible for service provision and delivery. Until those institutions are equally revitalized and energized, the nongovernmental organization sector in Bangladesh will remain an indispensable capacity resource for building social resilience.

Nonetheless, in going beyond local and community mobilization, further examination is needed of the aggregate impact that civil society and public activism can have on a country's governance institutions and overall development performance. This raises important observations about the ways that local and micro-level experiences of social mobilization can be scaled up in terms of impact and about how they relate to the macro-level issues.[107] Reviews of social mobilization experiences highlight the disconnect between such largely local initiatives and their wider development impact. This requires closely examining the barriers at the national level to substantial scaling up and devising new and creative models of civic engagement and social mobilization, such as social enterprises that engage the poor as investors and shareholders.[108]

Civil society and broader social mobilization can exercise voice in claiming intrinsic rights and in promoting progressive public actions and policies. Their resilience can be furthered by states that create an enabling environment and space for a vibrant and engaged civil society. Civil society neither can nor should replace state institutions. However, a positive and symbiotic relation between the two goes a long way in strengthening both. Civic participation therefore is an indispensable and central driver in activating formal and informal social institutions to respond to public needs and demands, making them equitable and efficient in their response to vulnerability.

Upgrading capacities to prepare for and recover from crises

The social and physical environments in which communities live and seek to thrive are wrought with complexity and unpredictability. Despite available knowledge on the earth's physical fault lines, the frequency and intensity of geophysical hazards remain largely unpredictable, and climate change is exposing parts of the world previously considered safe to the destructive effects of meteorological hazards. No matter how effective policies are at reducing inherent vulnerabilities, sudden onset hazards will occur, including low-probability high-impact disasters like the 2010 earthquake in Haiti. As the Arab Spring has shown, even in-depth knowledge of the factors that can trigger social unrest and violent conflict in a given society is no guarantee that violent conflict will always be predicted and prevented. Shocks like these can have inevitable and potentially destructive consequences for human development progress and resilience of countries, communities, families and individuals.

Vulnerabilities are exposed by shocks and underlying conditions. While it is natural to respond to a crisis when a shock occurs, there is equally a need to follow up by developing a more comprehensive response to future crises. Policies to prevent, respond to and recover from crises must become an integral part of human development policies and strategies, especially in noncrisis settings, rather than relying on ad hoc emergency relief in affected communities. When policies are oriented towards emergency response, mitigation can be overlooked, and shocks can re-emerge with potentially larger impact and greater subsequent costs of protection. Emergency response efforts are important and necessary, but comprehensive efforts to enable communities to better prepare for and recover from shocks and crises are a fundamental building block of resilience.

Disaster risk reduction and response

Natural disasters expose and exacerbate vulnerabilities, such as poverty, inequality, environmental degradation and weak governance. Countries and communities that are underprepared, that are unaware of risks and that have minimal preventive capacity suffer the impact of disasters far more severely. Poor countries also tend to suffer disproportionately. In the last 20 years at least 1.3 million people have been killed and 4.4 billion affected by disasters, which have cost the global economy at least $2 trillion.[109] However, the loss of lives owing to natural disasters has declined due to early warning and response systems. For example, in Bangladesh a severe cyclone in 1991 caused nearly 140,000 deaths, while a 2007 cyclone of similar magnitude killed 4,234 people. The reduction in cyclone-related deaths was achieved mainly by improving early warning systems, developing shelters and evacuation plans, constructing coastal embankments, maintaining and improving coastal forest cover and raising awareness at the community level.[110]

Greater efforts are needed to strengthen national and regional early warning systems. The key areas for action identified at the Second Conference on Early Warning in 2003 were better integration of early warning into development processes and public policies; better data availability for investigating, forecasting and managing risks on different time scales; better capacity and stronger early warning systems, particularly in developing countries; development of people-centred early warning systems; and programmes for when shocks occur.[111] Regional cooperation on early warning in particular can be highly effective, since natural hazards often affect multiple countries simultaneously. Early warning is a major element of disaster risk reduction. It saves lives and reduces economic and material losses from disasters. The Hyogo Framework for Action highlights the importance of, and makes clear commitments to, local, national and regional early warning mechanisms that provide real-time and understandable warnings to risks with clear directions for response actions.

No matter how well a country is prepared and how good its policy framework is, shocks occur, often with inevitable and highly destructive

Vulnerabilities are exposed by shocks and underlying conditions

consequences. The key objective is then to rebuild while increasing social, material and institutional resilience. Responses to extreme weather events have been complicated by weak institutions and conflict. The first response to any crisis is inevitably humanitarian. The way in which humanitarian assistance is delivered matters because it sets the foundation for transitioning to longer term rehabilitation and restoration. An early recovery approach needs to draw the main strands of the humanitarian and development responses together, ensuring that the response strategy can deliver early needs without compromising the longer term need for state capacity and responsive delivery.

The resilience of a country includes its capacity to recover quickly and well from disasters. This entails managing the immediate effects of the disasters as well as implementing specific measures to avoid further socioeconomic consequences. Societies unprepared to handle shocks often incur damages and losses that are much more extensive and prolonged. For instance, the Haitian earthquake cost the equivalent of 120 percent of Haiti's GDP, setting back decades of development investments.[112] Yet even this does not capture the full depth of impact nor the length of time required to fully recover. When recovery processes are partial and not oriented towards enhancing resilience, the impact of the disaster can be long lasting and have ongoing effects on entire generations.

Resilience is about transforming the structures and systems that perpetuate fragility and undermine resilience. External shocks can sometimes provide an incentive to initiate this transformation. This may require integrating measures of preparedness and recovery into laws, policies and institutional mechanisms that enable a country or community to operate. When backed up with budgets and resources, this allows for the inclusion of risk reduction concerns at each level of the development process, from the community to the national government. In this way, disaster risk reduction is not an additional expense or adjunct but a core component built into development from the onset.

Conflict prevention and recovery

An effective strategy for enhancing resilience in conflict-affected areas and for preventing conflict from occurring is to strengthen social cohesion. But building social cohesion in conflict-prone countries or in communities recovering from conflict is particularly challenging. Social fragmentation may be high, livelihoods may be threatened and institutions are often fragile and ill-equipped to devise and implement policies that reduce divisions (see box 4.4). That said, countries as diverse as Bolivia, Kenya, Nepal, Peru, Kyrgyzstan, Timor-Leste and Togo have invested in measures to build trust, collaborate and promote dialogue through credible intermediaries and 'infrastructures for peace'. These measures have led to positive results, including peaceful polls, fewer conflicts related to land and natural resources, and the mitigation of intergroup tension.[113]

While efforts to build social cohesion vary according to context and national circumstances, four common elements can be identified:

- *Increasing public awareness and access to information.* Efforts can be made to increase public advocacy in favour of peace, development and less-contentious politics. In 2006 Guyana experienced its first violence-free national election since independence. Instrumental to this outcome was the Social Cohesion Programme implemented in 2002 in response to past violence.[114] The programme was based on a national conversation around governance that was led by the president, systematic efforts at the community level to improve interethnic relations and a sustained public campaign aimed at creating a stronger and more peaceful sense of national identity. Subsequently, the 2011 election was also peaceful.
- *Credible internal intermediaries and mediators.* Independent, objective bodies can build trust and confidence among conflicted or polarized groups or sectors and facilitate consensus on specific issues of national importance. Ghana's national elections in 2008 and 2012 both saw an active role by the National Peace Council, a body first established in 2006 as an autonomous platform for facilitating dialogue and providing mediation in disputes over politics and identity and for supporting peaceful elections. This role was recognized publicly by all leaders in the country and in

When recovery processes are partial and not oriented towards enhancing resilience, the impact of the disaster can be long lasting and have ongoing effects on entire generations

the region by the West Africa Network for Peacebuilding.

More recently, Tunisia has been seeking to manage its post–Arab Spring transition. Sporadic political violence has not inflamed further tensions; secular and Islamist parties have found ways to work together within a pluralist political framework. An important factor in this transition has been the Tunisian General Labour Union's service as an intermediary. Founded in 1948 and having a deep reach into all segments of Tunisian society, the union has used its position to orient political discourse away from conflict and towards social and economic challenges.

- *Local committees and citizen groups.* Community groups can build trust at the local level by helping prevent conflict. In both Guyana and Tunisia citizen groups provided monitors and mediators who helped build trust and defuse tensions before larger issues arose and vitiated the political process. Ghana's National Peace Council is formally associated through legislation with similar bodies at the regional and district levels. In Yemen youth organizations have connected young people and offered social support in searching for jobs, dealing with financial problems and organizing community activities. Participation has helped build social cohesion by instilling habits of cooperation, solidarity and public spiritedness.[115]

- *Rebuilding livelihoods.* Experience has shown that support to livelihoods and economic recovery can build social cohesion. Livelihood support enables affected communities and individuals to recover in the short term and makes them more resilient to the challenges of future crises. Employment opportunities can create a sense of trust that is much needed in conflict areas. Cross-country analysis from Europe and Latin America suggests that employment can lead to trust in others and institutions.[110] Communities in crisis and post-crisis situations face many economic and social challenges, including at times the reintegration in the short term of ex-combatants in the aftermath of armed conflict and internally displaced persons and refugees. Re-creating employment opportunities and livelihoods can help stabilize communities and prevent subsequent lapses into violence.

Efforts to strengthen social cohesion are not reflected in any substantial manner in post-conflict peace-building, with the bulk of investment being in elections or the physical requirements for economic recovery. Essential as these investments are, the peaceful resolution of future disputes and crises will require systematic capacities for collaboration—and a new political culture—among groups that are used to advancing their interests through conflict and deadlock rather than negotiation. A growing emphasis on national dialogue processes is a welcome change in this direction. However, considerable investments in social cohesion, with systematic monitoring and assessment of impact, are needed to sustain these initial gains.

*　　　*　　　*

Like most of its analysis and data, this chapter's policy recommendations, important as they are, are all for national governments. But as has been seen many times, many threats and hazards go beyond national boundaries. It is time to ensure that national and international efforts are aligned, by getting governments and international bodies to work together better and with mutually supportive commitment towards reducing vulnerabilities.

Employment opportunities and livelihoods can help stabilize communities and prevent subsequent lapses into violence

"The difference between what we do and what we are capable of doing would suffice to solve most of the world's problems."

Mahatma Gandhi

"Stepping onto a brand-new path is difficult, but not more difficult than remaining in a situation, which is not nurturing to the whole woman."

Maya Angelou

5.

Deepening progress: global goods and collective action

This chapter focuses on the global aspects of vulnerability and how they link to national, community and individual vulnerabilities. It calls attention to the manifestations of vulnerability that accompany wider and deeper interdependence. And it takes the position that far more can be done to make globalization work for people.

Globalization as practised is not benefiting enough people, and in some cases integration is producing new vulnerabilities. Consider the chronic disparities in human development dimensions around the world, the very high share of people in vulnerable employment in some regions and the unpredictable shocks that can have global reach, such as pandemics, natural disasters, armed conflicts and financial instability. Globalization may have yielded many winners and overall gains. International links and multilateral agreements can foster knowledge sharing and mutual assistance—and in many cases enhance resilience. The dense global network of institutions and relationships characteristic of today's world can be taken advantage of to increase resilience. But not all people have had the voice or resources to influence the direction of change or benefit from global integration, and multilateral actions have been slow to respond to the world's growing challenges.

Today, an increasing number of insecurities require global and regional collective action. Financial systems can be better regulated. Trade talks can be unblocked. Markets can be subject to codes and standards. Climate change can be mitigated. Processes are under way to build more-resilient systems, but the provision of important public goods can be further improved, and global governance systems can be refined.

The chapter examines how transnational integration generates new vulnerabilities just as it provides new opportunities for greater human development and resilience. It underscores the commonalities among emerging vulnerabilities, such as the underprovision of public goods (including universal social protection and an effective climate regime), and the shortcomings in the architectures for global governance that permit threats like excessive financial volatility. It also considers existing global initiatives and contributes to the post-2015 agenda discussions by suggesting the types of public goods that can enhance the capacity of countries and people to cope with adverse events—and the types of governance improvements that will reduce the likelihood and impact of shocks.

All this is linked to the ways national governments can open policy space to make their countries and people more resilient. An overarching message is that greater systemic resilience needs an international commitment to the provision of public goods that make people more secure, achieved through collective action by individuals, communities and states.

Transnational vulnerabilities and common threads

Transnational integration of systems of trade, finance, migration and communications has supported progress in human development, offering opportunities to enter global markets, spur innovation through sharing knowledge and technology, and tap into transnational networks. Connecting people and pooling global resources and capacities afford tremendous opportunities to reinforce the resilience of individuals, countries and the world. But transnational risks appear to be intensifying. Chapters 1 and 2 warn against global trends that could undermine long-term human progress—from changing weather patterns and the increasing frequency and intensity of natural disasters to the spread of conflict and communicable diseases and to the volatility in financial asset prices, commodity prices and capital flows. Chapter 2 cautioned that food price volatility and financial volatility are threatening people's livelihoods and weakening social cohesion.

Each of these threats is unique, but they share some common aspects, and understanding them can orient collective action towards efficient and effective solutions. The scope and scale of connectivity and related insecurities are accelerating, and there are threats of global contagion. The national policy space to enhance coping capacities is increasingly constrained. And global systems are compromising individual capabilities. The underlying causes of most transnational vulnerabilities are the underprovision of public goods and the shortcomings of international governance. Public goods, and appropriate policies and institutions, can tilt the balance towards greater resilience.

Rising threats

Accelerated connections and insecurities. Transnational integration and its related threats are not new, but they are accelerating. Human beings have always been vulnerable to the spread of disease. In the 14th century caravans and merchant ships transported the Black Death across continents, inflicting huge losses of life across Asia and Europe. But the pace of transmission has increased dramatically, with jumbo jets transporting avian influenza across the world in hours.

The world has also long been characterized by global and regional economic, political and social connections now referred to as globalization. But such global connectivity has accelerated in recent years. Between 1999 and 2012 the global trade to GDP ratio increased from 37 percent to 51 percent.[1] Between 2000 and 2013 the number of international migrants rose from 175 million to 232 million.[2] Financial flows between countries increased from 31 percent of all flows in 1970 to over 180 percent in 2007.[3] Foreign exchange markets operate 24 hours a day, five days a week, and trades averaged $5.3 trillion a day in April 2013.[4] The production of many goods and services spans continents in globally integrated value chains. Social networks like Facebook and Twitter boost the potential to extend social spaces across wider geographies.

These trends have brought important benefits and opportunities to many. But in areas ranging from finance to security and to the environment, the pace and scale of connectivity have not been matched by measures to reduce emerging vulnerabilities—to prevent shocks, enhance capabilities and protect people's choices. For example, the integration of production along global value chains has brought much needed jobs, but competition to attract investment can also risk a race to the bottom for labour and environmental regulations (box 5.1).

Risks of contagion. Shocks—even policy changes—in one country can have global reach, with a direct bearing on individual capabilities and choices, potentially jeopardizing development progress in communities and countries far away. In 2008 the collapse of a bank in New York triggered a global financial crisis. In 2010 a volcano in Iceland disrupted air travel in Europe and left fresh produce rotting in Latin America and Africa, costing Kenya 5,000 farming jobs and $1.3 million a day in the flower sector alone.[5] In 2011 a tsunami off Japan cut the supply of car components to US automobile manufacturers, compounding recessionary employment insecurity for thousands of workers.[6] In 2012 conflict in the Democratic Republic of Congo, Mali, South Sudan, Sudan and the Syrian Arab Republic forced 1.1 million refugees into surrounding countries.[7] In 2013 the collapse of a building in Bangladesh unleashed civil protests against department stores in Europe and North America.

Constrained policy space. Global integration can shrink national policy space and constrain national capacities to address vulnerability. International competitive pressures may restrict government choices, making it more difficult to create and protect jobs or to provide universal education, health care and social protection. In the 1950s and 1960s states may have set their sights on full employment, but today they often limit their ambition to unemployment insurance, which, while important, offers much less social stability. As part of the post-2015 agenda, collective agreements on employment, social services and social protection could expand national policy space and empower governments to adopt the policies recommended in chapter 4 to reduce vulnerability.

Global exposure. People's livelihoods, personal security and well-being are exposed not only

BOX 5.1

Global value chains—pros and cons

Production processes have become highly dispersed and fragmented along global value chains. For many products the provision of raw materials, the production of components, and the assembly, marketing and delivery of finished goods take place in different countries, often in different regions of the world. Today, about 60 percent of global trade, or about $20 trillion, consists of trade in intermediate goods and services.[1] Participating countries can benefit from jobs, exports and foreign direct investment that can bring much needed capital and technology. This may enhance resilience, but these links are complex, and new vulnerabilities may also emerge.

Nice profits if you can get them

Global value chains may present distributional issues linked to wages, profits and the number of jobs. A study of Apple's iPod value chain found that most jobs were in Asia, while the majority of wages were paid in the United States. In 2006 China accounted for 30 percent of iPod-related jobs, but Chinese workers took home only 3 percent of iPod-related employee earnings.[2]

The share of profits and input costs for the iPhone follows a similar pattern. Evidence from 2010 shows that Apple is by far the biggest beneficiary of iPhone production. Chinese labour, while benefitting from access to jobs, gets less than 2 percent of the final sale value (see figure).[3]

Hazardous low-paid work

Poor working conditions are a reality for many workers who are not part of global supply chains, but competitive pressures in global production systems can exacerbate poor conditions, especially for low-skilled workers. While some workers may benefit from formal jobs in multinational corporations, the economics of value chains has encouraged the formation of third-party contractors that provide flexible low-cost workers, sometimes even through coercive means. In the worst cases these workers are victims of debt bondage and people smuggling.[4]

Governments understandably want to encourage private investment and job creation, but in the process they have tended to give industry a free rein, through deregulation, privatization, financial incentives and lax application of public ordinances. States may then be in a difficult position if they can attract investment and increase employment only by relaxing labour or environmental laws, which risks a global race to the bottom. Indeed, there is evidence that during the 1980s and 1990s the enforcement of labour laws

across countries declined in response to competition for foreign direct investment.[5] Many multinational companies have codes of conduct, but these encompass mainly their own branches and affiliates and do not always cover second-tier or other suppliers.[6]

The lax posture of governments and companies is now being challenged by investigative reporting, civil society advocacy and consumer backlash. In the apparel industry, civil society groups and trade unions have successfully challenged the corporate sector to improve the governance of supply chains: For example, more than 150 retailers have signed the legally enforceable Accord on Fire and Building Safety in Bangladesh, which was issued in 2013.[7]

Who profits from iPhones?

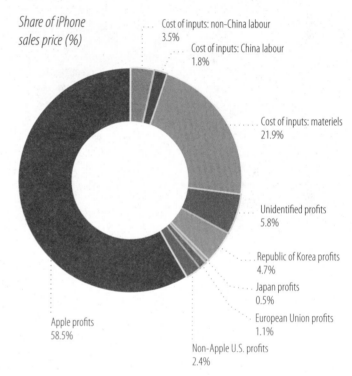

Share of iPhone sales price (%)

- Cost of inputs: non-China labour 3.5%
- Cost of inputs: China labour 1.8%
- Cost of inputs: materiels 21.9%
- Unidentified profits 5.8%
- Republic of Korea profits 4.7%
- Japan profits 0.5%
- European Union profits 1.1%
- Non-Apple U.S. profits 2.4%
- Apple profits 58.5%

Source: Human Development Report Office calculations based on Kraemer, Linden and Dedrick (2011).

Notes
1. UNCTAD 2013. 2. Calculated from tables 2 and 3 in Linden, Kraemer and Dedrick (2011). 3. Human Development Report Office calculations based on Kraemer, Linden and Dedrick (2011). 4. Barrientos 2013. 5. Davies and Vadlamannati 2013. 6. UNCTAD 2012a. 7. Bangladesh Accord Foundation 2013.

to changes in local conditions, but also to global and regional structures and events. Insecurities that transcend borders become relevant—whether the risk of losing a job during a global recession, uncertainty about access to sufficient sources of daily nutrition when global food prices suddenly shift or concerns about personal safety amid spreading social unrest and conflict. People are also moving across national borders in larger numbers and exposing

themselves to new insecurity and unfamiliar social contexts (box 5.2). Many threats that affect life cycle vulnerabilities, structural vulnerabilities and personal insecurities (chapter 3) can be linked to global events and systems. And building resilience requires, in addition to the national actions recommended in chapter 4, global action and coordination to increase national policy space and reduce the threat of global shocks.

BOX 5.2

International migration

Migrants are among the most vulnerable to myriad risks and obstacles. In 2013, 232 million people were living outside their home countries.[1] In both developed and developing countries migrants, particularly undocumented workers, find themselves in vulnerable situations. They may be excluded from normal worker protections and prohibited from joining local unions. They may lack access to social protection programmes that provide a buffer against the vicissitudes of the job market. And they may be subject to racial, ethnic and religious discrimination and social exclusion.

Even the process of migrating is rife with risk. Consider the 300 Eritrean migrants who perished when the boat ferrying them capsized near the Italian island of Lampedusa in October 2013—or the asylum seekers held in processing centres in Papua New Guinea and Nauru the same year.[2] Family structures and relationships at home can also be eroded. Of particular concern from a life cycle perspective are the impacts of migration on children: a higher likelihood of suffering abuse, more involvement in illegal activities, future drug and alcohol abuse and paying reduced attention in school.[3]

A special category of migration that leaves people especially vulnerable is caused by armed conflicts and populations fleeing harm and persecution. The number of people displaced by conflict has increased in recent years and is the highest in nearly two decades.[4] Additional groups of refugees are fleeing natural disasters, and numbers are likely to rise due to climate change. There have been discussions about where citizens of small island developing states will go if sea level rise makes their home country uninhabitable, and in many cases asylum status has been rejected.[5] On top of the vulnerability for undocumented migrants, refugees face the additional challenge of not being allowed to work in most receiving countries, and they are frequently housed in temporary settlements with poor services and insecure conditions.

Managed migration can reduce some of the risks facing migrants. For example, the Republic of Korea's Employment Permit System addresses home labour shortages while protecting migrant workers' rights and enhancing the transparency and security of the migration process.[6] But bilateral arrangements have limited reach, given the scale and scope of migration. And such programmes target mainly documented migrants rather than more-vulnerable undocumented migrants.

Migration-related vulnerability needs to be addressed collectively through an international migration regime. National regulations are insufficient for handling the multiple categories and risks of immigrants, refugees and displaced and stateless persons. Greater efforts are needed to develop consensus on treating migration as a global public good, to codify shared interests and common goals—particularly for protecting human rights and reducing the costs of migration and of sending remittances—and to improve public perceptions of immigrants and migration. Lowering the costs of sending remittances can also help receiving countries achieve greater macroeconomic stability.[7]

Civil society and nongovernmental organizations have engaged governments in dialogue and cooperation on particular issues (such as trafficking in people). A broader approach can build on this progress and include norm-setting and the elaboration of an international regime on migration. The recent UN dialogue on migration is a welcome initial step, and efforts to include migration in the post-2015 development agenda are encouraged.[8]

Notes
1. United Nations Population Division 2013. 2. UN News Centre 2013a, 2013b. 3. UNICEF 2007. 4. Internal Displacement Monitoring Centre 2013. 5. Welford 2013. 6. ILO 2010b. 7. Bettin, Presbitero and Spatafora 2014. 8. UN 2013a.

Common causes

Transnational vulnerabilities can all be viewed as expressions of the same problems: the underprovision of the types of public goods that enhance coping capabilities, and the mismatch between the extent of global integration and global challenges and the capacity of governance architectures to prevent or minimize shocks. A single country has limited capacity to independently reduce such vulnerability because global goods, such as climate stability, are best provided through global collective action. And yet, national policymaking is the primary avenue states take to address vulnerability. And in some cases the provision of important public goods is simply left to the market.[8] The national orientation of public policymaking is increasingly at odds with the global nature of policy challenges.

At a time when the international system of governance is called on to foster climate stability or reduce the likelihood of yet another financial crisis, cooperation is in many cases ad hoc, fragmented and dispersed across silos of governance organized around particular issues. The international community faces many distractions—economic troubles, armed conflicts and discord among major powers. International organizations are encumbered with funding shortfalls and escalating demands for humanitarian relief. While responses to natural disasters and humanitarian crises are often swift, there is less momentum towards solving longer term global issues. For this, collective action warrants a comprehensive view that extends beyond immediate threats and shocks and addresses underlying causes and longer term impacts.

Underprovision of global goods. How can the global community ensure the provision of goods that enhance resilience? Many goods have social value and can reduce vulnerability—malaria research, pollution reduction or agricultural innovations to reach poor farmers—but are undervalued by markets. Managing and controlling food price volatility, global recessions and climate change are also essential public goods that markets are ill-equipped to provide. The recent trend has been to encourage markets to generate private goods that achieve desired global goals. But private goods cannot sufficiently provide key public goods to reduce vulnerability.[9] The market is particularly unsuited to adjusting global governance architectures to reduce shocks and build resilience. Universally providing certain essential goods demands collective action among states, since no single country or community can alone resolve global market failures.

The need for global public goods is well documented.[10] The underprovision of global public goods—ranging from communicable disease control to adequate global market regulations—permits shocks that have regional and global reach. In addition to traditional global public goods to reduce vulnerability, there is a need for 'global merit goods' or 'universal social goods', goods essential for social stability and continuing progress.[11] Minimum levels of social protection and commitments to provide social services can be thought of as global merit goods—universally provided at the national or transnational level to improve equity and reinforce shared global values.[12] These types of goods offer protection to vulnerable groups, and when they are provided in combination with global public goods that reduce the likelihood of shocks, they can build resilience at the global level.

Multilateral efforts are facilitating cooperation to provide some of these goods, but they are weak in relation to the scope of the challenges and vulnerabilities. And they are weak in relation to the momentum of markets, the pace of commodification and the power of private interests. Global public goods and universal social goods that would correct or complement markets for more-inclusive and -sustainable growth remain largely underprovided.

Global collective action to provide public goods is clearly feasible. Take the eradication of smallpox. Beginning in 1966 the World Health Organization led a collective global programme of universal vaccination, vigilant surveillance of new cases and containment of sporadic outbreaks. The cost was low, but by 1980 the programme had eradicated the disease.[13] This example spurred similar collective action on other diseases and, thanks to medical advances and a worldwide effort of health preparedness, countries are more resilient to pandemics. There are also productive public-private cost-sharing initiatives to advance public health, such as those sponsored by the Bill and Melinda Gates Foundation[14] and the mobilization of private sources by Médecins Sans Frontières to support medical humanitarian aid and make antiretroviral drugs more accessible and available.[15]

The task now is to extend this kind of collective defence to other transnational risks—reconfiguring global systems and governance architectures so that they continue to provide connectivity and efficiency but also support the provision of essential global and national public goods. A global conversation is needed about what goods and which people markets leave behind and what goods might be brought into the public arena to build a more resilient global development trajectory.

Architectural deficits of global governance. Despite efforts to act and cooperate at the global level, structural deficits in governance architectures for handling global risks and making people more secure are limiting the pace of progress (box 5.3). There is a mismatch between governance mechanisms and the vulnerability and complexity of global processes. Today's fragmented global institutions are not accountable or fast-acting enough to address global challenges.[16] They typically work in an ad hoc manner with neither the mandates nor the resources to tackle global threats. Institutions and regulations also target particular issues, sometimes producing spillovers across policy domains—for example, trade policies can affect health by limiting access to certain types of drugs, and fiscal policies that exacerbate inequality can affect security.

In many respects, the shortcomings of global governance architectures in reducing vulnerability stem from deep asymmetries of power, voice and influence. Many international governance institutions and structures were designed for a post–Second World War order,

There is a mismatch between governance mechanisms and the vulnerability and complexity of global processes

BOX 5.3

Systemic barriers to collective action

The mismatch between the scale and urgency of global issues and the capacity of existing governance architectures to address these problems is not unique to any particular issue area. Gridlock in global governance is a systemic and historically contingent process, not an idiosyncratic phenomenon particular to a certain issue. But global issues are often discussed in silos, as if the barriers to collective action were unique to each problem. This perspective may undermine the search for solutions because it assumes that problems can be solved independently. In practice, of course, policies address specific issues. But the standstill in global governance across multiple issues, from slow progress on climate change to the stalemate in the Doha Round of trade negotiations, are systemic problems that can be summed up as growing multipolarity, institutional inertia, harder problems and institutional fragmentation.

Growing multipolarity

The number of states has grown over the last half century, as has the number whose cooperation is essential for resolving a global problem. The transaction costs of global governance have also grown. When the Bretton Woods organizations were formed in 1945, the rules of the world economy were essentially written by a small group of world powers. Today, the Group of 20 has become an important forum for global economic management, because problems cannot be solved without commitments from a larger group of countries. The inclusion of more countries in global decisionmaking should be celebrated, but the transaction costs of global governance are higher.

Institutional inertia

When key pillars of the post–Second World War governance order, including the UN Security Council and the Bretton Woods institutions, were designed, special privileges were granted to countries that were wealthy and powerful at the time. The objective was to ensure the participation of certain countries in global governance. Today, with the rise of the South, power has shifted away from the world order of the 1940s, so a broader range of participation and a more universally inclusive approach would be appropriate to deal with most global issues. But because few governance institutions were designed to naturally adjust to geopolitical fluctuations, institutions will not easily adapt.

Harder problems

The problems requiring transnational cooperation are more extensive, affecting a broader range of countries and individuals. They are also more intensive, permeating deeper into national policy space and daily interactions. For example, environmental problems have gone from chiefly local concerns about clean air and water to global and systemic issues such as climate change and biodiversity loss, characterized by deep interdependence. Shifts of this nature increase the complexity of incentives needed to progress towards global agreements.

Institutional fragmentation

Efforts to address transnational problems occur in a dense system of multilateral and transnational organizations. While this by itself is not a problem, it can increase the possibility of conflicting institutional mandates, uncoordinated interventions and competition for scarce resources. With such outcomes, the proliferation of institutions reduces the ability of multilateral institutions to provide public goods. Focal points could guide policy and help define the nature and form of cooperation.

Solving any problem at the global level requires first recognizing these challenges—and then acting collectively to overcome them. It is essential to think creatively and rigorously about how international cooperation might be strengthened under these adverse conditions.

Source: Hale 2014; Hale, Held and Young 2013.

---

and reforms have not reflected changing power relations or the changing nature of challenges (box 5.4). Meanwhile new regimes, such as those for global intellectual property rights, often disproportionately benefit private interests. Agendas and policies often underrepresent the interests and needs of less developed countries and the most vulnerable people—among them, unskilled workers, home-based workers, immigrants and the elderly. Those who have the least capacity to cope with shocks and to adjust to the speed of change are the least involved in creating the regulations, norms and goals of global governance. As a result, international rules and norms often reflect private interests rather than providing public goods and advancing social interests.[17] This is evident in financial governance. In the Basel Committee, which sets financial standards, private interests have privileged status unchecked by any countervailing power.[18]

Governance systems are not only short on offering protections and enhancing capabilities—in some cases they are producing new vulnerabilities. In finance, monetary policies that focus on deregulation and liberalization have increased the fragility of the financial system. And financial policies such as rigid loan to value ratios have encouraged banks to fuel property bubbles, whereas adjusting loans to reflect the state of the economy could have produced more financial stability.[19] The architectural deficits in governance systems leave a shortage of global public goods, merit goods and universal social goods that would correct or complement existing systems to build more-inclusive and -sustainable resilience.[20]

BOX 5.4

Gridlock in the global governance of security

International cooperation to manage violence and conflict is hampered by a mismatch between the global system of security agreements, institutions and policies and the most pressing security challenges of the day. These constraints limit the international community's capacity to ensure individual security, to reduce the emergence and spread of conflict and to assist in crisis recovery—all essential for reducing the acute vulnerability of people in such places as South Sudan, the Syrian Arab Republic, and the countries of the Sahel and the Great Lakes Region of East Africa, as well as surrounding countries and regions.

The origins of the problem can be traced to the institutional arrangements for security that emerged following the Second World War, and their mismatch with today's security threats. The United Nations was founded explicitly to uphold the collective security of sovereign states. Protection against foreign invasion was guaranteed to all member states, and the Security Council was given a mandate under Chapter VII of the UN Charter to take measures, including the use of force, against countries that threatened peace in this way.

This system helped prevent war between the Great Powers. But today, the security challenges have shifted, with internal conflicts and civil wars in the South, concentrated in the Arab States, South Asia and Sub-Saharan Africa, where the bulk of armed conflicts occur in a far greater number than in the 1940s (see figure 2.12 in chapter 2). The dominant structure of armed forces—based on a model of state military spending and war between nation states that has been in decline over the past half century—is ill-equipped to deliver in areas where security is most urgently needed today. Conflict resolution and post-crisis reconstruction demand cooperation and collaboration among armed forces and the international community, and focusing on the causes of internal conflict is essential.

Alongside the shift in security threats, there has been a transformation in the traditional concept of sovereignty as state autonomy to a far broader notion, including commitments to uphold the rights of citizens under a number of treaties. In 2005, at the largest ever meeting of UN member states, countries agreed unanimously to endorse a national and international 'responsibility to protect' every human being on the planet. But the consensus in adopting this principle has been broken by sharp disagreements over how to implement it.

The Security Council remains the key organ for upholding human security. But this institution was designed to uphold state security, and it retains a 1945 governance structure that relies on consensus among the Great Powers, so decisions will inevitably be influenced by their national interests. When permanent members disagree, no action is likely at the international level. Even when the Security Council can make decisions, it falls to national militaries, or such regional bodies as the North Atlantic Treaty Organization and the African Union, to implement the council's mandate, raising new possibilities to compromise actions.

The turn from interstate conflict to internal conflict has changed the focus of conflict prevention and recovery. This shift, combined with the emergence of the modern human rights regime, has radically changed the nature of sovereignty. At the same time, gridlock in global security governance—particularly multipolarity, more-challenging problems and institutional inertia—block the new institutions or reforms that could meet the goal of collective security. The resulting governance gap limits international capacity to address pressing security issues, passing the burden to the populations in conflict settings.

Source: Hale 2014.

Inaction risks social instability, whether induced by financial crises, climate-related disasters or mass unemployment and poverty. Indeed, recent numbers of local and global protests (843 recorded between 2006 and 2013) are similar in scale to the waves of rebellion in 1848, 1917 and 1968.[21] These protests are usually local and national, but they are directed against a common global experience: increasing insecurity and inequality. And they reflect opposition to the current architecture of globalization and its neglect of public goods and social welfare.

Collective action can restructure global systems in a way that instils people with new capabilities rather than generating new vulnerability and exacerbating existing insecurity. Cooperation is possible among states, international institutions, the private sector and civil society—including a global remit that would recognize the potential spillovers and feedback across countries and between different policy domains. Global governance systems can break the link between globalization and vulnerability, but this will be more likely if global policies and decisionmaking are inclusive, accountable and coordinated.

Putting people first in a globalized world

Enhancing capabilities and protecting choices can reduce vulnerability to transnational threats by enabling people to cope better. So can reducing the frequency, severity and scope of shocks or preventing them altogether. The means to accomplish these goals are twofold. First, providing certain types of public goods, those that could be considered elements of a global social contract, can open national policy space and help people cope with adverse events.

Second, enhancing systems of global governance can facilitate the provision of public goods and reduce the likelihood and scope of transnational shocks.

Elements of a global social contract

Capabilities can be enhanced and choices protected at the national level through the universal provision of such services as education, health care, water and electricity, as well as through universal social protection that empowers individuals with greater resources to withstand external shocks (chapter 4). Such public goods reduce pressure on individuals to make difficult decisions: People should not have to choose which of their children should leave school when jobs are lost and fees are too high or to enter demeaning and dangerous trades such as sex work or garbage scavenging to pay for food and shelter.

National measures are more easily enacted when global commitments are in place and global support is available. That is why the post-2015 agenda should include national universal public services, national social protection floors and full employment as key goals for the global community. These elements of a global social contract can balance maximizing the benefits of global integration and minimizing the costs and insecurities. Global commitments to these goals could open national policy space for states to determine the approaches for creating employment and providing social services and protections that work best in their particular contexts. But global agreements are essential because they can instigate action and commitment and generate financial and institutional support.

Policy norms have been heavily influenced by entrenched beliefs in the efficiency of markets and the power of privatization. Governments across the world have privatized public enterprises, reduced controls on the movement of capital, deregulated labour markets and introduced new intellectual property regimes.[22] Similar ideologies have taken root for individuals. People are expected to extol individualism, self-reliance and entrepreneurship; equate the pursuit of self-interest with freedom; and associate governments with inefficiency and corruption.[23] These beliefs are prevalent even among vulnerable groups that most need the protection of public goods and government support.

A global public domain that strikes a better balance between private and public interests can open national policy space. Policy norms that depict public provision of social protections as positive instruments can enable states to adopt and implement policies and programmes that protect people within their territories. Such norms could embolden states to commit to universal protections for labour that reduce the likelihood of exploitative work conditions while encouraging minimum social protections for workers and for people unable to work because they are between jobs, injured, disabled, elderly or pregnant. Today, only 20 percent of working-age people worldwide have adequate social security coverage, and many are without any type of social security.[24] A more positive view of the public domain would advance calls for universal public services and social protections that enhance people's capabilities to cope when crises hit.

The need for social services and social protection has already been established in international conventions and agreements, particularly in the Millennium Declaration.[25] Articles 22, 25 and 26 of the Universal Declaration of Human Rights (1948)[26] recognize the right to social security, as does Article 9 of the International Covenant on Economic, Social and Cultural Rights (1966).[27] In the 2007 Treaty of Lisbon the European Union identified measures for coordinating policies on social inclusion and social protection.[28] In 2009 the Social Protection Floor initiative brought together 19 UN bodies, several international financial institutions and 14 development partners to promote the goal of universal access to essential services such as health, education, housing, water and sanitation as well as social transfers to ensure income and food security and adequate nutrition.[29] Article 26 of the Convention on the Rights of the Child (1989) recognizes the right of every child to benefit from social security, including social insurance.[30] The Social Security (Minimum Standards) Convention (1952) of the International Labour Organization is among earlier initiatives requiring ratifying states to ensure a range of sickness, unemployment, old age, injury, invalidity and maternity benefits to their citizens.[31]

Most recently, the 2012 United Nations Conference on Sustainable Development in Rio called for a set of sustainable development goals.[32] These goals would produce a more stable public domain placing equality and sustainability at the centre of global development efforts. Together with the lead-up to the post-2015 agenda, the creation of the sustainable development goals presents an opportunity for the international community and member states to push forward the principle of universality—in public provision of social services, universal access to health care and education, and full employment and social protections—all essential elements of more-sustainable and -resilient human development.

Fragile states and conflict settings. How to protect people's choices in fragile states and conflict settings requires special consideration. Ensuring access to social protections, services such as health and education, and employment in fragile states is particularly important—and one of the most difficult development challenges. Inaction in fragile states can have repercussions for national, regional and international security, stability and prosperity.[33] Social contracts can be built within fragile states, and global commitments to universality and social protection can encourage more support for these efforts from the international community and greater commitment from elites in fragile states.[34]

The New Deal for Fragile States, a joint initiative of the 19 fragile countries of the G7+ and the donor community, is one platform for supporting elements of social contracts in fragile states.[35] It promotes solutions based on national ownership and a comprehensive approach to development and security. Recognizing that success is based on combined efforts and effective leadership, all members have committed to undertake collective action and reform to implement the New Deal. Since its inception in 2011, Afghanistan, the Central African Republic, the Democratic Republic of Congo, Liberia, Sierra Leone, Somalia, South Sudan and Timor-Leste have expressed interest in piloting the New Deal. Sierra Leone is one of the first countries to provide a fragility assessment, which reveals considerable progress but also challenges in terms of limited resources and human capital constraints.[36] Additional support for building and operationalizing social contracts in fragile states will be a critical part of universal commitments to social protection, services and employment.

Fiscal space. Where will the resources to provide universal social protection and social services come from? Some will be provided by traditional donors meeting their Millennium Development Goal commitments to increase official development assistance.[37] Several emerging economies also have vast international reserves that could finance public goods.[38] Individual states can raise funds through more-effective taxation of cross-border activities and reduction of illicit financial outflows. Governments lose revenue when companies transfer tax liabilities to low-tax jurisdictions, legally exploiting differences in national regulations. At 2013 public hearings in the United Kingdom and the United States legislators deplored corporate tax avoidance by global companies (such as Apple, Amazon and Starbucks) that legally exploit differences in national regulations to minimize payments to host governments.[39] Countries could arrive at a set of common rules to prevent competition for capital from driving down corporate taxes.[40] This could help many developing countries increase their tax base, leaving more funds for public investment.[41]

International action is also needed to stem illicit financial flows. For the least developed countries illicit financial flows increased from $9.7 billion in 1990 to $26.3 billion in 2008, with 79 percent of this due to trade mispricing. To put this in context, for every dollar of official development assistance that the least developed countries received, an average of 60 cents left in illicit flows between 1990 and 2008.[42] The tax revenue loss in developing countries to illicit flows was $98–$106 billion a year between 2002 and 2006.[43] Between 2008 and 2010 Africa lost $38 billion a year due to mispricing, or false invoicing, and another $25 billion to other illicit outflows—more than the region's receipt of official development assistance during the period.[44] Efforts to increase transparency have been put forward, but a global initiative could encourage and support transparent pricing across countries.

Inaction in fragile states can have repercussions for national, regional and international security, stability and prosperity

BOX 5.5

Can the Responsibility to Protect doctrine be broadened?

A key instrument for holding the international community and individual states accountable to vulnerable people is the Responsibility to Protect doctrine. This is a critical instrument, but it is narrowly constructed to address a specific set of vulnerabilities—holding states accountable for genocide, war crimes, ethnic cleansing and crimes against humanity.

While there has been much criticism and worry about how the Responsibility to Protect doctrine has been interpreted, there also are opportunities for adding to its scope in protecting vulnerable groups during crisis. Its main principle—that sovereignty is not a privilege, but a responsibility—should not be limited to mass atrocities like genocide, given the myriad other pervasive vulnerabilities that people face from financial crises to climate-related natural disasters. The doctrine could be extended to include the responsibility of states to protect vulnerable groups, including women, children and young people, the elderly and migrants. Indeed,

the International Covenant on Economic, Social and Cultural Rights already stipulates that states bear the responsibility to protect the rights to life, security, physical integrity, movement and property.[1]

The United Nations Population Fund has suggested that the Responsibility to Protect doctrine, at least in spirit, can promote institutions such as health and education services.[2] Other work is being done to mandate state responsibility to protect migrants—including, but not limited to, those who are trying to escape conflict at home.[3] The most essential part of broadening the doctrine's scope would be committing to agreed thresholds for intervention and establishing mechanisms for intervention and assistance.

This would be a bold step, not without controversy. But there is an urgent need for a collective and strong commitment towards protecting vulnerable groups, one that extends narratives and norms of protection beyond the scope of violent mass atrocities to include more-pervasive insecurities.

Notes
1. UN 1966. 2. UNFPA 2010. 3. Davies and Glanville 2010.

Among the Group of 20 countries harmonization is under way to reduce tax avoidance and evasion.[45] Other proposals deserve similar consideration, such as that of the Africa Progress Panel to address tax evasion on corporate revenues from oil, gas and mining operations. The Organisation for Economic Co-operation and Development is also encouraging voluntary compliance and disclosure through the Committee on Fiscal Affairs' Working Party on Tax Avoidance and Evasion.[46] A broader, more coherent effort across states and organizations towards an overarching international investment regime and harmonized tax regulations could be the next step. This could be part of the post-2015 agenda, with a focus on generating greater state policy space and enabling progress towards other goals.

Improving global governance

Social services and social protections will not reduce the frequency or scope of transnational threats. That requires changing the architecture of global systems in ways that reduce shocks and maximize positive social outcomes for all rather than promote profit or power for a few. Putting people first in a globalized world requires collective action to ensure that global and regional regulatory systems respond to insecurities and that public goods enhance people's capabilities to deal with transnational shocks.

As globalization deepens, multiple challenges are coming together to assume greater significance—from climate change to conflict to economic crises and social unrest. Past periods of change and uncertainty ushered in broad-based new institutions and norms for global interactions, including the rise of liberalism and free trade in the 19th century, a turn to Keynesian inspired public spending following the Great Depression of the 1930s and the establishment of the Bretton Woods system after the Second World War. Today there is an opportunity to reconfigure market arrangements and global government structures with similarly bold institutional changes so that globalization is balanced between maximizing the efficiencies of the market and protecting people (figure 5.1).

The list of global challenges is long, and the recommendations here are by no means exhaustive, but markets can be better regulated, financial and trade systems adjusted, and environmental threats reduced. These issues receive focus, but the governance of food, migration, public health and other global issue areas are equally important. Indeed, these areas are not mutually exclusive, and there are many overlaps whereby, for example, adjusting the financial architecture could reduce food price volatility and making changes to trade regimes could reduce vulnerability for migrants.

FIGURE 5.1

There is a mismatch between global challenges and global governance mechanisms

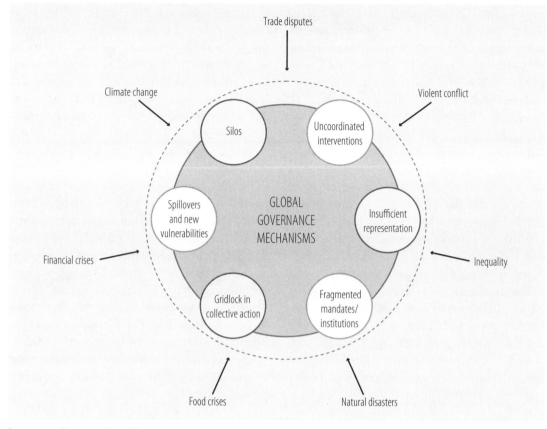

Source: Human Development Report Office.

Governance principles. Adjustments can be made across global issues to increase the likelihood that states will act collectively and to ensure cohesiveness in global governance (see box 5.3 for an overview of systemic problems in global governance). These principles are first-order changes that need to be made before policy and institutional progress is likely on specific problems such as financial volatility, imbalanced trade regimes or climate change.

First is the imperative to ensure equitable participation of developing countries in global governance by reforming the post–Second World War governance structures so that the needs of more-vulnerable countries, particularly the least developed countries and small island developing states, are not marginalized.[47] Second, participation can be extended to include perspectives from the private sector and civil society to ensure support for global collective action among states. Third, since collective action is most effective when it is

inclusive, decisions should be made in representative institutions, not in ad hoc groupings of countries like the Group of 20 or in selective meetings where decisionmaking lacks transparency.[48] Fourth, efforts can be made to increase coordination and cooperation among global governance institutions on various issues to reduce spillovers and better align goals.

Adhering to these principles would improve cooperation among countries that may be hesitant to pool their sovereignty for the collective good and among international institutions with overlapping and uncoordinated mandates, policies and programmes.

Finance. The international financial system is not well suited to minimizing vulnerabilities and protecting gains in human development. The effects of the 2008 global economic crisis on people and countries are a testament to this. The crisis was a consequence of insufficient regulation of complex instruments in the world's

The international financial system is not well suited to minimizing vulnerabilities and protecting gains in human development

leading financial centres.[49] But the impact was felt worldwide. Indeed, countries with otherwise sound financial systems suffered real declines in GDP and employment. Jobs were lost, and workers had to work shorter hours at lower wages. In the textile and apparel industry alone, upper estimates indicate that China lost 10 million jobs, India 1 million, Pakistan 200,000, Indonesia 100,000, Mexico 80,000, Cambodia 75,000 and Viet Nam 30,000.[50] In Bangladesh, Cambodia, Indonesia, Lao People's Democratic Republic, Mongolia, Thailand and Viet Nam workers' earnings dropped by as much as 50 percent.[51] In many countries young people, low-skilled labour and urban workers suffered the greatest employment losses.[52]

While economic shocks affect people in rich and poor countries alike—take the severe effects of the global recession in Greece and Spain—individuals in developing countries are often the most vulnerable. The recessionary downturn in US new car sales led to job cutbacks in Liberia, which supplies rubber for tyres.[53] US automobile workers were offered unemployment protection after the economic

downturn, but thousands of Liberian rubber tappers, most of them hired on contract, were laid off without alternative means of support.[54] Economic crises can also have lasting life cycle effects on future coping capacity. Many poor families that lose their livelihoods resort to taking their children out of school or reducing their food intake.[55] In Kazakhstan families cut back on meat, dairy products, and fresh fruits and vegetables and put off health care and medical procedures.[56]

Recent increases in private capital flows into developing countries, while important for development, leave many economies and people vulnerable. The vulnerability stems from volatile and countercyclical capital flows (figure 5.2).[57] Private capital is attracted by returns and deterred by risk, and cross-border financial flows tend to be pro-cyclical: During periods of economic growth capital pours in, and during downturns it gushes out. The procyclical flows can also be exacerbated by a loss of market confidence, undermining exchange rates and provoking economic contraction, with contagious effects across countries. That is what happened

FIGURE 5.2

Increases in net private capital flows into developing countries over 1980–2012 have left many economies and people vulnerable

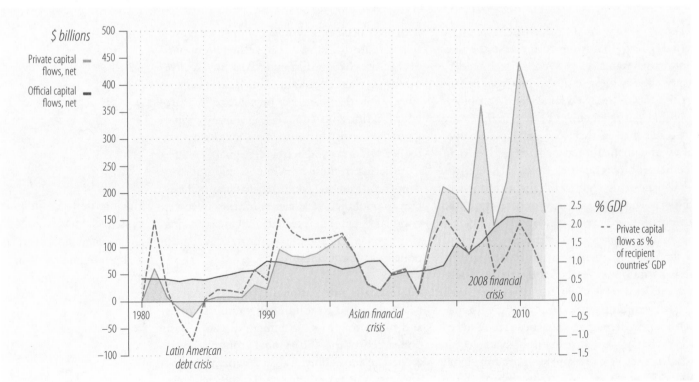

Source: Human Development Report Office calculations based on UNCTAD (2014).

in East Asia in July 1997. Market confidence was influenced particularly by the lower than expected assessments of rating agencies; downgrades triggered panic and destabilized markets.[58]

Instead of having a comprehensive governance system to manage exchange rates and capital controls, global financial institutions are ad hoc and piecemeal. Transgovernmental networks—quasi-formal institutions that bring national officials together to coordinate policy—address certain aspects of the problem, such as banking standards, insurance regulation and securities regulation. But as fundamentally technocratic institutions, they have limited mandates to pursue broad regulatory functions, often focusing more on facilitating financial flows than on managing their dangers. Indeed, they have only rarely pushed the industries they govern to adopt major behavioural changes, with the partial exception of the Basel Committee.[59] Some include considerable industry representation in their governance structures, as with the International Accounting Standards Board. Needed now is a financial system summoning the spirit of Bretton Woods—inclusive financial mechanisms and institutions that ensure access to liquidity, reduce the volatility of financial flows and minimize contagion.

- *Ensure access to liquidity.* Access to international and regional reserves during economic downturns and financial crises, when capital flight is most likely, can help countries cope with financial volatility. Many emerging economies self-insure and rely on their own large reserves of foreign exchange. But this approach has major opportunity costs in losses of development financing.[60] Many other developing countries face strong retrenchments of private capital during financial crises (when resources are most needed). Support from multilateral organizations (including regional institutions) as well as bilateral agencies is crucial to fund countercyclical spending and to ensure adequate funding for social protection programmes, employment policies and other national policies of protection. Regulations can also enable and encourage governments and financial institutions to avoid excessive financial risks during booms.

For individuals and communities, easing the flow of remittances can increase savings and enhance the ability to cope with economic downturns. In 2013 remittances to developing countries were estimated at $414 billion and may reach $540 billion by 2016.[61] These flows exceed the foreign exchange reserves in at least 14 developing countries.[62] Transaction costs to send money back home remain high, though. The average cost of sending $200 from one country to another reached as much as 27 percent in 2013.[63] Reducing this cost could greatly increase liquidity and should be a focus of financial reforms.

- *Reduce the volatility of financial flows.* A regulatory structure for global financial stability can reduce the volatility of cross-border capital flows. The International Monetary Fund has been moderately supportive of such provisions.[64] And the Group of 20 has pushed for countercyclical capital flow management that leaves space for national policymaking, noting that there is not a one size fits all set of capital flow management measures.[65] Policies may depend on the size of national financial sectors and the extent of regulatory capacity. Some countries have greater potential to affect others through national policy decisions, and when weighing policy options, potential spillovers can be taken into account. Take the threats facing emerging economies—high dollar interest rates and capital flight—in the light of imminent tapering by the US Federal Reserve.[66] Reserve currency issuers can affect capital flows with their macroeconomic policy decisions and can avoid excessive imbalances and sharp policy reversals.

- *Regional monetary funds.* Regional financial institutions can reduce the transmission of shocks and diminish the potential for global contagion.[67] They can also help stabilize bilateral exchange rates, provide regional expertise in addressing financial crises and provide liquidity during crises with countercyclical financing.[68] And they can give small countries a stronger voice. National policy space can be enlarged through macroeconomic coordination in regions where initiatives are already under way, including currency swap and regional pooling institutions such as the Chiang Mai Initiative Multilateralization, the nascent East African Community Monetary Union, the Latin American Reserve Fund,

A regulatory structure for global financial stability can reduce the volatility of cross-border capital flows

FIGURE 5.3

In recent years countries in all regions have become more reliant on imports and exports

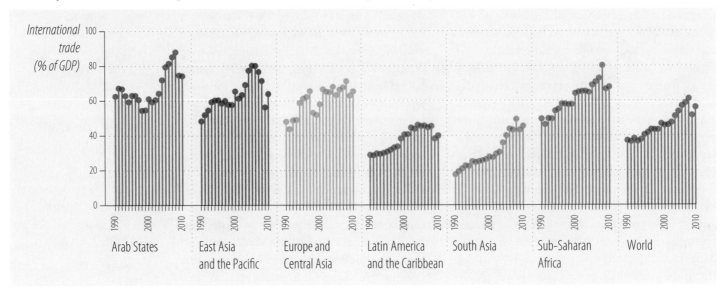

Source: Human Development Report Office calculations based on World Bank (2014b).

the Eurasian Economic Community's Anti-Crisis Fund and the Arab Monetary Fund.[69] The proposed BRICS Bank is another promising initiative.[70] The most ambitious project to date is the Chiang Mai Initiative Multilateralization and its currency swap arrangements among the central banks of member countries. Responding to lessons from the 1997 Asian Financial Crisis, it recognizes the value of regional policy dialogue in preventing contagion and providing liquidity in the face of speculative attacks.[71]

The time may have come for a full-fledged Asian Monetary Fund and Latin American Monetary Fund to pool reserves, stabilize exchange rates, provide countries with short-term funds and offer surveillance. Building on existing structures, other regions might then follow suit. Where membership is partial and the capacity to provide needed financial services low, the participation of developed or emerging economies can provide a rapidly growing pool of savings and reserves and increase creditworthiness.[72] Regional monetary funds can complement global funds, and a more competitive operating environment can strengthen the services of both.

Trade. In recent years countries have become more reliant on imports and exports (figure

5.3). Access to global markets has been an important driver of development, especially in countries that have invested heavily in human capabilities.[73] With a favourable external environment, countries can trade their way to growth. But when the global economy slows, export-oriented economies become vulnerable to fluctuations in commodity prices, terms of trade and external demand. The fallout from the 2008 financial crisis included declines in trade, employment and wages. In the first three quarters of 2009 world merchandise trade fell 30 percent and exports for all world regions more than 20 percent.[74] Employment rates also fell in all regions, and median growth in real wages for a sample of 53 countries plunged from 4.3 percent in 2007 to 1.4 percent in 2008.[75]

Adapting to a competitive international environment can produce insecurity for some individuals, enterprises and governments. Workers in some countries may gain as employment and exports grow, but in others people may lose their jobs as companies close and industries relocate. Adjustments are particularly hard for the more vulnerable segments of society whose bargaining positions are already weak.

Trade-related vulnerability is partly addressed by international trading agreements and rule-setting institutions like the World

Trade Organization. But the global trade architecture has shortcomings ranging from how decisions are made to a move towards more bilateral trade agreements and to asymmetries of negotiating power in setting policies for agriculture and intellectual property rights. Market access also takes priority over development concerns. These shortcomings demand attention if trade integration is to expand without generating additional shocks and vulnerability.

- *Flexible trade rules.* The main governance institution managing world trade remains the World Trade Organization, and despite some flaws, its multilateral rules offer flexibility to protect against trade's volatility. Countries can use the most favoured nation, antidumping and dispute settlement mechanisms to cushion their economies from other countries' actions. They can also use the enabling clause, which facilitates South–South trade agreements that are partial in scope, and can take temporary safeguarding measures against sudden price movements—such as spikes in the price of food imports. In addition, there is special protection for the least developed countries, which have been accorded differential and favourable treatment, including duty- and quota-free access, and grace periods for implementing their commitments. There have also been measures for expanding the least developed countries' trading opportunities such as technical assistance and Aid for Trade.[76] These protocols emerged over decades as countries realized that tariff reduction alone would not always promote equitable trade.

The recent shift towards bilateral trade agreements may reduce developing countries' capacities to respond to trade's risks and volatility and may undermine multilateral progress towards equitable trade. Many agreements include provisions not directly related to trade, such as those for patent protection, investment liberalization and government procurement.[77] The uneven negotiating power in forming bilateral agreements has even undermined the capacity of developing countries to adopt measures to manage capital flows.[78] If countries are to benefit in the long run, the trend towards reduced national policy space in trade agreements needs to be reversed—either by prioritizing multilateral agreements over bilateral agreements or by reducing the asymmetries in negotiating bilateral agreements.

- *Agricultural liberalization.* Despite protocols that allow countries to use temporary safeguards against sudden price movements, the global trading system still leaves countries and individuals vulnerable to shifts in prices, protection and production. The Doha Development Agenda acknowledges "the particular vulnerability of the least-developed countries and the special structural difficulties they face in the global economy".[79] During the World Trade Organization's Ninth Ministerial Conference in Bali, Indonesia, an agreement was reached that could allow developing countries more options for providing food security and boosting least developed countries' trade.[80] But after a decade of negotiations the 2013 agreement provided little protection for the least developed countries or agricultural workers in the South. In the meantime, spikes in the prices of food and other commodities are adding to hunger and starvation for the poor and vulnerable.[81]

Subsidy restrictions in agriculture have loopholes allowing developed countries to maintain and even increase subsidies.[82] Developing countries have to compete with subsidized food in their own markets and lose access to third markets, limiting their agricultural growth and leaving them more vulnerable to food price shocks.[83] Agricultural liberalization needs to be selective in targeting goods mainly exported by developing countries to avoid increasing prices of food staples of developing countries.[84] A review process could help ensure that trade rules and proposed reforms in agriculture enhance developing countries' food security and farmers' livelihoods.

- *Intellectual property rights.* The intellectual property rights regime favours the right to protect intellectual property rather than encouraging the widest possible dissemination and use of knowledge and technology.[85] But poorer countries and poorer people may not be able to afford medical and pharmaceutical products. This is a problem not only for trade, but also for global public health because disease burdens can remain

Despite protocols that allow countries to use temporary safeguards against sudden price movements, the global trading system still leaves countries and individuals vulnerable to shifts in prices, protection and production

high.[86] The current regime also impedes movement towards a low-carbon economy by constraining widespread dissemination of technological innovations.[87] Making things worse is the lack of national and international incentives for research and development to address the needs of poor and vulnerable groups.[88] Reforms to intellectual property rights regulations could encourage investment and enable wider access to the types of technologies and advances that enhance resilience.

- *Trade in services.* A review of the rules guiding trade in services is also in order. The General Agreement on Trade in Services includes opportunities to facilitate the movement of people (Mode 4), which could have spillovers for migrants by partially liberalizing migration. But its commitments to liberalize the movement of people have been minimal, limited largely to facilitating transfers and mobility of executives, managers and specialists. Commitments could be broadened to reduce the vulnerability of undocumented migrants.[89]

Climate change. Some of the expected effects of climate change will be abrupt, leaving very little time for adaptation. These include the disappearance of late-summer Arctic sea ice and the extinction of marine and terrestrial species. Heat waves and heavy precipitation events are very likely to increase in frequency and duration. And the incidence and magnitude of extreme high sea levels are also very likely to increase later in the 21st century. Global sea levels may rise as high as 80 centimetres above modern levels by 2100.[90] Today, more than 6 percent of the world's population—close to half a billion people—lives at an elevation lower than 5 metres.[91]

Feedback effects from changes in the reflectivity of the earth's surface and the extent of carbon sinks could also speed climate change. Reductions in snow cover and vegetation reduce the amount of heat that can be reflected from the earth's surface, leading to greater warming that is unrelated to greenhouse gases in the atmosphere. A warming climate can also speed the deterioration of terrestrial and marine carbon sinks, releasing large stores of carbon dioxide into the atmosphere.[92]

Vulnerability to extreme weather events and food crises has been a recurring threat (box 5.6). In the first half of 2012 Niger experienced a severe food and nutrition crisis. The trigger was a drought spanning the latter part of 2011 and the beginning of 2012. The country had been through a similar food crisis between February and August of 2010, with drought again the trigger. And this had been preceded by an even more severe food crisis, in 2005, a result of a 2004 drought. These droughts also affected neighbouring countries and others in the Sahel.[93] And events in other countries had a bearing on the crisis in Niger. For example, the 2012 crisis was compounded by instability in neighbouring Mali and the inflow of tens of thousands of people fleeing from the conflict there.[94]

The role of drought in contributing to the Syrian crisis is less well known. From 2006 to 2010 the Syrian Arab Republic suffered an unprecedented drought, devastating much of its rural society.[95] Impoverished farmers flooded into the slums of the cities. Observers estimate that 2–3 million of the country's 10 million rural inhabitants were reduced to extreme poverty.[96] These deprivations, combined with a lack of jobs and an inadequate state and international response, contributed to a rapid buildup of resentment and an acute awareness of group inequality, fertile ground for the civil war that started in 2011.

Humanitarian appeals and food and cash assistance can restore food entitlements, but they do not address the underlying vulnerability. The United Nations Integrated Strategy for the Sahel takes a multifaceted approach to humanitarian, development and security activities.[97] But it does not directly address the underlying driver—climate change. Urgent actions are needed on this front to reduce climate-related vulnerability. There are promising subnational actions, but multilateral action is the key to a resilient future for all.

- *Cities networks.* Subnational government bodies can be supported and encouraged. Cities, in particular, are increasingly taking action to mitigate climate change and become more resilient. Examples range from the C40 network of 58 megacities, to the ICLEI network of thousands of smaller municipalities, to sector- or region-specific

BOX 5.6

Who is vulnerable to climate change?

Beyond any doubt, climate change poses a current and growing disruption to nearly every person on the planet as well as to future generations.[1] But climate change is a complex phenomenon with differentiated impacts across countries, regions, sectors, income groups, age groups, ethnic groups and sexes. Even within households, climate change affects individuals differently. Those standing to lose most from climate change are those already very exposed.

- *Small island states.* The world's 51 small island developing states and their inhabitants face an existential threat. Most of their people live less than a metre or two above sea level, and sea level rise may make parts and in some cases all of their territory uninhabitable. These countries are already affected by more-frequent extreme weather events. Many small island states are exposed to Pacific typhoons or Atlantic hurricanes, which damage property and infrastructure and divert public finances from development. Weather events have also disrupted the tourism that many islands states rely on, while ocean acidification and coral bleaching have undercut traditional fishing lifestyles.[2]

- *Coastal cities.* Nearly 45 percent of the world's people live in coastal areas, mostly in large cities.[3] Even in the most developed countries, storms are already devastating coastal cities, often affecting the most vulnerable. Hurricanes Katrina and Sandy cost the United States $149 billion—50 percent more than the world is committed to spending on climate financing in developing countries.[4] The impact on coastal cities in developing countries will be greater, even as the resources available to fix the problems are fewer.

- *Smallholder farmers.* Changes in rainfall and temperature will be felt most acutely by the people who depend on natural systems for growing crops and raising livestock and by those who depend on them for food. In particular, farmers without access to irrigation will most immediately feel the impacts of unpredictable rainfall. Smallholder farmers in South Asia are particularly vulnerable—India alone has 93 million small farms.[5] These groups already face water scarcity. Some studies predict crop yields up to 30 percent lower over the next decades, even as population pressures continue to rise.[6]

Notes
1. IPCC 2007, 2012, 2013. 2. World Bank 2013b. 3. UN Atlas of the Oceans 2013. 4. NOAA 2013. 5. IFAD 2013. 6. World Bank 2013b.
Source: Hale 2014.

networks such as the Asian Cities Climate Change Resilience Network.[98] These municipalities pool knowledge and share best practices on how to develop low-carbon transportation systems or housing stocks and how to harden themselves against rising sea levels and fluctuating weather. Globally, cities account for up to 70 percent of total emissions,[99] so expanding these initiatives has extraordinary mitigation potential, even in countries slow to adopt national action plans. In the United States, national action has been blocked by Congress, but city- and state-level commitments cover nearly half of US emissions.[100]

- *Voluntary private sector disclosure and reduction.* Nongovernment actors are also taking steps to reduce carbon emissions. Firms and investors, often in partnership with civil society, are identifying climate risks in their supply chains and 'carbon proofing' their business models. For example, the World Wildlife Fund's Climate Savers programme helps large businesses develop emissions reduction strategies.[101] The Carbon Disclosure Project offers a tool through which companies can report their emissions footprints to investors—in 2013 the programme included 722 investors managing $87 trillion in assets—who can then pressure companies to reduce their climate risk.[102] The world's 500 largest companies produce 3.6 billion tonnes of greenhouse gases, so corporate emissions reductions hold great potential.[103] More actions can be taken to encourage and incentivize these voluntary efforts, and efforts can be made to map the extent of existing initiatives and assess their potential to increase in scope and ambition.

- *Urgent multilateral action.* Global efforts are essential for guiding action and offering incentives to subnational and nonstate actors (box 5.7). Unilateral approaches to climate change often focus on subsets of emitters and do not offer scope for a 'grand bargain'. They are still worthwhile, because every tonne of carbon mitigated means there is less adaptation required. But they are partial and second best in nature. They are also limited in their attention to adaptation, especially important to vulnerable groups and many populations in the least developed countries.

Multilateral bodies can engage such smaller initiatives and link them to multilateral processes to strengthen global governance of the environment more generally. Bringing the dynamism of bottom-up action into the multilateral process could build

BOX 5.7

Four essential global agendas

Four essential global agendas are tackling some of the world's greatest challenges: natural disasters, humanitarian crises, climate change and sustainable development. But they will produce durable change only if they tackle the architectural issues of global governance—such as ensuring more-equitable and -inclusive participation, pushing for coordination among global governance institutions and consciously developing norms of international cooperation and global citizenship.

Hyogo Framework for Action

The Hyogo Framework for Action, adopted by 168 countries in 2005, aims to reduce global disaster risk by 2015.[1] It puts forward a comprehensive set of tasks and actions that focus on building the capacity of local and national institutions, supporting early warning systems, supporting a culture of safety and resilience, reducing the drivers of vulnerability and strengthening disaster preparedness and response.

The framework has spearheaded collective action towards disaster risk reduction in national, regional and international agendas. But there is more to be done, and progress has not been uniform across countries or action areas. Remaining challenges include developing and using indicators and setting early warning systems in multihazard environments and enhancing the capacity of states to integrate disaster risk reduction into sustainable development policies and planning at the national and international levels.

World Humanitarian Summit

The World Humanitarian Summit, scheduled for 2016, aims to make humanitarian action more global, effective and inclusive—and more representative of the needs of a rapidly changing world.[2] It will be an opportunity to coordinate international humanitarian organizations around issues of vulnerability reduction and risk management.

Responding to the growing number of complex humanitarian emergencies will start by identifying and implementing approaches to reduce and manage humanitarian risks. The summit will be an opportunity to assess how humanitarian and development actors can take a more systematic, cohesive approach to planning, prioritizing and funding programmes—and

how action can be coordinated across economic, social and environmental domains. It will encourage collaboration among affected countries, donors and international organizations to jointly build humanitarian and development strategies.

Climate change—2 degree limit

In the 2009 Copenhagen Accord and 2010 Cancun Agreements 195 parties to the United Nations Framework Convention on Climate Change agreed to limit the average rise in global temperature to less than 2 degrees Celsius from preindustrial levels.[3] This commitment is based on the general scientific consensus that a 2 degree increase is the most the world can afford in order to limit dangerously disruptive impacts.

The international community's pledges and commitments are not yet sufficient to meet this goal. The Intergovernmental Panel on Climate Change's projections conclude that global temperatures will likely increase more than 1.5 degrees by the end of the 21st century and could easily exceed 2 degrees if major action is not taken to reduce emissions.[4] Achieving the objective is still technically and economically feasible, but political ambition is needed to close the gap between current emissions and the level that will set the world on a below 2 degrees trajectory by 2020.

Post-2015 agenda and sustainable development goals

In the run-up to the post-2015 agenda and the sustainable development goals, the international community has an unparalleled opportunity to make reducing vulnerability a priority in international development frameworks. The Millennium Development Goals helped reduce poverty and improve the lives of many. But continuing progress is not guaranteed unless the shocks are reduced and the capacities of people to cope are improved. Along these lines, the call for getting to zero poverty should be extended to staying at zero poverty, and progress needs to be maintained in other areas. Those most vulnerable to natural disasters, climate change and financial setbacks must be specifically empowered and protected. Making vulnerability reduction central in future development agendas is the only way to ensure that progress is resilient and sustainable.

Notes
1. UNISDR 2005. 2. UNOCHA 2014. 3. UNFCCC 2009, 2011. 4. IPCC 2013.

political coalitions to support a global treaty. In December 2011, under the Ad Hoc Working Group on the Durban Platform for Enhanced Action, countries agreed to negotiate by 2015 a new, legally binding treaty that would go into effect in 2020.[104] The United Nations Framework Convention on Climate Change can coordinate and channel the capacities of countries, cities, companies and civil society organizations through cooperative initiatives.[105] The Green Climate Fund, established in Cancun, Mexico, in 2010, could support these efforts financially.[106]

Collective action for a more secure world

The international system suffers from gridlock that limits international collective action across issue areas.[107] In the meantime, vulnerability intensifies as global bodies fail to agree on appropriate response mechanisms and fall short of introducing the right types of regulations to minimize risks and ensure that global systems support the common good. Reducing vulnerability to transnational threats, whether by fixing governance architectures to reduce shocks or taking steps to enable people to cope, requires greater leadership and cooperation among states and across international organizations. It also requires a more coherent approach that sets priorities and reduces spillovers—and more-systematic engagement with civil society and the private sector.

Cooperation

The lack of international coordination, cooperation and leadership stifles progress towards addressing global challenges and reducing vulnerability. This is not new. Over the years there have been various proposals for how to improve cooperation among states. In 2006 a Global Leaders Forum, comprising half the United Nations Economic and Social Council members, was proposed to upgrade the council's policy coordination towards meeting the Millennium Development Goals.[108] In 2009 the Stiglitz Commission proposed the Global Economic Coordination Council to identify gaps and spillovers in the current system of cooperation and propose how they might be filled.[109] Other proposals have been made to reform the United Nations Economic and Social Council.[110]

Emerging as a leading voice in global governance, the Group of 20 includes such emerging powers as Brazil, China, India and Mexico. But it is distinctly club-like and lacks the structure, mandate or accountability to provide public goods and restructure global governance architectures. The rise of the South presents an opportunity to make global governance more representative—and more effective.[111] But this will require new resolve for international cooperation and leadership. One option is to draw on past proposals and establish a Global Leaders Forum. Such a regular meeting of a representative group of heads of state could facilitate cooperation to reducing vulnerability among states and the UN system, including the UN Secretariat, funds and programmes; the International Monetary Fund; the International Labour Organization; the World Bank Group; the World Health Organization; and eventually the International Organization for Migration and the World Trade Organization.[112]

The High-level Political Forum on Sustainable Development created at the Rio+20 Conference in June 2012 also holds promise for political leadership and guidance to address critical global challenges. It has the legitimacy of being convened annually under the auspices of the United Nations Economic and Social Council and every four years under the auspices of the United Nations General Assembly. Starting in 2016 the forum will review sustainable development progress by developed and developing countries to enhance accountability and encourage action.[113]

Coherence

Global governance tends to be organized in silos, with separate institutions focusing on such issues as trade, climate, finance and migration. This makes it very difficult to take a systems perspective on global challenges or to identify spillovers and contradictions in the actions of states and international agencies.

Complete and thorough assessments of the multiple and at times overlapping architectural issues of global governance are needed to ensure that global cooperation is efficient and targeted towards the most critical areas. These could best be made by a nonpolitical body of independent experts who can take an objective systems perspective on global issues and provide advice and recommendations to governing bodies. An independent group of experts could set priorities for cooperation among states and international organizations. It could identify spillovers across the specialized bodies in the UN system—for example, the health effects of trade policies or the environmental effects of fiscal policies—and propose ways of addressing them. And it could assess global trends to determine whether urgent issues are being addressed and identify new challenges that should move onto global and national policy agendas.

Such a group could also carry out detailed cost-benefit studies showing the impact of policies across countries and population groups. That could encourage collective action, since countries often shy away from cooperation if they are uncertain about the potential outcomes. To reflect a diversity of views, ample voice would need to be given to experts from developing countries, and especially from vulnerable countries, including the least developed countries and small island developing states.

Complete and thorough assessments of the multiple and at times overlapping architectural issues of global governance are needed to ensure that global cooperation is efficient and targeted towards the most critical areas

Independent commissions can succeed. The Brundtland Commission made sustainability a common goal of development, and the Stiglitz-Sen-Fittousi Commission helped make well-being a more prominent topic on development agendas. However, these commissions were targeted towards particular issues. What would be useful now is a type of global stewardship council—tasked with the much broader challenge of keeping track of global trends to see whether the world is 'in balance', to confirm that issues requiring attention are getting resolved and to ensure that emerging concerns move onto global policy agendas.[114]

Engagement

Governance improves when citizens are directly involved. In close relationships with the public, governments can obtain accurate information about people's vulnerabilities and track the effects of policy interventions. Such engagement can result in efficient state interventions and public resources.[115] It occurs when people have the freedom, security, capability and voice to influence decisionmaking. They must also believe in their power to produce desired effects through collective action.[116] One example of widespread citizen engagement is participatory budgeting in Brazil.[117]

The International Labour Organization's tripartite structure indicates the possibilities for cooperation between state and nonstate actors. Governments, worker organizations and employer representatives freely and openly debate issues such as labour standards so that policy outcomes reflect the views of all parties. This structure differs from that of other international bodies, which do not give equal weight to nonstate actors. They generally limit consultative status to a selection of nongovernmental organizations, with access ranging from higher engagement within the United Nations Economic and Social Council to much lower representation and engagement at the International Monetary Fund.[118]

Previous global conventions and conferences have raised the rights and visibility of groups constrained by structural vulnerability The 1990 United Nations Convention on the Rights of the Child spelled out the need for special care and protection of children.[119]

The fourth World Conference on Women, in Beijing in 1995, committed states to specific actions to ensure women's rights.[120] The Convention on the Rights of Persons with Disabilities called on signatory states to remove barriers that prevent the full participation of disabled people in society.[121] The World Conference on Indigenous Peoples, scheduled for September 2014, aims to foster global cooperation to realize the rights of indigenous peoples.[122] Once international conventions are ratified, signatories agree to adopt relevant legislation and report periodically to the international community on progress. Even conferences at the consultative level can encourage state action to reduce structural vulnerability.

People are more likely to support the provision of global public goods when they view themselves as global citizens—part of a global community that benefits from capital controls, labour rights and women's rights.[123] In principle, this is now much more feasible as people connect across borders. For example, greater flows of migrants have created opportunities for new forms of solidarity, bringing together people with similar vulnerabilities but different citizenships in host countries.[124]

Collective action is built on personal interactions and trust, but today's communications technologies and social networks also hold potential for extending the scope of social and political communities across borders.[125] Mobile phone use is almost universal, with 6.8 billion subscriptions, and Internet use is on the rise, with average annual growth in Africa leading the way at 27 percent.[126] Communications technology can also increase the voices of the vulnerable—encouraging the political and social participation of groups that have historically been excluded from, or minimally represented in, public discourse, including the poor, women, minorities and other vulnerable groups.

*　　　*　　　*

The oft-postulated goal of more-inclusive, -sustainable and -resilient global growth and development requires a positive vision of the global public domain and recognition that 'the world we want' depends on successful provision of natural and human-made public goods. Markets, while important, cannot provide adequate social and environmental protections on their own. States, individually and collectively, have to be brought back in with a stronger, more forthcoming willingness to cooperate—through the harmonization of national policies or through international collective action. Governments need greater policy space to provide protections and employment for their people. Civil society can generate political will, but only if citizens recognize the value to the individual of cross-border collaboration and public goods.

Progress takes work. Many of the Millennium Development Goals are likely to be met at the national level by 2015, but success is not automatic, and the gains are not necessarily permanent. Taking development a step further requires protecting achievements against vulnerability and shocks, increasing resilience and deepening progress. Identifying and targeting vulnerable groups, reducing inequality and addressing structural vulnerability are essential to sustaining development over an individual's lifetime and across generations.

Notes

Overview

1 UNDP 2013a.
2 Stiglitz and Kaldor 2013a.
3 See, for example, World Bank (2013c).
4 UN General Assembly 2013b, p. 9.
5 UN System Task Team on the Post-2015 UN Development Agenda 2012b.
6 FAO, IFAD and WFP 2013.
7 ILO 2013d.
8 UNDESA 2009.
9 WHO 2011b.
10 CRED 2013.
11 UNDP 2011a.
12 World Bank 2010.
13 UNDP 2013c.
14 Cornia and Stewart 1993.
15 UN System Task Team on the Post-2015 UN Development Agenda 2012b.
16 ILO 2012b.
17 ILO 2010c.
18 Stiglitz and Kaldor 2013a.

Chapter 1

1 UNDP 1990.
2 Chambers 2006.
3 Choudhury 2013.
4 United Nations Global Pulse 2012; Conceição, Mukherjee and Nayyar 2011.
5 Stewart 2013.
6 Social competences are defined as what social institutions can be or do; they are in a sense the capabilities of institutions, as against those of individuals. See Stewart (2013).
7 UNDP 1994, p. 3.
8 UNDP 1994; Ogata and Sen 2003.
9 Macfarlane and Khong 2006.
10 As per UN General Assembly 2012 resolution 66/290 "the notion of human security includes the following: (a) The right of people to live in freedom and dignity, free from poverty and despair. All individuals, in particular vulnerable people, are entitled to freedom from fear and freedom from want, with an equal opportunity to enjoy all their rights and fully develop their human potential; (b) Human security calls for people-centred, comprehensive, context-specific and prevention-oriented responses that strengthen the protection and empowerment of all people and all communities; . . .".
11 Stiglitz and Kaldor 2013a.
12 Dutta, Foster and Mishra 2011, p. 1.
13 UN 2012a.
14 Based on available data from 91 countries.
15 Sundaram 2013.
16 Based on available data from 104 countries for 2000–2012, representing 5.4 billion people (Human Development Report Office

calculations based on data from the World Bank's PovcalNet (http://iresearch.worldbank.org/PovcalNet/, accessed 15 February 2014).
17 Data are available for eight countries.
18 ILO 2010c.
19 Sundaram 2013.
20 Sundaram 2013.
21 Stiglitz and Kaldor 2013a.
22 IPCC 2013.
23 UNDP 2011a.
24 La Trobe 2002.
25 UN General Assembly 2013c.
26 Kaul 2014.
27 Stiglitz and Kaldor 2013a.
28 Horizontal inequality is inequality between groups. See Stewart, Brown and Mancini (2005).
29 Minorities at Risk Project 2014.
30 Swiderska and others 2009.
31 WHO 2011b.
32 UNDESA 2009.
33 IPU 2013; Munyaneza 2013.
34 See Liem and Rayman (1982), Darity and Goldsmith (1996) and Muqtada (2010), among others.
35 See Burgard, Brand and House 2007; Sullivan and von Wachter 2009; Cutler and others 2002; Brand, Levy and Gallo 2008.
36 Zaidi 2014; Hardgrove and others 2014; Young 2014.
37 Nussbaum 2005.
38 Boudet and others 2012.
39 ILO n.d.
40 IMF 2014.
41 IMF 2014; ILO 2013e.
42 O'Sullivan, Mugglestone and Allison 2014.
43 Stiglitz and Kaldor 2013a.
44 Ismi 2013.
45 Østby 2008b; Stewart 2008.
46 Stewart 2008.
47 Stewart 2013.
48 Kelly and others 2008.
49 Fitoussi and Malik 2013.
50 Sen 1992.
51 Kant 1781.
52 Sen 1999, p. 8.
53 Sen, Stiglitz and Fitoussi 2009, p. 4.
54 The 1993 *HDR* (UNDP 1993) defines jobless growth as when output rises but increases in employment lag behind.
55 World Bank 2012.
56 HelpAge International 2013.
57 Ninth World Trade Organization Ministerial Conference (2013) website, https://mc9.wto.org.
58 Revkin 2012.
59 Polanyi 1944.

Chapter 2

1 UNDP 2013a.
2 Sen, Stiglitz and Fitoussi 2009, p. 7.

3 Developed countries are not included in regional aggregates, but they are included in the human development aggregates.
4 Some caveats: Since the HDI is bounded to a maximum of 1, it might be subject to declining marginal improvement; because the income component (a flow) is often more volatile than the health and education components (stocks), short-term changes might be driven mainly by income (particularly during an economic crisis); and the lack of recent data (especially on education and for the poorest countries) may hide overall progress. Nonetheless, the magnitude of the changes and the fact that the conclusions are fairly robust to different cutoff points (for instance, 2005 instead of 2008) suggest that more-meaningful factors are at play.
5 The smaller sample (compared with the 187 countries that have an HDI value for 2013) is due to the lack of a sufficiently long time series for several countries.
6 For instance, better access to skilled antenatal care and birth attendance contributed to sharply reduced maternal mortality in Nepal. Free universal access to education enhanced human development in Sri Lanka. And cash transfer programmes in several Latin American countries helped reduce poverty. See also the 2013 *HDR* (UNDP 2013a) for key drivers of progress.
7 UNDP 2010.
8 In some regions this might be due to the difficulty of raising educational attainment beyond a certain level—such as primary education in South Asia and Sub-Saharan Africa.
9 UNDP 2013a.
10 These data are not directly comparable with those in figure 2.4 since these data refer to the number of countries that experienced a specific trend in inequality (rather than providing a measure of inequality at the regional level) as well as having a longer timeframe.
11 UNDESA 2013b.
12 Lakner and Milanovic 2013. The authors adjust previous estimates—which pointed to a recent decline in global inequality—to address the likely underreporting of the highest incomes in surveys.
13 Milanovic 2012. The share of the richest 1 percent might be severely underestimated, given the difficulty of estimating their incomes.
14 Fuentes-Nieva and Galasso 2014.
15 Stiglitz 2012a.

16 *The Economist* 2013b.
17 Atkinson 2013.
18 Refers to 2000–2012 and is expressed in 2005 purchasing power parity terms (based on World Bank 2014a).
19 Refers to 2005–2012 (based on HDRO calculations).
20 UNDP 1993.
21 The International Labour Organization suggests that if the current trends in labour markets persist, employment rates will return to precrisis levels in 2015 in developing countries but only after 2017 in developed countries (ILO 2013e).
22 ILO 2013c.
23 Sen 2013.
24 UNDP 2011a, 2013. The 2011 *HDR* defined sustainable human development as "the expansion of the substantive freedoms of people today while making reasonable efforts to avoid seriously compromising those of future generations" (p. 18).
25 UN 2013b.
26 See Rockström and others (2009) and Fitoussi and Malik (2013).
27 UNDP 2013a.
28 Pineda 2013.
29 UNCTAD 2012b.
30 ILO 2013a.
31 Kim and Conceição 2010.
32 Molina and others 2014. An HDI downturn is defined as a slowdown in HDI growth with respect to its long-run trend. The study also finds that the nonincome components of human development are more resilient to shocks than the income component is (perhaps because the income component is a flow rather than a stock).
33 There is also evidence that capital account liberalization leads to a persistent increase in inequality (see Furceri and Loungani 2013).
34 World Bank 2013c.
35 This naturally depends on the source and type of economic growth.
36 Stiglitz 2012a. For instance, in the United States the stagnation of real wages for workers at the bottom of the distribution scale—when combined with easy credit—contributed to the housing bubble of the early 2000s. At the global level macroeconomic imbalances contributed to greater economic instability, which also played an important role in the global economic crisis.
37 Berg and Ostry 2011b.
38 Naylor and Falcon (2010) argue that commodity price variations in the 2000s were similar to the extreme volatility that was observed in the 1970s—and thus considerably larger than in the 1980s and 1990s.

Macroeconomic policy, exchange rates and petroleum prices were key determinants of price variability over 2005–2010.

39 The 2011 *HDR* (UNDP 2011a) argued that environmental risk can greatly increase global inequality.

40 Cutter and others 2009.

41 WHO 2011a.

42 IPCC 2013.

43 IPCC 2014.

44 UNDP 2013c.

45 The Uppsala Conflict Data Program/Peace Research Institute Oslo defines four types of armed conflict: interstate, which occurs between two or more states, internal, which occurs between the government of a state and one or more internal opposition groups without intervention from other states, internationalized internal, which occurs between the government of a state and one or more internal opposition groups with intervention from other states (secondary parties) on one or both sides, and extrasystemic, which occurs between a state and a nonstate group outside its own territory. Extrasystemic conflicts mainly relate to the colonial wars. To reduce the number of categories, extrasystemic conflicts are included in interstate conflicts, and internationalized internal conflicts are included in internal conflicts.

46 For the past three years income inequality has topped the World Economic Forum's Global Risks ranking in terms of likelihood (see World Economic Forum 2014).

47 OECD 2012.

Chapter 3

1 We are particularly concerned about the potential restriction of choices that people have reason to value.

2 See Young (2014).

3 Fuentes-Nieva and Galasso 2014.

4 Stiglitz 2012b.

5 Pineda and Rodríguez 2006a; Bénabou 2000; Alesina and others 1996.

6 UNDP 2013a.

7 Schroder-Butterfill and Marianti 2006.

8 Results also depend on the kind of indicator used. For example, the potential for catchup after early stunting is found to be positive for height *z* scores, but there is less evidence of catchup for height. This implies that there are cases in which reversal is possible but that the evidence is mixed and context specific (see Cameron, Preece and Cole 2005).

9 Shonkoff and Richter 2013.

10 Sub-Saharan Africa is the only region that has not substantially reduced the share of children under age 5 since 1970 (Human Development Report Office calculations based on Lutz and KC 2013).

11 See Young (2002).

12 Shonkoff and Phillips 2000; McCain, Mustard and McCuaig 2011; Shonkoff and others 2012.

13 Hertzman and Boyce 2010.

14 Early human development is an intricate and dynamic interaction between nature and nurture—that is, genes and the environment. Genes 'listen' to the environment, and the environment 'adapts' the genetic blueprint. The environment modifies expression of genes (for example, gene variants, phenotype) and can turn genes on and off through the epigenetic process. In this process, experiences leave a chemical signature, or epigenetic mark, that alters genetic expression without changing the DNA sequence. Many of these changes are temporary, but others seem to endure (see McCain, Mustard and McCuaig 2011 and Young 2013).

15 These results are not deterministic; they simply reflect that earlier adversity is associated with a higher likelihood of adverse effects in the future (see Anda and others 2006, Felitti and others 1998, Hertzman and Boyce 2010 and Young 2014).

16 Bhutta 2002; Engle and others 2007, 2011; Alderman and Engle 2008; Armecin and others 2006.

17 McEwen 2008. Exposure to a development risk increases the likelihood of compromised development, but it is not deterministic. It implies only that the child is more likely to face development challenges. The evidence also highlights that this could reduce the impact of the child's exposure to protective factors or interventions to promote early childhood development (see Wachs and Rahman 2013).

18 Heckman 2006.

19 Young 2014.

20 Many of the same risks that are commonly encountered by children growing up in poverty in low- and medium-income countries are also encountered by poor children growing up in high-income countries, even though risks are fewer for the latter (see Wachs and Rahman 2013).

21 Lack of birth registration may severely limit a child's right to full citizenship, and it may prevent a child from receiving most forms of child protection, such as health care. The region in which birth registration is most challenging is South Asia, which accounted for about half the 51 million children without birth registration in the world in 2007 (see Engle, Rao and Petrovic 2013).

22 Nutrition is a critical factor beginning at the early development stages. Both the quantity and quality of infants' nutrition have important effects on their growth. Feeding practices and weaning of infants affect their weight and their morbidity and mortality. Studies show that suboptimal breastfeeding and nonexclusive breastfeeding in the first 6 months of life account for 10 percent of the burden of disease in children under age 5 (Black and others 2008).

23 Young 2014.

24 Brooks-Gunn and Duncan 1997.

25 Engle and others 2007.

26 Hart and Risley 1995. Carneiro and Heckman (2003) also found differences in cognitive skills that correlated with socioeconomic class as early as age 6.

27 Ardila and others 2005. A few studies in developing countries are showing similar findings of the link between socioeconomic status and cognitive development (Naudeau and others 2011). A study in Ecuador (Paxson and Schady 2007) shows that household wealth (and parent education) is associated with higher scores on tests of receptive language and that the gaps among older children are larger.

28 Interactions include back-and-forth communication with caregivers, vocalization, gestures, facial expressions and body movements. The interactions may be warm expressions by mothers, physical contact and play, visual mutuality and vocal exchanges, and mothers' response to infants in timely and appropriate ways (Bornstein and others 2008). See also Bornstein and Putnick (2012) on cognitive and socioemotional positive caregiving activities.

29 NICHD 2006.

30 However, the effect was negative and small but not statistically different from zero for children ages 7–12 at the time of the crisis (Stevens and Schaller 2011; Falkingham 2000; Frankenberg, Duncan and Beege 1999).

31 Falkingham 2000.

32 Child labour is also an outcome of income insecurity and labour market vulnerability among working adults. Child labour is a coping mechanism of poor households—precisely those most vulnerable to adverse shocks to their livelihoods (Basu and Van 1998).

33 Young 2014.

34 Heckman 2013.

35 McCain, Mustard and Shanker 2007; Mustard 2006.

36 WHO 2002; Heise 1998; Abramsky and others 2011; Abrahams and Jewkes 2005.

37 However, some authors highlight that underreporting issues could make it difficult to have conclusive evidence (Berliner and Elliot 1996).

38 Pereda and others (2009), examining 65 studies from 22 countries.

39 Bos and others 2009.

40 Pinheiro 2006; Plan International 2012.

41 The International Labour Organization defines youth as people ages 15–24 (ILO 2013b).

42 Human Development Report Office calculations based on UN (2014b) and Lutz and KC (2013).

43 ILO 2013a.

44 Verick 2009; Ha and others 2010.

45 ILO 2012a.

46 Verick 2009.

47 Assaad and Levison 2013.

48 As documented in UNDP (2013a).

49 The 'youth bulge' is estimated to bring more than 120 million new young people a year into the job market, mostly in developing countries (see World Economic Forum 2014).

50 The World Bank estimates that more than 25 percent of young people in the world (around 300 million) have no productive work (see Newhouse 2013).

51 This is not only because of economic considerations, but also because of the lack of trust and social ties that exclusion from productive opportunities brings about (see Assaad and Levison 2013).

52 Under the base case scenario, youth unemployment is expected to be even slightly higher by 2050 (14.3 percent).

53 The gap will close in South Asia, albeit slowly, as supply begins to decrease around 2035.

54 Boyden, Hardgrove and Knowles 2012.

55 Pells 2011.

56 Ames, Rojas and Portugal 2009; Woldehanna, Jones and Tefera 2008. See also Vennam and others (2009).

57 Morrow 2013.

58 Rolleston and James 2011. These results are not driven by differences in school attendance, since in these countries girls are more likely to be in school at age 15 (see Hardgrove and others 2014).

59 Including the risk of social stigma to lesbian, gay, bisexual, transgendered and questioning young people in all societies.

60 Another vulnerability that comes with sexual experience is the exposure to risks of sexually transmitted infections.

61 Hardgrove 2012.

62 Bunting and McAuley 2004.

63 Pinheiro 2006.

64 Kelly 2010.

65 UNDP 2013b.

66 Krug and others 2002a.

67 Vulnerable employment is the sum of unpaid family workers and own-account workers.

68 International Labour Organization projections show that by 2017 the share of working poor among the total employed population is expected to decline to 17 percent in South Asia and 32 percent in Sub-Saharan Africa (ILO 2013a).

69 World Bank 2012.

70 ILO 2013e.

71 Von Wachter 2014. See also Stephens (1997); Schmieder, von Wachter and Bender (2009); Eliason and Storrie (2009); and Morissette, Zhang and Frenette (2007).

72 See Kaplan, Martinez and Robertson (2005) for the case of Mexico.

73 Frankenberg, Duncan and Beege 1999; Smith and others 2002; McKenzie 2003.

74 Burgard, Brand and House 2007; Sullivan and von Wachter 2009; Cutler and others 2002.

75 Brand, Levy and Gallo 2008.

76 For women, income disparity in old age depended particularly on age (younger cohorts do better), on education (having a higher level of educational attainment reduces the gender gap), and occupation and sector of employment when working (see Bardasi and Jenkins 2002).

77 ILO 2012c.

78 For category 3 categories the number of jobs fell, but the lowest quality jobs were lost first, resulting in improved overall job quality. For category 2 countries employment rates rose from 2007 but as a result of an increase in low-quality jobs.

79 ILO 2012b.

80 Heintz 2012.

81 Bargain and Kwenda 2009; von Wachter 2014.

82 Ono and Sullivan 2013; Keizer 2008.

83 ILO 2013a.

84 Arriagada 1994; Cerrutti 2000; Casale 2003.

85 Bahçe and Memiş 2013; Berik and Kongar 2013.

86 Heath 2012.

87 Stevens and Schaller 2011; Falkingham 2000.

88 Mejia-Mantilla 2012; Falkingham 2000.

89 World Bank 2012; Fischer 2013.

90 World Bank 2012.

91 Kuhn, Lavile and Zweimuller 2009.

92 Human Development Report Office calculations based on Lutz and KC (2013).

93 Barrientos 2006.

94 Those who have contributed to a pension scheme during their working life will have some income and are less vulnerable than those who have had poorly paid, part-time, insecure or informal employment (Zaidi 2013).

95 Kondkher, Knox-Vydmanov and Vilela 2013.

96 Some studies indicate that regularly and by right delivered social pensions, even where relatively small, improve the socioeconomic conditions of older people, supporting their role as family members that actively participate in taking decisions (see Beales 2012). The positive effects of social pensions could be extended to other family members, especially children. Children in families that include an older person in receipt of a social pension have been shown to benefit, in terms of nutrition and education, from the contribution of these relatively small payments to family income (see Duflo 2000).

97 Widowhood and the onset of disability are also important triggers that have an adverse impact on the financial well-being of older people (see Burkhauser, Holden and Feaster 1988; Burkhauser, Butler and Holden 1991; Emmerson and Muriel 2008; Holden, Burkhauser and Myers 1986; and McLaughlin and Jensen 2000).

98 UNFPA and HelpAge International 2012.

99 OECD 2011b.

100 ECLAC 2011.

101 WHO 2011b.

102 Masset and White 2004.

103 UNFPA and HelpAge International 2012.

104 Similarly, the World Health Organization (WHO 2007) found that particular groups of older women were more at risk of poverty in all countries, including those who are widowed, divorced or living with disabilities and those caring for grandchildren and children orphaned by AIDS.

105 The United Nations Children's Fund (UNICEF 2006) estimates that in East and Southern Africa 40–60 percent of orphaned and vulnerable children are cared for by their grandparents. Similarly, Beegle and others (2009) indicates that older people take care of as many as 81 percent of orphaned children.

106 Stewart, Brown and Mancini 2005.

107 DFID 2001.

108 Chambers 1989.

109 UN Enable 2013.

110 Around 1.5 million people (out of 10 million) became homeless and moved to camps after the earthquake. Because of the limited capacity of the state and public services to conduct reconstruction and protect the population, the vulnerability of the poorest households increased even further (with epidemics, inundations and the like), and their living conditions worsened (see Châtaigner 2014 and Herrera and others 2014).

111 Rentschler 2013.

112 The World Bank's PovcalNet database provides estimates of income poverty based on surveys from 2000–2012 for 104 countries representing 5.4 billion people. The number of people living on less than $1.25 a day is 1.2 billion, or 22 percent of the population in these 104 countries. International poverty lines are also expressed in 2005 purchasing power parity terms.

113 The population considered near multidimensional poverty has 20–33 percent of deprivations. This group can be called the 'near poor'. The population considered near poor in a monetary sense has an equivalent income of more than $1.25 a day but less than $2.50 a day.

114 Socially and geographically disadvantaged people who are exposed to persistent inequality, including horizontal inequality (for example, inequality based on gender, age, race, ethnicity and disability), have been found to be particularly negatively affected by climate change and climate-related hazards (see IPCC 2014).

115 World Bank 2013b.

116 UN Global Pulse 2012.

117 Stiglitz and Kaldor 2013a.

118 Frazer and Marlier 2012.

119 Hallegatte and others 2010; Rentschler 2013.

120 Rentschler 2013.

121 Rentschler 2013.

122 This simply reflects that the poorest households are exposed to a larger number and a wider range of types of shocks or adverse events than wealthier households are (see Boyden 2009; Woodhead, Dornan and Murray 2013).

123 Krutikova 2010.

124 UNDP 2011a.

125 Countries ranked in the top quintile of the Organisation for Economic Co-operation and Development's Social Institutions and Gender Index, which measures underlying discrimination against women by capturing and quantifying discriminatory social institutions (see OECD 2010).

126 The study used a large dataset of 59 countries, covering 1.5 million births between 1975 and 2004 (Conceição, Mukherjee and Nayyar 2011; Baird, Friedman and Schady 2007).

127 Friedman and Schady 2009.

128 European Parliamentary Research Service 2013.

129 Ferris, Petz and Stark 2013.

130 Supported by Swayam Shikshan Prayog, a Mumbai-based nongovernmental organization, and the Covenant Centre for Development, a Tamil Nadu–based nongovernmental organization, the women visited 13 villages in Nagapattinam and Cuddalore, the two worst affected districts. They identified ways to promote the villages' long-term housing and livelihood rehabilitation programmes and actively supported the population by talking with survivors, sharing stories and organizing meetings with women's groups, youth groups and fisher cooperatives (see Gupta and Leung 2011).

131 UNDESA 2009.

132 In view of the diversity of indigenous peoples, the UN system has not adopted an official definition of the term 'indigenous'. Instead it has developed a modern understanding of the term based on such criteria as self-identification as indigenous peoples; historical continuity with precolonial or presettler societies; strong links to territories and surrounding natural resources; distinct social, economic and political systems; distinct language, culture and beliefs; and resolve to maintain and reproduce ancestral environments and systems as distinctive peoples and communities.

133 Vinding and Kampbel 2007.

134 For example, during an August 2013 heat wave in the Hungarian town of Ozd, water supply was shut off in a large number of public water taps on which the Roma depend. This left thousands of them waiting to collect water from the public taps still working (see Dunai 2013).

135 Hughes and others 2012.

136 For example, wheelchair users may have no difficulty relating to general disaster risk reduction information. However, those same individuals may face severe barriers in safely protecting themselves during and evacuating after an earthquake.

137 Robinson, Scherrer and Gormally 2013.

138 Disability is also related to lower levels of education. Evidence shows a higher likelihood of experiencing a disability at lower levels of education. This is true for all regions, though to a varying degree (see KC and others 2014).

139 WHO 2011b.

140 Around a third of migration from developing countries is irregular migration (UNDP 2009b).

141 Female migrants accounted for 49.6 percent of international migrants in 2005 (UNFPA 2008).

142 UNFPA 2008.

143 UNDP 1994, p. 1.

144 Gasper and Gomez 2014.

145 WHO 2002.

146 Quite concretely, the cost to society of violence is sizeable. A 1992 study on the United States estimated the annual direct and indirect cost of gunshot wounds at $126 billion and of cutting or stab wounds at $51 billion (WHO 2002). In addition, a joint Inter-American Development Bank–United Nations Development Programme study found important costs of crime and violence as a percentage of GDP in five Latin American countries in 2010, ranging from 3 percent in Chile and Uruguay to over 10 percent in Honduras (see UNDP 2013b).

147 Gasper and Gomez 2014.

148 UNDP 2005, 2013b.

149 UNDP 2012b.

150 Stiglitz and Kaldor 2013a.

151 OECD 2011a.

152 Stewart 2010.

153 Excluded by mainstream society from participating fully in the economic, social and political life of their society, often because some group characteristics (for example, cultural, religious or racial). See Stewart and others (2006).

154 Zeitlyn 2004.

155 Stewart 2010.

156 Motives of group leaders may be lack of political power, while followers care more about social and cultural inequality (see Stewart 2008). See also OECD (2011a) for a discussion of some critical socioeconomic drivers of inequality in developing countries and their interaction.

157 Østby's (2008a) analysis of 55 countries over 1986–2003 finds a significant rise in the probability of conflict in countries with severe economic and social horizontal inequality. Mancini (2008) indicates that violent conflict is more likely to occur in areas with less economic development and greater religious polarization. He also finds that measures of (vertical) income inequality as well as other purely demographic indicators of ethnic diversity did not affect the likelihood of communal violence (see also Stewart 2008, 2010 and Hoeffler 2012). Other research has suggested considering social exclusion as vertically occurring processes of disadvantage, since this provides a more nuanced understanding of how social dislocations may lead to conflict in a way that avoids the tendency to blame inequality-induced conflict on the lower social strata without incorporating the role often played by the elites in many conflict episodes (see Fischer 2008).

158 The connection between social exclusion and conflict can be illustrated in many examples: the Muslim rebellions in the Philippines and Thailand; the separatist movements of Aceh, Timor-Leste and Papua in Indonesia; and the separatism of East Pakistan and Eritrea, among others (see Stewart 2010).

159 Evidence links some of these episodes to periods of economic policy reform (such as changes in trade policy). See Kanbur (2007).

160 Marc and others 2012.

161 Stewart and others 2006. See also Stewart (2010) for a typology of the different approaches to manage horizontal inequality.

162 Parlow 2012.

163 EWSCWA 2007.

164 UNHCR 2012.

165 Of this figure, 17.7 million were internally displaced persons and 10.5 million were refugees (2.3 million more than in 2011). The refugee figure was close to that of 2011 (10.4 million), and the number of internally displaced

persons increased 2.2 million since the end of 2011 (UNHCR 2012).

166 Conflict—in particular, civil wars—was found to be associated with underperformance on the Human Development Index (progress significantly below what could be expected given the initial conditions), since 60 percent of countries that experience this kind of conflict (28 of 46 countries in the sample) underperformed (see UNDP 2010).

167 Human Development Report Office calculation based on Uppsala Conflict Data Program data on battle deaths.

168 Other important services that may be severely affected by conflict are reproductive health services. For example, couples may not have access to family planning services, increasing unwanted pregnancies and unsafe abortions (see WHO 2000).

169 Sudanese children ages 7–12 who were living in northern Uganda and had been exposed to war were more likely to have behavioural problems, symptoms of depression and complaints similar to post-traumatic stress disorder than were Ugandan children who had not been affected by war (Paardekooper, De Jong and Hermanns 1999).

170 Using household data for Colombia, Engel and Ibanez (2007) show that perceptions of safety can have a decisive influence on migration.

171 Acts of gender-based and sexual violence against women and girls (including mass rape) are increasingly common features of war and conflict (see WHO 2000).

172 Gagro 2010.

Chapter 4

1 Bolsa Família evolved from Bolsa Escola as a conditional cash transfer programme with incentives for parents to keep children in school and regularly visit health centres. In 2006 Bolsa Família was estimated to cost 0.5 percent of Brazil's GDP and about 2.5 percent of total government expenditure, while covering about 11.2 million families, or about 44 million Brazilians.

2 Mkandawire 2001; Kumlin and Rothstein 2005.

3 UN General Assembly 2013b, p. 12.

4 UN General Assembly 2013a, p. 11.

5 Deacon and Cohen 2011.

6 Korpi and Palme (1998, p. 661) define the paradox as, "The more we target benefits at the poor and the more concerned we are with creating equality via equal public transfers to all, the less likely we are to reduce poverty and inequality."

7 Mkandawire 2001; Rothstein 2001.

8 Baldwin 1990.

9 Deacon and Cohen 2011.

10 Heller (2005) defines fiscal space as room in a government's budget that allows it to provide resources for a desired purpose without jeopardizing the sustainability of its financial position or the stability of the economy. The Nordic model could be financed precisely because it also included provisions to support full employment. Full employment generated the tax revenues needed to pay for the Nordic model.

11 UNICEF 2008.

12 ILO and UNDP 2011.

13 UNICEF 2008.

14 UNICEF 2008.

15 ILO 2011b.

16 Waters, Saadah and Pradhan 2003.

17 Waters, Saadah and Pradhan 2003.

18 Mok, Lawler and Hinsz 2009.

19 At the same time, the traditional familial and community networks and other social institutions in Thailand remained relatively stable, with the rural-urban links providing an informal safety net for the dispossessed.

20 UNDP 2011c.

21 Ringen 1988.

22 Esping-Andersen 1999; Palme 2006.

23 ILO 2011b.

24 Esping-Andersen and Myles 2008.

25 Jäntti and Bradbury 2001.

26 Nelson (2004) traced the high poverty reduction in Sweden to high redistribution by non–means tested provisions, such as universal provisions.

27 ILO and UNDP 2011.

28 UNDP 2013a.

29 Female literacy and education indicators for women can be better indicators of the coverage education since aggregate indicators may average out gender differences in education achievements. This is particularly true for patriarchal societies where women are likely to have less access to education and health care resources than men are.

30 Meng and Tang 2010.

31 Xinhua New Service 2013.

32 MacLeod and Urquiola 2012.

33 Young 2014.

34 Dalman and Bremberg 1999.

35 The advantages gained from effective early interventions are best sustained when they are followed by continued investments in high-quality education. The returns on school investment are higher for people with stronger cognitive skills, where cognitive development happens in the early years.

36 Heckman 2005.

37 Bornstein and others 2008.

38 Hackman, Farah and Meaney 2010; Nelson, Fox and Zeanah 2014.

39 For an overview of the literature on the correlation between socioeconomic status and early childhood development, see Young (2014).

40 ILO 2014.

41 Amsden 2001; Chang 1993.

42 ILO 2006a.

43 Heyer, Stewart and Thorp 1999; Thorp, Stewart and Heyer 2005.

44 For reviews of public works programmes, see Devereux and Solomon (2006) and Lal and others (2010).

45 Zepeda and others 2013.

46 Kostzer 2008.

47 Muqtada 1987; Ahmed and others 1995.

48 Marshall and Butzbach 2003; Devereux and Solomon 2006.

49 Langer and others 2012; Date-Bah 2003.

50 KC and others 2014.

51 Hausmann 2013.

52 The understanding of diversified rural livelihoods is one of the generic insights coming out of the literature on livelihoods.

53 In some cases development transitions may lead to new social security regimes, or there might be feedback effects between economic transitions and social protections.

54 China National Bureau of Statistics 2011.

55 UNRISD 2010.

56 UNDP 2011a.

57 Hoon 2011.

58 Stephan 2009.

59 Moreover, the point is also made that Germany's wage subsidies over the period seem to be fiscally beneficial. Estimated fiscal gains amount to €1,600–2,000 for men in East Germany and to €500–1,000 for men in West Germany and women in East Germany over the observation period of 3.5 years. Careful design and implementation are critical to avoid windfall gains to employers that do not produce net benefits.

60 Burns, Edwards and Pauw 2010.

61 Gupta and Larssen 2010, p. 26. Specifically, the researchers found "that for the long-term disabled with a working capacity reduction in the 18–49 age group, employment probability is raised by 33 pct. points after the scheme was introduced relative to a mean employment rate at a baseline of 44 percent."

62 Bonilla García and Gruat (2003, p. 13) define social protection "as the set of public measures that a society provides for its members to protect them against economic and social distress that would be caused by the absence or a substantial reduction of income from work as a result of various contingencies (sickness, maternity, employment injury, unemployment, invalidity, old age, and death of the breadwinner); the provision of health care; and, the provision of benefits for families with children."

63 Roxburgh and Mischke 2011

64 Paci, Revenga and Rijkers 2011.

65 ODI 2008.

66 Paci, Revenga and Rijkers 2011, p. 13.

67 Onyango, Hixson and McNally 2013.
68 Haughton and Khandker 2012.
69 Data on public social expenditures are derived from OECD (n.d.). The main social policy areas are old age, survivors, incapacity-related benefits, health, family, active labour market programmes, unemployment, housing and other social policy areas. Those areas can be further divided by type of expenditure (cash benefits, benefits in-kind), type of programme (active labour market programme, incapacity-related) and source (voluntary private, public).
70 Furceri 2009.
71 OECD 2013b.
72 Assimaidou, Kiendrebeogo and Tall 2013.
73 Von Wachter 2014.
74 World Bank 2012.
75 Fischer 2013.
76 Posel, Fairburn and Lund 2006.
77 ILO 2009.
78 ILO 2010c, 2011b.
79 ILO 2011a.
80 Gassmann and Behrendt 2006.
81 ILO 2010c.
82 ILO 2006b.
83 Burkina Faso, Cameroon, Ethiopia, Guinea, Kenya, Senegal, the United Republic of Tanzania, Bangladesh, India, Nepal, Pakistan and Viet Nam.
84 ILO 2008.
85 Easterly, Ritzen and Woolcock 2006.
86 The classification of less- and more-cohesive societies is the same as in Easterly, Ritzen and Woolcock (2006) and is based on measures of ethno-linguistic fractionalization and income share of the middle class (defined as the middle 60 percent of the income distribution). Easterly, Ritzen and Woolcock (2006) define more cohesive societies as those in the lower half of ethno-linguistic fractionalization and in the upper half of income share of the middle class and less cohesive societies as the reverse. Since 1980 more-cohesive societies have progressed faster than less cohesive societies, but the difference became much more pronounced after the recession in less cohesive societies in the 1980s and after the global crisis in 2008.
87 *The Economist* 2013a.
88 Telles 2004.
89 Carneiro 2013.
90 Naidoo and Kongolo 2004.
91 Maisonnave, Decaluwé and Chitiga 2009.
92 Burger and Jafta 2010.
93 Sander and Taylor 2012.
94 World Bank 2011.
95 To foster desired behaviours, economists emphasize material incentives provided through contracts, markets or policy. While these often work very effectively, there also many puzzling cases where incentives fail

to have the desired effects (crowding out) or where minor incentives have a disproportionately large impact (crowding in, shift in norms). Societies also sometimes persist with what seem like inefficiently costly forms of incentives (prison rather than fines or reparations) or renounce others that might be quite cheap or effective (public shaming). For a more detailed discussion, see Benabou and Tirole (2011).
96 Young 2007.
97 Kinzig and others 2013.
98 Benabou and Tirole 2011.
99 UNDP 2009a.
100 UNDP 2009a.
101 Rodrik 2000, p. 3.
102 Easterly and others 2006.
103 Evans and Heller forthcoming.
104 Stewart 2013.
105 International Policy Centre for Inclusive Growth 2009.
106 UNDP 2003.
107 Sobhan 2014.
108 UNISDR 2012b.
109 Haque and others 2012.
110 UNISDR n.d.
111 UN System Task Team on the Post-2015 UN Development Agenda 2012a.
112 UNDP 2013d.
113 Lund and Myers 2007.
114 Marc and others 2012.
115 World Bank 2012.

Chapter 5

1 World Bank 2014b.
2 United Nations Population Division 2013.
3 Hale 2014.
4 Bank for International Settlements 2013.
5 Wadhams 2010.
6 Canis 2011.
7 UNHCR 2012.
8 Kaul 2014.
9 Kaul 2014.
10 Kaul and others 2003; Kaul and Conceição 2006.
11 Universal social goods are goods and services that society decides should be guaranteed to all people, independent of their capacity to pay, and the rules that citizens should respect in their interaction with each other (such as nondiscrimination and protection of weaker members of society). See Ocampo (2013).
12 See Musgrave (1959) for the original theorization of merit goods. For an explanation of merit goods in the global context, see Sandler, Arce and Daniel (2002).
13 Fenner and others 1988.
14 WHO 2013a.
15 Médecins Sans Frontières 2013.
16 Held and Young 2013.
17 Stiglitz and Kaldor 2013b.
18 Held and Young 2011.

19 Stiglitz 2013.
20 See Kaul (2013, 2014) and Kaul and others (2003) for more on global public goods. See Musgrave (1959) for original theorization of merit goods. For explanation of merit goods in the global context, see Sandler, Arce and Daniel (2002). See Ocampo (2013) for a discussion of universal social goods (goods that aim to promote common social norms and standards and promote equality among individuals).
21 Ortiz and others 2013.
22 Crouch 2011.
23 Evans and Sewell 2013.
24 ILO 2010c.
25 UN 2000.
26 UN 1948.
27 UN 1966.
28 EU 2007.
29 UN 2009.
30 UN 1989.
31 ILO 1952.
32 See UNCSD (2012) for details of the proposal to develop an inclusive and transparent intergovernmental process on the sustainable development goals that is open to all stakeholders with a view to developing global sustainable development goals to be agreed by the UN General Assembly.
33 Naudé, Santos-Paulino and McGillivray 2011.
34 UNDP 2012c.
35 International Dialogue on Peacebuilding and Statebuilding 2011. The G7+ members are Afghanistan, Burundi, the Central African Republic, Chad, Côte d'Ivoire, the Democratic Republic of the Congo, Ethiopia, Guinea, Guinea-Bissau, Haiti, Liberia, Nepal, Papua New Guinea, Sierra Leone, the Solomon Islands, Somalia, South Sudan, Timor-Leste and Togo.
36 Sierra Leone 2013.
37 Targets 8.B and 8.C of the Millennium Development Goals encourage increasing official development assistance by developed countries but do not list specific targets. However, at the 2005 Group of Eight Summit in Gleneagles, Scotland, donor countries pledged to provide official development assistance at the level of 0.7 percent of gross national income by 2015. In 2012 official development assistance was less than half this goal, at only 0.29 percent of (UN 2013c).
38 UNDP 2013a.
39 Hamdani 2014.
40 OECD 2013a.
41 OECD 2013a.
42 UNDP 2011b.
43 Hollingshead 2010.
44 Africa Progress Panel 2013.
45 G20 2013.
46 OECD 2011c.
47 UNDP 2013a.
48 Ocampo 2010.
49 Stiglitz and Kaldor 2013b.
50 Cattaneo, Gereffi and Staritz 2010.

51 UN Global Pulse 2010.
52 Cho and Newhouse 2013.
53 Jansen and von Uexkull 2010.
54 Jansen and von Uexkull 2010.
55 Dureya and Morales 2011.
56 Gavrilovic and others 2009.
57 Bluedorn and others 2013.
58 Ferri, Liu and Stiglitz 1999.
59 The Basel Committee on Banking Supervision has introduced stringent regulatory standards, including increasing capital buffers to draw on during periods of financial stress, measures to improve the quality of bank capital and a global minimum debt to equity ratio. Promising though it is, the 2010 Basel III Accord is based on voluntary commitments and has yet to be fully implemented (see Held and Young 2011).
60 UNDP 2013a.
61 Ratha and others 2013.
62 Ratha and others 2013.
63 This cost was for transfers from Ghana to Nigeria (World Bank 2013a).
64 IMF 2012.
65 G20 2011.
66 Kynge 2014.
67 Ocampo 2006; Machinea and Titelman 2007.
68 Ocampo and Griffith-Jones 2007.
69 Grabel 2012.
70 The leaders of Brazil, China, India, the Russian Federation and South Africa agreed to pool their resources to establish a BRICS Bank during the March 2013 BRICS Summit in South Africa.
71 Park 2006.
72 Culpeper 2006.
73 UNDP 2013a.
74 Hamdani 2014.
75 Jansen and von Uexkull 2010.
76 Hamdani 2014.
77 Thrasher and Gallagher 2008.
78 Gallagher, Griffith-Jones and Ocampo 2012.
79 WTO 2001 p. 1.
80 WTO 2013.
81 Von Braun and Tadesse 2012; Hoekman and Martin 2012.
82 Khor and Ocampo 2011.
83 Ghaenm 2011.
84 Khor and Ocampo 2011.
85 Kennedy and Stiglitz 2013.
86 Odagir and others 2012; Pollock 2006.
87 Abdel-Latif 2012.
88 Hogerzeil and others 2013.
89 Khor and Ocampo 2011.
90 IPCC 2013.
91 World Bank 2014b.
92 IPCC 2013.
93 UNDP 2012a.
94 Hirsch 2012.
95 Polk 2013.
96 Polk 2013.
97 UN General Assembly 2013c.
98 Hale 2014.
99 UN-Habitat 2011.
100 Lutsey and Sperling 2008.
101 WWF 2007.

102 CDP 2013.

103 CDP 2013.

104 UNFCCC 2012.

105 Hale 2014.

106 UNFCCC 2011.

107 Hale, Held and Young 2013.

108 The proposal was forcefully rejected on the grounds that it risked further weakening the United Nations Economic and Social Council, the United Nations Conference on Trade and Development and the United Nations General Assembly. In response to the Global Leaders Forum proposal and a package of other recommendations, the developing countries suggested that rather than limiting the UN system to a secondary role and niche issues, the UN system should assert its leadership over the World Bank and the International Monetary Fund, which were considered to be dominated by developed countries (Müller 2010).

109 Ocampo and Stiglitz 2011.

110 See Chaterjee (2009), Weiss (2011), Abebe and others (2012) and UN (2013e).

111 UNDP 2013a.

112 Such a council would be similar to the Global Economic Coordination Council recommended in Stiglitz and others (2009).

113 UN 2012b, 2013d.

114 Kaul 2013.

115 Evans and Heller forthcoming.

116 Bandura 2000.

117 Evans and Heller forthcoming.

118 Reinalda 2013.

119 UN 1989.

120 UN 1995.

121 UN 2006.

122 UN 2014a.

123 Sassen 2006.

124 Sassen 2006.

125 Tarrow 2013.

126 ITU 2013.

References

Abdel-Latif, A. 2012. "Intellectual Property Rights and Green Technologies from Rio to Rio: An Impossible Dialogue?" Policy Brief 14. International Centre for Trade and Sustainable Development, Geneva.

Abebe, H., R. Dugan, M. McShane, J. Mellin, T. Patel, and L. Patentas. 2012. "The United Nations' Role in Global Economic Governance: A Research and Policy Brief for the Use of the NGO Committee on Financing for Development." www.ngosonffd.org/wp-content/uploads/2010/11/UN-Role-in-Global-Economic-Governance-2012.pdf. Accessed 27 March 2014.

Abrahams, N., and R. Jewkes. 2005. "Effects of South African Men's Having Witnessed Abuse of Their Mothers during Childhood on Their Levels of Violence in Adulthood." *American Journal of Public Health* 95(10): 1811–16. www.ncbi.nlm.nih.gov/pmc/articles/PMC1449441/. Accessed 20 March 2014.

Abramsky, T., C.H. Watts, C. Garcia-Moreno, K. Devries, L. Kiss, M. Ellsberg, H.A.F.M. Jansen, and L. Heise. 2011. "What Factors Are Associated with Recent Intimate Partner Violence? Findings from the WHO Multi-Country Study on Women's Health and Domestic Violence." *BMC Public Health* 11: 109. www.ncbi.nlm.nih.gov/pmc/articles/PMC3049145/pdf/1471-2458-11-109.pdf. Accessed 20 March 2014.

Africa Progress Panel. 2013. *Africa Progress Report 2013: Equity in Extractives: Stewarding Africa's Natural Resources for All.* Geneva. www.africaprogresspanel.org/wp-content/uploads/2013/08/2013_APR_Equity_in_Extractives_25062013_ENG_HR.pdf. Accessed 24 March 2014.

Ahmed, A.U., S. Zohir, S.K. Kumar, and O.H. Chowdury. 1995. "Bangladesh's Food for Work Programme and Alternatives to Food Security." In J. von Braun, ed., *Employment for Poverty Reduction and Food Security.* Washington, DC: International Food Policy Research Institute.

Alderman H., and P. Engle. 2008. "The Synergy of Nutrition and ECD Interventions in Africa." In M. Garcia, A. Pence, and J. Evans, eds., *Africa's Future, Africa's Challenge: Early Childhood Care and Development in Sub-Saharan Africa.* Washington, DC: World Bank.

Alesina, A., S. Ozler, N. Roubini, and P. Swagel. 1996. "Political Instability and Economic Growth." *Journal of Economic Growth* 1(2): 189–211.

Alliance Development Works. 2012. *World Risk Report 2012.* Berlin.

Ames, P., V. Rojas, and T. Portugal. 2009. "Starting School: Who is Prepared? Young Lives' Research on Children's Transition to First Grade in Peru." Young Lives Working Paper 47. University of Oxford, Department of International Development, Oxford, UK. www.younglives.org.uk/files/working-papers/wp47-starting-school-who-is-prepared-young-lives2019-research-on-children2019s-transition-to-first-grade-in-peru. Accessed 21 March 2014.

Amsden, A.H. 2001. *The Rise of the 'Rest': Challenges to the West from Late Industrializing Economies.* Oxford, UK: Oxford University Press.

Anand, S., and A. Sen. 2000. "Human Development and Economic Sustainability." *World Development* 28(12): 2029–49. www2.econ.iastate.edu/classes/tsc220/hallam/Readings/AnandSenHumanDevelopmentEconomicSustainability.pdf. Accessed 17 March 2014.

Anda R.F., V.J. Felitti, J. Walker, C.L. Whitfield, J.D. Bremner, B.D. Perry, S.R. Dube, and W.H. Giles. 2006. "The Enduring Effects of Abuse and Related Adverse Experiences in Childhood: A Convergence of Evidence from Neurobiology and Epidemiology." *European Archives of Psychiatry and Clinical Neuroscience* 56(3): 174–86.

Ardila, A., M. Rosselli, E. Matute, and S. Guajardo. 2005. "The Influence of the Parents' Educational Level on the Development of Executive Functions." *Developmental Neuropsychology* 28(1): 539–60. http://psy2.fau.edu/~rosselli/NeuroLab/pdfs/parents_effect_on_executive_function.pdf. Accessed 19 March 2014.

Armecin, G., J.R. Behrman, P. Duazo, S. Ghuman, S. Gultiano, E.M. King, and N. Lee. 2006. "Early Childhood Development through an Integrated Program: Evidence from the Philippines." Policy Research Working Paper 3922. World Bank, Washington, DC.

Arriagada, I. 1994. "Changes in the Urban Female Labour Market." *CEPAL Review* 53: 92–110.

Assaad, R., and D. Levison. 2013. "Employment for Youth—A Growing Challenge for the Global Economy." Background paper for the High Level Panel on the Post-2015 UN MDG Development Agenda. www.post2015hlp.org/wp-content/uploads/2013/06/Assaad-Levison-Global-Youth-Employment-Challenge-Edited-June-5.pdf. Accessed 21 March 2014.

Assimaidou K., Y. Kiendrebeogo, and A. Tall. 2013. "Social Protection for Poverty Reduction in Times of Crisis." Etudes et Documents 11. Centre d'Études et de Recherches sur le Développement International, Clermont-Ferrand, France. http://cerdi.org/uploads/ed/2013/2013.11.pdf. Accessed 15 May 2014.

Atkinson, A. 2013. "Ensuring Social Inclusion in Changing Labour and Capital Markets." European Economy—Economic Papers 481. European Commission, Directorate General Economic and Monetary Affairs, Brussels.

Bahçe, S.A.K., and E. Memiş. 2013. "Estimating the Impact of the 2008–09 Economic Crisis on Work Time in Turkey." *Feminist Economics* 19(3): 181–207. http://dx.doi.org/10.1080/13545701.2013.786182. Accessed 25 March 2014.

Baird, S., J. Friedman, and N. Schady. 2007. "Aggregate Income Shocks and Infant Mortality in the Developing World." Policy Research Working Paper 4346. World Bank, Washington, DC. http://elibrary.worldbank.org/doi/pdf/10.1596/1813-9450-4346. Accessed 28 March 2014.

Baldwin, P. 1990. *The Politics of Social Solidarity: Class Bases of the European Welfare State, 1875–1975.* Cambridge, UK: Cambridge University Press.

Bandura, A. 2000. "Exercise of Human Agency through Collective Efficacy." *Current Directions in Psychological Science* 9(3): 75–78.

Bangladesh Accord Foundation. 2013. "Accord on Fire and Building Safety in Bangladesh." http://bangladeshaccord.org/wp-content/uploads/2013/10/the_accord.pdf. Accessed 16 November 2013.

Bank for International Settlements. 2013. "Triennial Central Bank Survey: Foreign Exchange Turnover in April 2013: Preliminary Global Results." Monetary and Economic Department, Basel, Switzerland. www.bis.org/publ/rpfx13fx.pdf. Accessed 20 January 2014.

Bardasi, E., and S.P. Jenkins. 2002. *Income in Later Life: Work History Matters.* Bristol, UK: The Policy Press. www.jrf.org.uk/sites/files/jrf/jr111-income-later-life.pdf. Accessed 25 March 2014.

Bargain, O., and P. Kwenda. 2009. "The Informal Sector Wage Gap: New Evidence Using Quantile Estimations on Panel Data." Discussion Paper 4286. Institute for the Study of Labour, Bonn, Germany. http://d-nb.info/996172467/34. Accessed 25 March 2014.

Barrientos, A. 2006. "Ageing, Poverty and Public Policy in Developing Countries: New Survey Evidence." In P.A. Kemp, K. Van den Bosch, and L. Smith, eds., *Social Protection in an Ageing World.* International Studies on Social Security Vol. 13. Oxford, UK: Intersentia.

Barrientos, S.W. 2013. "'Labour Chains': Analysing the Role of Labour Contractors in Global Production Networks." *Journal of Development Studies* 49(8): 1058–71.

Basu, K., and P.H. Van. 1998. "The Economics of Child Labor." *American Economic Review* 88(3): 412–27. http://qed.econ.queensu.ca/pub/faculty/sumon/basu_childlabor.pdf. Accessed 20 March 2014.

Beales, S. 2012. "Empowerment and Older People: Enhancing Capabilities in an Ageing World." Paper prepared for the Expert Group Meeting on promoting people's empowerment in achieving poverty eradication, social integration and productive and decent work for all, 10–12 September, New York. www.un.org/esa/socdev/egms/docs/2012/SylviaBeales.pdf. Accessed 26 March 2014.

Beegle, K., D. Filmer, A. Stokes, and L. Tiererova. 2009. "Orphanhood and the Living Arrangements of Children in Sub-Saharan Africa." Policy Research Working Paper 4889. Washington, DC: World Bank. www-wds.worldbank.org/servlet/WDSContentServer/WDSP/IB/2009/07/24/000112742_20090724110307/Rendered/PDF/WPS4889.pdf. Accessed 26 March 2014.

Bénabou, R. 2000. "Unequal Societies: Income Distribution and the Social Contract." *American Economic Review* 90(1): 96–129.

Bénabou, R., and J. Tirole. 2011. *Laws and Norms.* NBER Working Paper 17579. Cambridge, MA: National Bureau of Economic Research.

Béné, C., R.G. Wood, A. Newsham, and M. Davies. 2012. "Resilience: New Utopia or New Tyranny? Reflection about the Potentials and Limits of the Concept of Resilience in Relation to Vulnerability Reduction Programmes." Working Paper 405. Institute of Development Studies, Brighton, UK.

Berg, A., and J. Ostry. 2011a. "Equality and Efficiency." *Finance & Development* 48(3): 12–15.

———. **2011b.** "Inequality and Unsustainable Growth: Two Sides of the Same Coin?" Staff Discussion Note 11/08. International Monetary Fund, Washington, DC.

Berg, J. 2009. "Brazil: The Minimum Wage as a Response to the Crisis." ILO Notes on the Crisis. International Labour Organization, Geneva.

Berik, G., and E. Kongar. 2013. "Time Allocation of Married Mothers and Fathers in Hard Times: The 2007–09 U.S. Recession." *Feminist Economics* 19(3): 208–37. http://dx.doi.org/10.1080/13545701.2013.798425. Accessed 25 March 2014.

Berliner, L., and D.M. Elliott. 1996. "Sexual Abuse of Children." In J. Briere, L. Berliner, J.A. Bulkley, C. Jenny, and T. Reid, eds., *The APSAC Handbook on Child Maltreatment*. Thousand Oaks, CA: Sage Publications.

Bettin, G., A.F. Presbitero, and N. Spatafora. 2014. "Remittances and Vulnerability in Developing Countries." Working Paper WP/14/13. International Monetary Fund, Washington, DC. www.imf.org/external/pubs/ft/wp/2014/wp1413.pdf. Accessed 27 March 2014.

Bhutta, Z.A. 2002. "Children of War: The Real Casualties of the Afghan Conflict." *British Medical Journal* 324(7333): 349–52.

Black, R.E., L.H. Allen, Z.A. Bhutta, L.E. Caulfield, M. de Onis, M. Ezzati, C. Mathers, and J. Rivera. 2008. "Maternal and Child Undernutrition Study Group. Maternal and Child Undernutrition: Global and Regional Exposures and Health Consequences." *Lancet* 371(9608): 243–60.

Bluedorn, M.J.C., R. Duttagupta, J. Guajardo, and P. Topalova. 2013. "Capital Flows are Fickle: Anytime, Anywhere." Working Paper WP/13/183. International Monetary Fund, Washington, DC. www.imf.org/external/pubs/ft/wp/2013/wp13183.pdf. Accessed 24 March 2014.

Bonilla García, A., and J.V. Gruat. 2003. "Social Protection: A Life Cycle Continuum Investment for Social Justice, Poverty Reduction and Sustainable Development." International Labour Organization, Social Protection Section, Geneva. www.ilo.org/public/english/protection/download/lifecycl/lifecycle.pdf. Accessed 15 May 2014.

Bornstein, M.H., and D. Putnick. 2012. "Cognitive and Socioemotional Caregiving in Developing Countries." *Child Development* 83(1): 46–61.

Bornstein, M.H., C.S. Tamis-Lemonda, C.S. Hahn, and O.M. Haynes. 2008. "Maternal Responsiveness to Young Children at Three Ages: Longitudinal Analysis of a Multidimensional, Modular, and Specific Parenting Construct." *Developmental Psychology* 44(3): 867–74.

Bos, K.J., N. Fox, C.H. Zeanah, and C.A. Nelson. 2009. "Effects of Early Psychosocial Deprivation on the Development of Memory and Executive Function." *Frontiers in Behavioral Neuroscience* 3: 16.

Boudet, A.M.M., P. Petesch, C. Turk, and A. Thumala. 2012. *On Norms and Agency: Conversations about Gender Equality with Women and Men in 20 Countries*. Washington, DC: World Bank.

Boyden, J. 2009. "Risk and Capability in the Context of Adversity: Children's Contributions to Household Livelihoods in Ethiopia." *Children, Youth and Environments* 19(2): 111–137. www.colorado.edu/journals/cye/19_2/19_2_07_Ethiopia.pdf. Accessed 27 March 2014.

Boyden, J., A. Hardgrove, and C. Knowles. 2012. "Continuity and Change in Poor Children's Lives: Evidence from Young Lives." In A. Minujin and S. Nandy, eds., *Global Child Poverty and Well-being: Measurement, Concepts, Policy and Action*. Bristol, UK: Policy Press.

Brand, J.E., B.R. Levy, and W.T. Gallo. 2008. "Effects of Layoffs and Plant Closings on Depression among Older Workers." *Research on Aging* 30(6): 701–21. www.ncbi.nlm.nih.gov/pmc/articles/PMC2792935/. Accessed 25 March 2014.

Brooks-Gunn, J., and G.J. Duncan. 1997. "The Effects of Poverty on Children." *The Future of Children* 7(2): 55–71.

Bunting, L., and C. McAuley. 2004. "Research Review: Teenage Pregnancy and Motherhood: The Contribution of Support." *Child and Family Social Work* 9(2): 207–15.

Burgard, S.A., J.E. Brand, and J.S. House. 2007. "Toward a Better Estimation of the Effect of Job Loss on Health." *Journal of Health and Social Behavior* 48(4): 369–84. http://sarahburgard.com/pdf/Burgard%20Brand%20and%20House%202007%20JHSB.pdf. Accessed 25 March 2014.

Burger, R., and R. Jafta. 2010. "Affirmative Action in South Africa: An Empirical Assessment of the Impact on Labour Market Outcomes." Working Paper 76. Oxford University, Centre for Research on Inequality, Human Security and Ethnicity, Oxford, UK.

Burkhauser, R.V., J.S. Butler, and K.C. Holden. 1991. "How the Death of a Spouse Affects Economic Well-being after Retirement: A Hazard Model Approach." *Social Science Quarterly* 72: 504–19.

Burkhauser, R.V., K.C. Holden, and D. Feaster. 1988. "Incidence, Timing and Events associated with Poverty: A Dynamic View of Poverty in Retirement." *Journal of Gerontology* 43(2): S46–S52.

Burns, J., L. Edwards, and K. Pauw. 2010. "Wage Subsidies to Combat Unemployment and Poverty: Assessing South Africa's Options." Discussion Paper 00969. International Food Policy Research Institute, Washington, DC.

Cameron, N., M.A. Preece, and T.J. Cole. 2005. "Catch-up Growth or Regression to the Mean? Recovery from Stunting Revisited." *American Journal of Human Biology* 17(4): 412–17.

Canis, B. 2011. "The Motor Vehicle Supply Chain: Effects of the Japanese Earthquake and Tsunami." Congressional Research Service, Washington, DC. www.fas.org/sgp/crs/misc/R41831.pdf. Accessed 19 March 2014.

Cannon, T., and D. Muller-Mahn. 2010. "Vulnerability, Resilience and Development Discourses in Context of Climate Change." *Natural Hazards* 55(3): 621–35.

Carneiro, J. 2013. "Brazil's Universities Take Affirmative Action." BBC Brasil, 28 August. www.bbc.co.uk/news/business-23862676. Accessed 15 May 2014.

Carneiro, P., and J. Heckman. 2003. *Human Capital Policy*. NBER Working Paper 9495. Cambridge, MA: National Bureau of Economic Research. www.nber.org/papers/w9495.pdf. Accessed 19 March 2014.

Casale, D. 2003. "The Rise in Female Labour Force Participation in South Africa: An Analysis of Household Survey Data, 1995-2001." Ph.D. dissertation. University of KwaZulu-Natal, Division of Economics, South Africa.

Cattaneo, O., G. Gereffi, and C. Staritz, eds. 2010. *Global Value Chains in a Postcrisis World: A Development Perspective*. Washington, DC: World Bank.

CDP (Carbon Disclosure Project). 2013. *Sector Insights: What Is Driving Climate Change Action in the World's Largest Companies? Global 500 Climate Change Report 2013*. London. https://www.cdp.net/cdpresults/cdp-global-500-climate-change-report-2013.pdf. Accessed 24 March 2014.

Cerrutti, M. 2000. "Economic Reform, Structural Adjustment and Female Labor Force Participation in Buenos Aires, Argentina." *World Development* 28(5): 879–91.

Chalabi, M., and J. Holder. 2013. "WHO Report into Violence against Women: Key Data." *The Guardian*. Datablog, 20 June. www.theguardian.com/news/datablog/2013/jun/20/women-violence-worldwide-statistics-who. Accessed 28 March 2014.

Chambers, R. 1989. "Editorial Introduction: Vulnerability, Coping and Policy." *IDS Bulletin* 20(2): 1–7.

———. 2006. "Vulnerability, Coping and Policy (Editorial Introduction)." *IDS Bulletin* 37(4): 33–40.

Chang, H. 1993. *The Political Economy of Industrial Policy*. New York: Palgrave Macmillan.

Châtaigner J.-M. 2014. *Fragilités et résilience ; les nouvelles frontières de la mondialisation*. Paris: Karthala.

Chatterjee, A. 2009. "The UN at Sixty Three: Problems and Prospects of Reforming a Veteran." *Journal of Management and Social Sciences* 5(1): 22–29. http://biztek.edu.pk/downloads/research/jmss_v5_n1/3%20The%20UN%20at%20Sixty%20three.pdf?origin=publication_detail. Accessed 27 March 2014.

Chen, S., and M. Ravallion. 2012. "Absolute Poverty Measures for the Developing World." In *Measuring the Real Size of the World Economy*. Washington, DC: World Bank.

China National Bureau of Statistics. 2011. *China Statistical Yearbook 2011*. Beijing.

Cho, Y., and D. Newhouse. 2013. "How Did the Great Recession Affect Different Types of Workers? Evidence from 17 Middle-Income Countries." *World Development* 41: 31–50.

Choudhury, C. 2013. "India Weathers Cyclone Phailin." Bloomberg, 16 October. www.bloomberg.com/news/2013-10-16/india-weathers-cyclone-phailin.html. Accessed 14 May 2014.

Conceição, P., S. Mukherjee, and S. Nayyar. 2011. "Impacts of the Economic Crisis on Human Development and the MDGs in Africa." *African Development Review* 23(4): 439–60.

Cornia, G.A., and F. Stewart. 1993. "Two Errors of Targeting." *Journal of International Development* 5: 459–96.

CRED (Centre for Research on the Epidemiology of Disasters). 2013. EM-DAT: The International Disaster Database: Disaster trends. Catholic University of Louvain, Belgium. www.emdat.be/disaster-trends. Accessed 12 April 2014.

Crouch, C. 2011. *The Strange Non-Death of Neo-Liberalism*. Cambridge, UK: Polity.

Culpeper, R. 2006. "Reforming the Global Financial Architecture: The Potential of Regional Institutions." In J. A. Ocampo, ed., *Regional Financial Cooperation*. Washington DC: Brookings Institution Press.

Cutler, D.M., F. Knaul, R. Lozano, O. Mendez, and B. Zurita. 2002. "Financial Crisis, Health Outcomes, and Aging: Mexico in the 1980s and 1990s." *Journal of Public Economics* 84(2): 279–303.

Cutter, S., C. Emrich, J. Webb, and D. Morath. 2009. "Social Vulnerability to Climate Variability Hazards: A Review of the Literature." Final Report to Oxfam America. University of South Carolina, Department of Geography, Hazards and Vulnerability Research Institute, Columbia, SC.

Dalman, C., and S. Bremberg. 1999. "How Do We Invest in the Children? Child Welfare Measures in the County of Stockholm, Measured in SEK." Centre for Child and Adolescent Health, Stockholm.

Darity, W., and A. Goldsmith. 1996. "Social Psychology, Unemployment and Macroeconomics." *Journal of Economic Perspectives* 10(1): 121–40.

Date-Bah, E. 2003. *Jobs after War: A Critical Challenge in the Peace and Reconstruction Puzzle.* Geneva: International Labour Office.

Davidson, D.J. 2010. "The Applicability of the Concept of Resilience to Social Systems: Some Sources of Optimism and Nagging Doubts." Society and Natural Resources 23(12): 1135–49.

Davies, R.B., and K.C. Vadlamannati. 2013. "A Race to the Bottom in Labor Standards? An Empirical Investigation." *Journal of Development Economics* 103: 1–14.

Davies, S.E., and L. Glanville. 2010. *Protecting the Displaced: Deepening the Responsibility to Protect.* Leiden, the Netherlands: Martinus Nijhoff Publishers.

Deacon, B., and S. Cohen. 2011. "From the Global Politics of Poverty Alleviation to the Global Politics of Social Solidarity." *Global Social Policy* 11(2–3): 233–249.

Devereux, S., and C. Solomon. 2006. "Employment Creation Programmes: The International Experience." Issues in Employment and Poverty Discussion Paper 24. International Labour Organization, Geneva.

DFID (UK Department for International Development). 2001. *Making Government Work for Poor People: Building State Capability.* London. www.gsdrc.org/docs/open/tsp.pdf. Accessed 28 March 2014.

———. **2010.** "Building Peaceful States and Societies." A DFID Practice Paper. London. www.gsdrc.org/docs/open/CON75.pdf. Accessed 15 May 2014.

Drèze J., and A. Sen. 1989. *Hunger and Public Action.* Oxford, UK: Clarendon Press.

Duflo, E. 2000. *Grandmothers and Granddaughters: Old Age Pension and Intra-Household Allocation in South Africa.* Working Paper 8061. Cambridge, MA: National Bureau of Economic Research. www.nber.org/papers/w8061.pdf?new_window=1. Accessed 26 March 2014.

Dunai, M. 2013. "Hungarian Roma Queue for Water in Heatwave after pumps shut down." Reuters, 9 August. www.reuters.com/article/2013/08/09/us-hungary-roma-water-heat-idUSBRE9760ZI20130809. Accessed 28 March 2014.

Duryea, S., and M. Morales. 2011. "Effects of the Global Financial Crisis on Children's School and Employment Outcomes in El Salvador." *Development Policy Review* 29(5): 527–46.

Dutta, I., J. Foster, and A. Mishra. 2011. "On Measuring Vulnerability to Poverty." *Social Choice and Welfare* 37(4): 743–61.

Easterly, W., J. Ritzen, and M. Woolcock. 2006. "Social Cohesion, Institutions, and Growth." *Economics and Politics* 18(2): 103–20. http://ssrn.com/abstract=909632 or http://dx.doi.org/10.1111/j.1468-0343.2006.00165.x. Accessed 15 May 2014.

EC (European Commission). 2013a. Eurostat database: General government deficit/surplus. http://epp.eurostat.ec.europa.eu/tgm/table.do?tab=table&init=1&language=en&pcode=tec00127&plugin=1. Accessed 9 December 2013.

———. **2013b.** Eurostat database: General government gross debt. http://epp.eurostat.ec.europa.eu/tgm/table.do?tab=table&init=1&language=en&pcode=tsdde410&plugin=1. Accessed 9 December 2013.

ECLAC (Economic Commission for Latin America and the Caribbean. 2011. "El Envejecimiento y las Personas de Edad. Indicadores para América Latina y el Caribe." Santiago de Chile. www.cepal.org/celade/noticias/documentosdetrabajo/3/39343/Separata_Indicadores_Envejecimiento.pdf. Accessed 28 March 2014.

***The Economist.* 2013a.** "Affirmative Action in Brazil: Slavery's Legacy." Americas View blog, 26 April. www.economist.com/blogs/americasview/2013/04/affirmative-action-brazil. Accessed 15 May 2014.

———. **2013b.** "Poverty: Not Always with Us." 1 June.

Eliason, M., and D. Storrie. 2009. "Does Job Loss Shorten Life?" *Journal of Human Resources* 44(2): 277–382.

Emmerson, C., and A. Muriel. 2008. "Financial Resources and Well-being." In J. Banks, E. Breeze, C. Lessof, and J. Nazroo, eds., *Living in the 21st Century: Older People in England. The 2006 English Longitudinal Study of Ageing (Wave 3).* London: Institute for Fiscal Studies.

Engel, S. and A.M. Ibanez. 2007. "Displacement Due to Violence in Colombia: A Household-Level Analysis." *Economic Development and Cultural Change* 55(2): 335–65.

Engle, P.L., M.M. Black, J.R. Behrman, M. Cabral de Mello, P.J. Gertler, L. Kapiriri, R. Martorell, and M.E. Young. 2007. "Strategies to Avoid the Loss of Developmental Potential in More than 200 Million Children in the Developing World." *Lancet* 369(9557): 229–42.

Engle, P.L, L.C. Fernald, H. Alderman, J. Behrman, C. O'Gara, A. Yousafzai, M. Cabral de Mello, M. Hidrobo, N. Ulkuer, I. Ertem, S. Iltus, and the Global Development Steering Group. 2011. "Strategies for Reducing Inequalities and Improving Developmental Outcomes for Young Children in Low-Income and Middle-Income Countries." *Lancet* 378(9799): 1339–53.

Engle, P.L., N. Rao, and O. Petrovic. 2013. "Situational Analysis of Young Children in a Changing World." In P. Rebello Britto, P.L. Engle, and C.M. Super, eds., *Handbook of Early Childhood Development. Research and Its Impact on Global Policy.* New York: Oxford University Press.

Equality Now. 2011. *Discrimination against Women in Law.* New York. www.equalitynow.org/sites/default/files/WG_Report_EN.pdf. Accessed 28 March 2014.

ESCWA (Economic and Social Commission for Western Asia). 2007. *The Impact of Armed Conflict on Women.* Beirut.

Esping-Andersen, G. 1999. *Social Foundations of Postindustrial Economies.* Oxford, UK: Oxford University Press.

Esping-Andersen, G., and J. Myles. 2008. "The Welfare State and Redistribution." Unpublished manuscript. http://dcpis.upf.edu/~gosta-esping-andersen/materials/welfare_state.pdf. Accessed 15 May 2014.

EU (European Union). 2007. "Treaty of Lisbon." http://europa.eu/lisbon_treaty/full_text/index_en.htm. Accessed 20 March 2014.

European Parliamentary Research Service. 2013. "Women in Politics: Background Notes on 12 Countries." Brussels. www.europarl.europa.eu/eplibrary/EPRS-Background-Notes.pdf. Accessed 28 March 2014.

Evans, P., and P. Heller. Forthcoming. "Human Development, State Transformation and the Politics of the Developmental State." In S. Leibfried, F. Nullmeier, E. Huber, M. Lange, J. Levy, and J.D. Stephens, eds., *The Oxford Handbook of Transformations of the State.* Oxford, UK: Oxford University Press.

Evans, P., and W.H. Sewell. 2013. "The Neo-Liberal Era: Ideology, Policy and Social Effect." In P.A. Hall and M. Lamont, eds., *Social Resilience in the Neoliberal Era.* Cambridge, UK: Cambridge University Press.

Falkingham, J. 2000. "From Security to Uncertainty: The Impact of Economic Change on Child Welfare in Central Asia." Working Paper 76. United Nations Children's Fund Innocenti Research Centre, Florence, Italy. www.unicef-irc.org/publications/pdf/iwp76.pdf. Accessed 25 March 2014.

Fang, C., D. Yang, and W. Meiyan. 2010. "Employment and Inequality Outcomes in China." Paper presented at the Organisation for Economic Co-operation and Development and European Union Joint High-Level Conference, 19 May, Paris. www.oecd.org/els/emp/42546043.pdf. Accessed 22 May 2014.

FAO (Food and Agriculture Organization of the United Nations). 2013. "FAO Food Price Index." www.fao.org/worldfoodsituation/foodpricesindex/. Accessed 18 February 2014.

FAO (Food and Agriculture Organization of the United Nations), IFAD (International Fund for Agricultural Development) and WFP (World Food Programme). 2013. *The State of Food Insecurity in the World 2013: The Multiple Dimensions of Food Security.* Rome.

Felitti, V.J., R.F. Anda, D. Nordenberg, D.F. Williamson, A.M. Spitz, V. Edwards, M.P. Koss, and J.S. Marks. 1998. "The Relationship of Childhood Abuse and Household Dysfunction to Many of the Leading Causes of Death in Adults: The Adverse Childhood Experiences (ACE) Study." *American Journal of Preventive Medicine* 14(4): 245–58.

Fenner, F., D.A. Henderson, I. Arita, Z. Ježek, and I.D. Ladnyi. 1988. *Smallpox and its Eradication.* Geneva: World Health Organization.

Ferri, G., L.G. Liu, and J. Stiglitz. 1999. "The Procyclical Role of Rating Agencies: Evidence from the East Asian Crisis." *Economic Notes* 28(3): 335–55.

Ferris, E., D. Petz, and C. Stark. 2013. "The Year of Recurring Disasters: A Review of Natural Disasters in 2012." Brookings Institution–London School of Economics, Project on Internal Displacement, Washington, DC. www.brookings.edu/research/reports/2013/03/natural-disaster-review-ferris. Accessed 28 March 2014.

Fischer, A.M. 2008. "Resolving the Theoretical Ambiguities of Social Exclusion with Reference to Polarisation and Conflict." DESTIN Working Paper 08-90. London School of Economics and Political Science, Development Studies Institute, London. www.lse.ac.uk/

internationalDevelopment/
pdf/WP/WP90.pdf. Accessed 20 March 2014.

———. 2013. "The Social Value of Employment and the Redistributive Imperative for Development." Occasional Paper. United Nations Development Programme, Human Development Report Office, New York.

Fitoussi, J.P., and K. Malik. 2013. "Choices, Capabilities and Sustainability." Occasional Paper. United Nations Development Programme, Human Development Report Office, New York.

Frankenberg, E., T. Duncan, and K. Beege. 1999. "The Real Cost of Indonesia's Economic Crisis: Preliminary Findings from the Indonesia Life Surveys." Labor and Population Program Working Paper 99-04. RAND, Santa Monica, CA. www.rand.org/content/dam/rand/pubs/drafts/2008/DRU2064.pdf. Accessed 20 March 2014.

Fraser, S., G. Leonard, I. Matsuo, and H. Murakami. 2012. "Tsunami Evacuation: Lessons from the Great East Japan Earthquake and Tsunami of March 11th 2011." GNS Science Report 2012/17. Institute of Geological and Nuclear Sciences, Lower Hutt, New Zealand.

Frazer, H., and E. Marlier. 2012. 2011 Assessment of Social Inclusion Policy Developments in the EU: Main Findings and Suggestions on the Way Forward. European Commission, Directorate General of Employment, Social Affairs and Inclusion, Brussels.

Friedman, J., and N. Schady. 2009. "How Many More Infants Are Likely to Die in Africa as a Result of the Global Financial Crisis?" Policy Research Working Paper 5023. World Bank, Washington, DC. http://econ.worldbank.org/external/default/main?pagePK=64165259&theSitePK=469372&piPK=64165421&menuPK=64166093&entityID=000158349_20090820140450&cid=decresearch%22. Accessed 28 March 2014.

Fuentes-Nieva, R., and N. Galasso. 2014. "Working for the Few: Political Capture and Economic Inequality." Briefing Paper 178. Oxfam, Oxford, UK. www.oxfam.org/sites/www.oxfam.org/files/bp-working-for-few-political-capture-economic-inequality-200114-en.pdf. Accessed 17 March 2014.

Funk, A., J.L. Lang, and J. Osterhaus. 2005. Ending Violence against Women and Girls: Protecting Human Rights. Good Practices for Development Cooperation. Deutsche Gesellschaft für Internationale Zusammenarbeit, Planning and Development Department Governance and Democracy, Eschborn, Germany. http://www2.gtz.de/dokumente/bib/05-1048.pdf. Accessed 26 March 2014.

Furceri, D. 2009. "Stabilization Effects of Social Spending: Empirical Evidence from a Panel of OECD Countries Overcoming the Financial Crisis in the United States." OECD Economics Department Working Paper 675. Organisation for Economic Co-operation and Development, Paris.

Furceri, D., and P. Loungani. 2013. "Who Let the Gini Out?" Finance & Development 50(4): 25–27.

G20 (Group of Twenty). 2011. "G20 Coherent Conclusions for the Management of Capital Flows Drawing on Country Experiences." 15 October. www.g20.utoronto.ca/2011/2011-finance-capital-flows-111015-en.pdf. Accessed 24 March 2014.

———. 2013. "Tax Annex to the St. Petersburg G20 Leaders' Declaration." http://en.g20russia.ru/news/20130906/782776427.html. Accessed 20 March 2014.

Gagro, S. 2010. "The Crime of Rape in the ICTY's and the ICTR's Case-Law." Zbornik PFZ 60(3): 1309–34.

Gallagher, K.P., S. Griffith-Jones, and J.A. Ocampo, eds. 2012. Regulating Global Capital Flows for Long-Run Development. Pardee Center Task Force Report. Boston, MA: Boston University, Fredrick S. Pardee Center for the Study of the Longer Range Future. http://stephanygj.net/papers/RegulatingGlobalCapitalFlowsForLongRunDevelopment2012.pdf. Accessed 24 March 2014.

Gallopín, G.C. 2006. "Linkages between Vulnerability, Resilience, and Adaptive Capacity." Global Environmental Change 16(3): 293–303.

Gallup. 2013. Gallup World Poll Database. http://worldview.gallup.com. Accessed 15 October 2013.

Gasper, D., and O. Gomez. 2014. "Evolution of Thinking and Research on Human Security and Personal Security 1994–2013." Human Development Research Paper. United Nations Development Programme, Human Development Report Office, New York.

Gassmann, F., and C. Behrendt. 2006. "Cash Benefits in Low-income Countries: Simulating the Effects on Poverty Reduction for Tanzania and Senegal." Issues in Social Protection Discussion Paper 15. International Labour Organization, Social Security Department, Geneva. www.gsdrc.org/docs/open/SP21.pdf. Accessed 15 May 2014.

Gavrilovic, M., C. Harper, N. Jones, R. Marcus, and P. Pereznieto. 2009. "Impact of the Economic Crisis and Food and Fuel Price Volatility on Children and Women in Kazakhstan." Report for UNICEF Kazakhstan Office. Overseas Development Institute, London.

Ghanem, H. 2011. "How to Stop the Rise in Food Price Volatility." 13 January. Carnegie Endowment for International Peace, Washington, DC. http://carnegieendowment.org/2011/01/13/how-to-stop-rise-in-food-price-volatility/3bs. Accessed 24 March 2014.

Global Footprint Network. 2014. National Footprint Accounts, 2014 Edition. Oakland, CA.

Grabel, I. 2012. "Financial Architectures and Development: Resilience, Policy Space, and Human Development in the Global South." Working Paper 281. University of Massachusetts Amherst, Political Economy Research Institute, Amherst, MA. www.peri.umass.edu/fileadmin/pdf/working_papers/working_papers_251-300/WP281.pdf. Accessed 24 March 2014.

Gupta, N.D., and M. Larssen. 2010. "Evaluating Labour Market Effects of Wage Subsidies for the Disabled—The Danish Flexjob Scheme." Working Paper 07:2010. Danish National Centre for Social Research, Copenhagen. http://pisa2012.dk/Files/Filer/SFI/Pdf/Working_papers/wp-07-2010.pdf. Accessed 15 May 2014.

Gupta, S., and I.S. Leung. 2011. "Turning Good Practices into Institutional Mechanisms: Investing in Grassroots Women's Leadership to Scale Up Local Implementation of the Hyogo Framework for Action." An In-depth Study for the HFA Mid-Term Review. Huairou Commission and GROOTS International, New York. www.unisdr.org/files/18197_201guptaandleung.theroleofwomenasaf.pdf. Accessed 28 March 2014.

Ha, B., C. McInerney, S. Tobin, and R. Torres. 2010. "Youth Employment in Crisis." Discussion Paper DP/201/2010. International Institute for Labour Studies, Geneva. www.ilo.org/wcmsp5/groups/public/---dgreports/---inst/documents/publication/wcms_192840.pdf. Accessed 21 March 2014.

Hackman, D.A., M.J. Farah, and M.J. Meaney. 2010. "Socioeconomic Status and the Brain: Mechanistic Insights from Human and Animal Research." Nature Reviews Neuroscience 11(9): 651–59.

Hale, T. 2014. "Improving Global Collective Action in a Connected World." Human Development Research Paper. United Nations Development Programme, Human Development Report Office, New York.

Hale, T., D. Held, and K. Young. 2013. Gridlock: Why Global Cooperation Is Failing When We Need It Most. Cambridge, UK: Polity.

Hall, P.A., and M. Lamont. 2013. Social Resilience in the Neoliberal Era. Cambridge, UK: Cambridge University Press.

Hallegatte, S., F. Henriet, A. Patwardhan, K. Narayanan, S. Ghosh, S. Karmakar, U. Patnaik, A. Abhayankar, S. Pohit, J. Corfee-Morlot, C. Herweijer, N. Ranger, S. Bhattacharya, M. Bachu, S. Priya, K. Dhore, F. Rafique, P. Mathur, and N. Naville. 2010. "Flood Risks, Climate Change Impacts and Adaptation Benefits in Mumbai: An Initial Assessment of Socio-Economic Consequences of Present and Climate Change Induced Flood Risks and of Possible Adaptation Options." Environment Working Paper 27. Organisation for Economic Co-operation and Development, Paris. http://dx.doi.org/10.1787/5km4hv6wb434-en. Accessed 27 March 2014.

Hamdani, K. 2014. "Trans-border Vulnerabilities" Human Development Research Paper. United Nations Development Programme, Human Development Report Office, New York.

Haque, U., M. Hashizume, K.N. Kolivras, H.J. Overgaard, B. Das, and T. Yamamoto. 2012. "Reduced Death Rates from Cyclones in Bangladesh: What More Needs to Be Done?" Bulletin of the World Health Organization 90: 150–56.

Hardgrove, A. 2012. "Life after Guns: The Life Chances and Trajectories of Ex-combatant and Other Post-war Youth in Monrovia, Liberia." DPhil thesis. University of Oxford, Department of International Development, Oxford, UK.

Hardgrove, A., K. Pells, P. Dornan, and J. Boyden. 2014. "Life Course Vulnerabilities for Youth: The Trouble in Transitions." Human Development Research Paper. United Nations Development Programme, Human Development Report Office, New York.

Hart, B., and T.R. Risley. 1995. Meaningful Differences in the Everyday Experience of Young American Children. Baltimore, MD: Paul H. Brookes Publishing.

Harvard Law and Policy Review. 2013. "India's Parliament Passes New Law on Sexual Offenses." 2 April. http://www3.law.harvard.edu/journals/hlpr/2013/04/indias-parliament-passes-new-law-on-sexual-offenses/#more-16. Accessed 27 March 2014.

Haughton, J., and S.H. Khandker. 2012. "The Surprising Effects of the Great Recession: Losers and Winners in Thailand in 2008-2009." Policy Research Working Paper 6255. World Bank, Washington, DC. http://elibrary.worldbank.org/doi/pdf/10.1596/1813-9450-6255. Accessed 15 May 2014.

Hausmann, R. 2013. "The Logic of the Informal Economy." Project Syndicate, 19 June. www.project-syndicate.org/commentary/the-logic-of-the-informal-economy-by-ricardo-hausmann. Accessed 15 May 2014.

Heath, R. 2012. "Women's Access to Labour Market Opportunities, Control of Household Resources, and Domestic Violence." Policy Research Working Paper 6149. World Bank, Washington, DC. http://econ.worldbank.org/external/default/main?pagePK=64165259&theSitePK=469372&piPK=64165421&menuPK=64166093&entityID=000158349_20120726090130. Accessed 25 March 2014.

Heckman, J. 2005. "Skill Formation and the Economics of Investing in Disadvantaged Children." *Science* 312(5782): 1900–02.

———. 2013. "The Economics of Inequality and Human Development." Keynote presentation at the First National Congress meeting on building a legal framework for public policies for early childhood, 16 April, Brasilia.

Heintz, J. 2012. "Informality, Inclusiveness, and Economic Growth: An Overview of Key Issues." Supporting Inclusive Growth Working Paper 2012/2. International Development Research Centre, Ottawa. www.idrc.ca/EN/Documents/SIG-WP2-Informality.pdf. Accessed 25 March 2014.

Heise, L.H. 1998. "Violence against Women: An Integrated, Ecological Framework." *Violence against Women* (4)3: 262–90.

Held, D., and K. Young. 2011. "Crises in Parallel Worlds: The Governance of Global Risks in Finance, Security and the Environment." In C.J. Calhoun and G.M. Derluguian, eds., *The Deepening Crisis: Governance Challenges After Neoliberalism.* Vol. 2. New York: New York University Press.

———. 2013. "Transforming Global Governance? Structural Deficits and Recent Developments in Security and Finance." In J. Stiglitz and M. Kaldor, eds., *The Quest for Security: Protection Without Protectionism and the Challenge of Global Governance.* New York: Columbia University Press.

Heller, P. 2005. "Understanding Fiscal Space." Policy Discussion Paper PDP/05/4. International Monetary Fund, Washington, DC. www.imf.org/external/pubs/ft/pdp/2005/pdp04.pdf. Accessed 21 April 2014.

———. 2014. "Challenges and Opportunities: Civil Society in a Globalizing World." Human Development Research Paper. United Nations Development Programme, Human Development Report Office, New York.

HelpAge International. 2013. *Global AgeWatch Index 2013: Insight Report.* London.

Herrera, J., D. Milbin, F. Roubaud, C. Saint-Macary, C. Torelli, and C. Zanuso. 2014. *Enquête sur les Conditions de Vie des Ménages Après Séisme ECVMAS-Haïti 2012.* Port au Prince: Institut Haïtien de Statistique et d'Informatique, and Paris: Développement, institutions et mondialisation.

Herztman, C., and T. Boyce. 2010. "How Experience Gets Under the Skin to Create Gradients in Developmental Health." *Annual Review of Public Health* 31: 329–47.

Heyer, J., F. Stewart, and R. Thorp. 1999. "Group Behaviour and Development." Research Paper 161. United Nations University, World Institute for Development Economics Research, Helsinki. http://wider.unu.edu/publications/working-papers/previous/en_GB/wp-161/_files/82530858921501417/default/wp161.pdf. Accessed 15 March 2014.

Hirsch, A. 2012. "Sahel Food Crisis Has Been Made Worse by the Widespread Unrest in Africa." *The Guardian,* 29 March.

Hoeffler, A. 2012. "On the Causes of Civil War." In M.R. Garfinkel and S. Skaperdas, eds., *The Oxford Handbook of the Economics of Peace and Conflict.* New York: Oxford University Press.

Hoekman, B., and W. Martin. 2012. "Reducing Distortions in International Commodity Markets: An Agenda for Multilateral Cooperation." Policy Research Working Paper 5928. World Bank, Poverty Reduction and Economic Management Network, International Trade Department, and Development Research Group, Washington, DC. www-wds.worldbank.org/external/default/WDSContentServer/IW3P/IB/2012/01/03/000158349_20120103113143/Rendered/PDF/WPS5928.pdf. Accessed 24 March 2014.

Hogerzeil, H.V., J. Liberman, V.J. Wirtz, S.P. Kishore, S. Selvaraj, R. Kiddell-Monroe, and T. von Schoen-Angerer. 2013. "Promotion of Access to Essential Medicines for Non-Communicable Diseases: Practical Implications of the UN Political Declaration." *Lancet* 381(9867): 680–89.

Holden, K.C., R.V. Burkhauser, and D.A. Myers. 1986. "Income Transitions at Older Stages of Life: The Dynamics of Poverty." *Gerontologist* 26(3): 292–97.

Holling, C.S. 1973. "Resilience and Stability of Ecological Systems." *Annual Review of Ecology and Systematics* 4: 1–23.

Hollingshead, A. 2010. "The Implied Tax Revenue Loss from Trade Mispricing." Global Financial Integrity, Washington, DC. www.gfintegrity.org/storage/gfip/documents/reports/implied%20tax%20revenue%20loss%20report_final.pdf. Accessed 24 March 2014.

Hoon, H.T. 2011. "Wage Subsidies in a Program for Economic Inclusion and Growth." Singapore Management University, Research Collection School of Economics, Singapore. http://ink.library.smu.edu.sg/cgi/viewcontent.cgi?article=2254&context=soe_research. Accessed 22 April 2014.

Hornborg, A. 2009. "Zero-Sum World Challenges in Conceptualizing Environmental Load Displacement and Ecologically Unequal Exchange in the World-System." International Journal of Comparative Sociology 50(3-4): 237–62.

Hughes, K., M.A. Bellis, L. Jones, S. Wood, G. Bates, L. Eckley, E. McCoy, C. Mikton, T. Shakespeare, and A. Officer. 2012. "Prevalence and Risk of Violence against Adults with Disabilities: A Systematic Review and Meta-analysis of Observational Studies." *Lancet* 379(9826): 1621–29.

IFAD (International Fund for Agricultural Development). 2013. "Climate Facts." www.ifad.org/climate/facts.htm. Accessed 7 November 2013.

ILO (International Labour Organization). 1952. "Social Security (Minimum Standards) Convention." www.ilo.org/dyn/normlex/en/f?p=NORMLEXPUB:12100:0::NO:12100:P12100_ILO_CODE:C102. Accessed 20 March 2014.

———. 2006a. Changing Patterns in the World of Work International Labour Conference. 95th Session. Geneva. http://www.ilo.org/public/english/standards/relm/ilc/ilc95/pdf/rep-i-c.pdf Accessed 22 May 2014

———. 2006b. "Social Security for All: Investing in Global Social and Economic Development: A Consultation." Issues in Social Protection Discussion Paper 16. Geneva.

———. 2008. "Can Low-income Countries Afford Basic Social Security?" Global Campaign on Social Security and Coverage for All Paper 3. Social Security Department, Geneva.

———. 2009. "Protecting People, Promoting Jobs: From Crisis Response to Recovery and Sustainable Growth." Communication to G20 Leaders by ILO Director-General, Pittsburgh Summit, 24–25 September, Pittsburgh, PA.

———. 2010a. *Constitution of the International Labour Organisation and Selected Texts.* Geneva: International Labour Office. www.ilo.org/public/english/bureau/leg/download/constitution.pdf. Accessed 25 March 2014.

———. 2010b. "Pioneering a System of Migration Management in Asia: The Republic of Korea's Employment Permit System Approach to Decent Work." Geneva. www.ilo.org/wcmsp5/groups/public/---asia/---ro-bangkok/documents/publication/wcms_145630.pdf. Accessed 20 March 2014.

———. 2010c. *World Social Security Report 2010/11.* Geneva: International Labour Office. www.ilo.org/wcmsp5/groups/public/---dgreports/---dcomm/---publ/documents/publication/wcms_146566.pdf. Accessed 20 March 2014.

———. 2011a. "Conclusions Concerning the Recurrent Discussion on Social Protection (Social Security)." Adopted at the 100th Session of the International Labour Conference, Geneva.

———. 2011b. *Social Protection Floor for a Fair and Inclusive Globalization.* Report of the Advisory Group chaired by Michelle Bachelet convened by the ILO with the collaboration of the WHO. Geneva: International Labour Office.

———. 2012a. *Global Employment Trends for Youth 2012.* Geneva: International Labour Office. www.ilo.org/w-msp5/groups/public/---dgreports/---dcomm/documents/publication/wcms_180976.pdf. Accessed 21 March 2014.

———. 2012b. "Statistical Update on Employment in the Informal Economy." International Labour Office, Geneva. http://laborsta.ilo.org/applv8/data/INFORMAL_ECONOMY/2012-06-Statistical%20update%-%20v2.pdf. Accessed 15 May 2014.

———. 2012c. *World of Work Report 2012.* Geneva: International Labour Office. www.ilo.org/wcmsp5/groups/public/@dgreports/@dcomm/@publ/documents/publication/wcms_179453.pdf. Accessed 25 March 2014.

———. 2013a. *Global Employment Trends 2013: Recovering from a Second Jobs Dip.* Geneva: International Labour Office. www.ilo.org/wcmsp5/groups/public/---dgreports/---dcomm/---publ/documents/publication/wcms_202326.pdf. Accessed 21 March 2014.

———. 2013b. *Global Employment Trends for Youth 2013: A Generation at Risk.* Geneva: International Labour Office. www.ilo.org/wcmsp5/groups/public/---dgreports/---dcomm/documents/publication/wcms_212423.pdf. Accessed 21 March 2014.

———. 2013c. *Global Wage Report 2012/2013: Wages and Equitable Growth.* Geneva: International Labour Office.

———. 2013d. *Key Indicators of the Labour Market.* 8th ed. Geneva: International Labour Office.

———. 2013e. *World of Work Report 2013: Repairing the Economic and Social Fabric.* Geneva: International Labour Office. www.ilo.org/wcmsp5/groups/public/---dgreports/

---dcomm/documents/publication/wcms_214476.pdf. Accessed 24 March 2014.

———. 2014. *Global Employment Trends 2014: The Risk of a Jobless Recovery.* www.ilo.org/wcmsp5/groups/public/ ---dgreports/---dcomm/---publ/documents/publication/ wcms_233953.pdf. Accessed 21 April 2014.

———. n.d. "Informal Economy." www.ilo.int/global/ topics/employment-promotion/informal-economy/. Accessed 14 May 2014.

ILO (International Labour Organization) and UNDP (United Nations Development Programme). 2011. "Inclusive and Resilient Development: The Role of Social Protection." Paper prepared for the G20 Development Working Group. Geneva.

IMF (International Monetary Fund). 2012. "The Liberalization and Management of Capital Flows: An Institutional View." Washington, DC. www.imf.org/ external/np/pp/eng/2012/111412.pdf. Accessed 24 March 2014.

———. 2014. *World Economic Outlook: April 2014.* Washington, DC.

Internal Displacement Monitoring Centre. 2013. *Global Overview 2012: People Internally Displaced by Conflict and Violence.* Geneva. www.internal-displacement.org/ publications/2013/global-overview-2012-people-internally -displaced-by-conflict-and-violence. Accessed 20 March 2014.

International Dialogue on Peacebuilding and Statebuilding. 2011. *A New Deal for Engagement in Fragile States.* www.newdeal4peace.org/wp-content/ uploads/2013/01/new-deal-for-engagement-in-fragile -states-en.pdf. Accessed 20 March 2014.

International Policy Centre for Inclusive Growth. 2009. "What Explains the Decline in Brazil's Inequality?" One Pager 89. Brasilia.

IPCC (Intergovernmental Panel on Climate Change). 2007. *Climate Change 2007: Impacts, Adaptation and Vulnerability.* Contribution of Working Group II to the Fourth Assessment Report of the Intergovernmental Panel on Climate Change. Cambridge, UK: Cambridge University Press.

———. 2012. *Managing the Risks of Extreme Events and Disasters to Advance Climate Change Adaptation: Special Report of the Intergovernmental Panel on Climate Change.* Cambridge, UK: Cambridge University Press.

———. 2013. *Climate Change 2013: The Physical Science Basis.* Working Group I Contribution to the Fifth Assessment Report of the Intergovernmental Panel on Climate Change. Cambridge, UK: Cambridge University Press. https://www.ipcc.ch/report/ar5/wg1/. Accessed 20 March 2014.

———. 2014. *Climate Change 2014: Impacts, Adaptation, and Vulnerability.* Working Group II Contribution to the Fifth Assessment Report. Cambridge, UK: Cambridge University Press.

IPU (Inter-Parliamentary Union). 2013. *Women in Parliament in 2013.* Geneva.

Ismi, Asad. 2013. "Maoist Insurgency Spreads to Over 40% of India. Mass Poverty and Delhi's Embrace of Corporate Neoliberalism Fuels Social Uprising." 20 December. Center for Research on Globalization, Montreal, Canada. www. globalresearch.ca/maoist-insurgency-spreads-to-over -40-of-india-mass-poverty-and-delhis-embrace-of -corporate-neoliberalism-fuels-social-uprising/5362276. Accessed 14 May 2014.

ITU (International Telecommunication Union). 2013. "The World in 2013: ICT Facts and Figures." Geneva. www.itu.int/en/ITU-D/Statistics/Documents/facts/ ICTFactsFigures2013-e.pdf. Accessed 24 March 2014.

Jansen, M., and E. von Uexkuell. 2010. *Trade and Employment in the Global Crisis.* Geneva: International Labour Office. www.ilo.org/wcmsp5/groups/public/ @dgreports/@dcomm/@publ/documents/publication/ wcms_141911.pdf. Accessed 24 March 2014.

Jäntti, M., and B. Bradbury. 2001. "Child Poverty across Industrialized Countries." *Journal of Population and Social Security* 1(Supplement): 385–410.

Jolly, R., G.A. Cornia, D. Elson, C. Fortin, S. Griffith-Jones, G. Helleiner, R. van der Hoeven, R. Kaplinsky, R. Morgan, I. Ortiz, R. Pearson and F. Stewart. 2012. "Be Outraged: There are Alternatives." Sussex, UK: Richard Jolly. http://policy-practice.oxfam.org.uk/ publications/be-outraged-there-are-alternatives-224184. Accessed 16 May 2014.

Kabeer, N. 2014. "Vulnerability, Capability and Citizenship: Addressing Violence against Women and Girls." Human Development Research Paper. United Nations Development Programme, Human Development Report Office, New York.

Kabeer, N., K. Huda, S. Kaur, and N. Lamhauge. 2012. "Productive Safety Nets for Women in Extreme Poverty: Lessons from Pilot Projects in India and Pakistan." Discussion Paper 28/12. University of London, School of Oriental and African Studies, Centre for Development Policy and Research, London. www.soas.ac.uk/cdpr/publications/ papers/file76193.pdf. Accessed 28 March 2014.

Kabeer, N., K. Mumtaz, and A. Sayeed. 2010. "Beyond Risk Management: Vulnerability, Social Protection and Citizenship in Pakistan." *Journal of International Development* 22: 1–19. www.researchcollective.org/ Documents/Beyond_Risk_Management_Vulnerability_ Social_Protection_and_Citizenship_in_Pakistan.PDF. Accessed 28 March 2014.

Kanbur, R. 2007. "Poverty and Conflict: The Inequality Link." Coping with Crisis Working Paper Series. International Peace Institute, New York. www.isn.ethz.ch/ Digital-Library/Publications/Detail/?id=126966. Accessed 21 March 2014.

Kant, E. 1781. *Critique of Pure Reason.* P. Guyer and A. Wood, trans. and eds, 1997. Cambridge, UK: Cambridge University Press.

Kaplan, D.S., G. Martinez, and R. Robertson. 2005. "What Happens to Wages after Displacement?" *Economía* 5(2): 197–242.

Karanikolos, M., P. Mladovsky, J. Cylus, S. Thomson, S. Basu, D. Stuckler, J. Mackenbach, and M. McKee. 2013. "Financial Crisis, Austerity, and Health in Europe." *Lancet* 381(9874): 1323–31.

Karoly, L.A., S.S. Everingham, J. Houbé, R. Kilburn, C.P. Rydell, M. Sanders, and P.W. Greenwood. 1997. "Benefits and Costs of Early-Childhood Interventions: A Documented Briefing." RAND Corporation, Santa Monica, CA.

Kaul, I. 2013. *Global Public Goods: A Concept for Framing the Post-2015 Agenda?* Bonn, Germany: Deutsche Institut für Entwicklungspolitik.

———. 2014. "Fostering Sustainable Human Development: Managing the Macro-Risks of Vulnerability." Human Development Research Paper. United Nations Development Programme, Human Development Report Office, New York.

Kaul, I., and P. Conceição, eds. 2006. *The New Public Finance: Responding to Global Challenges.* Oxford, UK: Oxford University Press.

Kaul, I., P. Conceição, K. Le Goulven, and R.U. Mendoza. 2003. *Providing Global Public Goods: Managing Globalization.* Oxford, UK: Oxford University Press.

KC, S., W. Lutz, E. Loichinger, R. Muttarak, and E. Striessnig. 2014. "Reducing Vulnerability in Critical Life Course Phases through Empowerment." Human Development Research Paper. United Nations Development Programme, Human Development Report Office, New York.

Keizer, A.B. 2008. "Non-regular Employment in Japan." *Work, Employment, and Society* 22(3): 407–25. http://wes. sagepub.com/content/22/3/407.abstract. Accessed 26 March 2014.

Kelly, S. 2010. "The Psychological Consequences to Adolescents for Exposure to Gang Violence in the Community: An Integrated Review of the Literature." *Journal of Child and Adolescent Psychiatric Nursing* 23(2): 61–73. http://middleschoolgangsandcliques.wikispaces. com/file/view/The+Psychological+Consequences+to+ Adolescents+of+Exposure+to+Gang+Violence+in+the+ Community-+An+Integrated+Review+of+the+Literaturejcap _225.pdf. Accessed 21 March 2014.

Kelly, T., W. Yang, C.S. Chen, K. Reynolds, and J. He. 2008. "Global Burden of Obesity in 2005 and Projections to 2030." *International Journal of Obesity* 32(9): 1431–37.

Kennedy, D., and J. Stiglitz, eds. 2013. *Law and Economics with Chinese Characteristics: Institutions for Promoting Development in the Twenty-First Century.* Oxford, UK: Oxford University Press.

Khor, M., and J.A. Ocampo. 2011. "The Unsettled Global Trade Architecture." *Queries* 1(4): 68–88.

Kim, N., and P. Conceição. 2010. "The Economic Crisis, Violent Conflict, and Human Development." *International Journal of Peace Studies* 15(1): 29–43.

Kinzig, A.P., P.R. Ehrlich, L.J. Alston, K. Arrow, S. Barrett, T.G. Buchman, G.C. Daily, B. Levin, S. Levin, M. Oppenheimer, E. Ostrom, and D. Saari. 2013. "Social Norms and Global Environmental Challenges: The Complex Interaction of Behaviors, Values, and Policy." *Bioscience* 63(3): 164–75.

Kondkher, B.H., C. Knox-Vydmanov, and A. Vilela. 2013. "Old Age Social Protection Options for Bangladesh." Dhaka University, Bureau of Economic Research, and HelpAge International. www.pension-watch.net/silo/ files/old-age-sp-options-for-bangladesh.pdf. Accessed 26 March 2014.

Korpi, W., and J. Palme. 1998. "The Paradox of Redistribution and Strategies of Equality: Welfare State Institutions, Inequality, and Poverty in the Western Countries." *American Sociological Review* 63(5): 661–87.

Kostzer, D. 2008. "Argentina: A Case study on the Plan Jefes y Jefas de Hogar Desocupados, or the Employment Road to Economic Recovery." Working Paper 534. The Levy Economics Institute, Annandale-on-Hudson, NY. www.

levyinstitute.org/pubs/wp_534.pdf. Accessed 21 April 2014.

Kraemer, K., G. Linden, and J. Dedrick. 2011. "Capturing Value in Global Networks: Apple's iPad and iPhone." Working Paper. University of California, Irvine, Paul Merage School of Business, Personal Computing Industry Center, Irvine, CA. http://pcic.merage.uci.edu/papers/2011/value_iPad_iPhone.pdf. Accessed November 2013.

Krug, E.G., L.L. Dahlberg, J.A. Mercy, A.B. Zwi, and R. Lozano, eds. 2002a. *World Report on Violence and Health*. Geneva: World Health Organization. http://whqlibdoc.who.int/publications/2002/9241545615_eng.pdf?ua=1. Accessed 30 March 2014.

Krug, E.G., J. Mercy, L. Dahlberg, and A. Zwi. 2002b. "The World Report on Violence and Health." *Lancet* 360: 1083–88.

Krutikova, S. 2010. "Who Gets to Stay in School? Long-run Impact of Income Shocks on Schooling in Rural Tanzania." Working Paper 36. University of Oxford, Department of Economics, Centre for the Study of African Economies, Oxford, UK. www.economics.ox.ac.uk/Centre-for-the-Study-of-African-Economies-Series/who-gets-to-stay-in-school-long-run-impact-of-income-shocks-on-schooling-in-rural-tanzania. Accessed 26 March 2014.

Kuhn, A., R. Lavile, and J. Zweimuller. 2009. "The Public Health Cost of Job Loss." *Journal of Health Economics* 28(6): 1099–1115.

Kumhof, M., and R. Rancière. 2010. "Leveraging Inequality." *Finance & Development* 47(4): 28–31.

Kumlin, S., and B. Rothstein. 2005. "Making and Breaking Social Capital: The Impact of Welfare-State Institutions." *Comparative Political Studies* 38(4): 339–65.

Kwak, S., and S. Smith. 2011. "Multidimensional Poverty and Interlocking Poverty Traps: Framework and Application to Ethiopian Household Panel Data." Working Paper 2011-04. George Washington University, Elliott School of International Affairs, Institute for International Economic Policy, Washington, DC.

Kynge, J. 2014. "'Fragile Five' Falls Short As Tapering Leaves More Exposed." *Financial Times*, 15 January. www.ft.com/intl/cms/s/0/a245c70e-7e0c-11e3-95dd-00144feabdc0.html#axzz2xBU9hUZg. Accessed 27 March 2014.

La Trobe, S. 2002. "Climate Change and Poverty." Discussion paper. Tearfund, Middlesex, UK.

Lakner, C., and B. Milanovic. 2013. "Global Income Distribution: From the Fall of the Berlin Wall to the Great Recession." Policy Research Working Paper 6719. World Bank, Washington, DC.

Lal, R., S. Miller, M. Lieuw-Kie-Song, and D. Kostzer. 2010. "Public Works and Employment Programmes: Towards a Long-Term Development Approach." Working Paper 66. International Policy Centre for Inclusive Growth, Brasilia, and United Nations Development Programme, New York. www.ipc-undp.org/pub/IPCWorkingPaper66.pdf. Accessed 21 April 2014.

Langer, A., F. Stewart, and R. Venugopal. 2012. "In Brief: Have Post-conflict Development Policies Addressed Horizontal Inequalities?" Centre for Research on Inequality, Human Security and Ethnicity, Oxford, UK. http://www.qeh.ox.ac.uk/pdf/pdf-research/crise-ib9. Accessed 22 May 2014.

Leach, M. 2008. "Re-Framing Resilience: A Symposium Report." Brighton, UK: STEPS Centre.

Liem, R., and R. Rayman. 1982. "Health and Social Costs of Unemployment: Research and Policy Considerations." *American Psychologist* 37(10): 1116–23.

Linden, G., K. Kraemer, and J. Dedrick. 2011. "Innovation and Job Creation in a Global Economy: The Case of Apple's iPod." *Journal of International Commerce and Economics* 3: 223–39.

Lund, M., and R. Myers. 2007. "Can Fostering a Culture of Dialogue Change the Course of a Nation? An Evaluation of the United Nations Social Cohesion Programme in Guyana." United Nations Development Programme, New York.

Lutsey, N., and D. Sperling. 2008. "America's Bottom-Up Climate Change Mitigation Policy." *Energy Policy* 36(2): 673–85.

Lutz, L., and S. KC. 2013. "Demography and Human Development: Education and Population Projections." In K. Malik and M. Kugler, eds., *Human Progress and the Rising South*. New York: United Nations Development Programme, Human Development Report Office.

Macfarlane, S.N., and Y.F. Khong. 2006. *Human Security and the UN: A Critical History*. Bloomington, IN: Indiana University Press.

Machinea, J.L., and D. Titelman. 2007. "Less Volatile Growth? The Role of Regional Financial Institutions." *Cepal Review* 91: 7–28.

MacLeod, W.B., and M. Urquiola. 2012. *Anti-lemons: Reputation and Educational Quality*. NBER Working Paper 15112. Cambridge, MA: National Bureau of Economic Research.

Maddison, A. 2010. "Statistics on World Population, GDP and Per Capita GDP, 1-2008 AD." Groningen Growth and Development Centre, the Netherlands. www.ggdc.net/maddison/oriindex.htm. Accessed 15 March 2014.

Maisonnave, H., B. Decaluwé, and M. Chitiga. 2009. "Does South African Affirmative Action Policy Reduce Poverty?" Working Paper 09-36. Centre interuniversitaire sur le risque, les politiques économiques et l'emploi, Montreal, Canada.

Mancini, L. 2008. "Horizontal Inequality and Communal Violence: Evidence from Indonesian Districts." In F. Stewart, ed., *Horizontal Inequalities and Conflict: Understanding Group Violence in Multiethnic Societies*. Basingstoke, UK: Palgrave Macmillan.

Marc, A., A. Willman, G. Aslam, M. Rebosio, and K. Balasuriya. 2013. *Societal Dynamics and Fragility: Engaging Societies in Responding to Fragile Situations*. Washington, DC: World Bank.

Marshall, K., and O. Butzbach, eds. 2003. *New Social Policy Agendas for Europe and Asia: Challenges, Experience, and Lessons*. Washington, DC: World Bank. http://www-wds.worldbank.org/external/default/WDSContentServer/WDSP/IB/2003/02/07/000094946_03012804015776/Rendered/PDF/multi0page.pdf. Accessed 22 May 2014.

Masset, E., and H. White. 2004. "Are Chronically Poor People Being Left out of Progress towards the Millennium Development Goals? A Quantitative Analysis of Older People, Disabled People and Orphans." *Journal of Human Development* 5(2): 279–97.

McCain, M.N., J.F. Mustard, and K. McCuaig. 2011. *Early Years Study 3: Making Decisions, Taking Action*. Toronto, Canada: Margaret & Wallace McCain Family Foundation. www.misatoronto.ca/index.php/learning/exploring/

resources/i_115_eys3_en_2nd_072412.pdf. Accessed 18 March 2014.

McCain, M.N., J.F. Mustard, and D.S. Shanker. 2007. *Early Years Study 2: Putting Science into Action*. Toronto, Canada: Council of Early Child Development. http://earlylearning.ubc.ca/media/publications/early_years_study_2.pdf. Accessed 20 March 2014.

McEwen, B.S. 2008. "Understanding the Potency of Stressful Early Life Experiences on Brain and Body Function." *Metabolism Clinical and Experimental* 57(2): S11–S15.

McGee, R., and J. Gaventa. 2011. "Shifting Power? Assessing the Impact of Transparency and Accountability Initiatives." Working Paper 383. Institute of Development Studies, Brighton, UK. http://r4d.dfid.gov.uk/PDF/Outputs/Mis_SPC/60827_Wp383McGeeGaventa.pdf. Accessed 24 April 2014.

McKenzie, D.J. 2003. "How Do Households Cope with Aggregate Shocks? Evidence from the Mexican Peso Crisis." *World Development* 31(7): 1179–99.

McLaughlin, D.K., and L. Jensen. 2000. "Work History and US Elders' Transitions into Poverty." *Gerontologist* 40(4): 469–79.

Mearns, R., and A. Norton, eds. 2010. *Social Dimensions of Climate Change: Equity and Vulnerability in a Warming World*. Washington, DC: World Bank.

Médecins Sans Frontières. 2013. *Untangling the Web of Antiretroviral Price Reductions*. Geneva. http://d2pd3b5abq75bb.cloudfront.net/2013/09/11/10/25/44/896/MSF_Access_UTW_16th_Edition_2013.pdf. Accessed 20 March 2014.

Mejia-Mantilla, C. 2012. "Mid-term and Long-term Effects of the 1998 Asian Crisis in Indonesia." University of California–Los Angeles.

Meng, Q., and S. Tang. 2010. "Universal Coverage of Health Care in China: Challenges and Opportunities." Background Paper 7 for *World Health Report 2010*. World Health Organization, Geneva.

Milanovic, B. 2012. "Global Income Inequality by the Numbers: In History and Now—An Overview." Policy Research Working Paper 6259. World Bank, Washington, DC.

Miller, F., H. Osbahr, E. Boyd, F. Thomalla, S. Bharwani, G. Ziervogel, B. Walker, J. Birkmann, S. Van der Leeuw, J. Rockström, J. Hinkel, T. Downing, C. Folke, and D. Nelson. 2010. "Resilience and Vulnerability: Complementary or Conflicting Concepts?" *Ecology and Society* 15(3): 11.

Minorities at Risk Project. 2014. Database. University of Maryland, Center for International Development and Conflict Management, College, Park, MD. www.cidcm.umd.edu/mar/data.asp. Accessed 28 April 2014.

Mkandawire, T. 2001. "Social Policy in a Development Context." Social Policy and Development Programme Paper 7. United Nations Research Institute for Social Development, Geneva.

Mok, K., J. Lawler, and S.B. Hinsz. 2009. "Economic Shocks in Education: Analysis of the 1997 Asian Financial Crisis and Lessons for Today." *Global Social Policy* 9(1 suppl): 145–79.

Molina, G., E. Ortiz, A. Reyes, and P. Garcia. 2014. "Human Development Outliers: Progress That is Resilient to Shocks." Human Development Research Paper. United Nations Development Programme, Human Development Report Office, New York.

Morissette, R., X. Zhang, and M. Frenette. 2007. "Earnings Losses of Displaced Workers: Canadian Evidence from a Large Administrative Database on Firm Closures and Mass Lay-offs." Analytical Studies Branch Research Paper. Catalogue no. 11F0019MIE—No. 291. Statistics Canada, Ottawa. www.statcan.gc.ca/pub/11f0019m/11f0019m2007291-eng.pdf. Accessed 24 March 2014.

Morrone, A., K. Scrivens, C. Smith, and C. Balestra. 2011. "Measuring Vulnerability and Resilience in OECD Countries." Paper prepared for the IARIW-OECD Conference on Economic Insecurity, 22–23 November, Paris.

Morrow, V. 2013. "Troubling Transitions? Young People's Experiences of Growing Up in Poverty in Rural Andhra Pradesh, India." *Journal of Youth Studies* 16(1): 86–100.

Müller, J. 2010. "UN System Coordination: The Challenge of Working Together." *Journal of International Organizations Studies* 1: 29–56.

Munyaneza, J. 2013. "Rwanda: Women Take 64 Percent Seats in Parliament." *The New Times*, 19 September. http://allafrica.com/stories/201309190110.html. Accessed 14 May 2014.

Muqtada, M. 1987. "Special Employment Schemes in Rural Bangladesh: Issues and Perspective." *Philippine Review of Economics* 24(3&4): 323–86.

———. **2010.** "The Crisis of Orthodox Macroeconomic Policy: The Case for a Renewed Commitment to Full Employment." Employment Working Paper 53. International Labour Organization, Geneva.

Musgrave, R.A. 1959. *Theory of Public Finance: A Study in Public Economy.* New York: McGraw-Hill.

Mustard, J.F. 2006. "Early Child Development and Experience-based Brain Development—The Scientific Underpinnings of the Importance of Early Child Development in a Globalized World." Paper prepared for the World Bank International Symposium on Early Child Development—A Priority for Sustained Economic Growth & Equity, 27–29 September, Washington, DC. www.brookings.edu/views/papers/200602mustard.pdf. Accessed 20 March 2014.

Naidoo, V., and M. Kongolo. 2004. "Has Affirmative Action Reached South African Women?" *Journal of International Women's Studies* 6(1): 124–36.

Narayan, A., J. Saavedra-Chanduvi, and S. Tiwari. 2013. "Shared Prosperity: Links to Growth, Inequality and Inequality of Opportunity." Policy Research Working Paper 6649. World Bank, Washington, DC.

Narayan, D., and P. Petesch, eds. 2007. *Moving out of Poverty: Cross-Disciplinary Perspectives.* New York: Palgrave Macmillan.

Narayan, D., R. Chambers, M.K. Shah, and P. Petesch. 2000. *Voices of the Poor: Crying Out for Change.* Oxford, UK: Oxford University Press.

Naudé, W., A.U. Santos-Paulino, and M. McGillivray, eds. 2011. *Fragile States: Causes, Costs, and Responses.* Oxford, UK: Oxford University Press.

Naudeau, S., S. Martinez, P. Premand, and D. Filmer. 2011. "Cognitive Development among Young Children in Low-Income Countries." In H. Alderman, ed., *No Small Matter: The Impact of Poverty, Shocks and Human Capital Investments in Early Childhood Education.* Washington, DC: World Bank. http://siteresources.worldbank.org/EXTAFRREGTOPEDUCATION/Resources/444707-1291071725351/nosmallmatter.pdf. Accessed 19 March 2014.

Naylor, R., and W. Falcon. 2010. "Food Security in an Era of Economic Volatility." *Population and Development Review* 36(4): 693–723.

Nayyar, D. 2012. "On Macroeconomics and Human Development." *Journal of Human Development and Capabilities* 13(1): 7–30.

Nelson, C.A., N.A. Fox, and C.H. Zeanah. 2014. *Romania's Abandoned Children: Deprivation, Brain Development, and the Struggle for Recovery.* Cambridge, MA: Harvard University Press.

Nelson, K. 2004. "Mechanisms of Poverty Alleviation: Anti-Poverty Effects of Non-Means-Tested and Means-Tested Benefits in Five Welfare States." *Journal of European Social Policy* 14(4): 371–90.

Newhouse, D. 2013. "New Estimates of Youth Idleness and Employment Outcomes in Developing Countries." Social Protection and Labor. World Bank, Washington, DC.

NICHD (National Institute of Child Health and Human Development) Early Child Care Research Network. 2006. "Child-Care Effect Sizes for the NICHD Study of Early Child Care and Youth Development." *American Psychologist* 61(2): 99–116. www.psy.miami.edu/faculty/dmessinger/c_c/rsrcs/rdgs/childcare/NICHD_EffectSizes_AmerPsy.2006.pdf. Accessed 20 March 2014.

NOAA (United States Department of Commerce, National Oceanic and Atmospheric Administration). 2013. "Hurricane Sandy Service Assessment." Washington, DC. www.nws.noaa.gov/os/assessments/pdfs/Sandy13.pdf. Accessed 20 March 2014.

Nussbaum, M.C. 2005. "Women's Bodies: Violence, Security, Capabilities." *Journal of Human Development* 6(2): 167–83. https://www.amherst.edu/system/files/media/1556/Picq-%2520nussbaum-women%2527s%2520bodies.pdf. Accessed 28 March 2014.

O'Keefe, P., K. Westgate, and B. Wisner. 1976. "Taking the Naturalness out of Natural Disasters." *Nature* 260(5552): 566–67.

O'Sullivan, R., K. Mugglestone, and T. Allison. 2014. "In This Together: The Hidden Cost of Young Adult Unemployment." Policy Brief. Young Invincibles, Washington, DC.

Ocampo, J.A., ed. 2006. *Regional Financial Cooperation.* Washington, DC: Brookings Institution Press.

———. **2010.** "Rethinking Global Economic and Social Governance." *Journal of Globalization and Development* 1(1): 1–29.

———. **2013.** "Global Economic and Social Governance and the United Nations System." Initiative for Policy Dialogue Working Paper. New York. http://policydialogue.org/files/publications/Global_Econ_and_UN_Ocampo_withCS.pdf. Accessed 20 March 2014.

Ocampo, J.A., and S. Griffith-Jones. 2007. "A Counter-Cyclical Framework for a Development-Friendly International Financial Architecture." Working Paper 39. United Nations Department of Economic and Social Affairs, New York. www.un.org/esa/desa/papers/2007/wp39_2007.pdf. Accessed 24 March 2014.

Ocampo, J.A., and J. Stiglitz. 2011. "From the G-20 to a Global Economic Coordination Council." *Journal of Globalization and Development* 2(2): 1–18.

Odagiri, H., A. Goto, A. Sunami, and R.R. Nelson. 2012. *Intellectual Property Rights, Development, and Catch Up: An International Comparative Study.* Oxford, UK: Oxford University Press.

ODI (Overseas Development Institute). 2008. "The Indian National Rural Employment Guarantee Act: Will It Reduce Poverty and Boost the Economy?" Project Briefing 7. London.

OECD (Organisation for Economic Co-operation and Development). 2010. "Gender Inequality and the MDGs: What Are the Missing Dimensions?" Paris. www.oecd.org/social/poverty/45987065.pdf. Accessed 28 March 2014.

———. **2011a.** "Growing Income Inequality in OECD Countries: What Drives It and How Can Policy Tackle It?" OECD Forum on Tackling Inequality, 2 May, Paris. www.oecd.org/social/soc/47723414.pdf. Accessed 31 March 2014.

———. **2011b.** *Pensions at a Glance 2011: Retirement-Income Systems in OECD and G20 Countries.* Paris. http://dx.doi.org/10.1787/pension_glance-2011-en. Accessed 26 March 2014.

———. **2011c.** *Tax Transparency 2011: Report on Progress.* Paris. www.oecd.org/tax/transparency/48981620.pdf. Accessed 20 March 2014.

———. **2012.** "Think Global, Act Global: Confronting Global Factors that Influence Conflict and Fragility." A Summary of the Berlin Policy Forum, 15–16 November, Berlin.

———. **2013a.** *Action Plan on Base Erosion and Profit Shifting.* Paris. http://dx.doi.org/10.1787/9789264202719-en. Accessed 24 March 2014.

———. **2013b.** "Crisis Squeezes Income and Puts Pressure on Inequality and Poverty: Results from the OECD Income Distribution Database (May 2013)." Paris. www.oecd.org/els/soc/OECD2013-Inequality-and-Poverty-8p.pdf. Accessed 15 May 2014.

———. **2013c.** *Education at a Glance 2013: OECD Indicators.* Paris.

———. **2013d.** *Employment Outlook 2013.* Paris.

———. **2013e.** *Health at a Glance 2013: OECD Indicators.* Paris.

———. **2013f.** "Unemployment Set to Remain High in OECD Countries through 2014 – Youth and Low-skilled Hit Hardest." www.oecd.org/employment/unemployment-set-to-remain-high-in-oecd-countries-through-2014youth-and-low-skilled-hit-hardest.htm. Accessed 14 May 2014.

———. **n.d.** Social Expenditure Database. Paris. www.oecd.org/social/expenditure.htm. Accessed 20 March 2014.

Ogata, S., and A. Sen. 2003. *Human Security Now: Protecting and Empowering People.* New York: Commission on Human Security.

Ono, Y., and D. Sullivan. 2013. "Manufacturing Plants' Use of Temporary Workers: An Analysis Using Census Micro Data." *Industrial Relations: A Journal of Economy and Society* 52(2): 419–43. ftp://tigerline.census.gov/ces/wp/2008/CES-WP-08-40.pdf. Accessed 24 March 2014.

Onyango, M.A., B.L. Hixson, and S. McNally. 2013. "Minimum Initial Service Package (MISP) for Reproductive Health during Emergencies: Time for a New Paradigm." *Global Public Health* 8(3): 342–56.

Ortiz, I., S. Burke, M. Berrada, and H. Cortés. 2013. "World Protests 2006-2013." Working Paper. Initiative for Policy Dialogue and Friedrich-Ebert-Stiftung, New York. http://policydialogue.org/files/publications/World_Protests_2006-2013-Complete_and_Final_4282014.pdf. Accessed 24 March 2014.

Østby, G. 2008a. "Inequalities, the Political Environment and Civil Conflict: Evidence from 55 Developing Countries." In F. Stewart, ed., *Horizontal Inequalities and Conflict: Understanding Group Violence in Multiethnic Societies.* Basingstoke, UK: Palgrave Macmillan.

———. **2008b.** "Polarization, Horizontal Inequalities and Violent Civil Conflict." *Journal of Peace Research* 45(2): 143–62.

Paardekooper, B., J.T.V.M. De Jong, and J.M.A. Hermanns. 1999. "The Psychological Impact of War and the Refugee Situation on South Sudanese Children in Refugee Camps in Northern Uganda: An Exploratory Study." *Journal of Child Psychology and Psychiatry* 40(4): 529–36.

Paci, P., A. Revenga, and B. Rijkers. 2011. "Coping with Crises: Policies to Protect Employment and Earnings." Vox, 19 April. www.voxeu.org/article/coping-crises-policies-protect-employment-and-earnings. Accessed 15 May 2014.

Palme, J. 2006. "Welfare States and Inequality: Institutional Designs and Distributive Outcome." *Research in Social Stratification and Mobility* 24(4): 387–403.

Pardee Center for International Futures. 2013. "Development-Oriented Policies and Alternative Human Development Paths." In K. Malik and M. Kugler, eds., *Human Progress and the Rising South.* New York: United Nations Development Programme.

Park, Y.C. 2006. "Regional Financial Integration in East Asia: Challenges and Prospects. Regional Financial Cooperation." In J.A. Ocampo, ed., *Regional Financial Cooperation.* Washington DC: Brookings Institution Press.

Parliament of India Rajya Sabha. 2013. *One Hundred and Sixty Seventh Report on the Criminal Law (Amendment) Bill, 2012.* New Delhi: Rajya Sabha Secretariat. www.prsindia.org/uploads/media/Criminal%20Law/SCR%20Criminal%20Law%20Bill.pdf. Accessed 28 March 2014.

Parlow, A. 2012. "Armed Conflict and Children's Health – Exploring New Directions: The Case of Kashmir." MPRA Paper 38033. Munich Personal RePEc Archive, Munich, Germany. http://mpra.ub.uni-muenchen.de/38033/1/MPRA_paper_38033.pdf. Accessed 28 March 2014.

Paxson, C., and N. Schady. 2007. "Cognitive Development among Young Children in Ecuador: The Roles of Wealth, Health and Parenting." Policy Research Working Paper 3605. World Bank, Washington, DC. https://openknowledge.worldbank.org/handle/10986/8929. Accessed 19 March 2014.

Pells, K. 2011. "Poverty and Gender Inequalities: Evidence from Young Lives." Young Lives Policy Paper 3. University of Oxford, Department of International Development, Oxford, UK.

Pereda, N., G. Guilera, M. Forns, and J. Gómez-Benito. 2009. "The Prevalence of Child Sexual Abuse in Community and Student Samples: A Meta-analysis." *Clinical Psychology Review* 29(4): 328–38.

Pick, S., and J. Sirkin. 2010. *Breaking the Poverty Cycle: The Human Basis for Sustainable Development.* New York: Oxford University Press.

Pineda, J. 2013. "Sustainability and Human Development: A Proposal for a Sustainability Adjusted Human Development Index." *Theoretical and Practical Research in Economic Fields* 3(2): 71–98.

Pineda, J., and F. Rodríguez. 2006a. "The Political Economy of Investment in Human Capital." *Economics of Governance* 7: 167–93.

———. **2006b.** "Public Investment in Infrastructure and Productivity Growth: Evidence from the Venezuelan Manufacturing Sector." Wesleyan Economics Working Paper 2006-010. Wesleyan University, Middletown, CT.

Pinheiro, P.S. 2006. *World Report on Violence against Children.* United Nations Secretary-General's Study on Violence against Children. New York: United Nations. www.unicef.org/lac/full_tex(3).pdf. Accessed 21 March 2014.

Plan International. 2012. *State of the World's Girls 2012: Learning for Life.* Report prepared for the "Because I Am a Girl" campaign. Woking, UK. http://plan-international.org/girls/pdfs/2012-report/The-State-of-the-World-s-Girls-Learning-for-Life-Plan-International-2012.pdf. Accessed 21 March 2014.

Polanyi, K. 1944. *The Great Transformation: The Political and Economic Origins of Our Time.* Boston, MA: Beacon Press.

Polk, W.R. 2013. *Humpty Dumpty: The Fate of Regime Change.* Stone, UK: Panda Press.

Pollock, R. 2006. *The Value of the Public Domain.* London: Institute for Public Policy Research. http://rufuspollock.org/papers/value_of_public_domain.ippr.pdf. Accessed 27 March 2014.

Posel, D., J.A. Fairburn, and F. Lund. 2006. "Labour Migration and Households: A Reconsideration of the Effects of the Social Pension on Labour Supply in South Africa." *Economic Modelling* 23(5): 836–53.

Raman, A.V., and J.W. Björkman. 2008. "Public-Private Partnership in Health Care Services in India." *Health Administrator* 21(1–2): 62–77.

Ratha, D., C. Eigen-Zucchi, S. Plaza, H. Wyss, and S. Yi. 2013. "Migration and Remittance Flows: Recent Trends and Outlook, 2013–2016." Migration and Development Brief 21. World Bank, Washington, DC. http://siteresources.worldbank.org/INTPROSPECTS/Resources/334934-1288990760745/MigrationandDevelopmentBrief21.pdf. Accessed 24 March 2014.

Reinalda, B., ed. 2013. *Routledge Handbook of International Organization.* London: Routledge.

Reinhart, C. 2012. *A Series of Unfortunate Events: Common Sequencing Patterns in Financial Crises.* Working Paper 17941. Cambridge, MA: National Bureau of Economic Research.

Rentschler, J.E. 2013. "Why Resilience Matters: The Poverty Impacts of Disasters." Policy Research Working Paper 6699. World Bank, Washington, DC. http://elibrary.worldbank.org/doi/pdf/10.1596/1813-9450-6699. Accessed 26 March 2014.

Revkin, A. 2012. "Beyond Rio: Pursuing 'Ecological Citizenship.'" *New York Times,* 25 June.

Ringen, S. 1988. "Direct and Indirect Measures of Poverty." *Journal of Social Policy* 17(3): 351–65.

Robinson, A., V. Scherrer, and A. Gormally. 2013. "Disability and Vulnerability: A Primer." Disability-inclusive DRR Network for Asia and the Pacific partners. www.didrrn.net/home/files/3613/8614/3327/DiDRRN_GP_vulnerability_primer_v.fin.pdf. Accessed 24 March 2014.

Rockström, J., W. Steffen, K. Noone, Å. Persson, F. Chapin, E. Lambin, T. Lenton, M. Scheffer, C. Folke, H. Schellnhuber, B. Nykvist, C. De Wit, T. Hughes, S. van der Leeuw, H. Rodhe, S. Sörlin, P. Snyder, R. Costanza, U. Svedin, M. Falkenmark, L. Karlberg, R. Corell, V. Fabry, J. Hansen, B. Walker, D. Liverman, K. Richardson, P. Crutzen, and J. Foley. 2009. "Planetary Boundaries: Exploring the Safe Operating Space for Humanity." *Ecology and Society* 14(2): 32.

Rodrik, D. 2000. "Participatory Politics, Social Cooperation, and Economic Stability." *American Economic Review* 90(2): 140–44. http://citeseerx.ist.psu.edu/viewdoc/download?doi=10.1.1.298.5443&rep=rep1&type=pdf. Accessed 15 May 2014.

Roemer, J.E. 1993. "A Pragmatic Approach to Responsibility for the Egalitarian Planner." *Philosophy and Public Affairs* 22(2): 146–66.

Rolleston, C., and Z. James. 2011. "The Role of Schooling in Skill Development: Evidence from Young Lives in Ethiopia, India, Peru and Vietnam." Paper commissioned for the *Education for All Global Monitoring Report 2012.* www.younglives.org.uk/files/policy-papers/role-of-schooling-in-skill-development. Accessed 21 March 2014.

Rothstein, B. 2001. "Social Capital in the Social Democratic Welfare State." *Politics and Society* 29(2): 207–41.

Roxburgh, C., and J. Mischke. 2011. *European Growth and Renewal: The Path from Crisis to Recovery.* McKinsey Global Institute. www.mckinsey.com/insights/europe/european_growth_and_renewal_path_to_recovery. Accessed 22 April 2014.

Sander, R., and S. Taylor Jr. 2012. *Mismatch: How Affirmative Action Hurts Students It's Intended to Help, and Why Universities Won't Admit It.* New York: Basic Books.

Sandler, T., M. Arce, and G. Daniel. 2002. "A Conceptual Framework for Understanding Global and Transnational Public Goods for Health." *Fiscal Studies* 23(2): 195–222.

Sassen, S. 2006. *Territory, Authority, Rights: From Medieval to Global Assemblages.* Vol. 7. Princeton, NJ: Princeton University Press.

Schmieder, J.F., T.M. von Wachter, and S. Bender. 2009. "The Effects of Unemployment Insurance on Labour Supply and Search Outcomes: Regression Discontinuity Estimates from Germany." Discussion Paper 0910-08. Columbia University, Department of Economics, New York. http://doku.iab.de/discussionpapers/2010/dp0410.pdf. Accessed 24 March 2014.

Schroder-Butterfill, E., and R. Marianti. 2006. "A Framework for Understanding Old-age Vulnerabilities." *Ageing & Society* 26(1): 9–35. http://journals.cambridge.org/action/displayFulltext?type=1&fid=371433&jid=ASO&volumeId=26&issueId=01&aid=371432&bodyId=&membershipNumber=&societyETOCSession. Accessed 17 March 2014.

Sebastian, H. 2009. "The Culture of Fear and Control in Costa Rica: Crime Statistics and Law Enforcement." Working Paper 104. German Institute of Global Affairs, Hamburg, Germany.

Seitz, S. 2013. "Indigenous Peoples and the Process of Decentralization: Conflicting Interests Regarding Upland Resource Management in Palawan Province/Philippines." Occasional Paper 13. University of Freiburg, Germany. https://areastudies.uni-freiburg.de/Content/files/occasional-paper-series/op13_seitz.pdf/at_download/file. Accessed 16 May 2014.

Sen, A. 1992. Inequality Reexamined. Oxford, UK: Oxford University Press.

———. 1999. "Democracy as a Universal Value." Journal of Democracy 10(3): 3–17.

———. 2013. "The Ends and Means of Sustainability." Journal of Human Development and Capabilities 14(1): 6–20.

Sen, A., J. Stiglitz, and J. Fitoussi. 2009. Report by the Commission on the Measurement of Economic Performance and Social Progress. Paris.

Sen, P. 1998. "Violence against Women." Gender and Development 6(3): 7–16.

Shonkoff, J.P., and D.A. Phillips. 2000. From Neurons to Neighborhoods: The Science of Early Childhood Development. Washington DC: National Academy Press.

Shonkoff, J.P., and L. Richter. 2013. "The Powerful Reach of Early Childhood Development." In P. Rebello Britto, P.L. Engle, and C.M. Super, eds., Handbook of Early Childhood Development. Research and Its Impact on Global Policy. New York: Oxford University Press.

Shonkoff, J.P., L. Richter, J. van der Gaag, and Z.A. Bhutta. 2012. "The Biology of Adversity: Building an Integrated Science of Child Survival, Early Childhood Development, and Human Capital Formation." Pediatrics 129(2): 1–13.

Sierra Leone, Ministry of Finance and Economic Development, Development Assistance Coordination Office. 2013. Republic of Sierra Leone Fragility Assessment. Freetown. www.newdeal4peace.org/wp-content/uploads/2013/05/Fragility-Assessment-SierraLeone-border-180313.pdf. Accessed 24 March 2014.

Sinclair, A.R.E., and J.M. Fryxell. 1985. "The Sahel of Africa: Ecology of a Disaster." Canadian Journal of Zoology 63: 987–94.

Smith, J.P., G. Teruel, T. Duncan, K. Beegle, and E. Frankenberg. 2002. "Wages, Employment and Economic Shocks: Evidence from Indonesia." Journal of Population Economics 15(1): 161–93. http://scholar.google.com/scholar_url?hl=it&q=http://www.dtic.mil/cgi-bin/GetTRDoc%3FAD%3DADA385386&sa=X&scisig=AAGBfm327yyptkliH6W6JPPHV92yhL2HFA&oi=scholarr. Accessed 24 March 2014.

Sobhan, R. 2014. "Vulnerability Traps and Their Effects on Human Development. Human Development Research Paper. United Nations Development Programme, Human Development Report Office, New York.

Somavia, J. 2013. The Meaning of Decent Work. Geneva: International Labour Office.

Stephan, G. 2009. "Employer Wage Subsidies and Wages in Germany: Some Evidence from Individual Data." Discussion Paper 9/2009. Federal Employment Agency, Institute for Employment Research, Nuremberg, Germany.

Stephens, A.H. 1997. "Persistent Effects of Job Displacement: The Importance of Multiple Job Losses." Journal of Labour Economics 15(1): 165–88. www.jstor.org/stable/2535319?seq=1. Accessed 24 March 2014.

Stevens, A.H., and J. Schaller. 2011. "Short-run Effects of Parental Job Loss on Children's Academic Achievement." Economics of Education Review 30(2): 289–99.

Stewart, F., ed. 2008. Horizontal Inequalities and Conflict. Understanding Group Violence in Multiethnic Societies. New York: Palgrave Macmillan.

———. 2010. "Horizontal Inequalities as a Cause of Conflict: A Review of CRISE Findings." Background paper for World Development Report 2011. World Bank, Washington, DC.

———. 2013. "Capabilities and Human Development: Beyond the Individual—the Critical Role of Social Institutions and Social Competencies." In K. Malik and M. Kugler, eds., Human Progress and the Rising South. New York: United Nations Development Programme.

Stewart, F., M. Barrón, G. Brown, and M. Hartwell. 2006. "Social Exclusion and Conflict: Analysis and Policy Implications." Policy Paper. Oxford University, Centre for Research on Inequality, Human Security and Ethnicity, Oxford, UK. www.qeh.ox.ac.uk/pdf/pdf-research/crise-pp1. Accessed 26 March 2014.

Stewart, F., G. Brown, and L. Mancini. 2005. "Why Horizontal Inequalities Matter: Some Implications for Measurement." Working Paper 19. Oxford University, Centre for Research on Inequality, Human Security and Ethnicity, Oxford, UK. http://r4d.dfid.gov.uk/pdf/outputs/inequality/wp19.pdf. Accessed 26 March 2014.

Stiglitz, J. 2012a. "Macroeconomic Fluctuations, Inequality, and Human Development." Journal of Human Development and Capabilities 13(1): 31–58.

———. 2012b. The Price of Inequality: How Today's Divided Society Endangers Our Future. New York: W. W. Norton & Company.

———. 2013. "Social Protection without Protectionism." In J. Stiglitz and M. Kaldor, eds., The Quest for Security: Protection Without Protectionism and the Challenge of Global Governance. New York: Columbia University Press.

Stiglitz, J., and M. Kaldor, eds. 2013a. The Quest for Security: Protection without Protectionism and the Challenge of Global Governance. New York: Columbia University Press.

———. 2013b. "Introduction." In J. Stiglitz, and M. Kaldor, eds., The Quest for Security: Protection Without Protectionism and the Challenge of Global Governance. New York: Columbia University Press.

Stiglitz, J., A. Bougrov, Y. Boutros-Ghali, J.P. Fitoussi, C.A. Goodhart, and R. Johnson. 2009. "Report of the Commission of Experts of the President of the United Nations General Assembly on Reforms of the International Monetary and Financial System." United Nations Conference on the World Financial and Economic Crisis and its Impact on Development, 24–26 June, New York. www.un.org/ga/president/63/interactive/financialcrisis/PreliminaryReport210509.pdf. Accessed 24 March 2014.

Stiglitz, J., A. Sen, and J. Fitoussi. 2010. Mismeasuring Our Lives: Why GDP Doesn't Add Up. New York: New Press.

Sullivan, D., and T. von Wachter. 2009. "Job Displacement and Mortality: An Analysis Using Administrative Data."

Quarterly Journal of Economics 124(3): 1265–1306. http://qje.oxfordjournals.org/content/124/3/1265.abstract. Accessed 24 March 2014.

Sulmasy, G., and J. Yoo. 2007. "Challenges to Civilian Control of the Military: A Rational Choice Approach to the War on Terror." UCLA Law Review 54. http://papers.ssrn.com/sol3/papers.cfm?abstract_id=1030761. Accessed 16 May 2014.

Sundaram, J. 2013. "A World of Vulnerability." Project Syndicate, 13 July. www.project-syndicate.org/commentary/poverty--vulnerability--and-social-protection-by-jomo-kwame-sundaram. Accessed 28 April 2014.

Swiderska, K. A. Argumedo, Y. Song, J. Li, R. Pant, H. Herrera, D. Mutta, P. Munyi, and S. Vedavathy. 2009. Protecting Community Rights over Traditional Knowledge: Implications of Customary Laws and Practices: Key Findings and Recommendations 2005–2009. London: International Institute for Environment and Development.

Tarrow, S. 2013. The Language of Contention: Revolutions in Words, 1688-2012. Cambridge, UK: Cambridge University Press.

Telles, E.E. 2004. Race in Another America: The Significance of Skin Color in Brazil. Princeton, NJ: Princeton University Press.

Temin, M. 2008. "Expanding Social Protection for Vulnerable Children and Families: Learning from an Institutional Perspective." Working Paper. Inter-Agency Task Team on Children and HIV and AIDS: Working Group on Social Protection, New York. www.unicef.org/aids/files/Expanding_Social_Protection.MTemin.May2008.pdf. Accessed 16 May 2014.

Thorp, R., F. Stewart, and A. Heyer. 2005. "When and How Far Is Group Formation a Route out of Chronic Poverty?" World Development 33(6): 907–20.

Thrasher, R., and K. Gallagher. 2008. 21st Century Trade Agreements: Implications for Long-Run Development Policy. Pardee Paper 2. Boston, MA: Boston University, Frederick S. Pardee Center for the Study of the Longer Range Future. http://ase.tufts.edu/gdae/Pubs/rp/KGPardeePolSpaceSep08.pdf. Accessed 24 March 2014.

Tshimpanga, J.M., E. Enfors, R. Biggs, and G. Peterson. 2011. "Maradi Agro-ecosystem." Regime Shifts Database. www.regimeshifts.org/component/k2/item/57-maradi-agro-ecosystem#. Accessed 28 April 2014.

UCDP (Uppsala Conflict Data Program). 2013. UCDP Non-State Conflict Dataset v. 2.5-2013, 1989–2012. Sweden. www.pcr.uu.se/research/ucdp/datasets/ucdp_non-state_conflict_dataset_/. Accessed 18 February 2014.

UCDP (Uppsala Conflict Data Program) and PRIO (Peace Research Institute Oslo). 2013. UCDP/PRIO Armed Conflict Dataset v.4-2013, 1946–2012. Sweden and Oslo. www.pcr.uu.se/research/ucdp/datasets/ucdp_prio_armed_conflict_dataset/. Accessed 18 February 2014.

UN (United Nations). 1948. "Universal Declaration of Human Rights." G.A. Res. 217A(III), U.N. GAOR, 3d Sess., U.N. Doc. A/810 (Dec. 10, 1948). www.un.org/en/documents/udhr/. Accessed 20 March 2014.

———. 1966. "International Convention on Economic, Social and Cultural Rights." G.A. res. 2200A (XXI), 21 U.N. GAOR Supp. (No. 16) at 49, U.N. Doc. A/6316 (1966). www.ohchr.org/EN/ProfessionalInterest/Pages/CESCR.aspx. Accessed 20 March 2014.

————. 1989. "Convention on the Rights of the Child." GA res. 44/25, annex, 44 UN GAOR Supp. (No. 49) at 167, U.N. Doc. A/44/49 (1989). www.un.org/documents/ga/res/44/a44r025.htm. Accessed 20 March 2014.

————. 1995. "Report of the Fourth World Conference on Women." 4–15 September, Beijing. www.un.org/womenwatch/daw/beijing/pdf/Beijing%20full%20report%20E.pdf. Accessed 20 March 2014.

————. 2000. "United Nations Millennium Declaration." www.un.org/millennium/declaration/ares552e.htm. Accessed 20 March 2014.

————. 2005. World Summit Outcome (A/60/L.I) 15 September, 2005. New York. www.un.org/womenwatch/ods/A-RES-60-1-E.pdf. Accessed 25 March 2014.

————. 2006. "Convention on the Rights of Persons with Disabilities." www.un.org/disabilities/default.asp?id=259. Accessed 20 March 2014.

————. 2009. "The Social Protection Floor." www.un.org/ga/second/64/socialprotection.pdf Accessed 20 March 2014.

————. 2012a. "Report of the UN Special Rapporteur on Extreme Poverty and Human Rights." A/67/278. New York.

————. 2012b. "Resolution Adopted by the General Assembly on 27 July 2012: Resolution 66/288. The Future We Want." Sixty-Sixth Session of the General Assembly. New York. www.un.org/ga/search/view_doc.asp?symbol=A/RES/66/288&Lang=E. Accessed 27 March 2014.

————. 2013a. "Declaration of the High-level Dialogue on International Migration and Development." Sixty-Eighth Session of the General Assembly. New York. www.iom.int/files/live/sites/iom/files/What-We-Do/docs/Final-Declaration-2013-En.pdf. Accessed 20 March 2014.

————. 2013b. A New Global Partnership: Eradicate Poverty and Transform Economies through Sustainable Development. Report of the High-Level Panel of Eminent Persons on the Post-2015 Development Agenda. New York.

————. 2013c. The Global Partnership for Development: The Challenge We Face. MDG Gap Task Force Report 2013. New York. www.un.org/en/development/desa/policy/mdg_gap/mdg_gap2013/mdg_report_2013_en.pdf Accessed 20 March 2014.

————. 2013d. "Resolution Adopted by the General Assembly on 9 July 2013: Resolution 67/290. Format and Organizational Aspects of the High-Level Political Forum on Sustainable Development." Sixty-Seventh Session of the General Assembly. New York. www.un.org/ga/search/view_doc.asp?symbol=A/RES/67/290. Accessed 27 March 2014.

————. 2013e. "Resolution Adopted by the General Assembly on 20 September 2013: Resolution 61/16 on 'Strengthening of the Economic and Social Council'." Sixty-Eighth Session of the General Assembly. New York. www.un.org/ga/search/view_doc.asp?symbol=A/RES/68/1. Accessed 27 March 2014.

————. 2014a. "World Conference on Indigenous Peoples." http://wcip2014.org/background. Accessed 20 March 2014.

————. 2014b. World Population Prospects: The 2012 Revision. New York. http://esa.un.org/wpp/Excel-Data/population.htm. Accessed 18 February 2014.

UN (United Nations) General Assembly. 2009. "Legal Empowerment of the Poor and Eradication of Poverty." Report of the Secretary General. A/64/133. New York. www.snap-undp.org/lepknowledgebank/Public%20Document%20Library/Legal%20empowerment%20of%20the%20poor%20and%20Eradication%20of%20Poverty.pdf. Accessed 16 May 2014.

————. 2013a. "Draft Resolution Referred to the High-Level Plenary Meeting of the General Assembly by the General Assembly at its Sixty-Fourth Session." A/65/L.1. www.un.org/en/mdg/summit2010/pdf/mdg%20outcome%20document.pdf. Accessed 16 May 2014.

————. 2013b. "A Life of Dignity for All: Accelerating Progress towards the Millennium Development Goals and Advancing the United Nations Development Agenda beyond 2015." Report of the Secretary-General. A/68/202. New York.

————. 2013c. "Report of the Secretary-General on the Situation in the Sahel Region." New York.

UN (United Nations) News Centre. 2013a. "States Must Prioritize Migrants' Human Rights, UN Independent Experts Reiterate." 7 October. www.un.org/apps/news/story.asp?NewsID=46206&Cr=Italy&Cr1=&Kw1=lampedusa&Kw2=&Kw3=#.U0XDET_XI25. Accessed 20 March 2014.

————. 2013b. "Australia's Transfer of Asylum-seekers to Pacific Islands Faulted in UN Reports." 26 November. www.un.org/apps/news/story.asp?NewsID=46596&Cr=asylum&Cr1. Accessed 20 March 2014.

UN Atlas of the Oceans. 2013. "Human Settlement on the Coasts." www.oceansatlas.org/servlet/CDSServlet?status=ND0xODc3JjY9ZW4mMzM9KiYzNz1rb3M~. Accessed 20 March 2014.

UN Enable. 2013. "Disability, Natural Disasters and Emergency Situations." www.un.org/disabilities/default.asp?id=1546. Accessed 30 March 2014.

UN Global Pulse. 2010. Voices of the Vulnerable: Recovery from the Ground Up. New York. www.unglobalpulse.org/sites/default/files/reports/Voices-of-the-Vulnerable_0.pdf. Accessed 24 March 2014.

————. 2012. "Monitoring Household Coping Strategies during Complex Crises." www.unglobalpulse.org/projects/rivaf-research-monitoring-household-coping-strategies-during-complex-crises. Accessed 30 March 2014.

UN System Task Team on the Post-2015 UN Development Agenda. 2012a. Disaster Risk and Resilience. New York. www.unisdr.org/files/27462_20120607unttpostmdgthinkpieceondrra.pdf. Accessed 16 May 2014.

————. 2012b. Social Protection: A Development Priority in the Post-2015 UN Development Agenda. New York. http://www.un.org/millenniumgoals/pdf/Think%20Pieces/16_social_protection.pdf. Accessed 27 March 2014.

UNCSD (United Nations Conference on Sustainable Development). 2012. "The Future We Want." Rio de Janeiro, Brazil. www.uncsd2012.org/content/documents/727The%20Future%20We%20Want%2019%20June%201230pm.pdf. Accessed 27 March 2014.

UNCTAD (United Nations Conference on Trade and Development). 2012a. Corporate Social Responsibility in Global Value Chains: Evaluation and Monitoring Challenges for Small and Medium Sized Suppliers in Developing Countries. New York and Geneva. http://unctad.org/en/PublicationsLibrary/diaeed2012d3_en.pdf. Accessed 19 March 2014.

————. 2012b. Development and Globalization: Facts and Figures 2012. Geneva.

————. 2013. World Investment Report: Global Value Chains: Investment and Trade for Development. New York and Geneva. http://unctad.org/en/publicationslibrary/wir2013_en.pdf. Accessed 19 March 2014.

————. 2014. UNCTADstat. http://unctadstat.unctad.org/ReportFolders/reportFolders.aspx?sCS_referer=&sCS_ChosenLang=en Accessed 20 March 2014.

UNDESA (United Nations Department of Economic and Social Affairs). 2009. State of the World's Indigenous Peoples. New York. www.un.org/esa/socdev/unpfii/documents/SOWIP_web.pdf. Accessed 28 March 2014.

————. 2013a. "LDC Information: The Criteria for Identifying Least Developed Countries." www.un.org/en/development/desa/policy/cdp/ldc/ldc_criteria.shtml. Accessed 14 May 2014.

————. 2013b. Report on World Social Situation 2013: Inequality Matters. New York.

UNDP (United Nations Development Programme). 1990. Human Development Report 1990. New York.

————. 1993. Human Development Report 1993: People's Participation. New York

————. 1994. Human Development Report 1994: New Dimensions of Human Security. New York.

————. 2003. Assessment of Micro-Macro Linkages in Poverty Alleviation: South Asia. Evaluation Office, New York.

————. 2005. Costa Rica National Human Development Report: Overcoming Fear: Citizen (In)security and Human Development in Costa Rica. New York. http://hdr.undp.org/sites/default/files/costa_rica_2005_en.pdf. Accessed 31 March 2014.

————. 2009a. Community Security and Social Cohesion: Towards a UNDP Approach. Geneva.

————. 2009b. Human Development Report 2009: Overcoming Barriers: Human Mobility and Development. New York: Palgrave Macmillian. http://hdr.undp.org/sites/default/files/reports/269/hdr_2009_en_complete.pdf. Accessed 31 March 2014.

————. 2010. Human Development Report 2010: The Real Wealth of Nations: Pathways to Human Development. New York.

————. 2011a. Human Development Report 2011: Sustainability and Equity: A Better Future for All. New York.

————. 2011b. "Illicit Financial Flows from the Least Developed Countries 1990-2008." Discussion Paper. New York. http://www.ginbot7.org/pdf/IFFs_from_LDCs_web.pdf. Accessed 24 March 2014.

————. 2011c. Sharing Innovative Experiences: Successful Social Protection Floor Experiences. New York.

————. 2011d. Towards Human Resilience: Sustaining MDG Progress in an Age of Economic Uncertainty. New York.

————. 2012a. Africa Human Development Report 2012: Towards a Food Secure Future. www.undp.org/content/dam/undp/library/corporate/HDR/Africa%20HDR/UNDP-Africa%20HDR-2012-EN.pdf. Accessed 20 March 2014.

———. 2012b. *Caribbean Human Development Report 2012: Human Development and the Shift to Better Citizen Security.* New York. www.undp.org/content/dam/undp/library/corporate/HDR/Latin%20America%20and%20Caribbean%20HDR/C_bean_HDR_Jan25_2012_3MB.pdf. Accessed 31 March 2014.

———. 2012c. *Governance for Peace: Securing the Social Contract.* New York. www.undp.org/content/dam/undp/library/crisis%20prevention/governance-for-peace_2011-12-15_web.pdf.pdf. Accessed 24 March 2014.

———. 2012d. *Seeing Beyond the State: Grassroots Women's Perspectives on Corruption and Anti-corruption.* New York.

———. 2012e. *Somalia National Human Development Report: Empowering Youth for Peace and Development.* New York. www.undp.org/content/dam/undp/library/corporate/HDR/Arab%20States/HDR-Somalia-2012-E.pdf. Accessed 21 March 2014.

———. 2013a. *Human Development Report 2013: The Rise of the South: Human Progress in a Diverse World.* New York.

———. 2013b. *Informe Regional de Desarrollo Humano 2013-2014: Seguridad Ciudadana con Rostro Humano: Diagnóstico y Propuestas para América Latina.* New York. www.undp.org/content/dam/rblac/img/IDH/IDH-AL%20Informe%20completo.pdf. Accessed 21 March 2014.

———. 2013c. *The Millennium Development Goals Report 2013.* New York.

———. 2013d. *Preventing Crisis, Enabling Recovery: A Review of UNDP's Work in Conflict and Disaster-Affected Countries: 2012.* New York. www.undp.org/content/dam/undp/library/crisis%20prevention/BCPR_isuu-sm.pdf. Accessed 15 May 2014.

———. 2014. *Humanity Divided: Confronting Inequality in Developing Countries.* New York.

UNDP (United Nations Development Programme), World Bank, and EC (European Commission). 2011. "Roma Data." www.eurasia.undp.org/content/rbec/en/home/ourwork/povertyreduction/roma-in-central-and-southeast-europe/roma-data/. Accessed 28 March 2014.

UNECA (United Nations Economic Commission for Africa). 2010. *Innovations and Best Practices in Public Sector Reforms: The Case of Civil Service in Ghana, Kenya, Nigeria and South Africa.* Addis Ababa. www.uneca.org/sites/default/files/publications/innovations_in_the_public_sector.pdf. Accessed 16 May 2014.

UNFCCC (United Nations Framework Convention on Climate Change). 2009. "Copenhagen Accord." FCCC/CP/2009/L.7. Bonn, Germany. http://unfccc.int/resource/docs/2009/cop15/eng/l07.pdf. Accessed 27 March 2014.

———. 2011. "Report of the Conference of the Parties on Its Sixteenth Session, Held in Cancun from 29 November to 10 December 2010." FCCC/CP/2010/7/Add.1. Bonn, Germany. http://unfccc.int/resource/docs/2010/cop16/eng/07a01.pdf. Accessed 27 March 2014.

———. 2012. "Report of the Conference of the Parties on Its Seventeenth Session, Held in Durban from 28 November to 11 December 2011." FCCC/CP/2011/9/Add.1. Bonn, Germany. http://unfccc.int/resource/docs/2011/cop17/eng/09a01.pdf. Accessed 27 March 2014.

UNFPA (United Nations Population Fund). 2008. "Linking Population, Poverty and Development. Migration: A World on the Move." www.unfpa.org/pds/migration.html. Accessed 30 March 2014.

UNFPA (United Nations Population Fund). 2010. *State of World Population 2010.* New York. www.unfpa.org/webdav/site/global/shared/documents/publications/2010/EN_SOWP10.pdf. Accessed 20 March 2014.

UNFPA (United Nations Population Fund) and HelpAge International. 2012. *Ageing in the Twenty-First Century: A Celebration and a Challenge.* New York and London: UNFPA and HelpAge.

UN-Habitat (United Nations Human Settlements Programme). 2011. *Cities and Climate Change: Global Report on Human Settlements 2011.* Nairobi. http://mirror.unhabitat.org/pmss/listItemDetails.aspx?publicationID=3086. Accessed 24 March 2014.

UNHCR (United Nations High Commissioner for Refugees). 2012. *UNHCR Global Trends 2012: Displacement. The New 21st Century Challenge.* Geneva. http://unhcr.org/globaltrendsjune2013/UNHCR%20GLOBAL%20TRENDS%202012_V08_web.pdf. Accessed 19 March 2014.

UNICEF (United Nations Children's Fund). 2006. *State of the World's Children Report 2007: Women and Children: The Double Dividend of Gender Equality.* New York.

———. 2007. *The Impact of International Migration: Children Left Behind in Selected Countries of Latin America and the Caribbean.* New York. www.unicef.org/videoaudio/PDFs/The_Impact_of_International_Migration_LAC.pdf. Accessed 20 March 2014.

———. 2008. *The State of Asia-Pacific's Children.* New York. www.unicef.org/pacificislands/SAPC_Full_Report.pdf. Accessed 22 May 2014.

UNISDR (United Nations International Strategy for Disaster Reduction). 2005. "Hyogo Framework for Action 2005-2015: Building the Resilience of Nations and Communities to Disasters." Geneva. www.unisdr.org/2005/wcdr/intergover/official-doc/L-docs/Hyogo-framework-for-action-english.pdf. Accessed 20 March 2014.

———. 2012a. "Japan's Success in Risk Reduction Highlighted on March 11 Anniversary." Press Release, 9 March. Geneva.

———. 2012b. "UNISDR Counts the Cost of 20 Years of Inaction on Climate Change and Risk Reduction." Press release, 13 June. Geneva.

———. n.d. "Key Focus Areas." www.unisdr.org/2006/ppew/iewp/iewp-introduction.htm. Accessed 16 May 2014.

United Nations Global Pulse. 2012. "Monitoring Household Coping Strategies during Complex Crises." www.unglobalpulse.org/projects/rivaf-research-monitoring-household-coping-strategies-during-complex-crises. Accessed 28 April 2014.

United Nations Population Division. 2013. "Trends in International Migrant Stock: The 2013 Revision." New York. http://esa.un.org/unmigration/TIMSA2013/migrantstocks2013.htm. Accessed 21 November 2013.

UNOCHA (UN Office for the Coordination of Humanitarian Affairs). 2014. "World Humanitarian Summit 2016 Concept Note." https://docs.unocha.org/sites/dms/Documents/WHS%20Concept%20Note.pdf. Accessed 20 March 2014.

UNOHCHR (Office of the High Commissioner for Human Rights). 2003. "Human Rights in the Administration of Justice: A Manual on Human Rights for Judges, Prosecutors and Lawyers." Geneva. www.ohchr.org/Documents/Publications/training9Titleen.pdf. Accessed 16 May 2014.

UNRISD (United Nations Research Institute for Social Development). 2010. *Combating Poverty and Inequality: Structural Change, Social Policy and Politics.* Geneva. www.unrisd.org/80256B3C005BCCF9%2F%28httpAuxPages%29%2F92B1D5057F43149CC125779600434441%2F. Accessed 16 May 2014.

UNSSC (United Nations System Staff College). 2010. *Indigenous Peoples and Peacebuilding: A Compilation of Best Practices.* Turin, Italy.

Välilä, T., and A. Mehrotra. 2005. "Evolution and Determinants of Public Investment in Europe." Economic and Financial Report 2005/01. European Investment Bank, Luxembourg.

Van de Gaer, D. 1993. "Equality of Opportunity and Investment in Human Capital." Ph.D. thesis. Catholic University of Louvain, Belgium.

Vennam, U., A. Komanduri, E. Cooper, G. Crivello, and M. Woodhead. 2009. "Early Childhood Education Trajectories and Transitions: A Study of the Experiences and Perspectives of Parents and Children in Andhra Pradesh, India." Young Lives Working Paper 52. University of Oxford, Department of International Development, Oxford, UK. www.younglives.org.uk/files/working-papers/wp52-early-childhood-education-trajectories-and-transitions-a-study-of-the-experiences-and-perspectives-of-parents-and-children-in-andhra-pradesh-india. Accessed 21 March 2014.

Verick, S. 2009. "Who Is Hit Hardest during a Financial Crisis? The Vulnerability of Young Men and Women to Unemployment in an Economic Downturn." Discussion Paper 4359. Institute for the Study of Labour, Bonn. http://ftp.iza.org/dp4359.pdf. Accessed 21 March 2014.

Vinding, D., and E.R. Kampbel. 2007. "Indigenous Women Workers with Case Studies from Bangladesh, Nepal and the Americas." Working Paper. International Labour Office, Geneva. www.ilo.org/wcmsp5/groups/public/---dgreports/---gender/documents/publication/wcms_173293.pdf. Accessed 28 March 2014.

Von Braun, J., and G. Tadesse. 2012. "Global Food Price Volatility and Spikes: An Overview of Costs, Causes, and Solutions." Discussion Paper on Development Policy 161. University of Bonn, Center for Development Research, Bonn, Germany. http://ageconsearch.umn.edu/bitstream/120021/3/DP161Rev.pdf. Accessed 24 March 2014.

Von Wachter, T. 2014. "The Effect of Labour-market Related Shocks on Worker and Family Outcomes in Developed and Developing Countries." Human Development Research Paper. United Nations Development Programme, Human Development Report Office, New York.

Wachs, T.D., and A. Rahman. 2013. "The Nature and Impact of Risk and Protective Influences on Children's Development in Low-Income Countries." In P.R. Britto, P. Engle, and C. Super, eds., *Handbook of Early Childhood Development Research and Its Impact on Global Policy.* New York: Oxford University Press.

Wadhams, N. 2010. "Iceland Volcano: Kenya's Farmers Losing $1.3m a Day in Flights Chaos." *The Guardian,* 18 April.

www.theguardian.com/world/2010/apr/18/iceland-volcano-kenya-farmers. Accessed 19 March 2014.

Waldron, J. 2013. "Separation of Powers in Thought and Practice?" *Boston College Law Review* 54: 433–68. www.bc.edu/content/dam/files/centers/clough/pdf/01_waldron.pdf. Accessed 16 May 2014.

Waters, H., F. Saadah, and M. Pradhan. 2003. "The Impact of the 1997–98 East Asian Economic Crisis on Health and Health Care in Indonesia in Health Policy Plan." *Health Policy and Planning* 18(2): 172–81.

Weiss, T.G. 2011. "ECOSOC and the MDGs: What Can Be Done?" In R. Wilkinson, and D. Humle, eds., *The Millennium Development Goals and Beyond: Global Development after 2015*. New York: Routledge. www.povertydialogue.org/wp-content/uploads/2011/01/26_ECOSOC_and_the_MDGs_What_can_be_Done_ThomasGWeiss.pdf. Accessed 27 March 2014.

Welford, R. 2013. "Climate Change Refugees." *CSR Asia Weekly.* http://csr-asia.com/csr-asia-weekly-news-detail.php?id=12312. Accessed 20 March 2014.

WHO (World Health Organization). 2000. "Reproductive Health during Conflict and Displacement: A Guide for Programme Managers." Geneva. http://whqlibdoc.who.int/hq/2001/WHO_RHR_00.13.pdf?ua=1. Accessed 20 March 2014.

———. **2002.** *World Health Report 2002: Reducing Risks, Promoting Healthy Life.* Geneva. www.who.int/whr/2002/en/whr02_en.pdf. Accessed 20 March 2014.

———. **2007.** *Women, Ageing and Health: A Framework for Action.* Geneva. http://whqlibdoc.who.int/publications/2007/9789241563529_eng.pdf. Accessed 26 March 2014.

———. **2010.** *Global Burden of Disease 2010.* Geneva.

———. **2011a.** *Gender, Climate Change and Health.* Geneva.

———. **2011b.** *World Report on Disability.* Geneva. http://whqlibdoc.who.int/publications/2011/9789240685215_eng.pdf. Accessed 30 March 2014.

———. **2013a.** "Global Leaders Support New Six-year Plan to Deliver a Polio-free World by 2018." News release. 25 April. www.who.int/mediacentre/news/releases/2013/polio_six_year_plan_20130425/en/. Accessed 20 March 2014.

———. **2013b.** "Global and Regional Estimates of Violence against Women: Prevalence and Health Effects of Intimate Partner Violence and Nonpartner Sexual Violence." Geneva. http://apps.who.int/iris/bitstream/10665/85239/1/9789241564625_eng.pdf. Accessed 28 March 2014.

Wisner, B., P. Blaikie, T. Cannon, and I. Davis. 2004. *At Risk: Natural Hazards, People's Vulnerability and Disasters.* 2nd ed. London: Routledge.

Woldehanna, T., N. Jones, and, B. Tefera. 2008. "The Invisibility of Children's Paid and Unpaid Work: Implications for Ethiopia's National Poverty Reduction Policy." *Childhood* 15: 177–201.

Woodhead, M., P. Dornan, and H. Murray. 2013. *What Inequality Means for Children, Evidence from Young Lives.* Oxford, UK: Young Lives. www.younglives.org.uk/files/policy-papers/what-inequality-means-for-children-evidence-from-young-lives. Accessed 27 March 2014.

World Bank. 2000. *World Development Report 2000/01.* Washington, DC.

———. **2010.** *World Development Report 2011: Conflict, Security and Development.* Washington, DC.

———. **2011.** "Malaysia Economic Monitor: Brain Drain." Bangkok.

———. **2012.** *World Development Report 2013: Jobs.* Washington, DC.

———. **2013a.** Remittance Prices Worldwide Databank. http://remittanceprices.worldbank.org. Accessed 27 March 2014.

———. **2013b.** *Turn Down the Heat: Climate Extremes, Regional Impacts, and the Case for Resilience.* Washington DC: World Bank. www.worldbank.org/content/dam/Worldbank/document/Full_Report_Vol_2_Turn_Down_The_Heat_%20Climate_Extremes_Regional_Impacts_Case_for_Resilience_Print%20version_FINAL.pdf. Accessed 20 March 2014.

———. **2013c.** *World Development Report 2014: Risk and Opportunity—Managing Risk for Development.* Washington, DC.

———. **2014a.** PovcalNet online database. Washington, DC. http://iresearch.worldbank.org/PovcalNet/. Accessed 15 February 2014.

———. **2014b.** World Development Indicators DataBank. http://databank.worldbank.org/data/views/variableSelection/selectvariables.aspx?source=world-development-indicators. Accessed 20 March 2014.

———. **n.d.** "Workers in the Informal Economy." http://go.worldbank.org/1PVGLNWYC0. Accessed 28 April 2014.

World Economic Forum. 2014. *Global Risks 2014: Ninth Edition.* Geneva. http://www3.weforum.org/docs/WEF_GlobalRisks_Report_2014.pdf. Accessed 21 March 2014.

WTO (World Trade Organization). 2001. "Ministerial Declaration." WT/MIN(01)/DEC/1. www.wto.org/english/thewto_e/minist_e/min01_e/mindecl_e.pdf. Accessed 13 May 2014.

———. **2013.** Ninth WTO Ministerial Conference. https://mc9.wto.org. Accessed 24 March 2014.

WWF (World Wildlife Fund). 2007. "Climate Savers." http://wwf.panda.org/what_we_do/how_we_work/businesses/climate/climate_savers/. Accessed 20 March 2014.

Xinhua News Service. 2013. "China Achieves 99% Rural Healthcare Coverage." 23 August. www.china.org.cn/china/2013-08/23/content_29808818.htm. Accessed 16 May 2014.

Young, H.P. 2007. "Social Norms and Public Policy." Brookings Institution, Washington, DC.

Young, I.M. 1990. *Justice and the Politics of Difference.* Princeton, NJ: Princeton University Press.

Young, M.E. 2002. *From Early Child Development to Human Development: Investing in Our Children's Future.* Washington, DC: World Bank.

———. **2014.** "Addressing and Mitigating Vulnerability across the Life Cycle: The Case for Investing on Early Childhood." Human Development Research Paper. United Nations Development Programme, Human Development Report Office, New York.

Zaidi, A. 2014. "Vulnerabilities in Old Age: A Review." Human Development Research Paper. United Nations Development Programme, Human Development Report Office, New York.

Zeitlyn, S. 2004. "Social Exclusion in Asia – Some Initial Ideas." UK Department for International Development, London.

Zepeda, E., S. McDonald, M. Panda, and G. Kumar. 2013. "Employing India: Guaranteeing Jobs for the Rural Poor." Carnegie Endowment for International Peace, Washington, DC. www.un.org/en/development/desa/policy/publications/seminars/india_rural_employment.pdf. Accessed 22 May 2014.

Statistical annex

Readers guide

The 17 statistical tables of this annex provide an overview of key aspects of human development. The first six tables contain the family of composite human development indices and their components estimated by the Human Development Report Office (HDRO). The remaining tables present a broader set of indicators related to human development.

Unless otherwise specified in the notes, tables use data available to the HDRO as of 15 November 2013. All indices and indicators, along with technical notes on the calculation of composite indices and additional source information, are available online at http://hdr.undp.org/en/data.

Countries and territories are ranked by 2013 Human Development Index (HDI) value. Robustness and reliability analysis has shown that for most countries the differences in HDI are not statistically significant at the fourth decimal place.[1] For this reason countries with the same HDI value at three decimal places are listed with tied ranks.

Sources and definitions

Unless otherwise noted, the HDRO uses data from international data agencies with the mandate, resources and expertise to collect national data on specific indicators.

Definitions of indicators and sources for original data components are given at the end of each table, with full source details in *Statistical references*.

Gross national income per capita in purchasing power parity terms

In comparing standards of living based on income across countries, the income component of the HDI uses gross national income (GNI) per capita converted into purchasing power parity (PPP) terms to eliminate differences in national price levels.

The International Comparison Programme (ICP) survey is the world's largest statistical initiative that produces internationally comparable price levels, economic aggregates in real terms and PPP estimates. Estimates from ICP surveys conducted in 2011 and covering 180 countries became publicly available on 7 May 2014 and were used to compute the 2013 HDI values.

Methodology updates

Over the past three years the HDRO has held intensive consultations with leading academic experts and policymakers to discuss approaches to development measurement, including the Report's family of composite indices. A key point of agreement among participants in these discussions was that the composite indices must be clearly and intuitively understandable to policymakers, media, civil society leaders and other audiences so that the indices will continue to be used for human development policy guidance and advocacy.

A formal policy on future modifications of human development indices is being elaborated. And the HDRO website (http://hdr.undp.org/en) provides access for the first time to the proprietary software programs used to calculate the indices in this Report.

The 2014 Report retains the HDI, the Multidimensional Poverty index (MPI), the Inequality-adjusted Human Development Index (IHDI) and the Gender Inequality Index (GII), with slight modifications to the HDI and MPI. The HDI now includes fixed maximum goalposts that we hope to maintain for at least five years. For details on the HDI goalposts, see *Technical note 1* at http://hdr.undp.org. For details on updates to the MPI, see *Technical note 5* at http://hdr.undp.org.

Comparisons over time and across editions of the Report

Because national and international agencies continually improve their data series, the data—including the HDI values and ranks—presented in this Report are not comparable to those published in earlier editions. For HDI comparability across years and countries, see table 2, which presents trends using consistent data calculated at five-year intervals for 1980–2013.

Discrepancies between national and international estimates

National and international data can differ because international agencies harmonize national data using a consistent methodology and occasionally produce estimates of missing data to allow comparability across countries. In other cases international agencies might not have access to the most recent national data.

When HDRO becomes aware of discrepancies, it brings them to the attention of national and international data authorities.

Country groupings and aggregates

The tables present weighted aggregates for several country groupings. In general, an aggregate is shown only when data are available for at least half the countries and represent at least two-thirds of the population in that classification. Aggregates for each classification cover only the countries for which data are available.

Human development classification

HDI classifications are based on HDI fixed cut-off points, which are derived from the quartiles of distributions of component indicators. The cut-off points are HDI of less than 0.550 for low human development, 0.550–0.699 for medium human development, 0.700–0.799 for high human development and 0.800 or greater for very high human development.

Regional groupings

Regional groupings are based on United Nations Development Programme regional classifications. Least Developed Countries and Small Island Developing States are defined according to UN classifications (see www.unohrlls.org).

Country notes

Data for China do not include Hong Kong Special Administrative Region of China, Macao Special Administrative Region of China or Taiwan Province of China.

Data for Sudan include data for South Sudan, unless otherwise indicated.

Symbols

A dash between two years, as in 2005–2013, indicates that the data are from the most recent year available in the period specified. A slash between years, as in 2005/2013, indicates average for the years shown. Growth rates are usually average annual rates of growth between the first and last years of the period shown.

The following symbols are used in the tables:

..	Not available
0 or 0.0	Nil or negligible
—	Not applicable

Statistical acknowledgements

The Report's composite indices and other statistical resources draw on a wide variety of the most respected international data providers in their specialized fields. HDRO is particularly grateful to the Centre for Research on the Epidemiology of Disasters; Economic Commission for Latin America and the Caribbean; Eurostat; Food and Agriculture Organization; Gallup; ICF Macro; Internal Displacement Monitoring Centre; International Labour Organization; International Monetary Fund; International Telecommunication Union; Inter-Parliamentary Union; Luxembourg Income Study; Organisation for Economic Co-operation and Development; Oxford Poverty and Human Development Initiative; United Nations Children's Fund; United Nations Conference on Trade and Development; United Nations Department of Economic and Social Affairs; United Nations Economic and Social Commission for West Asia; United Nations Educational, Scientific and Cultural Organization Institute for Statistics; Office of the United Nations High Commissioner for Refugees; United Nations Office on Drugs and Crime; United Nations World Tourism Organization; World Bank; and World Health Organization. The international education database maintained by Robert Barro (Harvard University) and Jong-Wha Lee (Korea University) was another invaluable source for the calculation of the Report's indices.

Statistical tables

The first seven tables relate to the five composite human development indices and their components.

Since the 2010 Human Development Report, four composite human development indices—the HDI, IHDI, GII and MPI—have been calculated. This year the Report introduces the Gender Development Index, which compares the HDI calculated separately for women and men.

The remaining tables present a broader set of human development related indicators and provide a more comprehensive picture of a country's human development.

Table 1, Human Development Index and its components, ranks countries by 2013 HDI value and details the values of the three HDI components: longevity, education (with two indicators) and income. The table also presents values for the 2012 HDI based on the most recent data available for that year, along with the change in rank between 2012 and 2013.

Table 2, Human Development Index trends, 1980–2013, provides a time series of HDI values allowing 2013 HDI values to be compared with those for previous years. The table uses the most recently revised historical data available in 2013 and the same methodology applied to compute the 2013 HDI. Along with historical HDI values, the table includes the change in HDI rank over the last five years and the average annual HDI growth rates across three different time intervals.

Table 3, Inequality-adjusted Human Development Index, contains two related measures of inequality—the IHDI and the loss in HDI due to inequality. The IHDI looks beyond the average achievements of a country in health, education and income to show how these achievements are distributed among its residents. The IHDI can be interpreted as the level of human development when inequality is accounted for. The relative difference between the IHDI and HDI is the loss due to inequality in distribution of the HDI within the country. The table also presents a new measure, the coefficient of human inequality, which is an unweighted average of inequalities in three dimensions. In addition, the table shows each country's difference in rank on the HDI and the IHDI. A negative value means that taking inequality into account lowers a country's rank in the HDI distribution. The table also presents three standard measures of income inequality: the ratio of the top and the bottom quintiles; the Palma ratio, which is the ratio of income of the top 10 percent and the bottom 40 percent; and the Gini coefficient.

Table 4, Gender Inequality Index, presents a composite measure of gender inequality using three dimensions: reproductive health, empowerment and labour market participation. Reproductive health is measured by two indicators: the maternal mortality ratio and the adolescent birth rate. Empowerment is measured by the share of parliamentary seats held by women and the share of population with at least some secondary education. And labour market is measured by participation in the labour force. A low GII value indicates low inequality between women and men, and vice-versa.

Table 5, Gender Development Index, measures disparities in HDI by gender. The table contains HDI values estimated separately for women and men; the ratio of which is the GDI. The closer the ratio is to 1, the smaller the gap between women and men. Values for the three HDI components—longevity, education (with two indicators) and income—are also presented by gender.

Table 6, Multidimensional Poverty Index, captures the multiple deprivations that people face in their education, health and living standards. The MPI shows both the incidence of nonincome multidimensional poverty (a headcount of those in multidimensional poverty) and its intensity (the relative number of deprivations people experience at the same time). Based on intensity thresholds, people are classified as near multidimensional poverty, multidimensionally poor or in severe poverty, respectively. The contributions of deprivations in each dimension to overall poverty are also included. The

table also presents measures of income poverty—population living on less than PPP $1.25 per day and population living below the national poverty line. This year's MPI includes some modifications to the original set of 10 indicators: height-for-age replaces weight-for-age for children under age 5 because stunting is a better indicator of chronic malnutrition. A child death is considered a health deprivation only if it happened in the five years prior to the survey. The minimum threshold for education deprivation was raised from five years of schooling to six to reflect the standard definition of primary schooling used in the Millennium Development Goals and in international measures of functional literacy, and the indicators for household assets were expanded to better reflect rural as well as urban households. The table also presents MPI estimates obtained under the earlier specifications for comparative purposes.

Table 6A, Multidimensional Poverty Index: Changes over time (select countries), presents estimates of MPI and its components for two or more time points for countries for which consistent data were available in 2013. Estimation is based on the revised methodology.

Table 7, Health: children and youth, presents indicators of infant health (percentage of infants who are exclusively breast-fed for the first six months of life, percentage of infants who lack immunization for DTP and measles, and infant mortality rate), child health (percentage of children under age 5 who are stunted, percentage of children who are overweight and child mortality rate) and HIV prevalence and prevention (number of children ages 0–14 living with HIV, youth HIV prevalence rate, condom use among young people, and percentage of pregnant women living with HIV not receiving treatment to prevent mother-to-child transmission). The table also includes data on antenatal coverage.

Table 8, Adult health and health expenditure, contains adult mortality rates by gender, age-standardized mortality rates from alcohol and drug use, and age-standardized obesity rates and HIV prevalence rates among adults. It also includes two indicators on life expectancy—life expectancy at age 60 and health-adjusted life expectancy at birth—and three indicators on quality of health care—number of physicians per 10,000 people, health expenditure as a share of GDP and out of pocket expenditure for health.

Table 9, Education, presents standard education indicators along with indicators on education quality, including average test scores on reading, mathematics and science for 15-year-old students. The table provides indicators of educational attainment—adult and youth literacy rates and the share of the adult population with at least some secondary education. Gross enrolment ratios at each level of education are complemented by primary school dropout rates. The table also includes two indicators on education quality—primary school teachers trained to teach and the pupil–teacher ratio—as well as an indicator on education expenditure as a percentage of GDP.

Table 10, Command over and allocation of resources, covers several macroeconomic indicators such as gross domestic product (GDP); gross fixed capital formation; taxes on income, profit and capital gain as percentage of total tax revenue; share of agriculture, hunting, forestry and fisheries in GDP; and consumer price index. Gross fixed capital formation is a rough indicator of national income that is invested rather than consumed. In times of economic uncertainty or recession, gross fixed capital formation typically declines. The consumer price index is a measure of inflation. General government final consumption expenditure (presented as a share of GDP and as average annual growth) and research and development expenditure are indicators of public spending. In addition, the table presents three indicators on debt—domestic credit provided by the banking sector, external debt stock and total debt service, all measured as a percentage of GDP—and two indicators related to the price of food—the price level index and the price volatility index.

Table 11, Social competencies, contains indicators on three components: employment and related vulnerabilities, social protection and suicide rates by gender. Indicators on vulnerabilities related to employment include vulnerable employment, youth and total unemployment, child labour and working poor as well as length of mandatory paid maternity leave. Social protection is represented by the percentage of children under age 5 with birth registration and the percentage of pension-age population actually receiving an old-age pension.

Table 12, Personal insecurity, reflects the extent to which the population is insecure. It presents number of refugees by country of origin and number of internally displaced people. It shows long-term unemployment rates, homicide rates, and the size of the homeless population, prison population and orphaned children population. And it includes the depth of food deficit and a perception-based indicator on justification of wife beating by gender.

Table 13, International integration, provides indicators of several aspects of globalization. International trade is captured by measuring the remoteness of world markets and international trade as share of GDP. Capital flows are represented by net inflows of foreign direct investment and private capital, official development assistance and inflows of remittances. Human mobility is captured by the net migration rate, the stock of immigrants and the number of international inbound tourists. International communication is represented by the share of population that uses the Internet and international incoming and outgoing telephone traffic.

Table 14, Environment, covers environmental vulnerability and effects of environmental threats. The table shows the proportion of fossil fuels and renewable energy sources in the primary energy supply, levels and annual growth of carbon dioxide emissions per capita and measures of ecosystem and natural resources preservation (natural resource depletion as a percentage of GNI, forest area and change in forest area and fresh water withdrawals). The table contains the under-five mortality rates due to outdoor and indoor air pollution and to unsafe water, unimproved sanitation or poor hygiene. The table also presents indicators of the direct impacts of natural disasters (number of deaths and population affected).

Table 15, Population trends, contains major population indicators, including total population, median age, dependency ratios and total fertility rates, which can help assess the burden of support that falls on the labour force in a country. Deviations from the natural sex ratio at birth have implications for population replacement levels, suggest possible future social and economic problems and may indicate gender bias.

Table 16, Supplementary indicators: perceptions of well-being, includes indicators that reflect individuals' opinions and self-perceptions about relevant dimensions of human development— quality of education, quality of health care, standard of living and labour market, personal safety and overall satisfaction with freedom of choice and life. The table also contains indicators regarding trust in other people and satisfaction with the community and a set of broader indicators reflecting perceptions about government policies on poverty alleviation and preservation of environment, and overall trust in national government.

Note

1. Aguna and Kovacevic (2011) and Høyland, Moene and Willumsen (2011).

Key to HDI countries and ranks, 2013

Afghanistan	169	Georgia	79	Norway	1
Albania	95	Germany	6	Oman	56
Algeria	93	Ghana	138	Pakistan	146
Andorra	37	Greece	29	Palau	60
Angola	149	Grenada	79	Palestine, State of	107
Antigua and Barbuda	61	Guatemala	125	Panama	65
Argentina	49	Guinea	179	Papua New Guinea	157
Armenia	87	Guinea-Bissau	177	Paraguay	111
Australia	2	Guyana	121	Peru	82
Austria	21	Haiti	168	Philippines	117
Azerbaijan	76	Honduras	129	Poland	35
Bahamas	51	Hong Kong, China (SAR)	15	Portugal	41
Bahrain	44	Hungary	43	Qatar	31
Bangladesh	142	Iceland	13	Romania	54
Barbados	59	India	135	Russian Federation	57
Belarus	53	Indonesia	108	Rwanda	151
Belgium	21	Iran (Islamic Republic of)	75	Saint Kitts and Nevis	73
Belize	84	Iraq	120	Saint Lucia	97
Benin	165	Ireland	11	Saint Vincent and the Grenadines	91
Bhutan	136	Israel	19	Samoa	106
Bolivia (Plurinational State of)	113	Italy	26	Sao Tome and Principe	142
Bosnia and Herzegovina	86	Jamaica	96	Saudi Arabia	34
Botswana	109	Japan	17	Senegal	163
Brazil	79	Jordan	77	Serbia	77
Brunei Darussalam	30	Kazakhstan	70	Seychelles	71
Bulgaria	58	Kenya	147	Sierra Leone	183
Burkina Faso	181	Kiribati	133	Singapore	9
Burundi	180	Korea (Republic of)	15	Slovakia	37
Cambodia	136	Kuwait	46	Slovenia	25
Cameroon	152	Kyrgyzstan	125	Solomon Islands	157
Canada	8	Lao People's Democratic Republic	139	South Africa	118
Cape Verde	123	Latvia	48	Spain	27
Central African Republic	185	Lebanon	65	Sri Lanka	73
Chad	184	Lesotho	162	Sudan	166
Chile	41	Liberia	175	Suriname	100
China	91	Libya	55	Swaziland	148
Colombia	98	Liechtenstein	18	Sweden	12
Comoros	159	Lithuania	35	Switzerland	3
Congo	140	Luxembourg	21	Syrian Arab Republic	118
Congo (Democratic Republic of the)	186	Madagascar	155	Tajikistan	133
Costa Rica	68	Malawi	174	Tanzania (United Republic of)	159
Côte d'Ivoire	171	Malaysia	62	Thailand	89
Croatia	47	Maldives	103	The former Yugoslav Republic of Macedonia	84
Cuba	44	Mali	176	Timor-Leste	128
Cyprus	32	Malta	39	Togo	166
Czech Republic	28	Mauritania	161	Tonga	100
Denmark	10	Mauritius	63	Trinidad and Tobago	64
Djibouti	170	Mexico	71	Tunisia	90
Dominica	93	Micronesia (Federated States of)	124	Turkey	69
Dominican Republic	102	Moldova (Republic of)	114	Turkmenistan	103
Ecuador	98	Mongolia	103	Uganda	164
Egypt	110	Montenegro	51	Ukraine	83
El Salvador	115	Morocco	129	United Arab Emirates	40
Equatorial Guinea	144	Mozambique	178	United Kingdom	14
Eritrea	182	Myanmar	150	United States	5
Estonia	33	Namibia	127	Uruguay	50
Ethiopia	173	Nepal	145	Uzbekistan	116
Fiji	88	Netherlands	4	Vanuatu	131
Finland	24	New Zealand	7	Venezuela (Bolivarian Republic of)	67
France	20	Nicaragua	132	Viet Nam	121
Gabon	112	Niger	187	Yemen	154
Gambia	172	Nigeria	152	Zambia	141
				Zimbabwe	156

TABLE 1

Human Development Index and its components

TABLE 1

HDI rank	Human Development Index (HDI) Value 2013	Life expectancy at birth (years) 2013	Mean years of schooling (years) 2012[a]	Expected years of schooling (years) 2012[a]	Gross national income (GNI) per capita (2011 PPP $) 2013	Human Development Index (HDI) Value 2012	Change in rank 2012–2013
VERY HIGH HUMAN DEVELOPMENT							
1 Norway	0.944	81.5	12.6	17.6	63,909	0.943	0
2 Australia	0.933	82.5	12.8	19.9	41,524	0.931	0
3 Switzerland	0.917	82.6	12.2	15.7	53,762	0.916	0
4 Netherlands	0.915	81.0	11.9	17.9	42,397	0.915	0
5 United States	0.914	78.9	12.9	16.5	52,308	0.912	0
6 Germany	0.911	80.7	12.9	16.3	43,049	0.911	0
7 New Zealand	0.910	81.1	12.5	19.4	32,569	0.908	0
8 Canada	0.902	81.5	12.3	15.9	41,887	0.901	0
9 Singapore	0.901	82.3	10.2 [b]	15.4 [c]	72,371	0.899	3
10 Denmark	0.900	79.4	12.1	16.9	42,880	0.900	0
11 Ireland	0.899	80.7	11.6	18.6	33,414	0.901	−3
12 Sweden	0.898	81.8	11.7 [b]	15.8	43,201	0.897	−1
13 Iceland	0.895	82.1	10.4	18.7	35,116	0.893	0
14 United Kingdom	0.892	80.5	12.3	16.2	35,002	0.890	0
15 Hong Kong, China (SAR)	0.891	83.4	10.0	15.6	52,383	0.889	0
15 Korea (Republic of)	0.891	81.5	11.8	17.0	30,345	0.888	1
17 Japan	0.890	83.6	11.5	15.3	36,747	0.888	−1
18 Liechtenstein	0.889	79.9 [d]	10.3 [e]	15.1	87,085 [f,g]	0.888	−2
19 Israel	0.888	81.8	12.5	15.7	29,966	0.886	0
20 France	0.884	81.8	11.1	16.0	36,629	0.884	0
21 Austria	0.881	81.1	10.8 [b]	15.6	42,930	0.880	0
21 Belgium	0.881	80.5	10.9 [b]	16.2	39,471	0.880	0
21 Luxembourg	0.881	80.5	11.3	13.9	58,695	0.880	0
24 Finland	0.879	80.5	10.3	17.0	37,366	0.879	0
25 Slovenia	0.874	79.6	11.9	16.8	26,809	0.874	0
26 Italy	0.872	82.4	10.1 [b]	16.3	32,669	0.872	0
27 Spain	0.869	82.1	9.6	17.1	30,561	0.869	0
28 Czech Republic	0.861	77.7	12.3	16.4	24,535	0.861	0
29 Greece	0.853	80.8	10.2	16.5	24,658	0.854	0
30 Brunei Darussalam	0.852	78.5	8.7	14.5	70,883 [h]	0.852	0
31 Qatar	0.851	78.4	9.1	13.8	119,029 [g]	0.850	0
32 Cyprus	0.845	79.8	11.6	14.0	26,771	0.848	0
33 Estonia	0.840	74.4	12.0	16.5	23,387	0.839	0
34 Saudi Arabia	0.836	75.5	8.7	15.6	52,109	0.833	0
35 Lithuania	0.834	72.1	12.4	16.7	23,740	0.831	1
35 Poland	0.834	76.4	11.8	15.5	21,487	0.833	−1
37 Andorra	0.830	81.2 [d]	10.4 [i]	11.7	40,597 [i]	0.830	0
37 Slovakia	0.830	75.4	11.6	15.0	25,336	0.829	1
39 Malta	0.829	79.8	9.9	14.5	27,022	0.827	0
40 United Arab Emirates	0.827	76.8	9.1	13.3 [k]	58,068	0.825	0
41 Chile	0.822	80.0	9.8	15.1	20,804	0.819	1
41 Portugal	0.822	79.9	8.2	16.3	24,130	0.822	0
43 Hungary	0.818	74.6	11.3 [b]	15.4	21,239	0.817	0
44 Bahrain	0.815	76.6	9.4	14.4 [l]	32,072 [h]	0.813	0
44 Cuba	0.815	79.3	10.2	14.5	19,844 [m]	0.813	0
46 Kuwait	0.814	74.3	7.2	14.6	85,820 [g]	0.813	−2
47 Croatia	0.812	77.0	11.0	14.5	19,025	0.812	0
48 Latvia	0.810	72.2	11.5 [b]	15.5	22,186	0.808	0
49 Argentina	0.808	76.3	9.8	16.4	17,297 [h]	0.806	0
HIGH HUMAN DEVELOPMENT							
50 Uruguay	0.790	77.2	8.5	15.5	18,108	0.787	2
51 Bahamas	0.789	75.2	10.9	12.6 [n]	21,414	0.788	0
51 Montenegro	0.789	74.8	10.5 [o]	15.2	14,710	0.787	1
53 Belarus	0.786	69.9	11.5 [o]	15.7	16,403	0.785	1
54 Romania	0.785	73.8	10.7	14.1	17,433	0.782	1
55 Libya	0.784	75.3	7.5	16.1	21,666 [h]	0.789	−5
56 Oman	0.783	76.6	6.8	13.6	42,191 [h]	0.781	0
57 Russian Federation	0.778	68.0	11.7	14.0	22,617	0.777	0
58 Bulgaria	0.777	73.5	10.6 [b]	14.3	15,402	0.776	0
59 Barbados	0.776	75.4	9.4	15.4	13,604	0.776	−1
60 Palau	0.775	72.4 [d]	12.2 [p]	13.7	12,823	0.773	0
61 Antigua and Barbuda	0.774	76.0	8.9 [p]	13.8	18,800	0.773	−1

TABLE
1

HDI rank		Human Development Index (HDI) Value 2013	Life expectancy at birth (years) 2013	Mean years of schooling (years) 2012[a]	Expected years of schooling (years) 2012[a]	Gross national income (GNI) per capita (2011 PPP $) 2013	Human Development Index (HDI) Value 2012	Change in rank 2012–2013
62	Malaysia	0.773	75.0	9.5	12.7	21,824	0.770	0
63	Mauritius	0.771	73.6	8.5	15.6	16,777	0.769	0
64	Trinidad and Tobago	0.766	69.9	10.8	12.3	25,325	0.765	0
65	Lebanon	0.765	80.0	7.9 [o]	13.2	16,263	0.764	0
65	Panama	0.765	77.6	9.4	12.4	16,379	0.761	2
67	Venezuela (Bolivarian Republic of)	0.764	74.6	8.6	14.2	17,067	0.763	−1
68	Costa Rica	0.763	79.9	8.4	13.5	13,012	0.761	−1
69	Turkey	0.759	75.3	7.6	14.4	18,391	0.756	0
70	Kazakhstan	0.757	66.5	10.4	15.0	19,441	0.755	0
71	Mexico	0.756	77.5	8.5	12.8	15,854	0.755	−1
71	Seychelles	0.756	73.2	9.4 [o]	11.6	24,632	0.755	−1
73	Saint Kitts and Nevis	0.750	73.6 [d]	8.4 [p]	12.9	20,150	0.749	0
73	Sri Lanka	0.750	74.3	10.8	13.6	9,250	0.745	2
75	Iran (Islamic Republic of)	0.749	74.0	7.8	15.2	13,451 [h]	0.749	−2
76	Azerbaijan	0.747	70.8	11.2 [o]	11.8	15,725	0.745	−1
77	Jordan	0.745	73.9	9.9	13.3	11,337	0.744	0
77	Serbia	0.745	74.1	9.5	13.6	11,301	0.743	1
79	Brazil	0.744	73.9	7.2	15.2 [q]	14,275	0.742	1
79	Georgia	0.744	74.3	12.1 [r]	13.2	6,890	0.741	2
79	Grenada	0.744	72.8	8.6 [p]	15.8	10,339	0.743	−1
82	Peru	0.737	74.8	9.0	13.1	11,280	0.734	0
83	Ukraine	0.734	68.5	11.3	15.1	8,215	0.733	0
84	Belize	0.732	73.9	9.3	13.7	9,364	0.731	0
84	The former Yugoslav Republic of Macedonia	0.732	75.2	8.2 [r]	13.3	11,745	0.730	1
86	Bosnia and Herzegovina	0.731	76.4	8.3 [o]	13.6	9,431	0.729	0
87	Armenia	0.730	74.6	10.8	12.3	7,952	0.728	0
88	Fiji	0.724	69.8	9.9	15.7	7,214	0.722	0
89	Thailand	0.722	74.4	7.3	13.1	13,364	0.720	0
90	Tunisia	0.721	75.9	6.5	14.6	10,440	0.719	0
91	China	0.719	75.3	7.5	12.9	11,477	0.715	2
91	Saint Vincent and the Grenadines	0.719	72.5	8.6 [p]	13.3	10,339	0.717	0
93	Algeria	0.717	71.0	7.6	14.0	12,555	0.715	0
93	Dominica	0.717	77.7 [d]	7.7 [p]	12.7 [n]	9,235	0.716	−1
95	Albania	0.716	77.4	9.3	10.8	9,225	0.714	2
96	Jamaica	0.715	73.5	9.6	12.5	8,170	0.715	−3
97	Saint Lucia	0.714	74.8	8.3 [p]	12.8	9,251	0.715	−4
98	Colombia	0.711	74.0	7.1	13.2	11,527	0.708	0
98	Ecuador	0.711	76.5	7.6	12.3 [n]	9,998	0.708	0
100	Suriname	0.705	71.0	7.7	12.0	15,113	0.702	1
100	Tonga	0.705	72.7	9.4 [b]	14.7	5,316	0.704	0
102	Dominican Republic	0.700	73.4	7.5	12.3 [l]	10,844	0.698	0
MEDIUM HUMAN DEVELOPMENT								
103	Maldives	0.698	77.9	5.8 [b]	12.7	10,074	0.695	0
103	Mongolia	0.698	67.5	8.3	15.0	8,466	0.692	3
103	Turkmenistan	0.698	65.5	9.9 [s]	12.6 [p]	11,533	0.693	1
106	Samoa	0.694	73.2	10.3	12.9 [t]	4,708	0.693	−2
107	Palestine, State of	0.686	73.2	8.9 [o]	13.2	5,168 [h,u]	0.683	0
108	Indonesia	0.684	70.8	7.5	12.7	8,970	0.681	0
109	Botswana	0.683	64.4 [v]	8.8	11.7	14,792	0.681	−1
110	Egypt	0.682	71.2	6.4	13.0	10,400	0.681	−2
111	Paraguay	0.676	72.3	7.7	11.9	7,580	0.670	0
112	Gabon	0.674	63.5	7.4	12.3	16,977	0.670	−1
113	Bolivia (Plurinational State of)	0.667	67.3	9.2	13.2	5,552	0.663	0
114	Moldova (Republic of)	0.663	68.9	9.8	11.8	5,041	0.657	2
115	El Salvador	0.662	72.6	6.5	12.1	7,240	0.660	0
116	Uzbekistan	0.661	68.2	10.0 [r]	11.5	5,227	0.657	0
117	Philippines	0.660	68.7	8.9 [b]	11.3	6,381	0.656	1
118	South Africa	0.658	56.9	9.9	13.1 [p]	11,788	0.654	1
118	Syrian Arab Republic	0.658	74.6	6.6	12.0	5,771 [h,u]	0.662	−4
120	Iraq	0.642	69.4	5.6	10.1	14,007	0.641	0
121	Guyana	0.638	66.3	8.5	10.7	6,341	0.635	0
121	Viet Nam	0.638	75.9	5.5	11.9 [n]	4,892	0.635	0
123	Cape Verde	0.636	75.1	3.5 [p]	13.2	6,365	0.635	−2

TABLE 1   Human Development Index and its components | 161

TABLE 1 HUMAN DEVELOPMENT INDEX AND ITS COMPONENTS

HDI rank	Human Development Index (HDI) Value 2013	Life expectancy at birth (years) 2013	Mean years of schooling (years) 2012[a]	Expected years of schooling (years) 2012[a]	Gross national income (GNI) per capita (2011 PPP $) 2013	Human Development Index (HDI) Value 2012	Change in rank 2012–2013
124 Micronesia (Federated States of)	0.630	69.0	8.8 [s]	11.4 [p]	3,662	0.629	0
125 Guatemala	0.628	72.1	5.6	10.7	6,866	0.626	0
125 Kyrgyzstan	0.628	67.5	9.3	12.5	3,021	0.621	1
127 Namibia	0.624	64.5	6.2	11.3	9,185	0.620	0
128 Timor-Leste	0.620	67.5	4.4 [w]	11.7	9,674	0.616	1
129 Honduras	0.617	73.8	5.5	11.6	4,138	0.616	0
129 Morocco	0.617	70.9	4.4	11.6	6,905	0.614	2
131 Vanuatu	0.616	71.6	9.0 [o]	10.6	2,652	0.617	−3
132 Nicaragua	0.614	74.8	5.8	10.5	4,266	0.611	0
133 Kiribati	0.607	68.9	7.8 [p]	12.3	2,645	0.606	0
133 Tajikistan	0.607	67.2	9.9	11.2	2,424	0.603	1
135 India	0.586	66.4	4.4	11.7	5,150	0.583	0
136 Bhutan	0.584	68.3	2.3 [w]	12.4	6,775	0.580	0
136 Cambodia	0.584	71.9	5.8	10.9	2,805	0.579	1
138 Ghana	0.573	61.1	7.0	11.5	3,532	0.571	0
139 Lao People's Democratic Republic	0.569	68.3	4.6	10.2	4,351	0.565	0
140 Congo	0.564	58.8	6.1	11.1	4,909	0.561	0
141 Zambia	0.561	58.1	6.5	13.5	2,898	0.554	2
142 Bangladesh	0.558	70.7	5.1	10.0	2,713	0.554	1
142 Sao Tome and Principe	0.558	66.3	4.7 [w]	11.3	3,111	0.556	−1
144 Equatorial Guinea	0.556	53.1	5.4 [p]	8.5	21,972	0.556	−3
LOW HUMAN DEVELOPMENT							
145 Nepal	0.540	68.4	3.2	12.4	2,194	0.537	0
146 Pakistan	0.537	66.6	4.7	7.7	4,652	0.535	0
147 Kenya	0.535	61.7	6.3	11.0	2,158	0.531	0
148 Swaziland	0.530	49.0	7.1	11.3	5,536	0.529	0
149 Angola	0.526	51.9	4.7 [w]	11.4	6,323	0.524	0
150 Myanmar	0.524	65.2	4.0	8.6	3,998 [h]	0.520	0
151 Rwanda	0.506	64.1	3.3	13.2	1,403	0.502	0
152 Cameroon	0.504	55.1	5.9	10.4	2,557	0.501	0
152 Nigeria	0.504	52.5	5.2 [w]	9.0	5,353	0.500	1
154 Yemen	0.500	63.1	2.5	9.2	3,945	0.499	0
155 Madagascar	0.498	64.7	5.2 [p]	10.3	1,333	0.496	0
156 Zimbabwe	0.492	59.9	7.2	9.3	1,307	0.484	4
157 Papua New Guinea	0.491	62.4	3.9	8.9 [p]	2,453	0.490	−1
157 Solomon Islands	0.491	67.7	4.5 [p]	9.2	1,385	0.489	0
159 Comoros	0.488	60.9	2.8	12.8	1,505	0.486	−1
159 Tanzania (United Republic of)	0.488	61.5	5.1	9.2	1,702	0.484	1
161 Mauritania	0.487	61.6	3.7	8.2	2,988	0.485	−2
162 Lesotho	0.486	49.4	5.9 [b]	11.1	2,798	0.481	1
163 Senegal	0.485	63.5	4.5	7.9	2,169	0.484	−3
164 Uganda	0.484	59.2	5.4	10.8	1,335	0.480	0
165 Benin	0.476	59.3	3.2	11.0	1,726	0.473	0
166 Sudan	0.473	62.1	3.1	7.3 [p]	3,428	0.472	0
166 Togo	0.473	56.5	5.3	12.2	1,129	0.470	1
168 Haiti	0.471	63.1	4.9	7.6 [p]	1,636	0.469	0
169 Afghanistan	0.468	60.9	3.2	9.3	1,904	0.466	0
170 Djibouti	0.467	61.8	3.8 [r]	6.4	3,109 [h]	0.465	0
171 Côte d'Ivoire	0.452	50.7	4.3	8.9 [p]	2,774	0.448	0
172 Gambia	0.441	58.8	2.8	9.1	1,557	0.438	0
173 Ethiopia	0.435	63.6	2.4 [w]	8.5	1,303	0.429	0
174 Malawi	0.414	55.3	4.2	10.8	715	0.411	0
175 Liberia	0.412	60.6	3.9	8.5 [p]	752	0.407	0
176 Mali	0.407	55.0	2.0 [b]	8.6	1,499	0.406	0
177 Guinea-Bissau	0.396	54.3	2.3 [r]	9.0	1,090	0.396	0
178 Mozambique	0.393	50.3	3.2 [w]	9.5	1,011	0.389	1
179 Guinea	0.392	56.1	1.6 [w]	8.7	1,142	0.391	−1
180 Burundi	0.389	54.1	2.7	10.1	749	0.386	0
181 Burkina Faso	0.388	56.3	1.3 [r]	7.5	1,602	0.385	0
182 Eritrea	0.381	62.9	3.4 [p]	4.1	1,147	0.380	0
183 Sierra Leone	0.374	45.6	2.9	7.5 [p]	1,815	0.368	1
184 Chad	0.372	51.2	1.5 [s]	7.4	1,622	0.370	−1
185 Central African Republic	0.341	50.2	3.5	7.2	588	0.365	0

TABLE 1

HDI rank	Human Development Index (HDI) Value 2013	Life expectancy at birth (years) 2013	Mean years of schooling (years) 2012[a]	Expected years of schooling (years) 2012[a]	Gross national income (GNI) per capita (2011 PPP $) 2013	Human Development Index (HDI) Value 2012	Change in rank 2012–2013
186 Congo (Democratic Republic of the)	0.338	50.0	3.1	9.7	444	0.333	1
187 Niger	0.337	58.4	1.4	5.4	873	0.335	−1
OTHER COUNTRIES OR TERRITORIES							
Korea, Democratic People's Rep. of	..	70.0	..	..	..	..	..
Marshall Islands	..	72.6	..	..	4,206	..	..
Monaco	..	..	..	..	..	..	..
Nauru	..	..	..	9.3	..	..	..
San Marino	..	..	..	15.3	..	..	..
Somalia	..	55.1	..	..	..	..	..
South Sudan	..	55.3	..	..	1,450	..	..
Tuvalu	..	..	..	10.8	5,151	..	..
Human Development Index groups							
Very high human development	0.890	80.2	11.7	16.3	40,046	0.889	—
High human development	0.735	74.5	8.1	13.4	13,231	0.733	—
Medium human development	0.614	67.9	5.5	11.7	5,960	0.612	—
Low human development	0.493	59.4	4.2	9.0	2,904	0.490	—
Regions							
Arab States	0.682	70.2	6.3	11.8	15,817	0.681	—
East Asia and the Pacific	0.703	74.0	7.4	12.5	10,499	0.699	—
Europe and Central Asia	0.738	71.3	9.6	13.6	12,415	0.735	—
Latin America and the Caribbean	0.740	74.9	7.9	13.7	13,767	0.739	—
South Asia	0.588	67.2	4.7	11.2	5,195	0.586	—
Sub-Saharan Africa	0.502	56.8	4.8	9.7	3,152	0.499	—
Least developed countries	0.487	61.5	3.9	9.4	2,126	0.484	—
Small island developing states	0.665	70.0	7.5	11.0	9,471	0.663	—
World	**0.702**	**70.8**	**7.7**	**12.2**	**13,723**	**0.700**	—

NOTES

a Data refer to 2012 or the most recent year available.

b Updated by HDRO based on data from UNESCO Institute for Statistics (2013b).

c Calculated by the Singapore Ministry of Education.

d Value from UNDESA (2011).

e Assumes the same adult mean years of schooling as Switzerland before the most recent update.

f Estimated using the purchasing power parity (PPP) rate and the projected growth rate of Switzerland.

g For the purpose of calculating the HDI, GNI per capita is capped at $75,000.

h Based on PPP conversion rates for GDP from World Bank (2014) and on GDP deflators and GNI per capita in national currency from United Nations Statistics Division (2014).

i Assumes the same adult mean years of schooling as Spain before the most recent update.

j Estimated using the PPP rate and the projected growth rate of Spain.

k Based on data from UNESCO Institute for Statistics (2011).

l Based on data on school life expectancy from UNESCO Institute for Statistics (2013a).

m Projected growth rate based on ECLAC (2013).

n Based on data on school life expectancy from UNESCO Institute for Statistics (2012).

o Based on the estimate of educational attainment distribution from UNESCO Institute for Statistics (2013b).

p Based on cross-country regression.

q HDRO calculations based on data from the National Institute for Educational Studies of Brazil (2013).

r Based on data from United Nations Children's Fund Multiple Indicator Cluster Surveys for 2005–2012.

s Based on data from household surveys in the World Bank's International Income Distribution Database.

t HDRO calculations based on data from Samoa Bureau of Statistics (n.d.).

u Based on projected growth rates from UNESCWA (2013).

v Unpublished provisional estimate from an October 2013 communication note from the United Nations Population Division.

w Based on data from Demographic and Health Surveys conducted by ICF Macro.

DEFINITIONS

Human Development Index (HDI): A composite index measuring average achievement in three basic dimensions of human development—a long and healthy life, knowledge and a decent standard of living. See *Technical note 1* at http://hdr.undp.org for details on how the HDI is calculated.

Life expectancy at birth: Number of years a newborn infant could expect to live if prevailing patterns of age-specific mortality rates at the time of birth stay the same throughout the infant's life.

Mean years of schooling: Average number of years of education received by people ages 25 and older, converted from education attainment levels using official durations of each level.

Expected years of schooling: Number of years of schooling that a child of school entrance age can expect to receive if prevailing patterns of age-specific enrolment rates persist throughout the child's life.

Gross national income (GNI) per capita: Aggregate income of an economy generated by its production and its ownership of factors of production, less the incomes paid for the use of factors of production owned by the rest of the world, converted to international dollars using PPP rates, divided by midyear population.

MAIN DATA SOURCES

Columns 1 and 6: HDRO calculations based on data from UNDESA (2013a), Barro and Lee (2013), UNESCO Institute for Statistics (2013b), United Nations Statistics Division (2014), World Bank (2014) and IMF (2014).

Column 2: UNDESA 2013a.

Column 3: Barro and Lee (2013), UNESCO Institute for Statistics (2013b) and HDRO estimates based on data on educational attainment from UNESCO Institute for Statistics (2013b) and on methodology from Barro and Lee (2013).

Column 4: UNESCO Institute for Statistics 2013b.

Column 5: HDRO calculations based on data from World Bank (2014), IMF (2014) and United Nations Statistics Division (2014).

Column 7: Calculations based on data in columns 1 and 6.

TABLE 1 Human Development Index and its components | 163

TABLE 2

Human Development Index trends, 1980–2013

TABLE 2

	Human Development Index (HDI)									HDI rank	Change	Average annual HDI growth (%)		
	Value													
HDI rank	1980	1990	2000	2005	2008	2010	2011	2012	2013	2012	2008–2013ᵈ	1980–1990	1990–2000	2000–2013
VERY HIGH HUMAN DEVELOPMENT														
1 Norway	0.793	0.841	0.910	0.935	0.937	0.939	0.941	0.943	0.944	1	0	0.59	0.80	0.28
2 Australia	0.841	0.866	0.898	0.912	0.922	0.926	0.928	0.931	0.933	2	0	0.29	0.37	0.29
3 Switzerland	0.806	0.829	0.886	0.901	0.903	0.915	0.914	0.916	0.917	3	1	0.29	0.66	0.27
4 Netherlands	0.783	0.826	0.874	0.888	0.901	0.904	0.914	0.915	0.915	4	3	0.53	0.57	0.35
5 United States	0.825	0.858	0.883	0.897	0.905	0.908	0.911	0.912	0.914	5	−2	0.39	0.29	0.26
6 Germany	0.739	0.782	0.854	0.887	0.902	0.904	0.908	0.911	0.911	6	−1	0.57	0.89	0.51
7 New Zealand	0.793	0.821	0.873	0.894	0.899	0.903	0.904	0.908	0.910	7	1	0.35	0.62	0.32
8 Canada	0.809	0.848	0.867	0.892	0.896	0.896	0.900	0.901	0.902	8	1	0.48	0.21	0.31
9 Singapore	..	0.744	0.800	0.840	0.868	0.894	0.896	0.899	0.901	12	14	..	0.72	0.92
10 Denmark	0.781	0.806	0.859	0.891	0.896	0.898	0.899	0.900	0.900	10	−1	0.31	0.63	0.37
11 Ireland	0.734	0.775	0.862	0.890	0.902	0.899	0.900	0.901	0.899	8	−6	0.54	1.08	0.32
12 Sweden	0.776	0.807	0.889	0.887	0.891	0.895	0.896	0.897	0.898	11	−1	0.38	0.98	0.08
13 Iceland	0.754	0.800	0.858	0.888	0.886	0.886	0.890	0.893	0.895	13	0	0.59	0.70	0.32
14 United Kingdom	0.735	0.768	0.863	0.888	0.890	0.895	0.891	0.890	0.892	14	−2	0.45	1.18	0.25
15 Hong Kong, China (SAR)	0.698	0.775	0.810	0.839	0.877	0.882	0.886	0.889	0.891	15	2	1.06	0.43	0.74
15 Korea (Republic of)	0.628	0.731	0.819	0.856	0.874	0.882	0.886	0.888	0.891	16	5	1.52	1.14	0.65
17 Japan	0.772	0.817	0.858	0.873	0.881	0.884	0.887	0.888	0.890	16	−2	0.57	0.48	0.28
18 Liechtenstein	..	..	..	..	..	0.882	0.887	0.888	0.889	16	..	..	..	..
19 Israel	0.749	0.785	0.849	0.869	0.877	0.881	0.885	0.886	0.888	19	−1	0.48	0.78	0.34
20 France	0.722	0.779	0.848	0.867	0.875	0.879	0.882	0.884	0.884	20	0	0.76	0.85	0.33
21 Austria	0.736	0.786	0.835	0.851	0.868	0.877	0.879	0.880	0.881	21	3	0.67	0.61	0.41
21 Belgium	0.753	0.805	0.873	0.865	0.873	0.877	0.880	0.880	0.881	21	1	0.68	0.81	0.07
21 Luxembourg	0.729	0.786	0.866	0.876	0.882	0.881	0.881	0.880	0.881	21	−6	0.75	0.98	0.13
24 Finland	0.752	0.792	0.841	0.869	0.878	0.877	0.879	0.879	0.879	24	−7	0.52	0.60	0.34
25 Slovenia	..	0.769	0.821	0.855	0.871	0.873	0.874	0.874	0.874	25	−2	..	0.66	0.48
26 Italy	0.718	0.763	0.825	0.858	0.868	0.869	0.872	0.872	0.872	26	−2	0.60	0.78	0.43
27 Spain	0.702	0.755	0.826	0.844	0.857	0.864	0.868	0.869	0.869	27	1	0.74	0.90	0.39
28 Czech Republic	..	0.762	0.806	0.845	0.856	0.858	0.861	0.861	0.861	28	1	..	0.56	0.52
29 Greece	0.713	0.749	0.798	0.853	0.858	0.856	0.854	0.854	0.853	29	−2	0.49	0.64	0.51
30 Brunei Darussalam	0.740	0.786	0.822	0.838	0.843	0.844	0.846	0.852	0.852	30	2	0.60	0.46	0.27
31 Qatar	0.729	0.756	0.811	0.840	0.855	0.847	0.843	0.850	0.851	31	−1	0.35	0.71	0.37
32 Cyprus	0.661	0.726	0.800	0.828	0.844	0.848	0.850	0.848	0.845	32	−1	0.95	0.96	0.43
33 Estonia	..	0.730	0.776	0.821	0.832	0.830	0.836	0.839	0.840	33	0	..	0.61	0.61
34 Saudi Arabia	0.583	0.662	0.744	0.773	0.791	0.815	0.825	0.833	0.836	34	13	1.28	1.17	0.90
35 Lithuania	..	0.737	0.757	0.806	0.827	0.829	0.828	0.831	0.834	36	1	..	0.28	0.75
35 Poland	0.687	0.714	0.784	0.803	0.817	0.826	0.830	0.833	0.834	34	3	0.38	0.94	0.48
37 Andorra	..	..	..	..	..	0.832	0.831	0.830	0.830	37	..	..	..	..
37 Slovakia	..	0.747	0.776	0.803	0.824	0.826	0.827	0.829	0.830	38	0	..	0.39	0.51
39 Malta	0.704	0.730	0.770	0.801	0.809	0.821	0.823	0.827	0.829	39	4	0.36	0.53	0.57
40 United Arab Emirates	0.640	0.725	0.797	0.823	0.832	0.824	0.824	0.825	0.827	40	−5	1.25	0.95	0.28
41 Chile	0.640	0.704	0.753	0.785	0.805	0.808	0.815	0.819	0.822	42	3	0.96	0.67	0.68
41 Portugal	0.643	0.708	0.780	0.790	0.805	0.816	0.819	0.822	0.822	41	3	0.96	0.97	0.41
43 Hungary	0.696	0.701	0.774	0.805	0.814	0.817	0.817	0.817	0.818	43	−3	0.08	0.99	0.43
44 Bahrain	0.677	0.729	0.784	0.811	0.810	0.812	0.812	0.813	0.815	44	−2	0.75	0.72	0.30
44 Cuba	0.681	0.729	0.742	0.786	0.830	0.824	0.819	0.813	0.815	44	−9	0.68	0.17	0.73
46 Kuwait	0.702	0.723	0.804	0.795	0.800	0.807	0.810	0.813	0.814	44	1	0.29	1.08	0.09
47 Croatia	..	0.689	0.748	0.781	0.801	0.806	0.812	0.812	0.812	47	−1	..	0.82	0.64
48 Latvia	..	0.710	0.729	0.786	0.813	0.809	0.804	0.808	0.810	48	−7	..	0.26	0.82
49 Argentina	0.665	0.694	0.753	0.758	0.777	0.799	0.804	0.806	0.808	49	4	0.43	0.81	0.55
HIGH HUMAN DEVELOPMENT														
50 Uruguay	0.658	0.691	0.740	0.755	0.773	0.779	0.783	0.787	0.790	52	5	0.49	0.69	0.50
51 Bahamas	..	..	0.766	0.787	0.791	0.788	0.789	0.788	0.789	51	−3	..	..	0.23
51 Montenegro	..	..	..	0.750	0.780	0.784	0.787	0.787	0.789	52	1	..	..	..
53 Belarus	..	..	..	0.725	0.764	0.779	0.784	0.785	0.786	54	7	..	..	..
54 Romania	0.685	0.703	0.706	0.750	0.781	0.779	0.782	0.782	0.785	55	−3	0.25	0.05	0.82
55 Libya	0.641	0.684	0.745	0.772	0.789	0.799	0.753	0.789	0.784	50	−5	0.65	0.85	0.40
56 Oman	..	..	..	0.733	0.714	0.780	0.781	0.781	0.783	56	6	..	..	..
57 Russian Federation	..	0.729	0.717	0.750	0.770	0.773	0.775	0.777	0.778	57	0	..	−0.17	0.64
58 Bulgaria	0.658	0.696	0.714	0.749	0.766	0.773	0.774	0.776	0.777	58	0	0.57	0.25	0.66
59 Barbados	0.658	0.706	0.745	0.761	0.776	0.779	0.780	0.776	0.776	58	−5	0.71	0.54	0.31
60 Palau	..	..	0.741	0.771	0.772	0.768	0.770	0.773	0.775	60	−4	..	..	0.34
61 Antigua and Barbuda	..	..	..	..	..	0.778	0.772	0.773	0.774	60	..	..	..	..
62 Malaysia	0.577	0.641	0.717	0.747	0.760	0.766	0.768	0.770	0.773	62	1	1.05	1.12	0.58

	Human Development Index (HDI)									HDI rank		Average annual HDI growth		
	Value										Change	(%)		
HDI rank	1980	1990	2000	2005	2008	2010	2011	2012	2013	2012	2008–2013ª	1980–1990	1990–2000	2000–2013
63 Mauritius	0.558	0.621	0.686	0.722	0.741	0.753	0.759	0.769	0.771	63	9	1.07	1.01	0.90
64 Trinidad and Tobago	0.658	0.658	0.697	0.745	0.764	0.764	0.764	0.765	0.766	64	−3	0.00	0.58	0.73
65 Lebanon	..	..	..	0.741	0.750	0.759	0.764	0.764	0.765	65	2	..	..	..
65 Panama	0.627	0.651	0.709	0.728	0.752	0.759	0.757	0.761	0.765	67	1	0.38	0.85	0.59
67 Venezuela (Bolivarian Republic of)	0.639	0.644	0.677	0.716	0.758	0.759	0.761	0.763	0.764	66	−2	0.08	0.50	0.93
68 Costa Rica	0.605	0.652	0.705	0.721	0.744	0.750	0.758	0.761	0.763	67	1	0.76	0.79	0.60
69 Turkey	0.496	0.576	0.653	0.687	0.710	0.738	0.752	0.756	0.759	69	16	1.50	1.27	1.16
70 Kazakhstan	..	0.686	0.679	0.734	0.744	0.747	0.750	0.755	0.757	70	−1	..	−0.09	0.84
71 Mexico	0.595	0.647	0.699	0.724	0.739	0.748	0.752	0.755	0.756	70	2	0.84	0.78	0.60
71 Seychelles	..	..	0.743	0.757	0.766	0.763	0.749	0.755	0.756	70	−12	..	..	0.14
73 Saint Kitts and Nevis	..	..	..	..	..	0.747	0.745	0.749	0.750	73	..	..	..	..
73 Sri Lanka	0.569	0.620	0.679	0.710	0.725	0.736	0.740	0.745	0.750	75	5	0.87	0.91	0.77
75 Iran (Islamic Republic of)	0.490	0.552	0.652	0.681	0.711	0.725	0.733	0.749	0.749	73	10	1.19	1.69	1.07
76 Azerbaijan	..	..	0.639	0.686	0.724	0.743	0.743	0.745	0.747	75	4	..	..	1.21
77 Jordan	0.587	0.622	0.705	0.733	0.746	0.744	0.744	0.744	0.745	77	−8	0.58	1.26	0.43
77 Serbia	..	0.726	0.713	0.732	0.743	0.743	0.744	0.743	0.745	78	−5	..	−0.19	0.34
79 Brazil	0.545	0.612	0.682	0.705	0.731	0.739	0.740	0.742	0.744	80	−4	1.16	1.10	0.67
79 Georgia	..	..	..	0.710	0.730	0.733	0.736	0.741	0.744	81	−3	..	..	..
79 Grenada	..	..	..	..	..	0.746	0.747	0.743	0.744	78	..	..	..	..
82 Peru	0.595	0.615	0.682	0.694	0.707	0.722	0.727	0.734	0.737	82	8	0.34	1.03	0.60
83 Ukraine	..	0.705	0.668	0.713	0.729	0.726	0.730	0.733	0.734	83	−5	..	−0.54	0.73
84 Belize	0.619	0.640	0.675	0.710	0.710	0.714	0.717	0.731	0.732	84	3	0.33	0.53	0.63
84 The former Yugoslav Republic of Macedonia	..	..	..	0.699	0.724	0.728	0.730	0.730	0.732	85	−3	..	..	..
86 Bosnia and Herzegovina	..	..	..	0.716	0.727	0.726	0.729	0.729	0.731	86	−7	..	..	..
87 Armenia	..	0.632	0.648	0.693	0.722	0.720	0.724	0.728	0.730	87	−4	..	0.26	0.92
88 Fiji	0.587	0.619	0.674	0.694	0.712	0.721	0.722	0.722	0.724	88	−4	0.53	0.86	0.55
89 Thailand	0.503	0.572	0.649	0.685	0.704	0.715	0.716	0.720	0.722	89	3	1.28	1.27	0.83
90 Tunisia	0.484	0.567	0.653	0.687	0.706	0.715	0.716	0.719	0.721	90	1	1.60	1.42	0.77
91 China	0.423	0.502	0.591	0.645	0.682	0.701	0.710	0.715	0.719	93	10	1.72	1.66	1.52
91 Saint Vincent and the Grenadines	..	..	..	..	..	0.717	0.715	0.717	0.719	91	..	..	..	..
93 Algeria	0.509	0.576	0.634	0.675	0.695	0.709	0.715	0.715	0.717	93	5	1.25	0.96	0.95
93 Dominica	..	..	0.691	0.708	0.712	0.717	0.718	0.716	0.717	92	−8	..	..	0.29
95 Albania	0.603	0.609	0.655	0.689	0.703	0.708	0.714	0.714	0.716	97	−1	0.10	0.74	0.69
96 Jamaica	0.614	0.638	0.671	0.700	0.710	0.712	0.714	0.715	0.715	93	−8	0.38	0.51	0.49
97 Saint Lucia	..	..	..	..	..	0.717	0.718	0.715	0.714	93	..	..	..	..
98 Colombia	0.557	0.596	0.655	0.680	0.700	0.706	0.710	0.708	0.711	98	−2	0.68	0.94	0.63
98 Ecuador	0.605	0.643	0.658	0.687	0.697	0.701	0.705	0.708	0.711	98	−1	0.61	0.24	0.59
100 Suriname	..	..	..	0.672	0.694	0.698	0.701	0.702	0.705	101	0	..	..	..
100 Tonga	0.602	0.631	0.672	0.695	0.696	0.701	0.702	0.704	0.705	100	−2	0.49	0.62	0.37
102 Dominican Republic	0.527	0.589	0.645	0.668	0.684	0.691	0.695	0.698	0.700	102	−1	1.12	0.91	0.63
MEDIUM HUMAN DEVELOPMENT														
103 Maldives	..	..	0.599	0.659	0.675	0.688	0.692	0.695	0.698	103	1	..	..	1.19
103 Mongolia	0.515	0.552	0.580	0.637	0.665	0.671	0.682	0.692	0.698	106	3	0.71	0.50	1.43
103 Turkmenistan	..	..	..	..	..	0.687	0.690	0.693	0.698	104	..	..	..	..
106 Samoa	..	..	0.654	0.681	0.683	0.688	0.690	0.693	0.694	104	−3	..	..	0.45
107 Palestine, State of	..	..	..	0.649	0.672	0.671	0.679	0.683	0.686	107	1	..	..	..
108 Indonesia	0.471	0.528	0.609	0.640	0.654	0.671	0.678	0.681	0.684	108	4	1.16	1.44	0.90
109 Botswana	0.470	0.583	0.560	0.610	0.656	0.672	0.678	0.681	0.683	108	2	2.18	−0.40	1.54
110 Egypt	0.452	0.546	0.621	0.645	0.667	0.678	0.679	0.681	0.682	108	−4	1.91	1.30	0.72
111 Paraguay	0.550	0.581	0.625	0.648	0.661	0.669	0.672	0.670	0.676	111	−3	0.55	0.73	0.61
112 Gabon	0.540	0.619	0.632	0.644	0.654	0.662	0.666	0.670	0.674	111	0	1.37	0.21	0.50
113 Bolivia (Plurinational State of)	0.494	0.554	0.615	0.636	0.649	0.658	0.661	0.663	0.667	113	2	1.17	1.04	0.63
114 Moldova (Republic of)	..	0.645	0.598	0.639	0.652	0.652	0.656	0.657	0.663	116	0	..	−0.76	0.80
115 El Salvador	0.517	0.529	0.607	0.640	0.648	0.652	0.657	0.660	0.662	115	1	0.22	1.38	0.67
116 Uzbekistan	..	..	..	0.626	0.643	0.648	0.653	0.657	0.661	116	2	..	..	..
117 Philippines	0.566	0.591	0.619	0.638	0.648	0.651	0.652	0.656	0.660	118	−1	0.45	0.46	0.49
118 South Africa	0.569	0.619	0.628	0.608	0.623	0.638	0.646	0.654	0.658	119	2	0.86	0.14	0.36
118 Syrian Arab Republic	0.528	0.570	0.605	0.653	0.658	0.662	0.662	0.662	0.658	114	−8	0.76	0.60	0.65
120 Iraq	0.500	0.508	0.606	0.621	0.632	0.638	0.639	0.641	0.642	120	−1	0.17	1.77	0.45
121 Guyana	0.516	0.505	0.570	0.584	0.621	0.626	0.632	0.635	0.638	121	0	−0.22	1.22	0.87
121 Viet Nam	0.463	0.476	0.563	0.598	0.617	0.629	0.632	0.635	0.638	121	2	0.28	1.70	0.96
123 Cape Verde	..	..	0.573	0.589	0.613	0.622	0.631	0.635	0.636	121	1	..	..	0.81
124 Micronesia (Federated States of)	..	..	..	..	..	0.627	0.627	0.629	0.630	124	..	..	..	..
125 Guatemala	0.445	0.483	0.551	0.576	0.601	0.613	0.620	0.626	0.628	125	3	0.82	1.34	1.01

TABLE 2   Human Development Index trends, 1980–2013 | 165

TABLE 2

TABLE 2 HUMAN DEVELOPMENT INDEX TRENDS, 1980–2013

	Human Development Index (HDI)									HDI rank		Average annual HDI growth		
	Value										Change	(%)		
HDI rank	1980	1990	2000	2005	2008	2010	2011	2012	2013	2012	2008–2013[a]	1980–1990	1990–2000	2000–2013
125 Kyrgyzstan	..	0.607	0.586	0.605	0.617	0.614	0.618	0.621	0.628	126	−2	..	−0.34	0.52
127 Namibia	0.550	0.577	0.556	0.570	0.598	0.610	0.616	0.620	0.624	127	3	0.48	−0.36	0.89
128 Timor-Leste	..	..	0.465	0.505	0.579	0.606	0.606	0.616	0.620	129	5	..	..	2.25
129 Honduras	0.461	0.507	0.558	0.584	0.604	0.612	0.615	0.616	0.617	129	−2	0.95	0.96	0.78
129 Morocco	0.399	0.459	0.526	0.569	0.588	0.603	0.612	0.614	0.617	131	3	1.41	1.37	1.23
131 Vanuatu	..	..	..	..	0.608	0.617	0.618	0.617	0.616	128	−5	..	..	..
132 Nicaragua	0.483	0.491	0.554	0.585	0.599	0.604	0.608	0.611	0.614	132	−3	0.17	1.22	0.79
133 Kiribati	..	..	..	..	..	0.599	0.599	0.606	0.607	133		..	..	..
133 Tajikistan	..	0.610	0.529	0.572	0.591	0.596	0.600	0.603	0.607	134	−2	..	−1.42	1.07
135 India	0.369	0.431	0.483	0.527	0.554	0.570	0.581	0.583	0.586	135	1	1.58	1.15	1.49
136 Bhutan	..	..	..	..	..	0.569	0.579	0.580	0.584	136		..	..	..
136 Cambodia	0.251	0.403	0.466	0.536	0.564	0.571	0.575	0.579	0.584	137	−1	4.83	1.47	1.75
138 Ghana	0.423	0.502	0.487	0.511	0.544	0.556	0.566	0.571	0.573	138	1	1.73	−0.30	1.26
139 Lao People's Democratic Republic	0.340	0.395	0.473	0.511	0.533	0.549	0.560	0.565	0.569	139	3	1.51	1.83	1.44
140 Congo	0.542	0.553	0.501	0.525	0.548	0.565	0.549	0.561	0.564	140	−2	0.19	−0.98	0.92
141 Zambia	0.422	0.407	0.423	0.471	0.505	0.530	0.543	0.554	0.561	143	7	−0.37	0.39	2.19
142 Bangladesh	0.336	0.382	0.453	0.494	0.515	0.539	0.549	0.554	0.558	143	2	1.29	1.71	1.62
142 Sao Tome and Principe	..	..	0.495	0.520	0.537	0.543	0.548	0.556	0.558	141	−1	..	..	0.92
144 Equatorial Guinea	..	..	0.476	0.517	0.543	0.559	0.553	0.556	0.556	141	−4	..	..	1.21
LOW HUMAN DEVELOPMENT														
145 Nepal	0.286	0.388	0.449	0.477	0.501	0.527	0.533	0.537	0.540	145	4	3.09	1.47	1.42
146 Pakistan	0.356	0.402	0.454	0.504	0.536	0.526	0.531	0.535	0.537	146	−1	1.22	1.21	1.30
147 Kenya	0.446	0.471	0.455	0.479	0.508	0.522	0.527	0.531	0.535	147	−1	0.55	−0.34	1.25
148 Swaziland	0.477	0.538	0.498	0.498	0.518	0.527	0.530	0.529	0.530	148	−5	1.20	−0.77	0.48
149 Angola	..	..	0.377	0.446	0.490	0.504	0.521	0.524	0.526	149	2	..	..	2.60
150 Myanmar	0.328	0.347	0.421	0.472	0.500	0.514	0.517	0.520	0.524	150	0	0.59	1.94	1.69
151 Rwanda	0.291	0.238	0.329	0.391	0.432	0.453	0.463	0.502	0.506	151	17	−2.01	3.31	3.35
152 Cameroon	0.391	0.440	0.433	0.457	0.477	0.493	0.498	0.501	0.504	152	2	1.19	−0.15	1.18
152 Nigeria	..	..	..	0.466	0.483	0.492	0.496	0.500	0.504	153	1	..	..	..
154 Yemen	..	0.390	0.427	0.462	0.471	0.484	0.497	0.499	0.500	154	2	..	0.90	1.22
155 Madagascar	..	..	0.453	0.470	0.487	0.494	0.495	0.496	0.498	155	−3	..	..	0.73
156 Zimbabwe	0.437	0.488	0.428	0.412	0.422	0.459	0.473	0.484	0.492	160	16	1.12	−1.30	1.08
157 Papua New Guinea	0.323	0.363	0.423	0.441	0.467	0.479	0.484	0.490	0.491	156	1	1.19	1.53	1.17
157 Solomon Islands	..	..	0.475	0.483	0.506	0.489	0.494	0.489	0.491	157	−10	..	..	0.25
159 Comoros	..	..	..	0.464	0.474	0.479	0.483	0.486	0.488	158	−4	..	..	..
159 Tanzania (United Republic of)	0.377	0.354	0.376	0.419	0.451	0.464	0.478	0.484	0.488	160	5	−0.64	0.59	2.04
161 Mauritania	0.347	0.367	0.433	0.455	0.466	0.475	0.475	0.485	0.487	159	−2	0.55	1.67	0.91
162 Lesotho	0.443	0.493	0.443	0.437	0.456	0.472	0.476	0.481	0.486	163	0	1.06	−1.06	0.72
163 Senegal	0.333	0.384	0.413	0.451	0.474	0.483	0.483	0.484	0.485	160	−6	1.44	0.72	1.25
164 Uganda	0.293	0.310	0.392	0.429	0.458	0.472	0.477	0.480	0.484	164	−4	0.55	2.38	1.63
165 Benin	0.287	0.342	0.391	0.432	0.454	0.467	0.471	0.473	0.476	165	−2	1.78	1.33	1.52
166 Sudan	0.331	0.342	0.385	0.423	0.447	0.463	0.468	0.472	0.473	166	−1	0.33	1.20	1.59
166 Togo	0.405	0.404	0.430	0.442	0.447	0.460	0.467	0.470	0.473	167	−1	−0.03	0.63	0.74
168 Haiti	0.352	0.413	0.433	0.447	0.458	0.462	0.466	0.469	0.471	168	−8	1.61	0.46	0.66
169 Afghanistan	0.230	0.296	0.341	0.396	0.430	0.453	0.458	0.466	0.468	169	1	2.56	1.42	2.46
170 Djibouti	..	..	..	0.412	0.438	0.452	0.461	0.465	0.467	170	−3	..	..	..
171 Côte d'Ivoire	0.377	0.380	0.393	0.407	0.427	0.439	0.443	0.448	0.452	171	0	0.10	0.33	1.08
172 Gambia	0.300	0.334	0.383	0.414	0.432	0.440	0.436	0.438	0.441	172	−4	1.08	1.37	1.08
173 Ethiopia	..	..	0.284	0.339	0.394	0.409	0.422	0.429	0.435	173	2	..	..	3.35
174 Malawi	0.270	0.283	0.341	0.368	0.395	0.406	0.411	0.411	0.414	174	0	0.46	1.88	1.50
175 Liberia	..	..	0.339	0.335	0.374	0.393	0.402	0.407	0.412	175	3	..	..	1.52
176 Mali	0.208	0.232	0.309	0.359	0.385	0.398	0.405	0.406	0.407	176	0	1.14	2.89	2.13
177 Guinea-Bissau	..	..	..	0.387	0.397	0.401	0.402	0.396	0.396	177	−4	..	..	..
178 Mozambique	0.246	0.216	0.285	0.343	0.366	0.380	0.384	0.389	0.393	179	1	−1.31	2.84	2.49
179 Guinea	..	..	..	0.366	0.377	0.380	0.387	0.391	0.392	178	−2	..	..	..
180 Burundi	0.230	0.291	0.290	0.319	0.362	0.381	0.384	0.386	0.389	180	0	2.37	−0.03	2.29
181 Burkina Faso	..	..	..	0.321	0.349	0.367	0.376	0.385	0.388	181	0	..	..	..
182 Eritrea	..	..	..	..	..	0.373	0.377	0.380	0.381	182		..	..	..
183 Sierra Leone	0.276	0.263	0.297	0.329	0.346	0.353	0.360	0.368	0.374	184	0	−0.49	1.23	1.79
184 Chad	..	..	0.301	0.324	0.338	0.349	0.365	0.370	0.372	183	1	..	..	1.66
185 Central African Republic	0.295	0.310	0.314	0.327	0.344	0.355	0.361	0.365	0.341	185	−1	0.50	0.13	0.61
186 Congo (Democratic Republic of the)	0.336	0.319	0.274	0.292	0.307	0.319	0.323	0.333	0.338	187	1	−0.53	−1.52	1.64
187 Niger	0.191	0.218	0.262	0.293	0.309	0.323	0.328	0.335	0.337	186	−1	1.34	1.86	1.95

| | Human Development Index (HDI) | | | | | | | | | HDI rank | | Average annual HDI growth | | |
| | Value | | | | | | | | | | Change | (%) | | |
HDI rank	1980	1990	2000	2005	2008	2010	2011	2012	2013	2012	2008–2013[a]	1980–1990	1990–2000	2000–2013
OTHER COUNTRIES OR TERRITORIES														
Korea, Democratic People's Rep. of	..	..	..	..	..	..	..	..	..	..	..	..	..	..
Marshall Islands	..	..	..	..	..	..	..	..	..	..	..	..	..	..
Monaco	..	..	..	..	..	..	..	..	..	..	..	..	..	..
Nauru	..	..	..	..	..	..	..	..	..	..	..	..	..	..
San Marino	..	..	..	..	..	..	..	..	..	..	..	..	..	..
Somalia	..	..	..	..	..	..	..	..	..	..	..	..	..	..
South Sudan	..	..	..	..	..	..	..	..	..	..	..	..	..	..
Tuvalu	..	..	..	..	..	..	..	..	..	..	..	..	..	..
Human Development Index groups														
Very high human development	0.757	0.798	0.849	0.870	0.879	0.885	0.887	0.889	0.890	—	—	0.52	0.62	0.37
High human development	0.534	0.593	0.643	0.682	0.710	0.723	0.729	0.733	0.735	—	—	1.04	0.81	1.04
Medium human development	0.420	0.474	0.528	0.565	0.587	0.601	0.609	0.612	0.614	—	—	1.22	1.09	1.17
Low human development	0.345	0.367	0.403	0.444	0.471	0.479	0.486	0.490	0.493	—	—	0.64	0.95	1.56
Regions														
Arab States	0.492	0.551	0.611	0.644	0.664	0.675	0.678	0.681	0.682	—	—	1.14	1.05	0.85
East Asia and the Pacific	0.457	0.517	0.595	0.641	0.671	0.688	0.695	0.699	0.703	—	—	1.23	1.42	1.29
Europe and Central Asia	..	0.651	0.665	0.700	0.716	0.726	0.733	0.735	0.738	—	—	..	0.21	0.80
Latin America and the Caribbean	0.579	0.627	0.683	0.705	0.726	0.734	0.737	0.739	0.740	—	—	0.79	0.87	0.62
South Asia	0.382	0.438	0.491	0.533	0.560	0.573	0.582	0.586	0.588	—	—	1.37	1.16	1.39
Sub-Saharan Africa	0.382	0.399	0.421	0.452	0.477	0.488	0.495	0.499	0.502	—	—	0.44	0.52	1.37
Least developed countries	0.319	0.345	0.391	0.429	0.457	0.472	0.480	0.484	0.487	—	—	0.79	1.26	1.70
Small island developing states	0.545	0.587	0.613	0.637	0.658	0.662	0.663	0.663	0.665	—	—	0.75	0.43	0.62
World	**0.559**	**0.597**	**0.639**	**0.667**	**0.685**	**0.693**	**0.698**	**0.700**	**0.702**	**—**	**—**	**0.66**	**0.67**	**0.73**

NOTES

a A positive value indicates an improvement in rank.

DEFINITIONS

Human Development Index (HDI): A composite index measuring average achievement in three basic dimensions of human development—a long and healthy life, knowledge and a decent standard of living. See *Technical note 1* at http://hdr.undp.org for details on how the HDI is calculated.

Average annual HDI growth: A smoothed annualized growth of the HDI in a given period, calculated as the annual compound growth rate.

MAIN DATA SOURCES

Columns 1–9: HDRO calculations based on data from UNDESA (2013a), Barro and Lee (2013),

UNESCO Institute for Statistics (2013b), United Nations Statistics Division (2014), World Bank (2014) and IMF (2014).

Columns 10–14: Calculated based on data in columns 1–9.

TABLE 2   Human Development Index trends, 1980–2013 | 167

TABLE 3

Inequality-adjusted Human Development Index

HDI rank		Human Development Index (HDI) Value	Inequality-adjusted HDI (IHDI) Value	Overall loss (%)	Difference from HDI rank[b]	Coefficient of human inequality Value	Inequality in life expectancy (%)	Inequality-adjusted life expectancy index Value	Inequality in education[a] (%)	Inequality-adjusted education index Value	Inequality in income[a] (%)	Inequality-adjusted income index Value	Income inequality Quintile ratio	Income inequality Palma ratio	Income inequality Gini coefficient
		2013	2013	2013	2013	2013	2013	2013	2013[c]	2013	2013[c]	2013	2003–2012	2003–2012	2003–2012
VERY HIGH HUMAN DEVELOPMENT															
1	Norway	0.944	0.891	5.6	0	5.5	3.4	0.914	2.4	0.888	10.7	0.871	..	..	25.8
2	Australia	0.933	0.860	7.8	0	7.5	4.2	0.921	1.8	0.910	16.6	0.760	..	..	..
3	Switzerland	0.917	0.847	7.7	−1	7.6	3.9	0.926	5.8	0.795	13.2	0.824	..	..	33.7
4	Netherlands	0.915	0.854	6.7	1	6.6	3.9	0.902	4.1	0.857	11.8	0.806	5.1	..	30.9
5	United States	0.914	0.755	17.4	−23	16.2	6.2	0.851	6.7	0.830	35.6	0.609	..	..	40.8
6	Germany	0.911	0.846	7.1	1	7.0	3.7	0.900	2.4	0.863	14.8	0.781	..	..	28.3
7	New Zealand	0.910	..	..	..	..	4.8	0.895	..	..	..	..	..	..	..
8	Canada	0.902	0.833	7.6	−2	7.5	4.6	0.902	4.0	0.816	13.9	0.785	..	..	32.6
9	Singapore	0.901	..	..	..	..	2.8	0.932	..	..	..	..	..	..	..
10	Denmark	0.900	0.838	6.9	0	6.8	4.0	0.877	3.1	0.846	13.3	0.794	..	..	..
11	Ireland	0.899	0.832	7.5	−1	7.4	3.7	0.899	5.2	0.841	13.3	0.761	..	..	34.3
12	Sweden	0.898	0.840	6.5	3	6.4	3.1	0.922	3.6	0.800	12.4	0.803	..	..	25.0
13	Iceland	0.895	0.843	5.7	5	5.6	2.8	0.928	2.5	0.826	11.6	0.783	..	..	..
14	United Kingdom	0.892	0.812	8.9	−4	8.6	4.5	0.890	2.6	0.838	18.8	0.719	7.2	..	36.0
15	Hong Kong, China (SAR)	0.891	..	..	..	..	2.8	0.948	..	..	..	..	..	..	..
15	Korea (Republic of)	0.891	0.736	17.4	−20	16.8	3.9	0.910	28.1	0.622	18.4	0.704	..	..	..
17	Japan	0.890	0.779	12.4	−6	12.2	3.2	0.947	19.8	0.648	13.5	0.772	..	..	..
18	Liechtenstein	0.889	..	..	..	..	..	..	..	..	..	..	..	..	..
19	Israel	0.888	0.793	10.7	−4	10.4	3.8	0.915	7.9	0.786	19.6	0.693	..	..	39.2
20	France	0.884	0.804	9.0	−2	8.9	4.0	0.913	8.6	0.745	14.2	0.765	..	..	..
21	Austria	0.881	0.818	7.2	4	7.1	3.7	0.906	3.7	0.765	13.8	0.789	..	..	29.2
21	Belgium	0.881	0.806	8.5	0	8.5	3.9	0.895	9.2	0.738	12.3	0.792	..	..	33.0
21	Luxembourg	0.881	0.814	7.6	3	7.5	3.3	0.901	6.0	0.716	13.1	0.837	..	..	30.8
24	Finland	0.879	0.830	5.5	9	5.5	3.5	0.899	2.1	0.798	10.8	0.798	..	..	26.9
25	Slovenia	0.874	0.824	5.8	9	5.7	3.8	0.882	2.7	0.840	10.6	0.755	4.8	..	31.2
26	Italy	0.872	0.768	11.9	−1	11.6	3.4	0.927	11.7	0.697	19.8	0.701	..	..	36.0
27	Spain	0.869	0.775	10.9	1	10.5	3.9	0.918	5.4	0.751	22.1	0.673	..	..	34.7
28	Czech Republic	0.861	0.813	5.6	9	5.5	3.7	0.855	1.4	0.854	11.3	0.737	..	..	..
29	Greece	0.853	0.762	10.6	0	10.5	4.0	0.898	11.3	0.707	16.2	0.697	..	..	34.3
30	Brunei Darussalam	0.852	..	..	..	..	4.4	0.861	..	..	..	..	..	..	..
31	Qatar	0.851	..	..	..	..	6.0	0.844	..	..	..	..	13.3	..	41.1
32	Cyprus	0.845	0.752	11.0	−3	10.9	3.7	0.887	14.0	0.668	14.9	0.719	..	..	..
33	Estonia	0.840	0.767	8.7	3	8.5	5.6	0.791	2.5	0.837	17.4	0.681	6.4	..	36.0
34	Saudi Arabia	0.836	..	..	..	..	8.7	0.779	..	..	..	..	..	..	..
35	Lithuania	0.834	0.746	10.6	−3	10.4	6.6	0.749	6.1	0.823	18.6	0.673	6.7	1.6	37.6
35	Poland	0.834	0.751	9.9	−2	9.7	5.7	0.818	5.6	0.779	17.9	0.666	5.2	1.3	32.7
37	Andorra	0.830	..	..	..	..	..	..	..	..	..	..	..	..	..
37	Slovakia	0.830	0.778	6.3	9	6.2	5.6	0.805	1.5	0.790	11.5	0.740	3.6	0.9	26.0
39	Malta	0.829	0.760	8.3	5	8.2	4.8	0.875	5.7	0.691	14.1	0.727	..	..	..
40	United Arab Emirates	0.827	..	..	..	..	5.5	0.826	..	..	..	..	..	..	..
41	Chile	0.822	0.661	19.6	−16	18.5	5.9	0.868	13.7	0.644	36.0	0.516	13.5	3.5	52.1
41	Portugal	0.822	0.739	10.1	0	9.8	3.9	0.886	5.7	0.686	19.9	0.664	..	..	..
43	Hungary	0.818	0.757	7.4	7	7.3	5.4	0.795	3.5	0.777	13.1	0.703	4.8	1.2	31.2
44	Bahrain	0.815	..	..	..	..	6.3	0.816	..	..	..	..	..	..	..
44	Cuba	0.815	..	..	..	..	5.1	0.865	11.0	0.661	..	..	..	..	..
46	Kuwait	0.814	..	..	..	..	7.2	0.775	..	..	..	..	..	..	..
47	Croatia	0.812	0.721	11.2	−2	11.1	5.2	0.832	10.4	0.690	17.6	0.653	5.2	1.4	33.7
48	Latvia	0.810	0.725	10.6	0	10.3	7.6	0.741	3.6	0.784	19.8	0.654	6.0	1.4	34.8
49	Argentina	0.808	0.680	15.8	−4	15.3	9.3	0.786	8.6	0.716	28.1	0.560	11.3	2.4	44.5
HIGH HUMAN DEVELOPMENT															
50	Uruguay	0.790	0.662	16.1	−8	15.7	9.2	0.799	10.9	0.635	27.1	0.573	10.3	2.5	45.3
51	Bahamas	0.789	0.676	14.3	−3	14.0	9.4	0.770	8.0	0.657	24.5	0.612	..	..	..
51	Montenegro	0.789	0.733	7.2	5	7.1	7.6	0.779	2.5	0.754	11.3	0.669	4.3	1.0	28.6
53	Belarus	0.786	0.726	7.6	6	7.5	6.8	0.716	4.8	0.781	11.1	0.685	3.8	0.9	26.5
54	Romania	0.785	0.702	10.5	4	10.4	8.8	0.755	5.0	0.710	17.3	0.645	4.1	1.0	27.4
55	Libya	0.784	..	..	..	..	10.1	0.765	..	..	..	..	..	..	..
56	Oman	0.783	..	..	..	..	7.0	0.809	..	..	..	..	..	..	..
57	Russian Federation	0.778	0.685	12.0	3	11.6	9.8	0.666	2.1	0.764	22.9	0.631	7.3	1.9	40.1
58	Bulgaria	0.777	0.692	11.0	5	10.8	7.9	0.759	5.8	0.706	18.8	0.618	4.3	1.0	28.2

HDI rank	Human Development Index (HDI) Value 2013	Inequality-adjusted HDI (IHDI) Value 2013	Inequality-adjusted HDI (IHDI) Overall loss (%) 2013	Inequality-adjusted HDI (IHDI) Difference from HDI rank[b] 2013	Coefficient of human inequality Value 2013	Inequality in life expectancy (%) 2013	Inequality-adjusted life expectancy index Value 2013	Inequality in education[a] (%) 2013[c]	Inequality-adjusted education index Value 2013	Inequality in income[a] (%) 2013[c]	Inequality-adjusted income index Value 2013	Income inequality Quintile ratio 2003–2012	Income inequality Palma ratio 2003–2012	Income inequality Gini coefficient 2003–2012
59 Barbados	0.776	..	..	..	..	8.1	0.783	..	..	..	..	..	..	..
60 Palau	0.775	..	..	..	..	..	..	12.0	0.692	23.0	0.565	..	..	..
61 Antigua and Barbuda	0.774	..	..	..	..	8.0	0.792	..	..	..	..	..	..	..
62 Malaysia	0.773	..	..	..	..	4.9	0.805	..	..	..	..	11.3	2.6	46.2
63 Mauritius	0.771	0.662	14.2	−2	14.1	9.2	0.749	13.2	0.623	19.8	0.621	..	..	..
64 Trinidad and Tobago	0.766	0.649	15.2	−6	15.0	16.4	0.641	6.6	0.654	21.9	0.653	..	..	..
65 Lebanon	0.765	0.606	20.8	−17	20.3	6.7	0.861	24.1	0.479	30.0	0.538	..	..	..
65 Panama	0.765	0.596	22.1	−18	21.4	12.1	0.778	16.3	0.550	35.8	0.494	17.1	3.6	51.9
67 Venezuela (Bolivarian Republic of)	0.764	0.613	19.7	−10	19.4	12.2	0.738	17.6	0.562	28.4	0.556	11.5	2.4	44.8
68 Costa Rica	0.763	0.611	19.9	−11	19.1	7.3	0.855	15.7	0.551	34.3	0.483	14.5	3.3	50.7
69 Turkey	0.759	0.639	15.8	−3	15.6	11.0	0.757	14.1	0.560	21.8	0.616	8.3	1.9	40.0
70 Kazakhstan	0.757	0.667	11.9	9	11.8	16.7	0.596	5.9	0.717	12.7	0.695	4.2	1.1	29.0
71 Mexico	0.756	0.583	22.9	−13	22.3	10.9	0.788	21.4	0.501	34.6	0.500	10.7	2.7	47.2
71 Seychelles	0.756	..	..	..	..	7.9	0.754	..	..	..	..	18.8	6.4	65.8
73 Saint Kitts and Nevis	0.750	..	..	..	..	..	..	..	..	..	..	..	..	..
73 Sri Lanka	0.750	0.643	14.3	1	14.2	8.3	0.766	14.6	0.630	19.6	0.550	5.8	1.6	36.4
75 Iran (Islamic Republic of)	0.749	0.498	33.6	−34	32.1	12.5	0.728	37.3	0.429	46.6	0.395	7.0	1.7	38.3
76 Azerbaijan	0.747	0.659	11.8	7	11.5	21.7	0.611	8.3	0.642	4.5	0.730	5.3	1.4	33.7
77 Jordan	0.745	0.607	18.6	−5	18.5	11.9	0.730	22.4	0.543	21.1	0.564	5.7	1.5	35.4
77 Serbia	0.745	0.663	10.9	12	10.9	8.5	0.761	10.7	0.621	13.5	0.618	4.6	1.1	29.6
79 Brazil	0.744	0.542	27.0	−16	26.3	14.5	0.709	24.7	0.498	39.7	0.452	20.6	4.3	54.7
79 Georgia	0.744	0.636	14.5	4	14.0	12.9	0.728	3.3	0.745	25.9	0.474	9.5	2.1	42.1
79 Grenada	0.744	..	..	..	..	8.4	0.744	..	..	..	..	..	..	..
82 Peru	0.737	0.562	23.7	−9	23.4	13.9	0.726	25.6	0.494	30.6	0.495	13.5	2.9	48.1
83 Ukraine	0.734	0.667	9.2	18	9.1	10.4	0.669	6.1	0.747	10.9	0.593	3.6	0.9	25.6
84 Belize	0.732	..	..	..	..	11.4	0.734	..	..	37.9	0.426	17.6	..	53.1
84 The former Yugoslav Republic of Macedonia	0.732	0.633	13.6	7	13.3	7.6	0.785	10.6	0.574	21.8	0.563	10.0	2.3	43.6
86 Bosnia and Herzegovina	0.731	0.653	10.6	13	10.4	6.7	0.809	5.2	0.621	19.2	0.555	6.5	1.5	36.2
87 Armenia	0.730	0.655	10.4	15	10.2	12.7	0.733	3.7	0.675	14.3	0.567	4.6	1.2	31.3
88 Fiji	0.724	0.613	15.3	6	15.1	12.3	0.672	10.5	0.686	22.6	0.500	8.0	2.2	42.8
89 Thailand	0.722	0.573	20.7	−2	20.0	9.8	0.755	16.1	0.510	34.0	0.488	6.9	1.8	39.4
90 Tunisia	0.721	..	..	..	..	10.6	0.768	..	..	..	..	6.4	1.5	36.1
91 China	0.719	..	..	..	..	9.8	0.768	..	..	29.5	0.505	10.1	2.1	42.1
91 Saint Vincent and the Grenadines	0.719	..	..	..	..	12.9	0.703	..	..	..	..	..	..	..
93 Algeria	0.717	..	..	..	..	16.7	0.654	..	..	..	..	..	..	..
93 Dominica	0.717	..	..	..	..	..	..	..	..	..	..	..	..	..
95 Albania	0.716	0.620	13.4	11	13.4	9.9	0.796	11.9	0.536	18.3	0.558	5.3	1.4	34.5
96 Jamaica	0.715	0.579	19.0	1	18.6	15.0	0.700	10.6	0.598	30.1	0.465	9.6	..	45.5
97 Saint Lucia	0.714	..	..	..	..	9.9	0.760	..	..	..	..	..	..	..
98 Colombia	0.711	0.521	26.7	−10	25.7	13.5	0.719	22.1	0.469	41.5	0.420	20.1	4.5	55.9
98 Ecuador	0.711	0.549	22.7	−3	22.4	13.4	0.752	21.6	0.466	32.1	0.472	12.5	3.1	49.3
100 Suriname	0.705	0.534	24.2	−6	23.5	13.6	0.678	19.5	0.474	37.3	0.475	17.9	..	52.9
100 Tonga	0.705	..	..	..	..	13.7	0.699	..	..	..	..	..	..	..
102 Dominican Republic	0.700	0.535	23.6	−4	23.4	16.9	0.683	24.0	0.449	29.3	0.500	11.3	2.7	47.2
MEDIUM HUMAN DEVELOPMENT														
103 Maldives	0.698	0.521	25.4	−7	24.2	8.1	0.819	41.2	0.322	23.2	0.535	6.8	..	37.4
103 Mongolia	0.698	0.618	11.5	16	11.4	16.6	0.610	5.2	0.658	12.3	0.588	6.2	1.6	36.5
103 Turkmenistan	0.698	..	..	..	..	26.0	0.517	..	..	..	..	..	..	..
106 Samoa	0.694	..	..	..	..	13.3	0.709	..	..	..	..	..	..	..
107 Palestine, State of	0.686	0.606	11.7	13	11.7	13.1	0.711	6.9	0.617	15.0	0.507	5.8	1.5	35.5
108 Indonesia	0.684	0.553	19.2	5	19.1	16.4	0.654	23.2	0.463	17.7	0.559	6.3	1.7	38.1
109 Botswana	0.683	0.422	38.2	−21	36.5	21.9	0.533	32.1	0.420	55.5	0.336	..	..	..
110 Egypt	0.682	0.518	24.0	−5	22.8	13.4	0.682	40.9	0.339	14.2	0.602	4.4	1.2	30.8
111 Paraguay	0.676	0.513	24.1	−5	23.7	19.2	0.650	17.2	0.486	34.6	0.428	17.3	3.7	52.4
112 Gabon	0.674	0.512	24.0	−5	24.0	28.0	0.482	23.5	0.451	20.4	0.617	7.8	2.0	41.5
113 Bolivia (Plurinational State of)	0.667	0.470	29.6	−10	29.4	24.5	0.549	27.6	0.488	36.1	0.388	27.8	4.8	56.3
114 Moldova (Republic of)	0.663	0.582	12.2	16	12.0	11.0	0.670	6.1	0.614	18.9	0.480	5.3	1.3	33.0
115 El Salvador	0.662	0.485	26.7	−7	26.2	14.5	0.692	30.2	0.386	34.0	0.427	14.3	3.0	48.3
116 Uzbekistan	0.661	0.556	15.8	14	15.3	24.3	0.562	1.4	0.642	20.1	0.478	6.2	1.6	36.7
117 Philippines	0.660	0.540	18.1	10	18.0	15.2	0.635	13.5	0.528	25.2	0.470	8.3	2.2	43.0

TABLE 3 Inequality-adjusted Human Development Index | 169

TABLE 3 INEQUALITY-ADJUSTED HUMAN DEVELOPMENT INDEX

HDI rank	Human Development Index (HDI) Value	Inequality-adjusted HDI (IHDI) Value	Overall loss (%)	Difference from HDI rank[b]	Coefficient of human inequality Value	Inequality in life expectancy (%)	Inequality-adjusted life expectancy index Value	Inequality in education[a] (%)	Inequality-adjusted education index Value	Inequality in income[a] (%)	Inequality-adjusted income index Value	Income inequality Quintile ratio	Income inequality Palma ratio	Income inequality Gini coefficient
	2013	2013	2013	2013	2013	2013	2013	2013[c]	2013	2013[c]	2013	2003–2012	2003–2012	2003–2012
118 South Africa	0.658	..	..	..	..	25.7	0.422	18.1	0.569	..	..	25.3	7.1	63.1
118 Syrian Arab Republic	0.658	0.518	21.2	4	20.8	12.6	0.734	31.5	0.379	18.3	0.500	5.7	..	35.8
120 Iraq	0.642	0.505	21.4	0	21.2	17.6	0.626	29.8	0.328	16.1	0.626	4.6	1.2	30.9
121 Guyana	0.638	0.522	18.2	10	18.0	19.2	0.575	10.5	0.521	24.4	0.474	..	..	..
121 Viet Nam	0.638	0.543	14.9	15	14.9	12.1	0.757	18.0	0.421	14.6	0.502	5.9	1.5	35.6
123 Cape Verde	0.636	0.511	19.7	4	19.4	12.0	0.746	18.2	0.395	28.0	0.452	..	..	50.5
124 Micronesia (Federated States of)	0.630	..	..	..	..	19.8	0.604	..	..	63.1	0.201	..	..	61.1
125 Guatemala	0.628	0.422	32.8	−8	32.0	17.4	0.662	36.1	0.309	42.5	0.367	19.6	4.5	55.9
125 Kyrgyzstan	0.628	0.519	17.2	10	16.9	20.0	0.585	6.6	0.613	24.1	0.391	5.4	1.3	33.4
127 Namibia	0.624	0.352	43.6	−22	39.3	21.7	0.536	27.8	0.376	68.3	0.216	21.8	..	63.9
128 Timor-Leste	0.620	0.430	30.7	−3	29.4	22.8	0.565	47.6	0.248	17.8	0.568	..	..	..
129 Honduras	0.617	0.418	32.2	−6	31.1	17.0	0.687	29.6	0.356	46.8	0.299	29.7	5.2	57.0
129 Morocco	0.617	0.433	29.7	0	28.5	16.8	0.652	45.8	0.254	23.0	0.493	7.3	2.0	40.9
131 Vanuatu	0.616	..	..	..	..	15.4	0.672	..	..	18.5	0.404	..	..	..
132 Nicaragua	0.614	0.452	26.4	4	25.8	13.2	0.732	33.3	0.323	31.0	0.391	7.6	1.9	40.5
133 Kiribati	0.607	0.416	31.5	−4	30.1	20.6	0.597	21.4	0.473	48.4	0.255	..	..	..
133 Tajikistan	0.607	0.491	19.2	9	18.8	29.3	0.514	12.2	0.561	15.0	0.409	4.7	1.2	30.8
135 India	0.586	0.418	28.6	0	27.7	25.0	0.536	42.1	0.274	16.1	0.500	5.0	1.4	33.9
136 Bhutan	0.584	0.465	20.4	9	20.2	22.2	0.578	13.3	0.365	25.1	0.477	6.8	1.7	38.1
136 Cambodia	0.584	0.440	24.7	7	24.6	25.3	0.597	28.3	0.355	20.3	0.401	5.6	1.5	36.0
138 Ghana	0.573	0.394	31.3	−1	31.2	30.8	0.438	35.6	0.356	27.2	0.392	9.3	2.2	42.8
139 Lao People's Democratic Republic	0.569	0.430	24.5	8	24.1	21.5	0.583	34.1	0.287	16.8	0.474	5.9	1.6	36.7
140 Congo	0.564	0.391	30.7	0	30.6	36.0	0.382	25.4	0.381	30.3	0.410	10.7	2.8	47.3
141 Zambia	0.561	0.365	35.0	−4	34.5	37.2	0.368	23.8	0.451	42.6	0.292	17.4	4.8	57.5
142 Bangladesh	0.558	0.396	29.1	4	28.7	20.1	0.623	37.8	0.278	28.3	0.357	4.7	1.3	32.1
142 Sao Tome and Principe	0.558	0.384	31.2	0	30.4	26.9	0.521	20.0	0.375	44.2	0.290	..	..	50.8
144 Equatorial Guinea	0.556	..	..	..	..	44.4	0.283	..	..	..	..	..	..	..
LOW HUMAN DEVELOPMENT														
145 Nepal	0.540	0.384	28.8	3	27.8	21.1	0.588	44.0	0.253	18.3	0.381	5.0	1.3	32.8
146 Pakistan	0.537	0.375	30.1	2	28.7	29.9	0.502	45.2	0.204	11.0	0.516	4.2	1.2	30.0
147 Kenya	0.535	0.360	32.8	0	32.7	31.5	0.440	30.7	0.357	36.0	0.297	11.0	2.8	47.7
148 Swaziland	0.530	0.354	33.3	−2	33.1	35.0	0.290	26.8	0.404	37.6	0.378	14.0	3.5	51.5
149 Angola	0.526	0.295	44.0	−17	43.6	46.2	0.264	34.6	0.310	50.0	0.313	9.0	2.2	42.7
150 Myanmar	0.524	..	..	..	..	27.1	0.507	19.4	0.299	..	..	..	..	..
151 Rwanda	0.506	0.338	33.2	−4	33.1	30.2	0.473	29.4	0.338	39.6	0.241	11.0	3.2	50.8
152 Cameroon	0.504	0.339	32.8	−2	32.4	39.4	0.327	34.8	0.317	23.1	0.377	6.9	1.8	38.9
152 Nigeria	0.504	0.300	40.3	−14	40.2	40.8	0.296	45.2	0.233	34.5	0.394	12.2	3.0	48.8
154 Yemen	0.500	0.336	32.8	−2	31.7	30.3	0.462	47.2	0.179	17.6	0.457	6.3	1.7	37.7
155 Madagascar	0.498	0.346	30.5	2	30.3	24.8	0.517	30.1	0.320	36.1	0.250	9.3	2.3	44.1
156 Zimbabwe	0.492	0.358	27.2	7	26.8	26.8	0.449	17.8	0.411	35.8	0.249	..	..	..
157 Papua New Guinea	0.491	..	..	..	..	26.5	0.480	11.5	0.333	..	..	..	..	..
157 Solomon Islands	0.491	0.374	23.8	11	23.8	22.3	0.570	22.8	0.313	26.3	0.293	..	..	..
159 Comoros	0.488	..	..	..	..	34.2	0.414	47.4	0.237	..	..	26.7	..	64.3
159 Tanzania (United Republic of)	0.488	0.356	27.1	8	26.9	30.4	0.445	29.5	0.300	20.9	0.339	6.6	1.7	37.6
161 Mauritania	0.487	0.315	35.3	−2	34.6	36.6	0.405	45.9	0.191	21.2	0.404	7.8	1.9	40.5
162 Lesotho	0.486	0.313	35.6	−2	34.9	33.5	0.301	24.3	0.382	47.0	0.267	19.0	3.9	52.5
163 Senegal	0.485	0.326	32.9	3	32.3	29.5	0.471	44.6	0.204	22.7	0.359	7.7	1.9	40.3
164 Uganda	0.484	0.335	30.8	5	30.8	33.8	0.399	31.2	0.329	27.3	0.285	8.7	2.3	44.3
165 Benin	0.476	0.311	34.6	0	34.2	37.0	0.381	42.0	0.240	23.6	0.329	6.6	1.8	38.6
166 Sudan	0.473	..	..	..	..	32.8	0.435	..	..	..	..	6.2	1.4	35.3
166 Togo	0.473	0.317	32.9	4	32.6	36.8	0.355	37.6	0.321	23.5	0.280	7.6	1.8	39.3
168 Haiti	0.471	0.285	39.5	−3	38.9	27.9	0.478	40.4	0.223	48.4	0.218	..	..	59.2
169 Afghanistan	0.468	0.321	31.4	7	30.0	34.3	0.414	45.0	0.201	10.8	0.397	4.0	1.0	27.8
170 Djibouti	0.467	0.306	34.6	2	33.7	32.5	0.434	47.0	0.162	21.7	0.406	..	..	40.0
171 Côte d'Ivoire	0.452	0.279	38.3	−2	37.9	40.2	0.283	45.4	0.213	28.1	0.361	8.5	2.0	41.5
172 Gambia	0.441	..	..	..	..	34.8	0.389	..	..	26.9	0.303	11.0	2.8	47.3
173 Ethiopia	0.435	0.307	29.4	5	28.0	30.2	0.469	44.3	0.176	9.5	0.351	5.3	1.4	33.6
174 Malawi	0.414	0.282	31.9	1	31.6	40.0	0.326	30.2	0.307	24.6	0.224	8.9	2.3	43.9
175 Liberia	0.412	0.273	33.8	−1	32.8	33.1	0.417	46.4	0.197	19.0	0.247	7.0	1.7	38.2
176 Mali	0.407	..	..	..	..	45.6	0.293	36.9	0.193	..	..	5.2	1.3	33.0

TABLE
3

HDI rank	Human Development Index (HDI) Value	Inequality-adjusted HDI (IHDI) Value	Overall loss (%)	Difference from HDI rank[b]	Coefficient of human inequality Value	Inequality in life expectancy (%)	Inequality-adjusted life expectancy index Value	Inequality in education[a] (%)	Inequality-adjusted education index Value	Inequality in income[a] (%)	Inequality-adjusted income index Value	Income inequality Quintile ratio	Palma ratio	Gini coefficient
	2013	2013	2013	2013	2013	2013	2013	2013[c]	2013	2013[c]	2013	2003–2012	2003–2012	2003–2012
177 Guinea-Bissau	0.396	0.239	39.6	−4	39.4	45.3	0.289	40.3	0.194	32.5	0.244	..	..	35.5
178 Mozambique	0.393	0.277	29.5	2	28.9	40.2	0.278	18.2	0.304	28.4	0.250	9.8	2.5	45.7
179 Guinea	0.392	0.243	38.0	−1	37.8	40.3	0.332	42.0	0.171	31.1	0.253	7.3	1.8	39.4
180 Burundi	0.389	0.257	33.9	2	32.6	43.6	0.296	41.0	0.218	13.2	0.264	4.8	1.3	33.3
181 Burkina Faso	0.388	0.252	35.0	2	34.6	41.1	0.329	38.5	0.154	24.2	0.318	7.0	1.9	39.8
182 Eritrea	0.381	..	..	..	..	24.7	0.496	..	..	..	..	..	..	..
183 Sierra Leone	0.374	0.208	44.3	−3	43.6	51.2	0.192	48.7	0.156	31.0	0.302	5.6	1.5	35.4
184 Chad	0.372	0.232	37.8	1	36.8	46.1	0.259	43.4	0.145	21.0	0.332	7.4	1.8	39.8
185 Central African Republic	0.341	0.203	40.4	−2	39.9	45.7	0.252	45.9	0.172	28.1	0.192	18.0	4.5	56.3
186 Congo (Democratic Republic of the)	0.338	0.211	37.6	1	36.8	49.9	0.231	29.4	0.262	31.2	0.155	9.3	2.4	44.4
187 Niger	0.337	0.228	32.4	3	31.8	37.9	0.367	39.5	0.120	17.9	0.269	5.3	1.4	34.6
OTHER COUNTRIES OR TERRITORIES														
Korea, Democratic People's Rep. of	..	..	..	..	..	15.4	0.651	..	..	..	..	..	..	..
Marshall Islands	..	..	..	..	..	..	..	..	..	..	..	70.0	..	..
Monaco	..	..	..	..	..	..	..	..	..	..	..	..	..	..
Nauru	..	..	..	..	..	..	..	..	..	..	..	..	..	..
San Marino	..	..	..	..	..	..	..	..	..	..	..	..	..	..
Somalia	..	..	..	..	..	42.1	0.312	..	..	..	..	..	..	..
South Sudan	..	..	..	..	..	40.8	0.321	..	..	..	..	..	..	45.5
Tuvalu	..	..	..	..	..	..	..	10.5	..	..	..	..	..	..
Human Development Index groups														
Very high human development	0.890	0.780	12.3	—	12.0	4.9	0.881	8.7	0.769	22.4	0.702	—	—	—
High human development	0.735	0.590	19.7	—	19.3	10.7	0.749	17.4	0.531	29.9	0.517	—	—	—
Medium human development	0.614	0.457	25.6	—	25.2	21.9	0.575	35.1	0.331	18.6	0.502	—	—	—
Low human development	0.493	0.332	32.6	—	32.4	35.0	0.394	38.2	0.241	23.9	0.387	—	—	—
Regions														
Arab States	0.682	0.512	24.9	—	24.2	17.4	0.639	38.0	0.334	17.3	0.629	—	—	—
East Asia and the Pacific	0.703	0.564	19.7	—	19.5	11.7	0.734	19.7	0.477	27.0	0.513	—	—	—
Europe and Central Asia	0.738	0.639	13.3	—	13.2	14.2	0.676	8.6	0.639	16.9	0.605	—	—	—
Latin America and the Caribbean	0.740	0.559	24.5	—	23.9	13.2	0.733	22.2	0.502	36.3	0.474	—	—	—
South Asia	0.588	0.419	28.7	—	28.0	24.4	0.549	41.6	0.274	18.0	0.489	—	—	—
Sub-Saharan Africa	0.502	0.334	33.6	—	33.5	36.6	0.359	35.7	0.276	28.1	0.375	—	—	—
Least developed countries	0.487	0.336	31.0	—	30.9	32.3	0.433	35.6	0.253	24.7	0.348	—	—	—
Small island developing states	0.665	0.497	25.3	—	24.9	18.5	0.626	22.1	0.433	34.2	0.452	—	—	—
World	**0.702**	**0.541**	**22.9**	**—**	**22.8**	**17.3**	**0.647**	**27.0**	**0.433**	**24.1**	**0.564**	**—**	**—**	**—**

NOTES

a See http://hdr.undp.org for the list of surveys used to estimate inequalities.

b Based on countries for which the Inequality-adjusted Human Development Index is calculated.

c Data refer to 2013 or the most recent year available.

DEFINITIONS

Human Development Index (HDI): A composite index measuring average achievement in three basic dimensions of human development—a long and healthy life, knowledge and a decent standard of living. See *Technical note 1* at http://hdr.undp.org for details on how the HDI is calculated.

Inequality-adjusted HDI (IHDI): HDI value adjusted for inequalities in the three basic dimensions of human development. See *Technical note 2* at http://hdr.undp.org for details on how the IHDI is calculated.

Overall loss: Percentage difference between the IHDI and the HDI.

Difference from HDI rank: Difference in ranks on the IHDI and the HDI, calculated only for countries for which the IHDI is calculated.

Coefficient of human inequality: Average inequality in three basic dimensions of human development. See *Technical note 2* at http://hdr.undp.org.

Inequality in life expectancy: Inequality in distribution of expected length of life based on data from life tables estimated using the Atkinson inequality index.

Inequality-adjusted life expectancy index: The HDI life expectancy index adjusted for inequality in distribution of expected length of life based on data from life tables listed in *Main data sources*.

Inequality in education: Inequality in distribution of years of schooling based on data from household surveys estimated using the Atkinson inequality index.

Inequality-adjusted education index: The HDI education index adjusted for inequality in distribution of years of schooling based on data from household surveys listed in *Main data sources*.

Inequality in income: Inequality in income distribution based on data from household surveys estimated using the Atkinson inequality index.

Inequality-adjusted income index: The HDI income index adjusted for inequality in income distribution based on data from household surveys listed in *Main data sources*.

Quintile ratio: Ratio of the average income of the richest 20% of the population to the average income of the poorest 20% of the population.

Palma ratio: Ratio of the richest 10% of the population's share of gross national income (GNI) divided by the poorest 40%'s share. It is based on the work of Palma (2011), who found that middle class incomes almost always account for about half of GNI and that the other half is split between the richest 10% and poorest 40%, though their shares vary considerably across countries.

Gini coefficient: Measure of the deviation of the distribution of income among individuals or households within a country from a perfectly equal distribution. A value of 0 represents absolute equality, a value of 100 absolute inequality.

MAIN DATA SOURCES

Column 1: HDRO calculations based on data from UNDESA (2013a), Barro and Lee (2013), UNESCO Institute for Statistics (2013b), United Nations Statistics Division (2014), World Bank (2014) and IMF (2014).

Column 2: Calculated as the geometric mean of the values in columns 7, 9 and 11 using the methodology in *Technical note 2* (available at http://hdr.undp.org).

Column 3: Calculated based on data in columns 1 and 2.

Column 4: Calculated based on data in column 2 and recalculated HDI ranks for countries for which the

IHDI is calculated.

Column 5: Calculated as the arithmetic mean of the values in columns 6, 8 and 10 using the methodology in *Technical note 2* (available at http://hdr.undp.org).

Column 6: Calculated based on abridged life tables from UNDESA (2013a).

Column 7: Calculated based on data in column 6 and the unadjusted life expectancy index.

Columns 8 and 10: Calculated based on data from the Luxembourg Income Study database, Eurostat's European Union Statistics on Income and Living Conditions, the World Bank's International Income Distribution Database, United Nations Children's Fund Multiple Indicator Cluster Surveys, and ICF Macro Demographic and Health Surveys using the methodology in *Technical note 2* (available at http://hdr.undp.org).

Column 9: Calculated based on data in column 8 and the unadjusted education index.

Column 11: Calculated based on data in column 10 and the unadjusted income index.

Columns 12 and 13: HDRO calculations based on data from World Bank (2013a).

Column 14: World Bank 2013a.

TABLE 3   Inequality-adjusted Human Development Index | 171

TABLE 4

Gender Inequality Index

TABLE 4

HDI rank	Gender Inequality Index		Maternal mortality ratio	Adolescent birth rate	Share of seats in parliament	Population with at least some secondary education (% ages 25 and older)		Labour force participation rate (% ages 15 and older)	
	Value	Rank	(deaths per 100,000 live births)	(births per 1,000 women ages 15–19)	(% held by women)	Female	Male	Female	Male
	2013	2013	2010	2010/2015[a]	2013	2005–2012[b]	2005–2012[b]	2012	2012
VERY HIGH HUMAN DEVELOPMENT									
1 Norway	0.068	9	7	7.8	39.6	97.4	96.7	61.5	69.5
2 Australia	0.113	19	7	12.1	29.2	94.3[c]	94.6[c]	58.8	71.9
3 Switzerland	0.030	2	8	1.9	27.2	95.0	96.6	61.2	75.3
4 Netherlands	0.057	7	6	6.2	37.8	87.7	90.5	79.9	87.3
5 United States	0.262	47	21	31.0	18.2	95.1	94.8	56.8	69.3
6 Germany	0.046	3	7	3.8	32.4	96.3	97.0	53.5	66.4
7 New Zealand	0.185	34	15	25.3	32.2	95.0	95.3	62.1	73.9
8 Canada	0.136	23	12	14.5	28.0	100.0	100.0	61.6	71.2
9 Singapore	0.090	15	3	6.0	24.2	74.1	81.0	59.0	77.5
10 Denmark	0.056	5	12	5.1	39.1	95.5[d]	96.6[d]	59.1	67.5
11 Ireland	0.115	20	6	8.2	19.5	80.5	78.6	52.7	67.9
12 Sweden	0.054	4	4	6.5	44.7	86.5	87.3	60.2	68.1
13 Iceland	0.088	14	5	11.5	39.7	91.0	91.6	70.6	77.3
14 United Kingdom	0.193	35	12	25.8	22.6	99.8	99.9	55.7	68.8
15 Hong Kong, China (SAR)	..	..	..	3.3	..	72.2	79.2	51.6	68.0
15 Korea (Republic of)	0.101	17	16	2.2	15.7	77.0[e]	89.1[e]	49.9	72.0
17 Japan	0.138	25	5	5.4	10.8	87.0	85.8	48.1	70.4
18 Liechtenstein	..	..	..	..	20.0	..	..	..	..
19 Israel	0.101	17	7	7.8	22.5	84.4	87.3	58.1	69.5
20 France	0.080	12	8	5.7	25.1	78.0	83.2	50.9	61.8
21 Austria	0.056	5	4	4.1	28.7	100.0	100.0	54.6	67.7
21 Belgium	0.068	9	8	6.7	38.9	77.5	82.9	46.9	59.4
21 Luxembourg	0.154	29	20	8.3	21.7	100.0[d]	100.0[d]	50.7	64.9
24 Finland	0.075	11	5	9.2	42.5	100.0	100.0	56.0	64.3
25 Slovenia	0.021	1	12	0.6	24.6	95.8	98.0	52.3	63.5
26 Italy	0.067	8	4	4.0	30.6	71.2	80.5	39.4	59.4
27 Spain	0.100	16	6	10.6	35.2	66.8	73.1	52.6	66.5
28 Czech Republic	0.087	13	5	4.9	20.6	99.9	99.7	50.1	67.8
29 Greece	0.146	27	3	11.9	21.0	59.5	67.0	44.2	62.6
30 Brunei Darussalam	..	..	24	23.0	..	66.6[e]	61.2[e]	52.9	75.6
31 Qatar	0.524	114	7	9.5	0.1[f]	66.7	59.0	50.8	95.6
32 Cyprus	0.136	23	10	5.5	10.7	72.2	79.6	55.8	70.8
33 Estonia	0.154	29	2	16.8	20.8	100.0[d]	100.0[d]	56.0	68.7
34 Saudi Arabia	0.321	56	24	10.2	19.9	60.5	70.3	18.2	75.5
35 Lithuania	0.116	21	8	10.6	24.1	89.1	94.3	55.8	66.3
35 Poland	0.139	26	5	12.2	21.8	79.4	85.5	48.9	64.8
37 Andorra	..	..	..	..	50.0	49.5	49.3	..	..
37 Slovakia	0.164	32	6	15.9	18.7	99.1	99.5	51.0	68.7
39 Malta	0.220	41	8	18.2	14.3	68.6	78.2	38.0	66.5
40 United Arab Emirates	0.244	43	12	27.6	17.5	73.1	61.3	46.6	91.0
41 Chile	0.355	68	25	55.3	13.9	73.3	76.4	49.0	74.6
41 Portugal	0.116	21	8	12.6	28.7	47.7	48.2	55.4	67.2
43 Hungary	0.247	45	21	12.1	8.8	97.9[d]	98.7[d]	44.7	59.9
44 Bahrain	0.253	46	20	13.8	18.8	74.4[e]	80.4[e]	39.4	87.2
44 Cuba	0.350	66	73	43.1	48.9	73.9[e]	80.4[e]	43.3	70.1
46 Kuwait	0.288	50	14	14.5	6.2	55.6	56.3	43.4	82.8
47 Croatia	0.172	33	17	12.7	23.8	85.0	93.6	44.8	58.5
48 Latvia	0.222	42	34	13.5	23.0	98.9	99.0	54.5	67.1
49 Argentina	0.381	74	77	54.4	37.7	57.0[e]	54.9[e]	47.3	75.0
HIGH HUMAN DEVELOPMENT									
50 Uruguay	0.364	70	29	58.3	12.3	54.4	50.3	55.5	76.8
51 Bahamas	0.316	53	47	28.5	16.7	91.2[e]	87.6[e]	69.3	79.3
51 Montenegro	..	..	8	15.2	17.3	84.2	94.7	..	..
53 Belarus	0.152	28	4	20.6	29.5	87.0	92.2	49.9	62.7
54 Romania	0.320	54	27	31.0	11.6	86.1	92.0	48.5	64.7
55 Libya	0.215	40	58	2.5	16.5	55.6[e]	44.0[e]	30.0	76.4
56 Oman	0.348	64	32	10.6	9.6	47.2	57.1	28.6	81.8
57 Russian Federation	0.314	52	34	25.7	12.1	89.6	92.5	57.0	71.4
58 Bulgaria	0.207	38	11	35.9	24.6	93.0	95.7	47.8	58.8
59 Barbados	0.350	66	51	48.4	21.6	89.5[e]	87.6[e]	65.9	76.7
60 Palau	..	..	..	..	10.3	..	..	..	..

HDI rank	Gender Inequality Index		Maternal mortality ratio (deaths per 100,000 live births)	Adolescent birth rate (births per 1,000 women ages 15–19)	Share of seats in parliament (% held by women)	Population with at least some secondary education (% ages 25 and older)		Labour force participation rate (% ages 15 and older)	
	Value	Rank				Female	Male	Female	Male
	2013	2013	2010	2010/2015[a]	2013	2005–2012[b]	2005–2012[b]	2012	2012
61 Antigua and Barbuda	..	..	..	49.3	19.4	..	..	..	..
62 Malaysia	0.210	39	29	5.7	13.9	66.0[e]	72.8[e]	44.3	75.3
63 Mauritius	0.375	72	60	30.9	18.8	49.4	58.0	43.5	74.3
64 Trinidad and Tobago	0.321	56	46	34.8	26.0	59.4	59.2	52.9	75.5
65 Lebanon	0.413	80	25	12.0	3.1	38.8	38.9	22.8	70.5
65 Panama	0.506	107	92	78.5	8.5	63.5[e]	60.7[e]	49.0	81.9
67 Venezuela (Bolivarian Republic of)	0.464	96	92	83.2	17.0	56.5	50.8	50.9	79.2
68 Costa Rica	0.344	63	40	60.8	38.6	54.5[e]	52.8[e]	46.4	79.0
69 Turkey	0.360	69	20	30.9	14.2	39.0	60.0	29.4	70.8
70 Kazakhstan	0.323	59	51	29.9	18.2	99.3	99.4	67.5	77.5
71 Mexico	0.376	73	50	63.4	36.0	55.7	60.6	45.0	80.0
71 Seychelles	..	..	..	56.3	43.8	66.9	66.6	..	..
73 Saint Kitts and Nevis	..	..	..	..	6.7	..	..	..	..
73 Sri Lanka	0.383	75	35	16.9	5.8	72.7	75.5	35.0	76.4
75 Iran (Islamic Republic of)	0.510	109	21	31.6	3.1	62.2	67.6	16.4	73.1
76 Azerbaijan	0.340	62	43	40.0	16.0	93.7	97.4	62.5	68.9
77 Jordan	0.488	101	63	26.5	12.0	69.5	78.5	15.3	66.2
77 Serbia	..	..	12	16.9	33.2	58.4	73.6	..	..
79 Brazil	0.441	85	56	70.8	9.6	51.9	49.0	59.5	80.9
79 Georgia	..	..	67	46.8	12.0	..	..	56.2	74.7
79 Grenada	..	..	24	35.4	25.0	..	..	..	..
82 Peru	0.387	77	67	50.7	21.5	56.3	66.1	68.0	84.4
83 Ukraine	0.326	61	32	25.7	9.4	91.5[e]	96.1[e]	53.0	66.6
84 Belize	0.435	84	53	71.4	13.3	35.2[e]	32.8[e]	49.1	82.3
84 The former Yugoslav Republic of Macedonia	0.162	31	10	18.3	34.1	40.2	55.6	42.9	67.3
86 Bosnia and Herzegovina	0.201	36	8	15.1	19.3	44.8	70.0	34.1	57.2
87 Armenia	0.325	60	30	27.1	10.7	94.1[e]	94.8[e]	51.6	73.4
88 Fiji	..	..	26	42.8	..	57.5	58.1	37.5	72.0
89 Thailand	0.364	70	48	41.0	15.7	35.7	40.8	64.4	80.8
90 Tunisia	0.265	48	56	4.6	26.7	32.8	46.1	25.1	70.6
91 China	0.202	37	37	8.6	23.4	58.7	71.9	63.8	78.1
91 Saint Vincent and the Grenadines	..	..	48	54.5	13.0	..	..	55.7	78.2
93 Algeria	0.425	81	97	10.0	25.8	20.9	27.3	15.0	71.9
93 Dominica	..	..	..	..	12.5	29.7	23.2	..	..
95 Albania	0.245	44	27	15.3	17.9	81.8	87.9	45.0	65.4
96 Jamaica	0.457	88	110	70.1	15.5	74.0[e]	71.1[e]	56.1	71.0
97 Saint Lucia	..	..	35	56.3	17.2	..	..	62.6	76.0
98 Colombia	0.460	92	92	68.5	13.6	56.9	55.6	55.7	79.7
98 Ecuador	0.429	82	110	77.0	38.7	40.1	39.4	54.4	82.6
100 Suriname	0.463	95	130	35.2	11.8	44.6	47.1	40.4	68.8
100 Tonga	0.458	90	110	18.1	3.6	87.5	88.3	53.5	74.8
102 Dominican Republic	0.505	105	150	99.6	19.1	55.6	53.1	51.2	78.7
MEDIUM HUMAN DEVELOPMENT									
103 Maldives	0.283	49	60	4.2	6.5	13.3	16.6	55.9	77.1
103 Mongolia	0.320	54	63	18.7	14.9	85.3[e]	84.1[e]	56.1	68.8
103 Turkmenistan	..	..	67	18.0	16.8	..	..	46.7	76.5
106 Samoa	0.517	111	100	28.3	4.1	64.3	60.0	23.4	58.4
107 Palestine, State of	..	..	64	45.8	..	31.5	32.2	15.2	66.3
108 Indonesia	0.500	103	220	48.3	18.6	39.9	49.2	51.3	84.4
109 Botswana	0.486	100	160	44.2	7.9	73.6[e]	77.3[e]	71.8	81.5
110 Egypt	0.580	128	66	43.0	2.8	43.4[e]	59.3[e]	23.6	74.6
111 Paraguay	0.457	88	99	67.0	18.4	36.8	40.8	55.4	84.8
112 Gabon	0.508	108	230	103.0	16.7	53.8[e]	34.7[e]	56.0	65.1
113 Bolivia (Plurinational State of)	0.472	97	190	71.9	30.1	47.6	59.1	64.1	80.9
114 Moldova (Republic of)	0.302	51	41	29.3	19.8	93.6	96.6	37.0	43.3
115 El Salvador	0.441	85	81	76.0	26.2	36.8	43.6	47.6	79.0
116 Uzbekistan	..	..	28	38.8	19.2	..	..	47.9	75.2
117 Philippines	0.406	78	99	46.8	26.9	65.9	63.8	51.0	79.7
118 South Africa	0.461	94	300	50.9	41.1[g]	72.7	75.9	44.2	60.0
118 Syrian Arab Republic	0.556	124	70	41.6	12.0	29.0	38.9	13.4	72.7
120 Iraq	..	..	63	68.7	25.2	..	..	14.7	69.7
121 Guyana	0.524	113	280	88.5	31.3	61.5[e]	48.8[e]	42.3	80.9

TABLE 4   Gender Inequality Index | 173

TABLE
4

TABLE 4 GENDER INEQUALITY INDEX

	Gender Inequality Index		Maternal mortality ratio	Adolescent birth rate	Share of seats in parliament	Population with at least some secondary education (% ages 25 and older)		Labour force participation rate (% ages 15 and older)	
	Value	Rank	(deaths per 100,000 live births)	(births per 1,000 women ages 15–19)	(% held by women)	Female	Male	Female	Male
HDI rank	2013	2013	2010	2010/2015[a]	2013	2005–2012[b]	2005–2012[b]	2012	2012
121 Viet Nam	0.322	58	59	29.0	24.4	59.4	71.2	72.8	81.9
123 Cape Verde	..	..	79	70.6	20.8	..	..	51.1	83.5
124 Micronesia (Federated States of)	..	..	100	18.6	0.1	..	..	..	..
125 Guatemala	0.523	112	120	97.2	13.3	21.9	23.2	49.1	88.2
125 Kyrgyzstan	0.348	64	71	29.3	23.3	94.5	96.8	55.7	79.0
127 Namibia	0.450	87	200	54.9	25.0	33.0[e]	34.0[e]	75.2	82.2
128 Timor-Leste	..	..	300	52.2	38.5	..	..	24.7	51.1
129 Honduras	0.482	99	100	84.0	19.5	28.0	25.8	42.5	82.9
129 Morocco	0.460	92	100	35.8	11.0	20.1[e]	36.3[e]	43.0	57.4
131 Vanuatu	..	..	110	44.8	0.1	..	..	61.5	80.3
132 Nicaragua	0.458	90	95	100.8	40.2	30.8[e]	44.7[e]	47.0	80.1
133 Kiribati	..	..	..	16.6	8.7	..	..	..	..
133 Tajikistan	0.383	75	65	42.8	17.5	89.9	95.0	58.7	76.9
135 India	..	..	200	32.8	10.9	..	..	28.8	80.9
136 Bhutan	0.495	102	180	40.9	6.9	34.0	34.5	66.4	76.9
136 Cambodia	0.505	105	250	44.3	18.1[h]	9.9	22.2	78.9	86.5
138 Ghana	0.549	122	350	58.4	10.9	45.2	64.7	67.2	71.2
139 Lao People's Democratic Republic	0.534	118	470	65.0	25.0	22.9[e]	36.8[e]	76.3	78.9
140 Congo	0.617	133	560	126.7	9.6	43.8[e]	48.7[e]	68.4	72.9
141 Zambia	0.617	133	440	125.4	11.5	25.7[e]	44.2[e]	73.2	85.7
142 Bangladesh	0.529	115	240	80.6	19.7	30.8[e]	39.3[e]	57.3	84.1
142 Sao Tome and Principe	..	..	70	65.1	18.2	..	..	44.9	77.5
144 Equatorial Guinea	..	..	240	112.6	18.8	..	..	80.6	92.3
LOW HUMAN DEVELOPMENT									
145 Nepal	0.479	98	170	73.7	33.2	17.9[e]	39.9[e]	54.3	63.2
146 Pakistan	0.563	126	260	27.3	19.7	19.3	46.1	24.4	82.9
147 Kenya	0.548	121	360	93.6	19.9	25.3	31.4	62.0	72.2
148 Swaziland	0.529	115	320	72.0	21.9	49.9[e]	46.1[e]	43.8	71.3
149 Angola	..	..	450	170.2	34.1	..	..	63.1	76.9
150 Myanmar	0.430	83	200	12.1	4.6	18.0[e]	17.6[e]	85.7	82.9
151 Rwanda	0.410	79	340	33.6	51.9	7.4[e]	8.0[e]	86.5	85.5
152 Cameroon	0.622	136	690	115.8	16.1	21.1[e]	34.9[e]	63.6	76.7
152 Nigeria	..	..	630	119.6	6.6	..	..	48.1	63.5
154 Yemen	0.733	149	200	47.0	0.7	7.6[e]	24.4[e]	25.2	71.8
155 Madagascar	..	..	240	122.8	15.8	..	..	86.8	90.6
156 Zimbabwe	0.516	110	570	60.3	35.1	48.8	62.0	83.2	89.7
157 Papua New Guinea	0.617	133	230	62.1	2.7	6.8[e]	14.1[e]	70.5	74.0
157 Solomon Islands	..	..	93	64.9	2.0	..	..	53.4	79.1
159 Comoros	..	..	280	51.1	3.0	..	..	35.0	80.2
159 Tanzania (United Republic of)	0.553	123	460	122.7	36.0	5.6[e]	9.2[e]	88.1	90.2
161 Mauritania	0.644	140	510	73.3	19.2	8.0[e]	20.8[e]	28.6	79.0
162 Lesotho	0.557	125	620	89.4	26.8	21.9	19.8	58.8	73.3
163 Senegal	0.537	119	370	94.4	42.7	7.2	15.4	65.9	88.0
164 Uganda	0.529	115	310	126.6	35.0	22.9	33.5	75.9	79.3
165 Benin	0.614	132	350	90.2	8.4	11.2[e]	25.6[e]	67.5	78.3
166 Sudan	0.628	138	730	84.0	24.1	12.8[e]	18.2[e]	31.2	76.0
166 Togo	0.579	127	300	91.5	15.4	15.3[e]	45.1[e]	80.7	81.2
168 Haiti	0.599	130	350	42.0	3.5	22.5[e]	36.3[e]	60.6	70.8
169 Afghanistan	0.705	147	460	86.8	27.6	5.8[e]	34.0[e]	15.7	79.7
170 Djibouti	..	..	200	18.6	12.7	..	..	36.1	67.3
171 Côte d'Ivoire	0.645	141	400	130.3	10.4	13.7[e]	29.9[e]	52.2	81.5
172 Gambia	0.624	137	360	115.8	7.5	16.9[e]	31.4[e]	72.2	83.0
173 Ethiopia	0.547	120	350	78.4	25.5	7.8	18.2	78.2	89.4
174 Malawi	0.591	129	460	144.8	22.3	10.4	20.4	84.7	81.3
175 Liberia	0.655	143	770	117.4	11.7	15.7[e]	39.2[e]	58.2	64.7
176 Mali	0.673	145	540	175.6	10.2	7.7	15.1	50.6	81.4
177 Guinea-Bissau	..	..	790	99.3	14.0	..	..	68.1	78.5
178 Mozambique	0.657	144	490	137.8	39.2	1.5[e]	6.0[e]	26.3	75.8
179 Guinea	..	..	610	131.0	..	..	..	65.5	78.3
180 Burundi	0.501	104	800	30.3	34.9	5.2[e]	9.3[e]	83.2	81.8
181 Burkina Faso	0.607	131	300	115.4	15.7	0.9	3.2	77.1	90.1
182 Eritrea	..	..	240	65.3	22.0	..	..	79.9	89.8

	Gender Inequality Index		Maternal mortality ratio	Adolescent birth rate	Share of seats in parliament	Population with at least some secondary education		Labour force participation rate	
						(% ages 25 and older)		(% ages 15 and older)	
	Value	Rank	(deaths per 100,000 live births)	(births per 1,000 women ages 15–19)	(% held by women)	Female	Male	Female	Male
HDI rank	2013	2013	2010	2010/2015[a]	2013	2005–2012[b]	2005–2012[b]	2012	2012
183 Sierra Leone	0.643	139	890	100.7	12.4	9.5[e]	20.4[e]	65.7	68.9
184 Chad	0.707	148	1,100	152.0	14.9	1.7	9.9	64.0	79.2
185 Central African Republic	0.654	142	890	98.3	12.5[i]	10.3[e]	26.2[e]	72.5	85.1
186 Congo (Democratic Republic of the)	..	..	540	135.3	8.3	..	..	70.7	73.2
187 Niger	0.674	146	590	204.8	13.3	44.5	49.5	39.9	89.8
OTHER COUNTRIES OR TERRITORIES									
Korea, Democratic People's Rep. of	..	..	81	0.6	15.6	..	..	72.3	84.2
Marshall Islands	..	..	..	..	3.0	..	..	..	..
Monaco	..	..	..	..	20.8	..	..	..	..
Nauru	..	..	..	..	5.3	..	..	..	..
San Marino	..	..	..	..	18.3	..	..	..	..
Somalia	..	..	1,000	110.4	13.8	..	..	37.2	75.6
South Sudan	..	..	..	75.3	24.3	..	..	..	..
Tuvalu	..	..	..	..	6.7	..	..	..	..
Human Development Index groups									
Very high human development	0.197	—	16	19.2	26.7	86.1	87.7	52.3	69.0
High human development	0.315	—	42	28.8	18.8	60.2	69.1	57.1	77.1
Medium human development	0.502	—	186	43.4	17.5	44.7	53.2	38.7	80.0
Low human development	0.586	—	427	92.3	20.0	15.2	29.1	55.7	78.4
Regions									
Arab States	0.545	—	164	45.4	13.8	33.9	46.7	24.7	73.2
East Asia and the Pacific	0.331	—	72	21.2	18.7	54.6	66.4	62.8	79.3
Europe and Central Asia	0.317	—	31	30.8	18.2	70.4	80.6	45.5	70.2
Latin America and the Caribbean	0.416	—	74	68.3	25.3	53.3	53.9	53.7	79.8
South Asia	0.531	—	202	38.7	17.8	33.4	48.5	30.7	80.7
Sub-Saharan Africa	0.575	—	474	109.7	21.7	24.2	32.6	63.6	76.3
Least developed countries	0.568	—	389	97.0	20.3	17.0	26.5	64.0	81.6
Small island developing states	0.478	—	195	61.5	23.0	50.4	55.2	52.8	73.3
World	**0.449**	—	**145**	**47.4**	**21.1**	**60.0**	**67.4**	**50.6**	**76.7**

NOTES

a Data are annual average of projected values for 2010–2015.

b Data refer to the most recent year available during the period specified.

c Refers to population ages 25–64.

d Refers to population ages 25–74.

e Barro and Lee (2013) estimate for 2010 based on data from the United Nations Educational, Scientific and Cultural Organization's Institute for Statistics.

f For calculating the Gender Inequality Index, a value of 0.1% was used.

g Does not include the 36 special rotating delegates appointed on an ad hoc basis.

h Refers to 2012.

i Refers to an earlier year than that specified.

DEFINITIONS

Gender Inequality Index: A composite measure reflecting inequality in achievement between women and men in three dimensions: reproductive health, empowerment and the labour market. See *Technical note 3* at http://hdr.undp.org for details on how the Gender Inequality Index is calculated.

Maternal mortality ratio: Number of deaths due to pregnancy-related causes per 100,000 live births.

Adolescent birth rate: Number of births to women ages 15–19 per 1,000 women ages 15–19.

Share of seats in national parliament: Proportion of seats held by women in the national parliament, expressed as percentage of total seats. For countries with bicameral legislative systems, the share of seats is calculated based on both houses.

Population with at least some secondary education: Percentage of the population ages 25 and older who have reached (but not necessarily completed) a secondary level of education.

Labour force participation rate: Proportion of a country's working-age population (ages 15 and older) that engages in the labour market, either by working or actively looking for work, expressed as a percentage of the working-age population.

MAIN DATA SOURCES

Column 1: HDRO calculations based on data from UN Maternal Mortality Estimation Group (2013), UNDESA (2013a), IPU (2013), Barro and Lee (2013), UNESCO Institute for Statistics (2013b) and ILO (2013a).

Column 2: Calculated based on data in column 1.

Column 3: UN Maternal Mortality Estimation Group 2013.

Column 4: UNDESA 2013a.

Column 5: IPU 2013.

Columns 6 and 7: UNESCO Institute for Statistics 2013b.

Columns 8 and 9: ILO 2013a.

TABLE 4   Gender Inequality Index | 175

TABLE 5

Gender Development Index

TABLE 5

HDI rank	Gender Development Index — Ratio of female to male HDI 2013	Rank[b] 2013	Human Development Index (HDI) Value — Female 2013	Male 2013	Life expectancy at birth (years) — Female 2013	Male 2013	Mean years of schooling (years) — Female 2002–2012[c]	Male 2002–2012[c]	Expected years of schooling (years) — Female 2000–2012[c]	Male 2000–2012[c]	Estimated gross national income per capita[a] (2011 PPP $) — Female 2013	Male 2013
VERY HIGH HUMAN DEVELOPMENT												
1 Norway	0.997	5	0.940	0.943	83.6	79.4	12.7	12.6	18.2	16.9	56,994	70,807
2 Australia	0.975	40	0.920	0.944	84.8	80.3	12.5	13.1	20.3	19.4	35,551	47,553
3 Switzerland	0.953	76	0.895	0.939	84.9	80.2	11.5	13.1	15.6	15.8	42,561	65,278
4 Netherlands	0.968	51	0.899	0.929	82.9	79.1	11.6	12.2	18.0	17.8	34,497	50,432
5 United States	0.995	7	0.911	0.915	81.3	76.5	13.0	12.9	17.4	15.7	41,792	63,163
6 Germany	0.962	61	0.892	0.928	83.1	78.3	12.6	13.3	16.2	16.4	33,028	53,445
7 New Zealand	0.971	47	0.896	0.923	83.0	79.2	12.5	12.6	20.2	18.5	26,695	38,656
8 Canada	0.986	24	0.893	0.906	83.6	79.3	12.3	12.2	16.2	15.4	34,612	49,272
9 Singapore	0.967	52	0.878	0.908	84.7	79.8	9.7[d]	10.7[d]	15.5[e]	15.3[e]	50,001	95,329[f]
10 Denmark	0.989	17	0.895	0.906	81.5	77.3	11.9	12.3	17.6	16.3	37,106	48,742
11 Ireland	0.965	56	0.881	0.913	82.9	78.6	11.7	11.5	18.5	18.7	23,872	43,092
12 Sweden	1.004	6	0.898	0.894	83.9	79.7	11.8[d]	11.4[d]	16.6	15.1	38,071	48,365
13 Iceland	0.982	30	0.883	0.899	83.9	80.3	10.8	10.0	19.9	17.6	27,612	42,520
14 United Kingdom	0.993	13	0.887	0.894	82.5	78.6	12.8	11.8	16.7	15.8	27,589	42,632
15 Hong Kong, China (SAR)	0.969	49	0.874	0.902	86.4	80.4	9.8	10.3	15.3	15.4	40,051	66,417
15 Korea (Republic of)	0.940	85	0.860	0.915	84.8	78.1	11.1	12.5	16.1	17.8	21,795	38,990
17 Japan	0.951	79	0.863	0.907	87.0	80.1	11.2	11.8	15.1	15.4	22,384	51,906
18 Liechtenstein	..	..	..	..	..	..	..	..	13.8	16.4	..	..
19 Israel	0.984	29	0.879	0.893	83.6	79.9	12.6	12.5	16.1	15.2	24,636	35,402
20 France	0.989	17	0.878	0.888	85.2	78.3	10.9	11.4	16.3	15.6	29,580	44,139
21 Austria	0.935	91	0.834	0.892	83.6	78.5	8.9	10.6	15.9	15.3	25,170	61,543
21 Belgium	0.977	38	0.866	0.887	83.1	78.0	10.5[d]	10.7[d]	16.5	16.0	30,213	49,077
21 Luxembourg	0.961	66	0.861	0.896	83.0	78.0	10.9	11.7	14.0	13.8	41,351	76,196[f]
24 Finland	1.006	8	0.881	0.876	83.7	77.4	10.3	10.2	17.6	16.4	32,123	42,795
25 Slovenia	1.006	8	0.876	0.871	82.8	76.4	11.8	12.0	17.9	15.8	21,762	31,916
26 Italy	0.962	61	0.852	0.886	85.0	79.6	9.7	10.6	16.8	15.8	22,303	43,640
27 Spain	0.985	25	0.861	0.874	85.3	78.9	9.5	9.7	17.5	16.8	23,487	37,804
28 Czech Republic	0.969	49	0.844	0.871	80.7	74.6	12.1	12.5	16.9	15.9	16,233	33,098
29 Greece	0.959	69	0.833	0.868	83.1	78.4	9.9	10.4	16.6	16.4	17,791	31,707
30 Brunei Darussalam	0.981	31	0.839	0.856	80.5	76.7	8.6	8.8	14.9	14.2	52,831	88,468
31 Qatar	0.979	32	0.838	0.856	79.5	77.8	10.1	8.7	14.0	13.9	45,863	141,468[f]
32 Cyprus	0.940	85	0.817	0.869	81.8	77.9	10.7	12.6	14.0	13.9	19,787	33,461
33 Estonia	1.042	70	0.856	0.821	79.6	69.1	12.3	11.7	17.5	15.5	19,410	27,985
34 Saudi Arabia	0.897	112	0.773	0.861	77.6	73.9	8.0	9.2	15.9	15.4	16,197	78,689
35 Lithuania	1.036	58	0.848	0.818	78.2	66.0	12.3	12.4	17.3	16.0	19,588	28,607
35 Poland	1.010	14	0.837	0.828	80.5	72.3	11.9	11.7	16.3	14.7	16,462	26,871
37 Andorra	..	..	..	..	..	..	..	..	..	..	..	..
37 Slovakia	1.000	1	0.829	0.829	79.2	71.5	11.6[g]	11.5[g]	15.6	14.5	19,450	31,554
39 Malta	0.954	75	0.807	0.846	82.0	77.5	9.5	10.3	14.7	14.3	18,832	35,217
40 United Arab Emirates	0.958	70	0.800	0.835	78.2	76.1	10.2	8.7	13.9[g]	12.9[g]	23,903	72,659
41 Chile	0.962	61	0.803	0.835	82.7	77.1	9.6	9.9	15.3	15.0	14,339	27,410
41 Portugal	0.970	48	0.808	0.833	82.9	76.9	8.0	8.5	16.5	16.1	17,846	30,817
43 Hungary	0.998	4	0.816	0.818	78.6	70.5	11.2[d]	11.4[d]	15.7	15.1	17,233	25,663
44 Bahrain	0.961	66	0.798	0.831	77.5	75.9	9.1	9.6	15.1[h]	13.7[h]	24,531	36,660
44 Cuba	0.962	61	0.796	0.827	81.3	77.3	10.1[g]	10.3[g]	15.1	13.9	13,302	26,319
46 Kuwait	0.987	22	0.801	0.812	75.5	73.5	7.9	6.8	15.2	14.2	43,134	114,532[f]
47 Croatia	0.987	22	0.807	0.818	80.4	73.7	10.5	11.6	15.2	13.9	15,777	22,509
48 Latvia	1.033	52	0.823	0.797	77.5	66.7	11.5[d]	11.5[d]	16.3	14.8	18,624	26,415
49 Argentina	1.001	2	0.806	0.805	79.9	72.6	10.0	9.6	17.5	15.4	11,975	22,849
HIGH HUMAN DEVELOPMENT												
50 Uruguay	1.015	25	0.793	0.781	80.6	73.7	8.7	8.2	16.6	14.4	13,789	22,730
51 Bahamas	..	..	..	..	78.2	72.1	11.1	11.1	..	..	17,934	25,047
51 Montenegro	..	..	..	..	77.2	72.5	9.9[i]	11.2[i]	15.5	14.8	..	..
53 Belarus	1.021	32	0.793	0.777	75.8	64.2	11.4[i]	11.7[i]	16.3	15.2	12,655	20,730
54 Romania	0.973	43	0.771	0.793	77.5	70.3	10.4	11.0	14.5	13.7	12,005	23,148
55 Libya	0.931	93	0.749	0.805	77.3	73.5	7.5	7.5	16.4	15.9	10,649	32,678
56 Oman	..	..	..	..	79.0	74.8	..	..	13.9	13.4	17,346	56,424
57 Russian Federation	1.038	61	0.792	0.763	74.4	61.8	11.7	11.8	14.5	13.5	18,228	27,741
58 Bulgaria	0.994	8	0.775	0.779	77.3	70.0	10.6[d]	10.5[d]	14.5	14.1	12,539	18,430
59 Barbados	1.021	32	0.784	0.767	77.8	73.0	9.5	9.2	17.2	13.8	11,165	16,054
60 Palau	..	..	..	..	..	..	12.2	12.6	14.6	12.9	..	..

HDI rank	Gender Development Index — Ratio of female to male HDI 2013	Rank[b] 2013	Human Development Index (HDI) — Value Female 2013	Male 2013	Life expectancy at birth (years) Female 2013	Male 2013	Mean years of schooling (years) Female 2002–2012[c]	Male 2002–2012[c]	Expected years of schooling (years) Female 2000–2012[c]	Male 2000–2012[c]	Estimated gross national income per capita[a] (2011 PPP $) Female 2013	Male 2013
61 Antigua and Barbuda	..	..	..	..	78.3	73.5	..	..	13.7	13.8	..	..
62 Malaysia	0.935	91	0.743	0.794	77.4	72.7	9.2	9.9	12.7	12.7	13,187	30,984
63 Mauritius	0.957	72	0.750	0.784	77.1	70.3	8.0	9.1	15.9	15.2	10,980	22,726
64 Trinidad and Tobago	0.994	8	0.763	0.767	73.6	66.4	10.9	10.6	12.5	12.1	19,079	31,713
65 Lebanon	0.900	110	0.715	0.794	82.3	78.1	7.6[i]	8.2[i]	13.0	13.3	7,199	25,038
65 Panama	0.978	36	0.753	0.770	80.5	74.8	9.6[g]	9.2[g]	12.9	11.9	10,798	21,850
67 Venezuela (Bolivarian Republic of)	0.999	2	0.759	0.760	77.7	71.7	8.7	8.4	15.3	13.1	11,924	22,180
68 Costa Rica	0.973	43	0.751	0.772	82.2	77.8	8.4	8.3	13.9	13.2	9,719	16,204
69 Turkey	0.884	118	0.704	0.796	78.7	71.8	6.4	8.7	13.8	15.0	8,813	28,318
70 Kazakhstan	1.015	25	0.762	0.751	72.3	61.0	10.2[g]	10.5[g]	15.4	14.7	14,369	24,902
71 Mexico	0.940	85	0.728	0.775	79.8	75.1	8.1	8.8	12.9	12.6	10,060	22,020
71 Seychelles	..	..	..	..	78.1	69.0	9.4[i]	9.4[i]	12.1	11.1	..	..
73 Saint Kitts and Nevis	..	..	..	..	..	..	..	..	13.4	12.4	..	..
73 Sri Lanka	0.961	66	0.720	0.749	77.4	71.2	10.7[g]	9.4[g]	13.9	13.4	5,078	13,616
75 Iran (Islamic Republic of)	0.847	128	0.672	0.793	76.1	72.2	7.1	8.6	15.0	15.3	4,159	22,631
76 Azerbaijan	0.952	77	0.723	0.759	73.9	67.6	10.5[i]	11.2[i]	11.6	11.9	10,968	20,541
77 Jordan	0.842	130	0.658	0.781	75.6	72.3	9.4	10.4	13.5	13.1	2,875	19,459
77 Serbia	..	..	..	..	76.9	71.3	9.2[g]	9.9[g]	14.1	13.2	..	..
79 Brazil	..	..	..	..	77.6	70.4	7.3[g]	7.2[g]	..	..	10,851	17,813
79 Georgia	0.941	84	0.713	0.758	77.8	70.5	11.9[i]	12.4[i]	12.8	12.8	4,231	9,871
79 Grenada	..	..	..	..	75.3	70.3	..	..	16.3	15.3	..	..
82 Peru	0.957	72	0.720	0.753	77.6	72.2	8.5	9.6	13.2	13.1	8,942	13,607
83 Ukraine	1.012	21	0.738	0.729	74.4	62.8	11.2	11.4	15.3	14.9	6,450	10,279
84 Belize	0.963	60	0.714	0.742	77.1	70.9	9.2[g]	9.3[g]	14.1	13.3	6,163	12,571
84 The former Yugoslav Republic of Macedonia	0.944	83	0.708	0.750	77.5	72.9	7.9[i]	8.5[i]	13.4	13.2	7,913	15,563
86 Bosnia and Herzegovina	..	..	..	..	78.9	73.8	7.2[i]	9.5[i]	..	..	6,381	12,628
87 Armenia	0.994	8	0.725	0.729	78.0	71.3	10.8[g]	10.8[g]	13.6	11.2	5,486	10,282
88 Fiji	0.937	89	0.679	0.725	73.0	67.0	9.8	10.0	14.1	13.7	4,100	10,214
89 Thailand	0.990	14	0.718	0.725	77.8	71.1	7.0	7.7	13.4	12.7	11,728	15,069
90 Tunisia	0.891	116	0.669	0.751	78.3	73.6	5.5	7.5	15.0	14.0	4,751	16,226
91 China	0.939	88	0.696	0.740	76.7	74.1	6.9	8.2	13.0	12.8	9,288	13,512
91 Saint Vincent and the Grenadines	..	..	..	..	74.7	70.4	..	..	13.4	13.1	7,541	13,085
93 Algeria	0.843	129	0.629	0.746	72.7	69.4	5.9	7.8	14.2	13.8	3,695	21,219
93 Dominica	..	..	..	..	..	..	..	..	..	..	..	..
95 Albania	0.957	72	0.694	0.725	80.6	74.6	9.1	9.5	10.3	10.3	6,704	11,734
96 Jamaica	0.989	17	0.703	0.711	76.1	71.0	9.8	9.2	12.4	11.5	6,406	9,990
97 Saint Lucia	..	..	..	..	77.5	72.2	..	..	12.5	11.8	7,597	10,966
98 Colombia	0.972	46	0.697	0.718	77.7	70.4	7.0	7.1	13.5	12.9	7,698	15,485
98 Ecuador	..	..	..	..	79.4	73.7	7.4	7.8[g]	..	..	7,045	12,951
100 Suriname	0.974	41	0.693	0.711	74.3	67.9	7.3	8.0	12.9	11.2	9,874	20,329
100 Tonga	0.966	54	0.682	0.706	75.7	69.8	9.2[d]	9.5[d]	14.0	13.4	3,983	6,642
102 Dominican Republic	..	..	..	..	76.7	70.4	7.7	7.2	..	..	7,514	14,172
MEDIUM HUMAN DEVELOPMENT												
103 Maldives	0.936	90	0.673	0.718	79.0	76.9	5.4[d]	6.2[d]	12.8	12.5	7,504	12,608
103 Mongolia	1.021	32	0.705	0.691	71.6	63.7	8.5	8.2	15.6	14.4	7,299	9,654
103 Turkmenistan	..	..	..	..	69.8	61.4	..	..	..	..	7,714	15,479
106 Samoa	0.948	81	0.670	0.707	76.5	70.2	10.3	10.3	13.3[k]	12.5[k]	2,868	6,436
107 Palestine, State of	0.974	41	0.612	0.628	75.0	71.5	8.4[i]	9.3[i]	14.0	12.5	1,651	8,580
108 Indonesia	0.923	98	0.654	0.709	72.9	68.8	6.9	8.1	12.8	12.7	5,873	12,030
109 Botswana	0.964	58	0.669	0.694	66.8	62.1	8.7	9.0	11.7	11.6	11,491	18,054
110 Egypt	0.855	125	0.617	0.722	73.6	68.8	5.3	7.5	12.7	13.3	4,225	16,522
111 Paraguay	0.966	54	0.664	0.687	74.6	70.1	7.5	7.9	12.2	11.7	5,984	9,150
112 Gabon	..	..	..	..	64.5	62.4	8.4	6.4	..	..	14,003	19,919
113 Bolivia (Plurinational State of)	0.931	93	0.642	0.690	69.5	65.1	8.4[g]	10.0[g]	12.9	13.4	4,406	6,701
114 Moldova (Republic of)	0.990	14	0.659	0.666	72.8	65.0	9.6[g]	10.0[g]	12.1	11.6	4,196	5,979
115 El Salvador	0.965	56	0.648	0.672	77.1	67.8	6.1	6.9	12.0	12.3	5,383	9,302
116 Uzbekistan	0.945	82	0.637	0.674	71.7	65.0	9.5[i]	9.9[i]	11.3	11.7	3,579	6,893
117 Philippines	0.989	17	0.652	0.659	72.2	65.4	8.8[d]	8.5[d]	11.5	11.1	4,987	7,771
118 South Africa	..	..	..	..	58.8	54.7	9.8	10.1	..	..	8,539	15,233
118 Syrian Arab Republic	0.851	127	0.588	0.691	77.8	71.8	6.1	7.1	12.0	12.1	1,922	9,478
120 Iraq	0.802	137	0.556	0.693	73.2	65.9	4.4	6.7	8.7	11.4	4,246	23,555

TABLE 5   Gender Development Index | 177

TABLE 5 GENDER DEVELOPMENT INDEX

HDI rank	Gender Development Index — Ratio of female to male HDI 2013	Gender Development Index — Rank[b] 2013	Human Development Index (HDI) Value — Female 2013	Human Development Index (HDI) Value — Male 2013	Life expectancy at birth (years) — Female 2013	Life expectancy at birth (years) — Male 2013	Mean years of schooling (years) — Female 2002–2012[c]	Mean years of schooling (years) — Male 2002–2012[c]	Expected years of schooling (years) — Female 2000–2012[c]	Expected years of schooling (years) — Male 2000–2012[c]	Estimated gross national income per capita[a] (2011 PPP $) — Female 2013	Estimated gross national income per capita[a] (2011 PPP $) — Male 2013
121 Guyana	0.985	25	0.629	0.638	68.9	63.6	9.0[g]	8.1[g]	11.7	9.9	3,993	8,613
121 Viet Nam	..	..	..	..	80.5	71.3	5.2	5.7	..	..	4,147	5,655
123 Cape Verde	..	..	..	..	78.8	71.1	..	..	13.6	12.9	4,266	8,480
124 Micronesia (Federated States of)	..	..	..	..	69.9	68.0	5.6	9.2	..	..	..	..
125 Guatemala	0.910	104	0.596	0.655	75.6	68.5	5.0	6.4	10.3	11.1	4,456	9,397
125 Kyrgyzstan	0.976	39	0.618	0.633	71.9	63.4	9.3[g]	9.3[g]	12.7	12.3	2,228	3,837
127 Namibia	0.978	36	0.616	0.631	67.1	61.7	6.3	6.1	11.4	11.3	7,288	11,196
128 Timor-Leste	0.875	122	0.574	0.656	69.1	66.0	3.6[i]	5.3[i]	11.3	12.0	5,634	13,582
129 Honduras	0.929	95	0.590	0.634	76.2	71.5	5.3	5.7	12.1	11.2	2,474	5,800
129 Morocco	0.828	132	0.545	0.658	72.7	69.1	3.2	5.6	10.6	11.6	3,215	10,692
131 Vanuatu	0.900	110	0.581	0.646	73.8	69.7	8.0	10.0	10.2	10.9	2,022	3,264
132 Nicaragua	0.912	102	0.583	0.639	77.9	71.8	4.8	6.7	10.8	10.3	2,821	5,743
133 Kiribati	..	..	..	..	71.8	66.1	..	..	12.7	11.9	..	..
133 Tajikistan	0.952	77	0.591	0.621	70.8	64.1	10.0[g]	9.7[g]	10.4	12.0	1,939	2,906
135 India	0.828	132	0.519	0.627	68.3	64.7	3.2	5.6	11.3	11.8	2,277	7,833
136 Bhutan	..	..	..	..	68.7	68.0	..	..	12.5	12.3	5,419	7,942
136 Cambodia	0.909	105	0.533	0.587	74.5	69.1	3.2[g]	5.0[g]	10.3	11.5	2,410	3,220
138 Ghana	0.884	118	0.537	0.607	62.1	60.2	5.9	8.1	10.9	12.1	2,937	4,138
139 Lao People's Democratic Republic	0.897	112	0.537	0.599	69.7	66.9	3.8	5.4	9.5	10.8	3,806	4,902
140 Congo	0.928	96	0.543	0.585	60.2	57.4	5.5	6.7	10.9	11.3	4,222	5,597
141 Zambia	0.913	101	0.534	0.585	60.0	56.3	5.8	7.2	13.0	13.9	2,344	3,455
142 Bangladesh	0.908	107	0.528	0.582	71.5	69.9	4.6	5.6	10.3	9.7	1,928	3,480
142 Sao Tome and Principe	0.894	115	0.524	0.586	68.3	64.3	4.0[i]	5.5[i]	11.4	11.2	2,001	4,248
144 Equatorial Guinea	..	..	..	..	54.6	51.7	..	..	6.9	10.0	17,769	25,977
LOW HUMAN DEVELOPMENT												
145 Nepal	0.912	102	0.514	0.564	69.6	67.3	2.4	4.2	12.5	12.2	1,857	2,554
146 Pakistan	0.750	145	0.447	0.596	67.5	65.7	3.3	6.1	6.9	8.4	1,707	7,439
147 Kenya	0.908	107	0.508	0.560	63.6	59.8	5.4[g]	7.1[g]	10.7	11.3	1,763	2,554
148 Swaziland	0.877	121	0.493	0.562	48.3	49.6	7.4	6.8	10.9	11.8	3,738	7,384
149 Angola	..	..	..	..	53.4	50.4	..	..	8.7	14.0	5,080	7,587
150 Myanmar	..	..	..	..	67.2	63.1	4.1	3.8	..	..	3,362	4,673
151 Rwanda	0.950	80	0.463	0.487	65.7	62.4	3.1	3.6	..	..	1,263	1,550
152 Cameroon	0.872	123	0.468	0.537	56.2	53.9	5.1	6.7	10.3	10.2	2,062	3,052
152 Nigeria	0.839	131	0.458	0.546	52.8	52.2	4.2[i]	6.3[i]	8.2	9.8	4,068	6,594
154 Yemen	0.738	146	0.415	0.562	64.5	61.8	1.2	3.8	7.7	10.6	1,775	6,080
155 Madagascar	0.917	99	0.476	0.519	66.2	63.2	4.8[k]	5.6[k]	10.2	10.5	1,102	1,566
156 Zimbabwe	0.909	105	0.468	0.515	60.8	58.8	6.7[g]	7.8[g]	9.1	9.5	1,124	1,496
157 Papua New Guinea	..	..	..	..	64.6	60.4	3.2	8.4	..	..	2,140	2,754
157 Solomon Islands	..	..	..	..	69.2	66.3	..	..	8.8	9.7	940	1,816
159 Comoros	..	..	..	..	62.3	59.5	..	..	12.3	13.2	798	2,201
159 Tanzania (United Republic of)	0.916	100	0.466	0.509	62.9	60.2	4.5	5.8	9.0	9.3	1,501	1,903
161 Mauritania	0.801	138	0.425	0.530	63.1	60.0	2.6	4.9	8.1	8.3	1,362	4,592
162 Lesotho	0.973	43	0.474	0.488	49.5	49.2	6.8[d]	4.6[d]	11.6	10.6	2,217	3,395
163 Senegal	0.864	124	0.449	0.520	64.9	61.9	3.4[g]	5.6[g]	7.8	8.1	1,642	2,717
164 Uganda	0.896	114	0.456	0.509	60.4	58.0	4.3	6.4	10.6	10.9	1,167	1,502
165 Benin	0.822	134	0.428	0.520	60.7	57.9	2.0	4.4	9.4	12.7	1,455	1,999
166 Sudan	..	..	..	..	63.9	60.3	2.5	3.8	..	..	1,692	5,153
166 Togo	0.803	136	0.401	0.499	57.4	55.6	3.3	6.7	8.5	11.9	998	1,263
168 Haiti	..	..	..	..	65.0	61.2	3.2	6.7	..	..	1,349	1,930
169 Afghanistan	0.602	148	0.330	0.549	62.2	59.7	1.2	5.1	7.2	11.3	503	3,265
170 Djibouti	..	..	..	..	63.4	60.2	..	..	5.9	6.9	1,907	4,300
171 Côte d'Ivoire	..	..	..	..	51.6	50.0	3.1	5.4	..	..	1,866	3,648
172 Gambia	..	..	..	..	60.2	57.5	2.0	3.6	..	..	1,309	1,811
173 Ethiopia	0.853	126	0.401	0.470	65.3	62.0	1.4[i]	3.6[i]	8.0	9.0	1,090	1,515
174 Malawi	0.891	116	0.389	0.437	55.4	55.1	3.4[g]	5.1[g]	10.8	10.7	652	777
175 Liberia	0.786	140	0.379	0.482	61.5	59.6	2.3	5.6	8.9	12.4	634	868
176 Mali	0.771	143	0.350	0.455	54.9	55.1	1.4[d]	2.6[d]	7.6	9.6	914	2,076
177 Guinea-Bissau	..	..	..	..	55.8	52.8	1.4[i]	3.4[i]	..	..	907	1,275
178 Mozambique	0.879	120	0.343	0.391	51.0	49.3	0.8[i]	1.7[i]	8.9	10.1	939	1,086
179 Guinea	0.785	141	0.344	0.439	56.9	55.3	0.8[i]	2.6[i]	7.4	10.1	913	1,370

TABLE 5

	Gender Development Index		Human Development Index (HDI)		Life expectancy at birth		Mean years of schooling		Expected years of schooling		Estimated gross national income per capita[a]	
	Ratio of female to male HDI	Rank[b]	Value		(years)		(years)		(years)		(2011 PPP $)	
			Female	Male	Female	Male	Female	Male	Female	Male	Female	Male
HDI rank	2013	2013	2013	2013	2013	2013	2002–2012[c]	2002–2012[c]	2000–2012[c]	2000–2012[c]	2013	2013
180 Burundi	0.904	109	0.370	0.410	56.1	52.2	2.2	3.3	9.6	10.7	685	815
181 Burkina Faso	0.924	97	0.376	0.407	56.9	55.7	1.9[j]	1.1[j]	7.0	8.0	1,335	1,871
182 Eritrea	..	..	..	..	65.2	60.5	..	..	3.7	4.6	986	1,309
183 Sierra Leone	0.799	139	0.329	0.412	45.8	45.3	2.0	3.8	6.1	8.4	1,617	2,016
184 Chad	0.762	144	0.319	0.419	52.1	50.3	0.6	2.3	5.9	8.9	1,289	1,953
185 Central African Republic	0.776	142	0.296	0.382	52.1	48.3	2.3	4.9	5.9	8.6	482	698
186 Congo (Democratic Republic of the)	0.822	134	0.304	0.369	51.8	48.2	2.1	4.1	8.4	10.9	390	499
187 Niger	0.714	147	0.275	0.385	58.6	58.3	0.8	2.1	4.8	6.1	471	1,268
OTHER COUNTRIES OR TERRITORIES												
Korea, Democratic People's Rep. of	..	..	..	..	73.4	66.4	..	..	..	..	..	..
Marshall Islands	..	..	..	..	..	..	..	..	12.0	11.4	..	..
Monaco	..	..	..	..	..	..	..	..	..	..	..	..
Nauru	..	..	..	..	..	..	..	..	9.9	8.9	..	..
San Marino	..	..	..	..	..	..	..	..	15.9	14.7	..	..
Somalia	..	..	..	..	56.7	53.4	..	..	..	..	..	..
South Sudan	..	..	..	..	56.3	54.2	..	..	..	..	..	..
Tuvalu	..	..	..	..	..	..	..	..	11.4	10.3	..	..
Human Development Index groups												
Very high human development	0.975	—	0.874	0.896	83.0	77.4	11.6	11.8	16.7	15.8	26,677	53,683
High human development	0.946	—	0.710	0.750	76.8	72.3	7.5	8.5	13.4	13.1	9,426	16,966
Medium human development	0.875	—	0.565	0.646	70.0	65.9	4.7	6.4	11.4	11.8	3,199	8,619
Low human development	0.834	—	0.446	0.535	60.5	58.2	3.1	5.1	8.3	9.8	2,011	3,789
Regions												
Arab States	0.866	—	0.626	0.722	72.2	68.4	4.9	6.7	12.1	12.8	6,991	23,169
East Asia and the Pacific	0.943	—	0.682	0.724	75.8	72.3	6.8	7.9	12.8	12.6	8,154	12,488
Europe and Central Asia	0.938	—	0.705	0.752	75.4	67.3	8.8	9.8	13.4	13.8	7,287	17,867
Latin America and the Caribbean	0.963	—	0.716	0.744	78.0	71.8	7.7	8.0	13.6	13.0	8,962	18,732
South Asia	0.830	—	0.522	0.629	68.9	65.7	3.5	5.8	10.8	11.4	2,384	7,852
Sub-Saharan Africa	0.867	—	0.460	0.531	58.0	55.6	3.7	5.4	8.8	10.1	2,492	3,812
Least developed countries	0.859	—	0.447	0.520	62.8	60.3	2.9	4.5	9.0	10.1	1,576	2,629
Small island developing states	..	—	..	..	72.4	67.7	..	..	13.5	12.8	6,993	12,017
World	**0.920**	—	**0.655**	**0.712**	**73.0**	**68.8**	**6.0**	**7.4**	**12.0**	**12.3**	**8,956**	**18,277**

TABLE
5

NOTES

a Because disaggregated income data are not available, data are crudely estimated. See *Definitions* and *Technical note 4* at http://hdr.undp.org for details on the methodology.

b Countries are ranked by absolute deviation from gender parity in HDI values.

c Data refer to the most recent year available during the period specified.

d HDRO update based on data on educational attainment from UNESCO Institute for Statistics (2013b) and methodology from Barro and Lee (2013).

e Calculated by the Singapore Ministry of Education.

f For the purpose of calculating the HDI for men, estimated earned income is capped at $75,000.

g Based on UNESCO Institute for Statistics (2011).

h Based on data on school life expectancy from UNESCO Institute for Statistics (2013a).

i Based on the estimate of educational attainment distribution from UNESCO Institute for Statistics (2013a) .

j HDRO calculations based on recent data from Multiple Indicator Cluster Surveys.

k HDRO calculations based on data from the 2011 population census from Samoa Bureau of Statistics (n.d.).

l HDRO estimate based on country's most recent Demographic and Health Survey data.

DEFINITIONS

Gender Development Index: A composite measure reflecting disparity in human development achievements between women and men in three dimensions—health, education and living standards. See *Technical note 4* at http://hdr.undp.org for details on how the Gender Development Index is calculated.

Ratio of female to male HDI: Ratio of female to male HDI values.

Human Development Index (HDI): A composite index measuring average achievement in three basic dimensions of human development—a long and

healthy life, knowledge and a decent standard of living. See *Technical note 1* at http://hdr.undp.org for details on how the HDI is calculated

Life expectancy at birth: Number of years a newborn infant could expect to live if prevailing patterns of age-specific mortality rates at the time of birth stay the same throughout the infant's life.

Mean years of schooling: Average number of years of education received by people ages 25 and older, converted from educational attainment levels using official durations of each level.

Expected years of schooling: Number of years of schooling that a child of school entrance age can expect to receive if prevailing patterns of age-specific enrolment rates persist throughout the child's life.

Estimated gross national income (GNI) per capita: Derived from the ratio of female to male wage, female and male shares of economically active population and GNI (in 2011 purchasing power parity terms). See *Technical note 4* at http://hdr.undp.org/ for details.

MAIN DATA SOURCES

Columns 1 and 2: Calculated based on data in columns 3 and 4.

Columns 3 and 4: HDRO calculations based on data from UNDESA (2013a), Barro and Lee (2013), United Nations Statistics Division (2014), UNESCO Institute for Statistics (2013b), World Bank (2014) and ILO (2014).

Columns 5 and 6: UNDESA 2013a.

Columns 7 and 8: Barro and Lee (2013), UNESCO Institute for Statistics (2013b) and HDRO estimates based on data on educational attainment from UNESCO Institute for Statistics (2013b) and on methodology from Barro and Lee (2013).

Columns 9 and 10: UNESCO Institute for Statistics 2013.

Columns 11 and 12: HDRO calculations based on ILO (2013a), UNDESA (2013a) and World Bank (2014).

TABLE 5 Gender Development Index | 179

TABLE 6

Multidimensional Poverty Index

	Year and survey[a]	Multidimensional Poverty Index[b] Revised specifications[c] Index Value	Revised specifications[c] Headcount (%)	2010 specifications[d] Index Value	2010 specifications[d] Headcount (%)	Population in multidimensional poverty[e] Headcount (thousands)	Intensity of deprivation (%)	Population near multidimensional poverty[e] (%)	Population in severe poverty[e] (%)	Contribution of deprivation in dimension to overall poverty (%) Education	Health	Living standards	Population below income poverty line (%) PPP $1.25 a day 2002–2012[f]	National poverty line 2002–2012[f]
Afghanistan	2010/2011 M	0.293 [g]	58.8 [g]	0.353 [g]	66.2 [g]	17,116 [g]	49.9 [g]	16.0 [g]	29.8 [g]	45.6 [g]	19.2 [g]	35.2 [g]	..	36
Albania	2008/2009 D	0.005	1.2	0.005	1.4	38	38.3	7.2	0.1	22.4	47.1	30.5	0.62	12.4
Argentina	2005 N	0.015 [h]	3.7 [h]	0.011 [h]	2.9 [h]	1,438 [h]	39.1 [h]	5.2 [h]	0.5 [h]	38.2 [h]	27.8 [h]	34.0 [h]	0.92	..
Armenia	2010 D	0.002	0.6	0.001	0.3	18	37.0	3.0	0.1	3.4	87.8	8.7	2.47	35.8
Azerbaijan	2006 D	0.009	2.4	0.021	5.3	210	38.2	11.5	0.2	20.0	50.7	29.3	0.43	6
Bangladesh	2011 D	0.237	49.5	0.253	51.2	75,610	47.8	18.8	21.0	28.4	26.6	44.9	43.25	31.51
Belarus	2005 M	0.001	0.4	0.000	0.0	41	34.5	1.1	0.0	2.6	89.7	7.7	0.07	6.3
Belize	2011 M	0.030	7.4	0.018	4.6	23	41.2	6.4	1.5	36.2	34.8	29.0	..	..
Benin	2006 D	0.401 [i]	69.8 [i]	0.412 [i]	71.8 [i]	5,897 [i]	57.4 [i]	18.8 [i]	45.7 [i]	35.0 [i]	24.9 [i]	40.1 [i]	47.33	36.2
Bhutan	2010 M	0.128	29.4	0.119	27.2	211	43.5	18.0	8.8	40.3	26.3	33.4	1.66	12
Bolivia (Plurinational State of)	2008 D	0.097	20.6	0.089	20.5	2,022	47.0	17.3	7.8	21.9	27.9	50.2	15.61	51.3
Bosnia and Herzegovina	2011/2012 M	0.006 [i]	1.7 [i]	0.002 [i]	0.5 [i]	65 [i]	37.3 [i]	3.2 [i]	0.0 [i]	7.8 [i]	79.5 [i]	12.7 [i]	0.04	14
Brazil	2012 N	0.012 [g,k]	3.1 [g,k]	..	..	6,083 [g,k]	40.8 [g,k]	7.4 [g,k]	0.5 [g,k]	27.7 [g,k]	38.4 [g,k]	33.9 [g,k]	6.14	21.4
Burkina Faso	2010 D	0.508	82.8	0.535	84.0	12,875	61.3	7.6	63.8	39.0	22.5	38.5	44.6	46.7
Burundi	2010 D	0.442	81.8	0.454	80.8	7,553	54.0	12.0	48.2	25.0	26.3	48.8	81.32	66.9
Cambodia	2010 D	0.211	46.8	0.212	45.9	6,721	45.1	20.4	16.4	25.9	27.7	46.4	18.6	20.5
Cameroon	2011 D	0.260	48.2	0.248	46.0	10,187	54.1	17.8	27.1	24.5	31.3	44.2	9.56	39.9
Central African Republic	2010 M	0.424	76.3	0.430	77.6	3,320	55.6	15.7	48.5	23.8	26.2	50.0	..	..
China	2009 N	0.026 [k,l]	6.0 [k,l]	..	..	80,784 [k,l]	43.4 [k,l]	19.0 [k,l]	1.3 [k,l]	21.0 [k,l]	44.4 [k,l]	34.6 [k,l]	11.8	..
Colombia	2010 D	0.032	7.6	0.022	5.4	3,534	42.2	10.2	1.8	34.3	24.7	41.0	8.16	32.7
Congo	2011/2012 D	0.192	43.0	0.181	39.7	1,866	44.7	26.2	12.2	10.6	32.8	56.6	54.1	46.5
Congo (Democratic Republic of the)	2010 M	0.399	74.4	0.392	74.0	46,278	53.7	15.5	46.2	18.5	25.5	55.9	87.72	71.3
Cote d'Ivoire	2011/2012 D	0.307	59.3	0.310	58.7	11,772	51.7	17.9	32.4	36.5	25.8	37.7	23.75	42.7
Djibouti	2006 M	0.127	26.9	0.139	29.3	212	47.3	16.0	11.1	36.1	22.7	41.2	18.84	..
Dominican Republic	2007 D	0.026	6.2	0.018	4.6	599	41.9	10.8	1.4	36.2	30.4	33.3	2.24	40.9
Egypt	2008 D	0.036 [m]	8.9 [m]	0.024 [m]	6.0 [m]	6,740 [m]	40.3 [m]	8.6 [m]	1.5 [m]	41.8 [m]	45.6 [m]	12.6 [m]	1.69	25.2
Ethiopia	2011 D	0.537	88.2	0.564	87.3	78,887	60.9	6.7	67.0	27.4	25.2	47.4	30.65	29.6
Gabon	2012 D	0.073	16.7	0.070	16.5	273	43.4	19.9	4.4	15.2	43.8	40.9	4.84	32.7
Gambia	2005/2006 M	0.329	60.8	0.324	60.4	901	54.1	15.7	35.9	34.0	30.5	35.5	33.63	48.4
Georgia	2005 M	0.008	2.2	0.003	0.8	99	37.6	4.1	0.1	7.4	67.4	25.2	17.99	24.7
Ghana	2011 M	0.144	30.5	0.139	30.4	7,559	47.3	18.7	12.1	27.7	27.1	45.2	28.59	28.5
Guinea	2005 D	0.548	86.5	0.506	82.5	8,283	63.4	7.7	68.6	34.4	22.3	43.3	43.34	55.2
Guinea-Bissau	2006 M	0.495	80.4	0.462	77.5	1,168	61.6	10.5	58.4	30.5	27.9	41.6	48.9	69.3
Guyana	2009 D	0.031	7.8	0.030	7.7	61	40.0	18.8	1.2	16.8	51.2	32.0	..	..
Haiti	2012 D	0.242	50.2	0.248	49.4	5,104	48.1	22.2	20.1	24.8	23.4	51.8	..	..
Honduras	2011/2012 D	0.098 [i]	20.7 [i]	0.072 [i]	15.8 [i]	1,642 [i]	47.4 [i]	28.6 [i]	7.2 [i]	36.6 [i]	23.1 [i]	40.3 [i]	17.92	60
India	2005/2006 D	0.282	55.3	0.283	53.7	631,999	51.1	18.2	27.8	22.7	32.5	44.8	32.68	21.9
Indonesia	2012 D	0.024 [g]	5.9 [g]	0.066 [g]	15.5 [g]	14,574 [g]	41.3 [g]	8.1 [g]	1.1 [g]	24.7 [g]	35.1 [g]	40.2 [g]	16.20	12
Iraq	2011 M	0.052	13.3	0.045	11.6	4,236	39.4	7.4	2.5	50.1	38.6	11.3	2.82	22.9
Jordan	2009 D	0.004	1.0	0.008	2.4	64	36.8	4.1	0.1	33.7	56.3	10.0	0.12	13.3
Kazakhstan	2010/2011 M	0.004	1.1	0.001	0.2	173	36.4	2.3	0.0	4.3	83.9	11.8	0.11	3.8
Kenya	2008/2009 D	0.226	48.2	0.229	47.8	19,190	47.0	29.1	15.7	11.2	32.4	56.4	43.37	45.9
Kyrgyzstan	2005/2006 M	0.013	3.4	0.019	4.9	173	37.9	10.1	0.3	5.0	63.9	31.2	5.03	38
Lao People's Democratic Republic	2011/2012 M	0.186	36.8	0.174	34.1	2,447	50.5	18.5	18.8	37.7	25.4	36.9	33.88	27.6
Lesotho	2009 D	0.227	49.5	0.156	35.3	984	45.9	20.4	18.2	14.8	33.8	51.4	43.41	56.6
Liberia	2007 D	0.459	81.9	0.485	83.9	2,883	56.1	12.9	52.8	30.4	21.8	47.8	83.76	63.8
Madagascar	2008/2009 D	0.420	77.0	0.357	66.9	15,774	54.6	11.7	48.0	31.6	24.5	43.9	81.29	75.3
Malawi	2010 D	0.332	66.7	0.334	66.7	10,012	49.8	24.5	29.8	18.9	27.7	53.4	61.64	50.7
Maldives	2009 D	0.008	2.0	0.018	5.2	6	37.5	8.5	0.1	27.8	60.2	11.9	1.48	..
Mali	2006 D	0.533	85.6	0.558	86.6	10,545	62.4	7.8	66.8	37.4	22.6	40.1	50.43	43.6
Mauritania	2007 M	0.362	66.0	0.352	61.7	2,197	54.9	12.8	42.3	33.5	18.2	48.3	23.43	42
Mexico	2012 N	0.024	6.0	0.011	2.8	7,272	39.9	10.1	1.1	31.4	25.6	43.0	0.72	52.3
Moldova (Republic of)	2005 D	0.005	1.3	0.007	1.9	49	38.8	5.2	0.2	17.7	46.6	35.6	0.39	16.6
Mongolia	2005 M	0.077	18.3	0.065	15.8	462	42.0	19.0	4.2	13.5	35.7	50.8	..	27.4
Montenegro	2005/2006 M	0.012 [i]	3.0 [i]	0.006 [i]	1.5 [i]	19 [i]	40.1 [i]	1.3 [i]	0.5 [i]	21.0 [i]	63.8 [i]	15.3 [i]	0.12	9.3
Mozambique	2011 D	0.390	70.2	0.389	69.6	17,246	55.6	14.8	44.1	30.4	22.3	47.3	59.58	54.7
Namibia	2006/2007 D	0.200	42.1	0.187	39.6	876	47.5	22.6	15.7	14.8	33.4	51.8	31.91	28.7
Nepal	2011 D	0.197	41.4	0.217	44.2	11,255	47.4	18.1	18.6	27.3	28.2	44.5	24.82	25.2
Nicaragua	2011/2012 D	0.088	19.4	0.072	16.1	1,146	45.6	14.8	6.9	37.8	12.6	49.6	..	..
Niger	2012 D	0.584	89.8	0.605	89.3	15,408	65.0	5.9	73.5	35.9	24.0	40.0	43.62	59.5
Nigeria	2011 M	0.239	43.3	0.240	43.3	71,014	55.2	17.0	25.7	26.9	32.6	40.4	67.98	46

	Year and survey[a]	Multidimensional Poverty Index[b]				Population in multidimensional poverty[e]		Population near multidimensional poverty[e]	Population in severe poverty[e]	Contribution of deprivation in dimension to overall poverty (%)			Population below income poverty line (%)	
		Revised specifications[c]		2010 specifications[d]										
		Index Value	Headcount (%)	Index Value	Headcount (%)	Headcount (thousands)	Intensity of deprivation (%)	(%)	(%)	Education	Health	Living standards	PPP $1.25 a day 2002–2012[f]	National poverty line 2002–2012[f]
Pakistan	2012/2013 D	0.237	45.6	0.230	44.2	83,045	52.0	14.9	26.5	36.2	32.3	31.6	21.04	22.3
Palestine (State of)	2006/2007 N	0.007	2.0	0.005	1.4	74	36.9	7.4	0.1	16.6	72.3	11.1	0.04	21.9
Peru	2012 D	0.043	10.4	0.043	10.5	3,132	41.4	12.3	2.1	19.4	29.8	50.8	4.91	25.8
Philippines	2008 D	0.038[g,n]	7.3[g,n]	0.064[g,n]	13.4[g,n]	6,559[g,n]	51.9[g,n]	12.2[g,n]	5.0[g,n]	37.1[g,n]	25.7[g,n]	37.2[g,n]	18.42	26.5
Rwanda	2010 D	0.352	70.8	0.350	69.0	7,669	49.7	17.9	34.6	23.8	27.2	49.0	63.17	44.9
Sao Tome and Principe	2008/2009 D	0.217	47.5	0.154	34.5	82	45.5	21.5	16.4	29.1	26.5	44.4	..	61.7
Senegal	2010/2011 D	0.390	69.4	0.439	74.4	9,247	56.2	14.4	45.1	36.7	33.1	30.2	29.61	46.7
Serbia	2010 M	0.001	0.3	0.000	0.1	25	39.9	3.1	0.0	24.7	48.6	26.7	0.21	9.2
Sierra Leone	2010 M	0.405	72.7	0.388	72.5	4,180	55.8	16.7	46.4	24.2	28.3	47.4	51.71	52.9
Somalia	2006 M	0.500	81.8	0.514	81.2	7,104	61.1	8.3	63.6	33.7	18.8	47.5	..	..
South Africa	2012 N	0.041	10.3	0.044	11.1	5,400	39.6	17.1	1.3	8.4	61.4	30.2	13.77	23
Suriname	2010 M	0.033[j]	7.6[j]	0.024[j]	5.9[j]	40[j]	43.1[j]	4.7[j]	2.0[j]	31.0[j]	37.2[j]	31.8[j]	..	..
Swaziland	2010 M	0.113	25.9	0.086	20.4	309	43.5	20.5	7.4	13.7	41.0	45.3	40.63	63
Syrian Arab Republic	2006 M	0.024	6.4	0.021	5.5	1,197	38.0	7.7	0.9	44.4	43.1	12.5	1.71	..
Tajikistan	2012 D	0.031	7.9	0.054	13.2	629	39.0	23.4	1.2	13.4	52.6	34.0	6.56	46.7
Tanzania (United Republic of)	2010 D	0.335	66.4	0.332	65.6	29,842	50.4	21.5	32.1	16.9	28.2	54.9	67.87	28.2
Thailand	2005/2006 M	0.004	1.0	0.006	1.6	664	38.8	4.4	0.1	19.4	51.3	29.4	0.38	13.2
The former Yugoslav Republic of Macedonia	2011 M	0.007[j]	1.7[j]	0.002[j]	0.7[j]	36[j]	38.4[j]	2.4[j]	0.1[j]	18.5[j]	57.2[j]	24.3[j]	0.6	19
Timor-Leste	2009/2010 D	0.322	64.3	0.360	68.1	694	50.1	21.4	31.5	20.0	30.4	49.6	..	49.9
Togo	2010 M	0.260	50.9	0.250	49.8	3,207	51.2	20.3	26.4	28.9	25.0	46.1	28.22	58.7
Trinidad and Tobago	2006 M	0.007[g]	1.7[g]	0.020[g]	5.6[g]	23[g]	38.0[g]	0.5[g]	0.2[g]	2.2[g]	86.1[g]	11.7[g]	..	..
Tunisia	2011/2012 M	0.006	1.5	0.004	1.2	161	39.3	3.2	0.2	33.7	48.2	18.1	..	..
Uganda	2011 D	0.359	70.3	0.367	69.9	24,712	51.1	20.6	33.3	18.0	30.2	51.9	38.01	24.5
Ukraine	2007 D	0.002[g]	0.6[g]	0.008[g]	2.2[g]	264[g]	34.3[g]	0.2[g]	0.0[g]	1.0[g]	95.1[g]	3.8[g]	0.02	2.9
Uzbekistan	2006 M	0.013	3.5	0.008	2.3	935	36.6	6.2	0.1	3.7	83.4	12.8	..	..
Vanuatu	2007 M	0.135	31.2	0.129	30.1	69	43.1	32.6	7.3	24.4	24.1	51.6	..	..
Viet Nam	2010/2011 M	0.026	6.4	0.017	4.2	5,796	40.7	8.7	1.3	35.9	25.7	38.4	16.85	20.7
Yemen	2006 M	0.191[g]	37.5[g]	0.283[g]	52.5[g]	7,741[g]	50.9[g]	16.7[g]	18.4[g]	33.4[g]	21.3[g]	45.3[g]	17.53	34.8
Zambia	2007 D	0.318	62.8	0.328	64.2	7,600	50.7	18.7	31.3	16.3	29.4	54.3	74.45	60.5
Zimbabwe	2010/2011 D	0.181	41.0	0.172	39.1	5,482	44.1	24.9	12.2	7.8	37.9	54.3	..	72.3

TABLE 6

NOTES

a *D* indicates data from Demographic and Health Surveys, *M* indicates data from Multiple Indicator Cluster Surveys, and *N* indicates data from national surveys (see http://hdr.undp.org for the list of national surveys).

b Not all indicators were available for all countries, so caution should be used in cross-country comparisons. Where data were missing, indicator weights are adjusted to total 100%.

c The revised specifications refer to somewhat modified definitions of deprivations in some indicators compared to the 2010 specifications. See *Technical note 5* at http://hdr.undp.org for details.

d The 2010 specifications are based on a methodology from Alkire and Santos (2010).

e Based on the revised specifications in *Technical note 5* (available at http://hdr.undp.org).

f Data refer to the most recent year available during the period specified.

g Missing indicators on nutrition.

h Refers only to the urban part of the country.

i Missing indicator on electricity.

j Missing indicator on child mortality.

k Missing indicator on type of floor.

l Refers only to a part of the country (nine provinces).

m Missing indicator on cooking fuel.

n Missing indicator on school attendance.

DEFINITIONS

Multidimensional Poverty Index: Percentage of the population that is multidimensionally poor adjusted by the intensity of the deprivations. See *Technical note 5* at http://hdr.undp.org for details on how the Multidimensional Poverty Index is calculated.

Multidimensional poverty headcount: Population with a weighted deprivation score of at least 33 percent.

Intensity of deprivation of multidimensional poverty: Average percentage of deprivation experienced by people in multidimensional poverty.

Population near multidimensional poverty: Percentage of the population at risk of suffering multiple deprivations—that is, those with a deprivation score of 20–33 percent.

Population in severe poverty: Percentage of the population in severe multidimensional poverty—that is, those with a deprivation score of 50 percent or more.

Contribution of deprivation to overall poverty: Percentage of the Multidimensional Poverty Index attributed to deprivations in each dimension.

Population below PPP $1.25 a day: Percentage of the population living below the international poverty line $1.25 (in purchasing power parity terms) a day.

Population below national poverty line: Percentage of the population living below the national poverty line, which is the poverty line deemed appropriate for a country by its authorities. National estimates are based on population-weighted subgroup estimates from household surveys.

MAIN DATA SOURCES

Column 1: Calculated from various household surveys, including ICF Macro Demographic and Health Surveys, United Nations Children's Fund Multiple Indicator Cluster Surveys and several national household surveys conducted between 2005 and 2012.

Columns 2, 3 and 6–12: HDRO calculations based on data on household deprivations in education, health and living standards from various household surveys listed in column 1 using the revised methodology described in *Technical note 5* (available at http://hdr.undp.org).

Columns 4 and 5: Alkire, Conconi and Seth 2014.

Columns 13 and 14: World Bank 2013a.

TABLE 6   Multidimensional Poverty Index | 181

Multidimensional Poverty Index: changes over time (select countries)

	Year and survey[a]	Multidimensional Poverty Index[b] Value	Population in multidimensional poverty[c] Headcount (%)	Population in multidimensional poverty[c] Headcount (thousands)	Intensity of deprivation (%)	Population near multidimensional poverty (%)	Population in severe poverty (%)	Contribution of deprivation to overall poverty (%) Education	Health	Living standards
Bangladesh	2011 D	0.237	49.5	75,610	47.8	18.8	21.0	28.4	26.6	44.9
Bangladesh	2007 D	0.294	59.5	87,185	49.3	18.7	27.2	26.0	26.5	47.5
Belize	2011 M	0.030	7.4	23	41.2	6.4	1.5	36.2	34.8	29.0
Belize	2006 M	0.028	6.9	19	40.8	6.5	1.2	13.8	52.6	33.6
Bosnia and Herzegovina	2011/2012 M	0.006[d]	1.7[d]	65[d]	37.3[d]	3.2[d]	0.0[d]	7.8[d]	79.5[d]	12.7[d]
Bosnia and Herzegovina	2006 M	0.013[d]	3.5[d]	134[d]	38.1[d]	5.3[d]	0.1[d]	7.9[d]	76.3[d]	15.8[d]
Brazil	2012 N	0.012[e,f]	3.1[e,f]	6,083[e,f]	40.8[e,f]	7.4[e,f]	0.5[e,f]	27.7[e,f]	38.4[e,f]	33.9[e,f]
Brazil	2006 N	0.017[g]	4.0[g]	7,578[g]	41.4[g]	11.2[g]	0.7[g]	41.4[g]	20.4[g]	38.2[g]
Burkina Faso	2010 D	0.508	82.8	12,875	61.3	7.6	63.8	39.0	22.5	38.5
Burkina Faso	2006 M	0.538	85.2	11,775	63.2	6.9	67.1	38.0	22.3	39.6
Burundi	2010 D	0.442	81.8	7,553	54.0	12.0	48.2	25.0	26.3	48.8
Burundi	2005 M	0.485[e]	87.9[e]	6,833[e]	55.2[e]	8.5[e]	53.5[e]	37.8[e]	11.1[e]	51.1[e]
Cambodia	2010 D	0.211	46.8	6,721	45.1	20.4	16.4	25.9	27.7	46.4
Cambodia	2005 D	0.282	58.0	7,746	48.7	17.5	26.4	29.0	26.3	44.7
Cameroon	2011 D	0.260	48.2	10,187	54.1	17.8	27.1	24.5	31.3	44.2
Cameroon	2006 M	0.304[d]	51.8[d]	9,644[d]	58.7[d]	14.0[d]	35.9[d]	24.8[d]	31.7[d]	43.5[d]
Central African Republic	2010 M	0.424	76.3	3,320	55.6	15.7	48.5	23.8	26.2	50.0
Central African Republic	2006 M	0.464	80.5	3,245	57.7	12.1	54.5	30.2	24.3	45.6
Congo	2011/2012 D	0.192	43.0	1,866	44.7	26.2	12.2	10.6	32.8	56.6
Congo	2009 D	0.154[e]	32.7[e]	1,308[e]	47.1[e]	29.9[e]	15.1[e]	16.2[e]	25.6[e]	58.2[e]
Cote d'Ivoire	2011/2012 D	0.307	59.3	11,772	51.7	17.9	32.4	36.5	25.8	37.7
Cote d'Ivoire	2005 D	0.269[e,g]	50.0[e,g]	8,693[e,g]	53.9[e,g]	22.7[e,g]	26.7[e,g]	42.8[e,g]	20.8[e,g]	36.5[e,g]
Ghana	2011 M	0.144	30.5	7,559	47.3	18.7	12.1	27.7	27.1	45.2
Ghana	2008 D	0.186	39.2	9,057	47.4	20.3	15.4	26.5	28.5	45.0
Guyana	2009 D	0.031	7.8	61	40.0	18.8	1.2	16.8	51.2	32.0
Guyana	2007 M	0.032	7.9	61	40.1	10.7	1.5	16.9	44.8	38.3
Haiti	2012 D	0.242	50.2	5,104	48.1	22.2	20.1	24.8	23.4	51.8
Haiti	2005/2006 D	0.315	59.3	5,566	53.2	18.1	32.8	28.8	22.8	48.5
Honduras	2011/2012 D	0.098[h]	20.7[h]	1,642[h]	47.4[h]	28.6[h]	7.2[h]	36.6[h]	23.1[h]	40.3[h]
Honduras	2005/2006 D	0.156[h]	31.5[h]	2,214[h]	49.6[h]	26.6[h]	13.3[h]	38.4[h]	22.6[h]	39.0[h]
Indonesia	2012 D	0.024[e]	5.9[e]	14,574[e]	41.3[e]	8.1[e]	1.1[e]	24.7[e]	35.1[e]	40.2[e]
Indonesia	2007 D	0.043[e]	10.1[e]	23,432[e]	42.4[e]	15.4[e]	2.3[e]	30.4[e]	21.0[e]	48.7[e]
Iraq	2011 M	0.052	13.3	4,236	39.4	7.4	2.5	50.1	38.6	11.3
Iraq	2006 M	0.077	18.5	5,182	41.8	15.0	4.3	45.7	33.9	20.4
Kazakhstan	2010/2011 M	0.004	1.1	173	36.4	2.3	0.0	4.3	83.9	11.8
Kazakhstan	2006 M	0.007	1.8	277	38.5	4.7	0.2	5.5	73.4	21.2
Lao People's Democratic Republic	2011/2012 M	0.186	36.8	2,447	50.5	18.5	18.8	37.7	25.4	36.9
Lao People's Democratic Republic	2006 M	0.320[d]	55.0[d]	3,242[d]	58.3[d]	11.1[d]	35.2[d]	32.3[d]	32.6[d]	35.2[d]
Mexico	2012 N	0.024	6.0	7,272	39.9	10.1	1.1	31.4	25.6	43.0
Mexico	2006 N	0.028	6.9	7,779	40.9	10.7	1.6	32.0	29.0	39.0
Mozambique	2011 D	0.390	70.2	17,246	55.6	14.8	44.1	30.4	22.3	47.3
Mozambique	2009 D	0.395[e]	70.0[e]	16,343[e]	56.5[e]	14.7[e]	43.2[e]	31.3[e]	20.3[e]	48.4[e]
Nepal	2011 D	0.197	41.4	11,255	47.4	18.1	18.6	27.3	28.2	44.5
Nepal	2006 D	0.314	62.1	15,910	50.6	15.5	31.6	26.0	28.0	46.0
Nicaragua	2011/2012 D	0.088	19.4	1,146	45.6	14.8	6.9	37.8	12.6	49.6
Nicaragua	2006/2007 D	0.137	27.9	1,561	49.2	15.3	12.9	38.1	12.3	49.7
Niger	2012 D	0.584	89.8	15,408	65.0	5.9	73.5	35.9	24.0	40.0
Niger	2006 D	0.677	93.4	12,774	72.5	3.4	86.1	35.2	24.5	40.3
Nigeria	2011 M	0.239	43.3	71,014	55.2	17.0	25.7	26.9	32.6	40.4
Nigeria	2008 D	0.294	53.8	81,357	54.7	18.2	31.4	27.2	30.8	42.0
Pakistan	2012/2013 D	0.237	45.6	83,045	52.0	14.9	26.5	36.2	32.3	31.6
Pakistan	2006/2007 D	0.218[e]	43.5[e]	71,378[e]	50.0[e]	13.2[e]	21.7[e]	43.0[e]	19.7[e]	37.3[e]
Peru	2012 D	0.043	10.4	3,132	41.4	12.3	2.1	19.4	29.8	50.8
Peru	2011 D	0.051	12.2	3,607	42.2	12.3	2.8	20.2	29.0	50.8
Peru	2010 D	0.056	13.2	3,859	42.1	14.3	3.1	18.3	30.3	51.4
Peru	2008 D	0.069	16.1	4,605	42.7	53.8	15.1	17.9	29.1	53.0
Rwanda	2010 D	0.352	70.8	7,669	49.7	17.9	34.6	23.8	27.2	49.0
Rwanda	2005 D	0.481	86.5	8,155	55.6	9.7	60.4	23.3	22.3	54.4
Senegal	2010/2011 D	0.390	69.4	9,247	56.2	14.4	45.1	36.7	33.1	30.2
Senegal	2005 D	0.436	71.1	8,018	61.3	11.7	51.6	38.4	26.1	35.5
Serbia	2010 M	0.001	0.3	25	39.9	3.1	0.0	24.7	48.6	26.7
Serbia	2005/2006 M	0.011[d]	3.0[d]	296[d]	38.3[d]	3.8[d]	0.3[d]	18.1[d]	60.1[d]	21.8[d]
Sierra Leone	2010 M	0.405	72.7	4,180	55.8	16.7	46.4	24.2	28.3	47.4

	Year and survey[a]	Multidimensional Poverty Index[b] Value	Population in multidimensional poverty[c] Headcount (%)	Population in multidimensional poverty[c] Headcount (thousands)	Intensity of deprivation (%)	Population near multidimensional poverty (%)	Population in severe poverty (%)	Contribution of deprivation to overall poverty (%) Education	Contribution of deprivation to overall poverty (%) Health	Contribution of deprivation to overall poverty (%) Living standards
Sierra Leone	2008 D	0.451	79.7	4,409	56.6	12.5	51.7	32.0	22.7	45.3
South Africa	2012 N	0.041	10.3	5,400	39.6	17.1	1.3	8.4	61.4	30.2
South Africa	2008 N	0.039[f]	9.4[f]	4,701[f]	41.5[f]	21.4[f]	1.4[f]	13.4[f]	45.6[f]	41.1[f]
Suriname	2010 M	0.033[d]	7.6[d]	40[d]	43.1[d]	4.7[d]	2.0[d]	31.0[d]	37.2[d]	31.8[d]
Suriname	2006 M	0.044	9.2	46	47.4	6.3	3.6	36.7	21.1	42.2
Tajikistan	2012 D	0.031	7.9	629	39.0	23.4	1.2	13.4	52.6	34.0
Tajikistan	2005 M	0.059	14.7	1,002	39.8	18.6	2.3	11.0	57.3	31.7
The former Yugoslav Republic of Macedonia	2011 M	0.007[d]	1.7[d]	36[d]	38.4[d]	2.4[d]	0.1[d]	18.5[d]	57.2[d]	24.3[d]
The former Yugoslav Republic of Macedonia	2005 M	0.013	3.0	64	42.2	7.1	0.7	50.7	22.3	27.0
Togo	2010 M	0.260	50.9	3,207	51.2	20.3	26.4	28.9	25.0	46.1
Togo	2006 M	0.277	53.1	3,021	52.2	20.3	28.8	31.4	23.2	45.4
Uganda	2011 D	0.359	70.3	24,712	51.1	20.6	33.3	18.0	30.2	51.9
Uganda	2006 D	0.399	74.5	22,131	53.6	18.2	41.5	17.1	30.4	52.5
Zimbabwe	2010/2011 D	0.181	41.0	5,482	44.1	24.9	12.2	7.8	37.9	54.3
Zimbabwe	2006 D	0.193	42.4	5,399	45.4	22.8	15.7	11.5	29.6	58.9

NOTES

a *D* indicates data from Demographic and Health Surveys, *M* indicates data from Multiple Indicator Cluster Surveys, and *N* indicates data from national surveys (see http://hdr.undp.org for the list of national surveys).

b Not all indicators were available for all countries, so caution should be used in cross-country comparisons. Where data were missing, indicator weights are adjusted to total 100%.

c Based on revised definitions of deprivations in some indicators compared to the 2010 specifications—outlined in *Technical note 5* at http://hdr.undp.org.

d Missing indicator on child mortality.

e Missing indicators on nutrition.

f Missing indicator on type of floor.

g Missing indicator on cooking fuel.

h Missing indicator on electricity.

DEFINITIONS

Multidimensional Poverty Index: Percentage of the population that is multidimensionally poor adjusted by the intensity of the deprivations. See *Technical note 5* at http://hdr.undp.org for details on how the Multidimensional Poverty Index is calculated.

Multidimensional poverty headcount: Population with a weighted deprivation score of at least 33 percent.

Intensity of deprivation of multidimensional poverty: Average percentage of deprivation experienced by people in multidimensional poverty.

Population near multidimensional poverty: Percentage of the population at risk of suffering multiple deprivations—that is, those with a deprivation score of 20–33 percent.

Population in severe poverty: Percentage of the population in severe multidimensional poverty—that is, those with a deprivation score of 50 percent or more.

Contribution of deprivation to overall poverty: Percentage of the Multidimensional Poverty Index attributed to deprivations in each dimension.

MAIN DATA SOURCES

Columns 1 and 2: Calculated from various household surveys, including ICF Macro Demographic and Health Surveys, United Nations Children's Fund Multiple Indicator Cluster Surveys and several national household surveys conducted between 2005 and 2012.

Columns 3–10: HDRO calculations based on data on household deprivations in education, health and living standards from various household surveys listed in column 1 using the revised methodology described in *Technical note 5* (available at http://hdr.undp.org).

TABLE
6A

TABLE **7**

Health: children and youth

	Infants exclusively breastfed	Infants lacking immunization		Mortality rates		Antenatal coverage	Child malnutrition		HIV prevalence			Condom use among young people with multiple partners		Pregnant women living with HIV not receiving treatment to prevent mother-to-child transmission[a]
		(% of one-year-olds)		(per 1,000 live births)			(% under age 5)		Child (ages 0–14)	Youth				
							Stunting (moderate or severe)	Overweight (moderate or severe)		(% ages 15–24)		(% ages 15–24)		
	(% ages 0–5 months)	DTP	Measles	Infant	Under-five	(% of live births)			(thousands)	Female	Male	Female	Male	(%)
HDI rank	2008–2012[b]	2012	2012	2012	2012	2008–2012[b]	2008–2012[b]	2008–2012[b]	2012	2012	2012	2008–2012[b]	2008–2012[b]	2011
VERY HIGH HUMAN DEVELOPMENT														
1 Norway	..	1	6	2	3	..	..	..	..	..	..	..	..	..
2 Australia	..	8	6	4	5	98.3	..	..	..	..	..	..	..	..
3 Switzerland	..	5	8	4	4	..	..	..	..	..	..	..	..	..
4 Netherlands	..	1	4	3	4	..	..	..	..	..	..	..	..	..
5 United States	..	2	8	6	7	..	3.3[c]	7.0[c]	..	..	..	..	..	..
6 Germany	..	3	3	3	4	100.0[c]	..	..	..	..	..	..	..	..
7 New Zealand	..	6	8	5	6	..	..	..	..	..	..	..	..	..
8 Canada	..	2	2	5	5	100.0[c]	..	..	..	..	..	..	..	..
9 Singapore	..	2	5	2	3	..	4.4[c]	2.6[c]	..	..	..	..	..	..
10 Denmark	..	3	10	3	4	..	..	..	..	..	..	..	..	..
11 Ireland	..	2	8	3	4	99.5[c]	..	..	..	..	..	..	..	..
12 Sweden	..	1	3	2	3	100.0[c]	..	..	..	..	..	..	..	..
13 Iceland	..	3	10	2	2	..	..	..	..	..	..	..	..	..
14 United Kingdom	..	1	7	4	5	..	..	..	..	..	..	..	..	..
15 Hong Kong, China (SAR)	..	..	..	..	..	..	..	..	..	..	..	..	..	..
15 Korea (Republic of)	..	1	1	3	4	..	..	..	..	..	..	..	..	..
17 Japan	..	1	4	2	3	..	..	..	..	..	..	..	..	..
18 Liechtenstein	..	..	..	..	..	..	..	..	..	..	..	..	..	..
19 Israel	..	4	4	3	4	..	..	..	..	..	..	..	..	..
20 France	..	1	11	3	4	99.8[c]	..	..	..	..	..	..	..	..
21 Austria	..	7	24	3	4	..	..	..	..	..	..	..	..	..
21 Belgium	..	1	4	3	4	..	..	..	..	..	..	..	..	..
21 Luxembourg	..	1	4	2	2	..	..	..	..	..	..	..	..	..
24 Finland	..	1	3	2	3	99.8[c]	..	..	..	..	..	..	..	..
25 Slovenia	..	2	5	3	3	99.5[c]	..	..	..	..	..	..	..	..
26 Italy	..	1	10	3	4	99.0[c]	..	..	..	..	..	..	..	..
27 Spain	..	1	3	4	5	..	..	..	..	..	..	..	..	..
28 Czech Republic	..	1	2	3	4	..	..	..	..	..	..	..	..	..
29 Greece	..	1	1	4	5	..	..	..	..	..	..	..	..	..
30 Brunei Darussalam	..	4	1	7	8	99.0	..	..	..	..	..	..	..	..
31 Qatar	..	6	3	6	7	100.0	..	..	..	..	..	..	..	..
32 Cyprus	..	1	14	3	3	99.2[c]	..	..	..	..	..	..	..	..
33 Estonia	..	4	6	3	4	..	..	..	..	..	..	..	..	..
34 Saudi Arabia	..	2	2	7	9	97.0	..	..	..	..	..	..	..	..
35 Lithuania	..	3	7	4	5	100.0[c]	..	..	..	..	..	..	..	5.0
35 Poland	..	1	2	4	5	..	..	..	..	..	..	..	..	..
37 Andorra	..	1	2	3	3	..	..	..	..	..	..	..	..	..
37 Slovakia	..	1	1	6	8	96.9[c]	..	..	..	..	..	..	..	..
39 Malta	..	1	7	6	7	100.0[c]	..	..	..	..	..	..	..	..
40 United Arab Emirates	..	6	6	7	8	100.0[c]	..	..	..	..	..	..	..	..
41 Chile	63.0	10	10	8	9	..	..	..	..	0.1	0.2	..	..	5.0[d]
41 Portugal	..	1	3	3	4	100.0[c]	..	..	..	..	..	..	..	..
43 Hungary	..	1	1	5	6	..	..	..	..	..	..	..	..	..
44 Bahrain	..	1	1	8	10	100.0[c]	..	..	..	..	..	..	..	..
44 Cuba	48.6	4	1	4	6	100.0	..	..	..	0.1[e]	0.1[e]	66.4	..	5.0[d]
46 Kuwait	..	1	1	10	11	100.0	..	..	..	..	..	..	..	..
47 Croatia	..	3	5	4	5	..	..	..	..	..	..	..	..	..
48 Latvia	..	5	10	8	9	91.8[c]	..	..	..	..	..	..	..	5.0[d]
49 Argentina	54.0	6	6	13	14	99.2[c]	8.2[c]	9.9[c]	..	0.1	0.2	..	..	5.0
HIGH HUMAN DEVELOPMENT														
50 Uruguay	65.2	2	4	6	7	96.2[c]	14.7[c]	10.0[c]	..	0.2	0.5	..	..	5.0
51 Bahamas	..	1	9	14	17	98.0[c]	..	..	..	..	..	..	..	..
51 Montenegro	19.0[c]	2	10	6	6	97.4[c]	7.0[c]	15.6[c]	..	..	..	..	..	..
53 Belarus	9.0[c]	2	2	4	5	99.4	4.0[c]	9.7[c]	..	0.2	0.3	..	..	..
54 Romania	16.0[c]	4	6	11	12	93.5[c]	13.0[c]	8.3[c]	..	..	..	..	..	5.0
55 Libya	..	1	2	13	15	93.0[c]	21.0[c]	22.4[c]	..	..	..	..	..	..
56 Oman	..	1	1	10	12	99.0	9.8	1.7	..	..	..	..	..	..

HDI rank	Infants exclusively breastfed (% ages 0–5 months)	Infants lacking immunization (% of one-year-olds)		Mortality rates (per 1,000 live births)		Antenatal coverage (% of live births)	Child malnutrition (% under age 5)		HIV prevalence			HIV prevention		Pregnant women living with HIV not receiving treatment to prevent mother-to-child transmission[a]
							Stunting (moderate or severe)	Overweight (moderate or severe)	Child (ages 0–14)	Youth (% ages 15–24)		Condom use among young people with multiple partners (% ages 15–24)		
		DTP	Measles	Infant	Under-five				(thousands)	Female	Male	Female	Male	(%)
	2008–2012[b]	2012	2012	2012	2012	2008–2012[b]	2008–2012[b]	2008–2012[b]	2012	2012	2012	2008–2012[b]	2008–2012[b]	2011
57 Russian Federation	..	3	2	9	10	..	..	..	..	..	..	..	..	5.0[d]
58 Bulgaria	..	4	6	11	12	..	..	..	..	..	..	..	..	65.4
59 Barbados	..	7	10	17	18	100.0[c]	..	..	..	..	..	..	..	..
60 Palau	..	1	9	15	21	90.3	..	..	..	..	..	..	..	..
61 Antigua and Barbuda	..	1	2	9	10	100.0	..	..	..	..	..	..	..	..
62 Malaysia	..	1	5	7	9	90.7	16.6[c]	5.1	..	0.1	0.1	..	..	5.0[d]
63 Mauritius	21.0	1	1	13	15	..	..	..	..	0.3	0.3	..	..	5.0[d]
64 Trinidad and Tobago	13.0[c]	3	15	18	21	95.7[c]	..	..	..	..	..	67.1[c]	..	..
65 Lebanon	14.8	16	20	8	9	95.6[c]	..	..	..	..	..	..	..	..
65 Panama	..	1	2	16	19	95.8	19.0	..	..	0.3	0.4	..	..	5.0[d]
67 Venezuela (Bolivarian Republic of)	..	10	13	13	15	94.1[c]	15.6[c]	6.1[c]	..	0.3	0.3	..	..	33.4
68 Costa Rica	18.7[c]	8	10	9	10	89.9	5.6	8.1	..	0.2	0.1	..	..	..
69 Turkey	41.6	2	2	12	14	92.0	12.3	..	..	..	..	..	..	..
70 Kazakhstan	31.8	1	4	17	19	99.9	13.1	0.6	..	..	..	73.5	76.2	5.0[d]
71 Mexico	18.6	1	1	14	16	95.8	13.6[c]	9.7[c]	..	0.1	0.1	..	..	30.8
71 Seychelles	..	2	2	11	13	..	..	..	..	..	..	..	..	..
73 Saint Kitts and Nevis	..	1	5	7	9	100.0[c]	..	..	..	..	..	..	..	..
73 Sri Lanka	76.0[c]	1	1	8	10	99.4[c]	17.0[c]	0.8	..	0.1[e]	0.1[e]	..	..	86.3
75 Iran (Islamic Republic of)	23.0[c]	1	2	15	18	98.3	..	..	..	0.1	0.1	..	..	75.4
76 Azerbaijan	12.0[c]	19	34	31	35	76.6	25.0[c]	12.9[c]	..	0.1	0.2	..	28.6	5.0[d]
77 Jordan	22.7	2	2	16	19	98.8	7.7	4.4	..	..	..	..	..	..
77 Serbia	13.7	9	13	6	7	99.0	6.6	15.6	..	..	..	64.5[f]	63.3	66.7
79 Brazil	41.0	1	1	13	14	98.2	7.0[c]	7.3[c]	..	..	..	..	..	5.0[d]
79 Georgia	54.8	6	7	18	20	97.6	11.3	19.9	..	0.1	0.3	..	..	5.0[d]
79 Grenada	..	1	6	11	14	100.0[c]	..	..	..	..	..	..	..	..
82 Peru	70.6	1	6	14	18	95.4	19.5	9.8	..	0.2	0.2	38.0[c,f]	..	5.0[d]
83 Ukraine	18.0[c]	24	21	9	11	98.5[c]	..	..	..	0.5	0.4	62.7[c]	63.7[c]	5.0[d]
84 Belize	14.7	1	4	16	18	94.0	19.3	7.9	..	0.6	0.5	25.5[c,d]	..	16.7
84 The former Yugoslav Republic of Macedonia	23.0	3	3	7	7	98.6	4.9	12.4	..	..	..	..	..	..
86 Bosnia and Herzegovina	18.5	5	6	6	7	98.9	8.9[c]	17.4[c]	..	..	..	..	67.4	..
87 Armenia	34.6	2	3	15	16	99.1	19.3	15.3	..	0.1[e]	0.1[e]	..	..	25.0
88 Fiji	39.8[c]	1	1	19	22	100.0	..	..	..	0.1	0.1	..	..	..
89 Thailand	15.1	1	2	11	13	99.1	16.0[c]	8.0[c]	..	0.3	0.3	..	..	5.0[f]
90 Tunisia	6.0	1	4	14	16	96.0	10.1	14.3	..	0.1[e]	0.1[e]	..	..	18.2
91 China	27.6	1	1	12	14	94.1	9.9	6.6	..	..	..	..	..	33.9
91 Saint Vincent and the Grenadines	..	2	6	21	23	99.5	..	..	..	..	..	..	..	..
93 Algeria	7.0	1	5	17	20	89.4[c]	15.0[c]	12.9[c]	..	..	..	..	..	24.7
93 Dominica	..	2	1	12	13	100.0	..	..	..	..	..	..	..	..
95 Albania	38.6[c]	1	1	15	17	97.3	19.0[c]	21.7[c]	..	..	..	..	54.9	..
96 Jamaica	15.0[c]	1	7	14	17	99.0	4.8	4.0	..	0.5	0.9	49.4	75.5	8.7
97 Saint Lucia	..	1	1	15	18	99.2[c]	..	..	..	..	..	..	..	..
98 Colombia	42.8	8	6	15	18	97.0	13.2	4.8	..	0.2	0.3	38.8	..	22.4
98 Ecuador	40.0[c]	1	6	20	23	84.2[c]	29.0[c]	5.1[c]	..	0.2	0.4	..	..	5.0[d]
100 Suriname	2.8	6	27	19	21	89.9	8.8[c]	4.0[c]	..	0.7	0.4	39.3[c]	..	5.0
100 Tonga	..	5	5	11	13	97.9	..	..	..	..	..	..	..	..
102 Dominican Republic	7.8[c]	8	21	23	27	98.9[c]	9.8[c]	8.3	..	0.2	0.1	33.9[c]	61.8[c]	5.0
MEDIUM HUMAN DEVELOPMENT														
103 Maldives	47.8	1	2	9	11	99.1	18.9	6.5	..	0.1[e]	0.1[e]	..	..	..
103 Mongolia	65.7	1	1	23	28	99.0	15.3	10.9[c]	..	0.1[e]	0.1[e]	..	68.9	84.2
103 Turkmenistan	11.0[c]	2	1	45	53	99.1[c]	19.0[c]	..	..	..	..	..	..	..
106 Samoa	51.3	1	15	15	18	93.0	..	..	..	..	..	..	..	..
107 Palestine, State of	27.0[c]	2	2	19	23	98.8	10.9	..	..	..	..	..	..	..
108 Indonesia	41.5	9	20	26	31	92.7	35.6	12.3	..	0.5	0.4	..	..	76.6
109 Botswana	20.0[c]	2	6	41	53	94.1[c]	31.4[c]	11.2[c]	11.0	6.7	3.7	..	..	5.0
110 Egypt	53.2	6	7	18	21	73.6	28.9	20.5	..	0.1[e]	0.1[e]	..	..	85.7
111 Paraguay	24.4	4	9[g]	19	22	96.3	17.5[c]	7.1[c]	..	0.3	0.2	51.3	..	12.9
112 Gabon	6.0	14	29	42	62	94.4	16.5	7.4	3.6	1.6	0.4	55.7	76.5	27.1
113 Bolivia (Plurinational State of)	60.4	15	16	33	41	85.8	27.1	8.5	..	0.1	0.1	..	40.7	5.0

TABLE 7   Health: children and youth | 185

TABLE 7

TABLE 7   HEALTH: CHILDREN AND YOUTH

	Infants exclusively breastfed	Infants lacking immunization (% of one-year-olds)		Mortality rates (per 1,000 live births)		Antenatal coverage	Child malnutrition (% under age 5)		HIV prevalence			Condom use among young people with multiple partners		Pregnant women living with HIV not receiving treatment to prevent mother-to-child transmission[a]
									Child (ages 0–14)	Youth (% ages 15–24)		(% ages 15–24)		
	(% ages 0–5 months)	DTP	Measles	Infant	Under-five	(% of live births)	Stunting (moderate or severe)	Overweight (moderate or severe)	(thousands)	Female	Male	Female	Male	(%)
HDI rank	2008–2012[b]	2012	2012	2012	2012	2008–2012[b]	2008–2012[b]	2008–2012[b]	2012	2012	2012	2008–2012[b]	2008–2012[b]	2011
114 Moldova (Republic of)	46.0[c]	3	9	15	18	98.0[c]	10.0[c]	9.1[c]	..	0.2	0.2	..	..	23.9
115 El Salvador	31.4	8	7	14	16	94.0	19.2	6.0	..	0.2	0.3	..	..	26.7
116 Uzbekistan	26.0[c]	1	1	34	40	99.0[c]	19.0[c]	12.8[c]	..	0.1[e]	0.1[e]	..	..	5.0
117 Philippines	34.0	10	15	24	30	91.1	32.0	4.3	..	0.1[d]	0.1[d]	..	..	92.1
118 South Africa	8.0[c]	30	21	33	45	97.1	33.0[c]	19.2[c]	410.0	13.9	3.9	..	..	5.0
118 Syrian Arab Republic	42.6	32	39	12	15	87.7	27.5	17.9	..	..	..	..	..	..
120 Iraq	19.6	13	31	28	34	83.8	22.6	11.8	..	..	..	..	..	..
121 Guyana	33.2	1	1	29	35	92.1	18.2	6.2	..	0.8	0.5	..	76.1	5.0
121 Viet Nam	17.0	1	4	18	23	93.7	22.7	4.4	..	0.1	0.2	..	..	58.1
123 Cape Verde	60.0[c]	1	4	19	22	97.6[c]	..	..	..	0.1[e]	0.1[e]	..	..	..
124 Micronesia (Federated States of)	..	3	9	31	39	80.0	..	..	..	..	..	..	..	..
125 Guatemala	49.6	2	7	27	32	93.2	48.0	4.9	..	0.2	0.3	27.3[f]	74.3	5.0
125 Kyrgyzstan	32.0[c]	4	2	24	27	96.9	22.6	4.4	..	0.1	0.2	..	75.7	65.7
127 Namibia	24.0[c]	11	24	28	39	94.6[c]	29.0[c]	4.6[c]	18.0	4.1	2.2	73.7	82.2	5.0
128 Timor-Leste	51.5	31	38	48	57	84.4	58.1	4.7	..	..	..	..	..	..
129 Honduras	31.2	12	7	19	23	91.7	22.6[c]	5.1[c]	..	0.2	0.2	38.0[c]	59.0	34.6
129 Morocco	31.0[c]	1	1	27	31	77.1	14.9	10.7	..	0.1	0.1	..	..	70.0
131 Vanuatu	40.0[c]	22	48	15	18	84.3[c]	26.3[c]	4.5[c]	..	..	..	..	..	..
132 Nicaragua	30.6[c]	1	1	21	24	90.2[c]	22.0[c]	6.2[c]	..	0.2	0.3	..	..	42.9
133 Kiribati	69.0	6	9	46	60	88.4	..	..	..	..	..	2.4[f]	29.6	..
133 Tajikistan	25.0[c]	4	6	49	58	88.8	26.2	5.9	..	0.1	0.1	..	..	51.9
135 India	46.4[c]	12	26	44	56	74.2[c]	48.0	1.9[c]	..	0.1	0.1	17.1[c,f]	32.4[c]	..
136 Bhutan	48.7	3	5	36	45	97.3	33.5	7.6	..	0.1	0.1	..	..	61.5
136 Cambodia	73.5	3	7	34	40	89.1	39.9	1.6	..	0.2	0.2	..	..	14.4
138 Ghana	45.7	8	12	49	72	96.4	22.7	2.6	28.0	0.5	0.3	27.2	39.3	9.8
139 Lao People's Democratic Republic	26.0[c]	13	28	54	72	35.1	44.2	2.0	..	0.2	0.2	..	..	73.7
140 Congo	19.0[c]	10	20	62	96	93.0	30.0[c]	3.3	13.0	1.3	0.8	44.0	55.0	93.0
141 Zambia	61.0[c]	14	17	56	89	93.7[c]	45.4[c]	7.9[c]	160.0	4.6	3.5	41.5[c,f]	43.1[c]	5.0
142 Bangladesh	64.1	1	4	33	41	54.6	41.3	1.5	..	0.1[e]	0.1[e]	..	..	25.0
142 Sao Tome and Principe	51.4	2	8	38	53	97.9	29.3	10.5	..	0.4	0.3	..	59.1	..
144 Equatorial Guinea	24.0[c]	35	49	72	100	86.1[c]	35.0[c]	8.3[c]	..	..	..	..	..	..
LOW HUMAN DEVELOPMENT														
145 Nepal	69.6	10	14	34	42	58.3	40.5	1.5	..	0.1[e]	0.1[e]	..	45.1	71.2
146 Pakistan	37.0[c]	12	17	69	86	60.9[c]	43.7	6.4	..	0.1[e]	0.1[e]	..	..	95.5
147 Kenya	32.0	11	7	49	73	91.5	35.3	4.7	200.0	3.6	1.8	37.1	67.3	25.0
148 Swaziland	44.1	3	12	56	80	96.8	30.9	10.7	22.0	20	10.3	68.6	84.5	5.0
149 Angola	11.0[c]	1	3	100	164	79.8[c]	29.0[c]	..	30.0	1.2	0.6	..	..	76.4
150 Myanmar	23.6	11	16	41	52	83.1	35.1	2.6	..	0.1[e]	0.1[e]	..	..	5.0
151 Rwanda	84.9	1	3	39	55	98.0	44.2	7.1	27.0	1.3	1	..	..	34.1
152 Cameroon	20.0	6	18	61	95	84.7	32.5	6.5	59.0	1.8	1.0	46.5	66.5	38.4
152 Nigeria	15.1	53	58	78	124	57.7	35.8	3.0	430.0	1.3	0.7	46.6	..	79.1
154 Yemen	12.0[c]	11	29	46	60	47.0[c]	57.7[c]	5.0[c]	..	0.1	0.1	..	..	97.8
155 Madagascar	50.7	4	31	41	58	86.3	50.1	..	..	0.3	0.3	6.6	8.8	83.7
156 Zimbabwe	31.4	5	10	56	90	89.8	32.0	5.5	180.0	6.3	3.9	38.5[f]	50.5	38.2
157 Papua New Guinea	56.0[c]	15	33	48	63	78.8[c]	43.6[c]	4.4[c]	3.1	0.1[e]	0.1[e]	..	..	74.9
157 Solomon Islands	74.0[c]	6	15	26	31	73.9[c]	32.8[c]	2.5[c]	..	..	..	18.0[c]	39.1	..
159 Comoros	..	9	15	58	78	75.0	30.1	9.3	..	1.6	2.8	..	52.3	..
159 Tanzania (United Republic of)	49.8	1	3	38	54	87.8	42.0	5.0	230.0	3.6	1.8	33.9	40.6	15.3
161 Mauritania	45.9	5	25	65	84	75.4	22.5	1.2	..	0.2	0.1	..	..	95.7
162 Lesotho	53.5	7	15	74	100	91.8	39.0	7.3	38.0	10.7	5.8	44.9	60.3	30.0
163 Senegal	39.0	3	16	45	60	93.3	26.5	2.5	..	0.3	0.1	..	..	60.8
164 Uganda	63.2	11	18	45	69	93.3	33.4	3.4	190.0	4	2.3	..	47.3	43.3
165 Benin	32.5	12	28	59	90	85.8	44.6	17.9	9.1	0.4	0.2	34.6	43.8	63.9
166 Sudan	41.0	1	15	49	73	55.9	35.0	..	..	..	..	..	..	..
166 Togo	62.4	6	28	62	96	71.6	29.7	1.6	17.0	0.9	0.5	39.2	54.4	21.0
168 Haiti	39.7	19	42	57	76	84.5	21.9[c]	3.6[c]	12.0	0.9	0.6	51.6[c]	61.8[c]	5.0
169 Afghanistan	..	14	32	71	99	47.9	59.0[c]	4.6[c]	..	0.1[e]	0.1[e]	..	..	99.0[g]
170 Djibouti	1.0[c]	15	17	66	81	92.3[c]	30.8	8.1	1.2	0.3	0.2	..	..	80.1

TABLE 7

HDI rank	Infants exclusively breastfed (% ages 0–5 months) 2008–2012[b]	Infants lacking immunization (% of one-year-olds) DTP 2012	Infants lacking immunization Measles 2012	Mortality rates (per 1,000 live births) Infant 2012	Mortality rates Under-five 2012	Antenatal coverage (% of live births) 2008–2012[b]	Child malnutrition (% under age 5) Stunting (moderate or severe) 2008–2012[b]	Child malnutrition Overweight (moderate or severe) 2008–2012[b]	HIV prevalence Child (ages 0–14) (thousands) 2012	HIV prevalence Youth Female (% ages 15–24) 2012	HIV prevalence Youth Male 2012	HIV prevention: Condom use among young people with multiple partners Female (% ages 15–24) 2008–2012[b]	Condom use Male 2008–2012[b]	Pregnant women living with HIV not receiving treatment to prevent mother-to-child transmission[a] (%) 2011
171 Côte d'Ivoire	12.1	2	15	76	108	90.6	29.8	3.0	63.0	1.2	0.7	34.2	56.5	18.6
172 Gambia	33.5	1	5	49	73	98.1	23.4	1.9	..	0.5	0.2	49.3[f]	..	5.0
173 Ethiopia	52.0	20	34	47	68	42.5	44.4	1.7	170.0	0.5	0.3	..	47.2	72.3
174 Malawi	71.4	1	10	46	71	94.7	47.1	8.3	180.0	4.5	2.7	31.4	40.5	39.4
175 Liberia	29.0[c]	14	20	56	75	79.3[c]	41.8	4.6	3.7	0.1[e]	0.1[e]	16.2	27.8	23.1
176 Mali	20.4	15	41	80	128	70.4	27.8[c]	1.0	..	0.3	0.2	7.9[f]	38.0	57.9
177 Guinea-Bissau	38.3	8	31	81	129	92.6	32.2	3.2	5.9	1.7	0.9	50.0	..	59.5
178 Mozambique	42.8	9	18	63	90	92.3	42.6	7.4	180.0	6.6	2.8	38.3	40.8	39.0
179 Guinea	48.0	14	42	65	101	88.4	34.5	3.6	14.0	0.8	0.4	37.0	54.0	44.9
180 Burundi	69.3	1	7	67	104	98.9	57.7	2.7	17.0	0.6	0.4	..	..	38.0
181 Burkina Faso	38.2	6	13	66	102	94.3	32.9	2.4	21.0	0.5	0.4	65.3	74.7	45.8
182 Eritrea	52.0	1	1	37	52	70.3[c]	44.0[c]	1.6[c]	3.1	0.2	0.2	..	..	5.0
183 Sierra Leone	31.6	6	20	117	182	93.0	44.4	9.6	5.8	1	0.3	12.4	..	86.0
184 Chad	3.4	36	36	89	150	53.1	38.7	2.8	34.0	1.1	0.6	57.1[f]	..	25.5
185 Central African Republic	34.3	31	51	91	129	68.3	40.7	1.8	..	..	..	34.0[c]	46.5[c]	..
186 Congo (Democratic Republic of the)	37.0	14	27	100	146	88.8	43.4	4.9	88.0	0.8	0.4	15.9	..	57.6
187 Niger	23.3	20	27	63	114	46.1	43.9	2.4	..	0.1[e]	0.1[d]	..	..	..
OTHER COUNTRIES OR TERRITORIES														
Korea, Democratic People's Rep. of	65.0	3	1	23	29	100.0	27.9	..	..	..	..	..	..	..
Marshall Islands	31.0[c]	3	22	31	38	81.2[c]	..	..	..	..	..	8.8[f]	22.6	..
Monaco	..	1	1	3	4	..	..	..	..	..	..	..	..	..
Nauru	67.0[c]	2	4	30	37	94.5[c]	24.0[c]	2.8[c]	..	..	..	8.2	16.7	..
San Marino	..	2	13	3	3	..	..	..	..	..	..	..	..	..
Somalia	9.0[c]	48	54	91	147	26.1[c]	42.0[c]	4.7	..	0.2	0.2	..	..	94.0
South Sudan	45.1	21	38	67	104	40.3	31.1	5.4	19.0	1.2	0.6	7.3	..	90.0
Tuvalu	35.0[c]	1	2	25	30	97.4[c]	10.0[c]	6.3[c]	..	..	..	..	..	..
Human Development Index groups														
Very high human development	..	2	6	5	6	..	..	..	..	..	..	..	..	..
High human development	..	2	3	13	15	94.9	..	..	..	..	..	..	..	..
Medium human development	..	10	20	37	46	78.7	40.3	5.3	..	..	..	..	..	8.3
Low human development	..	18	27	64	94	70.5	39.8	4.2	..	..	..	..	..	46.1
Regions														
Arab States	..	8	15	28	37	78.1	27.7	..	..	..	..	..	..	..
East Asia and the Pacific	..	4	6	17	21	93.4	18.4	7.0	..	..	..	..	..	..
Europe and Central Asia	..	6	7	20	23	95.2	15.5	9.7	..	..	..	..	..	..
Latin America and the Caribbean	..	4	5	16	19	96.1	14.6	..	..	..	..	..	..	11.9
South Asia	..	11	22	45	57	71.8	46.7	2.5	..	..	..	..	..	34.8
Sub-Saharan Africa	..	20	28	64	97	76.9	37.8	4.6	200.8	..	..	..	..	33.7
Least developed countries	..	10	20	57	84	69.1	41.1	3.8	..	..	..	..	..	..
Small island developing states	..	11	25	37	49	92.1	..	..	..	..	..	..	..	..
World	..	9	16	35	47	84.8	..	..	..	..	..	..	..	..

NOTES

a Estimates are upper limit.

b Data refer to the most recent year available during the period specified.

c Refers to an earlier year than that specified.

d 5 or less.

e 0.1 or less.

f Based on a small denominator (typically 25–49 unweighted cases).

g 99 or greater.

DEFINITIONS

Infants exclusively breastfed: Percentage of children ages 0–5 months who are fed exclusively with breast milk in the 24 hours prior to the survey.

Infants lacking immunization against DPT: Percentage of surviving infants who have not received their first dose of diphtheria, pertussis and tetanus vaccine.

Infants lacking immunization against measles: Percentage of surviving infants who have not received the first dose of measles vaccine.

Infant mortality rate: Probability of dying between birth and exactly age 1, expressed per 1,000 live births.

Under-five mortality rate: Probability of dying between birth and exactly age 5, expressed per 1,000 live births.

Antenatal coverage: Proportion of women who used antenatal care provided by skilled health personnel for reasons related to pregnancy at least once during pregnancy, as a percentage of live births.

Stunted children: Percentage of children ages 0–59 months who are more than two standard deviations below the median height-for-age of the World Health Organization (WHO) Child Growth Standards.

Overweight children: Percentage of children ages 0–59 months who are more than two standard deviations above the median weight-for-height of the WHO Child Growth Standards.

Children living with HIV: Estimated number of children (ages 0–14) living with HIV.

HIV prevalence, youth: Percentage of the population ages 15–24 who are living with HIV.

Condoms use among young people with multiple partners: Proportion of young people (ages 15–24) who reported having had more than one sexual partner in the past 12 months and who used a condom the last time they had sex with any partner, expressed as a percentage of all young people with multiple partners.

Pregnant women living with HIV not receiving treatment to prevent mother-to-child transmission: Proportion of pregnant women living with HIV who are not receiving antiretroviral medicines to prevent mother-to-child transmission, expressed as a percentage of all pregnant women living with HIV.

MAIN DATA SOURCES

Columns 1 and 6–13: UNICEF 2014.

Columns 2 and 3: HDRO calculations based on data from UNICEF (2014).

Columns 4 and 5: Inter-agency Group for Child Mortality Estimation 2013.

Column 14: WHO 2013a.

TABLE 7   Health: children and youth | 187

TABLE 8

Adult health and health expenditures

HDI rank	Adult mortality rate (per 1,000 people) Female 2011	Adult mortality rate (per 1,000 people) Male 2011	Age-standardized death rates (per 100,000 people) From alcohol use 2008	Age-standardized death rates (per 100,000 people) From drug use 2008	Age-standardized obesity rate, adult (% of population ages 20 and older) 2008	HIV prevalence rate, adult (% ages 15–49) 2012	Life expectancy At age 60 (years) 2010/2015[a]	Health-adjusted (years) Female 2010	Health-adjusted (years) Male 2010	Physicians (per 10,000 people) 2003–2012[b]	Health expenditure Total (% of GDP) 2011	Out of pocket (% of total health expenditure) 2011
VERY HIGH HUMAN DEVELOPMENT												
1 Norway	49	77	2.9	0.9	19.8	..	24.0	69.7	66.3	..	9.1	13.6
2 Australia	46	80	1.0	0.5	25.1	..	25.1	71.8	68.4	38.5	9.0	19.8
3 Switzerland	41	69	2.3	3.0	14.9	..	25.0	72.4	69.1	40.8	10.9	25.0
4 Netherlands	55	72	0.9	0.1	16.2	..	23.5	70.2	67.9	..	12.0	5.1
5 United States	77	131	2.1	1.6	31.8	..	23.2	69.5	66.2	24.2	17.9	11.3
6 Germany	51	96	4.3	0.9	21.3	..	23.5	70.9	67.1	36.9	11.1	12.4
7 New Zealand	55	85	0.4	0.3	27.0	..	24.1	70.7	67.7	27.4	10.1	10.5
8 Canada	53	84	1.6	1.2	24.3	..	24.4	70.9	68.3	20.7	11.2	14.4
9 Singapore	41	72	..	..	6.4	..	24.5	72.6	69.6	19.2	4.6	60.4
10 Denmark	62	103	6.9	0.5	16.2	..	22.4	69.5	66.3	..	11.2	13.2
11 Ireland	51	85	1.6	2.2	24.5	..	23.4	70.5	67.2	..	9.4	14.5
12 Sweden	44	71	2.8	1.5	16.6	..	24.1	71.2	68.0	38.7	9.4	16.9
13 Iceland	38	64	0.9	0.3	21.9	..	24.3	69.9	66.9	34.6	9.1	18.2
14 United Kingdom	57	91	1.4	1.8	24.9	..	23.5	70.1	67.1	27.7	9.3	9.2
15 Hong Kong, China (SAR)	..	..	..	..	..	..	25.4	..	..	..	..	..
15 Korea (Republic of)	42	102	2.2	0.2	7.3	..	24.0	72.6	67.9	20.2	7.2	32.9
17 Japan	46	84	0.3	0.0	4.5	..	26.1	75.5	70.6	21.4	9.3	16.4
18 Liechtenstein	..	..	..	..	..	..	..	..	..	..	..	..
19 Israel	44	75	0.8	1.4	25.5	..	24.3	70.9	68.3	31.1	7.7	21.4
20 France	53	113	4.2	0.5	15.6	..	25.1	71.9	67.0	33.8	11.6	7.5
21 Austria	49	94	3.2	2.6	18.3	..	23.9	71.2	67.0	48.6	10.6	16.3
21 Belgium	59	102	1.7	0.4	19.1	..	23.6	70.6	66.5	37.8	10.6	19.1
21 Luxembourg	52	84	3.7	1.0	23.4	..	23.4	69.9	66.9	27.8	7.7	11.4
24 Finland	51	116	3.5	0.7	19.9	..	23.8	69.6	65.0	..	8.9	19.2
25 Slovenia	51	118	4.1	0.3	27.0	..	22.8	70.7	65.7	25.4	9.1	13.0
26 Italy	40	73	0.2	0.7	17.2	..	24.7	71.9	68.3	38.0	9.5	19.9
27 Spain	41	91	0.6	1.4	24.1	..	24.8	73.0	68.8	39.6	9.4	20.1
28 Czech Republic	60	132	1.3	0.3	28.7	..	21.1	69.6	64.8	37.1	7.4	15.1
29 Greece	43	102	0.1	..	17.5	..	23.5	70.4	67.0	..	10.8	36.7
30 Brunei Darussalam	71	105	..	0.5	7.9	..	21.4	68.6	66.2	13.6	2.5	14.8
31 Qatar	52	74	..	0.0	33.1	..	21.2	67.4	66.2	27.6	1.9	13.6
32 Cyprus	38	79	0.0	0.1	23.4	..	22.0	70.6	67.1	27.5	7.4	49.4
33 Estonia	69	207	8.8	0.6	18.9	..	20.2	69.3	61.7	33.4	6.0	18.6
34 Saudi Arabia	52	71	0.4	0.2	35.2	..	19.2	66.6	63.9	9.4	3.7	18.0
35 Lithuania	92	267	0.7	0.4	24.7	..	19.1	68.4	60.0	36.4	6.6	27.9
35 Poland	72	191	3.7	0.1	23.2	..	21.1	69.3	62.8	20.7	6.7	22.9
37 Andorra	44	93	0.4	1.2	24.2	..	..	72.2	68.3	39.1	7.2	19.6
37 Slovakia	70	170	0.0	1.5	24.6	..	19.8	68.3	62.4	30.0	8.7	26.2
39 Malta	42	77	0.2	..	26.6	..	22.3	70.6	66.7	32.3	8.7	33.9
40 United Arab Emirates	64	85	1.1	0.3	33.7	..	19.8	66.2	64.7	19.3	3.3	16.2
41 Chile	58	113	3.0	0.8	29.1	0.4	23.6	71.0	66.2	10.3	7.5	37.2
41 Portugal	50	117	0.9	1.5	21.6	..	23.2	70.7	66.4	..	10.4	27.3
43 Hungary	93	208	3.3	1.5	24.8	..	19.9	67.3	61.1	34.1	7.7	26.2
44 Bahrain	51	69	0.5	0.5	32.6	..	19.5	65.2	64.3	14.9	3.8	16.6
44 Cuba	75	119	2.1	0.0	20.5	0.1[c]	22.9	66.9	63.5	67.2	10.0	5.3
46 Kuwait	44	61	0.1	..	42.8	..	17.6	67.0	65.3	17.9	2.7	16.1
47 Croatia	60	140	2.9	1.6	21.3	..	20.6	68.3	63.6	27.2	7.8	14.6
48 Latvia	89	237	1.9	1.5	22.0	..	19.1	67.2	60.0	29.0	6.2	39.6
49 Argentina	85	154	1.7	0.9	29.4	0.4	21.4	68.7	63.5	31.6	8.1	24.7
HIGH HUMAN DEVELOPMENT												
50 Uruguay	80	152	1.2	0.3	23.6	0.7	21.8	70.0	64.0	37.4	8.0	13.1
51 Bahamas	116	190	4.9	0.2	35.0	..	22.3	66.9	59.4	28.2	7.7	28.7
51 Montenegro	81	154	..	..	21.8	..	19.2	66.1	63.3	20.3	9.3	30.0
53 Belarus	103	307	3.1	2.3	23.4	0.4	17.1	65.6	56.4	37.6	5.3	26.7
54 Romania	84	209	2.9	0.0	17.7	..	19.4	67.3	61.4	23.9	5.8	19.4
55 Libya	134	411	0.0	6.9	30.8	..	19.7	63.6	62.2	19.0	4.4	31.2
56 Oman	78	157	0.4	0.2	22.0	..	20.5	66.4	63.6	20.5	2.3	11.4
57 Russian Federation	131	351	3.5	4.5	24.9	..	17.5	64.5	55.4	43.1	6.2	35.4

HDI rank	Adult mortality rate (per 1,000 people) Female 2011	Male 2011	Age-standardized death rates (per 100,000 people) From alcohol use 2008	From drug use 2008	Age-standardized obesity rate, adult (% of population ages 20 and older) 2008	HIV prevalence rate, adult (% ages 15–49) 2012	Life expectancy At age 60 (years) 2010/2015[a]	Health-adjusted (years) Female 2010	Male 2010	Physicians (per 10,000 people) 2003–2012[b]	Health expenditure Total (% of GDP) 2011	Out of pocket (% of total health expenditure) 2011
58 Bulgaria	86	194	0.8	0.1	21.4	..	18.8	66.8	61.5	37.6	7.3	43.2
59 Barbados	70	122	0.7	..	33.4	..	19.5	64.7	61.9	18.1	7.7	29.0
60 Palau	109	231	0.1	0.0	50.7	..	..	..	..	13.8	10.6	11.6
61 Antigua and Barbuda	164	203	5.5	..	25.8	..	21.5	65.5	61.2	..	5.9	28.2
62 Malaysia	90	174	0.9	0.4	14.1	0.4	19.0	66.4	62.6	12.0	3.6	41.7
63 Mauritius	94	208	4.1	0.5	18.2	1.2	19.3	66.8	61.2	10.6	5.9	53.0
64 Trinidad and Tobago	104	222	0.8	0.4	30.0	..	17.8	63.3	55.7	11.8	5.7	38.5
65 Lebanon	99	148	2.0	4.6	28.2	..	22.7	67.5	65.9	35.4	6.3	56.5
65 Panama	82	148	0.3	0.8	25.8	0.7	23.9	69.0	64.3	..	8.2	26.8
67 Venezuela (Bolivarian Republic of)	90	198	0.6	0.8	30.8	0.6	21.1	68.5	61.7	..	5.2	57.0
68 Costa Rica	66	114	1.3	0.4	24.6	0.3	23.8	70.5	67.3	..	10.9	27.2
69 Turkey	68	123	..	0.2	29.3	..	20.9	66.0	61.8	17.1	6.7	16.1
70 Kazakhstan	152	337	3.1	4.0	24.4	..	16.5	62.4	53.9	38.4	3.9	41.5
71 Mexico	95	177	1.1	0.2	32.8	0.2	22.7	69.1	64.7	19.6	6.2	46.5
71 Seychelles	101	220	4.5	0.5	24.6	..	19.4	62.7	54.2	15.1	3.8	5.4
73 Saint Kitts and Nevis	83	170	4.4	..	40.9	..	..	..	..	..	4.4	41.8
73 Sri Lanka	77	191	5.2	0.4	5.0	0.1	19.6	68.6	62.3	4.9	3.4	45.9
75 Iran (Islamic Republic of)	85	154	1.2	11.1	21.6	0.2	19.9	65.3	61.5	8.9	6.0	58.5
76 Azerbaijan	85	175	1.7	0.5	24.7	0.2	18.3	65.1	59.9	33.8	5.2	70.1
77 Jordan	99	146	0.7	1.7	34.3	..	19.0	63.2	64.8	25.6	8.4	24.7
77 Serbia	86	175	..	..	23.0	..	18.7	68.0	64.0	21.1	10.4	36.2
79 Brazil	100	202	4.8	0.5	19.5	..	21.8	66.6	61.1	17.6	8.9	31.3
79 Georgia	88	227	0.2	3.7	21.2	0.3	19.8	66.9	59.3	42.4	9.9	69.5
79 Grenada	122	196	3.7	0.9	24.0	..	18.5	61.7	57.4	6.6	6.2	50.5
82 Peru	93	119	1.0	1.0	16.5	0.4	21.5	66.6	64.8	9.2	4.8	38.4
83 Ukraine	120	310	3.6	2.3	20.1	0.9	17.4	64.9	56.6	35.2	7.2	45.2
84 Belize	139	210	2.0	0.3	34.9	1.4	21.5	61.5	57.3	8.3	5.7	23.4
84 The former Yugoslav Republic of Macedonia	74	137	1.8	1.0	20.3	..	19.1	66.4	63.2	26.2	6.6	38.3
86 Bosnia and Herzegovina	66	141	0.2	2.8	24.2	..	20.2	68.1	64.4	16.9	10.2	31.3
87 Armenia	94	228	1.3	0.6	23.4	0.2	20.0	67.2	59.9	28.5	4.3	57.4
88 Fiji	153	244	0.2	..	31.9	0.2	17.0	59.0	57.1	4.3	3.8	21.0
89 Thailand	102	207	1.9	0.9	8.5	1.1	21.4	67.8	62.7	3.0	4.1	13.7
90 Tunisia	72	134	1.6	4.6	23.8	0.1 [c]	20.2	67.5	64.6	12.2	6.2	39.5
91 China	81	112	0.9	0.0	5.6	..	19.5	70.4	65.5	14.6	5.2	34.8
91 Saint Vincent and the Grenadines	115	176	4.1	0.7	25.1	..	19.7	62.5	58.1	..	4.9	18.3
93 Algeria	100	123	0.5	0.2	17.5	..	17.9	64.6	63.8	12.1	3.9	18.2
93 Dominica	118	222	1.9	0.7	25.0	..	..	65.0	58.3	..	5.9	23.6
95 Albania	87	123	0.1	0.7	21.1	..	21.1	67.0	62.5	11.1	6.3	55.0
96 Jamaica	103	188	0.1	0.0	24.6	1.7	21.3	64.6	61.0	4.1	4.9	32.5
97 Saint Lucia	88	180	1.9	..	22.3	..	21.0	64.1	59.0	..	7.2	51.1
98 Colombia	76	154	0.0	1.2	18.1	0.5	21.3	67.1	62.4	14.7	6.1	17.0
98 Ecuador	89	162	3.7	1.2	22.0	0.6	23.6	68.5	64.4	16.9	7.3	49.4
100 Suriname	111	194	0.7	0.2	25.8	1.1	18.5	63.0	58.5	9.1	5.3	11.0
100 Tonga	242	123	0.0	0.2	59.6	..	18.6	63.2	58.9	5.6	5.3	11.1
102 Dominican Republic	148	165	1.8	0.1	21.9	0.7	21.9	64.5	60.1	..	5.4	40.0
MEDIUM HUMAN DEVELOPMENT												
103 Maldives	61	91	3.6	1.5	16.1	0.1 [c]	21.0	68.9	67.3	16.0	8.5	49.1
103 Mongolia	147	309	0.8	0.0	16.4	0.1 [c]	16.3	60.3	53.0	27.6	5.3	39.7
103 Turkmenistan	201	375	5.9	0.5	14.3	..	17.0	63.0	57.1	..	2.7	39.2
106 Samoa	105	177	0.1	0.2	55.5	..	18.9	63.2	59.8	4.8	7.0	7.1
107 Palestine, State of	..	..	..	..	..	..	18.7	64.0	60.5	..	..	..
108 Indonesia	166	200	1.0	1.0	4.7	0.4	17.8	62.5	59.3	2.0	2.7	49.9
109 Botswana	238	301	0.6	0.3	13.5	23.0	16.4	61.3	57.1	3.4	5.1	5.0
110 Egypt	85	141	0.4	13.5	34.6	0.1 [c]	17.5	60.8	57.5	28.3	4.9	58.2
111 Paraguay	97	176	3.2	0.3	19.2	0.3	20.8	64.4	61.3	..	9.7	56.1
112 Gabon	266	300	0.7	0.3	15.0	4.0	18.2	52.8	47.4	2.9	3.2	46.6
113 Bolivia (Plurinational State of)	165	222	1.5	1.2	18.9	0.3	18.6	61.5	60.1	..	4.9	25.8
114 Moldova (Republic of)	109	269	2.8	0.2	20.4	0.7	16.2	64.6	57.5	36.4	11.4	44.9
115 El Salvador	138	294	22.8	0.1	26.9	0.6	22.0	67.0	60.5	16.0	6.8	32.3

TABLE 8 Adult health and health expenditures | 189

TABLE 8

TABLE 8 ADULT HEALTH AND HEALTH EXPENDITURES

HDI rank	Adult mortality rate (per 1,000 people) Female	Male	Age-standardized death rates (per 100,000 people) From alcohol use	From drug use	Age-standardized obesity rate, adult (% of population ages 20 and older)	HIV prevalence rate, adult (% ages 15–49)	Life expectancy At age 60 (years)	Health-adjusted (years) Female	Male	Physicians (per 10,000 people)	Health expenditure Total (% of GDP)	Out of pocket (% of total health expenditure)
	2011	2011	2008	2008	2008	2012	2010/2015[a]	2010	2010	2003–2012[b]	2011	2011
116 Uzbekistan	132	213	0.3	1.0	17.3	0.1	18.3	61.7	57.1	25.4	5.4	43.9
117 Philippines	137	256	0.9	0.3	6.4	0.1 [c]	17.0	63.2	57.4	11.5	4.1	55.9
118 South Africa	407	474	0.9	0.4	33.5	17.9	16.0	52.7	49.1	7.6	8.5	7.2
118 Syrian Arab Republic	75	132	0.6	2.9	31.6	..	19.9	67.5	64.6	15.0	3.7	51.0
120 Iraq	116	207	0.3	6.9	29.4	..	17.5	60.9	60.8	6.1	8.3	19.3
121 Guyana	258	379	1.1	0.6	16.9	1.3	16.6	57.6	52.5	2.1	5.9	18.0
121 Viet Nam	87	128	0.9	1.7	1.6	0.4	22.4	69.1	62.6	12.2	6.8	55.7
123 Cape Verde	103	269	0.5	0.4	11.5	0.2	19.9	66.4	60.8	3.0	4.8	23.4
124 Micronesia (Federated States of)	152	177	0.1	0.2	42.0	..	17.3	58.6	55.2	1.8	13.4	9.0
125 Guatemala	155	282	14.7	9.4	20.7	0.7	21.5	63.8	58.1	9.3	6.7	53.4
125 Kyrgyzstan	135	279	1.7	1.3	17.2	0.3	16.8	61.4	54.1	24.7	6.5	34.4
127 Namibia	242	282	0.5	0.3	10.9	13.3	17.3	55.1	50.0	3.7	5.3	7.7
128 Timor-Leste	224	259	0.9	1.0	2.9	..	16.9	59.2	56.9	1.0	5.1	4.0
129 Honduras	114	163	13.7	0.3	19.8	0.5	22.1	62.2	61.0	3.7	8.6	47.9
129 Morocco	89	141	0.8	8.0	17.3	0.1	17.9	61.9	60.3	6.2	6.0	58.0
131 Vanuatu	117	166	0.1	0.3	29.8	..	18.0	57.4	54.3	1.2	4.1	6.9
132 Nicaragua	119	204	10.5	0.3	24.2	0.3	22.2	66.3	61.9	3.7	10.1	42.2
133 Kiribati	164	340	..	0.1	45.8	..	17.4	54.7	49.6	3.8	10.1	1.3
133 Tajikistan	156	180	0.5	3.4	9.9	0.3	18.2	61.0	56.5	19.0	5.8	60.1
135 India	159	247	1.2	1.9	1.9	0.3	17.0	57.7	54.9	6.5	3.9	59.4
136 Bhutan	157	210	1.1	2.2	5.5	0.2	19.5	61.5	58.2	0.7	4.1	15.3
136 Cambodia	220	260	1.2	7.1	2.3	0.8	23.8	60.0	55.9	2.3	5.7	56.9
138 Ghana	217	252	1.8	2.1	8.0	1.4	15.5	56.1	54.5	0.9	4.8	29.1
139 Lao People's Democratic Republic	164	204	1.2	8.9	3.0	0.3	17.1	57.8	54.1	1.9	2.8	39.7
140 Congo	287	332	0.7	0.2	5.3	2.8	17.1	51.6	48.4	1.0	2.5	31.5
141 Zambia	377	426	0.8	0.3	4.2	12.7	17.0	48.7	46.8	0.7	6.1	27.0
142 Bangladesh	136	163	1.0	2.3	1.1	0.1 [c]	18.4	59.8	57.1	3.6	3.7	61.3
142 Sao Tome and Principe	189	234	1.8	0.4	11.3	1.0	18.2	60.6	58.5	4.9	7.7	56.9
144 Equatorial Guinea	331	369	1.0	0.3	11.5	..	15.9	51.1	46.7	3.0	4.0	31.6
LOW HUMAN DEVELOPMENT												
145 Nepal	157	183	1.0	1.2	1.5	0.3	17.1	59.9	57.6	2.1	5.4	54.8
146 Pakistan	152	186	0.4	6.0	5.9	0.1 [c]	17.4	58.0	55.2	8.1	2.5	63.0
147 Kenya	294	346	0.7	0.2	4.7	6.1	17.8	56.8	54.2	1.8	4.5	46.4
148 Swaziland	504	558	0.7	0.3	23.4	26.5	16.3	43.3	40.4	1.7	8.0	13.1
149 Angola	331	383	1.3	0.3	7.2	2.3	15.7	54.0	49.7	1.7	3.5	27.3
150 Myanmar	181	231	1.1	3.8	4.1	0.6	16.6	58.3	53.2	5.0	2.0	80.7
151 Rwanda	291	344	0.9	0.0	4.3	2.9	17.8	56.4	53.2	0.6	10.8	21.4
152 Cameroon	372	415	0.8	0.3	11.1	4.5	16.4	51.4	49.0	0.8	5.2	65.1
152 Nigeria	360	393	0.9	1.7	7.1	3.1	13.7	50.8	50.0	4.0	5.3	60.4
154 Yemen	185	234	0.5	13.1	16.7	0.1	16.2	55.3	55.3	2.0	5.5	78.1
155 Madagascar	167	213	0.8	0.4	1.7	0.5	16.9	54.7	53.0	1.6	4.1	25.2
156 Zimbabwe	473	501	0.8	0.1	8.6	14.7	18.8	46.1	43.3	0.6	..	..
157 Papua New Guinea	235	312	1.1	1.0	15.9	0.5	14.9	51.5	49.6	0.5	4.3	11.7
157 Solomon Islands	159	201	0.1	0.2	32.1	..	16.9	55.3	53.0	2.2	8.8	3.0
159 Comoros	229	275	0.6	0.3	4.4	2.1	15.9	54.6	53.4	1.5	5.3	42.2
159 Tanzania (United Republic of)	322	363	0.8	0.0	5.4	5.1	17.9	52.6	51.8	0.1	7.3	31.7
161 Mauritania	218	287	0.8	0.3	14.0	0.4	16.4	55.0	53.5	1.3	5.4	37.3
162 Lesotho	541	583	0.5	0.4	16.9	23.1	15.5	42.6	37.7	0.5	12.8	17.9
163 Senegal	239	293	0.8	0.0	8.0	0.5	16.2	56.5	54.8	0.6	6.0	32.7
164 Uganda	363	410	0.8	0.1	4.6	7.2	17.5	52.8	50.1	1.2	9.5	47.8
165 Benin	270	326	0.8	0.2	6.5	1.1	15.6	55.1	52.2	0.6	4.6	42.6
166 Sudan	216	279	1.3	3.5	6.6	..	17.4	58.1	55.9	2.8	8.4	69.1
166 Togo	313	359	0.8	0.2	4.6	2.9	14.5	52.0	50.0	0.5	8.0	40.4
168 Haiti	223	258	9.2	0.3	8.4	2.1	17.2	37.1	27.8	..	7.9	22.1
169 Afghanistan	245	289	0.7	33.1	2.4	0.1 [c]	15.9	46.2	48.5	1.9	9.6	79.4
170 Djibouti	308	352	0.1	14.9	10.4	1.2	17.5	54.1	52.9	2.3	7.9	31.6
171 Côte d'Ivoire	310	348	1.1	0.3	6.7	3.2	13.9	50.6	45.4	1.4	6.8	64.3
172 Gambia	237	295	0.8	0.3	8.5	1.3	15.2	54.2	52.3	1.1	4.4	22.3
173 Ethiopia	265	306	0.7	0.0	1.2	1.3	17.8	53.5	51.4	0.3	4.7	33.8

HDI rank	Adult mortality rate (per 1,000 people)		Age-standardized death rates (per 100,000 people)		Age-standardized obesity rate, adult (% of population ages 20 and older)	HIV prevalence rate, adult (% ages 15–49)	Life expectancy			Physicians (per 10,000 people)	Health expenditure	
							At age 60 (years)	Health-adjusted (years)			Total (% of GDP)	Out of pocket (% of total health expenditure)
	Female	Male	From alcohol use	From drug use				Female	Male			
	2011	2011	2008	2008	2008	2012	2010/2015[a]	2010	2010	2003–2012[b]	2011	2011
174 Malawi	347	384	0.8	0.3	4.5	10.8	17.0	46.4	43.7	0.2	8.4	14.2
175 Liberia	292	331	0.9	0.3	5.5	0.9	15.4	47.9	47.6	0.1	19.5	17.7
176 Mali	304	369	0.9	0.3	4.8	0.9	15.4	48.4	48.8	0.8	6.8	54.3
177 Guinea-Bissau	352	405	0.9	0.3	5.4	3.9	14.9	49.5	46.7	0.3	6.3	41.3
178 Mozambique	421	457	0.7	0.3	5.4	11.1	16.8	46.1	42.9	0.3	6.6	9.0
179 Guinea	294	348	0.9	0.3	4.7	1.7	14.8	50.6	49.8	1.0	6.0	67.4
180 Burundi	321	370	0.9	0.2	3.3	1.3	16.0	46.8	45.5	0.3	8.7	43.6
181 Burkina Faso	236	298	0.9	0.3	2.4	1.0	15.1	48.8	45.4	0.5	6.5	36.6
182 Eritrea	259	347	0.6	0.2	1.8	0.7	15.1	52.0	50.3	0.5	2.6	51.2
183 Sierra Leone	438	459	1.2	0.0	7.0	1.5	12.5	50.7	47.6	0.2	18.8	74.9
184 Chad	311	373	1.0	0.3	3.1	2.7	15.6	48.6	45.1	0.4	4.3	70.5
185 Central African Republic	420	466	0.9	0.2	3.7	..	15.9	41.7	37.7	0.5	3.8	43.4
186 Congo (Democratic Republic of the)	358	411	0.9	0.2	1.9	1.1	15.2	48.1	44.7	1.1	8.5	43.5
187 Niger	272	312	1.1	0.3	2.5	0.5	15.5	49.4	48.5	0.2	5.3	37.6
OTHER COUNTRIES OR TERRITORIES												
Korea, Democratic People's Rep. of	131	203	0.8	0.6	3.8	..	16.8	64.4	60.3	32.9	..	..
Marshall Islands	392	433	0.2	0.2	46.5	..	..	55.8	53.1	4.4	16.5	12.6
Monaco	51	110	2.0	..	..	..	..	..	..	70.6	4.4	7.0
Nauru	57	105	0.9	..	71.1	..	..	..	..	7.1	..	8.0
San Marino	46	56	..	..	..	..	..	..	..	48.8	7.2	14.7
Somalia	316	399	2.1	6.4	5.3	0.5	16.1	48.2	46.8	0.4	..	..
South Sudan	344	378	..	..	..	2.7	16.4	..	..	..	1.6	55.4
Tuvalu	283	251	0.2	0.1	..	..	..	..	..	10.9	17.3	0.1
Human Development Index groups												
Very high human development	59	109	1.9	1.0	22.0	..	23.0	70.9	66.9	27.8	12.2	13.7
High human development	89	152	1.6	0.9	12.5	..	19.9	68.6	63.6	17.2	6.0	33.8
Medium human development	157	230	1.3	2.3	5.9	..	18.5	59.5	56.3	7.4	4.6	44.7
Low human development	270	313	0.9	2.9	5.4	..	16.2	53.0	50.7	2.8	5.2	52.7
Regions												
Arab States	111	160	0.7	6.6	25.5	..	19.0	61.8	60.0	13.7	4.3	31.1
East Asia and the Pacific	99	137	1.0	0.4	5.6	..	18.5	68.2	63.5	12.1	4.8	35.9
Europe and Central Asia	104	216	2.3	1.4	23.1	..	18.7	64.8	58.9	26.2	6.3	28.5
Latin America and the Caribbean	98	181	3.4	0.8	23.6	..	21.2	66.8	62.0	..	7.6	34.4
South Asia	153	228	1.1	3.2	3.2	..	18.6	58.3	55.5	6.3	4.2	59.7
Sub-Saharan Africa	327	372	0.9	0.6	7.6	..	16.6	51.6	49.4	1.8	6.3	27.6
Least developed countries	246	289	1.0	2.7	3.6	..	16.8	53.7	51.3	1.7	5.6	48.2
Small island developing states	155	206	3.0	0.3	18.6	..	19.3	57.1	52.5	25.5	5.6	33.6
World	**127**	**188**	**1.4**	**1.7**	**11.6**	..	**20.7**	**63.7**	**59.8**	**13.4**	**10.1**	**17.8**

NOTES

a Data are annual average of projected values for 2010–2015.

b Data refer to the most recent year available during the period specified.

c 0.1 or less.

DEFINITIONS

Adult mortality rate: Probability that a 15-year-old will die before reaching age 60, expressed per 1,000 people.

Age-standardized death rate from alcohol use: The weighted average of the age-specific mortality rates from alcohol use per 100,000 people, where the weights are the proportions of people in the corresponding age groups of the World Health Organization standard population.

Age-standardized death rate from drug use: The weighted average of the age-specific mortality rates from drug use per 100,000 persons, where the weights are the proportions of people in the corresponding age groups of the WHO standard population.

Age-standardized obesity rate, adult: The weighted average of the age-specific obesity rate (with obesity defined as having a body mass index of 30 kilograms per square meter or higher) among adults ages 20 and older, expressed as a percentage of the total population ages 20 and older.

HIV prevalence rate, adult: Percentage of the population ages 15–49 who are living with HIV.

Life expectancy at age 60: Additional number of years that a 60-year-old could expect to live if prevailing patterns of age-specific mortality rates stay the same throughout the rest of his or her life.

Health-adjusted life expectancy: Average number of years that a person can expect to live in full health, taking into account years lived in less than full health due to disease and injury.

Physicians per 10,000 people: Number of medical doctors (physicians), both generalists and specialists, expressed per 10,000 people.

Health expenditure, total: Current and capital spending on health from government (central and local) budgets, external borrowing and grants (including donations from international agencies and nongovernmental organizations) and social (or compulsory) health insurance funds, expressed as a percentage of GDP.

Out-of-pocket health expenditure: Household direct payments to public and private providers of health care services and nonprofit institutions and nonreimbursable cost sharing, such as deductibles, copayments and fee for services, expressed as a percentage of total health expenditure.

MAIN DATA SOURCES

Columns 1–6 and 10: WHO 2013a.

Column 7: UNDESA 2013a.

Columns 8 and 9: Salomon and others 2012.

Column 11: World Bank 2013a.

Column 12: WHO 2013b.

TABLE 8

TABLE 8   Adult health and health expenditures | 191

TABLE 9

Education

HDI rank		Literacy rates Adult (% ages 15 and older) 2005–2012	Literacy rates Youth (% ages 15–24) 2005–2012	Population with at least some secondary education (% ages 25 and older) 2005–2012	Gross enrolment ratios Pre-primary (% of children of pre-school age) 2003–2012	Primary (% of primary school-age population) 2003–2012	Secondary (% of secondary school-age population) 2003–2012	Tertiary (% of tertiary school-age population) 2003–2012	Primary school dropout rates (% of primary school cohort) 2003–2012	Primary school teachers trained to teach (%) 2003–2012	Education quality Performance Mathematics 2012	Reading 2012	Science 2012	Pupil–teacher ratio (number of pupils per teacher) 2003–2012	Education expenditure (% of GDP) 2005–2012
VERY HIGH HUMAN DEVELOPMENT															
1	Norway	..	..	97.1	99	99	113	73	0.7	..	489	504	495	..	6.9
2	Australia	..	..	94.4 e	95	104	133	83	..	..	504	512	521	..	5.1
3	Switzerland	..	..	95.7	100	103	96	54	..	..	531	509	515	..	5.4
4	Netherlands	..	..	89.0	90	108	128	76	..	..	523	511	522	..	6.0
5	United States	..	..	95.0	73	99	94	95	6.9	..	481	498	497	14	5.6
6	Germany	..	..	96.6	112	101	102	57	3.4	..	514	508	524	12	5.1
7	New Zealand	..	..	95.2	93	100	120	81	..	..	500	512	516	15	7.2
8	Canada	..	..	100.0	71	99	102	..	..	..	518	523	525	..	5.5
9	Singapore	95.9	99.8	77.4	..	..	..	..	1.3	94	573	542	551	17	3.3
10	Denmark	..	..	96.1 f	100	100	120	74	1.1	..	500	496	498	..	8.7
11	Ireland	..	..	79.6	67	105	118	73	..	..	501	523	522	16	6.5
12	Sweden	..	..	86.9	95	101	97	74	4.4	..	478	483	485	9	7.0
13	Iceland	..	..	91.3	97	99	109	81	2.9	..	493	483	478	10	7.8
14	United Kingdom	..	..	99.9	85	107	97	61	..	..	494	499	514	17	5.6
15	Hong Kong, China (SAR)	..	..	75.4	101	101	106	60	1.0	96	561	545	555	14	3.4
15	Korea (Republic of)	..	..	82.9 g	118	104	97	101	1.0	..	554	536	538	19	5.0
17	Japan	..	..	86.4	87	103	102	60	0.1	..	536	538	547	17	3.8
18	Liechtenstein	..	..	..	95	105	111	44	20.6	..	535	516	525	8	2.1
19	Israel	..	..	85.8	97	104	102	62	1.1	..	466	486	470	13	6.0
20	France	..	..	80.5	110	108	110	57	0.6	..	495	505	499	18	5.9
21	Austria	..	..	100.0	101	100	98	71	0.6	..	506	490	506	11	6.0
21	Belgium	..	..	80.1	119	104	106	69	6.7	..	515	509	505	11	6.6
21	Luxembourg	..	..	100.0 f	89	97	101	18	..	..	490	488	491	9	..
24	Finland	..	..	100.0	70	99	107	96	0.4	..	519	524	545	14	6.8
25	Slovenia	99.7	99.9	96.9	91	98	98	85	1.4	..	501	481	514	17	5.7
26	Italy	99.0	99.9	75.7	98	100	101	64	0.5	..	485	490	494	10	4.5
27	Spain	97.7	99.6	69.9	127	104	129	83	2.2	..	484	488	496	12	5.0
28	Czech Republic	..	..	99.8	103	102	96	65	0.8	..	499	493	508	19	4.2
29	Greece	97.3	99.4	63.1	76	103	111	91	2.6	..	453	477	467	10	4.1
30	Brunei Darussalam	95.4	99.7	63.8 g	92	95	108	24	3.6	88	..	..	..	11	3.3
31	Qatar	96.3	96.8	60.5	73	103	112	12	6.4	49	376	388	384	10	2.5
32	Cyprus	98.7	99.8	78.7	79	101	93	47	4.7	..	440	449	438	13	7.3
33	Estonia	99.8	99.8	100.0 f	90	98	109	72	2.5	..	521	516	541	12	5.7
34	Saudi Arabia	87.2	98.0	66.5	13	103	114	51	1.3	91	..	..	..	11	5.6
35	Lithuania	99.7	99.8	91.4	77	99	107	77	3.6	..	479	477	496	12	5.4
35	Poland	99.7	100.0	82.3	74	99	97	74	1.5	..	518	518	526	10	5.2
37	Andorra	..	..	49.4	112	..	..	..	35.4	100	..	..	..	10	3.0
37	Slovakia	..	..	99.3	90	102	94	55	1.9	..	482	463	471	15	4.2
39	Malta	92.4	98.3	73.3	114	96	95	39	3.7	..	..	..	..	13	5.4
40	United Arab Emirates	90.0	95.0	62.7	71	108	..	..	15.6	100	434	442	448	18	..
41	Chile	98.6	98.9	74.8	112	102	90	71	2.1	..	423	441	445	22	4.1
41	Portugal	95.4	99.7	48.0	83	112	110	66	..	..	487	488	489	11	5.8
43	Hungary	99.0	98.9	98.3 e	87	101	101	60	1.9	..	477	488	494	11	4.9
44	Bahrain	94.6	98.2	78.0 g	50	..	96	33	2.2	82	..	..	..	12	2.9
44	Cuba	99.8	100.0	77.1 g	109	99	90	62	3.5	100	..	..	..	9	12.9
46	Kuwait	93.9	98.6	56.0	81	106	100	22	5.9	78	..	..	..	9	3.8
47	Croatia	98.9	99.6	89.1 g	64	94	98	59	0.7	100	471	485	491	14	4.3
48	Latvia	99.8	99.7	98.9	90	105	99	67	6.9	..	491	489	502	11	5.0
49	Argentina	97.9	99.2	56.3 g	75	118	90	75	4.7	..	388	396	406	16	5.8
HIGH HUMAN DEVELOPMENT															
50	Uruguay	98.1	98.8	52.5	89	112	90	63	5.3	..	409	411	416	14	2.9
51	Bahamas	..	..	89.6	..	108	93	..	10.5	92	..	..	..	14	..
51	Montenegro	98.5	99.3	89.2 g	61	101	91	56	19.5	..	410	422	410	8	..
53	Belarus	99.6	99.8	89.3	103	99	106	91	0.9	100	..	..	..	15	5.2
54	Romania	97.7	97.2	88.9	78	96	96	52	5.2	..	445	438	439	17	4.2
55	Libya	89.5	99.9	49.6 g	10	114	104	61	..	..	..	..	..	..	..
56	Oman	86.9	97.7	53.9	55	109	94	16	6.4	..	..	..	..	20	4.3

		Literacy rates		Population with at least some secondary education	Gross enrolment ratios				Primary school dropout rates	Primary school teachers trained to teach	Education quality			Pupil–teacher ratio	Education expenditure
		Adult	Youth		Pre-primary	Primary	Secondary	Tertiary			Performance of 15-year-old students				
											Mathematics[a]	Reading[b]	Science[c]		
		(% ages 15 and older)	(% ages 15–24)	(% ages 25 and older)	(% of children of pre-school age)	(% of primary school-age population)	(% of secondary school-age population)	(% of tertiary school-age population)	(% of primary school cohort)	(%)	2012	2012	2012	(number of pupils per teacher)	(% of GDP)
HDI rank		2005–2012[d]	2005–2012[d]	2005–2012[d]	2003–2012[d]	2003–2012[d]	2003–2012[d]	2003–2012[d]	2003–2012[d]	2003–2012[d]	2012	2012	2012	2003–2012[d]	2005–2012[d]
57	Russian Federation	99.7	99.7	90.9	90	99	85	75	3.9	..	482	475	486	18	4.1
58	Bulgaria	98.4	97.9	94.3	85	101	93	60	3.4	..	439	436	446	17	4.1
59	Barbados	..	..	88.6 [g]	79	105	105	61	6.6	55	..	..	..	13	7.5
60	Palau	..	..	..	..	101	96	..	..	..	..	..	..	..	..
61	Antigua and Barbuda	99.0	..	..	83	101	106	14	8.7	65	..	..	..	15	2.5
62	Malaysia	93.1	98.4	69.4 [g]	78	101	67	37	0.8	..	421	398	420	13	5.1
63	Mauritius	88.8	96.8	53.6	120	108	96	40	2.7	100	..	..	..	21	3.7
64	Trinidad and Tobago	98.8	99.6	59.3	83	106	86	12	10.6	88	..	..	..	18	..
65	Lebanon	89.6	98.7	54.2	91	107	74	46	6.7	10	..	..	..	14	1.6
65	Panama	94.1	97.6	62.1 [g]	65	100	84	42	8.4	90	..	..	..	23	4.1
67	Venezuela (Bolivarian Republic of)	95.5	98.5	53.7	72	102	85	78	6.1	..	..	..	..	..	3.6
68	Costa Rica	96.3	98.3	53.6 [g]	73	107	101	47	9.0	91	407	441	429	17	6.3
69	Turkey	94.1	98.7	49.4	29	102	89	61	5.0	..	448	475	463	..	2.9
70	Kazakhstan	99.7	99.8	99.3	54	105	98	45	0.7	..	432	393	425	16	3.1
71	Mexico	93.5	98.5	58.0	99	104	84	28	5.0	96	413	424	415	28	5.3
71	Seychelles	91.8	99.1	66.8	110	107	101	1	6.0	99	..	..	..	13	4.8
73	Saint Kitts and Nevis	..	..	..	96	88	79	18	26.5	61	..	..	..	16	4.2
73	Sri Lanka	91.2	98.2	74.0	87	99	99	14	2.7	82	..	..	..	24	2.0
75	Iran (Islamic Republic of)	85.0	98.7	65.1	35	106	86	55	3.8	98	..	..	..	20	4.7
76	Azerbaijan	99.8	100.0	95.5	27	96	100	20	1.8	100	..	..	..	12	2.8
77	Jordan	95.9	99.1	74.1	34	99	89	40	2.1	..	386	399	409	20	..
77	Serbia	98.0	99.3	65.6	56	93	92	52	1.6	56	449	446	445	16	4.7
79	Brazil	90.4	97.5	53.6	..	..	..	..	..	..	391	410	405	..	5.8
79	Georgia	99.7	99.8	92.0	58	106	87	28	6.9	95	..	..	..	6	2.7
79	Grenada	..	..	..	99	103	108	53	..	65	..	..	..	16	..
82	Peru	89.6	97.4	61.1	77	105	91	43	18.5	..	368	384	373	20	2.6
83	Ukraine	99.7	99.8	93.5 [g]	101	106	98	80	1.9	100	..	..	..	16	5.3
84	Belize	..	..	76.1 [g]	47	121	84	26	9.1	54	..	..	..	22	6.6
84	The former Yugoslav Republic of Macedonia	97.4	98.7	47.8	26	90	82	41	2.5	..	..	..	..	16	..
86	Bosnia and Herzegovina	98.0	99.7	56.8	16	..	..	38	16.7	..	..	..	..	..	..
87	Armenia	99.6	99.8	94.4 [g]	51	102	96	46	4.4	77	..	..	..	19	3.1
88	Fiji	..	..	57.8	18	105	90	62	9.1	100	..	..	..	31	4.1
89	Thailand	93.5	98.1	38.1	112	97	87	51	..	..	427	441	444	16	5.8
90	Tunisia	79.1	97.2	39.3	..	110	91	35	5.3	100	388	404	398	17	6.2
91	China	95.1	99.6	65.3 [g]	62	128	87	24	..	..	613	570	580	17	..
91	Saint Vincent and the Grenadines	..	..	..	80	105	101	..	31.4	85	..	..	..	16	5.1
93	Algeria	72.6	91.8	24.1	79	117	98	31	7.2	99	..	..	..	23	4.3
93	Dominica	..	..	26.5	95	119	97	..	12.2	61	..	..	..	16	3.5
95	Albania	96.8	98.8	84.8	69	..	82	55	1.2	..	394	394	397	19	3.3
96	Jamaica	87.0	95.6	72.6 [g]	113	..	93	26	4.8	..	..	..	..	28	6.4
97	Saint Lucia	..	..	..	61	87	91	10	10.4	88	..	..	..	17	4.4
98	Colombia	93.6	98.2	56.3	49	107	93	45	15.3	100	376	403	399	25	4.5
98	Ecuador	91.6	98.7	39.8	150	114	87	39	8.6	84	..	..	..	18	5.2
100	Suriname	94.7	98.4	45.9	88	114	85	..	9.7	100	..	..	..	15	..
100	Tonga	99.0	99.4	87.9	35	110	91	6	9.6	..	..	..	..	21	..
102	Dominican Republic	90.1	97.0	54.4	37	105	75	33	25.2	85	..	..	..	25	2.2
MEDIUM HUMAN DEVELOPMENT															
103	Maldives	98.4	99.3	14.9	95	98	72	13	..	81	..	..	..	12	7.2
103	Mongolia	97.4	95.7	84.7 [g]	86	117	103	61	7.0	99	..	..	..	29	5.5
103	Turkmenistan	99.6	99.8	..	..	..	..	..	..	..	..	..	..	..	..
106	Samoa	98.8	99.5	62.1	34	105	86	..	10.0	..	..	..	..	30	5.8
107	Palestine, State of	95.3	99.3	56.7	42	94	83	49	0.7	100	..	..	..	24	..
108	Indonesia	92.8	98.8	44.5	42	109	81	27	12.0	..	375	396	382	16	2.8
109	Botswana	85.1	95.2	75.5 [g]	18	106	82	7	7.0	100	..	..	..	25	7.8
110	Egypt	73.9	89.3	51.2 [g]	27	109	76	29	1.1	..	..	..	..	28	3.8
111	Paraguay	93.9	98.6	38.8	35	97	68	35	17.4	..	..	..	..	28	4.1
112	Gabon	89.0	97.9	24.0 [g]	35	165	..	..	..	100	..	..	..	25	..
113	Bolivia (Plurinational State of)	91.2	99.4	53.1	51	94	77	38	13.8	..	..	..	..	24	7.6

TABLE 9 Education | 193

TABLE 9

TABLE 9   EDUCATION

HDI rank	Literacy rates		Population with at least some secondary education	Gross enrolment ratios				Primary school dropout rates	Primary school teachers trained to teach	Education quality Performance of 15-year-old students			Pupil-teacher ratio	Education expenditure
	Adult	Youth		Pre-primary	Primary	Secondary	Tertiary			Mathematics[a]	Reading[b]	Science[c]		
	(% ages 15 and older)	(% ages 15–24)	(% ages 25 and older)	(% of children of pre-school age)	(% of primary school-age population)	(% of secondary school-age population)	(% of tertiary school-age population)	(% of primary school cohort)	(%)				(number of pupils per teacher)	(% of GDP)
	2005–2012d	2005–2012d	2005–2012d	2003–2012d	2003–2012d	2003–2012d	2003–2012d	2003–2012d	2003–2012d	2012	2012	2012	2003–2012d	2005–2012d
114 Moldova (Republic of)	99.0	100.0	95.0	80	94	75	38	4.2	..	..	..	..	16	8.6
115 El Salvador	84.5	96.0	39.8	63	114	67	25	16.0	96	..	..	..	29	3.4
116 Uzbekistan	99.4	99.9	..	25	93	105	9	1.9	100	..	..	..	16	..
117 Philippines	95.4	97.8	64.8 g	51	106	85	28	24.2	..	..	..	..	31	2.7
118 South Africa	93.0	98.8	74.3	77	102	102	..	..	87	..	..	..	30	6.0
118 Syrian Arab Republic	84.1	95.3	34.1	11	122	74	26	6.8	..	..	..	..	..	5.1
120 Iraq	78.5	82.4	32.4 g	7	107	53	16	..	100	..	..	..	17	..
121 Guyana	85.0	93.1	31.2 g	63	80	105	13	16.5	68	..	..	..	25	3.6
121 Viet Nam	93.4	97.1	65.0	77	105	..	25	2.5	100	511	508	528	19	6.6
123 Cape Verde	84.9	98.4	..	75	112	93	21	10.7	95	..	..	..	23	5.6
124 Micronesia (Federated States of)	..	..	..	..	112	83	..	..	..	..	..	..	..	..
125 Guatemala	75.9	87.4	22.6	64	114	65	18	29.1	..	..	..	..	26	2.8
125 Kyrgyzstan	99.2	99.8	95.6 g	25	106	88	41	2.9	72	..	..	..	24	5.8
127 Namibia	76.5	87.1	33.5 g	30	109	65	9	15.5	98	..	..	..	41	8.4
128 Timor-Leste	58.3	79.5	..	10	125	57	18	16.4	..	..	..	..	31	10.1
129 Honduras	85.1	95.9	27.0	42	109	73	21	30.4	36	..	..	..	34	..
129 Morocco	67.1	81.5	28.0	59	116	69	16	8.4	100	..	..	..	26	5.4
131 Vanuatu	83.2	94.6	..	61	122	60	5	28.5	100	..	..	..	22	5.2
132 Nicaragua	78.0	87.0	37.6 g	55	117	69	18	51.6	75	..	..	..	30	4.7
133 Kiribati	..	..	..	..	116	86	..	..	85	..	..	..	25	..
133 Tajikistan	99.7	99.9	92.4	9	100	86	22	2.0	94	..	..	..	23	3.9
135 India	62.8	81.1	38.7 g	58	113	69	23	..	..	..	..	..	35	3.3
136 Bhutan	52.8	74.4	34.4	9	112	74	9	5.1	91	..	..	..	24	4.7
136 Cambodia	73.9	87.1	15.5	15	124	45	16	34.1	100	..	..	..	46	2.6
138 Ghana	71.5	85.7	54.3 g	114	110	58	12	27.8	52	..	..	..	33	8.2
139 Lao People's Democratic Republic	72.7	83.9	29.7 g	24	123	47	17	30.1	97	..	..	..	27	3.3
140 Congo	..	..	46.2	14	109	54	10	29.7	80	..	..	..	44	6.2
141 Zambia	61.4	64.0	35.0 g	..	114	101	..	46.9	..	..	..	..	49	1.3
142 Bangladesh	57.7	78.7	26.7 g	26	114	51	13	33.8	58	..	..	..	40	2.2
142 Sao Tome and Principe	69.5	80.2	..	50	118	71	8	33.9	48	..	..	..	29	..
144 Equatorial Guinea	94.2	98.1	..	73	91	..	..	27.9	49	..	..	..	26	..
LOW HUMAN DEVELOPMENT														
145 Nepal	57.4	82.4	28.3 g	82	139	66	14	38.3	93	..	..	..	28	4.7
146 Pakistan	54.9	70.7	33.2	49	93	37	10	39.0	84	..	..	..	41	2.4
147 Kenya	72.2	82.4	28.6	51	112	60	4	..	97	..	..	..	47	6.7
148 Swaziland	87.8	93.7	48.1 g	25	115	60	6	32.7	78	..	..	..	29	7.8
149 Angola	70.4	73.0	..	87	140	32	7	68.1	..	..	..	..	46	3.5
150 Myanmar	92.7	96.1	17.8 g	9	114	50	14	25.2	100	..	..	..	28	0.8
151 Rwanda	65.9	77.3	7.7 g	13	134	32	7	64.4	96	..	..	..	59	4.8
152 Cameroon	71.3	80.6	27.9	30	111	50	12	30.2	79	..	..	..	46	3.2
152 Nigeria	51.1	66.4	..	13	81	44	10	20.1	66	..	..	..	36	..
154 Yemen	65.3	86.4	16.0 g	2	97	47	10	..	..	..	..	..	30	5.2
155 Madagascar	64.5	64.9	..	9	145	38	4	59.3	95	..	..	..	43	2.8
156 Zimbabwe	83.6	90.9	55.4 g	..	..	38	6	..	..	..	..	..	39	2.5
157 Papua New Guinea	62.4	70.8	10.5 g	100	60	..	..	..	..	..	..	..	36	..
157 Solomon Islands	..	..	..	43	141	48	..	36.6	54	..	..	..	24	7.3
159 Comoros	75.5	86.0	..	24	117	73	11	..	55	..	..	..	28	7.6
159 Tanzania (United Republic of)	67.8	74.6	7.4 g	34	93	35	4	18.6	97	..	..	..	46	6.2
161 Mauritania	58.6	69.0	14.2 g	..	97	27	5	18.8	100	..	..	..	40	3.7
162 Lesotho	75.8	83.2	20.9	36	111	52	11	36.8	68	..	..	..	34	13.0
163 Senegal	49.7	65.0	10.8	14	84	41	8	38.6	65	..	..	..	32	5.6
164 Uganda	73.2	87.4	28.8	14	110	28	9	75.2	95	..	..	..	48	3.3
165 Benin	28.7	42.4	18.4 g	19	123	48	12	40.7	47	..	..	..	44	5.3
166 Sudan	71.9	87.3	15.5 g	..	..	..	..	9.1	60	..	..	..	38	..
166 Togo	60.4	79.9	29.8 g	11	133	55	10	48.3	83	..	..	..	42	4.6
168 Haiti	48.7	72.3	29.1 g	..	..	..	..	..	..	..	..	..	..	..
169 Afghanistan	..	..	20.3 g	..	97	52	4	..	..	..	..	..	44	..
170 Djibouti	..	..	..	4	70	44	5	..	100	..	..	..	35	8.4

	Literacy rates			Gross enrolment ratios				Primary school dropout rates	Primary school teachers trained to teach	Education quality			Pupil–teacher ratio	Education expenditure
			Population with at least some secondary education							Performance of 15-year-old students				
	Adult	Youth		Pre-primary	Primary	Secondary	Tertiary			Mathematics[a]	Reading[b]	Science[c]		
	(% ages 15 and older)	(% ages 15–24)	(% ages 25 and older)	(% of children of pre-school age)	(% of primary school-age population)	(% of secondary school-age population)	(% of tertiary school-age population)	(% of primary school cohort)	(%)				(number of pupils per teacher)	(% of GDP)
HDI rank	2005–2012[d]	2005–2012[d]	2005–2012[d]	2003–2012[d]	2003–2012[d]	2003–2012[d]	2003–2012[d]	2003–2012[d]	2003–2012[d]	2012	2012	2012	2003–2012[d]	2005–2012[d]
171 Côte d'Ivoire	56.9	67.5	22.1 g	5	94	..	8	17.8	99	..	..	..	42	4.6
172 Gambia	51.1	68.1	24.0 g	30	85	57	4	17.2	63	..	..	..	34	3.9
173 Ethiopia	39.0	55.0	12.5	18	95	37	8	63.4	57	..	..	..	54	4.7
174 Malawi	61.3	72.1	8.6 g	..	141	34	1	50.9	78	..	..	..	74	5.4
175 Liberia	42.9	49.1	27.3 g	..	102	45	..	32.2	56	..	..	..	27	1.9
176 Mali	33.4	46.9	10.9	4	88	51	7	38.4	52	..	..	..	48	4.7
177 Guinea-Bissau	55.3	73.2	..	7	116	34	3	..	39	..	..	..	52	..
178 Mozambique	50.6	67.1	3.6 g	..	105	26	5	69.4	84	..	..	..	55	5.0
179 Guinea	25.3	31.4	..	16	91	39	9	41.4	75	..	..	..	44	3.1
180 Burundi	86.9	88.9	7.1 g	5	137	28	3	56.2	95	..	..	..	47	6.1
181 Burkina Faso	28.7	39.3	2.0	4	85	26	5	31.0	95	..	..	..	48	3.4
182 Eritrea	68.9	90.1	..	13	42	30	2	31.0	90	..	..	..	41	2.1
183 Sierra Leone	43.3	61.0	14.8 g	9	131	..	..	..	55	..	..	..	33	2.7
184 Chad	35.4	47.9	5.5	1	95	23	2	61.9	62	..	..	..	61	2.6
185 Central African Republic	56.6	65.6	17.9 g	6	95	18	3	53.4	58	..	..	..	80	1.2
186 Congo (Democratic Republic of the)	61.2	65.8	16.5 g	4	111	43	8	29.3	94	..	..	..	35	2.5
187 Niger	28.7	36.5	48.3	6	71	16	2	30.7	97	..	..	..	39	4.5
OTHER COUNTRIES OR TERRITORIES														
Korea, Democratic People's Rep. of	100.0	100.0	..	..	..	..	..	..	..	..	..	..	..	..
Marshall Islands	..	..	..	48	105	103	43	16.5	..	..	..	..	..	..
Monaco	..	..	..	..	..	..	..	..	..	..	..	..	..	1.6
Nauru	..	..	..	94	93	63	..	..	74	..	..	..	22	..
San Marino	..	..	..	108	92	95	64	3.8	..	..	..	..	6	..
Somalia	..	..	..	..	29	7	..	..	..	..	..	..	36	..
South Sudan	..	..	..	..	..	..	..	..	..	..	..	..	..	..
Tuvalu	..	..	..	105	100	..	..	..	..	..	..	..	19	..
Human Development Index groups														
Very high human development	..	..	86.9	85	103	101	76	3.6	..	—	—	—	..	5.3
High human development	94.2	98.9	64.9	67	118	87	35	8.1	..	—	—	—	..	4.6
Medium human development	71.7	85.9	47.5	51	111	70	23	18.3	..	—	—	—	..	3.7
Low human development	58.2	70.2	22.1	24	98	39	8	42.7	..	—	—	—	..	3.7
Regions														
Arab States	77.0	89.9	41.1	32	105	76	28	5.8	..	—	—	—	..	..
East Asia and the Pacific	94.4	98.8	..	58	120	84	..	..	..	—	—	—	..	..
Europe and Central Asia	97.7	99.4	75.6	43	101	95	50	4.1	..	—	—	—	..	3.4
Latin America and the Caribbean	91.5	97.1	54.7	79	106	85	44	14.6	..	—	—	—	..	5.2
South Asia	62.9	80.6	38.4	54	110	64	22	21.2	..	—	—	—	..	3.4
Sub-Saharan Africa	58.9	69.2	28.1	24	100	43	8	37.7	..	—	—	—	..	5.2
Least developed countries	59.3	71.5	..	20	105	42	9	39.9	..	—	—	—	..	3.7
Small island developing states	..	..	..	67	96	79	..	15.8	..	—	—	—	..	..
World	**81.2**	**87.9**	**63.6**	**52**	**108**	**74**	**31**	**17.1**	..	—	—	—	..	**5.0**

NOTES

a Average score for Organisation for Economic Co-operation and Development (OECD) countries is 494.

b Average score for OECD countries is 496.

c Average score for OECD countries is 501.

d Data refer to the most recent year available during the period specified.

e Refers to population ages 25–64.

f Refers to population ages 25–74.

g Barro and Lee (2013) estimate for 2010 based on data from the United Nations Educational, Scientific and Cultural Organization Institute for Statistics.

DEFINITIONS

Adult literacy rate: Percentage of the population ages 15 and older who can, with understanding, both read and write a short simple statement on their everyday life.

Youth literacy rate: Percentage of the population ages 15–24 who can, with understanding, both read and write a short simple statement on their everyday life.

Population with at least some secondary education: Percentage of the population ages 25 and older that reached at least a secondary level of education.

Gross enrolment ratio: Total enrolment in a given level of education (pre-primary, primary, secondary or tertiary), regardless of age, expressed as a percentage of the official school-age population for the same level of education.

Primary school dropout rate: Percentage of students from a given cohort that have enrolled in primary school but that drop out before reaching the last grade of primary education. It is calculated as 100 minus the survival rate to the last grade of primary education and assumes that observed flow rates remain unchanged throughout the cohort life and that dropouts do not re-enter school.

Primary school teachers trained to teach: Percentage of primary school teachers that have received the minimum organized teacher training (pre-service or in-service) required for teaching at the primary level.

Performance of 15-year-old students in reading, mathematics and science: Score obtained in testing of skills and knowledge of 15-year-old students in these subjects essential for participation in society.

Pupil-teacher ratio: Average number of pupils per teacher in primary education in a given school year.

Education expenditure: Total public expenditure (current and capital) on education, expressed as a percentage of GDP.

MAIN DATA SOURCES

Columns 1–9 and 13: UNESCO Institute for Statistics 2013.

Columns 10–12: OECD 2013.

Column 14: World Bank 2013a.

TABLE 9 Education | 195

TABLE 9

Command over and allocation of resources

TABLE 10

HDI rank	GDP (2011 PPP $ billions) 2012	GDP per capita (2011 PPP $) 2012	Gross fixed capital formation (% of GDP) 2005–2012	General government final consumption expenditure Total (% of GDP) 2005–2012	General government final consumption expenditure Average annual growth (%) 2005–2012	Taxes on income, profit and capital gain (% of total tax revenue) 2005–2012	Research and development expenditure (% of GDP) 2005–2012	Share of agriculture, hunting, forestry and fisheries (% of GDP) 2012	Domestic credit provided by the banking sector (% of GDP) 2012	External debt stock (% of GNI) 2005–2012	Total debt service (% of GNI) 2012	Consumer price index (2005=100) 2012	Domestic food price level Index 2013	Domestic food price level Volatility index 2013
VERY HIGH HUMAN DEVELOPMENT														
1 Norway	315.5	62,858	20.6	21.3	1.8	33.0	1.7	1.2	87.0 b	..	..	114	1.2	6.8
2 Australia	960.6	42,278	27.9	17.9	3.4	63.6	2.4	2.4	154.4	..	..	122	1.2 b	12.7
3 Switzerland	410.2	51,293	20.4	11.1	2.0	24.2	3.0	0.7	192.6	..	..	104	1.1 b	9.2
4 Netherlands	711.3	42,453	16.8	28.4	0.0	25.2	1.8	1.7	216.0	..	..	113	0.9 b	4.2
5 United States	15,965.5	50,859	14.7	17.3	−2.6	54.9	2.9	1.1	231.6	..	..	118	1.0 b	..
6 Germany	3,375.2	41,966	17.6	19.5	1.2	15.4	2.8	0.9	123.6	..	..	113	1.1	13.8
7 New Zealand	143.5	32,360	18.8	20.1	0.3	45.8	1.3	6.3	157.8 b	..	..	121	1.3 b	13.0
8 Canada	1,410.6	40,588	22.0	20.9	0.8	53.3	1.8	1.5	177.6 b	..	..	114	1.3 b	9.4
9 Singapore	379.7	71,475	24.1	9.7	−3.6	34.4	2.4	0.0	99.5	..	..	125	1.3	15.8
10 Denmark	232.2	41,524	17.6	28.6	0.2	38.9	3.1	1.5	206.6	..	..	117	1.1 b	20.9
11 Ireland	196.9	42,919	10.0	17.6	−3.4	36.0	1.8	1.6	202.1	..	..	112	1.0 b	4.2
12 Sweden	398.3	41,840	18.8	26.9	0.7	11.2	3.4	1.6	144.8	..	..	112	1.1 b	10.0
13 Iceland	12.4	38,553	14.4	25.5	−0.2	28.5	2.6	7.8	143.2	..	..	163	1.1 b	39.2
14 United Kingdom	2,207.0	34,694	14.2	22.1	2.2	35.6	1.8	0.7	210.1	..	..	123	1.2	22.9
15 Hong Kong, China (SAR)	359.8	50,291	26.4	9.1	3.7	38.7	0.8	..	200.6	..	..	122	..	..
15 Korea (Republic of)	1,474.9	29,495	26.7	15.8	3.9	30.3	3.7	2.6	168.7	..	..	123	2.0 b	41.7
17 Japan	4,465.4	35,006	20.6	20.4	1.5	42.9	3.4	1.2	346.2	..	..	99	1.9	10.0
18 Liechtenstein	..	..	..	..	..	..	..	0.7	..	..	..	..	..	..
19 Israel	242.1	30,600	20.4	22.9	3.2	27.6	4.4	2.0	85.9 b	..	..	120	1.3 b	33.0
20 France	2,369.9	36,074	19.8	24.7	1.4	23.7	2.3	2.0	136.4	..	..	112	1.1 b	8.8
21 Austria	363.7	43,139	21.4	18.8	0.4	23.3	2.8	1.6	133.4	..	..	116	1.2	15.9
21 Belgium	439.5	39,498	20.7	24.9	0.4	35.4	2.0	0.8	116.6	..	..	118	1.1 b	8.4
21 Luxembourg	46.0	86,587	20.2	16.9	5.0	29.8	1.6	0.3	167.7	..	..	118	1.1	..
24 Finland	206.3	38,104	19.4	24.8	0.8	15.6	3.9	2.8	104.1	..	..	117	1.2	23.4
25 Slovenia	56.4	27,394	17.8	20.8	−1.3	11.2	2.1	2.7	93.8	..	..	120	1.4	20.2
26 Italy	2,004.6	33,668	18.2	20.1	−2.9	32.3	1.3	2.0	167.6	..	..	116	1.2 b	9.1
27 Spain	1,458.9	31,198	19.1	20.1	−0.5	21.7	1.4	2.5	221.5	..	..	119	1.1 b	19.8
28 Czech Republic	281.0	26,733	23.6	20.8	−1.2	14.5	1.6	2.4	68.7	..	..	121	1.2	46.0
29 Greece	281.7	25,391	13.1	17.8	−4.2	17.0	0.6	3.4	135.5	..	..	123	1.1 b	14.4
30 Brunei Darussalam	29.3	71,080	13.4	17.3	2.0	..	..	0.7	13.5	..	..	107	1.6 b	11.7
31 Qatar	274.2	133,713	33.8	12.3	..	40.2	..	0.1	77.5	..	..	141	0.8	52.1
32 Cyprus	25.9	29,698	18.4	19.7	0.5	28.4	0.5	2.5	344.1	..	..	119	1.3 b	10.7
33 Estonia	32.2	24,195	25.0	19.6	4.0	8.0	1.6	4.1	79.0	..	..	138	1.5 b	39.5
34 Saudi Arabia	1,436.8	50,791	22.2	20.4	..	..	0.1	1.9	−10.5	..	..	141	1.2 b	34.7
35 Lithuania	70.4	23,554	16.7	17.6	0.7	7.4	0.8	4.0	52.3	72.6	16.35	138	1.8 b	128.1
35 Poland	853.3	22,143	19.4	17.9	0.1	13.1	0.7	3.9	63.8	..	..	125	1.3 b	7.5
37 Andorra	..	..	..	..	..	..	..	0.6	..	..	..	..	..	..
37 Slovakia	138.1	25,537	21.5	17.6	−0.7	9.6	0.6	3.1	54.1 b	..	..	124	1.4	32.5
39 Malta	11.9	28,398	14.6	20.5	0.9	31.8	0.6	1.6	154.1	..	..	118	1.5	15.0
40 United Arab Emirates	525.1	57,045	21.9	6.9	3.6	..	..	0.7	76.5	..	..	116	..	..
41 Chile	368.5	21,099	24.1	12.1	3.9	27.2	0.4	3.6	74.3	41.0	6.52	108	1.6	23.1
41 Portugal	263.9	25,096	15.8	18.3	−4.4	21.7	1.6	2.3	198.7	..	..	116	1.1 b	15.4
43 Hungary	219.7	22,146	17.2	20.3	−2.5	12.5	1.2	4.7	68.2	..	..	143	1.5 b	37.0
44 Bahrain	53.6	40,658	19.5	14.6	..	0.5	..	0.3	73.1	..	..	117	1.2 b	17.2
44 Cuba	..	..	9.9	37.9	2.4	..	0.6	5.0	..	..	..	..	..	..
46 Kuwait	273.7 b	84,188 b	15.6	14.8	..	0.6	0.1	0.3	54.8 b	..	..	140	0.9	25.3
47 Croatia	85.1	19,946	18.8	19.9	−1.9	7.8	0.7	5.0	96.3	..	..	123	1.5	36.3
48 Latvia	43.2	21,229	23.7	15.3	−0.2	8.1	0.6	5.0	63.0	134.4	28.50	148	1.4	97.0
49 Argentina	..	..	21.8	16.6	5.2	..	0.6	9.0	37.3	26.3	3.57	111 b	1.3	29.3
HIGH HUMAN DEVELOPMENT														
50 Uruguay	61.0	17,966	20.6	12.2	5.4	18.0	0.4	7.7	32.0	31.6	3.26	166	1.4	28.2
51 Bahamas	8.4	22,705	28.1	14.8	3.5	..	..	2.0	105.0	..	..	119	..	..
51 Montenegro	8.7	14,040	18.4	22.1	..	..	1.1	8.8	57.9	45.6	5.00	126 b	..	..
53 Belarus	159.6	16,868	32.8	14.6	−1.2	3.3	0.6	9.5	32.2	54.6	3.33	396	1.8 b	62.4
54 Romania	346.0	17,234	26.7	6.6	2.3	17.6	0.5	6.0	54.3	72.3	10.20	148	1.4 b	24.2
55 Libya	..	..	27.9	9.3	..	..	..	2.3	−65.9 b	..	..	154	..	..
56 Oman	..	..	..	17.2	..	2.5	..	1.1	35.4	..	..	141	1.1 b	39.4
57 Russian Federation	3,327.7	23,184	22.0	18.6	−0.2	1.7	1.2	3.9	41.1	31.1	3.50	185	1.6 b	24.2

									Share of	DEBT			PRICES		
		GDP	GDP per capita	Gross fixed capital formation	General government final consumption expenditure		Taxes on income, profit and capital gain	Research and development expenditure	agriculture, hunting, forestry and fisheries	Domestic credit provided by the banking sector	External debt stock	Total debt service	Consumer price index	Domestic food price level	
		(2011 PPP $ billions)	(2011 PPP $)	(% of GDP)	Total (% of GDP)	Average annual growth (%)	(% of total tax revenue)	(% of GDP)	(% of GDP)	(% of GDP)	(% of GNI)	(% of GNI)	(2005=100)	Index	Volatility index
HDI rank		2012	2012	2005–2012[a]	2005–2012[a]	2005–2012	2005–2012[a]	2005–2012[a]	2012	2012	2005–2012[a]	2012	2012	2013	2013
58	Bulgaria	115.0	15,738	21.4	7.8	−0.4	15.5	0.6	6.4	71.0	77.9	8.75	148	1.3[b]	39.3
59	Barbados	4.3[b]	15,299[b]	14.6	20.3	..	31.6	..	1.6	136.3[b]	..	..	151	..	..
60	Palau	0.3	14,411	..	..	..	..	..	6.1	..	..	..	..	..	..
61	Antigua and Barbuda	1.8	19,714	29.3	17.8	..	..	..	2.1	94.5	..	..	120	..	..
62	Malaysia	640.3	21,897	25.6	13.5	5.0	52.0	0.6	10.2	134.5	34.8	3.87	120	1.6	7.6
63	Mauritius	20.9	16,194	24.0	13.5	2.3	18.2	0.4	3.5	113.6	12.5	1.43	152	1.8[b]	71.4
64	Trinidad and Tobago	38.9	29,086	9.7	9.5	−0.6	47.5	0.1	0.4	36.5	..	..	178	..	..
65	Lebanon	73.1	16,509	31.2	14.5	6.9	17.2	..	5.0	176.4	61.7	13.36	118	..	..
65	Panama	63.3	16,655	27.7	11.2	18.1	..	0.2	3.5	89.0	43.7	2.80	137	..	..
67	Venezuela (Bolivarian Republic of)	528.5	17,642	20.3	12.2	6.3	21.5	..	5.7	42.0	21.8	2.00	249	2.3	82.1
68	Costa Rica	62.9	13,091	20.2	17.9	1.7	15.5	0.5	5.9	53.3	25.7	3.98	173	..	..
69	Turkey	1,344.3	18,167	20.3	14.8	5.7	25.5	0.8	8.9	71.9	40.1	7.36	178	1.9	81.7
70	Kazakhstan	361.1	21,506	20.6	11.6	11.3	36.5	0.2	4.5	41.8	77.9	20.49	184	..	15.0
71	Mexico	1,950.9	16,144	20.7	11.5	1.5	..	0.4	3.5	47.1	25.2	3.69	134	1.3	6.7
71	Seychelles	2.0	23,152	..	..	..	31.5	0.3	2.6	38.8	184.4	3.43	203	..	..
73	Saint Kitts and Nevis	1.1	20,895	29.9	10.4	..	6.8	..	1.6	108.2	..	..	133	..	..
73	Sri Lanka	180.1	8,862	27.1	14.8	6.3	16.6	0.1	11.1	48.4	41.0	2.24	196	1.8[b]	33.9
75	Iran (Islamic Republic of)	1,181.6[b]	15,461[b]	25.8	11.2	−4.3	19.3	0.8	9.3	18.0[b]	..	0.74	316	2.6[b]	58.6
76	Azerbaijan	147.7	15,888	22.5	10.3	10.2	18.1	0.2	5.5	24.7	14.9	3.32	179	1.9[b]	66.4
77	Jordan	71.6	11,340	25.2	16.5	−13.5	12.3	0.4	3.0	113.4	61.5	3.25	147	1.3	20.5
77	Serbia	83.7	11,587	26.3	18.9	−2.2	8.8	0.9	10.2	62.4	71.8	12.34	183	..	..
79	Brazil	2,840.9	14,301	18.1	21.5	3.2	28.4	1.2	5.2	110.5	16.6	2.43	141	1.3[b]	25.2
79	Georgia	30.0	6,691	21.8	17.7	..	35.2	0.2	8.3	35.0	79.1	11.46	154	..	7.2
79	Grenada	1.2	11,786	21.9	17.1	..	15.2	..	5.6	92.4	73.8	3.41	127	..	..
82	Peru	347.9	11,603	26.6	10.3	9.4	34.5	..	7.0	17.8	25.8	2.03	123	1.7	9.1
83	Ukraine	379.9	8,332	18.9	19.4	2.4	12.8	0.9	8.9	80.2	83.3	17.02	212	1.2[b]	70.6
84	Belize	2.7[b]	8,438[b]	25.4	15.8	5.1	29.8	..	12.4	66.9[b]	96.0	9.99	116	..	..
84	The former Yugoslav Republic of Macedonia	24.7	11,708	20.6	18.3	−2.8	12.7	0.2	10.3	48.8	62.8	9.24	124	1.6[b]	38.8
86	Bosnia and Herzegovina	35.2	9,184	21.9	23.0	1.7	6.6	0.0	8.4	67.0	58.6	4.71	125	1.7[b]	17.5
87	Armenia	21.6	7,291	31.3	11.9	14.2	19.4	0.3	20.9	44.4	68.3	8.66	145	1.9	51.0
88	Fiji	6.6	7,552	20.7	14.8	..	32.5	..	12.2	117.1	23.6	5.19	144	1.4[b]	19.3
89	Thailand	907.3	13,586	28.5	13.6	7.5	38.0	0.2	10.4	168.5	24.0	3.14	124	1.9	16.4
90	Tunisia	114.4	10,612	22.7	13.8	3.3	29.0	1.1	8.9	82.2	50.4	6.03	134	1.8	19.3
91	China	14,548.6	10,771	46.1	13.5	9.7	23.1	1.7	10.1	152.7	9.4	1.07	125	2.0[b]	65.9
91	Saint Vincent and the Grenadines	1.1	10,271	25.2	16.2	..	23.6	..	7.1	56.8	42.1	4.47	131	..	..
93	Algeria	491.7	12,779	38.3	14.2	6.6	60.2	0.1	8.8	−2.1	3.4	0.35	139	..	..
93	Dominica	0.7	9,629	22.8	17.6	..	..	..	14.6	63.4	59.9	3.63	121	..	..
95	Albania	29.2	9,243	25.3	8.2	7.6	..	0.2	20.4	67.0	46.0	2.97	122	1.7	22.8
96	Jamaica	22.8[b]	8,421[b]	20.8	16.0	..	31.4	..	6.4	51.5	98.8	11.87	205	..	..
97	Saint Lucia	1.9	10,242	35.7	16.6	..	..	..	2.9	134.7	37.6	3.76	123	..	..
98	Colombia	557.5	11,687	23.6	16.1	770.6	22.0	0.2	6.5	69.6	24.3	3.15	134	1.7	30.3
98	Ecuador	153.4	9,900	26.6	13.5	7.7	..	0.3	9.4	24.3[b]	25.1	3.15	137	1.6	13.1
100	Suriname	8.1	15,174	24.9	23.3	..	..	..	9.1	26.9	..	..	179	..	..
100	Tonga	0.5	5,127	30.7	17.1	..	..	..	18.8	27.2	43.5	1.34	141	..	..
102	Dominican Republic	113.2	11,016	16.3	8.1	11.5	18.7	..	5.9	46.4	28.8	2.80	153	..	..
MEDIUM HUMAN DEVELOPMENT															
103	Maldives	3.8	11,270	40.4	16.8	..	3.1	..	4.1	70.3	50.2	5.12	174	1.7[b]	55.4
103	Mongolia	23.2	8,288	51.7	14.1	9.4	15.3	0.2	17.1	30.8	32.7	1.44	211	1.8[b]	59.0
103	Turkmenistan	64.5	12,460	54.1	9.5	..	..	..	13.8	..	2.0	0.49	..	..	..
106	Samoa	0.9	4,935	..	..	..	..	..	9.8	45.7	58.5	1.95	141	..	..
107	Palestine, State of	..	..	25.7	32.6	8.5	2.1	..	5.6	..	..	..	119[b]	..	..
108	Indonesia	2,186.3	8,856	33.1	8.9	2.3	35.6	0.1	14.4	42.6	26.0	3.80	160	2.0	23.5
109	Botswana	28.9	14,443	36.1	19.3	2.2	28.5	0.5	3.0	14.9	13.8	0.46	181	2.0	64.6
110	Egypt	862.5	10,685	16.0	11.6	3.1	29.7	0.2	14.8	79.3	15.7	1.51	204	2.0	102.7
111	Paraguay	48.3	7,215	14.7	12.2	21.0	13.8	0.1	20.9	37.2	25.7	1.83	157	1.7	66.7
112	Gabon	29.4	17,997	25.9	8.9	13.6	..	0.6	2.7	13.0	19.7	2.48	117	2.5[b]	19.7
113	Bolivia (Plurinational State of)	59.3	5,650	18.2	13.5	4.9	9.6	0.2	12.3	48.7	27.6	2.00	157	1.6[b]	35.9
114	Moldova (Republic of)	14.8	4,146	23.4	20.6	11.1	1.0	0.5	12.8	42.2	72.0	6.18	173	1.5	46.8
115	El Salvador	46.9	7,445	14.2	11.2	2.5	24.3	0.1	11.4	66.1	53.5	5.52	127	..	..

TABLE 10 Command over and allocation of resources | 197

TABLE **10**

TABLE 10 COMMAND OVER AND ALLOCATION OF RESOURCES

	GDP	GDP per capita	Gross fixed capital formation	General government final consumption expenditure		Taxes on income, profit and capital gain	Research and development expenditure	Share of agriculture, hunting, forestry and fisheries	Domestic credit provided by the banking sector	DEBT		PRICES		
										External debt stock	Total debt service	Consumer price index	Domestic food price level	
	(2011 PPP $ billions)	(2011 PPP $)	(% of GDP)	Total (% of GDP)	Average annual growth (%)	(% of total tax revenue)	(% of GDP)	(% of GDP)	(% of GDP)	(% of GNI)	(% of GNI)	(2005=100)	Index	Volatility index
HDI rank	2012	2012	2005–2012ª	2005–2012ª	2005–2012	2005–2012ª	2005–2012ª	2012	2012	2005–2012ª	2012	2012	2013	2013
116 Uzbekistan	140.1	4,705	23.5	22.7	..	..	..	19.8	..	17.8	1.32	..	..	..
117 Philippines	580.7	6,005	19.4	10.5	12.2	42.1	0.1	11.8	50.9	33.6	4.85	137	1.6	26.4
118 South Africa	626.7	11,989	19.2	22.4	4.2	50.2	0.9	2.6	187.2	28.4	1.66	155	1.5 ᵇ	35.6
118 Syrian Arab Republic	..	..	18.8	10.1	8.5	..	..	21.0	47.7 ᵇ	..	1.09	204	1.5 ᵇ	44.0
120 Iraq	473.3	14,527	..	..	..	..	..	4.1	−1.9	..	..	181 ᵇ	1.6	47.2
121 Guyana	4.8	6,054	23.9	15.4	..	..	..	18.0	50.6	..	1.78	146	..	..
121 Viet Nam	436.1	4,912	27.7	5.4	4.8	..	..	19.7	115.4	49.1	2.88	216	1.7 ᵇ	28.7
123 Cape Verde	3.1	6,311	36.5	20.7	7.7	18.2	..	9.4	76.8	55.5	2.15	130	1.5	9.1
124 Micronesia (Federated States of)	0.4	3,428	..	..	..	..	..	..	−19.0	..	..	..	..	..
125 Guatemala	105.4	6,990	14.7	10.7	6.8	29.6	0.1	11.5	39.2	35.9	4.54	148	..	..
125 Kyrgyzstan	16.0	2,847	24.0	18.2	2.2	20.3	0.2	19.5	14.0 ᵇ	..	7.24	200	..	0.0
127 Namibia	20.6	9,136	21.9	25.2	7.9	28.3	..	7.6	49.5	..	..	157	1.8	38.9
128 Timor-Leste	2.2	1,815	..	..	..	..	..	4.4	−52.7	..	..	171	..	..
129 Honduras	35.1	4,423	24.3	16.1	1.3	22.7	..	14.0	55.9	28.5	6.12	156	..	..
129 Morocco	227.5	6,878	31.4	19.2	7.9	25.4	0.6	13.7	115.4	29.4	3.36	114	1.6	19.8
131 Vanuatu	0.7	2,894	26.2	18.1	..	..	..	21.9	68.2 ᵇ	25.4	0.83	122	..	..
132 Nicaragua	25.5	4,254	25.2	6.9	4.5	29.6	..	20.0	44.0	101.0	7.02	184	..	..
133 Kiribati	0.2	1,772	..	..	..	..	..	25.7	..	..	..	..	..	..
133 Tajikistan	18.6	2,320	18.7	9.9	1.2	..	0.1	23.1	13.1	51.6	8.99	202	..	..
135 India	6,245.4	5,050	29.6	11.8	3.9	49.5	0.8	17.4	76.6	18.3	1.57	181	1.6 ᵇ	35.0
136 Bhutan	5.6	7,490	56.1	20.8	−2.1	15.9	..	18.1	50.4	65.0	4.90	160	1.8 ᵇ	28.2
136 Cambodia	41.5	2,789	16.0	6.0	7.8	12.1	..	35.6	33.8	35.3	0.63	160	1.2	101.3
138 Ghana	92.3	3,638	29.0	13.6	5.1	24.7	0.2	22.7	32.3	29.8	0.91	224	1.7	44.8
139 Lao People's Democratic Republic	29.2	4,388	27.7	9.9	11.8	15.8	..	31.7	26.5 ᵇ	80.3	3.63	143	2.2 ᵇ	25.9
140 Congo	24.4	5,631	25.1	10.0	2.8	4.9	..	3.6	−8.9	23.1	0.96	137	2.5 ᵇ	10.4
141 Zambia	42.1	2,990	23.4	20.6	38.8	44.0	0.3	18.2	18.5	24.7	1.05	189	1.4	19.0
142 Bangladesh	365.7	2,364	25.4	5.7	5.6	22.4	..	17.3	69.2	22.6	1.22	174	1.6 ᵇ	20.3
142 Sao Tome and Principe	0.5	2,837	..	..	..	..	..	20.5	35.1	92.2	0.67	321	2.4 ᵇ	39.0
144 Equatorial Guinea	27.6	37,479	40.0	3.7	3.4	..	..	2.0	−3.5	..	..	147	..	0.0
LOW HUMAN DEVELOPMENT														
145 Nepal	58.5	2,131	19.6	10.3	12.5	19.2	..	35.7	67.0	20.8	1.06	186	1.6 ᵇ	35.1
146 Pakistan	781.2	4,360	10.9	8.3	8.2	28.8	0.5	24.4	44.5	27.3	1.34	222	2.1	46.5
147 Kenya	91.1	2,109	20.4	17.2	9.3	42.5	0.4	29.6	52.3	30.4	1.27	225	2.4 ᵇ	57.3
148 Swaziland	7.3	5,912	9.6	15.3	−5.8	..	..	7.3	21.1	15.5	1.16	167	..	22.6
149 Angola	152.9	7,346	11.4	19.5	..	..	..	9.4	15.9	23.4	3.12	233	2.4 ᵇ	133.7
150 Myanmar	..	..	..	..	..	25.2	..	36.4	..	..	..	239	..	..
151 Rwanda	15.8	1,379	22.8	8.2	15.2	..	..	35.1	8.0 ᵇ	17.5	0.31	174	1.8 ᵇ	30.3
152 Cameroon	55.4	2,551	19.8	14.9	9.8	..	..	23.3	15.2	12.2	1.28	124	2.0 ᵇ	11.2
152 Nigeria	918.4	5,440	..	..	..	0.6	0.2	33.1	35.3	6.1	0.19	201	2.4 ᵇ	38.6
154 Yemen	95.3	3,996	11.7	11.8	−14.1	..	..	14.6	26.9	20.5	0.93	228	1.6 ᵇ	49.6
155 Madagascar	30.7	1,378	32.6	10.0	3.9	11.8	0.1	27.5	12.9	28.4	0.43	185	2.0	32.6
156 Zimbabwe	18.4	1,337	12.4	23.8	..	..	..	17.5	75.5 ᵇ	64.8	12.45	1,197 ᵇ	2.1	54.0
157 Papua New Guinea	17.1	2,382	..	..	..	..	..	29.1	38.3	101.2	9.86	144	..	..
157 Solomon Islands	1.1	1,964	13.4	39.2	..	..	..	28.9	12.0	37.9	2.27	167	..	..
159 Comoros	1.1	1,493	12.4	15.3	..	..	..	50.9	21.6	45.6	0.65	123	..	..
159 Tanzania (United Republic of)	76.8	1,654	36.1	16.4	14.2	..	0.4	28.3 ᶜ	24.8	42.6	0.64	197	2.2 ᵇ	20.7
161 Mauritania	11.2	2,938	38.9	15.2	6.4	..	..	23.6	36.8	70.8	2.72	147	1.8 ᵇ	55.7
162 Lesotho	4.9	2,368	31.8	38.1	17.6	17.4	0.0	8.2	3.1	27.1	1.40	157	2.0 ᵇ	31.7
163 Senegal	29.8	2,174	30.3	8.7	4.8	..	0.4	17.0	31.0	30.6	2.50	120	1.9	78.5
164 Uganda	48.5	1,334	24.4	11.3	3.3	39.1	0.4	24.2	16.4	23.5	0.44	203	2.0	54.0
165 Benin	17.0	1,687	17.6	11.9	2.9	17.1	..	35.3	19.7	19.5	0.53	130	..	..
166 Sudan	125.4	3,370	19.2	10.9	20.9	..	..	41.8 ᵈ	24.5	..	0.91	280	..	..
166 Togo	8.5	1,286	18.6	9.8	15.8	10.3	..	47.1	37.6	18.1	0.46	125	2.2 ᵇ	284.3
168 Haiti	16.0	1,575	..	9.1	..	..	..	18.8	19.6	10.6	0.07	173	..	..
169 Afghanistan	56.4 ᵇ	1,892 ᵇ	16.6	16.0	..	2.7	..	30.3	−3.0 ᵇ	..	0.06	164	..	..
170 Djibouti	..	..	37.5	25.1	8.0	..	..	3.7	26.5 ᵇ	..	..	145	..	..
171 Côte d'Ivoire	54.5	2,747	10.1	8.6	0.4	..	..	30.0	27.3	52.1	2.36	121	2.1 ᵇ	51.9
172 Gambia	2.8	1,565	19.2	9.6	−3.4	..	0.0	23.0	43.9	43.6	2.82	129 ᵇ	2.8 ᵇ	23.7
173 Ethiopia	111.8	1,218	25.5	8.1	−0.8	16.0	0.2	48.4	37.1 ᵇ	27.2	1.12	365	1.9	100.6

TABLE 10

	GDP	GDP per capita	Gross fixed capital formation	General government final consumption expenditure		Taxes on income, profit and capital gain	Research and development expenditure	Share of agriculture, hunting, forestry and fisheries	Domestic credit provided by the banking sector	DEBT External debt stock	Total debt service	PRICES Consumer price index	Domestic food price level	
	(2011 PPP $ billions)	(2011 PPP $)	(% of GDP)	Total (% of GDP)	Average annual growth (%)	(% of total tax revenue)	(% of GDP)	(% of GDP)	(% of GDP)	(% of GNI)	(% of GNI)	(2005=100)	Index	Volatility index
HDI rank	2012	2012	2005–2012a	2005–2012a	2005–2012	2005–2012a	2005–2012a	2012	2012	2005–2012a	2012	2012	2013	2013
174 Malawi	11.8	739	13.5	19.9	10.0	..	..	32.0	35.6	22.3	0.39	203	1.9 b	67.0
175 Liberia	3.3	782	25.0	15.2	2.9	25.5	..	70.7	33.3	42.9	0.24	188	..	..
176 Mali	23.9	1,607	22.2	17.1	3.8	21.8	0.2	42.3	19.9	29.1	0.67	126	2.0	24.0
177 Guinea-Bissau	1.9	1,164	..	..	..	..	..	46.4	18.6	29.2	0.53	127	2.0 b	11.7
178 Mozambique	24.5	971	24.7	14.0	14.7	..	0.2	30.0	28.1	32.1	0.46	175	2.1 b	23.5
179 Guinea	13.9	1,216	17.6	10.6	69.2	..	..	25.9	32.2 b	65.6	3.67	331	2.9 b	66.7
180 Burundi	7.3	737	20.0	28.0	2.3	..	..	39.7	26.1	26.9	0.36	211	..	0.0
181 Burkina Faso	25.1	1,528	16.7	19.3	9.5	19.2	0.2	35.0	19.8	23.8	0.68	123	2.1	34.8
182 Eritrea	7.2	1,180	10.0	21.1	−9.5	..	..	16.9	104.0 b	40.8	0.86	..	..	..
183 Sierra Leone	9.5	1,586	40.3	10.1	2.0	21.8	..	45.8	14.0	48.2	0.71	214	2.4 b	108.9
184 Chad	24.9	2,003	31.8	13.2	−0.9	..	..	18.7	6.2	21.4	0.81	122	2.7 b	60.6
185 Central African Republic	4.4	964	12.5	8.1	−2.2	..	..	54.3	26.8	26.5	0.03	132	..	11.2
186 Congo (Democratic Republic of the)	29.6	451	20.5	13.2	6.9	11.9	0.5	41.6	10.7	37.9	1.76	2,378 b	..	..
187 Niger	15.2	884	36.8	14.4	..	11.6	..	40.4	13.6	23.7	0.58	117	2.5 b	31.9
OTHER COUNTRIES OR TERRITORIES														
Korea, Democratic People's Rep. of	..	..	..	..	..	..	..	21.2	..	..	..	..	..	..
Marshall Islands	0.2	3,526	..	..	..	..	..	14.1	..	..	..	..	..	..
Monaco	..	..	..	..	..	..	0.0	..	..	..	..	..	..	..
Nauru	..	..	..	..	..	..	..	5.1	..	..	..	..	..	..
San Marino	..	..	..	..	..	16.9	..	0.1	..	..	..	120	..	..
Somalia	..	..	..	..	..	..	..	60.2	..	..	..	..	..	..
South Sudan	19.4	1,790	10.5	17.1	16.8	..	..	9.7	..	..	..	149 b	..	..
Tuvalu	0.0	3,489	..	..	..	..	..	22.8	..	..	..	..	..	..
Human Development Index groups														
Very high human development	45,473.5	40,397	18.2	19.2	0.7	37.2	2.5	1.5	203.4	..	..	—	—	—
High human development	31,426.4	12,920	33.0	14.9	21.9	23.5	..	7.8	109.5	20.7	2.74	—	—	—
Medium human development	12,959.8	5,875	27.4	12.0	6.3	..	..	14.4	72.5	23.8	2.17	—	—	—
Low human development	3,010.1	2,830	17.1	12.6	6.3	..	..	28.1	32.8	23.4	1.17	—	—	—
Regions														
Arab States	5,098.0	16,367	23.7	14.5	..	..	..	8.1	24.8	..	..	—	—	—
East Asia and the Pacific	19,423.3	10,151	..	..	..	..	..	10.7	139.8	..	..	—	—	—
Europe and Central Asia	2,879.7	12,453	22.0	15.0	4.5	23.8	0.7	9.0	62.8	50.0	9.19	—	—	—
Latin America and the Caribbean	7,482.5	13,554	20.1	16.6	37.0	..	..	5.6	73.0	22.7	3.18	—	—	—
South Asia	8,878.4	5,147	27.0	11.3	1.2	41.9	..	18.1	72.1	20.0	1.43	—	—	—
Sub-Saharan Africa	2,797.2	3,237	21.0	17.8	5.8	..	..	18.4	77.2	24.0	1.24	—	—	—
Least developed countries	1,602.4	1,971	21.6	12.4	6.1	..	..	24.6	31.5	27.4	1.22	—	—	—
Small island developing states	286.4	6,736	..	..	..	..	..	8.7	52.5	..	..	—	—	—
World	92,889.4	13,599	22.6	17.6	5.8	..	..	4.4	168.0	..	..	—	—	—

TABLE **10**

NOTES

a Data refer to the most recent year available during the period specified.

b Refers to a year earlier than that specified.

c Mainland Tanzania only.

d Excludes South Sudan.

DEFINITIONS

Gross domestic product (GDP): Sum of gross value added by all resident producers in the economy plus any product taxes and minus any subsidies not included in the value of the products, expressed in 2005 international dollars using purchasing power parity rates.

GDP per capita: GDP in a particular period divided by the total population for the same period.

Gross fixed capital formation: Value of acquisitions of new or existing fixed assets by the business sector, governments and households (excluding their unincorporated enterprises) less disposals of fixed assets, expressed as a percentage of GDP. No adjustment is made for depreciation of fixed assets.

General government final consumption expenditure: All government current expenditures for purchases of goods and services (including compensation of employees and most expenditures on national defense and security but excluding government military expenditures that are part of government capital formation), expressed as a percentage of GDP.

Taxes on income, profit and capital gain: Taxes levied on the actual or presumptive net income of individuals, on the profits of corporations and enterprises, and on capital gains, whether realized or not, on land, securities and other assets.

Research and development expenditure: Current and capital expenditures (both public and private) on creative work undertaken systematically to increase knowledge and the use of knowledge for new applications, expressed as a percentage of GDP. It covers basic research, applied research, and experimental development.

Shares of agriculture, hunting, forestry and fisheries: Gross value added in the agriculture, hunting, forestry and fishery sectors, expressed as a percentage of a GDP.

Domestic credit provided by the banking sector: Credit to various sectors on a gross basis, with exception of credit to the central government, which is net, expressed as a percentage of GDP.

External debt stock as a percentage of GNI: Debt owed to nonresidents repayable in foreign currency, goods or services, expressed as a percentage of gross national income.

Total debt service: Sum of principal repayments and interest actually paid in foreign currency, goods or services on long-term debt; interest paid on short-term debt; and repayments (repurchases and charges) to the International Monetary Fund, expressed as a percentage of GNI.

Consumer price index: Index that reflects changes in the cost to the average consumer of acquiring a basket of goods and services that may be fixed or changed at specified intervals, such as yearly.

Domestic food price level index: Food purchasing power parity (PPP) rate divided by the general PPP rate. The index shows the price of food in a country relative to the price of the generic consumption basket in the country.

Domestic food price level volatility index: A measure of variation of the domestic food price level index, computed as the standard deviation of the deviations from the trend over the previous five years.

MAIN DATA SOURCES

Columns 1 and 2: World Bank 2014.

Columns 3–7 and 9–12: World Bank 2013a.

Column 8: United Nations Statistics Division 2013a.

Columns 13 and 14: FAO 2013a.

TABLE 10 Command over and allocation of resources | 199

TABLE 11

Social competencies

		Employment and vulnerability							Birth registration	Old age pension recipients[a] (% of statutory pension-age population)			Suicide rate (per 100,000)	
		Employment to population ratio	Vulnerable employment	Youth unemployment	Unemployment rate	Child labour	Share of working poor (PPP $2 a day)	Mandatory paid maternity leave		Total	Female	Male	Female	Male
		(% ages 25 and older)	(% of total employment)	(% ages 15–24)	(% ages 15 and older)	(% ages 5–14)	(% of total employment)	(days)	(% under age 5)					
HDI rank		2012	2003–2012[b]	2008–2012[b]	2004–2013[b]	2005–2012	2003–2010[b]	2013	2005–2012[b]	2004–2013[b]	2004–2013[b]	2004–2013[b]	2003–2009[b]	2003–2009[b]
VERY HIGH HUMAN DEVELOPMENT														
1	Norway	65.5	..	8.6	3.1	..	..	..	100.0	100.0	100.0	100.0	6.5	17.3
2	Australia	62.3	9.0	11.7	5.2	..	..	..	100.0	83.0	87.6	77.5	3.6	12.8
3	Switzerland	65.9	9.1	8.4	4.2	..	..	98	100.0	100.0	100.0	100.0	11.4	24.8
4	Netherlands	61.0	11.5	9.5	5.3	..	..	112	100.0	100.0	100.0	100.0	5.5	13.1
5	United States	61.0	..	16.2	7.4	..	..	..	100.0	92.5	..	..	4.5	17.7
6	Germany	58.0	6.8	8.1	5.5	..	..	98	100.0	100.0	100.0	100.0	6.0	17.9
7	New Zealand	66.2	12.1	17.7	6.9	..	..	98	100.0	98.0	96.5	99.8	5.5	18.1
8	Canada	62.9	..	14.3	7.2	..	..	105	100.0	97.7	..	..	5.4	17.3
9	Singapore	72.5	9.3	6.7	3.1	..	..	112	..	..	..	..	7.7	12.9
10	Denmark	59.2	..	14.1	7.5	..	..	126	100.0	100.0	100.0	100.0	6.4	17.5
11	Ireland	55.6	11.7	30.4	14.7	..	..	182	100.0	90.5	66.3	100.0	4.7	19.0
12	Sweden	62.7	..	23.7	8.0	..	..	..	100.0	100.0	100.0	100.0	6.8	18.7
13	Iceland	71.2	..	13.6	6.0	..	..	90	100.0	100.0	100.0	100.0	7.0	16.5
14	United Kingdom	59.1	..	21.0	7.9	..	..	273	100.0	99.5	99.2	100.0	3.0	10.9
15	Hong Kong, China (SAR)	60.9	7.4	9.3	3.3	..	..	70	..	72.9	..	..	10.7	19.0
15	Korea (Republic of)	65.4	24.8	9.0	3.2	..	..	90	..	77.6	..	..	22.1	39.9
17	Japan	58.5	10.5	7.9	4.3	..	..	98	100.0	80.3	..	..	13.2	36.2
18	Liechtenstein	..	..	..	2.5[c]	..	..	..	100.0	..	..	..	..	..
19	Israel	63.4	7.2	12.1	6.8	..	..	98	100.0	73.6	..	..	1.5	7.0
20	France	54.4	7.1	23.8	9.9	..	..	112	100.0	100.0	100.0	100.0	8.5	24.7
21	Austria	58.9	8.6	8.7	4.3	..	..	112	100.0	100.0	93.7	77.5	7.1	23.8
21	Belgium	53.0	10.3	19.8	7.5	..	..	105	100.0	84.6	67.8	100.0	10.3	28.8
21	Luxembourg	60.5	5.7	18.8	5.1	..	..	..	100.0	90.0	56.4	100.0	3.2	16.1
24	Finland	57.6	..	17.7	7.7	..	..	147	100.0	100.0	100.0	100.0	10.0	29.0
25	Slovenia	56.4	12.8	20.6	8.8	..	..	105	100.0	95.1	85.9	100.0	9.4	34.6
26	Italy	47.1	18.2	35.3	10.7	..	..	150	100.0	81.1	69.2	100.0	2.8	10.0
27	Spain	47.9	..	53.2	25.0	..	..	112	100.0	68.2	46.6	97.4	3.4	11.9
28	Czech Republic	59.3	15.0	19.5	7.0	..	..	196	100.0	100.0	100.0	100.0	4.4	23.9
29	Greece	43.8	29.7	55.3	24.2	..	..	119	100.0	77.4	54.6	100.0	1.0	6.0
30	Brunei Darussalam	68.1	..	..	1.7	..	..	..	..	81.7	..	..	..	..
31	Qatar	89.8	0.4	1.3	0.4	..	..	..	..	7.9	..	..	..	..
32	Cyprus	62.4	12.5	27.8	11.8	..	..	..	100.0	85.2	57.2	100.0	1.7	7.4
33	Estonia	59.4	..	20.9	10.2	..	..	140	100.0	98.0	97.5	98.5	7.3	30.6
34	Saudi Arabia	60.4	..	28.3	5.6	..	..	70	..	..	..	..	..	..
35	Lithuania	58.5	8.9	26.4	13.2	..	..	126	100.0	100.0	100.0	100.0	10.4	61.3
35	Poland	55.5	18.2	26.5	10.1	..	..	182	100.0	96.5	94.9	100.0	4.1	26.4
37	Andorra	..	..	..	..	..	..	..	100.0	..	..	..	..	..
37	Slovakia	57.0	12.4	34.0	14.0	..	..	238	100.0	100.0	100.0	100.0	3.4	22.3
39	Malta	49.9	8.9	14.2	6.4	..	..	..	100.0	60.5	32.0	97.5	1.0	5.9
40	United Arab Emirates	84.4	1.0	12.1	4.2	..	..	45	100.0	..	..	..	..	..
41	Chile	64.8	24.4	16.3	6.0	2.9	0.0	126	99.8[d]	74.5	73.4	76.4	4.2	18.2
41	Portugal	55.5	16.7	37.6	15.7	3.4[d,e]	..	..	100.0	100.0	100.0	100.0	4.0	15.6
43	Hungary	50.7	..	28.1	10.9	..	..	168	100.0	91.4	87.6	97.7	10.6	40.0
44	Bahrain	72.5	2.0	5.0	1.1	4.6	..	..	..	40.1	..	..	3.5	4.0
44	Cuba	58.4	..	3.1	3.2	..	..	..	100.0[d]	..	..	..	5.5	19.0
46	Kuwait	76.3	2.2	..	3.6	..	..	70	..	27.3	..	..	1.7	1.9
47	Croatia	47.4	16.5	43.1	15.8	..	0.0	208	..	57.6	44.2	85.1	7.5	28.9
48	Latvia	55.0	..	28.4	14.9	..	..	112	100.0	100.0	100.0	100.0	8.2	40.0
49	Argentina	62.5	19.0	18.3	7.3	6.5[d]	1.8	90	99.0[d,e]	90.7	93.3	86.8	3.0	12.6
HIGH HUMAN DEVELOPMENT														
50	Uruguay	65.3	..	18.5	6.4	7.9[d]	0.0	84	100.0	68.2	64.4	73.6	6.3	26.0
51	Bahamas	70.8	..	30.8	14.7	..	..	..	..	84.2	..	..	0.6	1.9
51	Montenegro	44.9	..	41.1	19.7	9.9	..	45	99.0	52.3	..	..	..	..
53	Belarus	53.9	2.1	12.5	0.7	1.4	0.0	126	100.0	93.6	..	..	8.8	48.7
54	Romania	57.3	31.5	22.7	7.0	0.9[e]	..	126	..	98.0	88.0	100.0	3.5	21.0
55	Libya	55.4	..	..	..	..	..	..	..	43.3	..	..	..	..
56	Oman	67.6	..	..	..	..	..	42	..	24.7	..	..	..	..
57	Russian Federation	65.0	..	14.8	5.5	..	0.0	140	100.0	100.0	100.0	100.0	9.5	53.9

		Employment and vulnerability								Old age pension recipients[a]			Suicide rate	
		Employment to population ratio	Vulnerable employment	Youth unemployment	Unemployment rate	Child labour	Share of working poor (PPP $2 a day)	Mandatory paid maternity leave	Birth registration	(% of statutory pension-age population)			(per 100,000)	
		(% ages 25 and older)	(% of total employment)	(% ages 15–24)	(% ages 15 and older)	(% ages 5–14)	(% of total employment)	(days)	(% under age 5)	Total	Female	Male	Female	Male
HDI rank		2012	2003–2012[b]	2008–2012[b]	2004–2013[b]	2005–2012	2003–2010[b]	2013	2005–2012[b]	2004–2013[b]	2004–2013[b]	2004–2013[b]	2003–2009[b]	2003–2009[b]
58	Bulgaria	50.3	8.0	28.1	12.3	..	..	410	100.0	96.9	95.5	99.4	6.2	18.8
59	Barbados	67.5	14.0	..	11.6	..	..	..	..	68.3	..	..	0.0	7.3
60	Palau	..	..	..	..	..	..	..	..	48.0	..	..	..	..
61	Antigua and Barbuda	..	..	..	..	..	..	..	..	69.7	..	..	..	..
62	Malaysia	65.5	..	10.3	3.0	..	1.9	60	..	19.8	..	..	..	..
63	Mauritius	59.3	16.2	23.7	8.1	..	..	84	..	100.0	100.0	100.0	1.9	11.8
64	Trinidad and Tobago	64.5	15.6	10.5	5.0 f	0.7	..	..	97.0	98.7	..	..	3.8	17.9
65	Lebanon	50.0	33.9	16.8	9.0	1.9	..	49	99.5	0.0	..	..	..	..
65	Panama	68.8	29.2	10.3	6.5	5.6 d	6.8	98	..	37.3	28.9	49.4	1.9	9.0
67	Venezuela (Bolivarian Republic of)	68.2	31.8	17.1	7.5	7.7 e	8.2	182	81.0 d,e	59.4	50.2	70.0	1.2	5.3
68	Costa Rica	64.0	20.2	18.4	7.8	4.7	4.2	120	55.8	48.8	65.4	1.9	10.2	
69	Turkey	48.5	32.1	17.5	8.1	2.6 d	6.4	112	93.7	88.1	..	..	..	..
70	Kazakhstan	75.2	29.2	3.9	5.8	2.2	1.1	126	99.7	95.9	..	..	9.4	43.0
71	Mexico	63.9	..	9.4	4.8	6.3	6.5	84	93.4	25.2	17.2	34.6	1.5	7.0
71	Seychelles	..	..	..	..	..	..	..	..	100.0	..	..	0.0	8.9
73	Saint Kitts and Nevis	..	..	..	..	..	..	..	..	44.7	39.7	51.6	..	..
73	Sri Lanka	57.9	..	17.3	5.0	..	26.0	84	97.2	17.1	..	..	..	..
75	Iran (Islamic Republic of)	44.7	..	23.0	13.5	11.4	6.2	90	98.6	26.4	..	..	..	..
76	Azerbaijan	73.0	54.7	14.2	5.2	6.5 d	6.1	126	93.6	81.7	79.0	82.6	0.3	1.0
77	Jordan	44.3	9.7	29.3	12.2	1.9 d	2.8	70	99.1	42.2	11.8	82.3	0.0	0.2
77	Serbia	47.2	26.4	51.1	23.9	4.4	..	135	98.9	46.1	44.8	48.4	10.0	28.1
79	Brazil	68.4	..	15.4	6.2	8.6 d	5.9	120	93.4 d	86.3	83.0	90.6	2.0	7.7
79	Georgia	62.4	60.6	33.3	15.0	18.4	26.8	126	98.5	89.8	..	..	1.7	7.1
79	Grenada	..	..	..	..	..	..	..	..	34.0	..	..	0.0	0.0
82	Peru	78.9	46.3	9.5	6.8 g	33.5 d	13.5	90	96.0	33.2	26.1	41.4	1.0	1.9
83	Ukraine	58.2	..	17.3	7.5	7.3	0.0	126	99.8	95.0	..	..	7.0	37.8
84	Belize	66.9	..	..	14.4	5.8	..	..	95.2	64.6	..	..	0.7	6.6
84	The former Yugoslav Republic of Macedonia	42.9	22.1	53.9	31.0	12.5	3.4	270	99.7	52.2	..	..	4.0	9.5
86	Bosnia and Herzegovina	36.4	27.4	62.8	28.0	5.3	0.0	365	99.5	29.6	..	..	..	..
87	Armenia	58.6	..	39.2	28.6	3.9 d	9.0	140	99.6	80.0	..	..	1.1	2.8
88	Fiji	56.3	38.8	..	4.6	..	49.7	84	..	10.6	..	..	..	..
89	Thailand	77.0	53.5	2.8	0.6	8.3	10.1	45	100.0	81.7	84.6	77.9	3.8	12.0
90	Tunisia	47.1	28.8	42.3	17.6	2.1	..	30	99.2	68.8	..	..	..	..
91	China	72.2	..	..	4.1 h	..	..	98	..	74.4	..	..	..	..
91	Saint Vincent and the Grenadines	..	8.0	33.8	..	..	..	..	..	76.6	..	..	1.9	5.4
93	Algeria	45.4	29.5	22.4	9.8	4.7 d	..	98	99.3	63.6	..	..	..	..
93	Dominica	..	..	..	..	..	..	..	..	38.5	..	..	..	..
95	Albania	53.3	..	22.5	13.8	12.0	3.4	365	98.6	77.0	60.8	100.0	3.3	4.7
96	Jamaica	65.3	..	34.0	13.9	6.1	4.6	56	97.8	55.5	..	..	..	..
97	Saint Lucia	..	..	..	21.0	..	..	..	..	26.5	8.3	10.3	0.0	4.9
98	Colombia	68.2	..	21.9	11.8	13.0 d	22.6	98	96.5	23.0	18.4	28.3	2.0	7.9
98	Ecuador	72.2	..	11.1	5.0	7.5	12.1	84	90.0	53.0	50.8	55.5	3.6	10.5
100	Suriname	56.3	..	..	9.5	4.1	..	..	98.9	..	..	..	4.8	23.9
100	Tonga	..	55.2	..	1.1	..	..	..	..	1.0	..	..	..	..
102	Dominican Republic	63.2	..	29.4	14.7	12.9	10.7	84	82.4	11.1	6.2	16.5	0.7	3.9
MEDIUM HUMAN DEVELOPMENT														
103	Maldives	67.4	29.6	..	11.7	..	11.2	..	92.5	99.7	..	..	0.0	0.7
103	Mongolia	69.3	54.9	11.9	9.9	10.4	..	120	99.0	100.0	..	..	..	..
103	Turkmenistan	62.1	..	..	4.0	..	..	..	95.5	..	..	..	..	..
106	Samoa	..	38.1	16.1	..	..	..	..	47.7	49.5	..	..	..	..
107	Palestine, State of	40.3	26.7	38.8	22.9	5.7	..	70	99.3 d	8.0	..	..	..	..
108	Indonesia	70.7	57.2	22.2	6.2	6.9 d	52.0	90	67.0	8.1	..	..	..	..
109	Botswana	74.5	..	..	17.6	9.0 d	..	84	72.2	100.0	100.0	100.0	..	..
110	Egypt	51.2	23.1	24.8	9.0	9.3	14.4	90	99.0	32.7	8.0	61.7	0.0	0.1
111	Paraguay	71.5	..	11.2	5.7	14.6	11.0	63	76.0	22.2	20.0	24.9	2.0	5.1
112	Gabon	63.2	52.9	..	20.4	13.4	14.2	98	89.6 e	38.8	..	..	..	..
113	Bolivia (Plurinational State of)	78.5	..	6.2	5.2	26.4 d	23.4	84	75.8 d	100.0	100.0	100.0	..	..
114	Moldova (Republic of)	42.7	28.6	13.1	5.6	16.3	10.9	126	100.0 e	72.8	77.0	63.7	5.6	30.1
115	El Salvador	64.5	..	12.4	6.4	10.4 d	12.1	84	98.6	18.1	10.3	31.6	3.6	12.9

TABLE 11

TABLE 11 Social competencies | 201

TABLE 11   SOCIAL COMPETENCIES

	Employment and vulnerability								Old age pension recipients[a]			Suicide rate	
	Employment to population ratio	Vulnerable employment	Youth unemployment	Unemployment rate	Child labour	Share of working poor (PPP $2 a day)	Mandatory paid maternity leave	Birth registration	(% of statutory pension-age population)			(per 100,000)	
	(% ages 25 and older)	(% of total employment)	(% ages 15–24)	(% ages 15 and older)	(% ages 5–14)	(% of total employment)	(days)	(% under age 5)	Total	Female	Male	Female	Male
HDI rank	2012	2003–2012[b]	2008–2012[b]	2004–2013[b]	2005–2012	2003–2010[b]	2013	2005–2012[b]	2004–2013[b]	2004–2013[b]	2004–2013[b]	2003–2009[b]	2003–2009[b]
116 Uzbekistan	62.6	..	..	0.4[c]	..	66.5	126	99.9	98.1	..	..	2.3	7.0
117 Philippines	69.3	39.8	16.3	7.3	..	40.9	60	90.0[e]	28.5	..	..	..	..
118 South Africa	48.6	10.1	51.5	25.1[e]	..	19.7	120	95.0[e]	92.6	..	..	0.4	1.4
118 Syrian Arab Republic	47.0	32.9	19.2	8.6	4.0	12.9	120	96.0	16.7	..	..	..	..
120 Iraq	44.0	..	..	8.0[i]	4.7	16.6	..	99.2	56.0	..	..	..	..
121 Guyana	56.2	..	..	..	16.4	..	..	87.9	100.0	..	..	13.4	39.0
121 Viet Nam	80.9	62.5	5.5	1.8	6.9	37.3	180	95.0	34.5	..	..	..	..
123 Cape Verde	66.8	..	..	..	3.2[d,e]	..	..	91.4	55.7	52.8	59.8	..	..
124 Micronesia (Federated States of)	..	..	..	..	..	..	..	..	..	..	..	..	..
125 Guatemala	69.1	..	7.5	2.9	25.8[d]	..	84	96.7	14.1	10.3	18.2	1.7	5.6
125 Kyrgyzstan	70.7	47.3	..	8.4	3.6	25.5	126	96.0	100.0	100.0	100.0	3.6	14.1
127 Namibia	63.5	32.7	34.3	16.7	..	..	84	78.0	98.4	..	..	..	..
128 Timor-Leste	54.0	69.6	14.8	..	4.2	68.2	..	55.2	100.0	..	..	..	..
129 Honduras	66.6	..	8.0	4.3	15.6	29.6	84	93.6	8.4	5.8	13.8	..	..
129 Morocco	51.5	50.7	18.6	9.0	8.3	13.0	98	94.0[d,e]	39.8	..	..	..	..
131 Vanuatu	..	70.0	..	5.5	..	..	..	43.0	3.5	..	..	..	..
132 Nicaragua	65.5	..	11.9	7.8	14.5[e]	27.4	84	85.0[d]	23.7	16.2	42.3	2.6	9.0
133 Kiribati	..	..	..	30.6	..	..	..	93.5	..	..	..	..	..
133 Tajikistan	71.1	..	16.7	11.5	10.0	48.3	140	88.3	80.2	72.1	95.6	2.3	2.9
135 India	60.8	80.8	10.7	9.3	11.8	74.5	84	41.1	24.1	..	..	7.8	13.0
136 Bhutan	81.0	53.1	7.2	2.0	2.9	50.8	..	99.9	3.2	..	..	..	..
136 Cambodia	85.8	..	3.4	7.1[i]	36.1[d]	53.1	90	62.1	5.0	..	..	..	..
138 Ghana	81.6	76.8	..	5.3[e]	33.9	48.3	84	62.5	7.6	..	..	..	..
139 Lao People's Democratic Republic	85.0	..	..	1.4	10.1	64.0	90	74.8	5.6	..	..	..	..
140 Congo	78.6	75.1	..	10.0[i]	24.7	72.9	105	91.0[d]	22.1	4.7	42.4	..	..
141 Zambia	79.9	81.0	..	13.2[k]	40.6[d]	76.1	84	14.0	7.7	..	..	..	..
142 Bangladesh	73.4	85.0	..	4.5	12.8	80.1	112	30.5	39.5	..	..	..	..
142 Sao Tome and Principe	..	..	..	16.6	7.5	..	..	75.1	41.8	..	..	..	..
144 Equatorial Guinea	86.5	..	..	..	27.8[e]	14.0	..	37.0[e]	..	..	..	..	..
LOW HUMAN DEVELOPMENT													
145 Nepal	85.2	..	..	..	33.9[d]	74.1	52	42.3	62.5	..	..	..	..
146 Pakistan	56.3	..	7.7	5.5	..	57.0	84	26.5	2.3	..	..	..	..
147 Kenya	75.6	..	..	..	25.9[e]	33.6	90	60.0	7.9	..	..	..	..
148 Swaziland	56.1	..	..	28.2	7.3	..	..	49.5	86.0	..	..	..	..
149 Angola	75.5	..	..	..	23.5[e]	..	90	36.0[e]	14.5	..	..	..	..
150 Myanmar	83.1	..	..	..	..	60.8	..	72.4	..	..	..	..	..
151 Rwanda	92.6	..	..	..	28.5	87.4	84	63.2	4.7	..	..	..	..
152 Cameroon	80.5	..	..	3.8	41.7	..	98	61.4	12.5	5.9	20.2	..	..
152 Nigeria	61.7	..	..	23.9[i]	24.7	79.2	84	41.5	..	..	..	..	..
154 Yemen	50.0	..	33.7	16.2	22.7[e]	33.5	70	17.0	8.5	..	..	..	..
155 Madagascar	91.4	..	..	3.8	28.1[d]	88.1	98	79.7	4.6	..	..	..	..
156 Zimbabwe	88.6	..	..	5.4	..	87.1	98	48.8	6.2	..	..	..	..
157 Papua New Guinea	77.9	..	..	..	..	..	..	..	0.9	..	..	..	..
157 Solomon Islands	72.8	..	..	..	..	44.2	..	..	13.1	..	..	..	..
159 Comoros	62.4	..	..	..	27.1[e]	61.2	..	88.0[e]	..	..	..	..	..
159 Tanzania (United Republic of)	91.9	87.7	7.1	4.3	21.1[d]	84.7	84	16.3	3.2	..	..	..	..
161 Mauritania	44.5	..	..	10.1[e]	14.6	..	98	58.8	9.3[d]	..	..	..	..
162 Lesotho	59.9	..	34.4	24.4	22.9[e]	51.2	84	45.1	100.0	100.0	100.0	..	..
163 Senegal	75.5	..	..	10.4	16.5[d]	61.1	98	74.6	23.5	..	..	..	..
164 Uganda	86.8	..	5.4	9.1[g]	25.4[d]	61.7	60	29.9	6.6	..	..	..	..
165 Benin	80.8	89.9	..	..	45.6	71.3	98	80.2	9.7	..	..	..	..
166 Sudan	55.1	..	22.9	19.8	..	..	56	59.3	4.6	..	..	..	..
166 Togo	83.9	89.1	..	..	28.3	66.7	98	77.9	10.9	..	..	..	..
168 Haiti	75.5	..	..	..	24.4	..	42	79.7	1.0	..	..	0.0	0.0
169 Afghanistan	52.2	..	..	8.5	10.3	73.6	..	37.4	10.7	..	..	..	..
170 Djibouti	..	..	..	..	7.7	..	..	92.0	12.0[d]	..	..	..	..
171 Côte d'Ivoire	73.1	..	..	..	26.0	45.5	98	65.0	7.7	..	..	..	..
172 Gambia	80.4	..	..	..	19.2	54.5	..	52.5	10.8	..	..	..	..
173 Ethiopia	84.1	..	..	17.5[e,j]	27.4[e]	73.1	90	6.6	9.0	..	..	..	..

TABLE
11

	Employment and vulnerability								Old age pension recipients[a]			Suicide rate	
	Employment to population ratio	Vulnerable employment	Youth unemployment	Unemployment rate	Child labour	Share of working poor (PPP $2 a day)	Mandatory paid maternity leave	Birth registration	(% of statutory pension-age population)			(per 100,000)	
	(% ages 25 and older)	(% of total employment)	(% ages 15–24)	(% ages 15 and older)	(% ages 5–14)	(% of total employment)	(days)	(% under age 5)	Total	Female	Male	Female	Male
HDI rank	2012	2003–2012[b]	2008–2012[b]	2004–2013[b]	2005–2012	2003–2010[b]	2013	2005–2012[b]	2004–2013[b]	2004–2013[b]	2004–2013[b]	2003–2009[b]	2003–2009[b]
174 Malawi	91.8	..	..	..	25.7	89.3	56	..	4.1	..	..	..	..
175 Liberia	72.0	78.7	5.1	3.7	20.8	94.4	90	3.6[d]	..	..	..	..	..
176 Mali	65.5	82.9	..	7.3	21.4	77.7	98	80.8	5.7	3.7	8.5	..	..
177 Guinea-Bissau	77.8	..	..	..	38.0	..	..	24.1	6.2	..	..	..	..
178 Mozambique	89.4	87.8	..	22.5	22.2	81.1	60	47.9	17.3	15.9	20.0	..	..
179 Guinea	79.0	..	..	1.7	40.1	70.2	98	43.2	8.8	..	..	..	..
180 Burundi	87.8	94.6	..	..	26.3	89.8	84	75.2	4.0	2.0	6.8	..	..
181 Burkina Faso	85.5	89.6	..	2.3	39.2	81.1	98	76.9	3.2	0.5	7.1	..	..
182 Eritrea	83.9	..	..	..	..	73.1	..	..	..	..	..	..	..
183 Sierra Leone	76.7	..	..	2.8	26.0	78.2	84	78.0	0.9	..	..	..	..
184 Chad	76.7	..	..	..	26.1	80.4	98	15.7	1.6	..	..	..	..
185 Central African Republic	82.3	..	..	..	28.5	77.5	..	61.0	..	..	..	..	..
186 Congo (Democratic Republic of the)	82.2	..	..	..	15.0	82.2	98	27.8	15.0	..	..	..	..
187 Niger	66.0	84.8	..	..	42.8	73.7	98	31.8[d]	6.1	..	..	..	..
OTHER COUNTRIES OR TERRITORIES													
Korea, Democratic People's Rep. of	79.1	..	..	..	..	60.8	..	100.0	..	..	..	..	..
Marshall Islands	..	..	..	..	..	..	..	95.9	64.2	..	..	..	..
Monaco	..	..	..	..	..	..	..	100.0	..	..	..	..	..
Nauru	..	..	..	..	..	..	..	82.6	56.5	..	..	..	..
San Marino	..	..	..	..	..	..	..	100.0	..	..	..	..	..
Somalia	59.2	..	..	..	49.0	74.5	..	3.0	..	..	..	..	..
South Sudan	..	..	..	..	..	..	..	35.4	..	..	..	..	..
Tuvalu	..	..	..	..	..	..	..	49.9	19.5	..	..	..	..
Human Development Index groups													
Very high human development	58.7	..	18.3	7.9	..	..	—	99.9	..	87.5	97.5	6.6	20.5
High human development	68.1	..	16.2	5.4	..	..	—	..	..	..	..	..	..
Medium human development	63.7	..	..	8.3	11.8	60.5	—	57.2	..	..	..	..	..
Low human development	72.2	..	..	..	25.2	74.9	—	40.3	..	..	..	..	..
Regions													
Arab States	52.7	..	24.6	10.4	..	..	—	80.8	..	..	..	..	..
East Asia and the Pacific	72.8	..	..	..	..	..	—	79.0	..	..	..	..	..
Europe and Central Asia	56.5	..	19.2	8.3	4.7	19.7	—	96.5	..	..	..	5.5	23.9
Latin America and the Caribbean	67.3	..	14.0	6.6	11.1	..	—	92.5	..	..	..	2.0	8.1
South Asia	60.9	..	..	8.6	12.3	74.2	—	41.3	..	..	..	..	..
Sub-Saharan Africa	75.0	..	..	..	26.2	71.1	—	43.5	..	..	..	..	..
Least developed countries	77.8	..	..	..	23.5	77.8	—	38.1	..	..	..	..	..
Small island developing states	65.7	..	..	..	..	..	—	..	..	..	..	..	..
World	65.4	..	..	7.5	..	..	—	62.3	..	..	..	..	..

TABLE
11

NOTES

a Because data are based on statutory pension age, which differs by country, comparisons should be made with caution.

b Data refer to the most recent year available during the period specified.

c Registered unemployed people only.

d Refers to an earlier year than the period specified.

e Differs from standard definition or refers to only part of the country.

f Excludes first-time job seekers.

g Main cities and metropolitan areas only.

h Registered unemployed people in urban areas only.

i Includes those on nonstandard type of break.

j Includes young people ages 12–14.

k Urban areas only.

l Includes those working less than 40 hours a week.

DEFINITIONS

Employment to population ratio: Percentage of the population ages 25 and older that is employed.

Vulnerable employment: Percentage of employed people engaged as unpaid family workers and own-account workers.

Youth unemployment: Percentage of the labour force population ages 15–24 that is not in paid employment or self-employed but is available for work and has taken steps to seek paid employment or self-employment.

Unemployment rate: Percentage of the labour force population ages 15 and older that is not in paid employment or self-employed but is available for work and has taken steps to seek paid employment or self-employment.

Child labour: Percentage of children ages 5–11 who, during the reference week, did at least one hour of economic activity or at least 28 hours of household chores, or children ages 12–14 who, during the reference week, did at least 14 hours of economic activity or at least 28 hours of household chores.

Share of working poor: Employed people living on less than $2 (in purchasing power parity terms) per day, expressed as a percentage of the total employed population ages 15 and older.

Mandatory paid maternity leave: Length of paid time off work that a female employee is entitled to in order to take care of a newborn child.

Birth registration: Percentage of children under age 5 who were registered at the moment of the survey. It includes children whose birth certificate was seen by the interviewer and children whose mother or caretaker says the birth has been registered.

Old age pension recipient: People above the statutory pensionable age receiving an old age pension (contributory, noncontributory or both), expressed as a percentage of the eligible population.

Suicide rate: Number of deaths from purposely self-inflicted injuries, in the total population or of a given sex or age, divided by the total number of the reference population, expressed per 100,000 people.

MAIN DATA SOURCES

Columns 1, 2, 3 and 6: ILO 2013a.

Column 4: ILO 2014b.

Columns 5 and 8: UNICEF 2014.

Column 7: World Bank 2013b.

Columns 9–11: ILO 2014a.

Columns 12 and 13: WHO 2013c.

TABLE 11   Social competencies | 203

TABLE 12

Personal insecurity

		Vulnerable groups								Attitudes	
		Refugees by country of origin[a]	Internally displaced persons[b]	Homeless people	Orphaned children	Prison population	Long-term unemployment rate	Depth of food deficit	Homicide rate	Justification of wife beating	
		(thousands)	(thousands)	(% of population)	(thousands)	(per 100,000 people)	(% of the labour force)	(kilocalories per person per day)	(per 100,000)	(% of women ages 15–49)	(% of men ages 15–49)
HDI rank		2012	2012	2009	2012	2002–2013[c]	2005–2012[c]	2011/2013	2008–2011	2005–2012[c]	2005–2012[c]
VERY HIGH HUMAN DEVELOPMENT											
1	Norway	0.0	..	..	..	72	0.3	..	2.3	..	..
2	Australia	0.0	..	..	..	130	1.1	..	1.1	..	..
3	Switzerland	0.0	..	..	..	82	1.5	..	0.6	..	..
4	Netherlands	0.1	..	..	..	82	1.7	..	0.9	..	..
5	United States	4.5 [d]	..	..	..	716	2.4	..	4.7	..	..
6	Germany	0.2	..	..	..	79	2.5	..	0.8	..	..
7	New Zealand	0.0	..	..	..	192	0.8	..	0.9	..	..
8	Canada	0.1	..	..	..	118	0.9	..	1.5	..	..
9	Singapore	0.1	..	0.0	..	230	0.6	..	0.3	..	..
10	Denmark	0.0	..	..	..	73	4.7	..	0.8	..	..
11	Ireland	0.0	..	..	..	88	9.0	..	0.9	..	..
12	Sweden	0.0	..	..	..	67	1.3	..	0.9	..	..
13	Iceland	0.0	..	..	..	47	1.5	..	0.9	..	..
14	United Kingdom	0.2	..	..	..	148	2.7	..	1.2	..	..
15	Hong Kong, China (SAR)	0.0	..	..	..	128	..	..	0.2	..	..
15	Korea (Republic of)	0.6	..	0.4	..	99	0.0	6	2.6	..	..
17	Japan	0.2	..	..	..	51	1.6	..	0.3	..	..
18	Liechtenstein	..	..	..	..	24	..	..	0.0	..	..
19	Israel	1.3	..	0.0	..	223	0.8	..	2.0	..	..
20	France	0.1	..	..	..	98 [e]	3.9	..	1.2	..	..
21	Austria	0.0	..	..	..	98	1.1	..	0.8	..	..
21	Belgium	0.1	..	..	..	108	3.4	..	1.8	..	..
21	Luxembourg	..	..	..	..	122	1.6	..	0.8	..	..
24	Finland	0.0	..	..	..	58	1.6	..	2.2	..	..
25	Slovenia	0.0	..	..	..	66	4.2	..	0.8	..	..
26	Italy	0.1	..	..	..	106	5.6	..	0.9	..	..
27	Spain	0.1	..	..	..	147	11.1	..	0.8	..	..
28	Czech Republic	0.6	..	..	..	154	3.0	..	0.8	..	..
29	Greece	0.1	..	..	..	111	14.4	..	1.6	..	..
30	Brunei Darussalam	0.0	..	0.0	..	122	..	2	0.8	..	..
31	Qatar	0.1	..	0.0	..	60	0.1	..	0.9	..	..
32	Cyprus	0.0	208 [f]	..	..	106 [g]	3.6	..	0.8	..	..
33	Estonia	0.5	..	..	..	238	5.5	..	4.8	..	..
34	Saudi Arabia	0.8	..	0.0	..	162	..	12	..	..	..
35	Lithuania	0.5	..	..	..	329	6.5	..	6.4	..	..
35	Poland	1.6	..	..	..	217	3.5	..	1.2	..	..
37	Andorra	0.0	..	..	..	38	..	..	1.2	..	..
37	Slovakia	0.2	..	..	..	187	8.9	..	1.8	..	..
39	Malta	0.0	..	..	..	145	3.0	..	0.7	..	..
40	United Arab Emirates	0.6	..	0.0	..	238	..	25	..	..	..
41	Chile	1.2	..	0.6	..	266	..	23	3.7	..	..
41	Portugal	0.0	..	..	..	136	7.6	..	1.1	..	..
43	Hungary	1.1	..	..	..	186	5.1	..	1.4	..	..
44	Bahrain	0.3	..	0.0	..	275	..	..	0.5	..	..
44	Cuba	6.7	..	1.9	..	510	..	4	5.0	..	..
46	Kuwait	1.2	..	..	..	137	..	11	2.2	..	..
47	Croatia	62.6	0	..	..	108	10.2	..	1.1	..	..
48	Latvia	0.7	..	..	..	304	7.7	..	3.1	..	..
49	Argentina	0.4	..	0.4	..	147	2.0	23	5.5	..	..
HIGH HUMAN DEVELOPMENT											
50	Uruguay	0.2	..	0.4	..	281	..	42	5.9	..	..
51	Bahamas	0.2	..	0.6	..	444	7.1	40	36.6	..	..
51	Montenegro	4.1	..	..	..	208	15.8	..	3.6	10.9	..
53	Belarus	6.2	..	..	..	335	..	..	4.9	4.1	4.2
54	Romania	2.8	..	..	..	155	3.2	..	1.6	..	..
55	Libya	5.3	50 [h]	0.0	..	81	..	8	2.9	..	..
56	Oman	0.1	..	0.0	..	61	..	..	0.7	..	..
57	Russian Federation	110.7	9.9 [i]	..	..	475	1.7	..	9.7	..	..
58	Bulgaria	2.1	..	..	..	151	6.8	..	1.7	..	..
59	Barbados	0.1	..	1.0	..	521	2.3	23	11.3	..	..

	Vulnerable groups						Depth of food deficit	Homicide rate	Attitudes	
	Refugees by country of origin[a]	Internally displaced persons[b]	Homeless people	Orphaned children	Prison population	Long-term unemployment rate			Justification of wife beating	
	(thousands)	(thousands)	(% of population)	(thousands)	(per 100,000 people)	(% of the labour force)	(kilocalories per person per day)	(per 100,000)	(% of women ages 15–49)	(% of men ages 15–49)
HDI rank	2012	2012	2009	2012	2002–2013[c]	2005–2012[c]	2011/2013	2008–2011	2005–2012[c]	2005–2012[c]
60 Palau	..	..	..	..	295	..		0.0	..	..
61 Antigua and Barbuda	0.0	..	9.4	..	403	..	100	6.8	..	..
62 Malaysia	0.5	..	0.3	..	132	..	23	..	..	..
63 Mauritius	0.1	..	0.3	..	202	2.0	37	3.4	..	..
64 Trinidad and Tobago	0.3	..	0.0	..	281	..	53	26.1	7.6	..
65 Lebanon	15.1	44.6	0.1	..	118	..	20	2.2	9.7 i	..
65 Panama	0.1	..	0.5	..	411	..	57	21.3	..	..
67 Venezuela (Bolivarian Republic of)	8.2	..	0.7	..	161	..	14	45.1	.. i	.. i
68 Costa Rica	0.3	..	1.4	..	314	..	57	10.0	..	..
69 Turkey	135.4	954–1,201 i	1.6	..	179	2.3	5	3.3	24.7	..
70 Kazakhstan	3.6	..	..	..	295	..	3	8.8	12.2	16.7
71 Mexico	8.4	..	0.7	..	210	0.1	2	23.7	..	..
71 Seychelles	0.0	..	0.2	..	709	..	49	..	..	..
73 Saint Kitts and Nevis	0.0	..	0.2	..	714	..	72	38.2	..	..
73 Sri Lanka	132.8	90	12.1	..	132	1.5	200	3.6	53.2 i	..
75 Iran (Islamic Republic of)	75.6	..	0.5	..	284	..	29	3.0	..	..
76 Azerbaijan	15.9	600 k	..	..	413	..	9	2.2	49.0	58.3
77 Jordan	2.4	..	0.0	..	95	..	20	..	90.0 i	..
77 Serbia	157.9	225	..	..	142	18.7	..	1.3	2.9	6.6 i
79 Brazil	1.1	..	0.3	..	274	9.8	56	21.8	..	..
79 Georgia	9.3	280 l	..	..	225 m	..	..	2.5	6.9	..
79 Grenada	0.3	..	0.0	..	424	..	138	11.5	..	..
82 Peru	5.2	150	2.5	..	202	..	76	10.3	..	..
83 Ukraine	25.3	..	..	..	305	2.1	..	4.3	3.6	11.1
84 Belize	0.0	..	0.0	..	476	..	39	39.0	8.6	..
84 The former Yugoslav Republic of Macedonia	7.6	..	..	..	122	25.4	..	1.5	14.5	..
86 Bosnia and Herzegovina	51.9	113	..	..	80	25.4	..	1.3	4.8	6.0
87 Armenia	16.1	8.4	..	..	164	9.7	16	1.4	9.3	19.9
88 Fiji	1.3	..	1.9	..	174	2.6	18	..	..	..
89 Thailand	0.4	..	0.4	..	398	0.1	40	4.8	..	..
90 Tunisia	1.9	..	0.0	..	199	..	6	1.1	30.3	..
91 China	193.3	..	4.5	..	121 n	..	76	1.0	..	..
91 Saint Vincent and the Grenadines	1.3	..	0.0	..	376	16.9	38	19.2	..	..
93 Algeria	5.7	..	0.8	..	162	7.1	15	0.8	67.9	..
93 Dominica	0.1	..	7.4	..	391	..	14	22.1	..	..
95 Albania	12.6	..	..	..	158	10.6	..	4.4	29.8	36.4
96 Jamaica	1.4	..	0.1	..	152	..	60	41.2	2.9 i	21.5 i
97 Saint Lucia	0.6	..	0.2	..	317	..	88	25.2	..	..
98 Colombia	111.8	4,900–5,500	1.7	..	245	..	70	33.2	..	..
98 Ecuador	0.8	..	0.9	..	149	..	106	18.2	..	..
100 Suriname	0.0	..	0.0	..	186	..	70	4.6	12.5	..
100 Tonga	0.0	..	3.6	..	150	..	..	1.0	..	..
102 Dominican Republic	0.3	..	1.5	..	240	..	107	25.0	4.1	..
MEDIUM HUMAN DEVELOPMENT										
103 Maldives	0.0	..	13.9	..	307 o	..	35	1.6	30.8 i	14.3 i
103 Mongolia	2.1	..	0.0	..	287	3.4	188	9.5	10.1	8.8 i
103 Turkmenistan	0.7	..	..	..	224	..	15	..	37.7 i	..
106 Samoa	0.0	..	16.0	..	228	..	23	1.1	60.8	45.7
107 Palestine, State of	5,366.7 p	144.5	..	..	..	..	211	..	..	..
108 Indonesia	10.1	170	0.8	..	59	..	64	0.6	35.0 i	17.0 i
109 Botswana	0.1	..	2.0	160	205	10.4	187	14.5	..	..
110 Egypt	10.0	..	0.1	..	80	7.7	8	3.3	39.3	..
111 Paraguay	0.1	..	0.2	..	118	..	157	11.4	..	..
112 Gabon	0.2	..	0.0	61	196	..	35	13.8	50.2	39.7
113 Bolivia (Plurinational State of)	0.6	..	0.8	..	140	1.3	140	7.7	16.1	..
114 Moldova (Republic of)	6.1	..	..	..	188 q	1.7	..	8.6	20.8	21.7 i
115 El Salvador	8.2	..	0.0	..	422	..	78	70.2	..	..
116 Uzbekistan	7.1	3.4	..	..	152	..	38	3.1	69.6	59.4 i
117 Philippines	1.0	72 r	3.3	..	111	0.1	100	5.4	14.1	..
118 South Africa	0.4	..	0.1	4,000	294	8.1	13	30.9	..	..
118 Syrian Arab Republic	728.2	6500	0.0	..	58	..	38	2.3	..	..

TABLE
12

TABLE 12 Personal insecurity | 205

TABLE 12 PERSONAL INSECURITY

HDI rank	Refugees by country of origin[a] (thousands) 2012	Internally displaced persons[b] (thousands) 2012	Homeless people (% of population) 2009	Orphaned children (thousands) 2012	Prison population (per 100,000 people) 2002–2013[c]	Long-term unemployment rate (% of the labour force) 2005–2012[c]	Depth of food deficit (kilocalories per person per day) 2011/2013	Homicide rate (per 100,000) 2008–2011	Justification of wife beating (% of women ages 15–49) 2005–2012[c]	Justification of wife beating (% of men ages 15–49) 2005–2012[c]
120 Iraq	746.4 [s]	2,100	0.0	..	110	..	217	2.0	51.2	..
121 Guyana	0.8	..	1.4	..	260	..	33	17.2	16.3	19.3
121 Viet Nam	336.9 [t]	..	2.0	..	145 [o]	..	63	1.6	35.8	..
123 Cape Verde	0.0	..	1.1	..	267	..	66	..	17.3	16.3 [j]
124 Micronesia (Federated States of)	..	..	..	..	80	..	..	0.9	..	..
125 Guatemala	6.4	..	0.0	..	105	..	201	38.5	..	..
125 Kyrgyzstan	3.5	67	..	..	181	..	39	6.5	37.7	..
127 Namibia	1.1	..	0.0	130	191	30.9	212	..	35.2	40.8
128 Timor-Leste	0.0	..	0.2	..	25	0.4	254	6.9	86.2	80.7
129 Honduras	2.6	..	0.9	..	153	..	46	91.6	12.4	9.9
129 Morocco	2.4	..	0.0	..	220	5.8	31	1.4	63.9	..
131 Vanuatu	0.0	..	5.0	..	76	..	48	0.9	60.0	..
132 Nicaragua	1.5	..	0.4	..	153	..	144	12.6	13.7	..
133 Kiribati	0.0	..	4.8	..	114	..	48	7.3	75.6	59.7
133 Tajikistan	0.7	..	..	..	130	..	249	2.1	74.4 [j]	..
135 India	14.3	540	1.0	..	30	1.4	121	3.5	54.4	51.0
136 Bhutan	41.6	..	0.2	..	135	..	..	1.0	68.4	..
136 Cambodia	14.0	..	2.2	..	106	..	102	..	45.7 [j]	22.4 [j]
138 Ghana	24.3	..	1.2	1,000	54	..	18	15.7	44.1	25.7 [j]
139 Lao People's Democratic Republic	8.0	..	19.7	..	69	..	195	4.6	58.2	49.1
140 Congo	12.2	7.8	2.1	220	31	..	234	30.8	75.7	..
141 Zambia	0.2	..	0.1	1,400	119	..	306	1.8	61.9	49.3
142 Bangladesh	10.2	..	2.1	..	42	..	118	2.7	32.5	..
142 Sao Tome and Principe	0.0	..	0.0	..	128	..	45	3.6	19.5	21.7
144 Equatorial Guinea	0.2	..	0.0	..	95	..	..	20.7	..	..
LOW HUMAN DEVELOPMENT										
145 Nepal	7.6	..	0.9	..	48	1.0	112	2.8	23.2	21.5
146 Pakistan	33.6	758 [u]	6.2	..	39	1.1	131	7.8	..	..
147 Kenya	8.9	412 [v]	0.0	2,600	121	..	166	6.3	52.6	44.0
148 Swaziland	0.1	..	0.0	120	284	..	262	..	27.6	23.1 [j]
149 Angola	20.2	..	0.2	1,100	105	..	153	19.0	..	..
150 Myanmar	215.3	498	0.3	..	120	..	..	10.2	..	..
151 Rwanda	97.5	..	0.1	590	492 [w]	..	201	17.1	56.2	25.1
152 Cameroon	13.4	..	0.1	1,300	119	..	85	..	46.5	38.7
152 Nigeria	18.0	..	0.5	11,500	32	..	42	12.2	45.6	..
154 Yemen	2.6	307	1.2	..	55 [x]	4.0	188	4.2	..	..
155 Madagascar	0.3	..	3.8	..	87	..	176	8.1	32.3	30.1
156 Zimbabwe	22.1	..	0.5	1,200	129	..	226	7.7	39.6	33.7
157 Papua New Guinea	0.2	..	3.7	320	48	..	..	13.0	..	..
157 Solomon Islands	0.1	..	0.3	..	55	..	81	3.7	68.8	65.1
159 Comoros	0.5	..	0.1	..	16	..	655	12.2	..	..
159 Tanzania (United Republic of)	1.1	..	0.2	3,100	78	..	221	24.5	53.5	38.1
161 Mauritania	33.8	..	2.2	..	45	..	46	14.7	37.9	..
162 Lesotho	0.0	..	0.1	220	121	15.6	102	35.2	37.1	48.4
163 Senegal	18.7	10–40	0.6	..	64	..	142	8.7	60.0	24.7
164 Uganda	5.6	30	1.4	2,700	97	..	192	10.9	58.3	43.7
165 Benin	0.5	..	0.9	450	75	..	34	15.1	46.6	13.5
166 Sudan	558.5 [y]	2900	1.3	..	56	..	..	24.2	47.0	..
166 Togo	15.7	..	1.8	360	64	..	98	10.9	43.0	..
168 Haiti	38.6	360	1.6	430	96	..	431	6.9	16.7	14.9
169 Afghanistan	2,585.6	493	0.7	..	76	..	..	2.4	90.2	..
170 Djibouti	0.6	..	3.1	43	83	..	143	3.4	..	..
171 Côte d'Ivoire	100.7	40–80 [z]	0.4	1,300	34 [aa]	..	133	56.9	47.9	42.0
172 Gambia	3.1	..	0.4	..	56	..	102	10.8	74.5	..
173 Ethiopia	74.9	..	0.2	4,500	136	1.3	314	25.5	68.4	44.9
174 Malawi	0.3	..	1.9	1,300	76	..	119	36.0	12.6	12.9
175 Liberia	23.5	..	0.2	190	46	..	201	10.1	59.3	30.2
176 Mali	149.9	353.4	0.7	..	36	..	39	8.0	87.2	..
177 Guinea-Bissau	1.2	..	0.1	120	..	..	61	20.2	40.2	..
178 Mozambique	0.2	..	3.0	2,000	65	5.9	269	3.3	22.9	19.9
179 Guinea	14.2	..	0.0	670	25	..	91	22.5	85.6	..

TABLE
12

	Vulnerable groups						Depth of food deficit	Homicide rate	Attitudes	
	Refugees by country of origin[a]	Internally displaced persons[b]	Homeless people	Orphaned children	Prison population	Long-term unemployment rate			Justification of wife beating	
	(thousands)	(thousands)	(% of population)	(thousands)	(per 100,000 people)	(% of the labour force)	(kilocalories per person per day)	(per 100,000)	(% of women ages 15–49)	(% of men ages 15–49)
HDI rank	2012	2012	2009	2012	2002–2013[c]	2005–2012[c]	2011/2013	2008–2011	2005–2012[c]	2005–2012[c]
180 Burundi	73.6	78.8	1.0	680	72	..	581	4.1	72.9	44.3
181 Burkina Faso	1.5	..	0.4	980	28	..	178	18.0	43.5	34.1
182 Eritrea	247.8	10	0.4	160	..	..	488	17.8	70.7	..
183 Sierra Leone	7.4	..	0.4	370	52	..	209	14.9	73.3	..
184 Chad	15.8	90	1.1	960	41	..	216	29.3	79.6	80.3[j]
185 Central African Republic	162.4	533[ab]	2.2	..	19	..	196	21.7	75.9	..
186 Congo (Democratic Republic of the)	509.2	2,770	0.4	5,100	33	..	..	21.7	75.9	..
187 Niger	0.8	..	1.3	..	42	..	77	3.8	70.1	..
OTHER COUNTRIES OR TERRITORIES										
Korea, Democratic People's Rep. of	1.1	..	5.3	..	..	..	238	15.2	..	..
Marshall Islands	0.0	..	..	..	58	..	..	0.0	55.9	57.6
Monaco	0.0	..	..	..	73	..	..	9.8	..	..
Nauru	..	..	..	..	277	..	..	..	..	..
San Marino	0.0	..	..	..	6	..	..	1.5	..	..
Somalia	1,136.1	1,133	6.8	..	..	..	..	..	75.7[ac]	..
South Sudan	86.9[ad]	430	..	470	65	..	..	..	78.5	..
Tuvalu	0.0	..	5.5	..	120	..	..	..	70.0	73.1
Human Development Index groups										
Very high human development	86.9	—	..	..	283	3.1	..	2.3	..	..
High human development	1,136.6	—	3.2	..	186	..	62	6.4	..	..
Medium human development	7,369.0	—	1.1	..	63	..	104	4.7	46.8	..
Low human development	5,085.4	—	1.6	..	71	..	157	14.1	53.8	..
Regions										
Arab States	8,585.0	—	0.5	..	116	..	56	4.9	..	..
East Asia and the Pacific	784.3	—	3.6	..	123	..	76	1.8	..	..
Europe and Central Asia	463.9	—	..	..	220	..	..	3.8	26.8	..
Latin America and the Caribbean	207.9	—	0.7	..	230	..	57	22.7	..	..
South Asia	2,901.2	—	1.7	..	46	..	119	3.8	51.9	..
Sub-Saharan Africa	1,768.7	—	0.7	4,535	91	..	149	17.4	54.7	..
Least developed countries	6,185.7	—	1.3	..	77	..	187	12.8	52.0	..
Small island developing states	54.1	—	1.8	..	231	..	152	14.2	..	..
World	**14,902.2**	—	**2.1**	..	**145**	..	..	**6.5**	..	..

NOTES

a Data refer to those recognized under the 1951 UN Convention, the 1967 UN Protocol and the 1969 Organization of African Unity Convention. In the absence of government figures, the Office of the United Nations High Commissioner for Refugees (UNHCR) has estimated the refugee population in 25 industrialized countries based on 10 years of individual refugee recognition.

b For more detailed comments on the estimates, see www.internal-displacement.org.

c Data refer to the most recent year available during the period specified.

d A limited number of countries record refugee and asylum statistics by country of birth rather than country of origin. This affects the number of refugees reported as originating from United States.

e Excludes territories in Africa, the Americas and Oceania.

f Includes more than 200,000 Greek and Turkish Cypriots displaced in 1974.

g Does not include the internationally unrecognized Turkish Republic of Northern Cyprus.

h Excludes non-Libyans displaced within the country.

i Includes internally displaced persons from Chechnya and North Ossetia with forced migrant status in and outside the North Caucasus.

j Based on a Hacettepe University survey commissioned by the government.

k Includes internally displaced persons from Nagorno Karabakh and surrounding districts as well as children born during displacement.

l Includes people displaced in the 1990s and in 2008 as well as 10,000 people internally displaced in South Ossetia. Also includes people with internally displaced person status who have returned home or been relocated with their children.

m Excludes Abkhazia and South Ossetia, which have declared independence from Georgia.

n Excludes people in pretrial or administrative detention.

o Sentenced prisoners only.

p Includes Palestinian refugees under the responsibility of United Nations Relief and Works Agency for Palestine Refugees in the Near East.

q Excludes the internationally unrecognized Transnistria.

r Includes people in government-recognized camps and relocation sites and people displaced by armed conflict, clan violence and crime in 2012 but excludes internally displaced persons living with hosts and people whose return or settlement elsewhere has not been sustainable.

s Refugee figures for Iraqis in Jordan and Syrian Arab Republic are government estimates. UNHCR has registered and is assisting 90,500 Iraqis in both countries as of 31 December 2013.

t Some 300,000 Vietnamese refugees are well integrated and in practice receive protection from the government of China.

u Includes people displaced in Khyber Pakhtunkhwa province and federally administered tribal areas who meet official internally displaced person registration criteria.

v Includes people displaced by the 2007 post-election violence and people still displaced by earlier episodes of violence.

w Includes thousands of people sentenced or awaiting trial in connection with the 1994 genocide.

x Ministry of the Interior prisons only.

y May include citizens of South Sudan.

z Excludes people displaced during the 2002–2007 conflict.

aa Prisons under government control only.

ab Rough estimate, as access to affected populations is limited.

ac Differs from standard definition or refers to only part of the country.

ad An unknown number of refugees and asylum-seekers from South Sudan may be included in data for Sudan.

DEFINITIONS

Refugees by country of origin: Number of people who have fled their country of origin because of a well founded fear of persecution due to their race, religion, nationality, political opinion or membership in a particular social group and who cannot or do not want to return to their country of origin.

Internally displaced persons: Number of people who have been forced to leave their homes or places of habitual residence—in particular, as a result of or to avoid the effects of armed conflict, situations of generalized violence, violations of human rights or natural or human-made disasters—and who have not crossed an internationally recognized state border.

Homeless people: People who lack a shelter for living quarters as a result of natural disasters, who carry their few possessions with them and who sleep in the streets, in doorways or on piers, or in any other space, on a more or less random basis, expressed as a percentage of the total population.

Orphaned children: Number of children (ages 0–17) who have lost one or both parents due to any cause.

Prison population: Number of adult and juvenile prisoners (including pre-trial detainees, unless otherwise noted), expressed per 100,000 people.

Long-term unemployment rate: Percentage of the labour force (the employed and unemployed population) ages 15 and older who are not working but are available for work and have taken specific steps to seek paid employment or self-employment for at least 12 months.

Depth of food deficit: Number of kilocalories needed to lift the undernourished from their status, holding all other factors constant.

Homicide rate: Number of unlawful deaths purposefully inflicted on a person by another person, expressed per 100,000 people.

Justification of wife beating: Percentage of women and men ages 15–49 who consider a husband to be justified in hitting or beating his wife for at least one of the following reasons: if his wife burns the food, argues with him, goes out without telling him, neglects the children or refuses sexual relations.

MAIN DATA SOURCES

Column 1: UNHCR 2013.

Column 2: IDMC 2013.

Column 3: United Nations Statistics Division 2013.

Columns 4, 9 and 10: UNICEF 2014.

Column 5: International Centre for Prison Studies 2013.

Column 6: ILO 2013a.

Column 7: FAO 2013a.

Column 8: UNODC 2013.

TABLE 12

TABLE 12 Personal insecurity | 207

TABLE 13

International integration

	Trade		Financial flows				Total reserves minus gold	Human mobility			Communication		
	Remoteness	International trade	Foreign direct investment, net inflows	Private capital flows	Net official development assistance received[a]	Remittances, inflows	Total reserves minus gold	Net migration rate	Stock of immigrants	International inbound tourists	Internet users	International telephone traffic (minutes per person)	
	(kilometres)	(% of GDP)	(% of GDP)	(% of GDP)	(% of GNI)	(% of GDP)	(% of GDP)	(per 1,000 people)	(% of population)	(thousands)	(% of population)	Incoming	Outgoing
HDI rank	2012	2012[b]	2012[b]	2012[b]	2011	2011[c]	2012[b]	2010/2015[d]	2013	2011	2012	2006–2011[e]	2006–2011[e]
VERY HIGH HUMAN DEVELOPMENT													
1 Norway	5,709	68.2	1.5	12.8	−1.0	0.16	3.4	6.0	13.8[f]	4,963	95.0	..	251.0
2 Australia	13,506	42.6	4.8	−3.6	−0.4	0.14	0.7	6.5	27.7[g]	5,875	82.3	..	..
3 Switzerland	5,878	91.6	1.5	4.0	−0.5	0.50	..	8.0	28.9	8,534	85.2	..	422.2
4 Netherlands	5,741	165.9	−1.1	9.4	−0.8	0.21	1.6	0.6	11.7	11,300	93.0	..	99.9
5 United States	8,678	31.7	1.3	−2.3	−0.2	0.04	..	3.1	14.3	62,711	81.0	81.2	199.8
6 Germany	5,972	97.6	0.8	4.3	−0.4	0.37	10.3	1.3	11.9	28,374	84.0	..	180.5
7 New Zealand	14,121	59.0	2.7	−4.5	−0.3	0.55	0.4	3.3	25.1	2,572	89.5	..	174.0
8 Canada	7,000	62.1	2.5	−1.9	−0.3	..	0.6	6.3	20.7	16,014	86.8	..	..
9 Singapore	10,132	379.1	20.6	5.7	..	..	0.1	15.0	42.9	10,390	74.2	483.4	1,582.4
10 Denmark	5,696	104.6	0.4	6.4	−0.9	0.38	3.5	2.7	9.9	7,363	93.0	176.7	205.0
11 Ireland	5,796	192.4	15.7	−1.2	−0.5	0.34	..	2.2	15.9	7,630	79.0	..	430.5
12 Sweden	5,735	91.3	0.7	0.5	−1.0	0.14	..	4.2	15.9	5,006	94.0	..	173.7
13 Iceland	5,866	112.1	3.8	41.9	−0.2	0.15	13.4	3.3	10.4	566	96.0	209.5	131.3
14 United Kingdom	5,930	65.7	2.3	14.3	−0.6	0.07	..	2.9	12.4	29,306	87.0	..	143.2
15 Hong Kong, China (SAR)	8,740	447.2	38.7	4.2	..	0.14	..	4.2	38.9	22,316	72.8	492.3	1,700.7
15 Korea (Republic of)	8,000	109.9	0.4	0.8	..	0.76	..	1.2	2.5	9,795	84.1	22.4	51.2
17 Japan	8,956	31.2	0.0	2.7	−0.2	0.04	1.4	0.6	1.9	6,219	79.1	14.1	27.3
18 Liechtenstein	..	..	..	..	..	..	6.4	..	33.1	53	89.4	..	..
19 Israel	6,783	72.2	4.3	1.3	−0.1	0.23	1.6	−2.0	26.5	2,820	73.4	..	..
20 France	5,990	57.1	2.5	−1.6	−0.5	0.69	8.2	2.0	11.6	81,411	83.0	172.9	190.7
21 Austria	5,860	110.5	0.5	1.2	−0.3	0.64	3.1	3.5	15.7	23,012	81.0	..	211.3
21 Belgium	5,746	168.4	−0.4	−9.2	−0.5	2.12	2.9	2.7	10.4	7,494	82.0	..	257.5
21 Luxembourg	5,740	311.4	31.0	−449.3	−1.0	2.94	..	9.7	43.3	871	92.0	809.9	821.8
24 Finland	5,763	80.1	0.7	−2.2	−0.5	0.29	..	1.8	5.4	4,192	91.0	..	..
25 Slovenia	5,889	147.3	0.0	0.0	−0.1	0.86	0.5	2.1	11.3	2,037	70.0	85.6	101.4
26 Italy	6,224	59.3	0.4	−0.8	−0.2	0.32	..	3.0	9.4	46,119	58.0	..	162.2
27 Spain	6,320	63.4	2.7	1.7	−0.3	0.67	..	2.6	13.8[h]	56,694	72.0	..	118.1
28 Czech Republic	5,776	150.7	5.4	−5.8	−0.1	0.84	..	3.8	4.0	8,775	75.0	125.5	46.5
29 Greece	6,347	59.0	1.2	50.3	−0.1	0.41	2.7	0.9	8.9	16,427	56.0	88.1	168.1
30 Brunei Darussalam	10,034	112.5	7.4	−4.3	1.0	..	..	0.8	49.3	242	60.3	..	..
31 Qatar	7,409	96.5	−0.1	14.6	..	0.33	1.8	48.8	73.8	2,527	88.1	427.4	..
32 Cyprus	6,581	86.7	4.3	−32.2	..	0.51	4.5	6.2	18.2[i]	2,392	61.0	248.8	460.5
33 Estonia	5,743	184.4	7.4	−2.0	−0.1	1.84	..	0.0	16.3	2,665	79.0	127.0	85.0
34 Saudi Arabia	7,423	86.4	1.7	−0.6	..	0.04	1.1	2.1	31.4	17,498	54.0	106.6	632.4
35 Lithuania	5,785	167.9	1.6	−3.9	..	4.56	0.1	−1.9	4.9	1,775	68.0	81.4	37.3
35 Poland	5,814	92.0	0.6	−4.8	−0.1	1.48	1.5	−0.2	1.7	13,350	65.0	..	34.6
37 Andorra	..	..	..	..	..	..	..	..	56.9	1,948	86.4	641.0	711.5
37 Slovakia	5,843	186.3	3.8	−14.8	−0.1	1.83	3.0	0.6	2.7	1,460	80.0	100.2	73.3
39 Malta	6,380	185.5	4.7	22.9	..	0.40	5.7	2.1	8.0	1,412	70.0	..	141.5
40 United Arab Emirates	7,526	169.6	2.2	..	..	..	0.8	11.4	83.7	..	85.0	313.3	654.5
41 Chile	12,324	68.1	11.3	−2.2	0.0	0.00	3.4	0.3	2.3	3,070	61.4	22.7	11.5
41 Portugal	6,380	78.1	6.5	9.4	−0.3	1.59	2.2	1.9	8.4	7,264	64.0	..	115.6
43 Hungary	5,885	181.8	6.8	−4.0	−0.1	1.76	1.1	1.5	4.7	10,250	72.0	115.9	50.2
44 Bahrain	7,323	123.7	2.7	−18.8	0.1	..	5.2	3.4	54.7	6,732	88.0	285.7	1,585.8
44 Cuba	8,274	38.6	0.0	..	..	..	..	−2.5	0.1	2,688	25.6	32.2	2.9
46 Kuwait	7,114	95.7	0.2	9.6	..	..	1.5	18.3	60.2	269	79.2	..	..
47 Croatia	5,911	86.6	2.3	−6.7	..	2.23	0.3	−0.9	17.6	9,927	63.0	98.7	53.1
48 Latvia	5,749	125.7	3.2	−7.5	..	2.45	..	−1.0	13.8	1,493	74.0	..	..
49 Argentina	12,258	37.1	2.7	−2.4	0.0	0.15	2.1	−0.5	4.5	5,705	55.8	..	18.4
HIGH HUMAN DEVELOPMENT													
50 Uruguay	12,159	65.2	4.7	−8.9	0.0	0.22	0.5	−1.8	2.2	2,857	55.1	76.2	47.9
51 Bahamas	8,002	101.0	7.6	−4.0	0.3	..	1.9	5.2	16.3	1,346	71.7	..	..
51 Montenegro	..	106.4	12.4	−13.0	1.6	7.62	..	−0.8	8.2	1,201	56.8	..	..
53 Belarus	5,823	158.7	2.3	−1.8	0.5	1.27	..	−0.2	11.6	116	46.9	88.2	64.7
54 Romania	6,077	85.1	1.4	−4.0	..	2.13	0.8	−0.4	0.9	7,611	50.0	115.5	40.3
55 Libya	6,566	94.8	2.2	5.0	..	..	3.5	−7.7	12.2	34	19.9	..	..
56 Oman	7,626	94.5	1.1	0.8	..	0.06	..	59.2	30.6	1,048	60.0	247.9	215.8
57 Russian Federation	6,080	51.6	2.6	−1.0	..	0.26	9.0	1.5	7.7	24,932	53.3	..	59.3
58 Bulgaria	6,106	137.0	4.0	−0.8	0.8	2.77	1.8	−1.4	1.2	6,328	55.1	107.3	51.1

		Trade		Financial flows				Total reserves minus gold	Human mobility			Communication		
		Remoteness	International trade	Foreign direct investment, net inflows	Private capital flows	Net official development assistance received[a]	Remittances, inflows		Net migration rate	Stock of immigrants	International inbound tourists	Internet users	International telephone traffic (minutes per person)	
		(kilometres)	(% of GDP)	(% of GDP)	(% of GDP)	(% of GNI)	(% of GDP)	(% of GDP)	(per 1,000 people)	(% of population)	(thousands)	(% of population)	Incoming	Outgoing
HDI rank		2012	2012[b]	2012[b]	2012[b]	2011	2011[c]	2012[b]	2010/2015[d]	2013	2011	2012	2006–2011[e]	2006–2011[e]
59	Barbados	8,615	99.7	9.1	−10.4	0.1	2.22	2.4	1.4	11.3	568	73.3	..	..
60	Palau	10,216	153.2	0.9	..	20.7	..	3.6	..	26.7	109	..	157.6	180.0
61	Antigua and Barbuda	8,344	105.0	5.1	−6.6	1.4	1.82	4.3	−0.1	31.9	241	83.8	367.6	180.0
62	Malaysia	9,949	163.0	4.2	−3.9	0.0	0.42	..	3.1	8.3[j]	24,714	65.8	..	..
63	Mauritius	10,613	119.9	2.4	−96.7	1.7	0.00	14.5	0.0	3.6[k]	965	41.4	150.0	102.4
64	Trinidad and Tobago	8,835	91.9	2.4	..	..	0.39	..	−2.2	2.4	386	59.5	192.2	205.9
65	Lebanon	6,677	72.9	8.7	−2.8	1.1	18.26	..	21.3	17.6	1,655	61.2	314.6	86.3
65	Panama	9,308	147.5	9.3	−8.0	0.4	1.24	..	1.5	4.1	1,473	45.2	54.7	102.5
67	Venezuela (Bolivarian Republic of)	8,975	50.4	0.6	−1.2	0.0	0.04	1.5	0.3	3.9	595	44.0	34.2	21.8
68	Costa Rica	9,325	79.4	5.3	−8.8	0.1	1.27	2.3	2.7	8.6	2,192	47.5	85.5	43.0
69	Turkey	6,306	58.0	1.6	−6.2	0.1	0.14	5.6	0.9	2.5	34,038	45.1	58.3	16.1
70	Kazakhstan	6,933	78.5	7.1	2.6	0.1	0.10	1.2	0.0	21.1	3,393	53.3	45.1	41.5
71	Mexico	9,118	66.9	1.1	−5.2	0.1	2.04	..	−2.0	0.9	23,403	38.4	..	..
71	Seychelles	9,484	144.7	13.1	−11.2	2.1	2.41	..	−3.4	13.0	194	47.1	63.2	93.4
73	Saint Kitts and Nevis	8,346	72.6	15.2	−12.2	2.5	6.35	..	..	10.5	92	79.3	821.4	630.3
73	Sri Lanka	9,181	60.7	1.6	−3.3	1.0	8.71	0.3	−3.0	1.5	856	18.3	28.5	..
75	Iran (Islamic Republic of)	6,873	..	0.8	..	..	0.26	0.3	−0.8	3.4	3,354	26.0	..	..
76	Azerbaijan	6,592	74.3	7.7	−1.6	0.5	2.87	..	0.0	3.4[l]	1,562	54.2	78.7	19.9
77	Jordan	6,784	119.1	5.1	−5.7	3.3	11.97	2.2	11.3	40.2	3,975	41.0	108.0	143.4
77	Serbia	5,987	92.4	6.2	−6.6	1.3	7.56	..	−2.1	5.6[m]	764	48.1	99.4	40.5
79	Brazil	11,491	26.5	3.4	−3.4	0.2	0.11	1.0	−0.2	0.3	5,433	49.8	1.0	2.1
79	Georgia	6,448	96.2	5.0	−9.2	3.9	10.65	0.4	−5.8	4.4[n]	2,822	45.5	62.4	34.9
79	Grenada	8,726	73.8	5.3	−3.0	1.6	3.71	1.9	−8.1	10.7	118	42.1	487.2	315.3
82	Peru	10,907	49.9	4.7	−4.3	0.4	1.53	..	−2.0	0.3	2,598	38.2	92.1	19.7
83	Ukraine	5,943	110.3	4.4	−6.4	0.5	4.79	1.9	−0.2	11.4	21,415	33.7	..	..
84	Belize	8,870	130.8	6.6	−5.6	0.4	5.23	3.7	4.6	15.3	250	25.0	130.0	147.6
84	The former Yugoslav Republic of Macedonia	6,113	129.3	3.4	−2.5	1.6	4.17	..	−0.5	6.6	327	63.1	230.2	22.2
86	Bosnia and Herzegovina	6,005	110.8	3.7	−3.3	0.1	10.73	..	−0.3	0.6	392	65.4	200.1	43.8
87	Armenia	6,506	72.3	4.9	−4.8	3.5	19.66	0.0	−3.4	10.6	758	39.2	176.2	253.3
88	Fiji	12,589	105.6	5.4	−6.0	2.0	4.14	..	−6.6	2.6	675	33.7	..	..
89	Thailand	9,132	148.8	2.4	0.2	0.0	1.32	8.2	0.3	5.6	19,230	26.5	14.3	11.1
90	Tunisia	6,323	106.6	0.9	−3.4	1.5	4.32	1.2	−0.6	0.3	4,785	41.4	57.2	15.9
91	China	8,513	58.7	3.0	−2.9	0.0	0.55	0.2	−0.2	0.1	57,581	42.3	9.1	2.8
91	Saint Vincent and the Grenadines	8,632	82.9	15.9	−18.0	2.8	4.27	3.4	−9.1	9.4	74	47.5	439.1	146.4
93	Algeria	6,359	52.4	1.4	−1.0	0.1	0.10	0.7	−0.3	0.7	2,395	15.2	57.9	25.5
93	Dominica	8,475	89.6	7.2	−4.9	5.2	4.87	4.3	..	8.9	76	55.2	134.1	164.3
95	Albania	6,128	89.8	9.6	−6.9	2.4	8.96	..	−3.2	3.1	2,932	54.7	252.0	24.0
96	Jamaica	8,541	84.7	1.2	−2.7	0.4	14.60	2.4	−5.8	1.3	1,952	46.5	259.7	882.7
97	Saint Lucia	8,566	114.1	6.7	−11.6	3.0	2.43	..	0.0	6.7	312	48.6	284.5	200.8
98	Colombia	9,603	38.7	4.3	−5.8	0.4	1.25	2.1	−0.5	0.3	2,385	49.0	..	..
98	Ecuador	10,014	64.4	0.8	−0.9	0.3	3.49	..	−0.4	2.3	1,141	35.1	60.6	11.6
100	Suriname	9,093	..	3.4	−1.3	2.3	0.09	..	−1.9	7.7	220	34.7	..	..
100	Tonga	12,825	78.5	2.4	..	21.1	16.68	0.2	−15.4	5.2	46	34.9	..	..
102	Dominican Republic	8,371	58.9	4.1	−5.6	0.4	6.56	0.8	−2.7	3.9	4,306	45.0	123.9	21.0
MEDIUM HUMAN DEVELOPMENT														
103	Maldives	9,236	214.4	13.1	−12.8	2.7	0.14	0.8	0.0	24.4	931	38.9	..	327.6
103	Mongolia	7,108	127.8	53.8	−65.6	4.3	3.19	..	−1.1	0.6	457	16.4	38.6	19.1
103	Turkmenistan	6,842	123.2	11.4	..	0.1	..	..	−1.0	4.3	8	7.2	..	..
106	Samoa	12,241	90.5	2.3	−3.8	16.6	21.94	0.4	−13.4	3.0	121	12.9	..	..
107	Palestine, State of	..	..	..	..	..	..	1.0	−2.0	5.9[o]	449	..	..	..
108	Indonesia	10,862	50.1	2.3	−2.7	0.1	0.82	3.6	−0.6	0.1	7,650	15.4	..	..
109	Botswana	10,458	95.1	2.0	−1.5	0.2	0.41	26.3	2.0	7.2	2,145	11.5	..	31.3
110	Egypt	6,859	44.8	−0.2	−0.2	0.2	6.07	1.0	−0.5	0.4	9,497	44.1	69.8	6.9
111	Paraguay	11,491	93.5	1.6	−3.4	0.4	3.43	0.4	−1.2	2.7	524	27.1	76.5	14.3
112	Gabon	8,696	..	3.9	..	0.5	..	1.0	0.6	23.6	..	8.6	11.0	17.7
113	Bolivia (Plurinational State of)	11,042	85.1	3.6	−2.6	0.5	4.36	0.7	−2.4	1.4	807	34.2	83.7	6.8
114	Moldova (Republic of)	6,007	128.1	2.3	−2.1	6.0	22.81	..	−5.9	11.2[p]	11	43.4	224.1	62.7
115	El Salvador	9,153	74.9	1.1	−5.9	1.3	15.84	4.2	−7.1	0.7	1,184	25.5	258.4	234.8
116	Uzbekistan	6,879	64.4	3.1	..	0.5	..	0.3	−1.4	4.4	975	36.5	..	..
117	Philippines	9,442	64.8	1.1	−1.8	−0.1	10.25	1.4	−1.4	0.2	3,917	36.2	..	..

TABLE
13

TABLE 13 International integration | 209

TABLE 13 INTERNATIONAL INTEGRATION

		Trade		Financial flows					Human mobility			Communication		
		Remoteness	International trade	Foreign direct investment, net inflows	Private capital flows	Net official development assistance received[a]	Remittances, inflows	**Total reserves minus gold**	Net migration rate	Stock of immigrants	International inbound tourists	Internet users	International telephone traffic (minutes per person)	
													Incoming	Outgoing
		(kilometres)	(% of GDP)	(% of GDP)	(% of GDP)	(% of GNI)	(% of GDP)	(% of GDP)	(per 1,000 people)	(% of population)	(thousands)	(% of population)		
HDI rank		2012	2012[b]	2012[b]	2012[b]	2011	2011[c]	2012[b]	2010/2015[d]	2013	2011	2012	2006–2011[e]	2006–2011[e]
118	South Africa	11,090	59.6	1.5	−1.8	0.3	0.29	1.6	−0.4	4.5	8,339	41.0	..	..
118	Syrian Arab Republic	6,710	71.1	2.5	−2.2	..	2.74	..	−13.7	6.4	8,546	24.3	81.1	22.2
120	Iraq	6,848	..	0.8	1.3	1.7	0.21	1.2	2.7	0.3	1,518	7.1	..	..
121	Guyana	9,073	..	6:4	−6.7	6.2	14.48	1.3	−8.2	1.8	157	34.3	110.2	46.1
121	Viet Nam	8,671	180.0	6.0	−6.5	3.0	6.95	0.4	−0.4	0.1	6,014	39.5	..	..
123	Cape Verde	8,000	114.8	2.8	−3.7	0.1	9.28	4.0	−6.9	3.0	428	34.7	172.6	34.1
124	Micronesia (Federated States of)	10,636	..	2.5	..	41.2	..	1.5	−15.7	2.5	26	26.0	..	..
125	Guatemala	9,114	60.8	2.3	−3.7	0.9	9.45	3.3	−1.0	0.5	1,823	16.0	138.6	48.7
125	Kyrgyzstan	6,892	136.2	11.2	−5.8	9.2	27.57	..	−6.3	4.1	3,114	21.7	47.0	83.0
127	Namibia	10,276	95.0	7.7	−4.4	2.4	0.12	..	−0.3	2.2	984	12.9	41.1	28.9
128	Timor-Leste	11,254	..	4.3	216.3	..	11.99	4.3	−13.3	1.0	51	0.9	7.0	11.7
129	Honduras	9,074	120.6	5.9	−5.9	3.8	15.87	..	−1.2	0.3	871	18.1	91.1	186.1
129	Morocco	6,601	86.6	2.5	−2.6	1.3	7.31	0.0	−2.7	0.2	9,342	55.0	123.3	23.9
131	Vanuatu	12,466	95.0	7.4	−7.4	12.4	2.77	1.5	0.0	1.2	94	10.6	..	..
132	Nicaragua	9,205	98.2	7.7	−8.3	7.6	9.48	2.4	−4.0	0.7	1,060	13.5	..	..
133	Kiribati	11,212	..	2.3	..	27.1	..	..	−2.0	2.6	5	10.7	..	..
133	Tajikistan	6,986	73.9	0.2	−0.2	5.5	46.91	0.0	−2.5	3.4	183	14.5	..	..
135	India	7,843	55.4	1.7	−1.1	0.2	3.41	3.5	−0.4	0.4	6,309	12.6	20.4	7.6
136	Bhutan	7,944	87.3	0.9	..	0.2	0.57	4.8	2.7	6.7	66	25.4	..	..
136	Cambodia	9,332	113.6	7.0	−10.6	0.1	1.25	..	−2.3	0.5	2,882	4.9	..	..
138	Ghana	8,385	102.1	8.1	−8.7	4.8	0.38	..	−0.8	1.4	931	17.1	50.8	27.3
139	Lao People's Democratic Republic	8,816	82.3	3.7	−3.8	5.2	1.34	2.1	−2.2	0.3	1,786	10.7	..	..
140	Congo	9,012	122.1	20.3	..	2.4	..	0.0	−2.1	9.7	101	6.1	31.9	73.3
141	Zambia	9,846	83.1	10.3	−8.2	6.1	0.24	2.5	−0.6	0.7	815	13.5	8.7	4.9
142	Bangladesh	8,214	60.3	1.0	−0.9	0.9	10.78	1.6	−2.6	0.9	303	6.3	141.6	2.9
142	Sao Tome and Principe	8,714	68.8	8.5	−7.0	30.2	2.77	..	−1.6	3.3	8	21.6	46.2	21.8
144	Equatorial Guinea	8,465	139.9	4.4	..	0.2	..	1.8	5.3	1.3	..	13.9	..	..
LOW HUMAN DEVELOPMENT														
145	Nepal	7,855	42.4	0.5	..	4.7	22.22	3.7	−2.9	3.5	736	11.1	14.0	..
146	Pakistan	7,322	33.1	0.4	−0.4	1.6	5.82	..	−1.8	2.2	907	10.0	44.2	20.6
147	Kenya	8,954	71.8	1.0	−0.8	7.4	2.72	2.5	−0.2	2.2	1,470	32.1	14.6	15.3
148	Swaziland	10,604	141.3	2.4	−5.0	3.2	1.38	4.7	−1.0	2.0	879	20.8	339.8	22.7
149	Angola	9,343	108.3	−2.9	8.6	0.2	0.00	..	0.6	0.4	481	16.9	..	..
150	Myanmar	..	..	..	..	..	..	0.2	−0.4	0.2	391	1.1	2.7	0.2
151	Rwanda	8,925	46.0	1.7	−2.3	20.2	1.62	..	−0.8	3.8	619	8.0	3.2	9.0
152	Cameroon	8,455	65.4	1.4	−0.5	0.3	0.45	0.1	−0.5	1.3	573	5.7	22.1	5.2
152	Nigeria	8,326	75.2	3.6	−7.9	0.8	8.45	..	−0.4	0.7	715	32.9	18.6	7.9
154	Yemen	7,912	65.1	−2.2	1.9	1.5	4.43	5.4	−1.1	1.3	1,025	17.4	80.9	4.8
155	Madagascar	10,325	63.2	9.2	..	4.2	..	0.1	0.0	0.1	225	2.1	4.0	2.1
156	Zimbabwe	10,030	137.3	4.0	..	7.4	..	..	5.7	2.6	2,423	17.1	32.6	14.5
157	Papua New Guinea	11,638	..	−2.5	0.8	4.9	0.09	..	0.0	0.3	165	2.3	..	..
157	Solomon Islands	11,809	72.9	12.2	−16.3	49.6	0.19	..	−4.3	1.4	23	7.0	..	..
159	Comoros	9,758	67.1	1.1	..	8.5	..	4.5	−2.8	1.7	11	6.0	..	..
159	Tanzania (United Republic of)	9,370	81.3	4.6	−6.0	10.4	0.32	0.4	−0.6	0.6	795	13.1	3.7	3.1
161	Mauritania	7,690	152.3	1.1	..	9.2	..	3.0	−1.0	2.3	..	5.4	38.4	15.2
162	Lesotho	10,772	154.5	5.2	−5.4	9.0	25.72	..	−1.9	0.1	397	4.6	8.4	5.6
163	Senegal	7,941	68.0	2.0	−2.7	7.4	10.23	8.5	−1.4	1.5	1,001	19.2	77.0	26.3
164	Uganda	8,793	58.1	8.7	−8.7	9.6	5.64	0.7	−0.8	1.4	1,151	14.7	..	6.0
165	Benin	8,305	41.9	1.6	−1.1	0.1	2.53	3.2	−0.2	2.3	209	3.8	32.6	27.8
166	Sudan	7,763	34.8	4.8	−4.2	1.9	2.22	4.7	−4.3	1.2	536	21.0	34.7	12.6
166	Togo	8,327	97.6	1.5	−0.8	15.5	9.13	5.3	−0.3	3.0	300	4.0	33.4	9.8
168	Haiti	8,407	68.8	2.5	..	23.2	21.12	2.0	−3.4	0.4	349	10.9	..	..
169	Afghanistan	7,192	45.3	0.5	0.0	35.0	..	1.3	−2.6	0.3	..	5.5	5.4	2.6
170	Djibouti	..	..	..	..	..	..	..	−3.7	14.2	53	8.3	43.6	222.0
171	Côte d'Ivoire	8,429	85.3	1.4	−3.4	6.2	1.55	0.0	0.5	12.0	270	2.4	29.3	29.2
172	Gambia	8,008	76.0	4.0	..	15.6	10.09	..	−1.5	8.8	106	12.4	..	..
173	Ethiopia	8,268	48.7	2.0	..	11.8	1.62	0.8	−0.1	0.8	523	1.5	8.0	0.4
174	Malawi	9,792	69.1	1.6	−1.5	14.5	0.31	3.0	0.0	1.3	767	4.4	6.7	0.9
175	Liberia	8,424	120.8	84.9	..	53.6	23.29	..	−0.9	5.3	..	3.8	29.4	36.8
176	Mali	7,964	61.8	1.7	0.6	12.3	4.44	0.9	−4.0	1.3	160	2.2	45.4	19.5

TABLE 13

		Trade		Financial flows					Human mobility			Communication		
	Remoteness	International trade	Foreign direct investment, net inflows	Private capital flows	Net official development assistance received[a]	Remittances, inflows	Total reserves minus gold	Net migration rate	Stock of immigrants	International inbound tourists	Internet users	International telephone traffic (minutes per person)		
	(kilometres)	(% of GDP)	(% of GDP)	(% of GDP)	(% of GNI)	(% of GDP)	(% of GDP)	(per 1,000 people)	(% of population)	(thousands)	(% of population)	Incoming	Outgoing
HDI rank	2012	2012[b]	2012[b]	2012[b]	2011	2011[c]	2012[b]	2010/2015[d]	2013	2011	2012	2006–2011[e]	2006–2011[e]
177 Guinea-Bissau	8,103	..	2.0	−2.6	12.3	4.74	1.5	−1.2	1.1	30	2.9	..	..
178 Mozambique	10,596	75.7	16.5	−36.0	16.3	1.25	..	−0.2	0.8	1,718	4.8	5.8	13.9
179 Guinea	8,264	78.4	18.8	−22.9	4.5	1.27	..	−0.2	3.2	30	1.5	..	..
180 Burundi	9,017	47.0	0.1	..	1.0	1.93	7.0	−0.4	2.5	142	1.2	..	..
181 Burkina Faso	7,930	49.7	0.1	1.8	0.3	1.06	3.3	−1.5	4.1	238	3.7	..	..
182 Eritrea	7,842	37.5	0.7	..	6.3	..	0.1	1.8	0.2	107	0.8	47.5	1.7
183 Sierra Leone	8,304	69.9	24.3	−25.5	14.6	2.00	0.8	−0.7	1.6	52	1.3	..	..
184 Chad	7,888	66.2	17.5	..	4.9	..	0.7	−1.9	3.4	71	2.1	..	..
185 Central African Republic	8,423	35.6	5.0	..	0.5	..	4.7	0.4	2.9	54	3.0	..	7.3
186 Congo (Democratic Republic of the)	9,216	146.3	10.2	..	38.4	0.73	0.9	−0.2	0.7	186	1.7	4.1	5.6
187 Niger	7,825	76.5	16.8	−18.9	10.9	1.69	2.8	−0.3	0.7	82	1.4	..	..
OTHER COUNTRIES OR TERRITORIES													
Korea, Democratic People's Rep. of	..	..	..	..	..	..	0.1	0.0	0.2	..	..	..	..
Marshall Islands	10,788	..	4.2	..	38.2	..	1.3	..	3.2	5	10.0	..	..
Monaco	..	..	..	..	..	..	..	..	64.2	295	87.0	..	..
Nauru	..	..	..	..	..	..	..	..	20.6	..	..	..	..
San Marino	5,958	..	..	..	..	..	0.5	..	15.4	156	50.9	..	..
Somalia	..	..	..	..	..	..	..	−2.9	0.2	..	1.4	..	..
South Sudan	..	94.2	..	..	..	..	2.3	15.7	5.6	..	..	..	..
Tuvalu	11,948	..	5.0	..	76.9	..	6.7	..	1.5	1	35.0	..	..
Human Development Index groups													
Very high human development	7,825	63.1	1.9	0.4	−0.3	0.26	..	2.5	12.5	581,506	77.1	..	174.8
High human development	8,536	60.0	2.8	−3.0	0.1	0.82	..	−0.1	1.8	282,225	42.5	21.2	13.1
Medium human development	8,741	63.3	2.2	−1.9	0.5	3.67	2.7	−0.9	0.7	84,432	17.6	..	..
Low human development	8,360	66.1	2.5	..	5.1	5.03	2.4	−0.8	1.6	19,970	12.3	..	10.3
Regions													
Arab States	7,037	91.9	1.5	1.0	..	..	1.3	0.4	8.3	71,884	34.2	92.0	106.3
East Asia and the Pacific	8,809	66.2	3.0	..	0.1	0.93	0.9	−0.3	0.4	125,944	36.7	..	..
Europe and Central Asia	6,364	77.0	3.6	−4.5	0.5	2.06	..	−0.6	6.7	74,011	41.1	79.3	34.1
Latin America and the Caribbean	10,621	45.8	3.1	−3.8	0.3	1.11	1.5	−1.0	1.3	70,256	43.4	39.9	25.4
South Asia	7,845	53.5	1.4	−1.1	0.6	3.57	2.7	−0.9	0.9	13,462	12.3	34.1	..
Sub-Saharan Africa	9,496	76.9	3.3	..	3.8	2.73	2.2	−0.1	1.8	30,695	15.2	..	9.7
Least developed countries	8,646	74.3	3.2	..	6.9	4.67	2.4	−1.1	1.2	18,701	6.8	..	..
Small island developing states	9,133	69.2	2.5	−9.6	3.3	5.79	..	−2.8	1.9	16,456	25.1	..	..
World	**8,078**	**62.4**	**2.2**	**−0.7**	**0.1**	**0.71**	**2.9**	**0.0**	**3.2**	**968,591**	**35.5**	**..**	**42.4**

NOTES

a A negative value refers to net official development assistance disbursed by donor countries.

b Data refer to 2012 or the most recent year available.

c Data refer to 2011 or the most recent year available.

d Data are average of annual projected values for 2010–2015.

e Data refer to the most recent year available during the period specified.

f Includes Svalbard and Jan Mayen Islands.

g Includes Christmas Island, Cocos (Keeling) Islands and Norfolk Island.

h Includes Canary Islands, Ceuta and Melilla.

i Includes Northern Cyprus.

j Includes Sabah and Sarawak.

k Includes Agalega, Rodrigues and Saint Brandon.

l Includes Nagorno-Karabakh.

m Includes Kosovo.

n Excludes Abkhazia and South Ossetia.

o Includes East Jerusalem. Refugees are not part of the foreign-born migrant stock in the State of Palestine.

p Includes Transnistria.

DEFINITIONS

Remoteness: GDP-weighted average distance from world markets, calculated as the sum of all bilateral distance between the capitals of one country and all others, weighted by the partner country's share in world GDP.

International trade: A basic indicator of openness to foreign trade and economic integration. It indicates the dependence of domestic producers on foreign demand (exports) and of domestic consumers and producers on foreign supply (imports), relative to the country's economic size (GDP). Trade is the sum of exports and imports of goods and services measured as a share of gross domestic product.

Foreign direct investment, net inflows: Sum of equity capital, reinvestment of earnings, other long-term capital and short-term capital, expressed as a percentage of GDP.

Private capital flows: Net foreign direct investment and portfolio investment, expressed as a percentage of GDP.

Net official development assistance received: Disbursements of loans made on concessional terms (net of repayments of principal) and grants by official agencies to promote economic development and welfare in countries and territories on the Development Assistance Committee list of aid recipients, expressed as a percentage of the recipient country's GNI.

Remittances, inflows: Earnings and material resources transferred by international migrants or refugees to recipients in their country of origin or countries in which the migrant formerly resided.

Total reserves minus gold: Sum of special drawing rights, reserves of International Monetary Fund (IMF) members held by the IMF and holdings of foreign exchange under the control of monetary authorities, excluding gold holdings, expressed as a percentage of GDP.

Net migration rate: Ratio of the difference between the number of in-migrants and out-migrants from a country to the average population, expressed per 1,000 people.

Stock of immigrants: Ratio of the stock of immigrants into a country, expressed as a percentage of the country's population. The definition of immigrant varies across countries but generally includes the stock of foreign-born people or the stock of foreign people (according to citizenship) or a combination of the two.

International inbound tourists: Arrivals of nonresident visitors (overnight visitors, tourists, same-day visitors, excursionists) at national borders .

Internet users: Percentage of people with access to the worldwide network.

International telephone traffic, incoming: Effective (completed) telephone calls (fixed and mobile) originating outside a given country with a destination inside the country, expressed in minutes of traffic per person.

International telephone traffic, outgoing: Effective (completed) telephone calls (fixed and mobile) originating inside a given country with a destination outside the country, expressed in minutes of traffic per person.

MAIN DATA SOURCES

Column 1: HDRO calculations based on data on GDP from World Bank (2013a) and data on geo-distance from CEPII (2013).

Column 2: HDRO calculations based on data from World Bank (2013a).

Columns 3–7, 10 and 11: World Bank 2013a.

Column 8: UNDESA 2013a.

Column 9: UNDESA 2013c.

Columns 12 and 13: HDRO calculations based on data on incoming and outgoing telephone traffic from ITU (2013).

TABLE **13**

TABLE 13   International integration | 211

TABLE 14

Environment

	Primary energy supply		Electrification rate	Carbon dioxide emissions per capita		Natural resource depletion	Forest area		Fresh water withdrawals	Deaths of children under age 5 due to			Population living on degraded land	Impact of natural disasters	
	Fossil fuels	Renewable sources												Number of deaths	Population affected
										(per 100,000 children under age 5)					
	(% of total)		(% of population)	(tonnes)	Average annual growth (%)	(% of GNI)	(% of total land area)	(% change)	(% of total renewable water resources)	Outdoor air pollution	Indoor air pollution	Unsafe water, unimproved sanitation or poor hygiene	(%)	(per year per million people)	(per million people)
HDI rank	2012[a]	2012[a]	2010	2010	1970/2010	2010–2012[b]	2011	1990/2011	2007–2011[b]	2008	2004	2004	2010	2005/2012	2005/2012
VERY HIGH HUMAN DEVELOPMENT															
1 Norway	57.3	47.8	..	11.7	4.5	10.5	33.3	11.1	0.8	0	0	0	0.2	0	41
2 Australia	95.4	4.6	..	16.9	5.5	6.9	19.3	−4.0	4.6	0	0	0	9.0	3	1,503
3 Switzerland	51.1	49.7	..	5.0	2.3	0.0	31.1	8.1	4.9	0	0	0	0.5	0	92
4 Netherlands	91.4	6.7	..	11.0	4.3	0.8	10.8	5.9	11.7	0	0	0	5.4	7	0
5 United States	83.6	16.3	..	17.6	5.6	1.2	33.3	2.9	15.6	0	0	0	1.1	2	5,691
6 Germany	80.2	20.4	..	9.1	..	0.2	31.8	3.3	21.0	0	0	0	8.1	0	3
7 New Zealand	61.4	38.4	..	7.2	3.3	1.1	31.4	7.0	1.5	0	0	..	5.3	5	20,003
8 Canada	73.7	27.9	..	14.6	5.1	3.0	34.1	0.0	1.5	0	0	0	2.7	0	407
9 Singapore	97.2	2.8	100.0	2.7	0.7	0.0	3.3	−4.3	31.7	0	0	0	..	..	..
10 Denmark	70.6	26.8	..	8.3	3.6	1.9	12.9	22.6	10.8	0	0	1	8.5	0	0
11 Ireland	84.7	6.4	..	8.9	3.8	0.1	10.9	60.8	1.5	0	0	..	0.5	0	45
12 Sweden	31.7	70.5	..	5.6	2.6	0.4	68.7	3.4	1.5	0	0	0	0.3	0	0
13 Iceland	15.3	84.7	..	6.2	2.9	0.0	0.3	254.0	0.1	0	0	0	..	0	0
14 United Kingdom	85.1	14.4	..	7.9	3.5	1.3	11.9	10.6	8.8	0	0	..	2.7	0	1,049
15 Hong Kong, China (SAR)	94.8	0.4	..	5.2	2.4	0.0	..	..	..	..	..	..	..	0	558
15 Korea (Republic of)	82.8	17.2	..	11.5	4.5	0.0	64.0	−0.8	36.5	0	0	..	2.9	1	289
17 Japan	94.8	5.2	..	9.2	3.9	0.0	68.6	0.2	20.9	0	0	0	0.3	18	795
18 Liechtenstein	..	..	..	..	..	..	43.1	6.2	..	..	..	..	..	..	..
19 Israel	96.7	4.8	99.7	9.3	3.9	0.3	7.1	16.5	79.7	0	0	..	12.9	1	2,675
20 France	49.1	52.4	..	5.6	2.6	0.0	29.2	10.1	15.0	0	0	0	3.9	3	881
21 Austria	67.1	32.2	..	8.0	3.5	0.2	47.2	3.1	4.7	0	0	0	2.7	0	28
21 Belgium	70.1	28.3	..	10.0	4.1	0.0	22.4	..	34.0	0	0	0	10.5	10	13
21 Luxembourg	87.4	4.0	..	21.4	6.1	0.1	33.5	..	1.9	0	0	2	..	0	0
24 Finland	43.0	47.5	..	11.5	4.5	0.1	72.9	1.5	1.5	0	0	0	0.0	0	75
25 Slovenia	66.6	34.5	..	7.5	..	0.3	62.3	5.6	3.0	0	0	..	8.4	0	2,133
26 Italy	83.7	13.9	..	6.7	3.1	0.1	31.4	21.6	23.7	0	0	0	2.2	1	184
27 Spain	75.9	24.9	..	5.9	2.7	0.0	36.8	33.0	29.0	0	0	0	1.4	0	64
28 Czech Republic	76.9	26.5	..	10.6	..	0.6	34.4	1.2	12.9	0	0	1	4.2	1	241
29 Greece	90.6	8.8	..	7.7	3.4	0.4	30.5	19.2	12.7	0	0	..	1.1	1	218
30 Brunei Darussalam	100.0	0.0	99.7	22.9	6.3	29.9	71.8	−8.4	1.1	0	0	..	..	..	..
31 Qatar	100.0	0.0	98.7	40.3	7.8	..	..	..	381.0	1	0	6	0.1	..	..
32 Cyprus	94.9	5.1	..	7.0	3.2	0.0	18.8	7.5	19.3	0	0	13	11.4	0	0
33 Estonia	88.1	14.6	..	13.7	..	1.7	52.1	5.7	14.0	0	0	0	5.0	0	37
34 Saudi Arabia	100.0	0.0	99.0	17.0	5.5	36.0	0.5	0.0	936.2	2	0	..	4.3	1	63
35 Lithuania	74.0	14.5	..	4.1	..	0.8	34.6	11.5	9.6	0	0	..	4.8	1	0
35 Poland	90.7	9.6	..	8.3	3.6	1.6	30.8	5.5	19.4	0	0	..	13.2	3	310
37 Andorra	..	..	..	6.6	..	..	34.0	0.0	..	0	0	0	..	..	..
37 Slovakia	67.5	32.3	..	6.6	..	0.4	40.2	0.6	1.4	0	0	0	9.1	3	38
39 Malta	94.5	5.5	..	6.2	2.9	..	0.9	0.0	71.3	0	0	..	..	..	..
40 United Arab Emirates	101.0	0.1	100.0	19.9	5.9	..	3.8	29.9	1,867.0	1	0	10	1.9	..	..
41 Chile	75.6	24.2	99.4	4.2	1.9	12.4	21.9	6.6	2.9	0	0	1	1.1	4	25,719
41 Portugal	74.9	22.0	..	4.9	2.3	0.1	37.8	4.0	12.3	0	0	..	2.3	1	21
43 Hungary	71.1	26.0	..	5.1	2.3	0.5	22.5	12.3	5.4	0	0	0	17.1	7	522
44 Bahrain	99.9	0.0	99.4	19.3	5.8	18.1	0.7	145.1	205.8	0	0	..	..	..	..
44 Cuba	86.7	13.3	97.0	3.4	1.3	3.3	27.3	42.4	11.6	0	1	1	17.0	0	61,215
46 Kuwait	100.0	0.0	100.0	31.3	7.1	29.3	0.4	82.6	2,075.0	1	0	..	0.6	..	..
47 Croatia	81.6	10.6	..	4.7	..	1.0	34.4	3.9	0.6	0	0	0	17.5	1	130
48 Latvia	63.7	33.8	..	3.4	..	0.5	54.1	6.0	1.2	0	0	0	1.8	3	0
49 Argentina	89.7	9.3	97.2	4.5	2.0	4.9	10.7	−16.2	4.0	0	0	3	1.7	0	1,837
HIGH HUMAN DEVELOPMENT															
50 Uruguay	57.0	42.1	98.8	2.0	0.0	0.5	10.2	94.4	2.6	0	0	3	5.7	1	10,565
51 Bahamas	..	..	..	6.8	3.1	0.0	51.4	0.0	..	0	0	2	..	1	12,130
51 Montenegro	60.2	28.4	..	4.2	..	..	40.4	0.0	..	..	..	..	8.0	0	4,999
53 Belarus	90.4	5.9	..	6.6	..	1.4	42.7	11.4	7.5	0	0	1	4.7	0	349
54 Romania	77.7	22.8	..	3.7	1.5	1.8	28.7	3.4	3.2	1	6	..	13.5	3	778
55 Libya	98.7	1.3	99.8	9.8	4.0	29.0	0.1	0.0	615.4	3	2	..	8.5	..	..
56 Oman	100.0	0.0	98.0	20.4	6.0	31.1	0.0	0.0	86.6	1	0	..	5.8	3	2,528
57 Russian Federation	91.0	9.2	..	12.2	..	14.3	49.4	0.1	1.5	0	0	5	3.1	44	176

		Primary energy supply		Electrification rate	Carbon dioxide emissions per capita		Natural resource depletion	Forest area		Fresh water withdrawals	Deaths of children under age 5 due to			Population living on degraded land	Impact of natural disasters	
		Fossil fuels	Renewable sources												Number of deaths	Population affected
											(per 100,000 children under age 5)					
		(% of total)		(% of population)	(tonnes)	Average annual growth (%)	(% of GNI)	(% of total land area)	(% change)	(% of total renewable water resources)	Outdoor air pollution	Indoor air pollution	Unsafe water, unimproved sanitation or poor hygiene	(%)	(per year per million people)	(per million people)
HDI rank		2012[a]	2012[a]	2010	2010	1970/2010	2010–2012[b]	2011	1990/2011	2007–2011[b]	2008	2004	2004	2010	2005/2012	2005/2012
58	Bulgaria	75.0	29.4	..	5.9	2.8	2.4	36.7	22.0	28.7	1	2	2	7.8	2	1,145
59	Barbados	..	..	..	5.4	2.5	..	19.4	0.0	108.0	0	0	0	..	0	4,482
60	Palau	..	..	..	10.6	4.2	..	87.6	..	..	0	0	40	..	..	..
61	Antigua and Barbuda	..	..	..	5.9	2.7	..	22.3	−4.9	16.2	0	1	0	..	0	178,447
62	Malaysia	94.5	5.5	99.4	7.7	3.4	6.2	62.0	−9.0	1.9	0	0	33	1.2	1	2,054
63	Mauritius	..	..	99.4	3.2	1.2	0.0	17.3	−9.7	26.4	0	0	7	..	1	689
64	Trinidad and Tobago	99.9	0.1	99.0	38.2	7.7	30.9	44.0	−6.2	6.0	0	1	5	..	0	0
65	Lebanon	95.5	3.3	99.9	4.7	2.2	0.0	13.4	4.6	18.6	1	0	40	1.2	0	4
65	Panama	79.7	20.2	88.1	2.6	0.7	0.5	43.6	−14.6	0.6	0	16	55	4.1	2	2,749
67	Venezuela (Bolivarian Republic of)	88.9	11.2	99.5	6.9	3.2	20.8	52.1	−11.6	0.7	0	1	30	1.9	1	785
68	Costa Rica	48.3	51.8	99.2	1.7	−0.5	0.1	51.5	2.5	5.1	0	2	4	1.3	2	13,250
69	Turkey	89.5	10.3	..	4.1	1.8	0.5	14.9	18.3	18.5	2	11	85	5.5	1	242
70	Kazakhstan	98.9	1.0	..	15.2	..	28.0	1.2	−3.5	18.6	5	3	249	23.5	0	1,213
71	Mexico	90.1	9.9	..	3.8	1.6	7.0	33.3	−8.0	16.9	1	8	23	3.8	1	10,808
71	Seychelles	..	..	..	7.8	3.5	0.0	88.5	0.0	..	0	0	..	..	0	38,151
73	Saint Kitts and Nevis	..	..	..	4.8	2.2	..	42.3	0.0	..	0	0	28	..	0	..
73	Sri Lanka	48.7	51.3	76.6	0.6	−2.9	0.3	29.4	−21.5	24.5	0	8	42	21.1	5	33,200
75	Iran (Islamic Republic of)	99.5	0.7	98.4	7.7	3.4	19.6	6.8	0.0	67.9	6	3	..	25.1	2	954
76	Azerbaijan	97.9	2.6	..	5.1	..	33.9	11.3	0.7	35.2	2	132	269	3.8	0	3,632
77	Jordan	96.0	2.0	99.4	3.4	1.4	1.7	1.1	−0.6	99.4	3	0	59	22.0	0	..
77	Serbia	89.1	11.1	..	6.3	..	..	31.6	19.3	2.5	..	..	..	18.5	0	3,731
79	Brazil	54.6	44.2	98.7	2.2	0.2	3.6	61.2	−10.0	0.7	0	18	123	7.9	1	4,236
79	Georgia	72.8	28.3	..	1.4	..	0.5	39.4	−1.4	2.9	2	70	169	1.9	0	5,359
79	Grenada	..	..	..	2.5	0.5	..	50.0	0.0	..	0	12	5	..	1	7,910
82	Peru	76.0	24.0	85.5	2.0	0.0	9.9	53.0	−3.3	1.0	2	21	69	0.7	8	14,947
83	Ukraine	79.6	20.7	..	6.6	..	3.9	16.8	4.9	13.8	0	0	3	6.2	3	1,344
84	Belize	..	..	..	1.4	−0.9	0.0	60.6	−12.8	1.2	0	21	27	1.1	4	56,475
84	The former Yugoslav Republic of Macedonia	82.1	10.4	..	5.2	..	4.0	39.8	10.8	16.1	0	1	..	7.1	0	96,337
86	Bosnia and Herzegovina	93.9	7.9	..	8.1	..	..	42.8	−1.1	0.9	1	1	2	6.1	0	3,222
87	Armenia	71.5	32.7	..	1.4	..	1.7	9.1	−25.7	36.8	2	17	65	9.6	0	..
88	Fiji	..	..	..	1.5	−0.7	0.5	55.7	6.8	0.3	1	18	11	..	6	13,877
89	Thailand	80.4	18.9	87.7	4.4	2.0	3.5	37.2	−2.9	13.1	0	21	59	17.0	3	70,880
90	Tunisia	85.3	14.8	99.5	2.5	0.5	5.2	6.6	59.0	61.7	1	3	64	36.7	0	312
91	China	88.3	11.7	99.7	6.2	2.9	6.1	22.5	33.4	19.5	2	10	55	8.6	8	68,601
91	Saint Vincent and the Grenadines	..	..	..	1.9	−0.1	0.0	68.7	5.8	..	0	2	..	..	0	21,068
93	Algeria	99.9	0.1	99.3	3.3	1.3	18.4	0.6	−11.0	48.9	1	5	101	28.8	1	433
93	Dominica	..	..	..	1.9	−0.1	0.0	59.2	−11.2	..	0	1	0	..	3	54,721
95	Albania	60.5	26.6	..	1.4	−1.0	3.7	28.3	−1.8	3.1	0	5	50	5.7	0	41,348
96	Jamaica	82.1	17.9	92.0	2.6	0.7	1.1	31.1	−2.3	9.9	1	15	47	3.3	2	16,769
97	Saint Lucia	..	..	..	2.3	0.3	..	77.0	7.3	..	0	3	2	..	7	8,562
98	Colombia	75.6	24.8	97.4	1.6	−0.5	10.4	54.4	−3.4	0.6	1	6	33	2.0	4	19,920
98	Ecuador	86.3	12.9	92.2	2.2	0.2	16.4	38.9	−22.0	2.3	1	2	63	1.6	1	8,368
100	Suriname	..	..	..	4.5	2.1	8.5	94.6	−0.1	0.5	0	0	43	..	1	30,325
100	Tonga	..	..	..	1.5	−0.7	0.0	12.5	0.0	..	0	16	55	..	9	2,448
102	Dominican Republic	89.3	10.7	96.9	2.1	0.1	0.4	40.8	0.0	26.1	2	12	73	7.0	6	5,827
MEDIUM HUMAN DEVELOPMENT																
103	Maldives	..	..	..	3.3	..	0.0	3.0	0.0	15.7	1	41	167	..	1	4,596
103	Mongolia	95.4	4.1	86.2	4.2	1.9	32.2	7.0	−13.7	1.6	19	78	195	31.5	3	147,305
103	Turkmenistan	100.9	0.0	..	10.5	..	..	8.8	0.0	112.5	2	2	449	11.1	..	..
106	Samoa	..	..	..	0.9	−2.1	0.3	60.4	31.5	..	0	26	63	..	96	33,004
107	Palestine, State of	..	..	..	0.6	..	..	1.5	1.0	49.9	..	..	..	..	0	979
108	Indonesia	66.4	33.6	73.0	1.8	−0.3	7.2	51.7	−20.9	5.6	2	41	130	3.1	6	3,976
109	Botswana	65.4	22.3	45.4	2.7	..	3.1	19.8	−18.1	1.6	4	210	341	22.0	26	2,694
110	Egypt	96.5	3.7	99.6	2.6	0.7	9.1	0.1	60.5	96.6	2	2	86	25.3	0	18
111	Paraguay	33.8	147.8	97.4	0.8	−2.3	0.0	43.8	−17.7	0.1	1	21	56	1.3	2	41,164
112	Gabon	38.9	61.1	60.0	1.7	−0.5	34.7	85.4	0.0	0.1	9	33	102	..	0	16,269
113	Bolivia (Plurinational State of)	72.7	27.3	80.2	1.5	−0.7	14.7	52.5	−9.4	0.4	0	93	245	2.0	3	17,376
114	Moldova (Republic of)	94.9	3.4	..	1.4	..	0.1	11.9	22.5	9.1	1	13	15	21.8	1	13,802
115	El Salvador	47.9	51.9	91.6	1.0	−1.7	0.5	13.6	−25.0	7.3	1	24	82	6.3	9	11,704

TABLE 14 Environment | 213

TABLE **14**

TABLE 14 ENVIRONMENT

		Primary energy supply		Electrification rate	Carbon dioxide emissions per capita		Natural resource depletion	Forest area		Fresh water withdrawals	Deaths of children under age 5 due to (per 100,000 children under age 5)			Population living on degraded land	Impact of natural disasters	
		Fossil fuels	Renewable sources								Outdoor air pollution	Indoor air pollution	Unsafe water, unimproved sanitation or poor hygiene		Number of deaths	Population affected
		(% of total)		(% of population)	(tonnes)	Average annual growth (%)	(% of GNI)	(% of total land area)	(% change)	(% of total renewable water resources)				(%)	(per year per million people)	(per million people)
HDI rank		2012ᵃ	2012ᵃ	2010	2010	1970/2010	2010–2012ᵇ	2011	1990/2011	2007–2011ᵇ	2008	2004	2004	2010	2005/2012	2005/2012
116	Uzbekistan	98.2	1.8	..	3.7	..	17.5	7.7	7.4	100.6	1	192	325	27.0	0	29
117	Philippines	59.7	40.3	83.3	0.9	−2.1	2.7	25.9	17.5	17.0	1	37	96	2.2	12	68,576
118	South Africa	87.2	12.9	75.8	9.2	3.9	6.7	7.6	0.0	24.3	2	23	104	17.5	1	967
118	Syrian Arab Republic	98.7	1.4	92.7	2.9	0.9	13.3	2.7	33.7	86.4	2	12	54	33.3	0	30,906
120	Iraq	97.5	1.0	98.0	3.7	1.6	50.6	1.9	3.3	73.4	12	12	383	4.5	0	337
121	Guyana	..	..	..	2.2	0.2	10.5	77.2	0.0	0.7	0	38	132	..	5	131,160
121	Viet Nam	71.0	28.2	97.6	1.7	−0.4	9.6	45.0	56.3	9.3	1	27	65	8.0	3	17,587
123	Cape Verde	..	..	..	0.7	−2.5	0.1	21.0	46.7	6.8	0	26	93	..	2	41,479
124	Micronesia (Federated States of)	..	..	..	1.0	..	..	58.4	−0.4	..	0	30	83	..	0	0
125	Guatemala	33.5	66.2	80.0	0.8	−2.3	2.1	33.6	−24.2	3.1	2	57	126	9.1	15	51,710
125	Kyrgyzstan	68.4	39.4	..	1.2	..	9.7	5.1	16.1	32.6	1	115	245	9.7	2	47,549
127	Namibia	66.0	21.0	43.7	1.5	..	1.0	8.8	−17.6	1.6	1	11	21	28.5	14	79,190
128	Timor-Leste	..	..	38.0	0.2	..	..	49.1	−24.3	14.3	0	0	149	..	2	3,007
129	Honduras	51.6	48.8	79.9	1.1	−1.6	0.6	45.3	−37.7	2.2	1	49	106	15.0	5	13,635
129	Morocco	93.6	4.1	98.9	1.6	−0.6	2.6	11.5	1.8	43.5	6	8	114	39.1	0	619
131	Vanuatu	..	..	..	0.5	−3.4	0.0	36.1	0.0	..	0	9	41	..	0	13,300
132	Nicaragua	49.8	50.3	72.1	0.8	−2.3	1.2	25.3	−32.6	0.7	1	49	102	13.9	7	13,510
133	Kiribati	..	..	..	0.6	−2.8	..	15.0	0.0	..	0	0	206	..	0	883
133	Tajikistan	42.9	57.5	..	0.4	..	1.1	2.9	0.5	51.1	1	343	551	10.5	3	43,344
135	India	72.3	27.6	75.0	1.7	−0.5	4.9	23.1	7.3	33.9	5	131	316	9.6	1	11,130
136	Bhutan	..	..	..	0.7	−2.7	3.4	84.9	31.5	0.4	0	124	324	0.1	4	14,213
136	Cambodia	26.2	71.1	31.1	0.3	−4.7	0.1	56.5	−23.0	0.5	3	346	595	39.3	4	22,695
138	Ghana	37.4	63.1	60.5	0.4	−4.1	10.5	21.2	−35.2	1.8	3	152	226	1.4	2	3,586
139	Lao People's Democratic Republic	..	..	63.0	0.3	−4.7	10.5	67.9	−9.5	1.0	1	157	242	4.1	1	31,911
140	Congo	48.9	51.0	37.1	0.5	−3.4	67.8	65.6	−1.4	0.0	19	149	220	0.1	10	2,080
141	Zambia	8.8	91.8	18.5	0.2	−5.8	17.5	66.3	−6.6	1.5	12	378	503	4.6	3	33,251
142	Bangladesh	71.5	28.5	46.5	0.4	..	2.3	11.1	−3.7	2.9	2	142	334	11.3	5	29,222
142	Sao Tome and Principe	..	..	..	0.6	−3.2	0.7	28.1	0.0	0.3	9	225	428	..	..	..
144	Equatorial Guinea	..	..	..	6.7	3.1	40.4	57.5	−13.2	0.1	10	0	505	..	2	1,398
LOW HUMAN DEVELOPMENT																
145	Nepal	12.5	86.9	76.3	0.1	−6.4	2.2	25.4	−24.7	4.5	1	139	337	2.3	6	9,560
146	Pakistan	60.9	39.1	67.4	0.9	−1.9	2.6	2.1	−34.9	74.4	22	132	205	4.5	48	29,793
147	Kenya	19.7	80.3	18.1	0.3	−4.6	1.2	6.1	−6.8	8.9	4	217	362	31.0	3	47,765
148	Swaziland	..	..	..	0.9	−2.1	0.0	33.0	20.2	23.1	2	148	252	..	0	89,821
149	Angola	39.3	60.7	40.2	1.6	−0.6	35.0	46.8	−4.3	0.5	11	1,073	1,266	3.3	21	13,856
150	Myanmar	21.3	78.7	48.8	0.2	−5.9	..	48.2	−19.7	2.8	3	181	378	19.2	290	6,913
151	Rwanda	..	..	..	0.1	−8.6	2.9	18.0	39.9	1.6	2	803	970	10.1	2	14,103
152	Cameroon	26.8	73.2	48.7	0.4	−4.3	5.3	41.7	−19.0	0.3	14	361	497	15.3	5	702
152	Nigeria	17.4	82.6	50.3	0.5	−3.4	24.4	9.5	−49.9	4.6	14	370	559	11.5	3	7,126
154	Yemen	98.5	1.5	39.6	1.0	−1.8	15.6	1.0	0.0	168.6	5	174	377	32.4	2	239
155	Madagascar	..	..	17.4	0.1	−7.3	2.7	21.5	−8.7	4.9	2	390	540	0.0	3	13,101
156	Zimbabwe	28.3	70.3	36.9	0.7	−2.5	3.4	39.5	−31.0	21.0	5	168	256	29.4	37	43,309
157	Papua New Guinea	..	..	..	0.5	−3.6	23.1	63.1	−9.3	0.0	1	108	288	..	7	9,760
157	Solomon Islands	..	..	..	0.4	−4.0	15.1	78.9	−5.0	..	0	54	84	..	17	9,788
159	Comoros	..	..	..	0.2	−5.5	1.1	1.4	−78.3	0.8	2	108	177	..	5	106,714
159	Tanzania (United Republic of)	10.7	89.3	14.8	0.2	−6.2	4.4	37.3	−20.4	5.4	4	239	322	25.0	1	15,931
161	Mauritania	..	..	..	0.6	−2.9	39.2	0.2	−42.9	11.8	16	220	390	23.8	2	77,339
162	Lesotho	..	..	17.0	0.0	..	1.0	1.5	10.5	1.4	2	19	44	63.6	1	202,696
163	Senegal	53.2	46.4	53.5	0.5	−3.2	1.6	43.8	−9.8	5.7	14	292	530	16.2	3	13,748
164	Uganda	..	..	8.5	0.1	−7.0	5.0	14.5	−39.0	0.5	2	327	427	23.5	3	11,021
165	Benin	41.7	56.2	27.9	0.5	−3.2	0.3	40.0	−21.7	0.5	8	394	518	1.6	2	18,298
166	Sudan	29.5	70.5	35.9	0.3	−4.5	9.8	23.2	−27.9	42.8	11	181	255	39.9	8	31,574
166	Togo	15.2	82.4	27.9	0.2	−5.1	3.7	4.9	−61.0	1.2	5	302	419	5.1	2	9,785
168	Haiti	22.0	78.0	20.0	0.2	−5.4	0.6	3.6	−13.6	8.6	5	297	428	15.2	2,485	58,688
169	Afghanistan	..	..	30.0	0.3	−4.7	2.1	2.1	0.0	31.0	21	1,183	1,405	11.0	13	18,859
170	Djibouti	..	..	..	0.6	−2.8	0.3	0.2	0.0	6.3	31	41	454	7.5	1	223,142
171	Côte d'Ivoire	21.5	79.0	58.9	0.3	−4.6	4.4	32.7	1.8	1.9	9	370	561	1.3	1	176
172	Gambia	..	..	..	0.3	−4.8	0.7	47.6	9.0	1.1	7	197	286	17.9	1	59,517
173	Ethiopia	5.7	94.3	23.0	0.1	−7.9	5.2	12.2	−20.0	4.6	2	538	705	72.3	2	32,750

TABLE 14

TABLE 14 — Environment

HDI rank	Primary energy supply — Fossil fuels (% of total) 2012[a]	Primary energy supply — Renewable sources (% of total) 2012[a]	Electrification rate (% of population) 2010	Carbon dioxide emissions per capita (tonnes) 2010	Carbon dioxide emissions per capita — Average annual growth (%) 1970/2010	Natural resource depletion (% of GNI) 2010–2012[b]	Forest area (% of total land area) 2011	Forest area (% change) 1990/2011	Fresh water withdrawals (% of total renewable water resources) 2007–2011[b]	Deaths of children under age 5 — Outdoor air pollution 2008	Deaths of children under age 5 — Indoor air pollution 2004	Deaths of children under age 5 — Unsafe water, unimproved sanitation or poor hygiene 2004	Population living on degraded land (%) 2010	Impact of natural disasters — Number of deaths (per year per million people) 2005/2012	Impact of natural disasters — Population affected (per million people) 2005/2012
174 Malawi	..	..	8.7	0.1	−7.7	1.7	34.0	−17.8	7.9	3	498	617	19.4	2	61,541
175 Liberia	..	..	..	0.2	−5.6	4.7	44.6	−12.8	0.1	6	676	885	..	1	28,135
176 Mali	..	..	..	0.0	−9.1	9.8	10.2	−11.8	6.5	9	703	880	59.5	1	55,720
177 Guinea-Bissau	..	..	..	0.2	−6.3	0.5	71.6	−9.2	0.6	12	648	873	1.0	41	20,739
178 Mozambique	9.5	93.3	15.0	0.1	−6.8	2.8	49.4	−10.5	0.4	11	270	388	1.9	4	20,084
179 Guinea	..	..	..	0.1	−6.9	14.2	26.5	−10.4	0.2	11	324	480	0.8	4	1,704
180 Burundi	..	..	..	0.0	−9.7	9.6	6.6	−41.1	2.3	4	897	1,088	18.5	2	39,618
181 Burkina Faso	..	..	14.6	0.1	−7.0	7.8	20.4	−18.4	5.7	9	632	786	73.2	27	28,139
182 Eritrea	21.7	78.3	32.0	0.1	..	0.0	15.1	−5.8	9.2	3	237	379	58.8	0	305,872
183 Sierra Leone	..	..	..	0.1	−6.8	1.8	37.8	−13.2	0.1	11	1,207	1,473	..	11	1,069
184 Chad	..	..	..	0.0	−9.3	25.4	9.1	−12.7	2.0	14	488	618	45.4	11	54,883
185 Central African Republic	..	..	..	0.1	−8.4	0.1	36.2	−2.7	0.1	10	411	511	..	1	1,959
186 Congo (Democratic Republic of the)	4.2	95.8	15.2	0.0	−8.9	18.0	67.9	−4.1	0.1	16	644	786	0.1	4	604
187 Niger	..	..	..	0.1	−7.5	1.8	0.9	−38.7	2.9	6	1,023	1,229	25.0	5	122,010
OTHER COUNTRIES OR TERRITORIES															
Korea, Democratic People's Rep. of	88.4	11.6	26.0	2.9	..	..	46.0	−32.5	11.2	3	0	245	2.9	6	26,951
Marshall Islands	..	..	..	2.0	..	..	70.2	..	..	..	45	201	..	0	66,716
Monaco	..	..	..	..	..	..	..	..	..	0	0	2	..	..	..
Nauru	..	..	..	..	..	..	..	..	..	0	1	..	..	..	..
San Marino	..	..	..	..	..	..	..	..	..	0	0	..	..	..	..
Somalia	..	..	..	0.1	−8.3	..	10.6	−19.5	22.4	19	710	885	26.3	16	145,928
South Sudan	..	..	..	..	..	..	33.3	0.0	..	..	..	..	..	0	16,491
Tuvalu	..	..	..	..	..	..	..	..	..	0	18	148	..	0	0
Human Development Index groups															
Very high human development	82.0	17.9	..	11.2	..	2.4	27.6	1.7	8.5	0	0	..	3.3	3	2,989
High human development	87.2	12.8	..	5.8	..	7.8	36.6	−1.0	4.6	2	10	61	8.8	8	42,653
Medium human development	74.9	25.3	..	1.8	..	7.7	27.6	−8.7	13.9	4	106	261	10.3	3	14,518
Low human development	..	..	..	0.4	..	12.1	26.3	−13.9	6.5	10	396	542	20.2	48	24,030
Regions															
Arab States	96.8	3.2	87.8	4.6	..	24.7	5.9	−22.5	71.1	6	73	214	24.3	2	10,933
East Asia and the Pacific	..	..	..	4.9	..	..	29.7	2.6	..	2	28	90	..	15	54,689
Europe and Central Asia	89.4	10.5	..	5.4	..	7.2	9.1	7.7	34.8	2	63	169	10.7	1	5,389
Latin America and the Caribbean	74.2	25.8	..	2.9	..	6.9	46.7	−9.2	1.5	1	22	80	5.3	44	12,252
South Asia	76.3	23.7	72.0	1.7	..	6.1	14.6	3.3	26.8	7	153	328	10.0	7	14,621
Sub-Saharan Africa	..	..	..	0.9	..	14.8	28.3	−10.8	1.6	8	428	576	22.3	4	22,382
Least developed countries	..	..	..	0.3	..	8.7	28.9	−12.0	3.1	7	431	590	23.5	51	28,158
Small island developing states	..	..	..	2.7	..	4.9	63.0	−3.6	..	2	123	218	..	479	33,638
World	81.4	18.6	..	4.6	..	5.3	31.0	−3.5	7.6	5	140	258	10.2	12	24,203

Deaths of children under age 5 due to are per 100,000 children under age 5.

NOTES

a Data refer to 2012 or the most recent year available.

b Data refer to the most recent year available during the period specified.

DEFINITIONS

Fossil fuels: Percentage of total energy supply that comes from natural resources formed from biomass in the geological past (such as coal, oil and natural gas).

Renewable energy sources: Percentage of total energy supply that comes from constantly replenished natural processes, including solar, wind, biomass, geothermal, hydropower and ocean resources, and some waste. Excludes nuclear energy.

Electrification rate: Proportion of people with access to electricity, expressed as a percentage of the total population. It includes electricity sold commercially (both on grid and off grid) and self-generated electricity but excludes unauthorized connections.

Carbon dioxide emissions per capita: Human-originated carbon dioxide emissions stemming from the burning of fossil fuels, gas flaring and the production of cement, divided by midyear population. Includes carbon dioxide emitted by forest biomass through depletion of forest areas.

Natural resource depletion: Monetary expression of energy, mineral and forest depletion, expressed as a percentage of total gross national income (GNI).

Forest area: Land spanning more than 0.5 hectare with trees taller than 5 metres and a canopy cover of more than 10 percent or trees able to reach these thresholds in situ. Excludes land predominantly under agricultural or urban land use, tree stands in agricultural production systems (for example, in fruit plantations and agroforestry systems) and trees in urban parks and gardens. Areas under reforestation that have not yet reached but are expected to reach a canopy cover of 10 percent and a tree height of 5 meters are included, as are temporarily unstocked areas resulting from human intervention or natural causes that are expected to regenerate.

Fresh water withdrawals: Total fresh water withdrawn, expressed as a percentage of total renewable water resources.

Deaths due to outdoor air pollution: Deaths of children under age 5 due to respiratory infections and diseases, lung cancer and selected cardiovascular diseases attributable to outdoor air pollution.

Deaths due to indoor air pollution: Deaths of children of age under 5 due to acute respiratory infections attributable to indoor smoke from solid fuels.

Deaths due to unsafe water, unimproved sanitation or poor hygiene: Deaths of children under age 5 due to diarrhoea attributable to poor water, sanitation or hygiene.

Population living on degraded land: Percentage of the population living on severely or very severely degraded land. Land degradation estimates consider biomass, soil health, water quantity and biodiversity.

Number of deaths due to natural disaster: Number of people confirmed as dead and missing and presumed dead as a result of a natural disaster, expressed per million people. Natural disasters are classified as climatological, hydrological and meteorological disasters and include drought, extreme temperature, flood, mass movement, wet storm and wildfire.

Population affected by natural disasters: People requiring immediate assistance during a period of emergency as a result of a natural disaster, including displaced, evacuated, homeless and injured people, expressed per million people.

MAIN DATA SOURCES

Columns 1 and 2: HDRO calculations based on data on total primary energy supply from World Bank (2013a).

Columns 3–5 and 7: World Bank 2013a.

Column 6: HDRO calculations based on World Bank (2013a).

Column 8: HDRO calculations based on data on forest and total land area from World Bank (2013a)

Column 9: FAO 2013b.

Columns 10–12: WHO 2013a.

Column 13: FAO 2013a.

Columns 14 and 15: CRED EM-DAT 2013 and UNDESA 2013a.

TABLE
14

TABLE 14 Environment | 215

TABLE 15

Population trends

HDI rank	Population Total (millions)		Under age 5 (millions)	Ages 65 and older (millions)	Average annual growth rate (%)		Urban[a] (% of population)	Median age (years)	Dependency ratio (per 100 people ages 15–64) Young age (0–14)	Old age (65 and older)	Total fertility rate (births per woman)		Sex ratio at birth[b] (male to female births)
	2013[c]	2030[c]	2013[c]	2013[c]	2000/2005	2010/2015[c]	2013[c]	2015[c]	2015	2015	2000/2005	2010/2015[c]	2010/2015[c]
VERY HIGH HUMAN DEVELOPMENT													
1 Norway	5.0[d]	5.8[d]	0.3[d]	0.8[d]	0.6[d]	1.0[d]	79.9[d]	39.2[d]	28.6[d]	25.2[d]	1.8[e]	1.9[d]	1.06[d]
2 Australia	23.3[e]	28.3[e]	1.6[e]	3.3[e]	1.3[e]	1.3[e]	89.5[e]	37.4[e]	29.1[e]	22.7[e]	1.8[e]	1.9[e]	1.06[e]
3 Switzerland	8.1	9.5	0.4	1.4	0.7	1.0	73.8	42.3	21.9	27.1	1.4	1.5	1.05
4 Netherlands	16.8	17.3	0.9	2.9	0.6	0.3	84.0	42.4	25.8	27.8	1.7	1.8	1.06
5 United States	320.1	362.6	20.8	44.7	0.9	0.8	82.9	37.7	29.4	22.2	2.0	2.0	1.05
6 Germany	82.7	79.6	3.5	17.5	0.1	−0.1	74.2	46.3	19.7	32.7	1.4	1.4	1.06
7 New Zealand	4.5	5.2	0.3	0.6	1.4	1.0	86.3	37.3	30.8	22.5	1.9	2.1	1.06
8 Canada	35.2	40.6	2.0	5.3	1.0	1.0	80.9	40.5	24.4	23.7	1.5	1.7	1.06
9 Singapore	5.4	6.6	0.3	0.6	2.7	2.0	100.0	38.7	20.8	15.2	1.3	1.3	1.07
10 Denmark	5.6	6.0	0.3	1.0	0.3	0.4	87.2	41.5	27.0	29.1	1.8	1.9	1.06
11 Ireland	4.6	5.3	0.4	0.6	1.8	1.1	62.8	35.9	32.9	19.2	2.0	2.0	1.07
12 Sweden	9.6	10.7	0.6	1.8	0.4	0.7	85.5	41.2	27.6	31.8	1.7	1.9	1.06
13 Iceland	0.3	0.4	0.0	0.0	1.1	1.1	93.9	35.9	31.2	20.3	2.0	2.1	1.05
14 United Kingdom	63.1	68.6	4.0	11.0	0.5	0.6	79.9	40.5	27.4	28.1	1.7	1.9	1.05
15 Hong Kong, China (SAR)	7.2	7.9	0.3	1.0	0.2	0.7	100.0	43.2	16.0	20.5	1.0	1.1	1.07
15 Korea (Republic of)	49.3	52.2	2.4	6.0	0.5	0.5	83.8	40.5	19.5	17.9	1.2	1.3	1.07
17 Japan	127.1	120.6	5.4	31.9	0.2	−0.1	92.5	46.5	21.2	43.6	1.3	1.4	1.06
18 Liechtenstein	0.0	0.0	..	..	1.0	0.7	14.3	..	..	..	..	..	..
19 Israel	7.7	9.6	0.8	0.8	1.9	1.3	92.0	30.1	45.8	17.8	2.9	2.9	1.05
20 France	64.3	69.3	3.9	11.5	0.7	0.5	86.9	41.0	28.6	29.6	1.9	2.0	1.05
21 Austria	8.5	9.0	0.4	1.6	0.5	0.4	68.1	43.3	21.6	27.9	1.4	1.5	1.06
21 Belgium	11.1	11.7	0.7	2.0	0.5	0.4	97.5	41.9	26.7	29.0	1.7	1.9	1.05
21 Luxembourg	0.5	0.6	0.0	0.1	1.0	1.3	85.9	39.1	25.4	21.2	1.7	1.7	1.05
24 Finland	5.4[f]	5.6[f]	0.3[f]	1.0[f]	0.3[f]	0.3[f]	83.9[f]	42.6[f]	26.1[f]	32.3[f]	1.8[f]	1.9[f]	1.04[f]
25 Slovenia	2.1	2.1	0.1	0.4	0.1	0.2	49.8	43.0	21.4	26.4	1.2	1.5	1.05
26 Italy	61.0	61.2	2.9	12.9	0.6	0.2	68.7	45.0	21.8	33.8	1.3	1.5	1.06
27 Spain	46.9[g]	48.2[g]	2.5[g]	8.3[g]	1.5[g]	0.4[g]	77.7[g]	42.2[g]	23.4[g]	27.6[g]	1.3[g]	1.5[g]	1.06[g]
28 Czech Republic	10.7	11.1	0.6	1.8	0.0	0.4	73.4	40.9	23.0	26.3	1.2	1.6	1.06
29 Greece	11.1	11.0	0.6	2.2	0.1	0.0	61.9	43.5	22.6	31.1	1.3	1.5	1.07
30 Brunei Darussalam	0.4	0.5	0.0	0.0	2.1	1.4	76.7	31.1	34.6	6.9	2.3	2.0	1.06
31 Qatar	2.2	2.8	0.1	0.0	6.5	5.9	99.1	31.7	15.9	1.1	3.0	2.1	1.05
32 Cyprus	1.1[h]	1.3[h]	0.1[h]	0.1[h]	1.8[h]	1.1[h]	70.9[h]	35.9[h]	23.5[h]	18.1[h]	1.6[h]	1.5[h]	1.07[h]
33 Estonia	1.3	1.2	0.1	0.2	−0.6	−0.3	69.6	41.3	24.7	28.2	1.4	1.6	1.06
34 Saudi Arabia	28.8	35.6	2.9	0.8	4.1	1.8	82.7	28.4	41.2	4.4	3.5	2.7	1.03
35 Lithuania	3.0	2.8	0.2	0.5	−1.2	−0.5	67.3	39.7	22.4	22.8	1.3	1.5	1.05
35 Poland	38.2	37.4	2.1	5.5	−0.1	0.0	60.7	39.4	21.7	22.0	1.3	1.4	1.06
37 Andorra	0.1	0.1	..	..	4.3	0.8	86.2	..	..	..	..	..	..
37 Slovakia	5.5	5.4	0.3	0.7	0.0	0.1	54.6	38.9	21.4	19.1	1.2	1.4	1.05
39 Malta	0.4	0.4	0.0	0.1	0.4	0.3	95.2	41.4	20.8	26.0	1.4	1.4	1.06
40 United Arab Emirates	9.3	12.3	0.7	0.0	6.3	2.5	84.9	31.4	19.4	0.6	2.4	1.8	1.05
41 Chile	17.6	19.8	1.2	1.8	1.1	0.9	89.6	33.7	29.9	15.3	2.0	1.8	1.04
41 Portugal	10.6	10.4	0.5	2.0	0.6	0.0	62.1	43.0	21.8	29.3	1.5	1.3	1.06
43 Hungary	10.0	9.5	0.5	1.7	−0.3	−0.2	70.4	41.0	21.9	26.1	1.3	1.4	1.06
44 Bahrain	1.3	1.6	0.1	0.0	5.5	1.7	88.8	30.2	28.3	3.0	2.7	2.1	1.04
44 Cuba	11.3	10.8	0.5	1.5	0.3	−0.1	75.1	41.3	22.1	19.9	1.6	1.5	1.06
46 Kuwait	3.4	4.8	0.3	0.1	3.7	3.6	98.3	29.7	33.6	3.3	2.6	2.6	1.04
47 Croatia	4.3	4.0	0.2	0.8	−0.4	−0.4	58.4	43.1	22.0	28.6	1.4	1.5	1.06
48 Latvia	2.1	1.9	0.1	0.4	−1.3	−0.6	67.7	41.7	23.5	28.2	1.3	1.6	1.05
49 Argentina	41.4	46.9	3.4	4.5	0.9	0.9	92.8	31.6	36.7	17.3	2.4	2.2	1.04
HIGH HUMAN DEVELOPMENT													
50 Uruguay	3.4	3.6	0.2	0.5	0.0	0.3	92.7	34.8	33.4	22.3	2.2	2.1	1.05
51 Bahamas	0.4	0.4	0.0	0.0	2.0	1.4	84.6	32.5	29.4	11.7	1.9	1.9	1.06
51 Montenegro	0.6	0.6	0.0	0.1	0.2	0.0	63.7	37.6	26.9	20.2	1.8	1.7	1.07
53 Belarus	9.4	8.5	0.5	1.3	−0.6	−0.5	75.9	39.5	22.4	19.7	1.2	1.5	1.06
54 Romania	21.7	20.2	1.1	3.3	−0.2	−0.3	52.8	40.0	21.8	22.3	1.3	1.4	1.06
55 Libya	6.2	7.5	0.6	0.3	1.6	0.9	78.1	27.2	44.7	7.6	2.9	2.4	1.06
56 Oman	3.6	4.9	0.4	0.1	2.8	7.9	73.9	27.1	29.2	4.0	3.2	2.9	1.05
57 Russian Federation	142.8	133.6	8.3	18.6	−0.4	−0.2	74.2	38.5	23.4	18.8	1.3	1.5	1.06
58 Bulgaria	7.2	6.2	0.3	1.4	−0.8	−0.8	74.3	43.4	21.2	30.1	1.2	1.5	1.06
59 Barbados	0.3	0.3	0.0	0.0	0.5	0.5	45.4	37.4	26.7	16.2	1.8	1.9	1.04

		Population						Urban[a]	Median age	Dependency ratio (per 100 people ages 15–64)		Total fertility rate		Sex ratio at birth[b]
		Total		Under age 5	Ages 65 and older	Average annual growth rate				Young age (0–14)	Old age (65 and older)	(births per woman)		(male to female births)
		(millions)		(millions)	(millions)	(%)		(% of population)	(years)					
HDI rank		2013[c]	2030[c]	2013[c]	2013[c]	2000/2005	2010/2015[c]	2013[c]	2015[c]	2015	2015	2000/2005	2010/2015[c]	2010/2015[c]
60	Palau	0.0	0.0	..	..	0.8	0.8	85.8	..	..	..	..	..	..
61	Antigua and Barbuda	0.1	0.1	0.0	0.0	1.2	1.0	29.8	30.9	35.2	10.4	2.3	2.1	1.03
62	Malaysia	29.7[i]	36.8[i]	2.5[i]	1.6[i]	2.0[i]	1.6[i]	74.2[i]	28.2[i]	36.6[i]	8.3[i]	2.5[i]	2.0[i]	1.06[i]
63	Mauritius	1.2[j]	1.3[j]	0.1[j]	0.1[j]	0.5[j]	0.4[j]	41.8[j]	35.5[j]	26.4[j]	13.3[j]	1.9[j]	1.5[j]	1.04[j]
64	Trinidad and Tobago	1.3	1.3	0.1	0.1	0.5	0.3	14.2	34.2	29.9	13.8	1.8	1.8	1.04
65	Lebanon	4.8	5.2	0.3	0.4	4.2	3.0	87.5	30.7	27.1	12.3	2.0	1.5	1.05
65	Panama	3.9	4.9	0.4	0.3	1.9	1.6	76.5	28.5	42.5	11.7	2.8	2.5	1.05
67	Venezuela (Bolivarian Republic of)	30.4	37.2	3.0	1.9	1.8	1.5	93.9	27.7	42.6	10.1	2.7	2.4	1.05
68	Costa Rica	4.9	5.8	0.4	0.3	1.9	1.4	65.6	30.6	32.5	10.8	2.3	1.8	1.05
69	Turkey	74.9	86.8	6.4	5.5	1.4	1.2	73.4	30.1	37.0	11.4	2.3	2.1	1.05
70	Kazakhstan	16.4	18.6	1.7	1.1	0.7	1.0	53.4	29.7	39.4	10.1	2.0	2.4	1.07
71	Mexico	122.3	143.7	11.3	7.8	1.3	1.2	78.7	27.7	41.7	10.3	2.5	2.2	1.05
71	Seychelles	0.1	0.1	0.0	0.0	1.8	0.6	54.4	33.2	31.7	11.2	2.2	2.2	1.06
73	Saint Kitts and Nevis	0.1	0.1	..	..	1.5	1.1	32.1	..	..	..	..	..	..
73	Sri Lanka	21.3	23.3	1.9	1.8	1.1	0.8	15.2	32.0	38.1	13.7	2.3	2.4	1.04
75	Iran (Islamic Republic of)	77.4	91.3	7.1	4.1	1.2	1.3	69.3	29.5	34.2	7.8	2.0	1.9	1.05
76	Azerbaijan	9.4[k]	10.5[k]	0.8[k]	0.5[k]	1.1[k]	1.1[k]	54.1[k]	30.4[k]	30.8[k]	7.8[k]	2.0[k]	1.9[k]	1.15[k]
77	Jordan	7.3	9.4	1.0	0.3	1.9	3.5	83.2	24.0	53.0	5.8	3.9	3.3	1.05
77	Serbia	9.5[l]	8.6[l]	0.5[l]	1.4[l]	−0.6[l]	−0.5[l]	57.1[l]	39.3[l]	22.9[l]	21.7[l]	1.6[l]	1.4[l]	1.05[l]
79	Brazil	200.4	222.7	14.6	15.1	1.3	0.8	85.2	31.2	33.6	11.6	2.3	1.8	1.05
79	Georgia	4.3[m]	4.0[m]	0.3[m]	0.6[m]	−1.2[m]	−0.4[m]	53.0[m]	38.1[m]	27.6[m]	22.0[m]	1.6[m]	1.8[m]	1.11[m]
79	Grenada	0.1	0.1	0.0	0.0	0.3	0.4	39.8	27.2	40.0	10.7	2.4	2.2	1.05
82	Peru	30.4	36.5	2.9	1.9	1.3	1.3	77.9	27.1	42.9	10.3	2.8	2.4	1.05
83	Ukraine	45.2	39.8	2.5	6.8	−0.8	−0.6	69.3	39.9	21.4	21.2	1.2	1.5	1.06
84	Belize	0.3	0.5	0.0	0.0	2.6	2.4	44.3	23.7	52.1	6.5	3.4	2.7	1.03
84	The former Yugoslav Republic of Macedonia	2.1	2.1	0.1	0.3	0.4	0.1	59.5	37.8	23.2	18.3	1.6	1.4	1.05
86	Bosnia and Herzegovina	3.8	3.7	0.2	0.6	0.2	−0.1	49.3	40.1	21.2	22.9	1.2	1.3	1.07
87	Armenia	3.0	3.0	0.2	0.3	−0.4	0.2	64.2	33.4	29.2	15.0	1.7	1.7	1.14
88	Fiji	0.9	0.9	0.1	0.0	0.3	0.7	53.0	27.5	43.9	8.9	3.0	2.6	1.06
89	Thailand	67.0	67.6	3.6	6.5	1.0	0.3	34.8	38.0	24.2	14.5	1.6	1.4	1.06
90	Tunisia	11.0	12.6	0.9	0.8	1.0	1.1	66.7	31.2	33.4	10.8	2.0	2.0	1.05
91	China	1,385.6	1,453.3	90.2	123.0	0.6	0.6	53.2	36.0	25.1	13.1	1.6	1.7	1.16
91	Saint Vincent and the Grenadines	0.1	0.1	0.0	0.0	0.2	0.0	50.1	29.8	36.0	10.7	2.2	2.0	1.03
93	Algeria	39.2	48.6	4.6	1.8	1.4	1.8	74.7	27.5	42.4	7.0	2.4	2.8	1.05
93	Dominica	0.1	0.1	..	..	0.2	0.4	67.4	..	..	..	..	..	..
95	Albania	3.2	3.3	0.2	0.3	−0.7	0.3	55.6	33.5	28.1	16.3	2.2	1.8	1.08
96	Jamaica	2.8	2.9	0.2	0.2	0.8	0.5	52.2	28.2	39.5	12.3	2.5	2.3	1.05
97	Saint Lucia	0.2	0.2	0.0	0.0	1.1	0.8	16.1	31.2	34.1	13.2	2.1	1.9	1.03
98	Colombia	48.3	57.2	4.5	3.0	1.6	1.3	75.8	28.3	40.7	10.0	2.6	2.3	1.05
98	Ecuador	15.7	19.6	1.6	1.0	1.9	1.6	68.6	26.7	45.8	10.7	3.0	2.6	1.05
100	Suriname	0.5	0.6	0.0	0.0	1.4	0.9	70.5	29.1	39.6	10.2	2.6	2.3	1.08
100	Tonga	0.1	0.1	0.0	0.0	0.6	0.4	23.6	21.3	64.3	10.2	4.2	3.8	1.05
102	Dominican Republic	10.4	12.2	1.1	0.7	1.5	1.2	70.8	26.4	46.4	10.3	2.8	2.5	1.05
MEDIUM HUMAN DEVELOPMENT														
103	Maldives	0.3	0.4	0.0	0.0	1.7	1.9	43.4	26.0	42.2	7.3	2.8	2.3	1.06
103	Mongolia	2.8	3.4	0.3	0.1	1.0	1.5	70.4	27.5	40.4	5.6	2.1	2.4	1.03
103	Turkmenistan	5.2	6.2	0.5	0.2	1.1	1.3	49.4	26.4	41.7	6.1	2.8	2.3	1.05
106	Samoa	0.2	0.2	0.0	0.0	0.6	0.8	19.4	21.2	64.9	9.1	4.4	4.2	1.08
107	Palestine, State of	4.3[n]	6.4[n]	0.6[n]	0.1[n]	2.1[n]	2.5[n]	74.8[n]	19.7[n]	67.3[n]	5.3[n]	5.0[n]	4.1[n]	1.05[n]
108	Indonesia	249.9	293.5	24.0	13.1	1.4	1.2	52.2	28.4	42.2	8.2	2.5	2.4	1.05
109	Botswana	2.0	2.3	0.2	0.1	1.3	0.9	62.9	22.8	52.3	6.0	3.2	2.6	1.03
110	Egypt	82.1	102.6	9.3	4.7	1.6	1.6	43.8	25.8	48.8	9.4	3.2	2.8	1.05
111	Paraguay	6.8	8.7	0.8	0.4	2.0	1.7	63.0	24.4	50.8	9.1	3.5	2.9	1.05
112	Gabon	1.7	2.4	0.2	0.1	2.4	2.4	86.9	20.9	67.6	8.9	4.5	4.1	1.03
113	Bolivia (Plurinational State of)	10.7	13.7	1.3	0.5	1.9	1.6	67.7	22.8	56.1	8.3	4.0	3.3	1.05
114	Moldova (Republic of)	3.5[o]	3.1[o]	0.2[o]	0.4[o]	−1.7[o]	−0.8[o]	49.1[o]	36.3[o]	23.6[o]	16.4[o]	1.5[o]	1.5[o]	1.06[o]
115	El Salvador	6.3	6.9	0.6	0.5	0.4	0.7	65.8	24.7	45.2	11.5	2.6	2.2	1.05
116	Uzbekistan	28.9	34.1	3.0	1.2	1.0	1.4	36.3	26.0	41.5	6.4	2.6	2.3	1.05
117	Philippines	98.4	127.8	11.3	3.8	2.0	1.7	49.3	23.4	53.4	6.5	3.7	3.1	1.06
118	South Africa	52.8	58.1	5.4	2.9	1.5	0.8	62.9	26.5	45.1	8.8	2.8	2.4	1.03
118	Syrian Arab Republic	21.9	29.9	2.6	0.9	2.1	0.7	56.9	22.7	56.4	7.1	3.7	3.0	1.05

TABLE 15   Population trends | 217

TABLE 15 POPULATION TRENDS

		Population								Dependency ratio (per 100 people ages 15–64)		Total fertility rate		Sex ratio at birth[b]
		Total		Under age 5	Ages 65 and older	Average annual growth rate		Urban[a]	Median age	Young age (0–14)	Old age (65 and older)			
		(millions)		(millions)	(millions)	(%)		(% of population)	(years)			(births per woman)		(male to female births)
HDI rank		2013[c]	2030[c]	2013[c]	2013[c]	2000/2005	2010/2015[c]	2013[c]	2015[c]	2015	2015	2000/2005	2010/2015[c]	2010/2015[c]
120	Iraq	33.8	51.0	4.9	1.1	2.8	2.9	66.4	20.0	68.1	5.5	4.8	4.1	1.07
121	Guyana	0.8	0.9	0.1	0.0	0.4	0.5	28.5	23.0	55.7	5.7	2.7	2.6	1.05
121	Viet Nam	91.7	101.8	7.1	6.0	1.0	1.0	32.3	30.7	31.7	9.6	1.9	1.8	1.10
123	Cape Verde	0.5	0.6	0.0	0.0	1.6	0.8	64.1	25.2	42.4	7.9	3.3	2.3	1.03
124	Micronesia (Federated States of)	0.1	0.1	0.0	0.0	−0.2	0.2	22.8	21.5	55.3	7.1	4.1	3.3	1.07
125	Guatemala	15.5	22.6	2.3	0.7	2.5	2.5	50.7	19.7	71.3	8.4	4.6	3.8	1.05
125	Kyrgyzstan	5.5	6.9	0.7	0.2	0.4	1.4	35.5	25.1	47.6	6.3	2.5	3.1	1.06
127	Namibia	2.3	3.0	0.3	0.1	1.3	1.9	39.5	21.8	57.0	5.9	3.8	3.1	1.03
128	Timor-Leste	1.1	1.6	0.2	0.0	3.1	1.7	29.1	16.9	86.5	6.6	7.0	5.9	1.05
129	Honduras	8.1	10.8	1.0	0.4	2.0	2.0	53.3	22.5	56.1	7.5	3.7	3.0	1.05
129	Morocco	33.0	39.2	3.4	1.6	1.0	1.4	57.8	27.5	41.7	7.6	2.5	2.8	1.06
131	Vanuatu	0.3	0.4	0.0	0.0	2.5	2.2	25.5	22.1	60.3	6.7	4.1	3.4	1.07
132	Nicaragua	6.1	7.4	0.7	0.3	1.3	1.4	58.1	23.8	50.4	7.6	3.0	2.5	1.05
133	Kiribati	0.1	0.1	0.0	0.0	1.8	1.5	44.1	24.1	47.8	6.7	3.6	3.0	1.07
133	Tajikistan	8.2	11.4	1.2	0.3	1.9	2.4	26.6	22.0	59.4	5.2	3.7	3.9	1.05
135	India	1,252.1	1,476.4	121.3	66.0	1.6	1.2	32.0	26.9	42.9	8.3	3.0	2.5	1.11
136	Bhutan	0.8	0.9	0.1	0.0	2.8	1.6	37.1	26.7	39.9	7.3	3.1	2.3	1.04
136	Cambodia	15.1	19.1	1.7	0.8	1.8	1.7	20.3	25.0	49.0	8.9	3.5	2.9	1.05
138	Ghana	25.9	35.3	3.7	0.9	2.5	2.1	53.2	20.9	65.0	5.9	4.6	3.9	1.05
139	Lao People's Democratic Republic	6.8	8.8	0.9	0.3	1.4	1.9	36.5	22.0	55.6	6.2	3.7	3.1	1.05
140	Congo	4.4	6.8	0.7	0.2	2.5	2.6	64.5	18.7	78.5	6.3	5.1	5.0	1.03
141	Zambia	14.5	25.0	2.7	0.4	2.5	3.2	40.0	16.7	90.6	5.0	6.0	5.7	1.02
142	Bangladesh	156.6	185.1	15.1	7.5	1.6	1.2	29.4	25.8	43.8	7.3	2.9	2.2	1.05
142	Sao Tome and Principe	0.2	0.3	0.0	0.0	2.1	2.6	64.1	19.4	74.8	5.8	4.6	4.1	1.03
144	Equatorial Guinea	0.8	1.1	0.1	0.0	3.1	2.8	39.8	20.9	65.6	4.8	5.6	4.9	1.03
LOW HUMAN DEVELOPMENT														
145	Nepal	27.8	32.9	2.9	1.4	1.7	1.2	17.7	23.1	53.4	8.6	3.7	2.3	1.07
146	Pakistan	182.1	231.7	21.8	8.0	1.9	1.7	36.8	23.2	52.3	7.0	4.0	3.2	1.09
147	Kenya	44.4	66.3	7.0	1.2	2.7	2.7	24.8	19.0	75.4	5.0	5.0	4.4	1.03
148	Swaziland	1.2	1.5	0.2	0.0	0.8	1.5	21.2	20.5	63.1	6.1	4.0	3.4	1.03
149	Angola	21.5	34.8	4.0	0.5	3.4	3.1	60.7	16.4	92.9	4.8	6.8	5.9	1.03
150	Myanmar	53.3	58.7	4.4	2.8	0.7	0.8	33.8	29.8	34.4	7.7	2.2	2.0	1.03
151	Rwanda	11.8	17.8	1.9	0.3	2.3	2.7	19.7	18.4	74.1	4.5	5.6	4.6	1.02
152	Cameroon	22.3	33.1	3.6	0.7	2.6	2.5	53.2	18.5	78.4	5.9	5.5	4.8	1.03
152	Nigeria	173.6	273.1	30.5	4.8	2.6	2.8	50.9	17.7	83.9	5.1	6.1	6.0	1.06
154	Yemen	24.4	34.0	3.4	0.7	2.8	2.3	33.5	19.7	67.5	5.1	5.9	4.2	1.05
155	Madagascar	22.9	36.0	3.6	0.6	3.0	2.8	33.8	18.7	75.2	5.1	5.3	4.5	1.03
156	Zimbabwe	14.1	20.3	2.0	0.5	0.3	2.8	39.6	20.1	66.9	6.7	4.0	3.5	1.02
157	Papua New Guinea	7.3	10.0	1.0	0.2	2.5	2.1	12.6	21.2	62.2	5.0	4.4	3.8	1.08
157	Solomon Islands	0.6	0.8	0.1	0.0	2.6	2.1	21.4	19.9	69.4	5.9	4.6	4.1	1.07
159	Comoros	0.7	1.1	0.1	0.0	2.6	2.4	28.2	19.1	75.1	5.1	5.3	4.7	1.05
159	Tanzania (United Republic of)	49.3[p]	79.4[p]	8.7[p]	1.6[p]	2.6[p]	3.0[p]	27.6[p]	17.6[p]	85.9[p]	6.2[p]	5.7[p]	5.2[p]	1.03[p]
161	Mauritania	3.9	5.6	0.6	0.1	3.0	2.5	42.0	20.0	69.4	5.6	5.2	4.7	1.05
162	Lesotho	2.1	2.4	0.3	0.1	0.7	1.1	29.0	21.2	59.2	6.9	3.8	3.1	1.03
163	Senegal	14.1	21.9	2.4	0.4	2.7	2.9	43.1	18.2	80.5	5.4	5.4	5.0	1.04
164	Uganda	37.6	63.4	7.1	0.9	3.4	3.3	16.4	15.9	96.6	4.9	6.7	5.9	1.03
165	Benin	10.3	15.5	1.7	0.3	3.3	2.7	46.2	18.6	76.7	5.3	5.8	4.9	1.04
166	Sudan	38.0	55.1	5.7	1.2	2.6	2.1	33.5	19.4	72.1	5.9	5.3	4.5	1.04
166	Togo	6.8	10.0	1.1	0.2	2.6	2.6	39.0	19.0	74.6	4.9	5.1	4.7	1.02
168	Haiti	10.3	12.5	1.3	0.5	1.5	1.4	56.1	22.7	55.8	7.5	4.0	3.2	1.05
169	Afghanistan	30.6	43.5	4.9	0.7	3.8	2.4	24.1	17.0	85.4	4.7	7.4	5.0	1.06
170	Djibouti	0.9	1.1	0.1	0.0	1.4	1.5	77.2	23.4	53.9	6.6	4.2	3.4	1.04
171	Côte d'Ivoire	20.3	29.2	3.2	0.6	1.5	2.3	52.8	19.1	73.4	5.7	5.2	4.9	1.03
172	Gambia	1.8	3.1	0.3	0.0	3.1	3.2	58.4	17.0	87.9	4.5	5.9	5.8	1.03
173	Ethiopia	94.1	137.7	14.2	3.2	2.9	2.6	17.5	18.6	75.2	6.3	6.1	4.6	1.04
174	Malawi	16.4	26.0	2.9	0.5	2.6	2.8	16.0	17.3	86.3	6.3	6.1	5.4	1.03
175	Liberia	4.3	6.4	0.7	0.1	2.5	2.6	48.9	18.6	77.4	5.5	5.7	4.8	1.05
176	Mali	15.3	26.0	3.0	0.4	3.0	3.0	36.2	16.2	95.5	5.4	6.8	6.9	1.05
177	Guinea-Bissau	1.7	2.5	0.3	0.0	2.2	2.4	45.3	19.3	73.3	5.3	5.7	5.0	1.03
178	Mozambique	25.8	38.9	4.4	0.8	2.8	2.5	31.7	17.3	87.4	6.4	5.7	5.2	1.03
179	Guinea	11.7	17.3	1.9	0.4	1.8	2.5	36.4	18.8	75.9	5.6	5.8	5.0	1.02

TABLE 15

	Population						Urban[a]	Median age	Dependency ratio (per 100 people ages 15–64)		Total fertility rate		Sex ratio at birth[b]
	Total		Under age 5	Ages 65 and older	Average annual growth rate				Young age (0–14)	Old age (65 and older)	(births per woman)		(male to female births)
	(millions)		(millions)	(millions)	(%)		(% of population)	(years)					
HDI rank	2013[c]	2030[c]	2013[c]	2013[c]	2000/2005	2010/2015	2013[c]	2015[c]	2015	2015	2000/2005	2010/2015[c]	2010/2015[c]
180 Burundi	10.2	16.4	1.9	0.2	3.0	3.2	11.5	17.6	85.3	4.5	6.9	6.1	1.03
181 Burkina Faso	16.9	26.6	3.0	0.4	2.9	2.8	28.2	17.3	85.6	4.6	6.4	5.7	1.05
182 Eritrea	6.3	9.8	1.1	0.1	4.2	3.2	22.2	18.5	78.8	4.3	5.7	4.7	1.05
183 Sierra Leone	6.1	8.1	0.9	0.2	4.3	1.9	40.0	19.3	72.4	4.7	5.7	4.8	1.02
184 Chad	12.8	20.9	2.5	0.3	3.8	3.0	22.0	15.9	96.3	4.8	7.2	6.3	1.03
185 Central African Republic	4.6	6.3	0.7	0.2	1.7	2.0	39.5	20.0	68.7	6.7	5.3	4.4	1.03
186 Congo (Democratic Republic of the)	67.5	103.7	11.9	1.9	2.8	2.7	35.4	17.5	84.7	5.4	6.9	6.0	1.03
187 Niger	17.8	34.5	3.7	0.5	3.6	3.9	18.3	15.0	106.0	5.5	7.7	7.6	1.05
OTHER COUNTRIES OR TERRITORIES													
Korea, Democratic People's Rep. of	24.9	26.7	1.7	2.4	0.8	0.5	60.6	33.9	30.5	13.8	2.0	2.0	1.05
Marshall Islands	0.1	0.1	..	..	0.0	0.2	72.5	..	..	..	..	..	..
Monaco	0.0	0.0	..	..	1.0	0.8	100.0	..	..	..	..	..	..
Nauru	0.0	0.0	..	..	0.1	0.2	100.0	..	..	..	..	..	..
San Marino	0.0	0.0	..	..	2.0	0.6	94.2	..	..	..	..	..	..
Somalia	10.5	16.9	2.0	0.3	2.7	2.9	38.7	16.5	92.6	5.6	7.4	6.6	1.03
South Sudan	11.3	17.3	1.8	0.4	3.8	4.0	18.4	18.9	75.3	6.4	5.9	5.0	1.04
Tuvalu	0.0	0.0	..	..	0.6	0.2	51.4	..	..	..	..	..	..
Human Development Index groups													
Very high human development	1,189.7	1,276.5	69.4	193.9	0.7	0.6	81.6	40.2	26.1	25.7	1.7	1.8	1.05
High human development	2,485.5	2,662.3	176.8	215.9	0.7	0.7	61.4	34.2	28.7	12.9	1.8	1.8	1.06
Medium human development	2,262.1	2,716.0	228.7	115.9	1.6	1.3	38.3	26.5	44.6	8.1	3.0	2.6	1.05
Low human development	1,145.6	1,675.6	176.9	38.0	2.5	2.4	34.5	19.5	72.6	6.0	5.3	4.6	1.04
Regions													
Arab States	366.0	481.3	43.9	15.4	2.2	2.0	57.8	24.6	50.8	6.8	3.6	3.2	1.05
East Asia and the Pacific	2,035.9	2,211.9	149.2	160.7	0.8	0.8	50.8	33.7	29.5	11.8	1.8	1.9	1.05
Europe and Central Asia	233.4	251.0	18.9	21.2	0.4	0.7	60.5	32.2	33.4	13.4	2.0	2.0	1.07
Latin America and the Caribbean	611.3	711.1	53.6	44.0	1.3	1.1	79.5	29.0	39.4	11.4	2.5	2.2	1.05
South Asia	1,749.0	2,085.5	175.1	89.6	1.6	1.3	33.4	26.4	44.2	8.1	3.1	2.6	1.06
Sub-Saharan Africa	888.2	1,348.9	146.6	27.6	2.6	2.7	37.4	18.5	78.9	5.8	5.7	5.1	1.03
Least developed countries	898.4[T]	1,287.0[T]	132.1[T]	31.7[T]	2.4[T]	2.3[T]	29.4[T]	19.9[T]	69.1[T]	6.2[T]	4.9[T]	4.2[T]	1.04
Small island developing states	54.3	63.4	5.4	3.7	1.3	1.1	53.0	27.9	45.4	11.0	3.1	2.7	1.06
World	**7,162.1[T]**	**8,424.9[T]**	**659.0[T]**	**570.5[T]**	**1.2[T]**	**1.1[T]**	**53.0[T]**	**29.6[T]**	**39.5[T]**	**12.5[T]**	**2.6[T]**	**2.5[T]**	**1.07**

NOTES

a Because data are based on national definitions of what constitutes a city or metropolitan area, cross-country comparisons should be made with caution.

b The natural sex ratio at birth is commonly assumed and empirically confirmed to be 1.05 male births to 1 female births.

c Projections based on medium-fertility variant.

d Includes Svalbard and Jan Mayen Islands.

e Includes Christmas Island, Cocos (Keeling) Islands and Norfolk Island.

f Includes Åland Islands.

g Includes Canary Islands, Ceuta and Melilla.

h Includes Northern Cyprus.

i Includes Sabah and Sarawak.

j Includes Agalega, Rodrigues and Saint Brandon.

k Includes Nagorno-Karabakh.

l Includes Kosovo.

m Includes Abkhazia and South Ossetia.

n Includes East Jerusalem.

o Includes Transnistria.

p Includes Zanzibar.

T From original data source.

DEFINITIONS

Population: De facto population in a country, area or region as of 1 July.

Population under age 5: De facto population in a country, area or region under age 5 as of 1 July.

Population ages 65 and older: De facto population in a country, area or region ages 65 and older as of 1 July.

Population average annual growth rate: Average annual exponential growth rate for the period specified.

Urban population: De facto population living in areas classified as urban according to the criteria used by each country or area as of July 1.

Median age: Age that divides the population distribution into two equal parts—that is, 50 percent of the population is above that age and 50 percent is below it.

Young age dependency ratio: Ratio of the population ages 0–14 to the population ages 15–64, expressed as the number of dependants per 100 persons of working age (ages 15–64).

Old age dependency ratio: Ratio of the population ages 65 and older to the population ages 15–64,

expressed as the number of dependants per 100 people of working age (ages 15–64).

Total fertility rate: Number of children that would be born to a woman if she were to live to the end of her child-bearing years and bear children at each age in accordance with prevailing age-specific fertility rates.

Sex ratio at birth: Number of male births per female birth.

MAIN DATA SOURCES

Columns 1–6 and 8–13: UNDESA 2013a.

Column 7: UNDESA 2013b.

TABLE
15

TABLE 15 Population trends | 219

TABLE 16

Supplementary indicators: perceptions of well-being

HDI rank	Perceptions of individual well-being							Perceptions about community			Perceptions about government		
	Education quality	Health care quality	Standard of living	Job	Safety	Freedom of choice	Overall life satisfaction index	Local labour market	Trust in other people	Community	Efforts to deal with the poor	Actions to preserve the environment	Trust in national government
	(% satisfied)	(% satisfied)	(% satisfied)	(% satisfied)	(% answering yes)	(% satisfied)	(0, least satisfied, to 10, most satisfied)	(% answering good)	(% answering can be trusted)	(% answering yes)	(% satisfied)	(% satisfied)	(% answering yes)
	2012	2008–2012[a]	2007–2013[a]	2007–2012[a]	2007–2012	2007–2012	2007–2012[a]	2007–2012[a]	2009–2011[a]	2007–2012[a]	2007–2013[a]	2007–2013[a]	2007–2012[a]
VERY HIGH HUMAN DEVELOPMENT													
1 Norway	78	82	90	91	87	92	7.7	54	..	92	34	52	66
2 Australia	66	81	87	87	65	93	7.2	27	..	90	45	69	42
3 Switzerland	77	94	94	93	78	94	7.8	35	44	94	67	74	77
4 Netherlands	74	88	88	92	77	87	7.5	14	46	93	63	66	57
5 United States	64	73	72	85	74	82	7.0	28	37	85	43	59	35
6 Germany	60	86	90	91	79	90	6.7	46	31	94	50	67	52
7 New Zealand	71	83	87	86	64	90	7.2	29	..	89	53	77	61
8 Canada	74	75	86	90	84	92	7.4	43	42	91	45	60	52
9 Singapore	85	84	80	88	89	82	6.5	63	33	92	66	84	83
10 Denmark	72	81	88	92	80	92	7.5	18	60	94	57	70	53
11 Ireland	82	64	76	88	74	90	7.0	6	30	90	52	63	35
12 Sweden	65	81	90	90	81	93	7.6	32	55	94	30	57	63
13 Iceland	78	79	81	93	80	87	7.6	33	..	75	34	55	26
14 United Kingdom	73	86	80	88	75	88	6.9	9	35	88	51	71	42
15 Hong Kong, China (SAR)	46	54	79	81	88	87	5.5	46	29	82	38	38	50
15 Korea (Republic of)	55	68	72	73	67	59	6.0	25	26	79	33	33	23
17 Japan	55	75	71	79	77	70	6.0	16	33	85	33	41	17
18 Liechtenstein	..	..	..	..	..	..	..	..	..	..	..	..	..
19 Israel	62	69	68	80	63	65	7.1	26	26	79	14	42	34
20 France	67	78	83	81	67	83	6.6	16	20	86	44	53	44
21 Austria	72	93	95	93	82	90	7.4	35	29	94	54	61	38
21 Belgium	69	87	87	86	66	82	6.9	19	30	91	45	58	44
21 Luxembourg	65	88	92	91	73	91	7.0	18	26	94	72	76	74
24 Finland	81	65	82	91	77	91	7.4	24	58	92	42	57	60
25 Slovenia	76	81	71	86	85	89	6.1	9	15	92	44	58	24
26 Italy	62	55	66	83	66	55	5.8	3	20	75	30	32	28
27 Spain	63	74	80	86	78	74	6.3	5	22	88	42	41	34
28 Czech Republic	62	71	65	78	59	71	6.3	11	24	84	21	52	17
29 Greece	46	29	38	73	47	36	5.1	1	16	80	7	17	13
30 Brunei Darussalam	..	..	..	..	..	..	..	..	..	..	..	..	..
31 Qatar	72	90	84	88	92	90	6.7	66	23	92	91	91	89
32 Cyprus	66	62	69	88	68	69	6.2	11	11	85	39	49	34
33 Estonia	51	45	43	78	61	65	5.4	18	33	85	8	54	27
34 Saudi Arabia	65	56	77	90	77	59	6.5	73	36	93	80	56	..
35 Lithuania	54	51	29	73	45	46	5.8	14	25	84	18	42	15
35 Poland	60	42	66	83	68	75	5.9	18	25	90	22	47	27
37 Andorra	..	..	..	..	..	..	..	..	..	..	..	..	..
37 Slovakia	61	59	49	78	55	53	5.9	8	21	83	22	42	37
39 Malta	64	70	63	80	72	82	6.0	19	16	82	47	64	50
40 United Arab Emirates	83	82	87	87	90	88	7.2	47	18	93	85	89	..
41 Chile	49	35	72	82	57	72	6.6	57	15	82	35	38	34
41 Portugal	67	57	52	83	60	73	5.0	7	27	88	29	43	23
43 Hungary	60	64	40	75	56	55	4.7	7	13	74	17	45	21
44 Bahrain	82	70	66	77	60	63	5.0	44	11	90	57	57	..
44 Cuba	..	..	..	..	..	..	..	..	..	..	..	..	..
46 Kuwait	65	62	88	93	..	93	6.2	69	11	93	89	78	..
47 Croatia	62	63	39	73	66	46	6.0	5	16	75	9	40	31
48 Latvia	54	48	32	77	58	51	5.1	17	13	85	12	55	19
49 Argentina	64	63	67	81	45	73	6.5	34	23	82	34	42	42
HIGH HUMAN DEVELOPMENT													
50 Uruguay	62	76	79	83	51	85	6.4	56	27	82	58	58	58
51 Bahamas	..	..	..	..	..	..	..	..	..	..	..	..	..
51 Montenegro	60	48	37	59	74	43	5.2	7	21	69	9	35	36
53 Belarus	53	38	37	62	61	53	5.7	26	34	82	26	45	59
54 Romania	53	52	36	70	54	60	5.2	9	15	82	8	23	24
55 Libya	33	41	57	74	91	68	5.8	49	..	72	56	37	..
56 Oman	..	78	87	86	..	91	6.9	69	..	90	..	..	..
57 Russian Federation	39	27	42	70	39	51	5.6	26	24	72	12	17	45

		Perceptions of individual well-being						Perceptions about community			Perceptions about government		
	Education quality	Health care quality	Standard of living	Job	Safety	Freedom of choice	Overall life satisfaction index	Local labour market	Trust in other people	Community	Efforts to deal with the poor	Actions to preserve the environment	Trust in national government
	(% satisfied)	(% satisfied)	(% satisfied)	(% satisfied)	(% answering yes)	(% satisfied)	(0, least satisfied, to 10, most satisfied)	(% answering good)	(% answering can be trusted)	(% answering yes)	(% satisfied)	(% satisfied)	(% answering yes)
HDI rank	2012	2008–2012[a]	2007–2013[a]	2007–2012[a]	2007–2012	2007–2012	2007–2012[a]	2007–2012[a]	2009–2011[a]	2007–2012[a]	2007–2013[a]	2007–2013[a]	2007–2012[a]
58 Bulgaria	45	39	29	74	59	59	4.2	6	20	77	9	33	34
59 Barbados	..	..	..	..	..	..	..	..	..	..	..	..	..
60 Palau	..	..	..	..	..	..	..	..	..	..	..	..	..
61 Antigua and Barbuda	..	..	..	..	..	..	..	..	..	..	..	..	..
62 Malaysia	91	87	75	83	45	82	5.9	44	14	83	70	72	76
63 Mauritius	..	77	64	85	55	83	5.5	38	..	91	..	79	67
64 Trinidad and Tobago	..	63	71	90	69	77	6.5	46	..	87	34	44	52
65 Lebanon	63	46	45	63	62	61	4.6	13	7	81	19	27	37
65 Panama	68	61	79	89	48	73	6.9	57	21	87	37	46	36
67 Venezuela (Bolivarian Republic of)	77	64	79	89	26	78	7.1	57	13	81	60	63	54
68 Costa Rica	83	65	75	85	53	92	7.3	26	14	85	40	72	28
69 Turkey	55	60	55	71	55	45	5.3	32	8	78	41	45	53
70 Kazakhstan	59	47	64	75	51	75	5.8	38	33	80	32	40	73
71 Mexico	62	71	78	76	54	77	7.3	43	29	79	41	53	36
71 Seychelles	..	..	..	..	..	..	..	..	..	..	..	..	..
73 Saint Kitts and Nevis	..	..	..	..	..	..	..	..	..	..	..	..	..
73 Sri Lanka	80	78	60	84	77	77	4.2	50	17	90	58	70	78
75 Iran (Islamic Republic of)	61	52	67	67	55	57	4.6	22	..	76	58	61	56
76 Azerbaijan	50	34	49	66	69	54	4.9	27	27	73	22	48	71
77 Jordan	61	72	46	69	81	65	5.1	13	9	74	51	47	77
77 Serbia	50	43	34	65	62	45	5.2	3	17	65	10	25	22
79 Brazil	52	25	77	83	46	80	6.9	56	15	74	43	46	46
79 Georgia	67	48	24	50	91	60	4.3	12	16	77	36	53	61
79 Grenada	..	..	..	..	..	..	..	..	..	..	..	..	..
82 Peru	53	37	60	74	46	66	5.8	43	12	72	37	40	27
83 Ukraine	44	18	24	67	46	49	5.0	15	29	76	8	18	24
84 Belize	..	..	69	..	43	62	6.5	44	..	67	20	30	26
84 The former Yugoslav Republic of Macedonia	62	47	39	60	63	58	4.6	8	11	65	16	37	37
86 Bosnia and Herzegovina	54	42	32	59	65	40	4.8	5	18	66	6	19	19
87 Armenia	52	40	30	50	78	46	4.3	12	15	55	14	32	29
88 Fiji	..	..	..	..	..	..	..	..	..	..	..	..	..
89 Thailand	91	88	83	97	74	83	6.3	73	27	95	67	75	70
90 Tunisia	44	32	54	63	59	53	4.5	22	15	71	30	38	44
91 China	62	65	73	72	82	77	5.1	38	57	80	68	72	..
91 Saint Vincent and the Grenadines	..	..	..	..	..	..	..	..	..	..	..	..	..
93 Algeria	64	52	66	72	53	56	5.6	53	16	83	41	48	53
93 Dominica	..	..	..	..	..	..	..	..	..	..	..	..	..
95 Albania	60	38	48	68	59	58	5.5	12	7	71	13	27	36
96 Jamaica	..	58	42	68	56	75	5.4	20	..	72	21	32	36
97 Saint Lucia	..	..	..	..	..	..	..	..	..	..	..	..	..
98 Colombia	65	46	75	82	45	81	6.4	41	14	83	34	49	36
98 Ecuador	76	60	69	84	47	81	6.0	35	9	84	59	67	64
100 Suriname	82	78	64	83	60	87	6.3	34	..	90	61	65	72
100 Tonga	..	..	..	..	..	..	..	..	..	..	..	..	..
102 Dominican Republic	72	59	63	70	39	83	4.8	21	15	81	46	57	43
MEDIUM HUMAN DEVELOPMENT													
103 Maldives	..	..	..	..	..	..	..	..	..	..	..	..	..
103 Mongolia	55	40	59	81	46	59	4.9	12	14	76	16	22	31
103 Turkmenistan	..	64	89	86	77	63	5.5	57	27	94	38	61	..
106 Samoa	..	..	..	..	..	..	..	..	..	..	..	..	..
107 Palestine, State of	67	62	47	64	63	53	4.6	8	9	76	39	40	47
108 Indonesia	82	80	63	77	89	70	5.4	38	21	90	28	54	67
109 Botswana	68	56	36	52	35	79	4.8	32	9	61	74	67	66
110 Egypt	40	35	63	71	57	44	4.2	10	25	63	31	20	60
111 Paraguay	76	69	86	89	44	75	5.8	60	12	92	33	46	30
112 Gabon	36	29	29	50	35	56	4.0	35	..	45	26	49	36
113 Bolivia (Plurinational State of)	70	48	71	85	40	85	6.0	50	10	84	56	58	44
114 Moldova (Republic of)	55	40	45	64	46	55	6.0	6	12	73	18	19	21
115 El Salvador	78	67	72	80	53	67	5.9	35	18	85	43	50	31

TABLE 16

TABLE 16

TABLE 16 SUPPLEMENTARY INDICATORS: PERCEPTIONS OF WELL-BEING

	Perceptions of individual well-being							Perceptions about community			Perceptions about government		
	Education quality	Health care quality	Standard of living	Job	Safety	Freedom of choice	Overall life satisfaction index	Local labour market	Trust in other people	Community	Efforts to deal with the poor	Actions to preserve the environment	Trust in national government
	(% satisfied)	(% satisfied)	(% satisfied)	(% satisfied)	(% answering yes)	(% satisfied)	(0, least satisfied, to 10, most satisfied)	(% answering good)	(% answering can be trusted)	(% answering yes)	(% satisfied)	(% satisfied)	(% answering yes)
HDI rank	2012	2008–2012[a]	2007–2013[a]	2007–2012[a]	2007–2012	2007–2012	2007–2012[a]	2007–2012[a]	2009–2011[a]	2007–2012[a]	2007–2013[a]	2007–2013[a]	2007–2012[a]
116 Uzbekistan	83	86	64	89	84	88	6.0	55	26	93	67	82	..
117 Philippines	83	83	70	83	66	91	5.0	65	14	90	82	87	76
118 South Africa	67	46	43	55	27	58	5.1	29	17	54	25	42	43
118 Syrian Arab Republic	43	30	38	53	49	40	3.2	17	9	35	47	44	..
120 Iraq	50	30	45	60	41	29	4.7	40	15	64	8	15	34
121 Guyana	..	..	64	..	47	66	6.0	33	..	75	20	34	46
121 Viet Nam	83	59	68	82	67	73	5.5	35	26	81	59	50	86
123 Cape Verde	..	..	..	..	..	..	..	..	..	..	..	..	..
124 Micronesia (Federated States of)	..	..	..	..	..	..	..	..	..	..	..	..	..
125 Guatemala	74	49	66	85	53	84	5.9	33	15	88	41	49	50
125 Kyrgyzstan	64	53	62	69	51	66	5.2	38	34	87	35	44	51
127 Namibia	..	..	61	..	33	76	4.9	33	..	77	35	58	82
128 Timor-Leste	..	..	..	..	..	..	..	..	..	..	..	..	..
129 Honduras	64	49	56	82	49	69	4.6	31	13	84	32	47	26
129 Morocco	41	25	74	68	56	72	5.0	21	58	77	48	51	45
131 Vanuatu	..	..	..	..	..	..	..	..	..	..	..	..	..
132 Nicaragua	83	65	71	85	56	84	5.4	40	11	89	53	67	57
133 Kiribati	..	..	..	..	..	..	..	..	..	..	..	..	..
133 Tajikistan	76	68	81	84	86	67	4.5	58	31	91	53	58	92
135 India	69	48	47	67	61	57	4.6	30	20	75	39	40	54
136 Bhutan	..	..	..	..	..	..	..	..	..	..	..	..	..
136 Cambodia	92	83	49	84	63	95	3.9	55	9	92	89	92	83
138 Ghana	59	46	35	63	73	68	5.1	29	19	55	22	44	58
139 Lao People's Democratic Republic	73	66	73	85	75	87	4.9	66	..	94	66	90	98
140 Congo	56	38	42	63	51	77	3.9	53	..	67	28	61	54
141 Zambia	54	50	34	54	46	78	5.0	32	31	56	27	41	59
142 Bangladesh	84	63	74	80	81	64	4.7	35	15	90	57	60	71
142 Sao Tome and Principe	..	..	..	..	..	..	..	..	..	..	..	..	..
144 Equatorial Guinea	..	..	..	..	..	..	..	..	..	..	..	..	..
LOW HUMAN DEVELOPMENT													
145 Nepal	79	56	57	85	61	57	4.2	36	17	84	34	45	44
146 Pakistan	59	43	58	74	41	35	5.1	17	20	79	16	19	23
147 Kenya	69	57	33	50	50	61	4.5	34	10	65	26	51	40
148 Swaziland	..	58	45	55	42	61	4.9	25	..	62	..	56	35
149 Angola	..	30	50	65	45	57	5.6	44	..	50	60	42	23
150 Myanmar	69	54	45	71	89	65	4.4	32	..	90	51	50	..
151 Rwanda	76	65	30	43	86	84	3.3	44	30	60	66	90	95
152 Cameroon	67	48	43	63	60	76	4.2	33	13	60	29	53	53
152 Nigeria	55	47	49	64	61	63	5.5	31	13	69	15	35	30
154 Yemen	35	19	47	53	65	67	4.1	12	27	71	27	21	60
155 Madagascar	50	35	18	48	40	48	3.6	29	..	83	23	36	35
156 Zimbabwe	62	58	48	53	52	46	5.0	33	15	65	36	58	41
157 Papua New Guinea	..	..	..	..	..	..	..	..	..	..	..	..	..
157 Solomon Islands	..	..	..	..	..	..	..	..	..	..	..	..	..
159 Comoros	49	24	38	61	72	53	4.0	30	35	75	17	39	46
159 Tanzania (United Republic of)	35	28	40	66	58	57	4.0	32	26	60	26	36	41
161 Mauritania	30	30	43	56	63	48	4.7	32	30	64	26	37	38
162 Lesotho	..	21	27	47	38	62	4.9	21	..	52	..	23	40
163 Senegal	31	42	37	68	57	67	3.7	40	28	64	23	40	65
164 Uganda	48	41	38	59	41	64	4.3	21	17	65	21	44	40
165 Benin	52	44	20	51	71	77	3.2	27	..	63	25	46	58
166 Sudan	38	28	44	48	68	40	4.6	17	31	63	22	26	54
166 Togo	..	23	16	42	52	56	2.9	24	..	58	10	46	51
168 Haiti	39	24	17	38	40	43	4.4	17	30	40	15	38	37
169 Afghanistan	64	43	31	88	39	49	3.8	37	25	70	20	43	44
170 Djibouti	..	49	63	70	72	74	4.4	55	55	75	55	58	68
171 Côte d'Ivoire	..	21	17	..	47	76	4.2	25	13	41	8	32	42
172 Gambia	..	..	..	..	..	..	..	..	..	..	..	..	..
173 Ethiopia	..	..	..	..	..	..	..	..	..	..	..	..	..

	Perceptions of individual well-being							Perceptions about community			Perceptions about government		
HDI rank	Education quality	Health care quality	Standard of living	Job	Safety	Freedom of choice	Overall life satisfaction index	Local labour market	Trust in other people	Community	Efforts to deal with the poor	Actions to preserve the environment	Trust in national government
	(% satisfied)	(% satisfied)	(% satisfied)	(% satisfied)	(% answering yes)	(% satisfied)	(0, least satisfied, to 10, most satisfied)	(% answering good)	(% answering can be trusted)	(% answering yes)	(% satisfied)	(% satisfied)	(% answering yes)
	2012	2008–2012[a]	2007–2013[a]	2007–2012[a]	2007–2012	2007–2012	2007–2012[a]	2007–2012[a]	2009–2011[a]	2007–2012[a]	2007–2013[a]	2007–2013[a]	2007–2012[a]
174 Malawi	66	64	37	50	49	64	4.3	32	33	78	47	61	47
175 Liberia	..	32	43	63	43	87	4.2	53	12	63	17	34	53
176 Mali	35	31	26	60	67	70	4.3	31	45	60	13	42	49
177 Guinea-Bissau	..	..	..	..	..	..	..	..	..	..	..	..	..
178 Mozambique	..	47	38	63	42	64	5.0	45	..	83	35	55	63
179 Guinea	22	21	20	49	50	64	3.7	46	..	64	10	43	56
180 Burundi	..	41	26	65	65	49	3.7	17	38	76	27	71	85
181 Burkina Faso	66	42	35	56	70	62	4.0	27	26	78	23	61	62
182 Eritrea	..	..	..	..	..	..	..	..	..	..	..	..	..
183 Sierra Leone	..	34	32	61	50	77	4.5	30	16	52	11	46	58
184 Chad	58	47	42	71	33	56	4.0	37	21	68	19	67	30
185 Central African Republic	..	23	34	67	60	78	3.7	36	37	76	27	69	78
186 Congo (Democratic Republic of the)	40	32	42	55	48	54	4.6	35	39	60	27	40	44
187 Niger	47	37	57	72	86	73	3.8	45	40	77	34	57	53
OTHER COUNTRIES OR TERRITORIES													
Korea, Democratic People's Rep. of	..	..	..	..	..	..	..	..	..	..	..	..	..
Marshall Islands	..	..	..	..	..	..	..	..	..	..	..	..	..
Monaco	..	..	..	..	..	..	..	..	..	..	..	..	..
Nauru	..	..	..	..	..	..	..	..	..	..	..	..	..
San Marino	..	..	..	..	..	..	..	..	..	..	..	..	..
Somalia	..	..	..	..	..	..	..	..	..	..	..	..	..
South Sudan	..	..	..	..	..	..	..	..	..	..	..	..	..
Tuvalu	..	..	..	..	..	..	..	..	..	..	..	..	..
Human Development Index groups													
Very high human development	63	72	—	84	72	77	6.6	—	31	86	41	53	36
High human development	60	58	—	74	68	73	5.5	—	..	79	55	60	48
Medium human development	71	54	—	71	65	62	4.8	—	..	78	41	46	59
Low human development	..	42	—	64	55	56	4.6	—	..	70	24	39	40
Regions													
Arab States	48	39	—	68	60	53	4.8	—	25	71	39	36	..
East Asia and the Pacific	..	..	—	..	..	..	..	—	..	..	..	..	..
Europe and Central Asia	57	50	—	71	60	56	5.3	—	21	79	33	43	47
Latin America and the Caribbean	..	47	—	80	47	77	6.6	—	..	78	41	49	42
South Asia	69	49	—	70	60	55	4.6	—	20	77	39	41	52
Sub-Saharan Africa	..	42	—	59	53	63	4.6	—	..	65	24	44	44
Least developed countries	..	45	—	67	62	62	4.3	—	..	74	37	49	55
Small island developing states	..	..	—	..	..	..	..	—	..	..	..	..	..
World	64	57	—	74	66	68	5.3	—	30	78	44	51	48

NOTES

a Data refer to the most recent year available during the period specified.

DEFINITIONS

Satisfaction with education quality: Percentage of respondents who answered "satisfied" to the Gallup World Poll question, "Are you satisfied or dissatisfied with the education system?"

Satisfaction with health care quality: Percentage of respondents who answered "satisfied" to the Gallup World Poll question, "Are you satisfied or dissatisfied with the availability of quality health care?"

Satisfaction with standard of living: Percentage of respondents answering "satisfied" to the Gallup World Poll question, "Are you satisfied or dissatisfied with your standard of living, all the things you can buy and do?"

Satisfaction with job: Percentage of respondents answering "satisfied" to the Gallup World Poll question, "Are you satisfied or dissatisfied with your job?"

Perception of safety: Percentage of respondents answering "yes" to the Gallup World Poll question, "Do you feel safe walking alone at night in the city or area where you live?"

Satisfaction with freedom of choice: Percentage of respondents answering "satisfied" to the Gallup World Poll question, "In this country, are you satisfied or dissatisfied with your freedom to choose what you do with your life?"

Overall life satisfaction index: Average response to the Gallup World Poll question: "Please imagine a ladder, with steps numbered from zero at the bottom to ten at the top. Suppose we say that the top of the ladder represents the best possible life for you, and the bottom of the ladder represents the worst possible life for you. On which step of the ladder would you say you personally feel you stand at this time, assuming that the higher the step the better you feel about your life, and the lower the step the worse you feel about it? Which step comes closest to the way you feel?"

Satisfaction with local labour market: Percentage of respondents answering "good" to Gallup World Poll question, "Thinking about the job situation in the city or area where you live today, would you say that it is now a good time or a bad time to find a job?"

Trust in other people: Percentage of respondents answering "can be trusted" to the Gallup World Poll question, "Generally speaking, would you say that most people can be trusted or that you have to be careful in dealing with people?"

Satisfaction with community: Percentage of respondents answering "yes" to the Gallup World Poll question, "Are you satisfied or dissatisfied with the city or area where you live?"

Satisfaction with efforts to deal with the poor: Percentage of respondents who answered "satisfied" to Gallup World Poll question, "In this country, are you satisfied or dissatisfied with efforts to deal with the poor?"

Satisfaction with actions to preserve the environment: Percentage of respondents answering "satisfied" to Gallup World Poll question: "In this country, are you satisfied or dissatisfied with the efforts to preserve the environment?"

Trust in national government: Percentage of respondents answering "yes" to the Gallup World Poll question, "In this country, do you have confidence in the national government?"

MAIN DATA SOURCES

Columns 1–13: Gallup 2013.

TABLE **16**

TABLE 16 Supplementary indicators: perceptions of well-being | 223

Regions

Arab States (20 countries or territories)
Algeria, Bahrain, Djibouti, Egypt, Iraq, Jordan, Kuwait, Lebanon, Libya, Morocco, State of Palestine, Oman, Qatar, Saudi Arabia, Somalia, Sudan, Syrian Arab Republic, Tunisia, United Arab Emirates, Yemen

East Asia and the Pacific (24 countries)
Cambodia, China, Fiji, Indonesia, Kiribati, Democratic People's Republic of Korea, Lao People's Democratic Republic, Malaysia, Marshall Islands, Federated States of Micronesia, Mongolia, Myanmar, Nauru, Palau, Papua New Guinea, Philippines, Samoa, Solomon Islands, Thailand, Timor-Leste, Tonga, Tuvalu, Vanuatu, Viet Nam

Europe and Central Asia (17 countries)
Albania, Armenia, Azerbaijan, Belarus, Bosnia and Herzegovina, Georgia, Kazakhstan, Kyrgyzstan, Republic of Moldova, Montenegro, Serbia, Tajikistan, The former Yugoslav Republic of Macedonia, Turkey, Turkmenistan, Ukraine, Uzbekistan

Latin America and the Caribbean (33 countries)
Antigua and Barbuda, Argentina, Bahamas, Barbados, Belize, Plurinational State of Bolivia, Brazil, Chile, Colombia, Costa Rica, Cuba, Dominica, Dominican Republic, Ecuador, El Salvador, Grenada, Guatemala, Guyana, Haiti, Honduras, Jamaica, Mexico, Nicaragua, Panama, Paraguay, Peru, Saint Kitts and Nevis, Saint Lucia, Saint Vincent and the Grenadines, Suriname, Trinidad and Tobago, Uruguay, Bolivarian Republic of Venezuela

South Asia (9 countries)
Afghanistan, Bangladesh, Bhutan, India, Islamic Republic of Iran, Maldives, Nepal, Pakistan, Sri Lanka

Sub-Saharan Africa (46 countries)
Angola, Benin, Botswana, Burkina Faso, Burundi, Cameroon, Cape Verde, Central African Republic, Chad, Comoros, Congo, Democratic Republic of the Congo, Côte d'Ivoire, Equatorial Guinea, Eritrea, Ethiopia, Gabon, Gambia, Ghana, Guinea, Guinea-Bissau, Kenya, Lesotho, Liberia, Madagascar, Malawi, Mali, Mauritania, Mauritius, Mozambique, Namibia, Niger, Nigeria, Rwanda, São Tomé and Príncipe, Senegal, Seychelles, Sierra Leone, South Africa, South Sudan, Swaziland, United Republic of Tanzania, Togo, Uganda, Zambia, Zimbabwe

Note: Countries included in aggregates for Least Developed Countries and Small Island Developing States follow UN classifications, which are available at www.unohrlls.org.

Statistical references

Aguna, C., and M. Kovacevic. 2011. "Uncertainty and Sensitivity Analysis of the Human Development Index." Human Development Research Paper 2010/47. UNDP–HDRO, New York. http://hdr.undp.org/en/content/uncertainty-and-sensitivity-analysis-human-development-index.

Alkire, S., A. Conconi, and S. Seth. 2014. "Multidimensional Poverty Index 2014: Brief Methodological Note and Results." Oxford Poverty and Human Development Initiative, Oxford University, UK.

Akire, S., and M. Santos. 2010. "Acute Multidimensional Poverty: A New Index for Developing Countries." Human Development Research Paper 2010/11. UNDP-HDRO. New York. http://hdr.undp.org/en/content/acute-multidimensional-poverty.

Barro, R.J., and J.W. Lee. 2013. *A New Data Set of Educational Attainment in the World, 1950–2010.* National Bureau of Economic Research Working Paper 15902. Cambridge, MA: National Bureau of Economic Research. www.nber.org/papers/w15902. Accessed 15 November 2013.

CEPII (Centre d'Etudes Prospectives et d'Informations Internationales). 2013. GeoDist. www.cepii.fr/CEPII/en/bdd_modele/presentation.asp?id=6. Accessed 15 November 2013.

CRED EM-DAT (Centre for Research on the Epidemiology of Disasters). 2013. The International Disaster Database. www.emdat.be. Accessed 15 November 2013.

ECLAC (Economic Commission for Latin America and the Caribbean). 2013. *Preliminary Overview of the Economies of Latin America and the Caribbean.* Santiago. www.eclac.org/cgi-bin/getProd.asp?xml=/publicaciones/xml/4/41974/P41974.xml. Accessed 15 November 2013.

Eurostat. 2013. "European Union Statistics on Income and Living Conditions (EUSILC)". Brussels. http://epp.eurostat.ec.europa.eu/portal/page/portal/microdata/eu_silc. Accessed 15 September 2013.

FAO (Food and Agriculture Organization). 2013a. FAOSTAT database. http://faostat3.fao.org/faostat-gateway/go/to/home/E. Accessed 15 November 2013.

———. **2013b.** AQUASTAT database. www.fao.org/nr/water/aquastat/data. Accessed 15 December 2013.

Gallup. 2013. Gallup World Poll database. http://worldview.gallup.com. Accessed 15 December 2013.

Høyland, B., K. Moene, and F. Willumsen. 2011. "The Tyranny of International Index Rankings." *Journal of Development Economics* 97(1): 1–14.

ICF Macro. Various years. The DHS Program. www.dhsprogram.com. Accessed 15 November 2013.

IDMC (Internally Displaced Monitoring Centre). 2013. IDPs worldwide. www.internal-displacement.org. Accessed 15 December 2013.

ILO (International Labour Organization). 2013a. *Key Indicators of the Labour Market.* 7th edition. Geneva. www.ilo.org/empelm/what/WCMS_114240/lang--en/index.htm. Accessed 15 December 2013.

———. **2013b.** LABORSTA database. http://laborsta.ilo.org. Accessed 15 November 2013.

———. **2014a.** Social Protection Department database. www.social-protection.org/gimi/gess/RessourceDownload.action?ressource.ressourceId=37897. Accessed 15 February 2014

———. **2014b.** ILOSTAT database. www.ilo.org/ilostat. Accessed 15 February 2014.

IMF (International Monetary Fund). 2014. World Economic Outlook database. April 2014. www.imf.org/external/pubs/ft/weo/2014/01/weodata/index.aspx. Accessed 7 May 2014.

Inter-agency Group for Child Mortality Estimation. 2013. Child mortality estimates. www.childmortality.org. Accessed 15 December 2013.

International Centre for Prison Studies. 2013. World prison brief. www.prisonstudies.org. Accessed 15 September 2013.

IPU (Inter-Parliamentary Union). 2013. Women in national parliaments. www.ipu.org/wmn-e/classif.htm. Accessed 15 October 2013.

ITU (International Telecommunication Union). 2013. World Telecommunication/ICT Indicators database. www.itu.int/ITU-D/ict/statistics. Accessed 15 August 2013.

LIS (Luxembourg Income Study). 2013. Luxembourg Income Study Project. www.lisdatacenter.org/our-data/lis-database/. Accessed 15 September 2013.

National Institute for Educational Studies of Brazil. 2013. Correspondence on school life expectancy. Brasilia.

OECD (Organisation for Economic Co-operation and Development). 2013. PISA 2012 results. www.oecd.org/pisa/keyfindings/pisa-2012-results.htm. Accessed 15 December 2013.

Palma, J.G. 2011. "Homogeneous Middles vs. Heterogeneous Tails, and the End of the 'Inverted-U': The Share of the Rich Is What It's All About." Cambridge Working Papers in Economics 1111. Cambridge University, UK. www.econ.cam.ac.uk/dae/repec/cam/pdf/cwpe1111.pdf. Accessed 15 September 2013.

Salomon, J.A., H. Wang, M.K. Freeman, T. Vos, A.D. Flaxman, A.D. Lopez, and C.J.L. Murray. 2012. "Healthy Life Expectancy for 187 Countries, 1990–2010: A Systematic Analysis for the Global Burden Disease Study 2010." *Lancet* 380(9859): 2144–62.

Samoa Bureau of Statistics. n.d. Census tables. www.sbs.gov.ws. Accessed 15 November 2013.

UNDESA (United Nations Department of Economic and Social Affairs). 2011. *World Population Prospects: The 2010 Revision.* New York. www.un.org/en/development/desa/population/publications/trends/population-prospects_2010_revision.shtml. Accessed 15 October 2013.

———. **2013a.** *World Population Prospects: The 2012 Revision.* New York. http://esa.un.org/unpd/wpp. Accessed 15 October 2013.

———. **2013b.** *World Urbanization Prospects: The 2011 Revision.* New York. http://esa.un.org/unup/CD-ROM/Urban-Rural-Population.htm. Accessed 15 October 2013.

———. **2013c.** *Trends in International Migrant Stock: The 2013 Revision.* New York. http://esa.un.org/unmigration/migrantstocks2013.htm. Accessed 15 September 2013.

UNESCO Institute for Statistics. 2011. *Global Education Digest 2011.* Montreal.

———. **2012.** *Global Education Digest 2012.* Montreal.

———. **2013a.** Data Centre. http://stats.uis.unesco.org. Accessed 15 May 2013.

———. **2013b.** Data Centre. http://stats.uis.unesco.org. Accessed 15 December 2013.

UNESCWA (United Nations Economic and Social Commission for Western Asia). 2013. *Survey of Economic and Social Developments in Western Asia, 2012–2013.* Beirut. www.escwa.un.org/information/pubaction.asp?PubID=1370. Accessed 15 November 2013.

UNHCR (United Nations High Commissioner for Refugees). 2013. Correspondence on refugees, September 2013. Geneva.

UNICEF (United Nations Children's Fund). 2014. *The State of the World's Children 2014 in Numbers: Every Child Counts: Revealing Disparities, Advancing Children's Rights.* New York. www.unicef.org/sowc2014/numbers. Accessed 15 April 2014.

———. **Various years.** Multiple Indicators Cluster Surveys. New York. www.unicef.org/statistics/index_24302.html. Accessed November 2013.

United Nations Statistics Division. 2013. National reporting of household characteristics, living arrangements and homeless households. www.un.org/en/development/desa/policy/cdp/ldc/ldc_data.shtml. Accessed 15 November 2013.

———. **2014.** National Accounts Main Aggregate Database. http://unstats.un.org/unsd/snaama. Accessed 7 May 2014.

UNODC (United Nations Office on Drugs and Crime). 2013. Homicide statistics. www.unodc.org/unodc/en/data-and-analysis/homicide.html. Accessed 15 November 2013.

WHO (World Health Organization). 2013a. Global Health Observatory. www.who.int/entity/gho/mortality_burden_disease/mortality_adult/en/. Accessed 15 September 2013.

———. **2013b.** Global Health Expenditure database. http://apps.who.int/nha/database. Accessed 15 November 2013.

———. **2013c.** Mental health. www.who.int/gho/mental_health. Accessed 15 November 2013.

WHO (World Health Organization), UNICEF (United Nations Children's Fund), UNFPA (United Nations Population Fund) and the World Bank. 2013. Trends in estimates of maternal mortality ratio. www.childinfo.org/maternal_mortality_ratio.php. Accessed 15 November 2013.

World Bank. 2013a. World Development Indicators database. Washington, D.C. http://data.worldbank.org. Accessed 15 October 2013.

———. **2013b.** "Getting a Job." http://wbl.worldbank.org/Data/ExploreTopics/getting-a-job#Parental. Accessed 15 July 2013.

———. **2014.** World Development Indicators database. Washington, D.C. http://data.worldbank.org. Accessed 7 May 2014.